Cape
Hatteras

Bermuda

D1234749

baco

ew
rovidence
Eleuthera

BAHAMAS

Cat Island

San Salvador

uma

g Island

Little Inagua

Turks & Caicos
Islands

Great
Inagua

**DOMINICAN
REPUBLIC**

HAITI

Hispaniola

Virgin
Islands
(U.S.)

Virgin
Islands
(U.K.)

Sombrero

Anguilla

ATER ANTILLES

Puerto Rico

Saba

Barbuda

ICA

St. Eustatius

Antigua

St. Kitts & Nevis

Guadeloupe

Montserrat

Marie Galante

**LESSER
ANTILLES**

Dominica

ribbean Sea

Martinique

NETHERLANDS ANTILLES

St. Vincent &
The Grenadines

St. Lucia

Península de
la Guajira

Gulf of
Venezuela

Aruba

Curaçao

Bonaire

Bequia

Barbados

fo

Margarita

Grenada

á

Tobago

Trinidad

*Mouth of the
Orinoco*

VENEZUELA

GUYANA

SURINAME

COLOMBIA

BRAZIL

PERU

National Audubon Society®
Field Guide to

Tropical Marine Fishes

of the Caribbean, the Gulf of Mexico,
Florida, the Bahamas, and Bermuda

A Chanticleer Press Edition

National Audubon Society®
Field Guide to

Tropical Marine Fishes

of the Caribbean, the Gulf of Mexico,
Florida, the Bahamas, and Bermuda

C. Lavett Smith

Curator Emeritus
Department of Icthyology
American Museum of Natural History
New York

Alfred A. Knopf, New York

This is a Borzoi Book
Published by Alfred A. Knopf, Inc.

www.randomhouse.com

Prepared and produced by
Chanticleer Press, Inc., New York.

Printed and bound by
Toppan Printing Co., Ltd., Tokyo, Japan.

Published August 1997
Fifth printing, December 2007

Library of Congress Cataloging-in-Publication
Number: 97-7690
ISBN: 0-679-44601-X

CONTENTS

PART II SPECIES ACCOUNTS

APPENDICES

THE AUTHOR

C. Lavett Smith is Curator Emeritus, Department of Ichthyology, at the American Museum of Natural History in New York City, where he has pursued the study of coral reef fishes for more than 35 years. Before joining the staff of the museum he taught at the College of Guam and the University of Hawaii. While at the museum he has conducted field studies in the Bahamas, the Virgin Islands, and Belize, and has made collecting expeditions to Polynesia, Australia, the Indian Ocean, New Guinea, and the Galápagos Islands. Dr. Smith has been scuba diving since 1956. In 1970 he spent 17 days on the sea floor off St. John, in the Virgin Islands, as a scientist-aquanaut in the Tektite II Program, a government-sponsored expedition. His special interests are reproductive biology and community ecology of fishes. Dr. Smith also maintains an interest in North American freshwater fishes and is the author of *Inland Fishes of New York State* (New York State Department of Environmental Conservation, 1985) and *Fish Watching: An Outdoor Guide to Freshwater Fishes* (Cornell University Press, 1994).

ACKNOWLEDGMENTS

Since the appearance in the mid-18th century of the first American flora and fauna guide, Mark Catesby's *Natural History of Carolina, Florida, and the Bahama Islands,* a vast array of scientific publications on tropical fishes of the western Atlantic have been produced. More than 300 scientific publications were consulted during the preparation of this guide, including one of the best regional ichthyology books of all time, *Fishes of the Bahamas and Adjacent Tropical Waters,* by James E. Böhlke and Charles C. G. Chaplin (second edition, revised by Eugenia B. Böhlke and William F. Smith-Vaniz; University of Texas Press, 1993). Especially useful were two semi-technical series of works published by the Food and Agriculture Organization of the United Nations: *FAO Species Identification Sheets for Fishery Purposes* and the *FAO Fisheries Synopsis* series. Several excellent popular guides to tropical fishes of the Caribbean also served as references, including: *Caribbean Reef Fishes,* by John E. Randall (T.F.H. Publications Incorporated, 1968); *A Field Guide to Atlantic Coast Fishes of North America,* by C. Richard Robins, G. Carleton Ray, and John Douglass (Houghton Mifflin, 1986); *Divers and Snorkelers Guide to the Fishes and Sea Life of the Caribbean, Florida, Bahamas, and Bermuda,* by F. Joseph Stokes (Academy of Natural Sciences of Philadelphia, revised 1988 and 1990); and *Reef Fish Identification,* by Paul Humann (New World Publications Incorporated, 1994).

What I know about West Indian fishes I have learned over four decades from numerous teachers, but three individuals stand out as having pointed the way: Reeve M. Bailey, who taught me to love the study of fishes; James W. Atz, who taught me to love the literature of fishes; and James C. Tyler, who guided my field work in many parts of the world. I also wish to thank Irwin A. Levy and Sol Heiligman, volunteers at the museum who spent many hours running down references, reading drafts, and listening to my ideas as this book took shape. I owe a special debt to my favorite snorkeling companion, my wife, Marjorie.

Preparation of this guide has truly been a team effort. The general consultant, Dr. Carter R. Gilbert, a longtime friend and colleague, has applied his legendary memory and vast knowledge of fishes of the region with characteristic competence, diligence, and generosity of spirit. Andrew Stewart, publisher, and the staff of Chanticleer Press have made every step of the publication process a delight. Alicia Mills, production manager, skillfully ushered the book through production; Drew Stevens, art director, designed the book and tamed every crisis with a calm that belies his artistic talent; Teri Myers, photo editor, accomplished the nearly impossible task of gathering photographs from many sources; Kathryn Clark, editor, turned words into prose; and Kristina Lucenko, assistant editor, checked every facet of the manuscript with meticulous diligence. My thanks also go to editors Lisa Leventer, Pat Fogarty, and Miriam Harris; copy editor Holly Thompson; editorial assistant Michelle Bredeson; photo assistant Christine Heslin; and managing editor Edie Locke. Dolores Santoliquido prepared the elegant silhouettes that capture the essence of the fishes; John Norton created illustrations that are attractive, forthright, and truly useful; and Jon Daugherity and Gary J. Antonetti of Ortelius Design provided the detailed endpaper maps. I would also like to acknowledge the many hours spent by hundreds of amateur and professional photographers gathering the photographs that we reviewed. We wish we could have printed dozens more of the stunning pictures submitted.

Finally, Amy Hughes, Chanticleer's editor-in-chief, weighed every statement and implemented many improvements in the book's organization and presentation. Working with Chanticleer has been like taking an enjoyable full-time course in writing, and I hope that I have learned even a small part of what they practice.

INTRODUCTION

With the development of safe, efficient snorkeling and diving gear, thousands of people have taken to the warm, clear waters of the tropical western Atlantic and adjoining waters to witness some of the most beautiful underwater scenery in the world. Underwater, the environment becomes truly three dimensional, and as we allow ourselves to move with the sea's fluid rhythms, every sense is renewed. On coral reefs, where stone is alive and the trees are animals, we find beauty in forms unknown in the terrestrial world.

This guide focuses on marine fishes of the tropical waters of the western Atlantic: Bermuda; both coasts of Florida; the Gulf of Mexico; the Caribbean Sea, including the West Indies (the Bahamas and the Greater and Lesser Antilles); and the coasts of Central and South America to the mouth of the Orinoco River. The photographs and text in the guide will help you to identify the region's fishes alive and underwater, without harming them in any way. We emphasize recognition by sight, often from a distance, and concentrate on such obvious characteristics as size, shape, color, and easily noted features such as trailing fins and whiskerlike barbels. Some related species can be distinguished only by such details as the number of rays in the fins or the number of scale rows along the sides; in those cases our descriptions are likewise more detailed.

The Introduction consists of three main sections. "Organization of the Guide" explains how the guide works and gives a breakdown of what the user will find in the colorplates section and the species accounts. "Biology of Fishes" discusses the classification, anatomy, and life history of fishes, as well as counting and measuring systems. This section, which includes detailed illustrations, provides the user with all the information needed in order to understand the species descriptions. "Marine Habitats of the Region" describes the region's biogeology and its major habitat types, which are pictured in the color-plates section. A brief note on conservation concludes the Introduction.

ORGANIZATION OF THE GUIDE

The *National Audubon Society Field Guide to Tropical Marine Fishes* is composed of three main sections: the Introduction, the color photographs of the marine habitats and the fish species of our region (Part I), and the written descriptions of the fishes (the species accounts, Part II). These are supplemented by the appendices, which include a glossary of terms used throughout the guide, an index of the fishes, and photo credits.

Coverage

The guide covers nearly 1,200 species of fishes, from inch-long gobies to the 40-foot (12-m) Whale Shark. The more than 400 species selected for full coverage—with a complete description, a photograph or full-body illustration, and a range map—are primarily the more common and/or conspicuous species that are likely to be encountered by snorkelers and divers to depths of about 150 feet (45 m). Less common, smaller, more cryptic, or evasive species are described as similar or related species. A few representatives of major groups that occur only in deep water are also described for completeness and to introduce the groups to which they belong.

This field guide presents the fishes in full-color photographs rather than more traditional paintings or drawings. In artists' renderings the patterns and colors of fishes are often exaggerated and idealized, whereas a good photograph captures the true color pattern of the fish. The photographs are not only beautiful but are true to nature, presenting the fishes in their natural settings and often engaged in characteristic behavior.

We have obtained color photographs of 376 species for this guide and have attempted to use, as much as possible, photographs of live fishes in their natural environment. In a few cases we have had to use photographs of dead specimens. Some species for which a suitable photograph was unavailable are represented in detailed illustrations that appear with the species descriptions in the black-and-white text pages. At least one representative of each family that occurs in fairly shallow water in our region is shown in either a photograph or an illustration.

The Color Plates

Part I of the field guide is the color-plates section. It opens with "Organization of Part I," which is followed by an essay that explains how to use the guide to identify fishes, 28 photographs of the region's marine habitats, two tables—the Family Key and the Thumb Tab Key—and 389 photographs of the fishes.

The Species Accounts

Following the color plates is Part II of the guide, which is devoted mainly to the species accounts, text descriptions of the species. This section also includes discussions of the larger groupings of fishes: classes, orders, families, and genera. When reading about a fish, readers should review the order and family discussions, as well as the genus table, that precede the species account. These provide information about the basic features of the fishes in the group. The text is arranged phylogenetically, according to scientific classification, which reflects the general evolutionary history of fishes from the jawless hagfishes through the cartilaginous sharks and rays to the most advanced bony fishes.

Genus Tables

When a family is represented by more than one genus in shallow water in our region, we provide a table of the genera listing their most important identification features. These tables are organized as follows: If the genus has one outstanding feature that positively identifies it, that feature is listed first, so if it is present in your fish, you have identified the genus. Other features listed may also be unique to the genus, or may be shared by some other genera in the family.

Plate Numbers

Most of the species accounts begin with the number of the color plate (occasionally two color plates) on which that species is shown. Species that are depicted in a detailed illustration instead of a photograph have no plate number.

Names

Next to the plate number is the fish's name: the common name (if there is one) and the scientific name. The first word in the scientific name is the genus name; the second is the trivial or species name. The common names follow the recommendations of the American Fisheries Society (AFS) whenever possible. For species not on the AFS list, we have tried to follow the recommendations of the Food and Agriculture Organization of the United Nations. For species not included in either of these sources, we have referred to the original describer's notes or regional monographs.

Common names can be unreliable because the same species may be known by different common names in different areas, and because the same common name may be applied to more than one species. Scientific names are more precise because each species can have only one valid scientific name. However, scientific names continue to be modified as our knowledge and understanding of the biological relationships among fishes expand.

Identification

This section presents the basic characteristics that permit identification of a fish, including shape, color, distinctive markings, and anatomical features. The key distinguishing features appear in italic type. If they vary greatly, the coloration and body shape of males, females, and juveniles may be described separately. Drawings in the margin illustrate details and special features.

In many accounts we have used a type of comparative measurement known as a *step measurement* for certain features. This is useful in comparing, for instance, the size of the head to the length of the fish; if the head length goes into the standard length (SL) three times, this is expressed as "head 3 in SL." For information on step measurements as well as on how to count fin rays and scales in the lateral line, see the section "Counting and Measuring," further below.

Size

Every identification section concludes with the fish's known or expected *total length* (TL, measured from the tip of the snout to the tip of the tail), *standard length* (SL, measured from the tip of the snout to the base of the caudal fin), or *fork length* (FL, measured from the tip of the snout to the tips of the middle rays of the caudal fin). Width (W, measured from the tip of one pectoral fin to the tip of the other) is given for many skates and rays.

Size information should be used with caution: Fishes may keep growing throughout their lives, and occasionally an unusually large individual is encountered. It might be thought that a better measure would be the "usual" or most common size, but such figures vary from place to place and probably from year to year. The real function of the sizes provided here is to give a general idea of how big the species gets. But since all fish start out as tiny embryos, most of the individuals you encounter will be smaller than the expected maximum lengths.

Habitat

We have compiled habitat information, often including depth, for each species. Some species have rather general habitats and might be found almost anywhere. Others are very restricted, and so the habitat provides an important clue to identification. Most species are most commonly seen at certain depths, are rare in other depths, and are never found in still others. For many species, especially those that live in relatively deep water, the habitat is unknown, and the best we can provide is an approximation of the depths at which these fishes have been caught.

Range

The geographic range of each species is described and shown on an accompanying map. Ichthyologists determine ranges by studying confirmed records of fishes in different areas. Records of a species are often scattered, and the range has to be estimated based on habits and habitat. The geographic distribution given is the normal range where the species occurs, although strays may occur beyond these limits. The range information is often most accurate if used in conjunction with the habitat description.

Most of the species in this book have a larval life stage during which they drift with the ocean currents. Many larvae ride the Gulf Stream and associated currents northward, and each fall "tropical strays" appear along the Atlantic coast as far north as New England, where they eventually succumb to falling temperatures or lack of food.

In the range section, abbreviations are used for northern (n), southern (s), eastern (e), western (w), central (c), and compounds of these words, such as northeast (ne).

Notes

In this section we provide additional information about the species such as its living habits, the foods it eats, and whether it is aggressive, has sharp or venomous spines, or is toxic to ingest. There might also be further information to help you confirm an identification, such as color variations, a discussion of seasonal migrations, or perhaps comments on alternate names that you might encounter in further readings.

Similar and Related Species

Species that may be confused with the subject as well as some related species that are less likely to be seen are discussed at the end of the species account. If the similar species does not have its own text account in this guide, we give its scientific name as well as its common name (if there is one), and its range and habitat, if known. When there are numerous similar or related species, they are presented in tables. We generally give a brief description (this often presents features that contrast with those of the main species covered) and the range. Size is given if the species is unusually large or small for its family. These tables are best used in conjunction with the genus tables and the family description.

BIOLOGY OF FISHES

Fishes are cold-blooded vertebrates that have evolved for an aquatic existence. Their gills extract dissolved oxygen from water, and their streamlined shapes allow them to slip easily through the water. Fishes move by the action of both their fins and their bodies. As a fish swims, the body is thrown into a series of curves that move rearward as waves, propelling the fish forward. The dorsal and anal fins also propel the fish by a series of wave-like flexing movements, and the pectoral, pelvic, and caudal fins make both wave-like and paddle-like motions.

Classification of Fishes

There is some argument over the classification of living fishes, but they are generally divided into three major groups: the jawless fishes (hagfishes and lampreys), the cartilaginous fishes (sharks, skates, rays, and related fishes), and the bony fishes. The bony fishes are divided into two types: lobe-finned fishes and ray-finned fishes. There are about 20,000 known fish species worldwide, 97 percent of them bony fishes. More than 1,000 species can be found in the geographic and depth ranges covered by this guide.

Biologists divide living organisms into major groups called phyla. The phylum Chordata includes the vertebrates, which encompasses fishes, mammals, birds, amphibians, and reptiles. Phyla are divided into classes, classes into orders, orders into families, families into genera (singular: genus), and genera into species. The species is the basic unit of classification and is generally what we have in mind when we talk about a "kind" of fish.

The formal definition of a *species* is rather abstruse, but in practical terms species are groups of organisms that breed successfully, producing fertile offspring. *Subspecies,* or races, are populations of a species that differ from one another in some way or are isolated geographically and that may be developing into new species.

Life History of Fishes

Fishes have a wide variety of life-history patterns. Some, such as damselfishes, attach their eggs to hard bottom and guard them until they hatch. Cardinalfishes and jawfishes carry their eggs in their mouths during the embryonic period. Some sharks give birth to live young. Most marine fishes, however, release eggs and sperm in the water column and have nothing further to do with them. These free-floating eggs then become part of the plankton, carried along to remote parts by the currents.

Nearly all marine fishes have a planktonic larval stage when the larvae are dispersed. Some species have larval stages that are so different from the adults that they were first thought to be different species or to belong to different genera or even families.

The length of time spent as larvae is highly variable and usually is not known. After the larval period is a post-larval stage, when the fish have the shape of adults but lack complete pigment patterns; next they become juveniles, which may or may not resemble the adults. Finally the juveniles mature and are ready to reproduce. Quite a few fishes start their reproductive life as one sex and then transform into the other, and a few species are hermaphroditic throughout their lives.

General Fish Anatomy and Coloration

Fishes are generally streamlined; the transition from head to body is imperceptible. The head is generally considered to end at the gill opening, the body at the anus. The surfaces of a fish are referred to as *dorsal* (the top, or back), *ventral* (the bottom, or belly), and *lateral* (the sides). The front of a fish is referred to as *anterior,* the rear as *posterior.*

Body Shapes

The *body shape* is the shape of a fish in profile. We use the following terms to describe body shapes: *fusiform* (tapering at both ends), *tapering* (narrowing toward the tail), *rectangular* (not tapering, narrowing abruptly right before the caudal peduncle), *oval, disk shaped* (rounded), and *eel-like.*

The *cross section* is the shape of the fish viewed head-on; the terms are: *oval, terete* (round), *compressed* (flattened from side to side), and *depressed* (flattened from top to bottom). The head can be depressed while the body is compressed.

The proportion of a fish's length (from snout to tail) to its depth (from back to belly) is also important in identification. A fish is said to be *elongate* if the measurement of the depth is small in comparison to that of the length. A fish is *deep* if the depth measurement is high compared to the length.

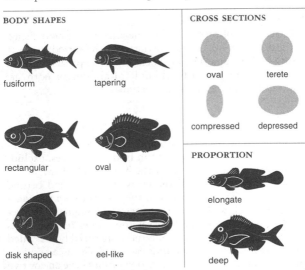

BODY SHAPES

fusiform

tapering

rectangular

oval

disk shaped

eel-like

CROSS SECTIONS

oval

terete

compressed

depressed

PROPORTION

elongate

deep

PATTERNS

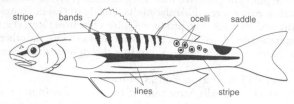

Color and Pattern

The majority of fishes are countershaded—dark above and paler below. In most fishes the transition is gradual, but sometimes there is a sharp line of demarcation between the dark upperparts and the pale undersurface.

Reef fishes are often colorful, and color can be very important in identifying fishes. However, color can also be misleading, as fishes can change color with age, sex, breeding period, and time of day. The coloration of certain fishes changes with the depth at which they live. Some fishes undergo a color change while they are being cleaned by "cleaner fishes," and others change color at times of stress or while they sleep.

Pattern is often more diagnostic than color when identifying a fish. In general, *stripes* are bands of color that run lengthwise (head to tail); *lines* are narrow stripes. *Bands* or *bars* are vertical, usually extending from back to belly. *Spots* are distinct and sharp edged; *blotches* are diffuse. *Saddles* are spots or blotches that extend from the dorsal surface down onto the sides. *Ocelli* (singular: ocellus), or *ocellated spots,* are spots with a margin of contrasting color.

Anatomy of Bony Fishes

The text that follows describes the anatomy of bony fishes. The anatomy of sharks is illustrated in the introduction to sharks, and the anatomy of skates and rays appears with the text describing the batoids (order Rajiformes); both are found in the species accounts section.

Head

The fish's head, the area from the tip of the snout to the gill opening, can be divided into a number of regions for identification. The *snout* is the area in front of the eyes, excluding the lower jaw. The top of the head is called the *frontal region;* behind the frontal region is the *occiput* and behind that the *nape.* The area between the eyes is called the *interorbital* area; below the eyes is the *suborbital* region; the anterior part of the suborbital area is sometimes referred to as the *preorbital* region. A ring of rather superficial bones called the *circumorbital bones* surrounds each eye. The area between the eye and the gills is the *cheek.* Bony fishes have one or two pairs of *nostrils* (sometimes tubular in shape) that are usually ahead of the eyes. The nostrils of fishes are olfactory organs, used only for smell.

Gill Area

Gills are the respiratory organs of fishes. The movable plate covering the gills is the *operculum,* or *gill cover,* which is supported by two main bones, the *opercle* and the *subopercle.* On each side of the head there is a J- or L-shaped bone called the *preopercle.* The ventral and posterior edges of the preopercle meet at an angle and are usually "free"—that is, the skin folds under the edge of the bone; sometimes the edge is serrate or bears one or more *preopercular spines.* Beneath the preopercle is another small bone called the *interopercle.* The slit-like opening behind the operculum is the *gill opening,* which marks the posterior limit of the head. On the underside of the body, the triangular part that extends forward between the gill covers is the *isthmus.* The arrangement of the gill membranes and the isthmus varies in bony fishes: In some fishes the gill membranes are separate ventrally, and the isthmus is exposed; in others the gill membranes are joined to one another across the isthmus; and in still others the gill membranes are joined to the isthmus.

THE HEAD

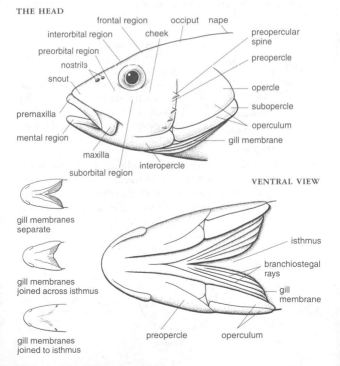

frontal region occiput nape
interorbital region cheek
preopercular spine
preorbital region
preopercle
nostrils
snout
opercle
subopercle
premaxilla
operculum
mental region
gill membrane
maxilla
interopercle
suborbital region

gill membranes separate

gill membranes joined across isthmus

gill membranes joined to isthmus

VENTRAL VIEW

isthmus
branchiostegal rays
gill membrane
preopercle operculum

GILLS: INTERIOR VIEW

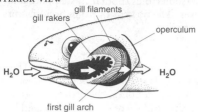

With rare exceptions, fish breathe by taking water in through the mouth, forcing it past the gills and out through the gill opening. The *gill membrane,* located along the edge of the operculum, prevents water from entering the gill chamber through the gill opening. Ventrally, the gill membranes are supported by bony rods called *branchiostegal rays.* The gills are supported by bony *gill arches.* Usually there are four pairs of gill arches, each with two rows of *gill filaments* along its posterior surface; the gill filaments, finger-like projections that take oxygen from the water, are the "lungs" of the fish. In most fishes a row of bony, finger-like *gill rakers* along the front of the gill arches protects the gills and prevents prey from escaping past the gills and out the gill opening. In some fishes the gill rakers are long, slender, and numerous, and are used for straining plankton for food.

Mouth and Jaws

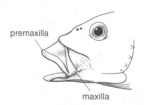

PROTRUSIBLE JAWS

The front part of the lower jaw is called the *mental region.* Usually a groove separates the upper lip from the tip of the snout. The upper outer jaws are supported on each side by two bones, the *premaxilla* and the *maxilla.* In higher fishes the premaxillae alone form the edges of the jaws, and the maxillae are located between them and the circumorbital bones, which may cover all but the tip of the maxillae. The premaxillae may also have projections at the front that extend toward the interorbital region. In some fishes the premaxillae may slide forward, displacing the upper jaw into a sort of a tube; such jaws are said to be *protrusible.*

MOUTH POSITIONS

terminal

superior

inferior

The position of the mouth varies among species. It is described as *terminal* if it is at the very front of the head; *superior* if the lower jaw projects beyond the upper; and *inferior* if the mouth is underneath the head with the upper jaw, or snout, projecting (an inferior mouth is sometimes described as *subterminal* when the upper jaw projects only slightly beyond the lower).

Scales

The scales of most bony fishes are thin plates made up of concentric bony ridges embedded in flexible connective tissue. Such scales are very different from the tooth-like scales of cartilaginous fishes (described and illustrated in the sharks section of the species accounts). Bony fish scales are usually described as cycloid or ctenoid. *Cycloid scales* are smooth all over, while *ctenoid scales* have small spines on the part of the scale that is exposed, that is, not covered by adjacent overlapping scales. These tiny spines give the fish a rough surface texture. Some bony fishes have scales on only part of the body, while others lack scales entirely.

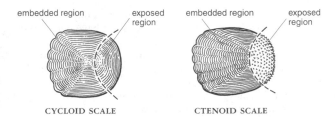

embedded region | exposed region   embedded region | exposed region

CYCLOID SCALE　　　　**CTENOID SCALE**

Lateral Line

A conspicuous landmark on the body of most fishes is the lateral line, typically a tube that runs along the length of the fish at mid-side just beneath the scales. Branch tubes reach the surface through the scales, where they open to the outside through small pores. The lateral line is a sensory organ that responds to vibrations in the water. Sound waves striking the fish set up vibrations in the fluid within the tube, and these stimulate tiny, hair-like projections along the tube. Extensions of the lateral line called *head canals* occur on various regions of the head. The patterns of the pores are sometimes important identification features, and the number of pored scales in the lateral line is often used as an indication of the relative size of the scales (the more scales in the lateral line, the smaller they are, and vice versa). Some fishes have no lateral line on the body, while others have several lateral lines. (See the section "Counting and Measuring," below, for information on counting lateral-line scales.)

PARTS OF A BONY FISH

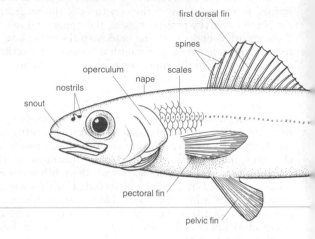

Fins

Fins are double membranes supported by bony (or, rarely, horny) rods called *fin rays*. Typically, fishes have one or two *dorsal fins* along the midline of the back, an *anal fin* on the ventral side behind the anus, a pair of *pectoral fins* just behind the gill openings, a pair of *pelvic fins* somewhere on the belly, and a *caudal fin* (tail fin).

Some fishes have a fatty *adipose fin,* usually with no rays, between the dorsal fin and the upper base of the caudal fin. The dorsal, anal, and caudal fins, all located on the midline of the body, are unpaired and are collectively referred to as *median fins;* the pectoral and pelvic fins are called *paired fins,* as there is one of each on each side of the body.

The place where a fin joins the body is called the *base;* the forward-most limit of the fin base is referred to as its *origin.* The *length* of a fin is the measure of its base, while the *height* of a fin is determined by the length of its rays. Thus, a fin can be described as short or long and high or low.

PARTS OF A FIN

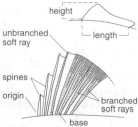

Fin rays are of two types: *soft rays,* which are usually segmented and branched toward their tips, and which consist of right and left halves; and *spines,* which are solid, single, unsegmented rods that do not branch. The more primitive fishes, such as the herrings, have only soft rays, while most relatively advanced fishes have

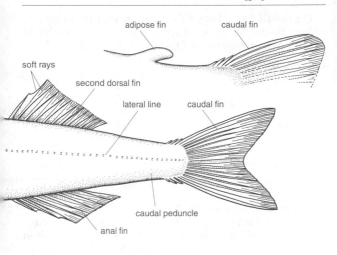

spines as well as soft rays. When spines are present they are nearly always at the anterior (front) part of the dorsal, anal, or pelvic fins. Sometimes one or more spines or rays are longer than the rest of the rays and extended as long filaments.

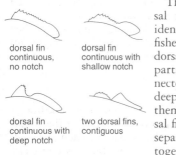

dorsal fin continuous, no notch

dorsal fin continuous with shallow notch

dorsal fin continuous with deep notch

two dorsal fins, contiguous

The arrangement of the dorsal fins is important in the identification of many types of fishes. In species with a single dorsal fin, the spiny and soft parts are continuous (connected), but there may be a deep or shallow notch between them. In species with two dorsal fins, the fins may be widely separated or they may be close together, or contiguous.

Some fishes have an enlarged scaly structure along the base of each pectoral or pelvic fin, or along both, that apparently serves to streamline or lessen the drag of the folded fin. This structure is called an *axillary process.*

Tail

The tail of most bony fishes is described as *homocercal* (nearly or completely symmetrical and supported by a complex internal V-shaped bony plate). In the tails of cartilaginous fishes, described as *heterocercal,* the spinal column extends into the larger upper lobe. Anatomically, the tail begins at the end of the body cavity. The narrow part of the tail that supports the caudal fin is the *caudal peduncle.*

The caudal fins of bony fishes come in a variety of shapes: *forked, lunate* (crescent shaped), *emarginate* (shallowly forked), *truncate* (squared-off), *rounded,* and *pointed.*

TAIL SHAPES

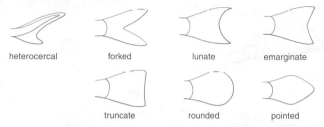

heterocercal   forked   lunate   emarginate

truncate   rounded   pointed

Counting and Measuring

Some of the descriptions in the species accounts list countable characteristics, such as the number of spines or rays in the fins or the number of scales along the side of the body. (Usually you must have a specimen in hand to note these features, but such close examination is sometimes necessary to identify the species precisely.)

Counting Spines and Rays

To count dorsal fin rays, simply count from front to back, starting with the first well-developed ray in soft-rayed fishes, or the first spine in spiny-rayed fishes. Count rays from the base; the last two ray elements count as one (they arise from one root). In pectoral and pelvic fins count all spines and rays; in the caudal fin count all branched rays and then add two.

Counting Scales

To count scales in the *lateral line,* look for a dark line or ridge running along the length of the fish from the shoulder just above the opercle to the caudal fin. Each pore will appear as a little hole, and you may be able to see or feel a ridge, indicating the canal underneath. It may be helpful to lift each scale as you count, using a needle or a thin-bladed knife. On some fishes the scales may be difficult to see and may require a magnifying glass. Begin by counting the first

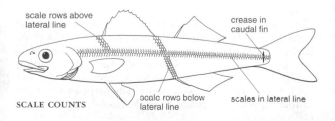

scale rows above lateral line

crease in caudal fin

scale rows below lateral line

scales in lateral line

SCALE COUNTS

scale behind the opercle and continue to the last vertebra, located at the crease made by flexing the caudal fin. Some fishes do not have a visible lateral line, so you will need to determine the number of scales in the *lateral series* by counting oblique (diagonal) rows of scales, beginning at the junction of the upper side of the opercle and the head, counting along a line to the base of the caudal fin.

To count the number of *scale rows* between the lateral line and the dorsal fin base, start at the front of the first dorsal fin and count the number of scales in an oblique row downward and backward to the lateral line. For the number of scale rows below the lateral line, begin at the front of the anal fin and count scales in an oblique row upward and forward to the lateral line.

Step Measurements

Differences in body proportions are very important identification clues. The relative depth, length, and width of the body are often distinctive, and sometimes the comparative size of the eye to the interorbital region or the snout to the rest of the head can help determine an identification. Ichthyologists usually express such proportions as step measurements, which are taken with expandable calipers or a drawing compass. To measure the head length in proportion to the entire body length, for example, place one point of the calipers at the tip of the snout and the other at the edge of the gill cover. With the calipers spread to this distance, which represents the head length, see how many times this length goes into the standard length (or SL, the distance from the tip of the snout to the base of the caudal fin rays). No attempt is made to compensate for curvature in either part. If the head measurement goes into the standard length three and a half times, it is expressed as "head 3.5 in SL." A short measurement goes into the standard more times than a large one. If one fish has "head 3 in SL" and another has "head 5 in SL," it is the former that has the larger head.

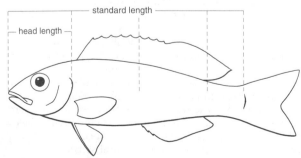

STEP MEASUREMENTS   Fish with head 3.5 in SL.

MARINE HABITATS OF THE REGION

Most people consider coral reefs the primary fish habitat of the tropical western Atlantic and the Caribbean Sea, and it is true that healthy coral reefs offer some of the most spectacular scenery in the world. However, peripheral habitats such as sea-grass beds, rocky shorelines, open sandy bottoms, and channels in mangrove swamps are home to some extremely interesting and highly specialized fishes in our region and should not be ignored.

Fish-watching in All Habitats

Start your fish-watching on the shore, before you even get wet. Position yourself on a dock at a time when the sun is behind you and the water is glass-calm, and simply watch the bottom for a few minutes. Even in harbors where the bottom is littered with discarded conch shells, bottles, old tires, and other debris, there are fishes to be seen. One of the first likely to be seen is the conspicuous black-and-yellow-banded Sergeant Major. A closer look will surely reveal the more somber-hued Dusky Damselfish, or some other species of damselfish, guarding its nest by rushing at any other fish that comes close. Fifteen or twenty minutes of gazing into the water will be well rewarded.

Most of your fish-watching, however, will be done in the water. A good, well-fitting face mask, a snorkel, and a pair of swim fins are all you need to get started. Even non-swimmers can see a variety of fishes in water that is no more than waist deep. If you are snorkeling or diving, you must discipline yourself to spend time looking, rather than chasing fish that are already at the limit of your underwater vision. Your best bet is to let the fish come to you. Be sure to search the entire water column. Some species never leave the bottom, and others nearly always hover just below the surface.

When fish-watching in coral reefs, examine the surface of living corals—but avoid touching the coral itself, for its live part is a thin, delicate layer that can be seriously damaged by the slightest contact. Look in caves and holes and under ledges. This means getting close enough to see into deep shadows; the best way to do this is to dive down so that you can get your face mask into the shade. Be careful where you put your hands and feet, not only to protect the coral, but also because long-spined sea urchins hide in deep crevices during the day. Their sharp, brittle spines easily puncture human skin and cause painful wounds.

Remember that the warm waters of our region are teeming with life. Explore each different habitat described below and you will find myriad communities of colorful and fascinating fishes interacting in their natural settings.

Benthic and Pelagic Habitats

In general, marine habitats are described as *benthic* (referring to the sea bottom) or *pelagic* (waters above the bottom). Benthic habitats are divided into the *littoral,* or *intertidal,* zone, which is the region that is covered at high tide and exposed at low tide, and the *sublittoral* zone, which extends seaward beyond the littoral zone. In the Caribbean, tidal ranges are small, on the order of one or two feet (30–60 cm), and the littoral zone is most evident along rocky shorelines and shallow flats.

The *continental shelf* is an underwater plain that surrounds the continents and gently slopes to depths of about 650 feet (200 m). The shelf around islands is called the *insular shelf;* many islands of our region, such as the Lesser Antilles and Bermuda, have little shelf, and the depth reaches 650 feet (200 m) close to shore, sometimes only a few yards out. The Bahamas sit on an extensive shelf.

Beyond the edge of the continental shelf is the *continental slope,* where the bottom falls away more quickly, from 650 feet (200 m) to 13,000 feet (4,000 m). Below the slope lie the *abyssal plains,* great expanses on the sea floor. The floors of the world's oceans are marked with a network of ridges where the edges of lithospheric plates (large sections of the earth's crust) meet. The sea floor is actually spreading at the ridges as magma pushes up from the deeper layers of the earth's interior. Closer to continents and island arcs the sea floor is interrupted by *subduction trenches,* where one crustal plate is sliding beneath another. The Puerto Rico Trench, which has some of the greatest depths in the Atlantic Ocean (more than 28,000 feet/8,500 m), is a classic example of a subduction trench.

BENTHIC AND PELAGIC HABITATS

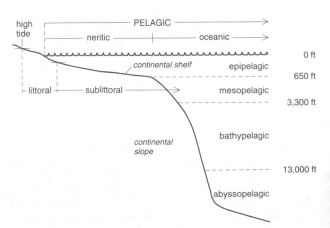

The pelagic region of oceans and seas encompasses all waters above the bottom. The waters over the continental shelf are termed *neritic;* those beyond the edge of the shelf are *oceanic.* Oceanographers divide the pelagic region into an *epipelagic* zone, which extends from the surface to a depth of about 650 feet (200 m; this is the part of the ocean where enough light penetrates to support photosynthesis); a *mesopelagic* zone, beginning at 650 feet (200 m) and extending to 3,300 feet (1,000 m); a *bathypelagic* zone, which extends from 3,300 to 13,000 feet (1,000–4,000 m); and below that the *abyssopelagic* zone.

Islands

The islands in our region were created by a variety of geologic forces. *Bermuda* is a group of islands mainly made up of marine limestone deposited on top of a vast volcanic mountain that rises from the sea floor. Most of Bermuda's hills are formed of sand that was piled up by the wind during times when the sea level was much lower than it is now.

The *Bahamas* are marine islands on blocks of limestone thrust up from the bottom of the sea. The hills, like those of Bermuda, are hardened sand dunes formed at times of lower sea level. A veneer of modern coral reef sediments and active coral reefs covers the underlying older marine rocks.

The large islands of the *Greater Antilles* are complex land masses of volcanic mountains, uplifted marine sediments, and sediments derived from erosion of the volcanic cores. The *Lesser Antilles* constitute an island arc of volcanoes, some still active, formed behind the edge of the Caribbean plate where it overrides the adjacent Atlantic plate. Anguilla, Barbados, and parts of Antigua are sea-floor remnants from the plate's subduction.

Shorelines

The shorelines along the edges of the continents and larger islands of our region—including beaches, offshore islands, sand bars, coastal lagoons, and estuaries—are the results of ocean water acting on land sediments as well as marine sediments derived from the sea floor itself. Natural shorelines in our region are either rocky shores, sandy beaches, or mangrove swamps.

Sandy Shorelines

Most *sandy beaches* (plates 1 and 2) of the Caribbean are made of calcareous (lime-based) sands that are the remains of the skeletons of plants and animals that built the coral reefs. If you examine a handful of sand you may be able to distinguish fragments of mollusk shells, corals, and certain red algae that also extract calcium carbonate from sea water to build their supporting "skeletons." You may also see tiny ovoid particles of calcium carbonate called oolites. The remains of other animals such as foraminifera and bryozoans contribute to the sands.

Offshore from sandy beaches the sea bottom is also sand and usually has definite low ridges or *ripple marks* formed as the moving water piles the sand into miniature dunes a few inches high (plate 3). Although such areas may seem empty of life, a number of interesting fishes occur there, including large rays, tonguefishes and other flatfishes, mojarras, and cruising predators such as barracudas.

Beach Rock

Along the region's sandy beaches you will see patches of *beach rock* (plates 4 and 5), which is a special kind of limestone that forms at the intertidal level under sandy beaches. Rain and sea water dissolve calcium carbonate in the beach's upper layers and deposit it in the deeper layers, where it binds the sand grains into firm rock. Beach rock is often exposed as shifting currents sweep it free of sand. Its irregular layers may be undercut, leaving deep horizontal crevices that provide excellent habitats for some fishes. The upper surface of the beach rock slopes gently seaward at an angle that is somewhat less steep than the slope of the beach itself. Often the beach rock surface just below the intertidal zone is pitted with short channels made by rock-boring sea urchins. Several species of fishes are found in association with these urchins.

Rocky Shorelines

Some of the region's rocky shorelines are *volcanic* in origin (plate 6), with large boulders of igneous rock formed by past eruptions. Other rocky shorelines are of native *limestone* that was formed above sea level. This limestone, ultimately derived from coral reefs, is made of sands that were blown by the wind into substantial dunes on land and subsequently consolidated by water trickling down through the loose sands, cementing them into a grainy limestone. Where the ocean meets the land, layers of limestone may be carved into cliffs. Limestone shorelines typically have a deep notch at sea level, called the *intertidal nip* (seen in profile at the seaward end of the limestone ledge in plate 7), formed by erosion from wave action and organisms such as sponges and mollusks that constantly dissolve and scrape away the rock as they feed on algae growing there. Rocky shorelines, both volcanic and limestone, provide shelter in the cracks and crevices of the rock for invertebrates and the fishes that prey on them. These shorelines often have sparse coral growth that will eventually envelop the rock and form a reef.

Mangrove Shorelines

Mangroves are small, salt-tolerant trees that grow in dense clumps. The red mangrove, the most salt-tolerant species, grows at the shoreline, often forming extensive areas of *mangrove swamps and shorelines* (plate 8). Red mangroves are characterized by dangling aerial roots (these allow the tree to "breathe" through pores) that eventually grow downward, forming large, intertangled loops called prop roots along the shore. Snorkeling along mangrove roots requires special care: Any disturbance will shake loose clouds of organic silt and impede visibility. Move your arms and flippers slowly and glide along the edge of the roots and you will be rewarded by some of the most intriguing scenery in the tropical marine world. Schoolmasters, Gray Snappers, and Sergeant Majors are among the fishes that you might encounter.

Coral Reefs

Coral reefs, by far the most spectacular environments in the region, are built of the skeletal matter of organisms that extract calcium carbonate from sea water and use it to build their skeletons. Although corals are the most conspicuous and largest reef builders, many other organisms contribute to reef formation, including foraminifera, mollusks, bryozoans, polychaete worms, and several kinds of plants. The underlying limestone rock consists of the remains of these organisms' skeletons ground by wave action and cemented together by biological and chemical processes into a solid limestone that in time loses all resemblance to the original skeletons.

Coral reefs have a clear organization of distinct zones that parallel the shoreline. This zonation is described in the following paragraphs; however, each area is unique, and not all of the features can be found everywhere. Plate 13 is an aerial view of a coral reef in which the different *zones* can be seen beneath the water surface.

CORAL REEF STRUCTURE

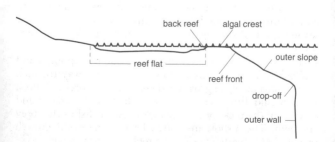

Reef Flats

The first zone, moving seaward from the shore, is the *reef flat,* which consists of areas of open sand interspersed with beds of *turtle grass* and other *sea grasses* (plate 9). Dense stands of sea grasses occur in shallow areas throughout the region. Sea-grass beds are the primary habitat for a few specially adapted fish species and serve as feeding grounds for many other fishes. Sandy bottom areas with sparse sea-grass and algae growth are often dotted with *mounds* about a foot (30 cm) high next to shallow pits (plate 10). These mounds are produced by burrowing invertebrates, including some worms and callianassid shrimps. The Orangespotted Goby is associated with these mounds.

Reef flats also have small, isolated coral reefs called *patch reefs* (plate 11) that are surrounded by sea-grass beds. These are excellent places for certain fishes that remain close to the shelter of the reef during the day and venture into the sea grasses to feed at night. Herbivores, both fishes and invertebrates, often crop the sea grasses around a patch reef, leaving an area bare of grasses in a conspicuous *halo* shape around the reef that is visible from the surface (plate 12). These halos are also called *Randall zones,* after Dr. John E. Randall, an ichthyologist who investigated their origin.

In a few places, for example the eastern margins of some of the outer islands of the Bahamas, patch reefs become very numerous and give rise to an interesting marine habitat. Because coralline algae grow best near the surface where sunlight penetrates, the patch reef expands most vigorously at the top, and the reef develops a mushroom shape. When this growth continues long enough, the tops of neighboring "mushrooms" begin to fuse to one another, forming a false bottom just below the water surface. Underwater, the original "stems" of the patch reefs remain as columns, or pillars, and the fused tops form a roof over a series of "rooms." The entire structure is known as a *pillar and gallery reef* (plates 19 and 20).

Toward the outer, seaward edge of the reef flat there may be a *rubble zone* (plate 16), a band of sandy patches littered with fragments of broken coral skeletons, old conch shells, and other reef debris that have washed down from the reef. The rubble zone provides habitat for a variety of fishes including the Sailfin Blenny, jawfishes, and the Sand Tilefish, which builds a nest from the rubble.

Algal Crest and Reef Front

The top of a coral reef is a band of dense limestone in which coralline algae has cemented the coral skeletons into a vast monolithic form called the *algal crest* (plate 15 shows a part of the crest exposed to the air). If you snorkel along the inside of the algal crest you will be able to see stages of its development. In some spots the remnants of the coral colonies are clearly visible; elsewhere they are less and less distinct as the algae cover them with a dense limestone. What appears to be a purplish stone is actually the coralline algae. The landward side of the algal crest is often marked by a zone of healthy corals that constitutes a *back reef* (plate 14). Reefs of the Indo-Pacific region often have a deep lagoon behind the reef crest and consequently have much better developed back reefs. In the West Indian region, back reefs are much more subtle.

In places, some of the algal crest is exposed at low tide. Pieces of large coral colonies that have been torn loose and thrown shoreward by powerful storm waves wash up here. If enough fragments accumulate they begin to trap sand and ultimately may form a *reef island*, also known as a *motu* (plate 17).

The outer, seaward side of the algal crest is the *reef front*, where the waves of the open sea end their long journey in lines of white surf. Coral growth is most vigorous on this side of the crest. Because the reef-building corals contain symbiotic algae that assist in the extraction of calcium carbonate from sea water, the corals grow fastest just below the surface where the most sunlight penetrates. The shallow water of the reef front supports the luxuriant growth of the tree-like *elkhorn coral* (*Acropora palmata;* plate 18). This part of the reef is called the *Acropora palmata zone,* or the *forereef.* Seaward of this zone the reef front slopes more or less steeply downward as the *outer slope* (plate 23), reaching a sharp *drop-off* (plate 24) at depths of 90 to 135 feet (30–40 m). Beyond the drop-off is the *outer wall* (plate 25), which plunges almost vertically to depths of hundreds of feet. The outer slope is often crossed by channels, or grooves, that run perpendicular to the edge of the reef. This is called the *groove and spur zone* (plates 21 and 22). In the western Atlantic the groove and spur zone is quite variable: In some areas the grooves are very conspicuous, elsewhere they might be hardly noticeable.

Other Habitats
Other special habitats of our region include *stromatolites* (plate 26), barrel-shaped structures built by blue-green algae and trapped sediments that are associated with coral reefs. They usually occur in channels where tidal currents are quite strong, often in breaks in the reefs between motus. Stromatolites are of special interest, because similar structures have been found as fossils dating back more than 570 million years to Precambrian times.

Many fishes, especially those that live around coral reefs, depend heavily on shelter, where they can hide and be safe from predators. Shelter sites also attract the invertebrates that many fishes feed on. For these reasons fishes are quick to take advantage of any type of shelter, including man-made structures. *Shipwrecks* are good places to see a variety of fishes, as are structures such as pier pilings, seawalls and jetties, and offshore oil-drilling platforms. Often these structures become nearly unrecognizable as they are encrusted with colorful marine life forms (plates 27 and 28).

Biogeography of the Region

Endemic species and subspecies (animals that are unique or particular to a geographical region) are much more common among terrestrial animals and freshwater fishes than marine fishes. In some areas, islands or groups of islands may support distinctive subspecies or even full species of certain birds or other creatures. Marine fishes, however, are less isolated, and the majority of species show little or no difference from island to island. Nevertheless, our region can be divided into several subregions that are distinguished either by the presence of species that occur nowhere else or by the limits of the occurrence of certain species. A regional barrier to species is referred to as a faunal break.

Bermuda: A rather isolated outpost of the West Indian faunal region, Bermuda has fewer species than areas farther south, as well as fewer endemics.

Atlantic Coast: A number of species have northern ranges extending from New England to Cape Hatteras, with a few records of members straying farther south. Other species have usual ranges from Florida to Cape Hatteras, with occasional strays reaching farther north.

Florida: The southern tip of Florida serves as a barrier between the Atlantic Ocean and the Gulf of Mexico. Some species are found on both sides of the Florida peninsula but not around its southern end. Some Gulf of Mexico species reach their limit at the northern part of the Gulf coast of Florida. Some Atlantic coast species reach their southern limit at the northern part of Florida's Atlantic coast.

Gulf of Mexico: In the northeastern Gulf, Mobile Bay and the Mississippi Delta form another limit. Some species range westward from the Mississippi Delta/Mobile Bay, and others range eastward to northern Florida. At the Texas–Mexico border, the Rio Grande Delta marks a break that separates the northwestern Gulf from the southern Gulf. Some southern Gulf species reach their northern limit at the Rio Grande, and others rarely venture east of the Yucatán Peninsula.

Caribbean Coastline: The western Caribbean is the region from the northeastern tip of the Yucatán Peninsula to Panama and Colombia. The South American coast and offshore islands from Panama to Trinidad form the southern rim of the Caribbean proper. Minor faunal breaks occur at the mouths of the Orinoco and Amazon Rivers, where fresh water runs into the ocean (deep-water species, which swim beneath the freshwater layer, are not hindered by these barriers).

Bahamas: The Bahamas are isolated by strong currents from Florida and the Greater Antilles. A number of species are known only from the Bahamas, but it is hard to be sure if these are true endemics or if they simply have not been collected in other areas.

Greater Antilles: These large and geologically complex islands—including Cuba, Jamaica, Hispaniola, and Puerto Rico—form the northern rim of the Caribbean Sea. High and mountainous, these islands have some brackish and freshwater environments.

Lesser Antilles: The rather small volcanic islands of the Lesser Antilles, which extend from the Virgin Islands south and then west to Aruba, have rugged coastlines with little shallow water surrounding them. Coral development is patchy, spectacular in some areas and scattered in others; consequently, the fish life is somewhat less diverse than in other coastal areas.

Conservation Note

The waters of the tropical western Atlantic, the Caribbean Sea, and the Gulf of Mexico are susceptible to environmental problems that plague many marine areas: overfishing, destruction of habitat, and pollution. Fish-watchers are encouraged to enter these areas with respect for the fragility and uniqueness of the ecosystems, especially the coral reefs, and the great diversity of life within them. Do as little as possible to disturb the wildlife: Do not touch live coral, avoid chasing fishes and other creatures, and do not collect specimens of plants or animals, some of which may be endangered. Those who fish in the region are reminded to follow local laws regarding licensing, seasons, and catch limits. The best way to conserve marine habitats and the flora and fauna within them is to look but don't touch, and leave no traces behind.

PART I
COLOR PLATES

ORGANIZATION OF PART I

Part I, the color-plates section of this guide, has five parts. The first, "How to Identify Fishes," explains how to use the guide to identify the fishes you see. This essay is followed by photographs of habitats of the tropical western Atlantic Ocean, the Caribbean Sea, and the Gulf of Mexico; these habitats are described in the Introduction to the guide. The third part is the Family Key (printed on white paper), which presents silhouette illustrations of typical representatives of the families of fishes found in the region, grouped according to shape and other shared physical characteristics. The fourth part is the Thumb Tab Key (printed on black paper), a guide to the fish silhouettes that are used in the thumb tabs on the left-hand pages of the fish species photographs. This key also serves as a visual index to the color plates.

The last and largest part of the color section is the fish species photographs. Each photograph has a caption that provides the common name of the species, its maximum length (width [w] is given for some batoids), and the page number on which it is described in the text. If the sex (male ♂, female ♀) or the phase (juvenile, supermale, etc.) of the individual is known, that information is also noted in the caption.

The species photographs are subdivided into 21 sections, each represented by a different thumb tab. The photographs are mainly presented in their taxonomic sequence, which is based on phylogenetic relationships (for the most part they follow the sequence used in the text). The order Perciformes, because of its large size, has been subdivided further; we have grouped the fishes within it by physical appearance.

HOW TO IDENTIFY FISHES

As experienced divers and snorkelers know, it is not always easy to identify a fish. The fish may dart away before you get a good look at it, or it may be a species with so many similar relatives that you are able to identify only the family or genus it belongs to. Unrelated fishes may share similar characteristics. The Flying Gurnard, for example, has large pectoral fins much like those of a flyingfish. An Escolar looks very much like some of the mackerels. The Tripletail might be mistaken for some kind of grouper. Some species (anchovies, for example) cannot be positively identified without physically examining specimens and even looking at X rays to check internal characteristics.

Also keep in mind that individuals of a species vary. If you see a fish that's an inch longer or has one more spine in the dorsal fin than the description says, that species should not necessarily be eliminated from consideration. It may just be an exceptional individual. Color, which would seem to be the most obvious identifying feature, can vary substantially with age, sex, breeding period, water depth, coloration of the surrounding habitat, time of day, and even with "mood."

Even the most experienced ichthyologist cannot identify every individual fish. With practice and experience, however, you will become familiar with many types of fishes and will learn what sorts of features and behaviors to focus on when you encounter a species unknown to you.

Using the Guide

This guide contains many features that will assist you in identifying a species of fish. The Introduction discusses fish structure and anatomy and the habitats of the western Atlantic and adjoining waters. The Family Key (on the white pages following the habitat photographs) arranges fish families by shape and other features and may enable you to find at a glance the family a fish belongs to. The color plates of the fishes are arranged in family groups and by overall appearance to help you find a fish using visual cues. The thumb tabs, which show a silhouette of a representative of each group, help you turn quickly to the photographs you are looking for. The caption beneath each species photograph gives the page number on which that species is described in the text in Part II of the guide.

The order and family introductions in Part II of the guide define the characteristics of the fishes in these categories. Genus tables outline the distinguishing features of the genera of each family that has more than one genus in shallow water in the region. The species accounts provide details including size, coloration, structural features, habitat and range, enabling you to identify a fish down to the species level. Tables of similar and related species outline the distinguishing features of some less-common relatives. Black-and-white illustrations provide detailed close-ups of certain features that are key to identification. Range maps and descriptions of ranges and habitats give additional information. In the Appendices are a glossary and an index.

Underwater Observation

When you see an unfamiliar fish while snorkeling or diving, look at it carefully, paying particular attention to its size, shape, and general coloration. Look especially for conspicuous markings on the body, head, and fins. Take careful notice of any structural peculiarities, such as elongated rays on the dorsal fin or tail, scales on the fins, or spines on the cheeks or elsewhere on the head. Other features, such as the placement, size, and shape of the fins, mouth, and eyes, can also be important clues. If the fish you see looks a lot like another fish that you can positively identify, determine how the fish you are observing differs. Take note of the habitat and whether the fish is on the bottom, near the surface, or somewhere in between. Keep an eye out for behavioral clues as well, such as whether the species travels in a school or in a pair. Many fish-watchers use slates or underwater notebooks to write down their observations.

Identifying a Fish

Often when you see a fish you will have some idea of what type it might be. A shark, for instance, is instantly recognizable as such by its shape, but discovering what species of shark it is may take a bit of detective work. Suppose you see a shark swimming over a coral reef in the Bahamas. Take note of its shape, its fin placement, and its tail. You might also be able to see the size and placement of its mouth (this is determined by observing how far back the mouth extends in relation to the eyes). When you are ashore, flip to the Family Key. You may be able to identify the family to which your species belongs immediately. If at first you are able only to narrow it down to a few families, turn to the page on which each is described (page numbers are given in the Family Key) and read the information. Once you have placed the shark in its family, flip through the photographs to see if you recognize your species. If you are unable to make the identification from a survey of the photographs, refer to the genus table, which follows the family introduction, and see if you can narrow it down further. Finally, read the individual species accounts and the similar species tables to see if you can identify the species. Remember to read the habitat and range descriptions, which often offer the final clue to identification.

While snorkeling or diving you may encounter a fish that is completely unknown to you. In that case, proceed in the same way as described above. Take note of as many features as you can, especially the shape. Suppose it is a highly compressed, deep-bodied, colorful fish. Start with the Family Key, where you will find a category for deep-bodied fishes with six different choices: spadefishes, butterflyfishes, angelfishes, butterfishes, triggerfishes, and filefishes. By quickly scanning the color plates of the fishes in those families (the numbers are given in the Family Key), you may be able to identify your fish. If you find a match, proceed to the family and species accounts and see if your fish matches the description. If it does not, go back and try again. When you find a species that seems to agree with both the picture and the description, check the range statement and map, and finally consult the similar species section or table to confirm your identification.

HABITATS

The tropical areas of the western Atlantic Ocean, Caribbean Sea, and Gulf of Mexico contain a wide array of marine habitats ranging from wide sweeps of sandy beaches to rugged volcanic shorelines, and from murky mangrove swamps to spectacularly colorful coral reefs. Plates 1–28 depict an assortment of these habitats, in underwater, terrestrial, and aerial views. Each color plate's caption identifies the type of habitat shown and provides its geographic location. The habitats of the region are discussed in the Introduction to this guide.

1 Sandy beach at Sandy Cay, British Virgin Islands

2 Sandy beach at Quintana Roo, Mexico

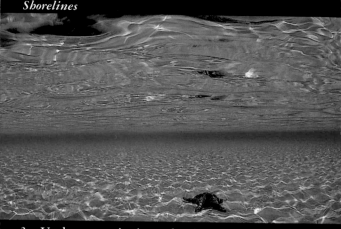

3 Underwater ripple marks, Grand Bahama Island

4 Beach with beach rock, Lighthouse Reef, Belize

5 Beach with slabs of beach rock, Bahamas

6   Volcanic shoreline, Saba, Netherlands Antilles

7   Limestone shoreline with intertidal nip, Aruba

8   Mangrove shorelines, Everglades, Florida

9   Reef flat with turtle grass, Bahamas

10   Reef flat with chord grass and mounds formed by
     burrowing invertebrates, Bahamas

11 Patch reef in reef flat area, Bahamas

12 Reef flat with halo where sea grasses have been
    cropped by herbivores, Bahamas

13 Aerial view of coral reef showing zonation, Belize

14 Back reef, on landward side of algal crest of coral reef, Grand Cayman Island

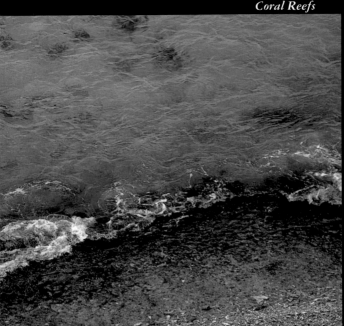

15 Algal crest of coral reef, formed of algae, debris, and coral skeletons, Bonaire

16 Rubble zone of broken coral, shells, and other debris, Honduras

17   Motu, or reef island, formed of accumulated sand and debris on Belize Barrier Reef

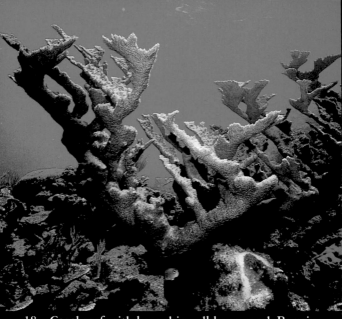

18   Coral reef with branching elkhorn coral, Bonaire

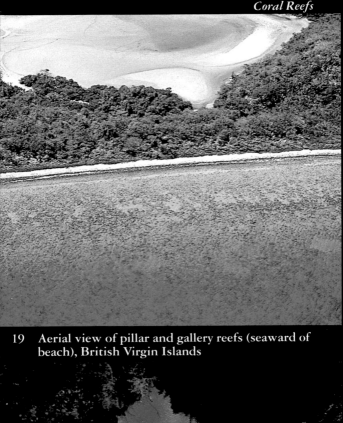

19 Aerial view of pillar and gallery reefs (seaward of beach), British Virgin Islands

20 Pillar and gallery reef, formed of interconnecting patch reefs, Cozumel

21   Groove in groove and spur zone of coral reef,
      Cayman Brac

22   Aerial view of groove and spur zone,

23 Outer slope, seaward side of coral reef, Belize

24 Drop-off, seaward of outer slope of coral reef, Bonaire

25 Outer wall, vertical drop below drop-off,
    Cayman Islands

26 Stromatolites, formed of algae and trapped
    sediments, Bahamas

27 Sunken wreck encrusted with flora and fauna,
Key Largo, Florida

28 Fish in sunken wreck, Key West, Florida

THE FAMILY KEY

The silhouettes in the following key show the typical shapes of fish families that live in the tropical western Atlantic Ocean, Caribbean Sea, and Gulf of Mexico. The silhouettes are grouped by general physical similarities, such as body shape and position; placement, number, and shape of fins; and other features. The key is designed to help you quickly determine the family a particular fish belongs to. Once the family is known, you are well on your way to identifying the species.

For each family a "typical" fish is shown in the key; this shape is repeated next to the family description in the text in Part I. Remember that in each family some genera or species may be atypical and may not resemble the silhouettes at all. For example, although most species in a family may have two separate dorsal fins, a few may have only one dorsal fin. Similarly, body shape may vary within a family, often significantly. For this reason some families have more than one silhouette and appear in more than one section of the key. This is the case with the pipefishes, which have a slender shape and tube-like snout, and the seahorses, with their unmistakable upright posture, both of the family Syngnathidae.

Remember that the key is based on superficial resemblance, which often reflects adaptations for a particular way of life. Families that look similar are not necessarily closely related. The hagfishes, for instance, though eel-like in shape, are extremely primitive jawless fishes not closely related to the eels.

How to Use the Family Key
Fishes that have very distinctive shapes are grouped first by body shape and are then further divided by characteristics such as fin shape. Other families that are not distinctively shaped are grouped mainly by fin characteristics. The scientific and common names of each family are given above the representative shape, along with the page number for the family description and the plate numbers of the family members that are shown in photographs. Once you have found the silhouette that seems to match the shape of your fish, turn to the page of the family description and read it carefully to determine if you have successfully identified the family to which your fish belongs.

**Primitive-looking.
One gill slit.
Pointed tail.**

Chimaeras
Chimaeridae
p. 246

**Shark-like.
Mouth in front
of eye.**

Whale Shark
Rhincodontidae
Pl. 29, *p. 253*

Nurse Sharks
Ginglymostomatidae
Pl. 30, *p. 254*

**Shark-like.
Eye with
nictitating
membrane.**

Cat Sharks
Scyliorhinidae
Pl. 34, *p. 261*

Requiem Sharks
Carcharhinidae
Pl. 35–45, *p. 262*

**Shark-like.
No nictitating
membrane.**

Thresher Sharks
Alopiidae
p. 257

Mackerel Sharks
Lamnidae
Pl. 32, 33, *p. 258*

**Shark-like.
No anal fin.**

Dogfish Sharks
Squalidae
Pl. 51, *p. 279*

Angel Sharks
Squatinidae
Pl. 52, *p. 280*

**Ray-like.
Tail pointed;
no caudal fin.**

Butterfly Rays
Gymnuridae
p. 291

Stingrays
Dasyatidae
Pl. 58–60, *p. 288*

Hound Sharks
Triakidae
Pl. 46, *p. 275*

Hammerhead Sharks
Sphyrnidae
Pl. 47–50, *p. 276*

Sand Tigers
Odontaspididae
Pl. 31, *p. 256*

Sawfishes
Pristidae
Pl. 53, *p. 283*

Guitarfishes
Rhinobatidae
Pl. 55, *p. 285*

Eagle Rays
Myliobatidae
Pl. 62, 63, *p. 292*

Mantas
Mobulidae
Pl. 64, *p. 295*

| Ray-like. Caudal fin present. | **Skates** Rajidae Pl. 56, 57, *p. 286* | **Electric Rays** Narcinidae Pl. 54, *p. 284* |

| Single dorsal fin; no fin spines. Large or moderate size. | **Tarpons** Megalopidae Pl. 66, *p. 301* | **Bonefishes** Albulidae Pl. 67, *p. 303* |

Pristigasterids
Pristigasteridae
p. 337

| Single dorsal fin; no fin spines. Small. | **Killifishes** Cyprinodontidae Pl. 113, *p. 395* | **Killifishes** Cyprinodontidae Pl. 114, 115, *p. 395* |

Subfamily Fundulinae   Subfamily Cyprinodontinae

Foureyed Fishes
Anablepidae
Pl. 117, *p. 401*

| Single dorsal fin. Ventral sucking disk. | **Clingfishes** Gobiesocidae Pl. 101–103, *p. 378* |

Round Stingrays
Urolophidae
Pl. 61, *p. 290*

Tenpounders
Elopidae
Pl. 65, *p. 300*

Herrings
Clupeidae
Pl. 82–84, *p. 331*

Anchovies
Engraulidae
p. 339

Livebearers
Poeciliidae
Pl. 116, *p. 399*

Rivulins
Aplocheilidae
Pl. 112, *p. 394*

male

female

Single dorsal fin. Body inflatable or enclosed in rigid, bony case. No pelvic fins.	**Boxfishes** Ostraciidae Pl. 403–407, *p. 678*	**Puffers** Tetraodontidae Pl. 408–412, *p. 680*

Small, fleshy adipose fin behind dorsal fin.	**Sea Catfishes** Ariidae Pl. 85, 86, *p. 345*	**Lizardfishes** Synodontidae Pl. 87–89, *p. 348*

Single, short dorsal fin with low spines.	**Sweepers** Pempheridae Pl. 277, *p. 538*

Single, long dorsal fin.	**Tilefishes** Malacanthidae Pl. 275, *p. 470*	**Dolphins** Coryphaenidae Pl. 276, *p. 492*

Two dorsal fins; first fin short, with no spines.	**Phycid Hakes** Phycidae Pl. 91, *p. 354*

Two dorsal fins; first fin short, spiny.	**Toadfishes** Batrachoididae Pl. 93, 94, *p. 364*	**Stargazers** Uranoscopidae Pl. 346, 347, *p. 583*

**Porcupinefishes
and Burrfishes**
Diodontidae
Pl. 413–416, *p. 684*

Lanternfishes
Myctophidae
Pl. 90, *p. 353*

Flashlightfishes
Anomalopidae
Pl. 118, *p. 403*

| Two well-developed dorsal fins nearly or completely separated. | **Snooks** Centropomidae Pl. 142, *p. 429* | **Barracudas** Sphyraenidae Pl. 278, *p. 643* |

| | **Snake Mackerels** Gempylidae *p. 644* | **Threadfins** Polynemidae *p. 582* |

| | **Mullets** Mugilidae Pl. 279, 280, *p. 579* | |

| Two dorsal fins. Small. | **Cardinalfishes** Apogonidae Pl. 182–192, *p. 463* | **Gobies** Gobiidae Pl. 351–372, *p. 612* |

| | **Bonnetmouths** Inermiidae Pl. 230, 231, *p. 517* | **Silversides** Atherinidae Pl. 106, 107, *p. 382* |

| First dorsal fin specialized: free spines. | **Cobia** Rachycentridae Pl. 272, *p. 473* | |

Bluefish
Pomatomidae
Pl. 271, *p. 472*

Jacks
Carangidae
Pl. 252–270,
p. 477

Mackerels
Scombridae
Pl. 377–383, *p. 646*

Drums
Sciaenidae
Pl. 194–202,
p. 525

Squirrelfishes
Holocentridae
Pl. 119–125,
p. 404

Goatfishes
Mullidae
Pl. 281–284, *p. 536*

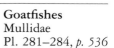

Sleepers
Eleotridae
Pl. 373, 374,
p. 638

Driftfishes
Nomeidae
Pl. 384, *p. 656*

Ariommatids
Ariommatidae
p. 658

Dragonets
Callionymidae
Pl. 348, *p. 611*

First dorsal fin specialized: sucker.

Remoras
Echeneidae
Pl. 273, 274, *p. 474*

Single dorsal fin with numerous well-developed spines in front.

Sea Basses
Serranidae
Pl. 143–174, *p. 431*

Tripletails
Lobotidae
Pl. 193, *p. 501*

Sea Chubs
Kyphosidae
Pl. 312, *p. 539*

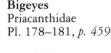

Bigeyes
Priacanthidae
Pl. 178–181, *p. 459*

Jawfishes
Opistognathidae
Pl. 349, 350, *p. 558*

Basslets
Grammatidae
Pl. 175–177, *p. 457*

Single dorsal fin with numerous spines in front. Large, smooth scales.

Wrasses
Labridae
Pl. 285–297, *p. 560*

Parrotfishes
Scaridae
Pl. 298–311, *p. 570*

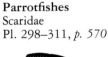

Dorsal fin spiny in front. Pelvic fin reduced to 2–4 rays. Small.

Sand Stargazers
Dactyloscopidae
p. 584

Triplefins
Tripterygiidae
Pl. 329, *p. 588*

Snappers
Lutjanidae
Pl. 203–212,
p. 493

Grunts
Haemulidae
Pl. 216–229,
p. 506

Porgies
Sparidae
Pl. 232–239, *p. 518*

Mojarras
Gerreidae
Pl. 213–215,
p. 502

Surgeonfishes
Acanthuridae
Pl. 326–328,
p. 640

Hawkfishes
Cirrhitidae
Pl. 240, *p. 557*

Damselfishes
Pomacentridae
Pl. 241–251, *p. 549*

Pikeblennies
Chaenopsidae
Pl. 330–334,
p. 589

Labrisomids
Labrisomidae
Pl. 335–340,
p. 598

**Combtooth
Blennies**
Blenniidae
Pl. 341–345, *p. 606*

Large pectoral fins.	**Scorpionfishes** Scorpaenidae Pl. 135–139, *p. 421*	**Flying Gurnards** Dactylopteridae Pl. 133, 134, *p. 420*

Body elongate. Elongate snout or lower jaw.	**Halfbeaks** Hemiramphidae Pl. 108, *p. 385*	**Needlefishes** Belonidae Pl. 109–111, *p. 391*

Body elongate. Small mouth at tip of tubular face.	**Cornetfishes** Fistulariidae Pl. 132, *p. 411*	**Pipefishes** Syngnathidae Pl. 126–129, *p. 412*

Body eel-like.	**Hagfishes** Myxinidae *p. 244*	**Freshwater Eels** Anguillidae Pl. 74, *p. 306*

	Conger Eels Congridae Pl. 80, 81, *p. 327*	**Spaghetti Eels** Moringuidae *p. 308*

Body elongate, nearly eel-like.	**Pearlfishes** Carapidae Pl. 92, *p. 357*	**Cusk-eels and Brotulas** Ophidiidae *p. 358*

Searobins
Triglidae
Pl. 140, 141,
p. 426

Flyingfishes
Exocoetidae
Pl. 104, 105,
p. 387

Swordfish
Xiphiidae
p. 652

Billfishes
Istiophoridae
Pl. 375, 376, p. 653

Trumpetfishes
Aulostomidae
Pl. 131, p. 410

Morays
Muraenidae
Pl. 68–73, p. 311

**Snake Eels and
Worm Eels**
Ophichthidae
Pl. 75–79, p. 320

False Morays
Chlopsidae
p. 309

Swamp Eels
Synbranchidae
p. 419

**Viviparous
Brotulas**
Bythitidae
p. 361

**Wormfishes and
Dartfishes**
Microdesmidae
p. 636

Cutlassfishes
Trichiuridae
p. 645

Body deep, compressed, disk-like.	**Spadefishes** Ephippidae Pl. 313, *p. 540*	**Butterflyfishes** Chaetodontidae Pl. 314–319, *p. 541*

	Triggerfishes Balistidae Pl. 392–395, *p. 670*	**Filefishes** Monacanthidae Pl. 396–402, *p. 673*

Body flattened.	**Lefteye Flounders** Bothidae Pl. 385–388, *p. 661*	**American Soles** Achiridae Pl. 389, 390, *p. 666*

Head with lure.	**Goosefishes** Lophiidae *p. 370*	**Frogfishes** Antennariidae Pl. 95–99, *p. 372*

Unusual body shapes.	**Seahorses** Syngnathidae Pl. 130, *p. 412*	**Sturgeons** Acipenseridae *p. 298*

Angelfishes
Pomacanthidae
Pl. 320–325,
p. 545

Butterfishes
Stromateidae
p. 659

Tonguefishes
Cynoglossidae
Pl. 391, *p. 667*

Batfishes
Antennariidae
Pl. 100, *p. 376*

Molas
Molidae
Pl. 417, *p. 686*

THE THUMB TAB KEY

The table on the following pages provides a key to the photographs of the fish species. The photographs have been arranged in 21 groupings according to the taxonomic relationships of the fishes, and mainly follow the same sequence as the species descriptions in the text in Part II. The fishes in the very large order Perciformes have been organized within that group by their overall shapes.

One family silhouette illustration has been chosen to represent each of the 21 groups. These silhouettes appear on the thumb tabs at the left-hand edge of each double page of color plates, providing a quick and convenient index to the color section.

The Thumb Tab Key serves as a visual index to the color plates. In the key, the silhouette that represents the group appears in the left-hand column. The silhouettes of all the families that are included in that group are on the right, along with their common names and plate numbers. The Bass-like Fishes, for instance, are represented by the silhouette of the sea bass family; the drums and the grunts, among other families, are also included in this group.

Thumb Tab	Family	Typical Shape
Sharks	Whale Shark Pl. 29	
	Nurse Sharks Pl. 30	
	Sand Tigers Pl. 31	
	Mackerel Sharks Pl. 32, 33	
	Cat Sharks Pl. 34	
	Requiem Sharks Pl. 35–45	
	Hound Sharks Pl. 46	
	Hammerhead Sharks Pl. 47–50	
	Dogfish Sharks Pl. 51	
	Angel Sharks Pl. 52	
Batoids	Sawfishes Pl. 53	
	Electric Rays Pl. 54	
	Guitarfishes Pl. 55	

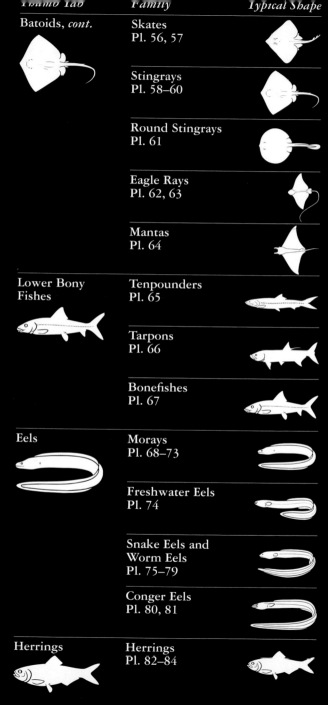

Thumb Tab	Family	Typical Shape
Batoids, *cont.*	Skates Pl. 56, 57	
	Stingrays Pl. 58–60	
	Round Stingrays Pl. 61	
	Eagle Rays Pl. 62, 63	
	Mantas Pl. 64	
Lower Bony Fishes	Tenpounders Pl. 65	
	Tarpons Pl. 66	
	Bonefishes Pl. 67	
Eels	Morays Pl. 68–73	
	Freshwater Eels Pl. 74	
	Snake Eels and Worm Eels Pl. 75–79	
	Conger Eels Pl. 80, 81	
Herrings	Herrings Pl. 82–84	

Thumb Tab	Family	Typical Shape
Catfishes, Lizardfishes, and Kin	Sea Catfishes Pl. 85, 86	
	Lizardfishes Pl. 87–89	
	Lanternfishes Pl. 90	
Hakes, Anglerfishes, Clingfishes, and Kin	Phycid Hakes Pl. 91	
	Pearlfishes Pl. 92	
	Toadfishes Pl. 93, 94	
	Frogfishes Pl. 95–99	
	Batfishes Pl. 100	
	Clingfishes Pl. 101–103	
Flyingfishes, Silversides, Killifishes, and Kin	Flyingfishes Pl. 104, 105	
	Silversides Pl. 106, 107	
	Halfbeaks Pl. 108	
	Needlefishes Pl. 109–111	

Thumb Tab	Family	Typical Shape
Flyingfishes, Silversides, Killifishes, and Kin, *cont.*	Rivulins Pl. 112	
	Killifishes, subfamily Fundulinae Pl. 113, 115	
	Killifishes, subfamily Cyprinodontinae Pl. 114	
	Livebearers Pl. 116	
	Foureyed Fishes Pl. 117	
Flashlightfishes and Squirrelfishes	Flashlightfishes Pl. 118	
	Squirrelfishes Pl. 119–125	
Pipefishes, Trumpetfishes, and Kin	Pipefishes Pl. 126–129	
	Seahorses Pl. 130	
	Trumpetfishes Pl. 131	
	Cornetfishes Pl. 132	
Flying Gurnards and Scorpionfishes	Flying Gurnards Pl. 133, 134	
	Scorpionfishes Pl. 135–139	
	Searobins Pl. 140–141	

Thumb Tab	Family	Typical Shape
Perciformes: Bass-like Fishes	Snooks Pl. 142	
	Sea Basses Pl. 143–174	
	Basslets Pl. 175–177	
	Bigeyes Pl. 178–181	
	Cardinalfishes Pl. 182–192	
	Tripletails Pl. 193	
	Drums Pl. 194–202	
	Snappers Pl. 203–212	
	Mojarras Pl. 213–215	
	Grunts Pl. 216–229	
	Bonnetmouths Pl. 230, 231	
	Porgies Pl. 232–239	
	Hawkfishes Pl. 240	
	Damselfishes Pl. 241–251	

Thumb Tab	Family	Typical Shape
Perciformes: Jack-like Fishes	Jacks Pl. 252–270	
	Bluefish Pl. 271	
	Cobia Pl. 272	
	Remoras Pl. 273, 274	
	Tilefishes Pl. 275	
	Dolphins Pl. 276	
	Sweepers Pl. 277	
Perciformes: Barracudas, Mullets, and Goatfishes	Barracudas Pl. 278	
	Mullets Pl. 279, 280	
	Goatfishes Pl. 281–284	
Perciformes: Wrasses and Parrotfishes	Wrasses Pl. 285–297	
	Parrotfishes Pl. 298–311	

Thumb Tab	Family	Typical Shape
Perciformes: Angelfish-like Fishes	Sea Chubs Pl. 312	
	Spadefishes Pl. 313	
	Butterflyfishes Pl. 314–319	
	Angelfishes Pl. 320–325	
	Surgeonfishes Pl. 326–328	
Perciformes: Blenny-like Fishes	Triplefins Pl. 329	
	Pikeblennies Pl. 330–334	
	Labrisomids Pl. 335–340	
	Combtooth Blennies Pl. 341–345	
	Stargazers Pl. 346, 347	
	Dragonets Pl. 348	
	Jawfishes Pl. 349, 350	

Thumb Tab	Family	Typical Shape
Perciformes: Goby-like Fishes	**Gobies** Pl. 351–372	
	Sleepers Pl. 373, 374	
Perciformes: Mackerel-like Fishes	**Billfishes** Pl. 375, 376	
	Mackerels Pl. 377–383	
	Driftfishes Pl. 384	
Flatfishes	**Lefteye Flounders** Pl. 385–388	
	American Soles Pl. 389, 390	
	Tonguefishes Pl. 391	
Filefishes, Puffers, Molas, and Kin	**Triggerfishes** Pl. 392–395	
	Filefishes Pl. 396–402	
	Boxfishes Pl. 403–407	
	Puffers Pl. 408–412	
	Porcupinefishes and Burrfishes Pl. 413–416	
	Molas Pl. 417	

SHARKS

Sharks are powerful cartilaginous fishes, often prized by sport fishermen. They are mostly white to gray, and have a characteristic fusiform shape, an asymmetrical tail, an inferior mouth, and five to seven pairs of gill slits on each side. Some species of sharks are quite small (2–5 feet/60–150 cm long), though most are about 10 to 15 feet (3–4.5 m) long, and one or two can exceed 30 feet (10 m) in length. Most sharks must swim constantly to keep from sinking and to force water over the gills for respiration. Although certain sharks are peaceable, others can be extremely aggressive. All sharks are best viewed from a safe distance.

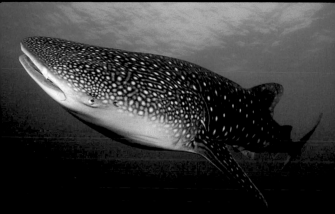

29   Whale Shark, 40′, *p. 253*

30   Nurse Shark, 13′, *p. 254*

31   Sand Tiger, 10′, *p. 256*

32 White Shark, 21′, *p. 259*

33 Shortfin Mako, 13′, *p. 260*

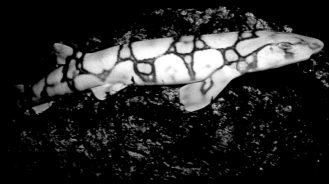

34 Chain Dogfish, 19″, *p. 261*

35   Tiger Shark, 23′, *p. 263*

36   Lemon Shark, 11′, *p. 264*

37   Atlantic Sharpnose Shark, 3′8″, *p. 265*

38 Blue Sharks, 13′, *p. 266*

39 Oceanic Whitetip Shark, 13′, *p. 269*

40 Silky Shark, 11′, *p. 270*

41 Night Shark, 9′, *p. 271*

42 Reef Shark, 10′, *p. 271*

43 Sandbar Shark, 10′, *p. 272*

44　Bull Shark, 11′, *p. 273*

45　Blacktip Shark, 8′4″, *p. 274*

46　Smooth Dogfish, 5′, *p. 275*

47 Great Hammerhead, 20′, *p. 277*

48 Scalloped Hammerhead, 14′, *p. 277*

49 Scalloped Hammerhead, *p. 277*

50   **Bonnethead**, 5′, *p. 278*

51   **Cuban Dogfish**, 3′7″, *p. 280*

52   Atlantic Angel Shark, 5′, *p. 281*

BATOIDS

Batoids constitute a major group of bottom-dwelling cartilaginous fishes that includes skates, rays, sawfishes, and mantas. Most are easily recognized by their flattened, disk-like bodies and their wing-like pectoral fins, although a few species are shark-like in shape. The mouth is on the under-side of the body, and the eyes are on the upper side. While most species are small to moderate in size, with disks about 1½ to 3 feet (50–100 cm) wide, the Manta can reach a width of 22 feet (6.7 m). Several types of batoids, including stingrays, have dangerous spines, and electric rays can give electric shocks.

53 Smalltooth Sawfish, 20′, *p. 283*

54 Lesser Electric Ray, 17¾″, *p. 285*

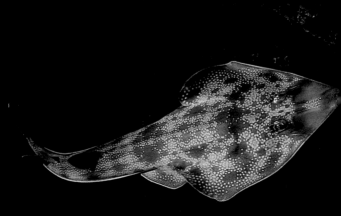

55 Atlantic Guitarfish, 30″, *p. 285*

56 Roundel Skate, 21″, *p. 286*

57 Clearnose Skate, 3′, *p. 287*

58 Bluntnose Stingray, *w.* 3′, *p. 289*

59 Southern Stingray, *w. 5', p. 288*

60 Southern Stingray buried in sand, *p. 288*

61 Yellow Stingray, *w. 14", p. 290*

62 Spotted Eagle Ray, *w. 9′, p. 293*

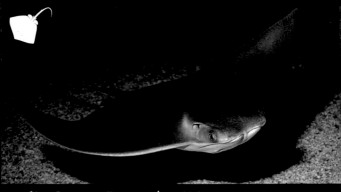

63 Cownose Ray, *w. 7′, p. 294*

64 Manta (with Remora below eye), *w. 22′, p. 295*

LOWER BONY FISHES

The fishes in this group—the Ladyfish, the Tarpon, and the Bonefish—are among the more primitive of the bony fishes and are actually the closest relatives of the eels (although they do not resemble eels as adults, their larval stages are very similar). These fishes are slender and elongate, have a single dorsal fin, and lack fin spines. The Ladyfish and the Tarpon, very closely related, have a bony structure between the lower jaws called a gular plate. The Bonefish lacks the gular plate and has a conical snout with which it roots in soft bottoms in search of small invertebrates. All three species are highly prized game fishes. The Tarpon is the largest, reaching record weights in excess of 280 pounds (128 kg), and the Bonefish record is close to 20 pounds (9 kg). The Ladyfish, although reaching only about 6 pounds (2.7 kg), is a strong fighter

65   Ladyfish, 3′3″, *p. 300*

66   Tarpon, 8′, *p. 302*

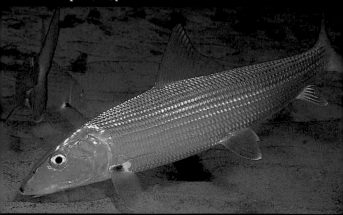

67   Bonefish, 31″, *p. 303*

EELS

While all eels have a characteristically elongate, snake-like shape, they vary significantly in size, coloration, and habitat. Moray eels are usually large and boldly patterned, and are often seen peering out of coral reefs and baring their fearsome-looking teeth, while small, dull-colored Brown Garden Eels can be seen by the dozens poking their heads out of burrows, forming a living garden on the sandy ocean floor. All eels lack pelvic fins. In most species the dorsal and anal fins are continuous with the caudal fin, and the tail ends in a point. Nearly all species are scaleless. Some eels have sharp teeth and may bite a diver poking into dark holes in the reef, but most are harmless to humans.

68   Chain Moray, 28″, *p. 313*

69   Viper Moray, 35″, *p. 314*

70   Goldentail Moray, 22″, *p. 315*

71   **Green Moray,** *6', p. 315*

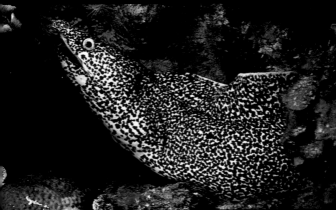

72   **Spotted Moray,** *3'3", p. 316*

73   **Purplemouth Moray,** *34", p. 317*

74   American Eels, 4′, *p. 306*

75   Speckled Worm Eel, 13¾″, *p. 322*

76   Goldspotted Eel, 3′7″, *p. 323*

77 Sharptail Eel, 31″, *p. 324*

78 Spotted Snake Eel, 7′, *p. 325*

79 Blackspotted Snake Eel, 28″, *p. 324*

80   Brown Garden Eels, 19″, *p. 329*

81   Manytooth Conger, 29″, *p. 329*

HERRINGS

Herrings, a group that includes pilchards, shads, and sardines, are moderately small, compressed, silvery fishes with a single dorsal fin and no fin spines. Most have enlarged scales, called scutes, along the belly, and some have fleshy tabs on the shoulder region. Herrings travel in large schools, and many are migratory, entering fresh water to spawn in large numbers. The closely related anchovies (not pictured here), also small, silvery schooling fishes, have protruding conical snouts, very large mouths, and only a single scute between the pelvic fins; most species have a bright silver stripe along each side of the body.

82   Dwarf Herring, 2½″, *p. 333*

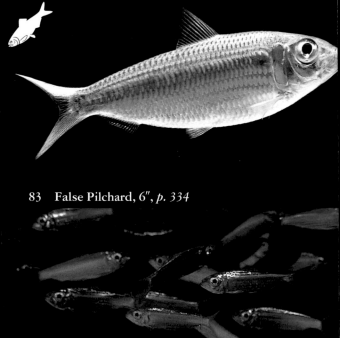

83   False Pilchard, 6″, *p. 334*

84   Redear Sardine, 4″, *p. 334*

CATFISHES, LIZARDFISHES, and KIN

The fishes of this group—the catfishes, lizardfishes, and lanternfishes—share a common feature, a small, fleshy adipose fin behind the dorsal fin. Catfishes are bottom dwellers with prominent whisker-like barbels on the head, smooth skin, forked tails, and hardened, spine-like rays at the front of the dorsal and pectoral fins. Most catfishes live in fresh water, but a few live in estuaries and coastal areas. Lizardfishes are characterized by a pointed, scaly head and conspicuous teeth that give them a reptilian aspect. They often rest motionless on the bottom. Lantern-fishes are small, dark-colored fishes with light-producing organs called photophores on their heads and bodies. They live in deep seas at mid-water level and are usually seen at night, when they travel up to the surface to feed.

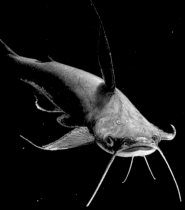

85 Gafftopsail Catfish, 3′3″, *p. 346*

86 Hardhead Catfish, 14″, *p. 347*

87 Sand Diver, 15″, *p. 349*

88 Red Lizardfish, 6″, *p. 350*

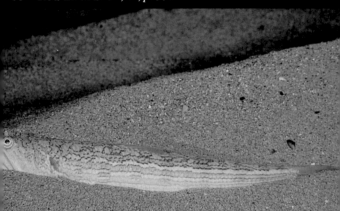

89 Snakefish, 10″, *p. 351*

90 Metallic Lanternfish, 2⅜″, *p. 353*

HAKES, ANGLERFISHES, CLINGFISHES, and KIN

This grouping includes a diverse variety of fishes—phycid hakes, pearlfishes, toadfishes, anglerfishes, and clingfishes—united by internal technical features that are beyond the scope of this field guide. Outwardly they vary greatly in shape and features; most lack spines in their fins. Phycid hakes have two or three dorsal fins—the first one quite short and the second very long—a long anal fin, and long-rayed pelvic fins situated far forward on the underside of the body. Pearlfishes are elongate fishes with no pelvic fins; single, long-based dorsal and anal fins; and pointed tails. Most pearlfishes live as inquilines inside such invertebrates as sea cucumbers. Toadfishes are bottom-dwelling, slow-moving fishes with broad heads, large mouths, and two or three strong spines in front of the long soft dorsal fin. Some toadfishes have venom glands associated with the dorsal fin spines. Anglerfishes, including the frogfishes and the batfishes, have the first dorsal spine modified into a small rod and lure—called an illicium and an esca—with which they lure prey within swallowing distance. They are often colorful and highly camouflaged. Clingfishes are small fishes with a sucker-like disk on the belly with which they attach themselves to rocks or plants. They may be more closely related to dragonets and blennies than to the other fishes grouped here.

91 Southern Hake, 12″, *p. 355*

92 Pearlfish, 8″, *p. 357*

93 Gulf Toadfish, 12″, *p. 366*

94   Coral Toadfish, 9½″, *p.* 367

95   Longlure Frogfish, 4⅜″, *p.* 372

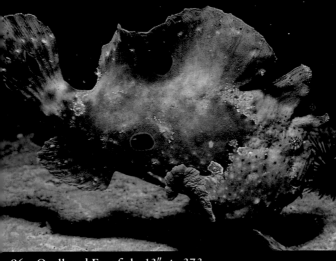

96　Ocellated Frogfish, 13″, *p. 373*

97　Dwarf Frogfish, 1⅜″, *p. 374*

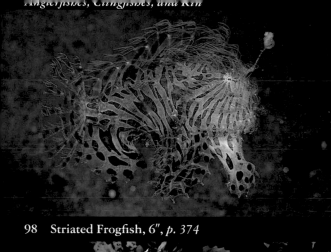

98 Striated Frogfish, 6″, *p. 374*

99 Sargassumfish, 5½″, *p. 375*

100 Shortnose Batfish, 9½″, *p. 377*

101   Red Clingfish, 1⅜″, *p. 379*

102   Skilletfish, dorsal view, 3⅛″, *p. 380*

103   Skilletfish, *p. 380*

FLYINGFISHES, SILVERSIDES, KILLIFISHES, and KIN

The fishes in the following plates—flyingfishes, silversides, halfbeaks, needlefishes, rivulins, killifishes, livebearers, and foureyed fishes—are surface-feeding fishes that are united by technical internal characteristics. Silversides, small fishes that travel in large schools, have large eyes, small oblique mouths, and two dorsal fins; most have a bright silver stripe along the side. Flyingfishes, halfbeaks, and needlefishes are all long, slender fishes with a single dorsal fin. Flyingfishes have short jaws and enlarged pectoral—and sometimes pelvic—fins that enable them to glide through the air. Halfbeaks have an elongate lower jaw, and needlefishes have very long, beak-like upper and lower jaws; both often skip along the surface of the water but never sustain flight as the flyingfishes do. Rivulins, killifishes, and livebearers, which are mostly freshwater fishes, are small and have a single dorsal fin far back on the body and a rounded or squared-off tail fin. Foureyed fishes, which have the dorsal fin even farther back on the body, have eyes divided into an upper and a lower part, providing them with simultaneous aerial and underwater vision.

104   Spotfin Flyingfish, 12″, *p. 388*

105   Juvenile four-winged flyingfish, *p. 388*

106   Reef Silversides, 4″, *p. 383*

107   Hardhead Silverside, 4″, *p. 383*

108   Ballyhoo, 15¾″, *p. 386*

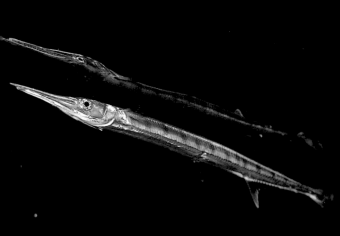

109   Flat Needlefish, 3′7″, *p. 392*

110   Atlantic Needlefish, 24″, *p. 392*

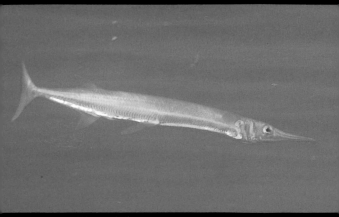

111   Houndfish, 4′4″, *p. 393*

112　Mangrove Rivulus, 2⅜″, *p. 395*

113　Gulf Killifish, 7″, *p. 396*

114　Sheepshead Minnow ♂, 3⅛″, *p. 398*

115 Diamond Killifish ♂, 1⅝″, *p. 398*

116 Pike Killifish ♀, 5½″, *p. 400*

117 Striped Foureyed Fish, 12″, *p. 402*

FLASHLIGHTFISHES
and SQUIRRELFISHES

The fishes of this group have large eyes, prominent fin spines, and very rough scales. Flashlightfishes are usually black and have a prominent light-producing organ beneath each eye. Squirrelfishes, mainly red in color, have very spiny dorsal fins, and most have spines on the head.

118   Atlantic Flashlightfish, 5⅛", *p. 403*

119   Squirrelfish, 12", *p. 405*

120   Longspine Squirrelfish, 10″, *p. 406*

121   Longjaw Squirrelfish, 7″, *p. 407*

122   Dusky Squirrelfish, 7″, *p. 407*

123   Reef Squirrelfish, 4″, *p. 408*

124   Cardinal Soldierfish, 5″, *p. 408*

125   Blackbar Soldierfish, 8¼″, *p. 409*

PIPEFISHES, TRUMPETFISHES, and KIN

The fishes of this group—pipefishes, seahorses, trumpetfishes, and cornetfishes—are all elongate, with tiny mouths at the ends of tube-shaped heads. Trumpetfishes, cornetfishes, and pipefishes are slender and elongate, while seahorses have an unmistakable, curling, upright profile with a horse-like head. Trumpetfishes have a row of free dorsal spines, similarly shaped dorsal and anal fins opposite each other, and a bluntly pointed tail. Cornetfishes have a long, slender filament at the end of the tail. Seahorses and pipefishes, though dissimilar in shape, both have bony rings encircling the body, and lack pelvic fins and fin spines. Seahorses have curling, prehensile tails and no caudal fins, while pipefishes have small but distinct tail fins.

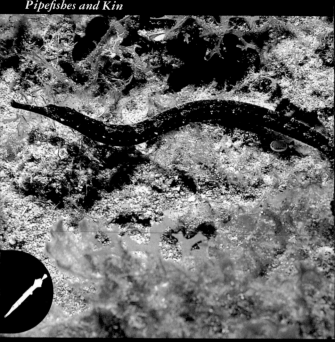

126 Dusky Pipefish, 9¾", *p. 415*

127 Gulf Pipefish, 7⅛", *p. 415*

128 Sargassum Pipefish, 7⅛″, *p. 416*

129 Whitenose Pipefish, 8¼″, *p. 416*

130   Lined Seahorse, 6″, *p. 414*

131   Trumpetfish, 30″, *p. 410*

132   Bluespotted Cornetfish, 6′6″, *p. 411*

FLYING GURNARDS
and SCORPIONFISHES

These fishes—of two separate orders—are grouped together because of a shared characteristic: a strut of bone that extends from the eye to the preopercle. The flying gurnards are bottom dwellers with enormously expanded pectoral fins and a head encased in bony armor. Scorpionfishes have large, spiny heads, usually with deep pits and ridges, and large, fan-like pectoral fins. Searobins, members of the scorpionfish order, have grooves and pits in the superficial bones of the head, deeply notched dorsal fins, and enlarged, wing-like pectoral fins with the lower rays free and extended; they use these finger-like rays to walk along the sea floor and poke about for food.

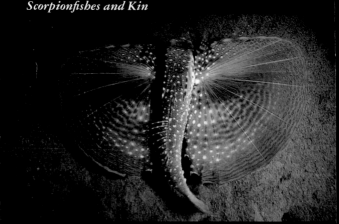

133 Flying Gurnard, 17¾″, *p. 420*

134 Flying Gurnard, *p. 420*

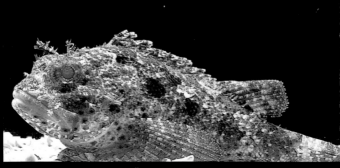

135 Barbfish, 6⅜″, *p. 422*

136   Mushroom Scorpionfish, 4⅜″, *p. 424*

137   Spotted Scorpionfish, 13¾″, *p. 424*

138   Spotted Scorpionfish, display behavior, *p. 424*

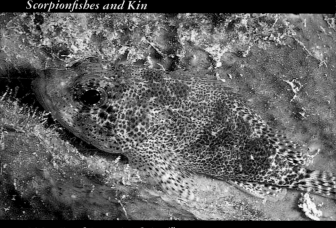

139   Reef Scorpionfish, 4″, *p. 425*

140   Horned Searobin, 5⅛″, *p. 426*

141   Bandtail Searobin, 9″, *p. 427*

PERCIFORMES:
BASS-LIKE FISHES

This diverse group of spiny-rayed fishes includes the snooks, sea basses, groupers, basslets, bigeyes, cardinalfishes, tripletails, drums, snappers, mojarras, grunts, bonnetmouths, porgies, hawkfishes, and damselfishes. In these fishes the spiny part of the dorsal fin is well developed, the pelvic fin is far forward and typically has one spine and five soft rays, and the anal fin generally has one to three spines. They range from the large robust groupers to the slender bonnetmouths. Snooks, tripletails, most groupers, and some snappers are large; bigeyes, many snappers, grunts, porgies, mojarras, and most drums are moderate size; and basslets, cardinalfishes, damselfishes, some sea basses, and the region's one species of hawkfish are small.

142 Common Snooks, 4′3″, *p. 430*

143 Sand Perch, 12″, *p. 434*

144 Butter Hamlet, 4″, *p. 435*

145   Shy Hamlet, 4″, *p. 435*

146   Barred Hamlet, 4″, *p. 436*

147   Indigo Hamlet, 5¾″, *p. 436*

148   Black Hamlet, 4″, *p. 437*

149   Lantern Bass, 2″, *p. 437*

150   Belted Sandfish, 4″, *p. 438*

151 Tobaccofish, 5⅛″, *p. 439*

152 Harlequin Bass, 3⅛″, *p. 440*

153 Chalk Bass, 2⅜″, *p. 440*

154 Coney, bicolor phase, 15″, *p. 442*

155 Graysby, 9″, *p. 442*

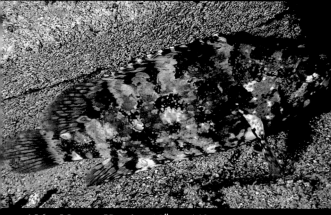

156 Mutton Hamlet, 10″, *p. 443*

157 Marbled Grouper, 32", *p. 443*

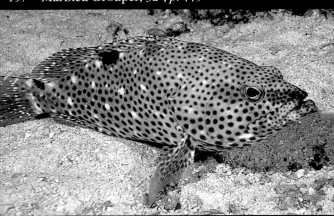

158 Rock Hind, 24", *p. 444*

159 Red Hind, 24", *p. 445*

160   Jewfish (with Sharksucker), 8′, *p. 445*

161   Red Grouper, 3′, *p. 446*

162   Misty Grouper juvenile, 3′3″, *p. 447*

163 Snowy Grouper, 4′, *p. 447*

164 Nassau Grouper, 3′3″, *p. 448*

165 Creole-fish, 12″, *p. 449*

166   Black Grouper, *4′3″, p. 450*

167   Yellowfin Grouper, *3′, p. 450*

168   Yellowmouth Grouper, *30″, p. 451*

169   Tiger Grouper, 3′3″, *p. 452*

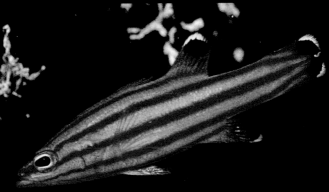

170   Peppermint Bass, 3½″, *p. 453*

171   Reef Bass, 3″, *p. 453*

172   Freckled Soapfish, 6″, *p. 454*

173   Greater Soapfish, 9″, *p. 455*

174   Spotted Soapfish, 5⅛″, *p. 455*

175 Royal Gramma, 3⅛″, *p. 457*

176 Blackcap Basslet, 4″, *p. 458*

178   Short Bigeye, 10½″, *p. 461*

179   Bulleye, 19¾″, *p. 461*

180   Glasseye Snapper, 10″, *p. 462*

181 Bigeye, 15″, *p. 463*

182 Oddscale Cardinalfish, 2⅜″, *p. 464*

183 Flamefish, 2¾″, *p. 465*

184   Whitestar Cardinalfish, 2⅜″, *p. 465*

185   Barred Cardinalfish, 5⅛″, *p. 466*

186   Belted Cardinalfish, 2½″, *p. 466*

187 Pale Cardinalfish, 4⅛″, p. 467

188 Sawcheek Cardinalfish, 2⅜″, p. 467

189 Freckled Cardinalfish, 3½″, p. 468

190   **Dusky Cardinalfish,** 3⅛″, *p. 468*

191   **Conchfish,** 3⅛″, *p. 469*

192   **Blackfin Cardinalfish,** 3⅛″, *p. 469*

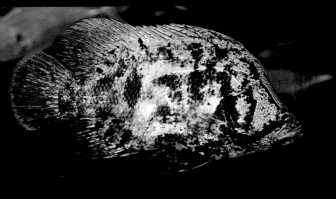

193   Tripletail, 3′, *p. 501*

194   Jackknife-fish, 10″, *p. 527*

195   Spotted Drum, 10″, *p. 528*

196   Cubbyu, 10″, *p. 529*

197   High-hat, 9″, *p. 529*

198   Gulf Kingfish, 18″, *p. 530*

199 Atlantic Croaker, 20″, p. 530

200 Reef Croaker, 8″, p. 531

201 Black Drum, 5′6″, p. 531

202   Red Drum, 4′11″, *p. 532*

203   Lane Snapper, 19¾″, *p. 494*

204   Mahogany Snapper, 19″, *p. 495*

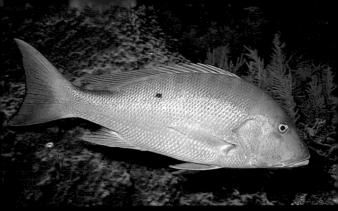

205 Mutton Snapper, 31″, *p. 495*

206 Schoolmaster, 25″, *p. 496*

207 Dog Snapper, 30″, *p. 497*

208 Gray Snapper, 35", *p. 497*

209 Cubera Snapper, 5', *p. 498*

210 Red Snapper, 3'3", *p. 498*

211 Yellowtail Snapper, 28″, *p. 499*

212 Vermilion Snapper, 24″, *p. 500*

213 Spotfin Mojarra, 8″, *p. 503*

214   Bigeye Mojarra, 7″, *p. 504*

215   Yellowfin Mojarra, 15½″, *p. 504*

216   Black Margate, 24″, *p. 507*

217   Porkfish, 15″, *p. 508*

218   Margate, 16½″, *p. 508*

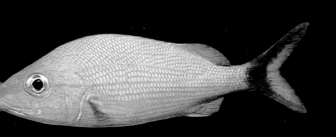

219   Tomtate, 10″, *p. 509*

220 Caesar Grunt, 13¾″, *p. 510*

221 Smallmouth Grunt, 9″, *p. 510*

222 French Grunt, 8¾″, *p. 511*

223 Spanish Grunt, 17″, *p. 511*

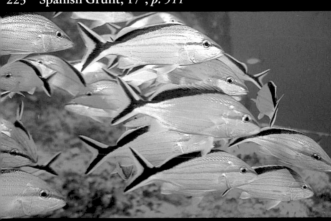

224 Cottonwick, 13″, *p. 512*

225 Sailors Choice, 16¼″, *p. 513*

226   White Grunt, 17¾", *p. 513*

227   Bluestriped Grunt, 14¾", *p. 514*

228   Striped Grunt, 8¾", *p. 515*

229 Pigfish, 15″, *p. 515*

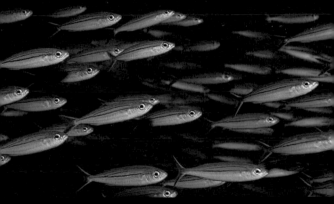

230 Bonnetmouths, 4½″, *p. 518*

231 Boga, 9″, *p. 517*

232   Sheepshead, 3′, *p. 519*

233   Sea Bream, 12¾″, *p. 520*

234   Pinfish, 15¾″, *p. 520*

235   **Grass Porgy**, 8¾″, *p. 521*

236   **Saucereye Porgy**, 14″, *p. 522*

237   **Knobbed Porgy**, 16¾″, *p. 522*

238   Jolthead Porgy, 27″, *p. 523*

239   Silver Porgy, 11″, *p. 524*

240   Redspotted Hawkfish, 3⅛″, *p. 558*

241   Yellowtail Damselfish, 8″, *p. 550*

242   Sergeant Major, 8″, *p. 551*

244   Blue Chromis, 4¾″, *p. 552*

245   Brown Chromis, 5⅜″, *p. 552*

246　Dusky Damselfish, *6″, p. 553*

247　Longfin Damselfish, *5″, p. 554*

248 Threespot Damselfish, 5″, *p. 555*

249 Cocoa Damselfish, 5″, *p. 555*

250 Beaugregory juvenile, 4", *p. 556*

251 Bicolor Damselfish, 4", *p. 557*

PERCIFORMES: JACK-LIKE FISHES

This section includes the jacks, tilefishes, remoras, dolphins, sweepers, the Bluefish, and the Cobia. These fishes are generally jack-like in shape, with a narrow caudal peduncle and a flaring caudal fin. Except for the tilefishes, which build nests on the sea floor, the fishes in this section are not closely associated with the bottom. Jacks are moderate-size to large fishes, usually silvery and often compressed. Most have the first two anal spines separated from the rest of the fin, and large scutes in some part of the lateral line. The Cobia is a large, rugged fish with a protruding lower jaw, a flat head, and short dorsal spines not connected by membrane. It resembles some remoras, but remoras are smaller and have a sucker-like disk on the head with which they sometimes attach themselves to sharks and other large fishes. The most common species of tilefish in our area is very elongate, with filaments at the tips of the caudal fin in larger fish. The Bluefish is a large, streamlined schooling fish often encountered close to shore. Dolphins are colorful fishes of open water with a deep head that gives them a superficial resemblance to the mammals of the same name. Sweepers are small coppery fishes that live in caves around reefs and rocky shorelines.

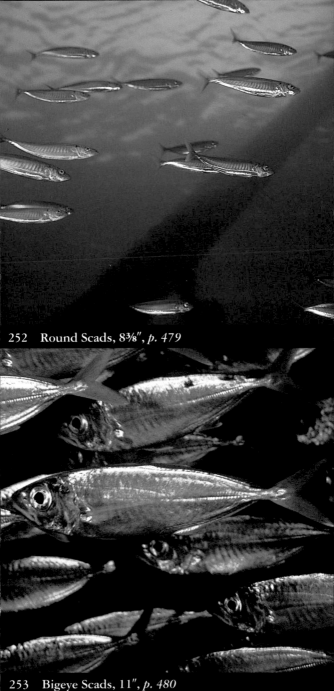

252 Round Scads, 8⅜″, *p. 479*

253 Bigeye Scads, 11″, *p. 480*

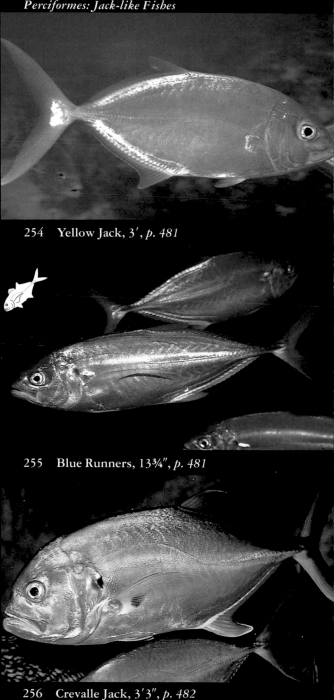

254   Yellow Jack, 3′, *p. 481*

255   Blue Runners, 13¾″, *p. 481*

256   Crevalle Jack, 3′3″, *p. 482*

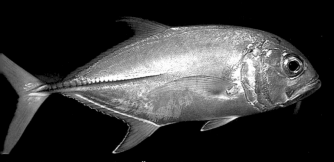

257 Horse-eye Jack, 31″, *p. 483*

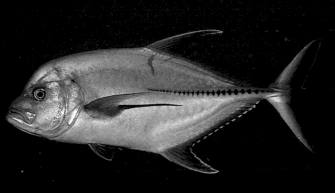

258 Black Jack, 3′, *p. 483*

259 Bar Jack, 15¾″, *p. 484*

260   Atlantic Bumper, 10¼", *p. 485*

261   African Pompano juvenile, 4′3″, *p. 485*

262   Atlantic Moonfish, 13″, *p. 486*

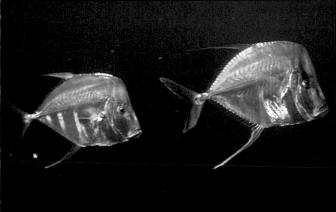

263   Lookdowns, 15¾″, *p. 487*

264   Lookdown juvenile, *p. 487*

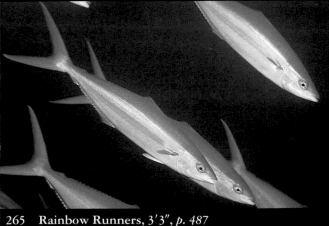

265   Rainbow Runners, 3′3″, *p. 487*

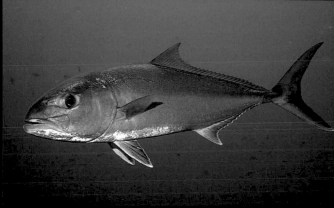

266   Greater Amberjack, 5′, *p. 488*

267   Leatherjack, 12″, *p. 489*

268   Florida Pompano, 13¾″, *p. 490*

269   Permits, 3′3″, *p. 490*

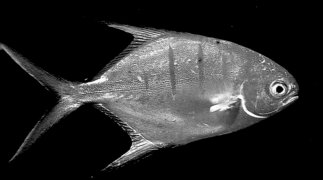

270   Palometa, 13¾″, *p. 491*

271   Bluefish, 3′7″, *p. 473*

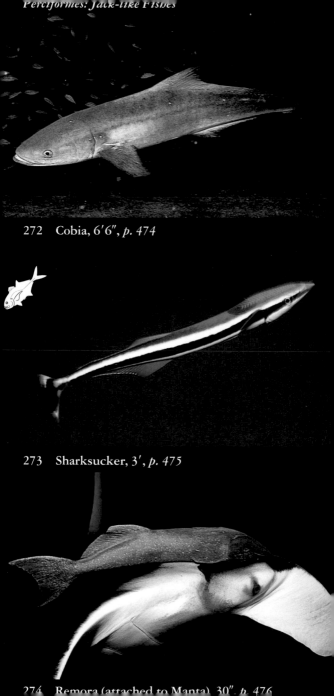

272   Cobia, 6′6″, *p. 474*

273   Sharksucker, 3′, *p. 475*

274   Remora (attached to Manta), 30″, *p. 476*

275 Sand Tilefish, 24″, *p. 471*

276 Dolphin, 6′6″, *p. 492*

277 Glassy Sweepers, 5⅜″, *p. 539*

PERCIFORMES:
BARRACUDAS, MULLETS,
and GOATFISHES

The fishes in this section are not closely related but are somewhat similar in shape, with forked tails and two dorsal fins (the first rather short) separated by a wide space. The goatfishes, distinguished by the presence of barbel-like appendages on the lower jaw, are often observed stirring up the sandy bottom with their "whiskers" in search of food. Barracudas, with their arrow-shaped bodies, are efficient and voracious predators but are generally regarded as harmless to humans. They are probably related to the mackerels. Some authorities now believe that the mullets, which have the pelvic fins placed behind the pectoral fins, are primitive spiny-rayed fishes that should not even be included in the order Perciformes.

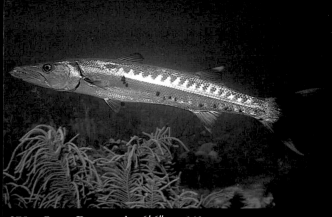

278 Great Barracuda, 6′6″, *p. 643*

279 Striped Mullets, 24″, *p. 580*

280 White Mullets, 15″, *p. 580*

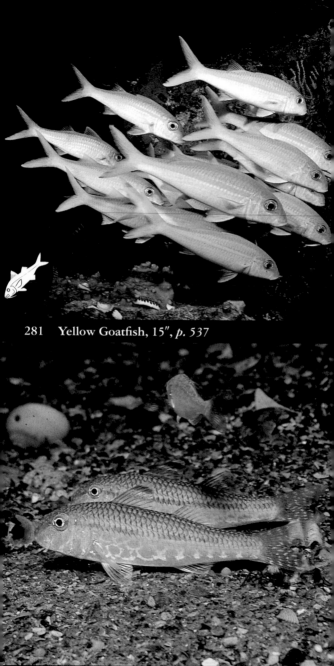

281   Yellow Goatfish, 15″, *p. 537*

282   Dwarf Goatfish, 12″, *p. 538*

283   Spotted Goatfish, night coloration, 12″, *p.* 537

284   Spotted Goatfish (Bar Jack in background), *p.* 537

PERCIFORMES:
WRASSES and PARROTFISHES

Wrasses and parrotfishes fit the image of the quintessential "tropical fish," and are favorites of divers. They are colorful, abundant, and easy to observe on coral reefs and adjacent sea-grass areas. All have a single long dorsal fin and large scales. The parrotfishes have fused teeth that give the impression of bird-like beaks, while the wrasses have canine teeth that are never beak-like. Many wrasses and parrotfishes have distinctive color phases at various times of their lives, including juveniles, young adults (both sexes) and older females, and terminal males, or supermales. If the phase or sex of the fish is evident in the photograph, it is noted in the caption.

285 Spanish Hogfish, 15", *p. 562*

286 Spotfin Hogfish, 9½", *p. 562*

287 Hogfish, 3', *p. 563*

288   Creole Wrasse, 12″, *p. 563*

289   Bluehead supermale, 5″, *p. 564*

290   Slippery Dick, 7″, *p. 565*

291 Yellowcheek Wrasse supermale, 8″, *p. 565*

292 Yellowhead Wrasse supermale, 6½″, *p. 566*

293 Clown Wrasse supermale, 5½″, *p. 566*

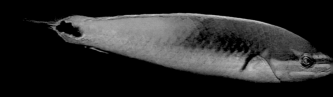

294   Rainbow Wrasse supermale, 3¾″, *p. 567*

295   Blackear Wrasse young adult, 6¾″, *p. 568*

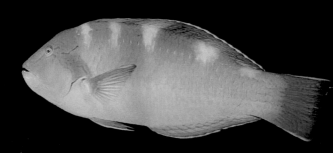

296   Puddingwife adult, 20″, *p. 568*

297   Pearly Razorfish, 7⅛″, *p. 569*

298   Queen Parrotfish adult, 20″, *p. 572*

299   Queen Parrotfish supermale, *p. 572*

300　Bluelip Parrotfish, 4″, *p. 571*

301　Princess Parrotfish juvenile, 13″, *p. 573*

302　Princess Parrotfish supermale, *p. 573*

303 Striped Parrotfish supermale, 11″, *p. 573*

304 Blue Parrotfish adult, 3′, *p. 574*

305 Rainbow Parrotfish adult, 4′, *p. 575*

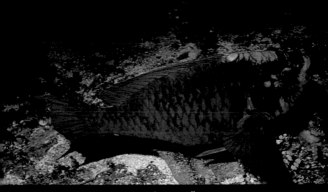

306   Midnight Parrotfish, 30″, *p.* 576

307   Bucktooth Parrotfish, 8″, *p.* 576

308   Redhead Parrotfish adult, 11″, *p.* 577

309 Redtail Parrotfish supermale, 18″, *p. 577*

310 Stoplight Parrotfish supermale, 22″, *p. 578*

311 Stoplight Parrotfish ♀, *p. 578*

PERCIFORMES:
ANGELFISH-LIKE FISHES

All of the fishes in this section—sea chubs, spadefishes, butterflyfishes, angelfishes, and surgeonfishes—are highly compressed, deepbodied fishes. Butterflyfishes and angelfishes, colorful and easily approached by divers, are favorite subjects for underwater photographers. The one spadefish that occurs in our area is a strikingly marked species often seen in schools along the outer edge of the reef. Sea chubs are herbivores that often feed near the top of the reef. Surgeonfishes, named for the protective spine on either side of the caudal peduncle, are also herbivores. They travel in large schools, grazing like herds of cattle.

312   Bermuda Chub, 13¾", *p. 540*

313   Atlantic Spadefish, 3′, *p. 541*

314   Longsnout Butterflyfish, 2⅞", *p. 542*

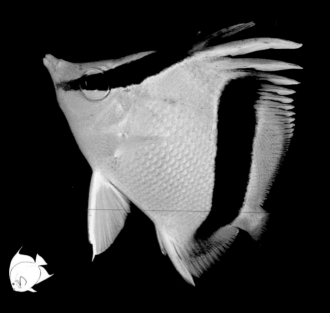

315 Bank Butterflyfish, 6″, *p. 542*

316 Foureye Butterflyfish, 2⅞″, *p. 543*

317 Spotfin Butterflyfish, 8″, *p. 543*

318 Reef Butterflyfish, 6″, *p. 544*

319   Banded Butterflyfish, 6″, *p. 544*

320   Cherubfish, 2″, *p. 546*

321 Blue Angelfish, 17½", *p. 546*

322 Queen Angelfish, 12", *p. 547*

323　Rock Beauty, 12″, *p. 547*

324　French Angelfish, 13½″, *p. 548*

325　Gray Angelfish, 14″, *p. 549*

326　Ocean Surgeon, 14″, *p. 641*

327　Doctorfish, 13¾″, *p. 642*

328　Blue Tang, 14″, *p. 642*

PERCIFORMES: BLENNY-LIKE FISHES

This section includes many species of tiny to small bottom-dwelling fishes that are somewhat similar in shape and generally have fan-shaped tails: triplefins, pikeblennies, labrisomids, combtooth blennies, stargazers, dragonets, and jawfishes. The triplefins, pikeblennies, labrisomids, and combtooth blennies, all generally referred to as blennies, are especially abundant on coral reefs and hard bottoms. Most have only two or three rays in the pelvic fin. Stargazers spend much of their time buried in the sand with only their eyes showing. Dragonets, which inhabit sandy bottoms, are characterized by dorsally bulging eyes, small, protrusible mouths, and large hook-like spines on the preopercle. The jawfishes have large heads and mouths; they characteristically live in holes they build in sand or in rocky crevices that they augment by placing stones around the openings.

329 Redeye Triplefin, 1¼", *p. 588*

330 Papillose Blenny, 1⅝", *p. 590*

331 Bluethroat Pikeblenny ♂, 5″, *p. 592*

332 Arrow Blenny, 1½″, *p. 593*

333 Wrasse Blenny, 4″, *p. 593*

334   Sailfin Blenny ♂, 2″, *p. 594*

335   Hairy Blenny, 7″, *p. 598*

336   Saddled Blenny, 3″, *p. 600*

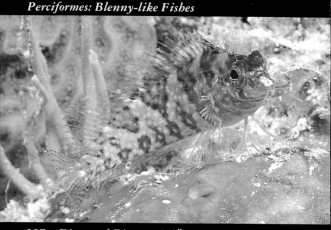

337   Diamond Blenny, 2½″, *p. 601*

338   Rosy Blenny, 2⅛″, *p. 601*

339   Goldline Blenny, 2¼″, *p. 602*

340   Blackcheek Blenny, 1¼", *p. 603*

341   Striped Blenny, 3⅛", *p. 607*

342   Redlip Blenny, 4½", *p. 608*

343   Seaweed Blenny, 3⅜″, *p. 608*

344   Molly Miller, 4″, *p. 609*

345   Tessellated Blenny, 1⅞″, *p. 609*

346 Southern Stargazer, 17¼", *p. 583*

347 Southern Stargazer buried in sand, *p. 583*

348 Lancer Dragonet, 4½", *p. 612*

349   Yellowhead Jawfish, 4″, *p. 559*

350   Banded Jawfish ♂, 8″, *p. 559*

PERCIFORMES:
GOBY-LIKE FISHES

Gobies and sleepers are a diverse group of mostly small fishes (only a few gobies reach more than a few inches in length) with two dorsal fins. Sleepers have separate pelvic fins, but most gobies have the inner rays of the pelvic fins joined by a membrane to form a cup-like sucking disk. There are more species of gobies than of any other marine fish; they inhabit almost every part of coral reefs and other tropical marine habitats.

351   Frillfin Goby, 6″, *p. 616*

352   Colon Goby, 1½″, *p. 617*

353   Bridled Goby, 2¼″, *p. 618*

354 Peppermint Goby, 1¼″, *p. 619*

355 Masked Gobies, 1⅜″, *p. 619*

356 Lyre Goby, 3″, *p. 623*

357   Darter Goby, 2⅞″, *p. 620*

358   Freshwater Goby, 3⅛″, *p. 620*

359   Dash Goby, 2″, *p. 621*

360 Tiger Goby, 2", *p. 628*

361 Leopard Goby, ⅝", *p. 628*

362 Greenbanded Goby, 1¾", *p. 629*

363   Neon Goby, 1⅝″, *p. 629*

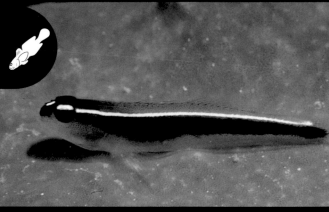

364   Yellowline Goby, 1⅞″, *p. 630*

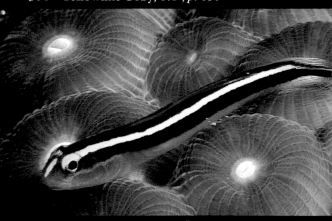

365   Yellowprow Goby, 1¼″, *p. 630*

366   Sharknose Goby, 1⅛″, p. 631

367   Goldspot Goby, 2¾″, p. 617

369   Orangespotted Goby with shrimp, 3¼", *p. 626*

370   Clown Goby, 2¾", *p. 627*

371   Rusty Goby, 1⅝", *p. 623*

372 Hovering Goby, 3½″, *p. 624*

373 Fat Sleeper, 15″, *p. 639*

374 Bigmouth Sleeper, 24″, *p. 639*

MACKEREL-LIKE FISHES

The fishes of this group—mackerels, billfishes, and driftfishes—are generally mackerel-like in shape, with slender caudal peduncles and forked tails. Powerful open-water fishes, the mackerels and billfishes are moderate-size to large, torpedo shaped, and usually blue above and silvery white below. Billfishes are the ultimate big-game fishes, characterized (as their name implies) by a long, pointed, spike-like upper jaw. Mackerels, including tunas, have deeply forked tails and a row of isolated finlets behind the dorsal and anal fins. Driftfishes are rather small, open-water fishes often associated with floating sargassum weed.

375 Sailfish, 7′10″, *p. 654*

376 Blue Marlin, 12′1″, *p. 655*

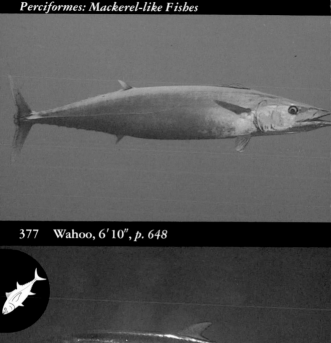

377   Wahoo, 6′10″, *p. 648*

378   Spanish Mackerel, 28″, *p. 649*

379   Cero, 34″, *p. 649*

380　Bullet Mackerel, 19¾″, *p. 650*

381　Little Tunny, 3′3″, *p. 650*

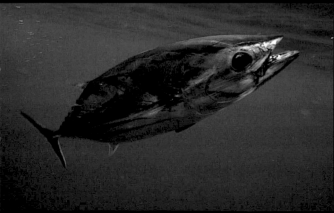

382　Skipjack Tuna, 3′3″, *p. 651*

383   Yellowfin Tuna, 6′10″, *p. 651*

384   Man-of-War Fish, 8″, *p. 657*

FLATFISHES

These fishes—flounders, soles, and tongue-fishes—have flattened bodies with the eyes on one side of the head. They swim sideways and rest on the bottom on their sides. Lefteye flounders have the eyes on the left side of the body, while American soles have the eyes on the right side. Tonguefishes have the eyes on the left but, unlike soles and flounders, have continuous dorsal, anal, and caudal fins ending in a point at the tail.

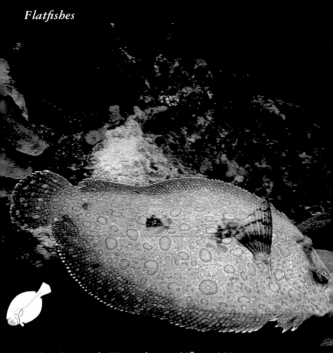

385 Peacock Flounder, 17¾", *p. 662*

386 Eyed Flounder, 6", *p. 663*

387   Ocellated Flounder, 10″, *p. 663*

388   Gulf Flounder, 28″, *p. 664*

389   Hogchoker, 8″, *p. 666*

390   Naked Sole, 8½″, *p. 667*

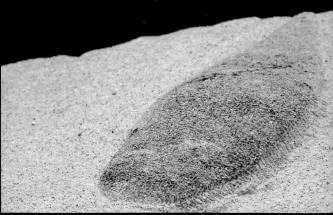

391   Blackcheek Tonguefish, 7½″, *p. 668*

TRIGGERFISHES, FILEFISHES, PUFFERS, MOLAS, and KIN

The fishes of this group—the triggerfishes, filefishes, boxfishes, puffers, porcupinefishes, burrfishes, and molas—are among the most bizarre-looking in the sea. They are tough skinned, usually have specialized teeth, and have either no pelvic fins or very small ones. Triggerfishes and filefishes are compressed and deep bodied, with a reduced number of dorsal spines. Triggerfishes have a large first dorsal spine that can be locked into an upright position by the second spine, and thick, plate-like scales all over the head and body. Filefishes have inconspicuous, bristle-like scales. Boxfishes are named for the shell-like cuirass of modified scales that encases the body. Puffers, porcupinefishes, and burrfishes have bristles or spines on the body and are able to inflate themselves with water or air. The puffers have the teeth fused into two plates in each jaw, while the other two groups have a single beak-like plate in each jaw. Molas, represented in our region by the Ocean Sunfish, are enormous, very deep-bodied fishes that look as if they have been chopped in half just behind the very high dorsal and anal fins. They often drift on the surface on their sides.

392 Queen Triggerfish, 19¾″, *p. 670*

393 Black Durgon, 19¾″, *p. 671*

394   Sargassum Triggerfish, 10", *p. 672*

395   Ocean Triggerfish, 24", *p. 672*

396   Whitespotted Filefish, 18″, *p. 674*

397   Orangespotted Filefish, 8″, *p. 674*

398 Fringed Filefish, 8", *p. 675*

399 Slender Filefish, 3½", *p. 675*

400   Planehead Filefish, 8″, *p. 676*

401   Pygmy Filefish, 8″, *p. 676*

402 Scrawled Filefish, 3′, *p. 677*

403 Scrawled Cowfish, 13¾″, *p. 678*

404 Honeycomb Cowfish, 14″, *p. 679*

405 Smooth Trunkfish, 12″, *p. 679*

406   Spotted Trunkfish, 17¾″, *p. 679*

407   Trunkfish, 17¾″, *p. 680*

408   Sharpnose Puffer, 4⅜″, *p. 681*

409   Sharpnose Puffer, *p. 681*

410   **Amazon Puffer,** 5″, *p. 682*

411   **Bandtail Puffer,** 6″, *p. 682*

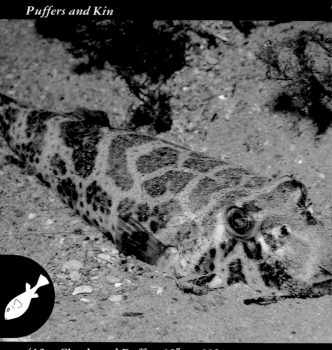

412   **Checkered Puffer,** 12″, *p. 682*

413   **Balloonfish,** 19¾″, *p. 684*

414 Porcupinefish, 24″, *p. 685*

415 Bridled Burrfish, 15″, *p. 685*

416   Web Burrfish, 12″, *p. 686*

417   Ocean Sunfish, 10′, *p. 687*

PART II
SPECIES ACCOUNTS

In the following pages, fish species that have a photograph are given a complete description with habitat notes and a range map. The number preceding each species description corresponds to the number of the photograph (occasionally two photographs) of that species in the color plates section. Families for which no photographs were available have a complete description and detailed illustration of a representative species.

In addition to the individual species illustrations, there are a variety of drawings of special features. Many of the shark descriptions are accompanied by illustrations of an upper tooth (on the left) and a lower tooth (on the right).

HAGFISHES
Class Myxini

The most primitive of all living fishes, hagfishes are the only vertebrates whose body fluids are isotonic, the same density as sea water. Because hagfishes have few hard parts, their presence in the fossil record is poor, but comparison with certain heavily armored fossil agnathan fishes indicates that their ancestors arose in late Precambrian times, more than 550 million years ago.

Hagfishes are similar to the lampreys in that both are jawless, lack paired fins, and have a single anterior nostril. They were once grouped together in the class Agnatha, but recent research has revealed that lampreys are more closely related to jawed vertebrates than to hagfishes. (Lampreys have a mainly northern distribution and are not covered in this guide.)

ORDER MYXINIFORMES

Hagfishes lack jaws and have primitive inner ears and rudimentary eyes without a lens or iris. A single nostril at the tip of the snout opens internally in the mouth and conducts water to the gills for breathing. They have two pairs of barbels at the sides of the nostril and one or two pairs at the sides of the mouth. Their bodies are eel-like and scaleless, without dorsal fins or paired fins. The anal fin is connected to the caudal fin, and the caudal fin extends forward onto the dorsal surface. A conspicuous row of mucous pores runs along the lower side of the body. Hagfishes generate large amounts of slime and are often called slime eels. They produce about 30 large, yolky ovoid eggs, each in a horny shell with hooked anchor filaments.

Unlike the lampreys, which use the jawless mouth as a suction disk to hold on to prey, the hagfishes use the mouth for biting, working the teeth on the tongue against the teeth on the roof of the mouth. Hagfishes feed on carrion, including the bodies of fishes and other animals that sink into deep water. They enter their prey through body orifices and also use a bizarre knot-tying behavior to tear out pieces of flesh. They tie themselves in a knot near the tail, and by pulling their own body through the knot gain leverage to pull their mouth—and the flesh in its grasp—away from the prey. In some areas where they are common, hagfishes may destroy fishes that have been caught in nets, leaving only skin and bones.

HAGFISHES
Family Myxinidae

There is only one family of hagfishes, Myxinidae, with six genera and about 43 species, all of which live in salt water. Nine species of two genera are known from deep waters of our region.

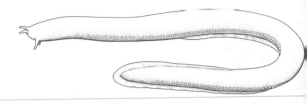

Caribbean Hagfish

Caribbean Hagfish
Myxine mcmillanae

Identification: Scaleless, eel-like, gray body; contrasting white head. 7 internal gill pouches connected to *single gill opening on each side*. No dorsal fin, but anal fin joined to caudal fin, which in turn extends onto dorsal surface. No paired fins. No jaws. 101–119 mucous pores along each side. TL to 18½" (47 cm).

Habitat: Burrows in mud in very deep water, usually at depths of 2,300–4,950' (700–1,500 m).

Range: Puerto Rico and Virgin Islands.

Notes: Although most people are unlikely to see a Caribbean Hagfish because of the great depths at which it lives, we have included it here as a representative of an important major group of jawless fishes.

Similar Species: Species of hagfishes are distinguished by technical characteristics such as number and shape of teeth on tongue. *Eptatretus* species, which also live over soft bottoms in deep water in w Atlantic and West Indian region, have 5–14 pairs of external gill openings.

CARTILAGINOUS FISHES
Chondrichthyes

Among the fishes with jaws there are two major lines. One, Chondrichthyes, is the cartilaginous fishes and includes the sharks, sawfishes, skates, rays, and chimaeras. The other, Osteichthyes, includes all of the bony fishes.

The first cartilaginous fishes were probably shark-like creatures that arose some 450 million years ago in Paleozoic times. Between 400 million and 350 million years ago, sharks diverged rapidly into a number of diverse groups, two of which dominated the world's oceans until about 150 million years ago, when they were replaced by modern sharks. Some modern sharks date back at least 180 million years, and most modern groups can be traced back about 100 million years.

As the name suggests, the cartilaginous fishes have no bone in their skeletons, although there may be considerable calcification of the cartilage. The fin rays are fine, numerous, and horny, made of keratin rather than bone. The tail is *heterocercal,* with the spinal column extending into the caudal fin. While a few lack scales, most cartilaginous fishes have *placoid* scales, which consist of a flat base with one or more spines; each scale has a dentine core and an enamel surface, like a tiny tooth.

Male cartilaginous fishes have modifications of the pelvic fins called *claspers* that are used to transfer sperm to the female's reproductive tract. Fertilization occurs internally in all cartilaginous fishes. Some species are *oviparous,* laying fertilized eggs enclosed in a horny shell; other species, termed *ovoviviparous,* retain the eggs internally until the embryonic period is complete, although the eggs receive no nutrients from the mother; still others are *viviparous,* with the embryo receiving nutrients from the mother through a placenta that develops from the membrane of the yolk sac and attaches to the uterine wall.

Chondrichthyes is split into two subgroups (some ichthyologists consider them classes, others subclasses): Holocephali, the chimaeras, which are characterized by a pointed tail and a single pair of gill openings; and Elasmobranchii, the sharks and batoids (skates and rays), which have five to seven pairs of gill slits and usually an upturned, asymmetrical tail, with the spinal column extending into the larger upper lobe of the caudal fin. Some rays have no caudal fin at all, with the tail simply ending in a blunt point.

CHIMAERAS
Subclass Holocephali
Order Chimaeriformes

Chimaeras are distinctive cartilaginous fishes with a single gill opening low on each side of the body and prominent sensory grooves or canals on the head that look like sewn seams. At the front of the first of their two dorsal fins is a stout spine with a posterior groove filled with venom glands. The heterocercal tail is symmetrical and pointed (thus chimaeras are measured in total length [TL], from the tip of the snout to the tip of the tail). Chimaeras have distinctive plate-like teeth with sharp cutting edges, two pairs in the upper jaw and a single pair in the lower jaw. Male chimaeras have a unique spiny, club-shaped appendage between the eyes as well as pelvic claspers similar to those of sharks and rays. Chimaeras lay eggs enclosed in a horny shell with a distinctive flange around its edge.

Currently three families of chimaeriforms—Chimaeridae, Callorhynchidae, and Rhinochimaeridae—are recognized, encompassing six genera and 33 species worldwide. All three families are represented in our region, but most are deepwater fishes beyond the scope of this guide.

CHIMAERAS
Family Chimaeridae

Members of this family have bluntly rounded snouts, while members of the other two chimaeriform families have elaborate elongate, pointed, or hoe-shaped snouts. These chimaeras have pointed tails, and the lateral-line canals are open grooves.

The family Chimaeridae has two genera and about 23 species, five of which are known from our area. Most chimaeras live in very deep water.

Cuban Ratfish
Chimaera cubana

Identification: A weird-looking, tapering fish, with *a blunt, rounded snout, seam-like sensory grooves on head, large pectoral fin, and a long, sharp spine at front of first dorsal fin.* Silver gray above, shading to white below. Tip of first dorsal and upper half of second dorsal blackish. Anal and caudal fins black. Pectoral and pelvic

Cuban Ratfish

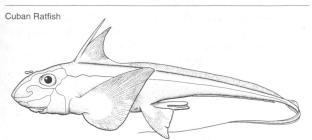

fins have dark edges. *Separate anal fin present, its tip not extending past level of end of second dorsal fin.* Males have curved, spiny, club-shaped appendage between eyes. Lateral-line canals in open grooves. TL to about 30″ (75 cm).

Habitat: Apparently bottom dwelling, in water 1,200–3,000′ (360–900 m) deep.

Range: Known only from Cuba, off Matanzas.

Notes: Included here as a representative of a major group of cartilaginous fishes, the Cuban Ratfish lives in very deep water and is unlikely to be seen by divers.

Similar Species: There are 4 other chimaeras from deep waters of continental slope (none has an official common name): *Hydrolagus alberti* and *H. mirabilis* have short snouts and long, filamentous caudal fins. *Rhinochimaera atlantica* and *Neoharriotta carri* (both family Rhinochimaeridae) have long, pointed snouts.

SHARKS AND BATOIDS
Subclass Elasmobranchii

Sharks, sawfishes, skates, and rays are cartilaginous fishes with five to seven pairs of *gill slits.* The gill slits are on the sides of the head more or less above the pectoral fins in sharks and usually on the underside of the head in the skates, rays, and sawfishes (collectively called batoids). In sharks the leading edge of the pectoral fin is free, while in batoids it is attached to the side of the head, forming a round or diamond-shaped disk. These distinctions are rather superficial, and recent studies have shown that some sharks may be more closely related to rays than to other families of sharks.

Elasmobranchs typically have placoid scales, which look like tiny teeth, although some, including the electric rays, lack scales altogether. They have no *swim bladders,* which are gas- or fat-filled sacs found in bony fishes, but large oily livers provide buoyancy in some species. The intestinal tract is rather short, but its absorptive surface is increased by either a series of rings, a central flap, or a spiral valve in the large intestine. The upper jaws of elasmobranchs are not fused to the skull, and in many sharks both jaws can be thrust outward for more efficient biting. Because elasmobranchs usually have pointed or strongly asymmetrical tails, their size is measured as total length (TL), i.e., from the tip of the snout to the tip of the longest part of the tail.

About 360 species of sharks and more than 450 species of batoids are known worldwide, but there are indications that a considerable number of species remain to be described. Authorities currently recognize eight orders of sharks but disagree about the classification of batoids. Some combine all batoids in a single order, Rajiformes—which includes the sawfishes, electric rays, guitarfishes, skates, stingrays, butterfly rays, eagle rays, and mantas—as we have done here. Others, however, recognize four separate orders for these groups. Batoids are further discussed in the section on the order Rajiformes, following the sharks species accounts. Sharks as a group are discussed in detail below.

SHARKS

Sharks are immediately recognizable by their characteristic elongate or fusiform shape, five to seven pairs of gill slits, and, in most species, strongly asymmetrical heterocercal tail. Because they have no swim bladders, most sharks that live in open water need to swim constantly to avoid sinking. Many also have a poorly developed mechanism for pumping water over the gills and must rely on their motion to force water over them. In sharks, as in other cartilaginous fishes, the inner parts of the pelvic fins of males are modified into elaborate *claspers* that are used for transferring sperm to the reproductive tract of the females.

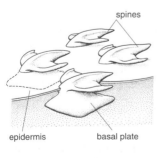

spines

epidermis   basal plate

PLACOID SCALES

Scales

The body of all sharks is covered with a thick skin that is embedded with *placoid scales,* each of which resembles a tiny tooth, with a basal plate and one or more spines. These spines may be conical or they may flare at the tips to form a secondary plate-like shield, which in turn may have keels or other features.

The Head

In most species of sharks the snout protrudes and the mouth is *inferior,* that is, on the underside of the head. The relative length and shape of the snout and the position and size of the mouth can be important features in shark identification. The nostrils, also on the underside of the head, are in front of the mouth. In some sharks there is a distinct flap, called the *nasal flap,* on the edge of the nostril. There may also be *nasoral grooves* between the mouth and each nostril. Grooves called *labial furrows* extend forward from the corners of the mouth; those on the lower jaw are the lower labial furrows, and those at the sides of the mouth are the upper labial furrows. Their relative length is important for distinguishing some species.

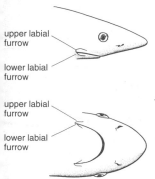

upper labial furrow

lower labial furrow

upper labial furrow

lower labial furrow

LABIAL FURROWS

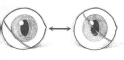

NICTITATING MEMBRANE

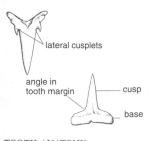

lateral cusplets

angle in tooth margin

cusp

base

TOOTH ANATOMY

Some sharks have a small opening behind each eye called a *spiracle.* Most skates and rays have large spiracles through which water is taken in and pumped over the gills for respiration, but in sharks the spiracles are vestigial and not used for breathing. The carcharhiniform sharks (order Carcharhiniformes) have an inner eyelid called the *nictitating membrane* that can be pulled across the eye, probably to provide extra protection to the eye while the sharks are feeding.

Teeth

Shark teeth are extremely variable, and are very important keys to shark identification. Sometimes they differ little from the scales of the body, often they are blade-like, and in a few species they are needle-like. Blade-like teeth can be triangular or they may have a central cusp that is differentiated from the base of the tooth by a definite angle in the tooth margin. Some sharks have teeth with multiple central cusps, and some have small accessory cusps called *lateral cusplets* on

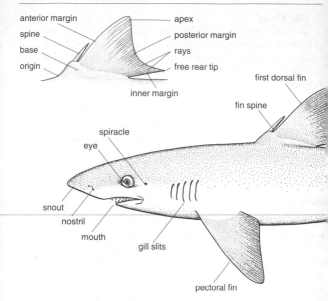

each side of the main cusp. The teeth of the upper and lower jaws can be quite different, and the teeth at the front of the jaw may differ from those at the sides in shape and, especially, in size. Shark teeth are regularly replaced, and several rows of replacement teeth are present at all times.

Gills

Sharks have five to seven gill slits on each side of the head. These are mostly in front of and above the level of the pectoral fins, although the ventral (or lower) ends of the gill slits may extend below the pectoral fin. Some sharks have the last two or even three gill slits over the pectoral fin base. All of the coastal sharks in our area have five pairs of gill slits; the sharks of our region with six or seven gill slits live in very deep water.

Fins

As in bony fishes, the dorsal, anal, and caudal fins (also called the *median fins*) of sharks are located on the midline of the body and do not occur in pairs, and the pectoral and pelvic fins do occur in pairs, one of each on each side of the body. The place where a fin joins the body is called the *base* of the fin; the forward-most limit of the fin base is referred to as its *origin.* The length of a fin is the measure of its base, while the height of a fin is determined by the length of its rays. Thus, a fin can be both short (with a short base) and high (with long rays) or both long and low.

PARTS OF A SHARK

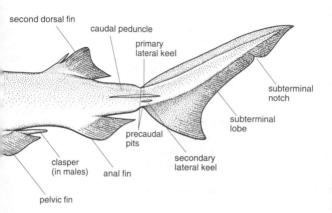

second dorsal fin

caudal peduncle

primary
lateral keel

subterminal
notch

subterminal
lobe

secondary
lateral keel

precaudal
pits

clasper
(in males)

anal fin

pelvic fin

The leading edge of a fin is called its *anterior margin.* The edge formed by the tips of the fin rays is referred to as the *posterior margin.* The rear edge of the fin, bounded by its last ray, is called its *inner margin,* and the tip of the last ray is the *free rear tip* of the fin.

The size, shape, and placement of the fins are important for identifying sharks. Key features are the number of dorsal fins (one or two) and the presence or absence of an anal fin. Some sharks have strong fin *spines* at the anterior margins of the dorsal fins. The origin of the first dorsal fin (and sometimes the second), in relation to the pelvic and pectoral fins, is of particular importance in distinguishing species. The pectoral fins vary in length and width; in some species they are *falcate,* long and curved like a sickle.

Tail and Caudal Fin

Sharks have *heterocercal tails,* with the spinal column bent upward to form the upper, or dorsal, lobe of the caudal fin. The dorsal margin of the caudal fin is merely an extension of the body, and the caudal fin rays are attached to the underside of the dorsal lobe. Usually some of the rays near the tip of the upper lobe are separated by an indentation—the *subterminal notch*—to form the *subterminal lobe.* The lower lobe of the caudal fin is formed by elongate fin rays.

The slender part of the body just ahead of the caudal fin is called the *caudal peduncle.* Some strong-swimming species have prominent longitudinal ridges—referred to as *lateral keels*—on either side of the caudal peduncle; there may be shorter secondary keels above or below the main keel. Some sharks have deep grooves or squarish indentations—*precaudal pits*—at the beginning of the tail.

Shark Orders

Five of the eight orders of sharks currently recognized occur in coastal waters in our region and are included in this guide: Orectolobiformes, Lamniformes, Carcharhiniformes, Squaliformes, and Squatiniformes. Not discussed here are the order Hexanchiformes, which includes the Sixgill Shark *(Hexanchus griseus)*, the Sevengill Shark *(Notorynchus cepedianus)*, and the Frill Shark *(Chlamydoselachus anguineus)*; the order Pristiophoriformes, the sawsharks; or the order Heterodontiformes, the bullhead sharks, because they do not live in the western Atlantic or their representatives in our region occur only in deep water.

It is relatively easy to distinguish among the different shark orders. The number of dorsal fins, presence or absence of an anal fin and fin spines, and position of the mouth are key features, while some groups also have special features that distinguish them, such as more than five gill slits, nictitating membranes, or a rostrum (long, extended snout). The following table outlines key features of each order.

Shark orders

Hexanchiformes	6–7 gill slits. 1 dorsal fin. Anal fin. No fin spines.
Heterodontiformes	2 dorsal fins, each with 1 stout spine. Anal fin.
Orectolobiformes	2 dorsal fins. Anal fin. No spines. Mouth far forward, entirely in front of eye.
Lamniformes	2 dorsal fins. Anal fin. No spines. Mouth fairly far back, at least partly below eye.
Carcharhiniformes	2 dorsal fins. Anal fin. No spines. Mouth far back, at least partly below eye. Nictitating membranes.
Squaliformes	2 dorsal fins, each with stout spine. No anal fin.
Pristiophoriformes	Long, flat, tapering toothed rostrum with pair of long barbels. 2 dorsal fins. No anal fin.
Squatiniformes	Flattened, ray-like body. 2 dorsal fins. No anal fin.

ORDER ORECTOLOBIFORMES

This order encompasses seven families with 33 species that are collectively referred to as carpet sharks. Two families, Rhincodontidae (the Whale Shark) and Ginglymostomatidae (the nurse sharks), have representatives in our region, although some authorities recognize the two as a single family (Rhincodontidae). Carpet sharks have an anal fin and two dorsal fins but no fin spines. The mouth is very far forward on the snout, entirely in front of the eyes. They have five pairs of gill openings.

WHALE SHARK
Family Rhincodontidae

The Whale Shark is so distinctive that it usually is placed in its own family. A huge shark, it is the largest fish in the world. Its gills are modified for straining plankton from water as it passes through the gill openings.

29 Whale Shark
Rhincodon typus

Identification: A huge shark with a flat, blunt head, a humped back, and distinct longitudinal ridges on back and upper sides. *Blue-gray, fading to white or yellow below, with rectangular grid of contrasting white spots and lines on dorsal surface. Mouth terminal and very large; teeth small and scale-like.* Caudal fin almost symmetrical, with high lower lobe (with long rays), and no subterminal lobe or notch. Prominent keel on either side of caudal peduncle. TL to at least 40′ (12 m); unconfirmed reports to 60′ (18 m).

Habitat: Near surface in open oceans, but sometimes seen cruising near outer wall along coral reefs.

Range: Occurs in all warm seas; records along Atlantic coast from New York to Brazil. Rare in Bermuda.

Notes: Despite its size, the Whale Shark is harmless to humans. It has small, scale-like teeth and feeds by filtering plankton with special sieve-like modifications of the gill bars (the structure separating the gill openings). The genus name is sometimes incorrectly spelled *Rhiniodon* or *Rhineodon.*

Similar Species: Basking Shark (*Cetorhinus maximus,* family Cetorhinidae, order Lamniformes) is similar in size but lacks flat head and humped back, has pointed nose, very long gill slits that reach well onto top of head, and nearly lunate tail, and generally is blue-gray without prominent markings. A plankton feeder, it cruises near surface in coastal waters, sometimes in schools; in w Atlantic it is usually found between Newfoundland and Florida.

NURSE SHARKS
Family Ginglymostomatidae

The nurse sharks are bottom-dwelling sharks with conspicuous barbels next to the nostrils, and small, scale-like teeth. Equipped with a more efficient gill pump than many other sharks, nurse sharks are able to rest at the bottom without moving. Eggs are retained in the uterus until they hatch; litters of 20 to 30 have been reported.

The family includes two genera and about three species; one species occurs in our region.

30 Nurse Shark
Ginglymostoma cirratum

Identification: A rather heavy-bodied shark, rich brown above, slightly paler below. Young tawny with small black spots. *Head blunt; mouth inferior. Pair of conspicuous barbels between nostrils. 2 dorsal fins, nearly equal in size, placed far back on body;* origin of first dorsal over or ahead of middle of pelvic fin base. Caudal fin has small lower lobe, well-developed subterminal lobe, and distinct subterminal notch. Caudal peduncle lacks keels on sides. No ridges on back. Minute spiracle behind eye. Teeth small, resembling slightly enlarged scales. TL to about 13' (4 m).

teeth

Habitat: Common in waters less than 40' (12 m) deep over shallow sand flats, in channels, and around coral reefs. Young may be found among prop roots of red mangroves.

Range: Bermuda; Atlantic coast from North Carolina to Florida (plus one record off Rhode Island); Gulf of Mexico, Antilles, and Caribbean to s Brazil.

Notes: The Nurse Shark often rests motionless on the ocean bottom, frequently under ledges and sometimes with its head sheltered and its tail exposed. Although its teeth are small and scale-like, the Nurse Shark has a tenacious grip, and divers who bother it risk serious skin abrasions. Nurse Sharks feed mostly on invertebrates, including spiny lobsters.

Similar Species: Lemon Shark and Sand Tiger also have dorsal fins nearly equal in size, but both have first dorsal farther forward on body, lack conspicuous barbels between nostrils, and have well-developed teeth.

ORDER LAMNIFORMES

This order includes some of the best-known predaceous sharks, such as the makos and the "Great White Shark" (its official name is actually just White Shark) made famous by the movie *Jaws*. Lamniform sharks have an anal fin and two dorsal fins but no fin spines. There are five pairs of gill slits; in some species the last two or three are over the pectoral fin base. The mouth extends backward so that its corners reach beyond the front of the eyes. A minute spiracle is usually present behind each eye. Lamniform sharks display *intra-uterine cannibalism:* One or two embryos of a litter develop faster and actually eat other embryos and undeveloped eggs while they are in the uterus.

The 15 or 16 species of lamniform fishes are assigned to seven families; four families have species in western Atlantic coastal waters and are included here (Cetorhinidae is discussed above in the Whale Shark account). We do not cover the families Mitsukurinidae (the Goblin Shark) and Megachasmidae (the Megamouth), which are rare deepwater sharks unlikely to be seen in shallow waters in our area, or Pseudocarchariidae (the Crocodile Shark), which occurs in the Pacific and the eastern Atlantic.

SAND TIGERS
Family Odontaspididae

Sand tigers are large, rather slow-moving sharks. The caudal fin is asymmetrical, with the upper lobe much longer than the lower, and there are no lateral keels on the caudal peduncle. These sharks have large, pointed teeth that are visible when the mouth is closed, giving them a fearsome appearance, although there are few documented attacks on humans. Four species are currently recognized, one of which occurs in our area.

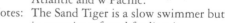

31	Sand Tiger
	Odontaspis taurus

Identification:

teeth

A rather humpbacked, heavy-bodied shark. Light brown or grayish; may have scattered small darker spots. Snout tapers to rounded point. *Teeth large, with narrow pointed central cusps and prominent lateral cusplets; visible when mouth is closed. 2 dorsal fins and anal fin about equal in size.* First dorsal fairly far back on body, closer to pelvic than pectoral origin. All gill openings short and ahead of pectoral fin. TL to about 10′ (3 m).

Habitat: Common in shallow water near shore, sometimes as deep as 630′ (190 m).

Range: Gulf of Maine to Florida, n Gulf of Mexico. One old record from Bermuda. Also from s Brazil to Argentina, and e Atlantic and w Pacific.

Notes: The Sand Tiger is a slow swimmer but is sometimes found feeding in coordinated groups that surround schools of prey, cutting off avenues of escape. It feeds on fishes smaller than itself and occasionally on invertebrates such as squids. Its conspicuous teeth give it a fearsome look, but it is not inclined to attack humans unless provoked. Eggs leave the ovaries in groups of about 20 and are retained in the reproductive tract. One individual in each uterus survives by feeding on the other eggs and embryos, reaching about 3 feet (1 m) in length by the time it is

born eight or nine months later. This
species has also been called *Eugomphodus
taurus* and *Carcharias taurus.*

Similar Species: Lemon Shark and Nurse Shark also
have dorsal fins nearly equal in size.
Nurse Shark has dorsal fins farther
back on body and conspicuous barbels
between nostrils. Lemon Shark is
more streamlined, with blunter snout
and smaller teeth that lack lateral
cusplets and are concealed when mouth
is closed.

THRESHER SHARKS
Family Alopiidae

The thresher sharks are immediately recognizable by their extremely long tails, which are longer
than the combined length of the head and body. It is be-
lieved that the tail is used to herd schooling fish into a tight
ball and then as a whip to stun the prey.

The family includes three species, two of which are found
in our area.

Bigeye Thresher

Bigeye Thresher
Alopias superciliosus

Identification: An easily identifiable shark with *an
extremely long tail and very large eyes that
extend onto top of head.* Gray above,
sharply delimited from whitish belly;
pale color of belly does not extend above
pectoral fin. Deep grooves on each side
of head above gill region. Gill openings
short, last three over pectoral fin base.
Snout moderately long and conical. TL
to 15′ (4.5 m).

Habitat: Open water, sometimes close to land.

Range: Warm seas: in w Atlantic from New York to Florida and Greater Antilles. Also Venezuela and s Brazil.

Notes: The Bigeye Thresher is an ovoviviparous species (eggs are retained in the female reproductive tract until hatching) with intrauterine cannibalism. A brood consists of only two to four young, each of which may be slightly more than 3 feet (1 m) long at birth. This shark feeds on smaller fishes, apparently herding them into a tight group before attacking. It may also use the tail to stun seabirds and other prey. Thresher sharks are not known to attack humans.

Similar Species: Thresher Shark (*A. vulpinus*) has much smaller eyes on sides of head and no grooves above gills; white color of belly extends up sides to level above pectoral fin; Newfoundland south to Florida, n Bahamas, and n Gulf of Mexico; also Pacific and Mediterranean Sea.

MACKEREL SHARKS
Family Lamnidae

In the mackerel sharks the lower lobe of the caudal fin has long rays, making the tail nearly symmetrical, and there are prominent keels on the caudal peduncle. The second dorsal and anal fins are very small. Lamnids have five pairs of rather long gill slits, all in front of the origin of the pectoral fin, and large, blade-like teeth.

The mackerel shark family consists of five species, three of which are found in our area.

Genera of family Lamnidae

Isurus	Teeth smooth; upper teeth narrow, without lateral cusplets. Body rather slender.
Carcharodon	Teeth serrate; upper teeth broadly triangular. Body chunky.
Lamna	Teeth smooth; upper teeth narrow, with lateral cusplets. Secondary keel below primary lateral keel on caudal peduncle.

32 White Shark
Carcharodon carcharias

teeth

Identification: A large, stout, spindle-shaped shark with *a pointed snout.* Blue or brownish above, turning abruptly white on lower side and onto belly; *dusky spot behind pectoral fin. Teeth serrate; upper teeth broadly triangular.* Gill openings rather large but not extending onto back or belly. Second dorsal and anal fins small. Origin of anal fin well behind second dorsal. Origin of first dorsal over free rear tip of pectoral fin. Caudal fin lunate, with upper and lower lobes nearly equal in size. Large lateral keel on each side of caudal peduncle but no secondary keels on caudal fin base. TL commonly to 17′5″ (5.3 m); maximum recorded TL 21′ (6.4 m).

Habitat: Coastal waters, usually near surface. May make long migrations across open seas.

Range: Temperate waters of all oceans. In w Atlantic records from Newfoundland to Florida, n Gulf of Mexico, Bahamas, Cuba, and Lesser Antilles. Also reports from s Brazil, Argentina, s Australia, and New Zealand.

Notes: A voracious predator known to attack humans, the White Shark (often called the Great White Shark) is sometimes considered the most dangerous shark in the world. Forty-one attacks on humans by White Sharks occurred off California between 1950 and 1982, but only four of these were fatal. This shark feeds on a variety of fish, including other sharks, as well as sea lions, birds, and sea turtles, carrion, and, occasionally, undigestible garbage. Little is known about its reproduction, although it probably retains the eggs in the uterus until they hatch; intrauterine cannibalism is likely. Females are rarely seen. The White Shark can grow quite massive—a 21-foot (6.4 m) specimen taken off Cuba weighed 7,100 pounds (3,220 kg)—but reports of a 36-foot (11 m) White Shark are certainly erroneous.

Similar Species: Mako sharks (genus *Isurus*) are similar
but have smooth-edged teeth and
more slender bodies, with first dorsal
origin well behind pectoral fin base,
and lack spot behind pectoral fin.

33 Shortfin Mako
Isurus oxyrinchus

Identification: A slender, spindle-shaped shark with a
long, acutely pointed snout and *tiny
second dorsal and anal fins.* Grayish blue
to deep blue above, shading to white on
belly; underside of snout white. *Teeth
smooth edged; upper teeth narrowly triangular.*
First dorsal origin behind free rear tip of
pectoral fin. Origin of anal fin behind
origin of second dorsal. Pectoral fin
shorter than head. Caudal peduncle
flattened, with broad keel on each side
but no secondary keel on caudal base. TL
to about 13′ (4 m).

Habitat: Offshore, near surface waters down to
about 500′ (150 m).

Range: All warm and temperate seas, from
Alaska in Pacific and British Isles in
Atlantic, south to tips of Africa, South
America, and s Australia.

Notes: The fast-swimming Shortfin Mako (like
its relative the Longfin Mako) is a prized
game fish that often jumps out of the
water when hooked. It is also a valuable
commercial species esteemed for its
high-quality flesh. A voracious predator,
the Shortfin feeds on fishes but rarely on
marine mammals. Although there are
few reported attacks on humans, it is
regarded as dangerous. Hooked makos
have been known to attack boats.

Similar Species: Longfin Mako *(I. paucus)* has pectoral fin
longer than head, underside of snout and
mouth dusky, and short secondary keels
at base of caudal fin. A tropical oceanic
species, it occurs in Gulf Stream from
New England to Florida and Cuba; also
in e Atlantic and in Pacific and w Indian
oceans. Porbeagle *(Lamna nasus),* a
temperate species that occurs outside of

our region, has first dorsal origin
above free rear tip of pectoral fin,
cusplets on teeth, and secondary keel
on caudal fin base below main keel on
caudal peduncle. White Shark, usually
larger, has serrate teeth with no cusplets.

ORDER CARCHARHINIFORMES

This is the largest order of sharks, containing nearly 200
species in eight families. Four of these families have representatives in our region. Carcharhiniforms have two dorsal
fins and an anal fin but no fin spines. The mouth extends
back to beyond the eyes. The eyes have nictitating membranes. Two families, Carcharhinidae and Sphyrnidae, have
precaudal pits.

CAT SHARKS
Family Scyliorhinidae

This is the largest family of sharks,
containing more than 100 species. Nearly a dozen species
of cat sharks occur in our area, but as they usually occur
in water more than 500 feet (150 m) deep, they are unlikely
to be seen. Members of this family have the dorsal fins
far back on the body; the origin of the first dorsal fin is over
or behind the pelvic fin base. They lack precaudal pits, and
the lower lobe of the caudal fin is only weakly developed.
There are five pairs of gill slits, the last one to three over the
pectoral fin base. Some have bold patterns of spots or dark
reticulations.

34 Chain Dogfish
Scyliorhinus retifer

Identification: A small, slender, boldly marked shark
with *a pattern of distinct black lines on a
pale brownish background;* some of these
lines surround dusky saddles, others
extend onto side as a network of fine
lines. *Origin of first dorsal fin behind free
rear tip of pelvic fin.* Snout short and
slightly flattened. Spiracle behind each
eye. Gill openings short. Teeth small,
with high central cusp and well-
developed cusplets. TL to 19″ (48 cm).

Habitat: Near and on bottom in waters
250′–1,800′ (75–550 m) deep over
continental shelf and upper continental
slope.

Range: Atlantic coast from Cape Cod to Florida
and Gulf of Mexico, and w Caribbean
from Yucatán to Nicaragua.

Notes: This species lays eggs in flat horny cases
with tendrils at the corners (similar to
the egg cases of skates) that probably get
tangled with objects on the bottom and
hold the developing eggs in place.
Nothing is known of the food habits of
the Chain Dogfish, although small
pebbles have been found in the stomachs
of individuals, suggesting that they feed
on the bottom. Other cat sharks in our
area, all of which occur in deep water,
lack reticulated color pattern.

REQUIEM SHARKS
Family Carcharhinidae

This is a family of 12 genera and 49
species of "ordinary looking" sharks; about 21 species occur
in our area. Requiem sharks have *precaudal pits,* transverse
grooves across the body that mark the beginning of the caudal fin. The dorsal fins are fairly far forward, with the first
dorsal origin in front of the pelvic fin origin. Internally they
differ from other sharks in having a *scroll valve,* which is a
longitudinal flap in the large intestine, rather than a *spiral
valve.* The Tiger Shark is ovoviviparous; all other members
of the family are viviparous, with a yolk-sac placenta.

It is difficult to distinguish many of the species of requiem
sharks. One approach is by getting to know key features:
The Tiger Shark has a unique banded pattern; the Lemon
Shark has dorsal fins almost equal in size; the Daggernose
Shark has a blade-like snout; the milk sharks (genus *Rhizoprionodon*) have the edge of the anal fin straight rather than
concave; the Blue Shark is slender and blue in color and has
long, pointed pectoral fins. The 14 regional species of requiem sharks in the genus *Carcharhinus,* characterized by a
deeply concave posterior anal fin margin, fall into two
groups—those that have a low ridge on the midline of the
back between the dorsal fins (called the *interdorsal ridge*) and
those that do not. Within these two groups identification is
made on the basis of more subtle features, such as the place-

ment of the fins, the shape of the snout, the form of the teeth, and color patterns. A table of the *Carcharhinus* species appears further below. Immediately following is a table outlining the key features of the Carcharhinidae genera.

Genera of family Carcharhinidae

Galeocerdo	Pattern of vertical bars. Snout short and blunt. Prominent lateral keels on caudal peduncle.
Negaprion	Yellowish. Body stout, snout blunt. Second dorsal fin nearly as large as first. No keels on caudal peduncle.
Rhizoprionodon	Origin of second dorsal fin well behind origin of anal fin. Posterior edge of anal fin nearly straight. No keels on caudal peduncle.
Prionace	Slender, blue, with pointed snout. Weak lateral keels on caudal peduncle.
Carcharhinus	Second dorsal fin much smaller than first, with origin over or close to level of anal origin. Posterior margin of anal fin deeply concave. No keels on caudal peduncle.
Isogomphodon	Snout long, triangular, and very flat. No keels on caudal peduncle.

35 Tiger Shark
Galeocerdo cuvier

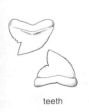

teeth

Identification: A large, heavy-bodied shark with *a striking pattern of dark gray vertical bands on a paler gray background* (less prominent in large adults). Small spiracle behind each eye. *Snout very short and blunt.* Upper labial furrows twice as long as lower, reaching forward almost to below eye. Teeth blade-like, curved, with strong serrations. Prominent interdorsal ridge between dorsal fins. Prominent lateral keels on caudal peduncle. TL to 18–23′ (5.5–7 m).

Habitat: Usually near surface to depths of 460′ (140 m).

Range: Worldwide in tropical and temperate
          seas, mainly in coastal and pelagic
          waters but also around remote islands.

Notes: The color pattern of the Tiger Shark
          makes it unmistakable. It is ovovivi-
          parous, retaining the eggs in the uterus
          until hatching. Litters are very large,
          sometimes as many as 80 young. An
          omnivorous feeder, the Tiger Shark
          consumes a variety of fishes, birds,
          mammals, and reptiles, including sea
          turtles and sea snakes. It also feeds on
          carrion and garbage, including cans,
          pieces of metal, and burlap bags. It is
          considered one of the most dangerous
          sharks and is said to be responsible for
          more attacks on humans than any other
          shark except the White Shark, possibly
          because it frequently enters very shallow
          water. This is one of the few species of
          requiem sharks that has spiracles,
          although they are not used for respiration.

36 Lemon Shark
Negaprion brevirostris

Identification: A stout brownish shark with yellow
                   overtones but no conspicuous markings.
                   Large second dorsal fin nearly same size as
                   first dorsal. First dorsal fin origin behind
                   inner corner of pectoral fin. Snout short
                   and blunt. Anal fin also large, with
                   concave outer margin. Teeth awl-like,
                   narrow, and generally smooth edged,
                   although large individuals may have
                   some serrations at base, but no lateral
                   cusplets. TL to 11′ (3.4 m).

teeth

Habitat: Inshore waters, from shoreline to depths
            of 300′ (90 m). Commonly encountered
            in mangrove areas; enters fresh water
            rarely in Florida.

Range: In w Atlantic from New Jersey to Brazil,
          throughout Caribbean and Gulf of
          Mexico. Also in e Pacific and possibly in
          e Atlantic.

Notes: The Lemon Shark bears up to 17
          young per litter. It feeds on fishes and
          large invertebrates, such as crabs and

conchs. This species has a reputation for aggressiveness and should be approached with caution.

Similar Species: Two other species have large second dorsal fins: Nurse Shark, which has dorsal fins far back on body (beginning over pelvic fin), and Sand Tiger, which has distinctive humpbacked shape and teeth visible when mouth is closed.

Lemon Shark range

37 Atlantic Sharpnose Shark
Rhizoprionodon terraenovae

Identification: A small, rather streamlined shark, with a long, somewhat pointed snout. *Posterior margin of anal fin straight or only slightly concave.* Generally gray; large individuals have small white spots, white posterior and inner margins on pectoral fin, and dusky tips on dorsal fins. First dorsal origin over or in front of free rear tip of pectoral fin. *Second dorsal fin origin well behind anal fin origin.* No keels on sides of caudal peduncle. Gill slits short, last two above pectoral fin. Teeth have strongly asymmetrical cusps; develop serrations in adults. Prominent upper labial furrows. TL to about 3′8″ (1.1 m).

teeth

Habitat: Surf zone and mouths of estuaries; to depths of 920′ (280 m), but usually less than 33′ (10 m) deep.

Range: New Brunswick to Florida and Gulf of Mexico.

Notes: The Atlantic Sharpnose Shark usually produces four to six young per litter. It feeds on small fishes and invertebrates and is considered harmless to people. Members of the genus *Rhizoprionodon* are sometimes called milk sharks.

Similar Species: Replaced in Caribbean Sea (Bahamas, Antilles, and along coast from Mexico to Uruguay) by Caribbean Sharpnose Shark *(R. porosus),* which has more vertebrae but is otherwise identical. Brazilian Sharpnose Shark *(R. lalandii),* which occurs on South American continental shelf from Panama to s Brazil, is a smaller species (TL less than 26"/66 cm) with even more vertebrae. Daggernose Shark *(Isogomphodon oxyrhynchus),* a very distinctive species with small eyes and a long, narrow, flattened, acutely triangular head, occurs from Trinidad to c Brazil, often around river mouths; it reaches 5' (1.5 m) TL, feeds on small schooling fishes, and is not considered dangerous to humans.

38　Blue Shark
Prionace glauca

teeth

Identification: A slender shark with *a pointed snout and long, pointed pectoral fins.* Dark blue above, shading to bright blue on side, white below. First dorsal origin about same distance from pelvic origin as from pectoral base. Posterior margin of anal fin deeply concave. Weak keels on side of caudal peduncle. Teeth serrate. TL to about 13' (4 m).

Habitat: Usually open ocean to at least 500' (150 m) deep; occasionally near shore.

Range: Worldwide in tropical and temperate seas.

Notes: A live-bearing species with a yolk-sac placenta, the Blue Shark produces from four to 135 young per litter. It feeds on fishes and squids, and occasionally birds and carrion. Although it is not particularly aggressive it often circles divers and has attacked on occasion.

Similar Species: This very distinctive species is unlikely to be confused with other sharks. Oceanic Whitetip Shark is another pelagic species, but it lacks keels on caudal peduncle and has bluntly rounded first dorsal and pectoral fins.

Genus *Carcharhinus*

Carcharhinus is a large genus, and the species are difficult to identify. One feature that serves to divide the species into two groups is the presence of an interdorsal ridge, a low, fleshy, keel-like ridge on the midline of the back between the dorsal fins. Once this division is made, identification of these sharks relies on combinations of characters, such as fin origin, shape, and size, snout length, and other details.

The following table divides members of the genus based on presence or absence of the interdorsal ridge, and then summarizes key features of each species. Following the table are full accounts for seven *Carcharhinus* species. Sizes and ranges are given in the table for those species that do not have a full account. The accompanying drawings of the heads as seen from below show the shape of the snout and the position of the eyes, nostrils, and mouth.

Carcharhinus species with interdorsal ridge

Oceanic Whitetip Shark

(C. longimanus) Large, robust. Snout short and blunt. Eye small. Paddle-shaped pectoral fin, rounded first dorsal fin; both with white tips. Origin of first dorsal fin over pectoral fin, between base and free rear tip.

Silky Shark

(C. falciformis) Large, slender. First dorsal origin well behind free rear tip of pectoral fin (farther forward in all other species). Second dorsal fin with long inner margin.

Dusky Shark

(C. obscurus) Large (to 13'/4 m), rather slender. Snout short and rounded. Gray or gray-brown, paler below, with inconspicuous pale stripe along side. First dorsal fin moderate-size with rounded front margin, its origin over free rear tip of pectoral fin. Second dorsal, with nearly straight rear margin, has origin over or in front of anal fin. Pectoral fin sickle-shaped. Massachusetts to Florida, Bahamas, Cuba, n Gulf of Mexico, Nicaragua to Brazil.

Night Shark

(C. signatus) Large, slender. Snout very long and pointed. First dorsal fin small, its origin over free rear tip of pectoral fin. Upper teeth broad based, with prominent cusplets.

Reef Shark

(*C. perezi*) Large. Snout short and blunt. First dorsal fin small, with short rear tip, its origin over rear end of pectoral fin base. Upper teeth without serrations or cusplets.

Galápagos Shark

(*C. galapagensis*) Large (to 12'/3.7m), gray. Snout rounded; rudimentary nasal flap. First dorsal high, origin behind end of pectoral fin base. Posterior margin of second dorsal fin concave. Worldwide, around offshore islands.

Bignose Shark

(*C. altimus*) Large (to 10'/3 m). Snout long and pointed; well-developed nasal flap. First dorsal origin over or ahead of end of pectoral fin base. Second dorsal fin, with concave rear margin, has origin over or just in front of anal origin. Worldwide in deep water.

Sandbar Shark

(*C. plumbeus*) Large, stout. Snout short and blunt. First dorsal fin very high (more than half the distance between tip of snout and first dorsal origin), its origin over end of pectoral fin base.

Carcharhinus species without interdorsal ridge

Bull Shark

(*C. leucas*) Large. Snout very short and rounded. First dorsal origin behind rear of pectoral fin base. Second dorsal fin fairly large, its origin just in front of anal fin origin.

Blacktip Shark

(*C. limbatus*) Fairly large, stout. Snout moderately long and pointed. White stripe on side; black tips on some fins. First dorsal fin large, its origin over or behind pectoral fin base.

Spinner Shark

(*C. brevipinna*) Large (to 9'/2.7m). Eye small. Snout very long and pointed. White stripe on side; black tip on pectoral fin. First dorsal origin over free rear tip of pectoral fin. North Carolina to Florida, n Gulf of Mexico, Bahamas, Cuba, Guyana.

Blacknose Shark

(*C. acronotus*) Small (to 5′/1.5 m). Black spot at tip of snout. First dorsal origin over free rear tip of pectoral fin. North Carolina to Florida, Bahamas, throughout Gulf of Mexico, Caribbean, including Antilles, to s Brazil.

Smalltail Shark

(*C. porosus*) Small (to 5′/1.5 m). Eye large. Snout long and pointed. First dorsal origin beyond pectoral fin base. Second dorsal origin over middle of anal fin base. N Gulf of Mexico, along continental coast to s Brazil.

Finetooth Shark

(*C. isodon*) Small (to 7′/1.9 m), with smooth or weakly serrate teeth. Long gill slits (about one-half length of first dorsal fin base). North Carolina to Florida, n Gulf of Mexico, s Brazil.

39 Oceanic Whitetip Shark
Carcharhinus longimanus

Identification:

teeth

A robust shark with *a rounded first dorsal fin and broad, paddle-shaped pectoral fin.* Low interdorsal ridge. Bronze-gray above, abruptly lighter below. In adult, tips of first dorsal and pectoral fins white. In juvenile, tips of pelvic, second dorsal, anal, and caudal fins black; 2 dark saddles across top of caudal peduncle. Snout bluntly rounded and short (about as long as distance between nostrils). Eye small. Origin of first dorsal fin over pectoral fin between end of base and free rear tip. Teeth triangular with serrate edges; lower teeth narrower than upper; central cusp of upper teeth not delimited by angle in tooth margin. Gill slits short, last three over pectoral fin. TL to 10–13′ (3–4 m).

Habitat: Well offshore, from surface to depths of at least 500′ (150 m), in areas where water is more than 600′ (180 m) deep.

Range: Worldwide in tropics and warm temperate oceans. In Atlantic from Maine to Argentina, including Gulf of Mexico and Caribbean.

Notes: Considered a dangerous species, the Oceanic Whitetip is capable of tearing chunks of meat from large animals. It has been implicated in deaths of shipwreck victims.

Similar Species: No other requiem shark has blunt, rounded first dorsal and pectoral fins. Silvertip Shark *(C. albimarginatus)* has conspicuous white edges on dorsal, pectoral, pelvic, and caudal fins, but its occurrence in w Atlantic is uncertain. Blue Shark, a slender, open-water species with a narrow, pointed snout, is dark blue above, shading to bright blue on side and white below.

---

40   Silky Shark
Carcharhinus falciformis

teeth

Identification: A large, slender shark with an interdorsal ridge and *first dorsal fin far back on body, its origin well behind free rear tip of pectoral fin.* Gray or gray-brown above, with tips of fins dusky but not sharply marked; no other conspicuous markings. Inner margin of second dorsal fin longer than height of fin. Last three gill slits over pectoral fin. Upper teeth have angled serrate central cusp delimited from strongly serrate base by angle in tooth margin; lower teeth have narrow, straight central cusp and no serrations. Scales small; skin feels silky. TL to 11′ (3.4 m).

Habitat: Oceanic, at edges of continental and insular shelves and offshore at depths of 60–1,650′ (18–500 m).

Range: Circumtropical. In w Atlantic from Massachusetts to s Brazil.

Notes: The Silky Shark is the only *Carcharhinus* species with an interdorsal ridge that has the dorsal fin origin behind the free rear tip of the pectoral fin. An offshore shark, it feeds on fishes and often damages fishing nets. It is considered dangerous, although there are no verified records of it attacking humans.

41 Night Shark
Carcharhinus signatus

Identification:

teeth

A large slender shark with an interdorsal ridge and *a long, pointed snout* (nearly twice as long as distance between nostrils). Gray, without conspicuous markings. First dorsal fin small, its origin over free rear tip of pectoral fin. Upper teeth have narrow oblique cusps delimited from broad base; prominent cusplets on base. Lower teeth have narrow cusps, smooth or weakly serrate. TL to 9′ (2.7 m).

Habitat: Coastal waters to depths of 130′ (40 m).

Range: Delaware to Florida, Bahamas, and n Cuba. Not in Gulf of Mexico, Caribbean, or Lesser Antilles. Also in s Brazil and e Atlantic.

Notes:

This is a shark of rather deep water that makes vertical migrations and is usually caught near the surface at night or near dawn. A schooling species that feeds on small fishes, it is considered harmless to people. It is sometimes placed in the genus *Hypoprion*.

Similar Species: Dusky Shark, Silky Shark, and Reef Shark, also larger species with interdorsal ridges, have short blunt snouts. Silky Shark has first dorsal origin behind free rear tip of pectoral fin, while Reef and Dusky have it anterior to or over free rear tip of pectoral fin.

42 Reef Shark
Carcharhinus perezi

Identification:

teeth

A fairly large shark with an interdorsal ridge and a short blunt snout (about as long as distance between nostrils). Gray, with no conspicuous markings. *First dorsal fin small, with short rear tip,* its origin over or ahead of free rear tip of pectoral ray. Upper side teeth have narrow cusps, delimited from base by angle in tooth margin; base without large serrations or cusplets. Gill slits short, last three over pectoral fin. TL less than 10′ (3 m).

Habitat: Reefs, usually in water less than 100′ (30 m) deep.

Range: Bermuda, Florida, Bahamas, Gulf of Mexico, Caribbean, and s Brazil. Distribution along coast of South America uncertain.

Notes: The most common shark around coral reefs, this species sometimes lies on the ocean bottom in caves. Although a fish eater, it has been implicated in attacks on divers in the Caribbean. It was formerly known as *C. springeri*.

Similar Species: Dusky Shark and Night Shark also have interdorsal ridges and first dorsal origin over rear tip of pectoral fin, but both have broad-based upper teeth, and Night Shark has long, pointed snout.

43 Sandbar Shark
Carcharhinus plumbeus

Identification: A large, rather stout shark with a low interdorsal ridge and a blunt, rounded snout (about as long as distance between nostrils). Gray overall, lighter below, with no conspicuous markings. *First dorsal fin very high* (height about equal to distance from eye to second or third gill opening), its origin over end of pectoral fin base. Upper side teeth have serrate, broad-based, triangular cusps, not delimited from base by angle in tooth margin. Lower teeth more slender and straight, with very weak serrations. TL to 10′ (3 m).

teeth

Habitat: Inshore waters (not in fresh water) to depths of 925′ (280 m).

Range: Tropical and subtropical waters of Atlantic, Pacific, and Indian Oceans. In w Atlantic, Atlantic coast (straying north to Massachusetts), Gulf of Mexico, Bahamas, Cuba, and s and w Caribbean.

Notes: No other requiem shark in our area has as high a dorsal fin as the Sandbar Shark. Although it is a fairly large shark, it is not known to attack people and is considered relatively harmless. It feeds on fishes and invertebrates and avoids carrion and garbage. Litters range from one to 14 young. This species was formerly known as *C. milberti*.

44 Bull Shark
Carcharhinus leucas

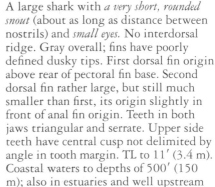

teeth

Identification: A large shark with *a very short, rounded snout* (about as long as distance between nostrils) and *small eyes*. No interdorsal ridge. Gray overall; fins have poorly defined dusky tips. First dorsal fin origin above rear of pectoral fin base. Second dorsal fin rather large, but still much smaller than first, its origin slightly in front of anal fin origin. Teeth in both jaws triangular and serrate. Upper side teeth have central cusp not delimited by angle in tooth margin. TL to 11' (3.4 m).

Habitat: Coastal waters to depths of 500' (150 m); also in estuaries and well upstream into fresh water.

Range: Coastal tropical and subtropical waters worldwide. In w Atlantic, sometimes strays north to Massachusetts; Bermuda, Bahamas, Gulf of Mexico, Greater Antilles, and continental coasts of Central and South America to s Brazil.

Notes: The Bull Shark gives birth to litters of up to 13 young. Although this widespread shark enters fresh water and travels far up rivers in many parts of the world, most notably to Lake Nicaragua in Central America, there are very few freshwater records in U.S. waters. It feeds on a wide variety of fishes, invertebrates, birds, mammals, carrion, and even garbage. Because of its size and its occurrence in fresh water and close inshore, it may be one of the three most dangerous sharks in the world (along with the White Shark and the Tiger Shark). The short snout, large size, triangular teeth, and lack of interdorsal ridge are sufficient to distinguish this species.

45 Blacktip Shark
Carcharhinus limbatus

teeth

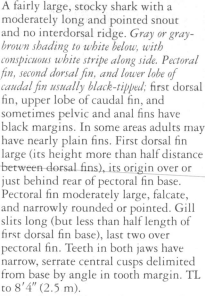

Identification: A fairly large, stocky shark with a moderately long and pointed snout and no interdorsal ridge. *Gray or gray-brown shading to white below, with conspicuous white stripe along side. Pectoral fin, second dorsal fin, and lower lobe of caudal fin usually black-tipped;* first dorsal fin, upper lobe of caudal fin, and sometimes pelvic and anal fins have black margins. In some areas adults may have nearly plain fins. First dorsal fin large (its height more than half distance between dorsal fins), its origin over or just behind rear of pectoral fin base. Pectoral fin moderately large, falcate, and narrowly rounded or pointed. Gill slits long (but less than half length of first dorsal fin base), last two over pectoral fin. Teeth in both jaws have narrow, serrate central cusps delimited from base by angle in tooth margin. TL to 8'4" (2.5 m).

Habitat: Tropical and subtropical continental waters from estuaries and river mouths to outer edges of coral reefs, usually in water less than 100' (30 m) deep. Also offshore, but not truly oceanic.

Range: All tropical and subtropical continental waters. In w Atlantic: Massachusetts to s Brazil, including Gulf of Mexico and Caribbean. Also e Atlantic and e Pacific.

Notes: The Blacktip Shark often travels in large schools and pursues its prey close to the surface, where its momentum sometimes carries it out of the water, a tendency that it shares with the closely related Spinner Shark. It normally feeds on fish and some invertebrates, such as crabs and lobsters. Although it is not especially aggressive and not likely to attack without provocation, the Blacktip has been implicated in attacks on people, particularly divers spearfishing or people dangling their feet in the water. It produces litters of one to 10 young.

Similar Species: Spinner Shark has smaller first dorsal fin
that originates farther back (over free
rear tip of pectoral fin) and long, pointed
snout (1½ to 2 times as long as distance
between nostrils).

HOUND SHARKS
Family Triakidae

Hound sharks are rather small sharks,
usually less than 4 feet (1.2 m) long, with an anal fin, two
dorsal fins, and no fin spines. The first dorsal origin is ahead
of the pelvic fin origin. There are moderately long labial
furrows at the corners of the mouth. Unlike the requiem
sharks (family Carcharhinidae), the hound sharks do not
have precaudal pits at the base of the tail.

The family, which occurs in all warm and temperate
coastal seas, includes nine genera and 35 species; one genus
(Mustelus) and three species are found in our region. The
different species of the genus *Mustelus* have characteristically shaped scales that are flattened on top.

46 Smooth Dogfish
Mustelus canis

Identification: A small, slender shark. *Well-separated
dorsal fins, second nearly as large as first.* Pale
gray overall, lighter below; no spots or
dark bars. Scales lance-shaped, with 3 or
4 parallel keel-like ridges. Origin of first
dorsal fin over inner margin of pectoral
fin. Upper labial furrows distinctly
longer than lower. Teeth molar-like.
Scale-like denticles on tongue and front
of palate. TL to 5′ (1.5 m).

Habitat: Coastal populations to depths of 60′ (18
m); deeper in island waters.

Range: Bermuda, Massachusetts to Florida,
Bahamas, n and w Gulf of Mexico,
Antilles; coast of Venezuela. Also from s
Brazil to Argentina but absent from the
region between Venezuela and s Brazil.

Notes: The Smooth Dogfish bears litters of four
to 20 young. Feeding primarily on small
fishes, crustaceans (including lobsters in
northern waters), and other invertebrates,
it does not attack humans.

Similar Species: Smalleye Smoothhound *(M. higmani),* a small species (TL to 16–25"/41–64 cm), has 3 cusps and curved ridges on crowns of scales; it ranges from Venezuela to s Brazil. Florida Smoothhound *(M. norrisi),* also small (TL to about 3'/1 m), has lance-shaped scales and upper labial furrows shorter than lower; it ranges from Florida and Gulf of Mexico to w Caribbean and Venezuela; also s Brazil.

HAMMERHEAD SHARKS
Family Sphyrnidae

Hammerhead sharks are immediately recognizable by the shape of the head, which has flat, wing-like expansions on each side, with the eyes at the outer edges of the "wings." It has been suggested that the increased distance between the eyes enhances binocular vision and that the extra surface area may allow room for more electro-receptor structures and enlarged olfactory organs. Hammerheads can be distinguished by differences in the outline of the head, mainly in the shape of the front margin—the presence or absence of *median* and *lateral notches* there—and the degree to which the wings are angled backward. Some species have well-defined grooves—termed *prenarial grooves*—along the anterior edge of the head, which probably channel water to the nostrils. Hammerheads have precaudal pits and, like all carcharhiniforms, have two dorsal fins and an anal fin but no fin spines. Some species of hammerheads have been implicated in attacks on humans.

HAMMERHEAD SHAPES

Great Hammerhead
S. mokarran

Scalloped Hammerhead
S. lewini

Bonnethead
S. tiburo

Smooth Hammerhead
S. zygaena

Smalleye Hammerhead
S. tudes

Scoophead
S. media

Except for the extreme modification of the head, hammerheads are very similar to carcharhinid sharks, and some authorities have assigned them to that family. Here we recognize them in their traditional family, Sphyrnidae, which encompasses about nine species worldwide in one or two genera. Six species of one genus occur in our region.

The drawings of the heads as seen from above show the differences in the shape of the wing-like extensions and in the outline of the front of the head.

47   Great Hammerhead
Sphyrna mokarran

Identification:
: A very large hammerhead with a high, pointed, strongly falcate first dorsal fin. Gray-brown above, paler below. *Front margin of head gently curved in juveniles, becoming nearly straight in adults, with slight median notch.* Second dorsal fin much smaller than first, but size difference not as great as in other hammerheads. Pelvic fin strongly falcate. Teeth strongly serrate. TL to 20' (6 m).

Habitat:
: From coast to well offshore in water up to 260' (80 m) deep.

Range:
: North Carolina to Brazil, Gulf of Mexico, and Caribbean; also e Atlantic, Indo–west Pacific, and e Pacific.

Notes:
: The Great Hammerhead is considered dangerous, although there have been few documented attacks on humans. It is a viviparous species that produces 13 to 42 young. No other species of hammerhead is so large or has the front of the head nearly straight.

48, 49   Scalloped Hammerhead
Sphyrna lewini

Identification:
: A large hammerhead, gray-brown above, shading to white below; pectoral fin tip dusky to black. *Front margin of head broadly arched, with prominent median notch. Side wings of head narrow, rear margins swept backward.* Second dorsal fin smaller than anal fin. Margin of anal fin deeply notched. Teeth weakly serrate. TL to 14' (4.3 m).

Habitat: Inshore and offshore waters to depths of about 900' (275 m).

Range: Worldwide in tropical and warm-temperate waters; from New Jersey to Brazil, including Bermuda, Bahamas, Gulf of Mexico, Antilles, and coasts of Central and South America.

Notes: The Scalloped Hammerhead bears live young in litters of 15 to 31. A yolk-sac placenta connects the mother and the young during the embryonic period. It feeds on fishes and invertebrates such as squids, octopuses, crabs, and lobsters. It is sometimes found in large schools, and while it is not especially aggressive, it is considered potentially dangerous.

Similar Species: Great Hammerhead has front of head almost straight, with only slight median notch, and second dorsal fin about same size as anal fin. Smooth Hammerhead *(S. zygaena),* also large (TL to 13'/4 m), has rear margins of head swept backward and front of head broadly arched, but lacks median notch; in w Atlantic it lives from Nova Scotia to Florida and from s Brazil to tip of South America; absent from Gulf of Mexico and w Caribbean.

50   Bonnethead
Sphyrna tiburo

Identification: A small hammerhead with *front of head semicircular in outline,* without notches along its front edge. Gray or gray-brown above, paler below, sometimes with small dark spots on side. First dorsal fin moderately falcate, its origin over inner margin of pectoral fin. Anal fin larger than second dorsal fin. Anterior teeth have short stout cusps; posterior teeth blunt, molar-like. TL to 5' (1.5 m).

Habitat: Shallow waters, often close inshore, at times as deep as 260' (80 m).

Range: Coastal waters from Rhode Island to s Brazil, Caribbean, and Gulf of Mexico. Rare in Bermuda.

Notes: The Bonnethead has small teeth and feeds primarily on crustaceans and some mollusks and small fishes. This hammerhead is not dangerous to people. It bears young in litters of four to 16. Yolk-sac placentas provide nourishment for the developing embryos.

Similar Species: No other hammerhead has front of head in semicircle. Smalleye Hammerhead *(S. tudes),* which occurs only in w Atlantic along South American coast from Venezuela to Uruguay, has moderately arched head with pronounced notch in center and indentations on sides, and has well-defined prenarial grooves along front of head. Scoophead *(S. media)* has moderately arched head with shallow center and side indentations; it ranges from Panama to s Brazil, and in e Pacific from Gulf of California to Ecuador.

ORDER SQUALIFORMES

Squaliform sharks are distinguished by the absence of an anal fin, a feature shared with the sawsharks (which have a blade-like rostrum armed with teeth), the angel sharks (which are flattened and ray-like), and the batoids (skates and rays). They have two dorsal fins and five pairs of gill slits.

There are four families of squaliform sharks: Echinorhinidae (bramble sharks, two species), Dalatiidae (sleeper sharks, 18 genera and about 49 species), Centrophoridae (gulper sharks, two genera and 13 species), and Squalidae (dogfish sharks, two genera and 10 species). Three of these are beyond the scope of this guide: Bramble sharks occur north and south of our region, while gulper sharks, with two species in our area, and sleeper sharks, with about 14 species in our area, live in very deep water.

DOGFISH SHARKS
Family Squalidae

This family includes some of the smallest sharks in the world as well as some very large species. There are about five species of dogfish sharks in our area, although there is considerable disagreement as to their classification. Two species might be encountered in shallow water, but one of these reaches just the fringes of our region. These two are immediately recognizable by the presence of a strong spine at the front of each dorsal fin and the lack of an anal fin.

51 Cuban Dogfish
Squalus cubensis

Identification: A slender gray shark, darker above, with *tips of dorsal fins black* and edges of pectoral, pelvic, and caudal fins white. *2 dorsal fins, each with strong, ungrooved spine at front edge.* Origin of first dorsal in front of free rear tip of pectoral fin. No anal fin. Precaudal pits well developed; weak keel on each side of caudal peduncle. Teeth have cutting edges and very oblique cusp. TL to 3′7″ (1.1 m).

Habitat: Outer continental shelf in water 200–1,250′ (60–380 m) deep.

Range: North Carolina to Florida, Cuba, and Hispaniola; n Gulf of Mexico. Also s Brazil and Argentina.

Notes: The Cuban Dogfish produces litters of about 10 young. Occurring in dense schools, it feeds on small fishes and invertebrates and is harmless to humans. It is taken in trawls in the northern Gulf of Mexico, and its liver is used for oil and vitamins.

Similar Species: Spiny Dogfish *(S. acanthias)* has white spots, lacks black tips on dorsal fins, and has first dorsal fin farther back, behind pectoral fin. A widespread temperate species and possibly the world's most abundant shark, in w Atlantic it reaches its southern limit in Florida.

ORDER SQUATINIFORMES

Members of this order are bottom dwellers with flat bodies similar to those of rays. The order consists of a single family, Squatinidae.

ANGEL SHARKS
Family Squatinidae

These flattened, ray-like sharks are called angel sharks because of their wing-shaped pectoral fins, the front margins of which are not connected to the head (as those of rays are). Angel sharks have two dorsal fins but no anal fin. The lower lobe of the caudal fin is longer than the upper. The mouth is subterminal. There are five pairs of gill slits, all in front of the pectoral fin, and a large spiracle behind each eye.

The family contains one genus and about a dozen species, one of which occurs in our area.

---

52 Atlantic Angel Shark
Squatina dumeril

Identification: *A ray-shaped shark.* Brown or gray above, paler below, with spots on rather sharply angled, wing-like pectoral fins. Head flat and broad, narrowing to *distinct neck at base of pectoral fins.* Gill openings on lower sides of head, not visible from above. Small spines on snout; row of moderately large spines on midline of back in front of and between dorsal fins. No anal fin. TL to about 5′ (1.5 m).

Habitat: Ocean bottom, from shoreline to depths of 4,500′ (1,375 m).

Range: Atlantic coast from New England to n Gulf of Mexico, Jamaica, Columbia, and Venezuela.

Notes: The Atlantic Angel Shark feeds on bottom fishes, mollusks, and crustaceans, moving to deeper water during the colder months. An ovoviviparous species, it retains its eggs in the uterus until they hatch. Although it is not considered dangerous to humans, it may try to bite anglers who catch it. Nothing else in our area resembles this ray-like shark.

ORDER RAJIFORMES

Another main group of cartilaginous fishes is the batoids, which includes the sawfishes, skates, and rays. They all have flattened bodies, and the front margins of the pectoral fins are attached to the head, so that the head and body form a circular or diamond-shaped disk. The gill openings are on the underside; all batoids in our region have five pairs of gill slits. The pectoral fins are often referred to as "wings," which is appropriate, for most batoids (with the exception of sawfishes and guitarfishes, which swim like sharks) use wave-like undulations of the pectoral fins to "fly" through the water. Some batoids have elongate bodies and are almost shark-like; others have long slender tails or very short tails. The tail exceeds the disk in length in all batoid families except the Urolophidae (round stingrays) and Gymnuridae (butterfly rays). Batoids do not have anal fins. Some species have only a spine where the dorsal fin normally would be; others have one or two dorsal fins. Because of their shapes, batoids are often measured along the width of the disk. Otherwise the lengths given are total length (TL).

Most batoids live on the bottom and breathe by taking water in through the *spiracles,* a pair of openings behind or near the eyes, and passing it over the gills and out through

PARTS OF A BATOID

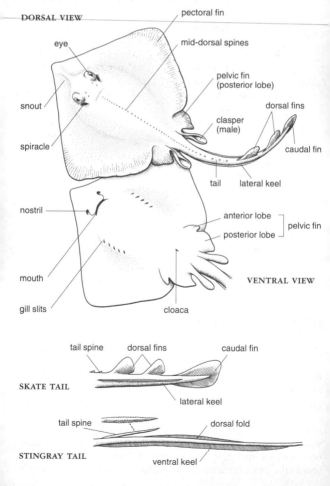

the gill slits. A few open-water species, such as the eagle rays and mantas, probably breathe through their mouths.

Batoids fall into four subgroups, which are recognized by some ichthyologists as suborders under the single order Rajiformes, and by others as separate orders (we treat them as suborders): Pristiformes, the sawfishes, contains a single family, Pristidae. Torpediniformes, the electric rays, has two families, Torpedinidae and Narcinidae, both of which are represented in our area, although the members of the family Torpedinidae are rare south of North Carolina and are not covered here. Rajiformes, the guitarfishes and skates, encompasses three families, two of which are represented in our area (Rhinobatidae and Rajidae). Myliobatiformes, the stingrays, round stingrays, eagle rays, butterfly rays, and mantas, has six families worldwide, five in our region (Dasyatidae, Urolophidae, Gymnuridae, Myliobatidae, and Mobulidae).

SAWFISHES
Family Pristidae

Sawfishes are unlike any other fishes except the sawsharks, which belong to the shark family Pristiophoridae and are found in very deep water. The bodies of sawfishes are generally elongate and shark-like, except that the front margins of the pectoral fins are fused to the head, and the five pairs of gill openings are on the underside of the head. The snout is extended into a flat *rostrum* (the "saw") armed with large horny teeth, uniform in size, along its sides. Sawfishes have two dorsal fins but lack an anal fin and have no fin spines.

The family has two genera and six species; two species occur in our region.

---

53 Smalltooth Sawfish
Pristis pectinata

Identification: An elongate, almost shark-like but flattened batoid. Brownish gray, with white belly. *Long, flat, blade-like rostrum, with 24–32 pairs of teeth along edges.* Gill slits on underside of head. 2 large, well-spaced dorsal fins, nearly equal in size. Origin of first dorsal fin over pelvic fin origin. Caudal fin large and obliquely triangular, with *no lower lobe.* TL to 20′ (6 m).

Habitat: Estuaries and coastlines, usually in shallow water.

Range: Atlantic coast from Chesapeake Bay to Florida (summer visitor north of n Florida); Gulf of Mexico and Caribbean to c Brazil. Rare in Bermuda.

Notes: The Smalltooth Sawfish is a live-bearer, producing 15 to 20 young at a time. The sawfish feeds on small fishes, which it impales with quick side-to-side slashes of the saw. It then wipes the saw on the bottom to remove the victims from its teeth so they can be swallowed.

Similar Species: Largetooth Sawfish *(P. pristis,* formerly *P. perotteti)* has 16–20 pairs of rostral teeth, definite lower lobe on caudal fin, and origin of first dorsal fin in front of pelvic fin origin; it occurs in coastal waters from Florida and Gulf of Mexico to Brazil and enters freshwater parts of rivers. Bahamas Sawshark *(Pristiophorus schroederi,* family Pristiophoridae), which is much smaller (TL to 31"/80 cm) and lives in very deep water (2,000–3,000'/ 600–915 m) off Florida, Cuba, and Bahamas, has flat, tapering rostrum with 22–24 long teeth alternating with shorter teeth along each side and pair of long, filamentous barbels near midpoint; also has short gill slits in front of pectoral fin.

ELECTRIC RAYS
Family Narcinidae

Electric rays have rounded disks, two dorsal fins, moderately stout tails, and small caudal fins. They are powerful electric fishes, able to produce shocks strong enough to stun their prey. Large torpedo rays of the genus *Torpedo* (family Torpedinidae), which rarely come south into our region, can produce in excess of 200 volts, and Lesser Electric Rays up to about 37 volts, enough to jolt a person who comes into contact with one in the water. The electric organs are kidney-shaped structures behind the eyes that usually are not visible through the skin of living individuals but can be felt in dead specimens.

The family Narcinidae contains nine genera and 24 species. One species is included here, although three others occur in deep water in our area.

54 Lesser Electric Ray
Narcine brasiliensis

Identification: *A pale sand-colored ray, often with ellipses of dark spots on dorsal side of rounded disk;* underside white or yellowish. Outlines of kidney-shaped electric organs may be visible behind eyes. Spiracles next to eyes, with rounded tubercles along their edges. 2 well-developed dorsal fins. Tail stout, about as long as disk, with fleshy keel along each side. Caudal fin triangular. TL to 17¾″ (45 cm).

Habitat: Sand bottoms from shoreline to depths of 130′ (40 m).

Range: North Carolina to Florida, n Gulf of Mexico, Jamaica, c Lesser Antilles, Yucatán, and n coast of South America from Colombia and Venezuela.

Notes: The only electric ray in shallow water in our area, the Lesser Electric Ray can deliver 14 to 37 volts of electricity, probably employing the shock to stun prey as well as for defense. A live-bearer, this ray produces broods of four to 15 young. It feeds on bottom-dwelling invertebrates, especially annelid worms.

GUITARFISHES
Family Rhinobatidae

Guitarfishes are named for their shape, which really does resemble a guitar. The body is elongate, almost like that of a shark, with a heart-shaped disk tapering to a pointed snout and a stout tail. There are two dorsal fins and a caudal fin. Guitarfishes swim like sharks, rather than "flying" like most rays.

This family contains seven genera and 45 species worldwide; three species are found in our area.

55 Atlantic Guitarfish
Rhinobatos lentiginosus

Identification: An elongate ray with *a heart-shaped disk terminating in a wedge-shaped snout with a few enlarged tubercles on tip.* Head concave between eyes. Gray to brown above, with small white spots. Mid-dorsal row of larger tubercles extends from spiracles to region between dorsal fins. Tail not sharply narrower than body. Caudal fin short, crescent-shaped, with vertebral column bent upward into upper lobe. TL to 30" (75 cm).

Habitat: Shallow water and along beaches from shoreline to depths of 100' (30 m).

Range: North Carolina to Yucatán.

Notes: In this ovoviviparous species, the eggs are retained in the uterus but have no placental connection with the mother. The Atlantic Guitarfish feeds on small sand-dwelling crustaceans.

Similar Species: Brazilian Guitarfish *(R. horkelii)* has flat or slightly convex head with no tubercles on snout; it occurs along Atlantic coast of Brazil, possibly as far north as Lesser Antilles. Southern Guitarfish *(R. percellens)* also lacks tubercles on tip of snout; it occurs in s Caribbean and south to n Argentina.

SKATES
Family Rajidae

Skates have diamond-shaped disks with two small dorsal fins (without spines), placed well back on the slender tail, and a small caudal fin. Most skates have some enlarged spines or tubercles on the dorsal surface of the disk. The mouth and the five pairs of gill slits are on the underside of the disk. Skates lay eggs in rectangular horny cases with tendrils. These are often found on beaches and are known as mermaids' purses.

Worldwide there are 18 genera and more than 200 species of skates. Three genera and about 30 species occur in our area, but only two species are common in shallow water.

---

56 Roundel Skate
Raja texana

Identification: Disk diamond-shaped, with outer corners abruptly rounded. Upper surface brown, with scattered indistinct pale spots; *round dark spot surrounded by pale ring on base of each pectoral fin.* Translucent area on either side of midline of snout. Lower surface white. Single row of short spines along mid-dorsal ridge. TL to 21″ (54 cm).

Habitat: Shallow bays to depths of more than 300′ (90 m).

Range: West coast of Florida and n Gulf of Mexico to Tampico, Mexico.

Notes: The Roundel Skate feeds on mollusks and bottom-dwelling annelid worms. Young Roundel Skates are common in shallow water; adults tend to live offshore.

Similar Species: Ocellate Skate *(R. ackleyi),* from deeper water in Gulf of Mexico, has elliptical spots on upper surface of pectoral fins.

57 Clearnose Skate
Raja eglanteria

Identification: A small skate with a diamond-shaped disk and a pointed snout. Light brown above, white below, with *irregular darker spots and bars on dorsal surface. Translucent area on each side of mid-dorsal ridge on snout.* Patch of 1–5 thorn-like tubercles on each side of dorsal midline at about middle of disk; additional patches of thorns around eyes and spiracles. Single row of small spines along mid-dorsal ridge. Tail about as long as disk, with rows of strong spines. TL to about 3′ (1 m).

Habitat: From saltwater parts of estuaries and bays to depths of 1,080′ (330 m).

Range: New England to Florida and e and n Gulf of Mexico.

Notes: This species is abundant in the northern parts of its range during the warmer months, when it moves inshore. It feeds on fish, squid, polychaete worms, crabs, and shrimp. The eggs are contained in rectangular cases with short tendrils at the corners.

Similar Species: Other shallow-water rays in our area have conspicuous ocellated spots on dorsal surface or several rows of spines down middle of back.

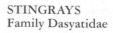

STINGRAYS
Family Dasyatidae

Stingrays have diamond-shaped or rounded disks, with the mouth and gills well back on the underside of the disk. They have long, slender tails with no caudal fin and also lack dorsal fins, but most have a strong, doubly serrate dorsal spine, usually near the base of the tail. The spine, which can be 5 to 6 inches (13–15 cm) long in large individuals, can inflict a serious wound. Not only does it cause physical damage, but each side of the spine has a groove with venom cells, causing an extremely painful sting. Like other rays, stingrays are ovoviviparous (they bear live young); the developing young have no placental connection with the mother but are nourished by a fluid secreted by vascular filaments in the uterine wall.

Many stingrays spend much of their time lying motionless on the bottom, covered with sand. They accomplish this by fanning the sand with their pectoral fins as they land on the bottom and allowing the sand to fall over their backs. They also fan the bottom to uncover their invertebrate prey.

There are nine genera and approximately 70 species of stingrays. Two genera and seven species occur in our area; we include the species that are reasonably common in shallow water.

Genera of family Dasyatidae

Dasyatis	Longitudinal membranous keel on lower surface of tail at rear. Disk somewhat diamond shaped.
Himantura	No prominent keel on lower tail surface. Disk nearly circular.

59, 60 Southern Stingray
Dasyatis americana

Identification: A large ray. Gray, olive, or brown above, depending on color of surroundings; underside white, with brown or gray along edges. *Disk has sharp outer corners* and irregular row of short spines on upper surface. Snout does not project beyond margin of disk. Tail has large, doubly serrate dorsal spine near its base, low fleshy fin fold on upper surface, and well-developed longitudinal membranous keel on lower, both usually dark. Disk width: female to 5′ (1.5 m); male to about 24″ (60 cm).

Habitat: Shallow water over sand and around reefs.

Range: Cape Hatteras to Florida, Bahamas, Gulf of Mexico, and Caribbean to Brazil. Strays farther northward.

Notes: The Southern is the most commonly seen stingray around coral reefs. It feeds on small fishes and invertebrates, including clams, worms, crabs, shrimps, and mantis shrimps. The eggs are retained in the female until hatching, but there is no placental connection with the mother. Some divers have found areas where stingrays congregate, and make special trips to feed them by hand.

Similar Species: Roughtail Stingray *(D. centroura)*, which also has sharp corners on disk, has irregular row of prominent mid-dorsal spines and is generally found along Atlantic coast from Florida northward. Longnose Stingray *(D. guttata)*, another species with sharp corners on disk, has pointed snout and row of blunt tubercles on middle of disk; it occurs in s Gulf of Mexico and Caribbean to s Brazil.

58 Bluntnose Stingray
Dasyatis say

Identification: A moderate-size stingray with a short blunt snout. Gray to brownish or greenish above, white below; tail and margins of disk and pelvic fins dusky in large individuals. *Disk has rounded corners,* few tubercles and spines along midline, and 1 or 2 short rows of tubercles on either side of midline. Well-developed folds on upper and lower surfaces of tail behind dorsal spine. Disk width to 3′ (1 m).

Habitat: Generally in shallow water near shore, to depths of 30′ (10 m).

Range: Chesapeake Bay to s Brazil, occasionally north to New Jersey. Throughout Antilles; scattered records in Gulf of Mexico.

Notes: The Bluntnose Stingray is a bottom feeder, with fish, clams, worms, and shrimps making up most of its diet. Moderately large and common in shallow water, it causes a considerable number of injuries to bathers and waders.

Similar Species: Atlantic Stingray *(D. sabina)*, also with rounded disk corners, has conspicuous projecting snout and mid-dorsal row of spines on disk. It runs up rivers and estuaries into fresh water, from Chesapeake Bay to Florida and Gulf of Mexico; it is common in Florida's St. Johns River. Chupare Stingray *(Himantura schmardae)*, from s Gulf of Mexico, Caribbean coast to Suriname, Antilles, and Great Exuma, Bahamas, has large round disk; tail is much longer than disk and has no fleshy folds.

ROUND STINGRAYS
Family Urolophidae

The stingrays of this family have rounded disks, without noticeable angles at the outer edges. They have no dorsal fin, but do have a caudal fin and a doubly serrate spine near the base of the tail. The tail is stout and does not exceed the disk in length, as it does in most other batoid families.

The family includes two genera *(Urolophus* and *Urotrygon)* and possibly 35 species. One species of *Urolophus* is common in shallow water throughout our region.

Genera of family Urolophidae

Urolophus	Caudal fin 4 times as long as high. Tail about equal to body in length.
Urotrygon	Caudal fin slender, about 6 times as long as high. Tail longer than body length.

61 Yellow Stingray
Urolophus jamaicensis

Identification: A small, frying-pan-shaped ray, variable in color, often with yellow spots and darker reticulations on upper surface.

Edge of disk has no sharp angles. *No dorsal fin. Well-developed caudal fin extends around tip of tail; doubly serrate spine near caudal fin base.* Disk width to about 14" (35 cm).

Habitat: Shallow reefs and associated habitats.

Range: Southern Florida, Bahamas, Yucatán, and throughout Caribbean.

Notes: The Yellow Stingray is commonly encountered by snorkelers and divers. In spite of its small size, it should be treated with respect, for a wound from its doubly serrate venomous spine is very painful, although perhaps not as serious as a wound from a larger stingray. A live-bearing species, it gives birth to three or four young. It feeds on shrimps and other bottom-dwelling invertebrates.

Similar Species: Two species of *Urotrygon* have been reported off Venezuela but are apparently very rare. Chupare Stingray (family Dasyatidae) also has round disk without sharp angles but is larger and has much longer tail with no caudal fin.

BUTTERFLY RAYS
Family Gymnuridae

Butterfly rays are very broad, diamond-shaped rays with the disk more than one and a half times as wide as it is long. They have very short tails without caudal fins, and the species in our range have no dorsal fins.

There are two genera of butterfly rays containing about 12 species; one species lives in our area, and a second sometimes strays into our region.

Smooth Butterfly Ray

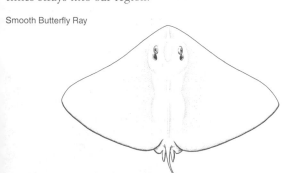

Smooth Butterfly Ray
Gymnura micrura

Identification: A rather small, *broad, diamond-shaped ray with a very short tail lacking a dorsal spine.* No dorsal or caudal fins. Pale brownish gray with irregular light and dark spots. Disk width to 4'–4'6" (1.2–1.4 m).

Habitat: Sandy shallows.

Range: Chesapeake Bay to Florida, Gulf of Mexico, and n South America to Brazil. Seasonal in north.

Notes: The extremely broad, shortened disk of the butterfly rays makes them look like flying delta-wing aircraft underwater.  Like other rays, the Smooth Butterfly Ray feeds on a variety of bottom-dwelling small invertebrates. Because it has no tail spine it is not dangerous to humans. A live bearer, it produces two to six young per litter.

Similar Species: Spiny Butterfly Ray *(G. altavela)* is much larger (disk width more than 6'/1.8 m) and has spine on tail and tentacle-like structure on inner rear margin of spiracle; it occurs in coastal waters up to 200' (60 m) deep in e Atlantic; scattered records in w Atlantic (Massachusetts to Brazil) may be strays.

EAGLE RAYS
Family Myliobatidae

In the eagle rays the disk is wider than it is long. The pectoral fins become abruptly narrow at the level of the eyes, so that the head extends in front of the anterior margins of the disk. The pectoral fins have anterior subdivisions that continue around the snout as a low ridge. The eyes and spiracles are on the sides of the head rather than on the dorsal surface as in the stingrays. There is a single dorsal fin near the base of the tail followed by one or more doubly serrate spines. These spines have venom cells in grooves along their length and can cause painful wounds. The tail is very long and lacks a caudal fin.

The family includes about four genera and 24 species; three genera and four species occur in our area.

Genera of family Myliobatidae

Aetobatus	Single row of tile-like teeth in each jaw. Upper side brown with white spots; underside white.
Myliobatis	7 rows of tile-like teeth in each jaw. Upper side more uniformly colored, with vague spots.
Rhinoptera	7 rows of tile-like teeth in each jaw. Upper side uniformly colored, no spots. Deep groove along side of head and across snout; snout deeply grooved in center beneath groove.

62 Spotted Eagle Ray
Aetobatus narinari

Identification: A beautiful, graceful ray with a very long, whip-like tail. Disk diamond shaped; head extends beyond front margins of disk. Tips of pectoral fins pointed, rear margins concave. *Brown above, with round white spots; white below. Single row of teeth in each jaw; each tooth a crescent shaped plate joined into a band.* Dorsal fin small, its origin over middle of pelvic fins, and followed by doubly serrate spine. Otherwise skin is smooth, with no spines or prickles. Disk width to about 9′ (2.7 m).

Habitat: Shallow coastal waters, frequently around coral reefs.

Range: Worldwide in tropical and warm temperate waters. In w Atlantic: Bermuda; from North Carolina to Brazil; throughout Gulf of Mexico and Caribbean, including Antilles.

Notes: The Spotted Eagle Ray, frequently seen by snorkelers and divers, sometimes travels in small schools. A powerful swimmer, it often leaps out of the water. Its occurrence at remote islands suggests that it can make long migrations across open water. The tail spines can cause serious wounds. This ray feeds mainly on bivalve mollusks, crushing them and neatly separating the meat from the shells, probably with the aid of a series of papillae in the back of the mouth. Very few shell fragments are found in its stomach. It bears young in litters of four.

Similar Species: Southern Eagle Ray *(Myliobatis goodei)* and Bullnose Ray *(M. freminvillei),* both with 7 rows of teeth in each jaw (1 wide row in middle and 3 rows of smaller diamond-shaped teeth on each side), are plain gray to reddish brown with diffuse white spots on upper surface, and white on lower surface; and have steep profile in front of eyes that makes projecting snout resemble duck bill. Southern Eagle Ray, which has dorsal fin beginning well behind level of rear margins of pelvic fins, occurs worldwide in tropical waters. Bullnose Ray, with dorsal fin origin close to level of rear margins of pelvic fins, occurs from Massachusetts to Brazil but is absent from w Gulf of Mexico and most of Caribbean.

63 Cownose Ray
Rhinoptera bonasus

Identification: A large broad, diamond-shaped ray; brownish above, white below. Head extends beyond front margin of disk. Tips of wings acutely pointed; posterior margins concave. *Deep groove around front of head below eyes; "forehead" above groove indented, snout below groove is distinctly bilobed,* resembling cow's nose. Dorsal fin originates over anterior part of pelvic fins and is followed by 1 or 2 doubly serrate spines. Tail 2–3 times as long as body. 7 rows of tile-like teeth in each jaw: 3 middle rows fairly broad (middle one widest); 2 rows of smaller diamond-shaped teeth on each side. Disk width to 6–7′ (1.8–2.1 m).

Habitat: Shallow coastal waters.
Range: New England to Florida, n Cuba, and n Gulf of Mexico. Also from Venezuela to Brazil.

Notes: The Cownose Ray sometimes occurs in large aggregations of several hundred individuals. It feeds on lobsters, crabs, and mollusks, crushing the hard shells with its tooth plates. This distinctive genus, which contains five species, is sometimes placed in a separate family, Rhinopteridae. No other rays in our region have a deep groove around the face.

MANTAS
Family Mobulidae

Mantas are the largest and most spectacular of all batoids. Their diamond-shaped disks may be as much as 22 feet (6.7 m) across. The distinctive pair of lobes that protrude forward and vertically downward from the front of the head on either side of the mouth are known as *cephalic fins.* The eyes are on the sides of the head at the base of the cephalic fins. Mantas have a small dorsal fin near the base of the tail, but no dorsal spines or caudal fin. Mantas live near the surface of the open ocean and, unlike the bottom-dwelling rays, have small spiracles that are probably not used in respiration. They feed on plankton strained from the water as it passes over a sieve-like series of small plates on their specialized gills.

The family includes two genera and about 13 species. Two species, one from each genus, occur in our area. Some authorities consider the mantas a subfamily within the eagle ray family, Myliobatidae.

Genera of family Mobulidae

Manta	Mouth terminal.
Mobula	Mouth subterminal, on ventral surface.

64 Manta
Manta birostris

Identification: A giant ray with a diamond-shaped disk that is wider than it is long. Dorsal surface dark reddish or olive-brown to black, sometimes with whitish shoulder blotches or oblique whitish stripes. Lower surface white, sometime blotched with gray or black. Pectoral fins pointed. *Mouth terminal, flanked by large cephalic fins,* which extend vertically downward when feeding but are rolled into a spiral that points forward when swimming. Tail very slender but shorter than body. Teeth on lower jaw only. Disk width to 22′ (6.7 m).

Habitat: Usually open coastal waters, sometimes shallows close to shore, and sometimes far offshore.

Range: Probably worldwide in tropical and temperate waters. In Atlantic from Bermuda and South Carolina to Brazil, occasionally farther north.

Notes: Mantas often feed at the surface and sometimes make spectacular leaps out of the water. Feeding on plankton and small schooling fishes, they are not dangerous to humans. The cephalic fins apparently serve to direct water into the mouth, so that plankton can be strained out by sieve-like modifications of the gill arches. The cephalic fins are also used to grasp objects that come into contact with the front of the head.

Similar Species: All other rays in our region are much smaller. Devil Ray *(Mobula hypostoma),* which reaches only about 4′ (1.2 m) wide, has mouth on underside of head; it is known from North Carolina, Florida, and Santos, Brazil.

BONY FISHES
Osteichthyes

As they are presently understood, bony fishes, Osteichthyes, fall into two groups, Sarcopterygii, or lobe-finned fishes, and Actinopterygii, ray-finned fishes. All bony fishes differ from cartilaginous fishes (sharks, rays, and chimaeras) in having bony skeletons and no pelvic claspers. A major innovation of bony fishes is the presence of a swim bladder, although some modern fishes have lost the swim bladder. Sarcopterygii includes the lungfishes, the coelacanths, and their derivatives, the tetrapods. They first appeared in the fossil record about 400 million years ago in the Silurian period. No sarcopterygian fishes occur in our region.

RAY-FINNED FISHES
Class Actinopterygii

Most of the living fishes of the world are bony fishes of the class Actinopterygii. The earliest actinopterygian fossils are of the Silurian period. They differ from the Sarcopterygii in many skeletal details but perhaps most obviously in the structure of the pectoral fins. In sarcopterygians there is a prominent lobe at the base of the pectoral fin with a single bone attached to the pectoral girdle with several series of smaller bones between it and the fin rays. In the Actinopterygii a single row of several bones called *actinosts* attaches to the pectoral girdle and supports the fin rays.

Bony fishes have a single pair of gill slits covered by a complex bony gill cover (sharks and rays have five to seven pairs of gill slits, and chimaeras have a single pair of gill openings but no gill cover). With the exception of the primitive sturgeons and paddlefishes, which have heterocercal tails (with the vertebral column extending into the upper lobe of the caudal fin) and keratinous (horny) fin rays like those of sharks, bony fishes have bony rays supporting the fins, and nearly or completely symmetrical tail fins (homocercal) supported by a bony plate. Bony fishes are measured either to the tip of the tail, or total length (TL), or to the base of the tail, known as standard length (SL). The anatomy of bony fishes is described in detail in the Introduction of this guide.

Most bony fishes lay eggs and fertilize them outside of the body. Internal fertilization and viviparity (live birth) have developed several times in different groups of bony fishes, but in these cases the sperm are transferred by some structure other than the pelvic fins (which is the case in the cartilaginous fishes), usually a modification of the anal fin.

ORDER ACIPENSERIFORMES

Fishes of this order are the most primitive of the actinopterygian fishes; this is evident in their heterocercal tails and fins with numerous, horny rays (both features of the more primitive cartilaginous fishes), and in the way their jaws are connected to the skull. Acipenseriform fishes have poorly ossified skeletons and bony, plate-like scales or no scales. The order includes two families: Acipenseridae, the sturgeons, with four genera and 24 species, and Polyodontidae, the paddlefishes, with two genera and two species. One species of sturgeon occurs in our region.

STURGEONS
Family Acipenseridae

The sturgeons are large, fusiform fishes with five rows of bony plates, called *scutes,* along the body: a mid-dorsal row, along the midline of the back; two dorso-lateral rows, one on each side of the midline; and two ventral lateral rows, one on each side of the midline of the belly. The snout is flattened and conical, with four barbels on the underside, and the inferior mouth is protrusible into a short tube. The dorsal and anal fins are far back on the body, and the pelvic fins are abdominal. Most sturgeons live in fresh water or are anadromous, living in salt water and moving into fresh water to spawn.

Atlantic Sturgeon

Atlantic Sturgeon
Acipenser oxyrinchus

Identification: An elongate fish, *pentagonal in cross section, with a heterocercal tail and shark-like fins.* Top of head and back bluish black, shading to white on belly. Mid-dorsal scutes oval, longer than broad, and without pronounced hooks on their keels; spines and keels on mid-dorsal scutes white, contrasting with dark-colored back. Upper half of dorso-lateral scutes matching background, lower half paler than background. Front edges of pectoral and pelvic fins and lower lobe of caudal fin white. Snout moderately long, with transverse row of 4 barbels on underside. Mouth narrow, less than half as wide as distance between eyes. TL: female to 14′ (4.3 m), male to 8′3″ (2.5 m).

Habitat: Usually close to shore in coastal waters, occasionally farther out on continental shelf and offshore banks. Moves into fresh water to spawn.

Range: Generally confined to Atlantic coast from Labrador to e Florida, and n Gulf of Mexico. Reports from French Guiana may be erroneous, and a record from Bermuda is more than 100 years old.

Notes: Sturgeons are spectacular fish highly valued for their caviar and for their flesh. They grow quite large: A record female was 14 feet (4.3 m) long and weighed 811 pounds (368 kg). Sturgeons are usually taken in nets during their spring spawning runs. The exact time of spawning depends on temperature and can begin as early as February in the south, June or July in the northern part of the range. Females take eight to 30 years to reach sexual maturity (the farther north they live the longer it takes) and spawn only every three to five years. Sturgeons are bottom feeders and consume a variety of invertebrates. The Atlantic is the only sturgeon in our area. The Gulf of Mexico population, considered a subspecies *(A. o. desotoi),* is very poorly known but is now under study. Its mid-dorsal scutes are squarish and usually have two strong hooks on their central keel.

TENPOUNDERS, TARPONS, BONEFISHES, and EELS
Subdivision Elopomorpha

Although they do not look much like them, the ten-pounders, tarpons, and their allies, the bonefishes, are closely related to the eels. Perhaps the best evidence for this association is that they all have similar larvae, called *leptocephali*

Bonefish leptocephalus

(sing. leptocephalus), which are translucent, ribbon-shaped, planktonic creatures with specialized, forward-directed teeth. Other fish larvae may be long and slender, but no others are ribbon-like.

ORDER ELOPIFORMES

The elopiform fishes encompass the tenpounders (also called ladyfishes) and the tarpons. Some authorities consider them to belong to a single family; others recognize two families, as we do here. There are about eight species, six tenpounders and two tarpons.

Elopiform fishes have a typical fish shape rather than the specialized, snake-like shape that distinguishes the related eels. They are slender, elongate, and somewhat compressed, with deeply forked tails and abdominal pelvic fins. There is a narrow superficial bony plate, called a *gular plate,* between the bones of the lower jaw.

TENPOUNDERS
Family Elopidae

Tenpounders, or ladyfishes, are slender fishes, only slightly compressed, with small scales and large tails. They have a well-developed gular plate and 23 to 35 branchiostegal rays. The single dorsal fin is short and without spines, and the last ray is not elongate.

The family contains one genus with about six species; two species probably occur in our area.

65 Ladyfish
Elops saurus

Identification: An elongate, fusiform, slightly compressed fish with a large, deeply forked caudal fin. Silvery overall, bluish above, shading to pale yellow below; fins dusky with yellowish tinge. *Scales small, more than 100 in lateral line.* Eye large, mostly covered by adipose tissue. Mouth terminal, with maxilla reaching well

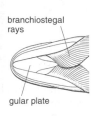

branchiostegal rays

gular plate

behind eye. *Gular plate narrow.* Single short dorsal fin, with origin near middle of body. Anal fin short, far back on body. Conspicuous scaly sheaths at bases of dorsal and anal fins. Pelvic fin abdominal, below dorsal fin; pectoral fin low on side of body. Prominent axillary processes at bases of pectoral and pelvic fins. TL to 3′3″ (1 m).

Habitat: Shallow coastal waters, including brackish lagoons; rarely over coral reefs. Enters fresh water in Florida.

Range: Western Atlantic from Cape Cod and Bermuda to Brazil. Widespread in Gulf of Mexico and w and s Caribbean, but uncommon in Antilles.

Notes: Although not valued as a food fish, the Ladyfish is sought by sport fishers. It feeds on crustaceans and small fishes, and sometimes occurs in schools. The Ladyfish spawns in the open sea, and the leptocephali move into lagoons and mangrove nursery areas. A study of leptocephali has revealed that there are two forms of Ladyfish in the western Atlantic, a northern form with 79 to 86 body segments and a southern form with 74 to 78 segments. If the difference can be confirmed in adult specimens, it is likely that the southern form represents a new species that is unnamed at present.

Similar Species: Tarpon is larger and more compressed, with much larger scales, and has last ray of dorsal fin extended. Other species of *Elops* live in Indo-Pacific region.

TARPONS
Family Megalopidae

Tarpons are big, robust fishes with very large scales. The last ray of the single dorsal fin is extended as a heavy filament, and the tail is moderately forked. The mouth is large, with heavy, bony jaws; like the related ten-pounders, the tarpons have a gular plate.

This family contains two species, one in the Atlantic and the other in the Indo-Pacific region. Some authorities consider them to be in the same genus, *Megalops,* while others put the Atlantic species in the genus *Tarpon.*

66 **Tarpon**
Megalops atlanticus

Identification:
A very large, elongate, moderately compressed fish. Generally silvery in color; darker, olive tinted above. *Large scales,* 37–42 in lateral line. Single dorsal fin short, its origin at about middle of body, with *last ray extended as heavy filament.* Anal fin longer, well behind dorsal fin. No fin spines. Pelvic fin abdominal; pectoral fin low on side. Pectoral and pelvic fins have large axillary scales. Caudal fin deeply forked. Large, terminal mouth with heavy, bony jaws, lower jaw projecting beyond upper; maxilla reaches to well behind eye. Gular plate slender. TL to about 8′ (2.4 m).

Habitat:
Inshore waters; common around mangrove areas; enters brackish estuaries and marshes, sometimes into fresh water.

Range:
North Carolina to Brazil, occasionally farther north. Throughout Gulf of Mexico and Caribbean.

Notes:
The Tarpon, formerly called *Tarpon atlanticus,* is a popular game fish famous for its spectacular jumps. Its bony jaws make it hard to hook and a challenge for skilled fishermen. Although it is not esteemed as a food fish, it is eaten in some areas. The swim bladder of the Tarpon is modified so that it can breathe air and thus survive in water with very little oxygen, such as some marshes and estuaries. Although no other fish in our area can be confused with the Tarpon, a smaller species, *M. cyprinoides,* is widespread in the Indo-Pacific region.

ORDER ALBULIFORMES

This is a small order encompassing the bonefishes (family Albulidae) and Notacanthoids, a group that includes two families of eel-like deep-sea fishes. Only the bonefishes occur in shallow water and are covered here. Albuliform fishes have conical snouts and inferior mouths with conical teeth. They do not have a gular plate on the lower jaw.

BONEFISHES
Family Albulidae

Bonefishes are large, slender, fusiform fishes, easily recognized by the protruding conical snout and inferior mouth. They have a single short dorsal fin, with no spines, and a deeply forked caudal fin.

The family contains a single genus, *Albula,* with at least two species. *Albula vulpes,* which occurs in all warm seas, may actually be more than one species, as indicated by recent biochemical studies.

---

67 Bonefish
Albula vulpes

Identification: A slender, fusiform fish, almost round in cross section, only slightly compressed. *Bluntly conical snout extends beyond inferior mouth.* Bluish above, shading to silvery white on side; dark streaks between scales of upper side. Snout has median, small, oval, dark spot on underside and pair of diagonal dark marks at tip. Juvenile has 7 or 8 indistinct saddle-shaped bars across back. Scales moderately large (65–71 in lateral line) and regular. Pelvic fin abdominal; pectoral fin low on side of body. Caudal fin deeply forked. Adipose tissue covers most of eye. 3 elongate patches of molar-like teeth on roof of mouth; similar patches on tongue and floor of mouth. Maxilla lacks teeth, does not reach to below eye. No gular plate. TL to about 31″ (79 cm).

Habitat: Shallow flats, mangrove areas, and river mouths.

Range: Tropical and warm temperate waters worldwide. In w Atlantic: North Carolina (occasionally farther north) to Florida, Bahamas, Gulf of Mexico, Antilles, and Caribbean to Brazil.

Notes: Bonefish root in the bottom for their invertebrate prey, often in water so shallow that the caudal and dorsal fins break the surface. Esteemed for its wariness and fighting qualities, this species is one of the most important game fishes of the world.

Similar Species: Shafted Bonefish *(A. nemoptera)*, which
has longer snout, larger mouth with tip
of maxilla reaching to below eye, and
last ray of dorsal fin extended as
filament, occurs from Panama to
Venezuela; also e Pacific.

ORDER ANGUILLIFORMES

This order includes 15 families of eels, all of which are represented in the western Atlantic Ocean. Nine of these occur
only in deep water and are not considered here. Fishermen
and divers commonly encounter morays and a few species of
snake eels, but most eels are secretive and rarely seen. Recent research on eels has resulted in a number of changes in
scientific names; different names may be encountered in
older references.

Eels are extremely elongate fishes with cylindrical, snake-
like bodies. They lack pelvic fins, and the pectoral fins are
small, vestigial, or absent. In most eels the dorsal and anal
fins are continuous with the caudal fin, although in most
snake eels the caudal fin is absent and the tail ends in a
sharp point. All eels lack fin spines, and most eels lack
scales, except members of the family Anguillidae, which
have tiny embedded scales arranged in a herringbone pattern. Eels have short gill openings on the sides of the body,
and two pairs of nostrils that are usually widely separated.
The anterior nostrils are near the tip of the snout, sometimes at the ends of short tubes. The posterior nostrils can

PARTS OF AN EEL

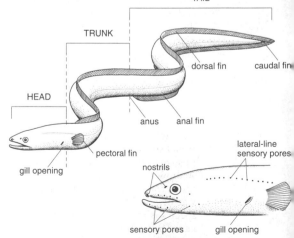

be round, slit-like, or tubular, and their location can vary from inside the upper lip to high on the sides of the head or even on the top of the head. As with other fishes, the head ends at the gill openings, the body (trunk) is the region from the gill openings to the anus, and the tail is the rest of the eel, including the caudal fin. The position of the anus—i.e., the relative length of the head and body vs. the tail length—is important in the identification of eels. Other features used to distinguish the species of eels are rather technical and often require close examination of specimens for such details as the location of the anus, the precise positions of the beginning of the dorsal and anal fins, the size and shape of the gill openings, and the shape and position of the nostrils. For some species the number and position of *sensory pores* on the head and body are important characteristics. These pores are small openings of the lateral-line system, employed to detect vibrations in the water.

The leptocephalic larvae of eels are translucent and ribbon-like, with rounded tail fins. They are attracted to lights and come to the surface at night, where they can often be caught in dip nets. Identification of leptocephali is beyond the scope of this guide.

Keep in mind that while all eels look like eels, there are some other fishes that are eel-like, such as the hagfishes, cuskeels, brotulas, gobies, and wormfishes. The synbranchiform fishes, although they are called swamp eels, are not eels at all.

We cover six eel families below; the key features of each family are outlined in the following table. The related family Heterenchelyidae is represented in our region by *Pythonichthys sanguineus*, a rare scaleless eel that resembles the Spaghetti Eel *(Moringua edwardsi)* and is discussed briefly in that account.

Eel families

Anguillidae	Large, with scales. Well-developed pectoral fin.
Moringuidae	No scales. Anus well behind mid-body. Dorsal origin at or behind mid-body. Fins low; pectoral fin very small. Caudal fin rays short; end of tail soft.
Chlopsidae	Small, without scales. Pectoral fin present or absent. Posterior nostril low on side of head, sometimes inside mouth. Anus in front of mid-body.

| *Muraenidae* | Large, colorful, without scales. No pectoral fin. Posterior nostril high on head. Mouth large. |

| *Ophichthidae* | No scales. Tail ends in sharp point (snake eels) or in flexible reduced caudal fin (worm eels). Posterior nostril low on side of head. |

| *Congridae* | No scales. Pectoral fin present. Lateral line complete, with pores for most of its length. Anus at or ahead of mid-body. |

FRESHWATER EELS
Family Anguillidae

    Freshwater eels are large, rather heavy-bodied eels with well-developed pectoral fins, a complete lateral line, and crescent-shaped gill openings on the sides of the body. They have small, non-overlapping scales deeply embedded in the thick skin. The dorsal and anal fins are well developed and connected to the caudal fin. The dorsal fin begins between the back of the head and the anus. Freshwater eels are catadromous, spending most of their adult lives in fresh water but returning to the sea to spawn (anadromous species live in the ocean and ascend rivers to spawn in fresh water). In general, males tend to remain near the coast, whereas females move far upstream into fresh water. The family contains one genus and about 15 species, only one of which is known from our area.

74 **American Eel**
Anguilla rostrata

Identification: A heavy-bodied eel, terete anteriorly, somewhat compressed posteriorly. Color variable: yellowish or brownish green above, paler below. Head and trunk slightly shorter than tail. Dorsal origin somewhat ahead of anus. *Caudal fin rounded, joined to dorsal and anal fins. Gill opening on side in front of lower half of well-developed pectoral fin.* Mouth terminal, horizontal; *lower jaw longer than upper.*

Snout rather pointed. Anterior nostril tubular, on side of snout; posterior nostril round, in front of eye. Small, non-overlapping scales in herringbone pattern, deeply embedded in skin. 103–111 vertebrae. TL: female to 4′ (1.2 m), male to 16″ (41 cm).

Habitat: Along coast in estuaries and marshes. Spawning grounds in Sargasso Sea.

Range: Bermuda, mainland coast to Florida, n and w Gulf of Mexico, Bahamas, Antilles south to Trinidad. Probably not in mainland South America.

Notes: The American Eel is a catadromous species, living in fresh water and traveling to the ocean to spawn in the Sargasso Sea, a vast area southeast of Bermuda. Although no adults or eggs have been collected in the spawning area, the smallest larvae are found there, and progressively larger larvae are found closer to the coast. As they reach the coast the ribbon-like leptocephali (larvae) transform into small elvers that are transparent at first, then develop their pigment as they settle to the bottom. Males tend to stay near the coast, where they are abundant in estuaries and marshes. Females ascend streams; they can even make their way around low dams and are often found in surprisingly small tributaries. At sexual maturity both sexes develop a more silvery coloration, and the eyes enlarge. They migrate downstream to the ocean and leave the coast for the spawning grounds. No adults return, and it is assumed that they die after spawning. In streams American Eels are generally bottom feeders, consuming small invertebrates, detritus, and carrion. They sometimes feed on fish caught in commercial gill nets.

Similar Species: European Eel *(A. anguilla)*, which is very similar but has 110–119 vertebrae, occurs in Europe, although its larvae are common near Bermuda, where they occur with American Eel.

SPAGHETTI EELS
Family Moringuidae

Spaghetti eels are moderate-size to large burrowing eels with no scales. They have no pectoral fins or very small ones (usually in adult males). Their slender, elongate bodies are round in cross section but compressed near the tail. The dorsal and anal fins are low and confined to the rear of the body, and the tail is very small, except in mature males of the genus *Moringua*. The anus is well behind the midpoint of the body. Spaghetti eels have two pairs of nostrils; the anterior nostrils are non-tubular and are located near the tip of the snout; the posterior nostrils, round and also non-tubular, are in front of the eyes. The eyes are very small except in mature adults. The family contains two genera: *Neoconger*, with three species, and *Moringua*, with six species. Most are uncommon in our region.

Genera of family Moringuidae

Neoconger	Upper jaw longer than lower. Dorsal fin begins in front of anus.
Moringua	Lower jaw longer than upper. Dorsal fin begins behind level of anus.

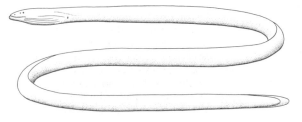

Spaghetti Eel female

Spaghetti Eel
Moringua edwardsi

male

Identification: *A very slender, elongate, cylindrical eel with a projecting lower jaw.* Juveniles uniformly orange-yellow above, white below. Mature males and females gray to black above, abruptly pale below. Anus behind mid-body. Tail slightly compressed; caudal fin small and pointed in juveniles and females, slightly forked in adult males. Dorsal and anal fins originate far back on body. Lateral line complete, ending at base of tail. Eye very small in non-reproductive individuals, well developed in mature adults. TL to 19¾" (50 cm).

Habitat: Sandy bottoms, to depths of 73' (22 m).

Range: Bermuda, Florida, Bahamas, Caribbean to Venezuela. Scarce in w Gulf of Mexico.

Notes: Spaghetti Eels feed on burrowing invertebrates that live in the sand. They are unusual in displaying extreme changes in color, fin shape, and eye size with maturity. Immature individuals seem to spend their time buried in the sand, but adults emerge at night and sometimes come to lights at the surface.

Similar Species: Ridged Eel *(Neoconger mucronatus),* a smaller species, has incomplete lateral line ending above anus and pointed snout that projects beyond lower jaw; it occurs in Gulf of Mexico and Caribbean south to Brazil. *Pythonichthys sanguineus* (family Heterenchelyididae) is a rare species known from Cuba, Puerto Rico, Colombia, and Guyana; moderately long (TL to 32"/80 cm), pink or reddish, with tiny eyes and large mouth, it has no pectoral fin and no lateral line, and its dorsal fin begins above gill opening, which is low on side of body.

FALSE MORAYS
Family Chlopsidae

False morays are superficially similar to true morays (family Muraenidae) but are smaller and differ in several internal features. Externally they can be recognized by the location of the posterior nostrils, which are near the upper lip or sometimes inside the mouth rather than in front of the eyes. In both families the anterior nostrils are near the tip of the snout at the ends of short tubes that are directed forward and outward. Some false morays have pectoral fins, while true morays never do. Some species can be distinguished by the arrangement of teeth on the roof of the mouth. Almost nothing is known about the spawning habits of false morays. Formerly called Xenocongridae, the family includes eight genera and 18 species; six genera occur in our area. In addition to the species listed here, there are several species from deep water in our region belonging to three other genera.

Genera of family Chlopsidae

Chilorhinus	Lower lip with downturned flange. Pectoral fin vestigial or absent. Posterior nostril opens inside mouth.
Kaupichthys	Lower lip without flange. Pectoral fin present. Posterior nostril outside mouth.
Chlopsis	Lower lip without flange. Pectoral fin absent. Posterior nostril outside mouth.

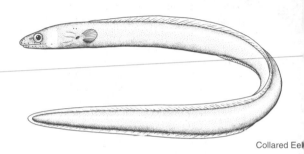

Collared Eel

Collared Eel
Kaupichthys nuchalis

Identification: A moderately slender eel with anus well ahead of mid-body. Brownish overall; underside of head and throat pale, with *pale band around head behind eyes.* Gill opening in front of well-developed pectoral fin. Dorsal fin origin over or slightly behind gill opening. Posterior nostril on side of head in front of lower rim of eye, without flap along dorsal edge. Vomerine teeth in 2 parallel rows. TL to 6¼″ (16 cm).

Habitat: In and around coral reefs, sometimes in sponges, from shoreline to depths of 250′ (75 m), sometimes deeper.

Range: Bermuda, Bahamas, nw Gulf of Mexico, and Antilles to Caribbean.

Notes: Although it is common around coral reefs, the Collared Eel is seldom seen. Apparently it sometimes lives in tubular sponges, and it has been suggested that this is its primary habitat. Nothing is known of its life history.

Similar Species: Morays are similar but larger, lack pectoral fins, and have posterior nostril high on side of head, above level of middle of eye. Reef Eel *(K. hyoproroides)* lacks pale ring around head; its posterior nostril is outside mouth and has fleshy flap on its dorsal rim; it occurs in Bermuda, s Florida, Bahamas, Caribbean to Venezuela; also in Indo-Pacific.

Other species of false morays

Bicolor Eel	*(Chlopsis bicolor)* Dark brown above, abruptly changing to white below. Widely scattered localities on both sides of Atlantic, including North Carolina, South Carolina, s Florida, Florida Keys, Yucatán Peninsula, s Brazil.
Chlopsis dentatus	Mottled color pattern. Posterior nostril covered by flap on its dorsal margin. Deep water. Cuba, w Caribbean, Colombia, Barbados; also e Atlantic, possibly w Pacific.
Seagrass Eel	*(Chilorhinus suensoni)* Rather stout, with short snout and distinctive downturned flange on outer edge of lower lip. Generally brownish; white ring around gill opening (on mid-side). Dorsal origin behind gill opening. Anus slightly ahead of mid-body. Vomerine teeth in rows that diverge posteriorly. Bermuda, Bahamas, w Caribbean from Yucatán to Honduras, south to Brazil. Not in Florida or Gulf of Mexico.

MORAYS
Family Muraenidae

Morays are robust, heavy-bodied, moderate-size to very large eels with no pectoral fins. They are often colorfully and boldly patterned. The caudal fin is joined to the dorsal and anal fins. Most morays have small, roundish gill openings on the sides of the head, although the gill openings are slit-like in some species. *Sensory pores,* small openings leading to the lateral line, are present only on the head, not on the body as in many other fishes. The number and position of these pores is sometimes useful for distinguishing closely similar species. The sensory pores occur in groups: three pairs of *supraorbital pores,* located over the eyes; three

or four pairs of *infraorbital pores,* below the eyes and along
the upper jaw; six *mandibular pores,* on the lower jaw; and
one to four (usually two) *branchial pores,* above the gill area.

The anterior nostrils are in short tubes near the tip of the
snout and directed outward. The posterior nostrils, usually
without tubes, are high on the sides of the head immediately in front of the upper part of the eyes. Most morays
have long sharp teeth along the edges of both jaws, although members of the genus *Echidna* have stout, conical, or
molar-like teeth. In some morays the teeth on the roof of the
mouth are hinged so that they fold down as food is ingested.

Morays are the eels that the snorkeler is most apt to see.
They seem to spend most of the daylight hours in holes with
their heads poking out. As long as the diver does not disturb
them, moray eels are harmless. However, it is unwise to reach
into holes or under ledges without looking first; with powerful jaws and needle-sharp teeth, morays can inflict serious in-
jury. Although morays are sometimes eaten, they have been
known to cause the tropical fish poisoning called ciguatera.

Worldwide the moray family includes 15 genera and perhaps as many as 200 species. Eight genera and about 23
species occur in the western Atlantic. Three genera, placed in
the subfamily Uropteryginae, have short dorsal and anal fins
that extend only a short distance forward from the end of the
tail. The rest of the morays (subfamily Muraeninae) have long
dorsal fins originating over or ahead of the gill openings, and
anal fins originating near the middle of the body. In all morays
the dorsal and anal fins are continuous with the caudal fin.

Genera of family Muraenidae
Subfamily Uropteryginae

Dorsal and anal fins short, confined to end of tail.

Channomuraena	Large, banded morays, with eye far for-ward, over anterior third of mouth. Pos-terior nostril in short tube, without contiguous sensory pore.
Uropterygius	Posterior nostril without contiguous sensory pore.
Anarchias	Posterior nostril contiguous with sensory pore so that it appears double.

Subfamily Muraeninae

Dorsal and anal fins longer, not confined to end of tail.

Echidna

Dorsal origin in front of gill opening. Teeth blunt, molar-like.

Enchelycore

Dorsal origin near gill opening. Jaws curved, meeting only near their tips.

Gymnothorax

Dorsal origin near gill opening; anal fin origin near anus (mid-body). Jaws straight, close completely. Posterior nostril usually non-tubular.

Monopenchelys

Dorsal origin slightly behind anus. Head and body shorter than tail.

Muraena

Dorsal origin near gill opening. Posterior nostril tubular.

68 Chain Moray
Echidna catenata

Identification: A rather heavy-bodied eel with a short blunt snout. Dark brown with *yellow, chain-like markings.* Head and body equal to or shorter than tail in length. Posterior nostril, above front of eye, has low, scalloped, fleshy rim. *Teeth bluntly pointed or molar-like, especially on roof of mouth.* TL to 28″ (71 cm).

Habitat: Shallow water around reefs, to depths of 65′ (20 m).

Range: Bermuda, Bahamas, Caribbean, including Antilles. Also s Atlantic islands.

Notes: The Chain Moray feeds primarily on small crabs and is often seen by snorkelers and divers. The life history of this species is a special mystery, for even its leptocephali larvae have not been found, although the larvae of most other eels in our region are known. The blunt teeth and conspicuous reticulated pattern make this species easily identifiable.

69 Viper Moray
Enchelycore nigricans

Identification: A slender, slightly compressed, brown moray, sometimes slightly mottled, with *arched jaws that touch only at their tips when mouth is closed.* Head and trunk shorter than or equal to tail in length. Posterior nostril large and elongate, well in front of eye. Sensory pores of lower jaw not surrounded by white spots. TL to 35" (89 cm).

Habitat: Coral reefs and rocky shorelines to depths of 80' (25 m).

Range: Bermuda, Bahamas, and w and s Caribbean, including Antilles. Also s Atlantic islands.

Notes: The Viper Moray is a common and wide-ranging, but secretive, species sometimes seen under ledges around coral reefs.

Similar Species: Chestnut Moray *(E. carychroa)* and Fangtooth Moray *(E. anatina)* have similarly arched jaws but rounded posterior nostrils. Chestnut Moray, a small (TL to 13"/33 cm), uniformly brown species with sensory pores of lower jaw surrounded by white rings, occurs in Bermuda, Bahamas, s Florida, n Gulf of Mexico, and Caribbean, including Antilles; also in e Atlantic. Adults are difficult to distinguish from those of Viper Moray. Fangtooth Moray, a large species (TL to 3'7"/1.1 m) known from Bermuda, Florida, Brazil, and e Atlantic islands (usually in deep water in w Atlantic), is brown with white spots and blotches.

Viper Moray range

70 Goldentail Moray
Gymnothorax miliaris

Identification:

A stout moray with a short blunt snout and an extremely variable color and pattern; usually dark with small yellow dots, but may even be pale pink with irregular brown blotches. *Tip of tail always pale, usually deep yellow in life.* Dorsal and anal fins long, not confined to tail. *Posterior nostril in short tube* (shorter than tube of anterior nostril) above front of eye. Front teeth short and pointed or wedge-shaped (not serrate); jaw teeth in 2 rows. TL to 22″ (55 cm).

Habitat: Usually around coral reefs, to depths of 200′ (60 m).

Range: Bermuda, Bahamas, Florida Keys, Caribbean, including Antilles, and se Brazil. Also mid-Atlantic islands.

Notes: The Goldentail is one of the most common and most easily recognized morays of the West Indian reefs. This species has been called *Muraena miliaris.*

Similar Species: Other species of morays in our area with tubular posterior nostrils are Marbled Moray *(Uropterygius macularius),* which has dorsal and anal fins confined to tip of tail, and species of genus *Muraena,* which also have dorsal origin ahead of gill opening but have posterior nostril in tube about as long as anterior nostril tube.

71 Green Moray
Gymnothorax funebris

Identification:

A very large moray, uniformly dark green to brown. Young blackish with white chin. Snout long and pointed; eye well forward, its center slightly before mid-jaw. Teeth smooth; front teeth canine-like. Posterior nostril not tubular. 4 infraorbital pores. TL to 6′ (1.8 m).

Habitat: Coral reefs and rocky tide pools, usually shallower than 100′ (30 m).

Range: Bermuda, Bahamas, around Caribbean, and n South America to mouth of Amazon; also s Brazil.

Notes: This is the largest moray apt to be encountered by a snorkeler in our region. There have been reports that it has attacked divers without provocation, but such behavior must be unusual. Used for food in some areas, the Green Moray has been reported to cause ciguatera (tropical fish poisoning).

Similar Species: Small Green Morays, rarely seen, could be confused with Purplemouth Moray, which has less uniform (somewhat mottled with darker flecks) green color and white margins on dorsal, caudal, and anal fins.

---

72 Spotted Moray
Gymnothorax moringa

Identification: A moderate-size moray with a pattern of *distinct small, round, overlapping dark brownish to purplish-black spots on white or pale yellow background.* Number of spots varies with individuals; some are quite pale with fewer dots, others are densely spotted and appear quite dark. Spotted pattern continues out to near edge of fins; margins of dorsal, anal, and caudal fins white in pale and small specimens, dark in dark and large specimens. Juveniles up to 4″ (10 cm) long are uniformly brown with pale fins and white lower jaws. Snout long and pointed; eye well forward, center before mid-jaw. Front teeth canine-like; teeth not serrate. Posterior nostril not tubular. 4 infraorbital pores. TL to 3′3″ (1 m), possibly longer.

Habitat: Common around rocky shorelines and shallow coral reefs, occasionally to depths of 660′ (200 m). Also in seagrass beds under overhangs, and rocky boulders and outcrops.

Range: Bermuda, South Carolina, e Gulf of Mexico, and around Caribbean to French Guiana and s Brazil. Also mid- and e Atlantic islands.

Notes: The Spotted Moray is probably the most common moray in shallow water in our region. It is usually seen with its head protruding from a hole and the rest of its body concealed.

Similar Species: Purplemouth Moray has freckled or mottled pattern and white margins on anal and caudal fins and rear third of dorsal fin.

73 Purplemouth Moray
Gymnothorax vicinus

Identification: A medium-size moray, usually *mottled greenish or brown overall,* often with darker flecks. *Anal and caudal fins have white margins that continue onto rear third and sometimes entire length of dorsal fin.* Dark slash at each corner of mouth; lining of mouth dusky or purplish black. Snout long and pointed; eye well forward, center of eye before mid-jaw. Teeth smooth; front teeth canine-like. 4 infraorbital pores. TL to 34″ (85 cm).

Habitat: Coral reefs and shallow waters to 250′ (75 m) deep.

Range: Bermuda, Bahamas, Florida, e Gulf of Mexico, throughout Caribbean, and south to sc coast of Brazil. Also e Atlantic islands.

Notes: The Purplemouth Moray is common around coral reefs and is likely to be seen by snorkelers. It is usually found in holes in rocks and around corals with just the head protruding. It can be approached closely, but you shouldn't attempt to touch it.

Similar Species: Green Moray is larger, has more uniform color pattern, and lacks distinct white margins on dorsal, anal, and caudal fins.

Other *Gymnothorax* species

Teeth smooth. Center of eye ahead of mid-jaw.

Polygon Moray   (*G. polygonius*) Similar color pattern to Spotted Moray: spotted polygons separated by darker lilac-brown reticulations. Rare; Bermuda, North Carolina, Cuba, Puerto Rico, Campeche Bank, Brazil.

Teeth serrate. Eye small, center over or behind mid-jaw. 4 pores below eye.

Lichen Moray	*(G. hubbsi)* Small. Short blunt snout. Pale branching marks on brownish background over entire body and fins. Only 11 specimens known, from North Carolina, Florida, Great Bahama Bank, Cuba.
Sharktooth Moray	*(G. maderensis)* Large. Blunt snout. Dark brown reticulations on paler yellowish background; head dusky; prominent white margins on fins. Scattered records: Bermuda, North Carolina, Cuba, Puerto Rico, Virgin Islands; also e Atlantic.

Teeth serrate. Snout short and blunt. Center of eye over or behind mid-jaw. 3 pores below eye.

Ocellated Moray	*(G. ocellatus)* Brown overall, with striking pattern of scattered white spots on body and alternating black and white markings on dorsal and anal fins. Caribbean, n South America to s Brazil.
Honeycomb Moray	*(G. saxicola)* Similar to Ocellated Moray but has prominent black saddles on edge of dorsal fin. North Carolina to s Florida; e Gulf of Mexico from Florida Keys to Mobile Bay.
Saddled Moray	*(G. conspersus)* Large. Dark brown with white spots on body and slash marks across outer half of dorsal fin. North Carolina, Florida, Antilles, Colombia to s Brazil.
Blacktail Moray	*(G. kolpos)* Large. Greenish brown with white ocellated spots that are small on head and anterior, becoming larger and fewer posteriorly, ending in single mid-lateral row of larger white spots toward darker brown tip of tail. North Carolina, Georgia, Gulf of Mexico from Straits of Florida to Louisiana, Campeche Bank.
Blackedge Moray	*(G. nigromarginatus)* Brown, with small yellow or white spots on body and lower half of fins; dorsal and anal fins with black margins; tip of tail pale. W Gulf of Mexico from Mobile Bay to ne Mexico, Yucatán, Honduras.

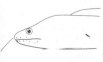

Other species of morays

Dorsal and anal fins long, not confined to end of tail.

Reticulate Moray — *(Muraena retifera)* Reticulated pattern of light brown blotches on dark brown background. North Carolina to Florida, e Gulf of Mexico, Yucatán, Venezuela.

Stout Moray — *(Muraena robusta)* Very large (TL to 6'2"/ 1.9 m). Pattern of large dark spots, with dark blotch around gill opening. Common in e Atlantic; infrequent off North Carolina, Florida, Panama.

Redface Eel — *(Monopenchelys acuta)* Small, slender, somewhat compressed. Snout long and broad. Uniformly brown, with red head and tail tip. Gill opening low on side. Posterior nostril round, non-tubular, above front of eye. Scattered localities, including Bahamas, Grand Cayman, Lesser Antilles, Cozumel, Venezuela. Also Ascension Island in s Atlantic, Indian and Pacific Oceans.

Dorsal and anal fins short, confined to end of tail.

Broadbanded Moray

— *(Channomuraena vittata)* Large, heavy-bodied. Head and body tannish gray to olive; 13–16 broad, reddish-brown bands around body. Posterior nostril above front of eye in short tube about one-third length of anterior nostril tube. Mouth large. Anus well behind mid-body. Bermuda, Bahamas, Antilles, Yucatán, Curaçao; also e Atlantic, possibly Pacific.

Pygmy Moray — *(Anarchias similis)* Small. Varies from uniformly dark brown to blotched. Irregular pattern of pale marks on lower side of head and chin; white spots around sensory pores. Sensory pore and posterior nostril appear as double opening. Bermuda, Georgia, both coasts of Florida, Bahamas, Nicaragua, Lesser Antilles, s Brazil.

Marbled Moray — *(Uropterygius macularius)* Small. Usually mottled, sometimes almost uniformly dark; always has pale marks on head and pale rims on sensory pores on head. Nostrils in short tubes; anterior nostril near tip of snout; posterior nostril above front of eye. Gill opening a small, oblique slit. Short jaws close completely. Anus slightly ahead of mid-body. Bermuda, Bahamas, Florida Keys, Caribbean south to Brazil.

SNAKE EELS and WORM EELS
Family Ophichthidae

Ophichthidae is an extremely diverse family of elongate, scaleless eels, many of which resemble snakes. Some are quite colorful, and a number are active in the daytime. Some ophichthids have pectoral fins, others do not. Some have the dorsal fin originating on the head, others have the dorsal origin behind the anus, and some lack fins altogether. In those species in which a caudal fin is present, it is contiguous with the dorsal and anal fins. The gill openings may be on the sides of the body or on the ventral surface. The posterior nostrils are located on or near the upper lip, and like the anterior nostrils can be simple openings or at the ends of tubes. The teeth are fang-like in some species and blunt in others. The family is divided into two subfamilies: Myrophinae, the worm eels, which have flexible tail tips and short but externally visible caudal fin rays; and Ophichthinae, the snake eels, which have hard-tipped tails with no rays visible externally (except in some species from the Pacific).

Ophichthidae is a very large family, with some 55 genera and 255 species worldwide; 25 genera and 55 species are found in the western Atlantic. We include here only a few species that divers or anglers are apt to encounter in shallow water. Others may be common but are seldom seen because of their burrowing habits.

Genera of family Ophichthidae
Subfamily Myrophinae

Tip of tail flexible; caudal fin rays visible externally.

Myrophis	Dorsal fin origin between gill opening and anus. Teeth on vomer.
Ahlia	Dorsal fin origin above or behind anus. No vomerine teeth.

Subfamily Ophichthinae

Tail ends in hard point.

Apterichtus	No fins. Anterior nostril tubular. Eye moderate in size.
Ichthyapus	No fins. Anterior nostril non-tubular, with convoluted opening. Eye tiny.
Myrichthys	Pectoral fin well developed but short, with broad base. Underside of snout has short median groove. Anterior nostril tubular; posterior nostril inside mouth. Teeth molar-like.
Aplatophis	Pectoral fin present. Anterior teeth fang-like, extending out of closed mouth. Mouth terminal. Anterior and posterior nostrils tubular.
Letharchus	No pectoral or anal fins. Anterior nostril non-tubular; posterior nostril inside mouth.
Caralophia	No pectoral fins. Underside of snout not grooved. Anterior nostril non-tubular; posterior nostril inside mouth.
Callechelys	No pectoral fins. Underside of snout has median groove. Anterior nostril tubular; posterior nostril on underside of snout. Tip of tail pointed.
Gordiichthys	No pectoral fins. Underside of snout has median groove. Anterior nostril tubular or surrounded by groove; posterior nostril inside mouth, from side appearing as slit below eye. Tip of tail blunt.
Aprognathodon	No pectoral fins. No groove on underside of snout. Dorsal fin origin on nape. Anterior nostril tubular; posterior nostril inside mouth. Tip of tail pointed.
Ethadophis	No pectoral fins. No groove on underside of snout. Anterior nostril tubular; posterior nostril inside mouth. Tip of tail blunt.
Bascanichthys	Minute pectoral fin present at upper end of gill opening. Dorsal fin origin on head. Underside of snout has median groove. Anterior nostril tubular; posterior nostril inside mouth.

Quassiremus	Pectoral fin minute, shorter than eye diameter. Dorsal fin origin behind gill opening. Underside of snout has short median groove. Anterior nostril tubular; posterior nostril inside mouth.
Echiophis	Pectoral fin well developed. Mouth terminal. Snout short, underside without groove. Anterior and posterior nostrils tubular, close together.
Ophichthus	Pectoral fin well developed. Dorsal fin origin above or behind gill opening. Snout long, conical, with groove on underside. Anterior nostril tubular; posterior nostril inside mouth or on edge of lip.

75 Speckled Worm Eel
Myrophis punctatus

Identification:	A slender, moderately compressed eel with *dorsal fin origin midway between gill opening and anus.* Pale tan to yellowish brown overall, paler ventrally, with *squarish brown freckles* on upper surface and chin. Pectoral fin has broad base. Gill opening small, on mid-side. Single pore behind each eye. Anterior nostril tubular; posterior nostril along edge of mouth and covered by flap so that it opens inside mouth. Upper jaw longer than lower. Teeth moderately sharp. TL to 13¾" (35 cm).
Habitat:	Tidal creeks and brackish estuaries, offshore to depths of 22′ (7 m) over mud and sand bottoms.
Range:	Bermuda, Carolinas to Florida, e Gulf of Mexico, throughout Caribbean.
Notes:	Worm eels are secretive, burrowing fishes that really do resemble worms. This species is the most abundant worm eel in the western Atlantic. It is frequently taken in trawls and sometimes comes to lights at the surface, but because of its burrowing habits it is unlikely to be seen by divers.

Other species of worm eels

Flexible tail tip with visible caudal fin rays.

Broadnose Worm Eel	*(Myrophis platyrhynchus)* Small. Pale with widely spaced small black spots on back and side. Dorsal fin origin midway between gill opening and anus. 2 pores behind each eye. Bermuda, Bahamas, Antilles, w Caribbean, s Brazil.
Leaden Worm Eel	*(Myrophis plumbeus)* Moderate-size. Pale tan to gray with tiny black spots; sometimes abruptly darker above. Dorsal fin origin closer to gill opening than to anus. Inshore brackish and fresh water. Suriname, French Guiana, south to Brazil; also e Atlantic.
Longfin Worm Eel	*(Myrophis anterodorsalis)* Small. Pale yellow to tan with tiny dark spots on snout, nape, and body above lateral line. Dorsal fin origin only 1–2 pectoral fin lengths behind gill opening. Islands off coast from Colombia to Tobago.
Key Worm Eel	*(Ahlia egmontis)* Pale tan with scattered tiny spots. Mature individuals darker, with red-brown band at back of head and red-brown lower jaw. Dorsal fin origin above or just behind anus. Bermuda, North Carolina, both sides of Florida, Bahamas, Caribbean, s Brazil.

76 Goldspotted Eel
Myrichthys ocellatus

Identification: A slender eel with a distinctive pattern of *diffuse dark spots, each with a pale center (bright yellow in life),* on a pale tan or greenish-brown background, shading to pale green ventrally. Dorsal fin origin on head. Pectoral fin well developed, with broad base. TL to 3'7" (1.1 m).

Habitat: Sea-grass beds and areas with sand and coral rubble, as well as coral reefs to depths of 23' (7 m).

Range: Bermuda, Florida Keys, Bahamas, Antilles, South American coast to Guyana.

Notes: The Goldspotted Eel is often seen during daylight hours moving along the bottom as it hunts small prey under small coral fragments and in algae and sea grasses. Occasionally it will come to lights at the surface at night. Although it is similar to the Sharptail Eel, it can be distinguished by its dark spots with pale centers.

77 Sharptail Eel
Myrichthys breviceps

Identification: An elongate eel with a well-developed pectoral fin. *Light brown to grayish brown, darker above, with pale spots.* Dorsal fin origin on head. TL to 31″ (78 cm).

Habitat: Shallow sea-grass beds and coral reefs to depths of 30′ (9 m).

Range: Bermuda, Bahamas, Florida Keys, Antilles, and South American coast from Panama to Brazil.

Notes: The Sharptail Eel feeds mainly on crabs, and is often seen hunting during the day. The Goldspotted Eel is very similar but has a pattern of dark spots with pale centers.

79 Blackspotted Snake Eel
Quassiremus ascensionis

Identification: A slender snake eel with *a minute pectoral fin.* Salmon-buff above, abruptly white ventrally, with row of *dark spots along dorsal midline and alternating spots and blotches below lateral line.* Dorsal fin origin behind gill opening. Eye behind middle of upper jaw. TL to 28″ (70 cm).

Habitat: Sand and turtle grass, to depths of 40′ (12 m).

Range: Bermuda; scattered records in Bahamas and Lesser Antilles. Also Brazil and Ascension Island in s Atlantic.

Notes: The Blackspotted Snake Eel has been observed buried in the sand with only the head showing. Because it lives around turtle grass and sandy areas, it is often overlooked by divers and snorkelers.

Similar Species: Spotted Snake Eel is similar but has large pectoral fin and is larger. Some *Callechelys* species are also similar but have dorsal fin origin on head, well in front of gill opening.

---

78 Spotted Snake Eel
Ophichthus ophis

Identification: A large snake eel. *Body pale,* with about 20 large dark spots on midline, 25–35 pairs of smaller spots along base of dorsal fin, *dark band across back of head,* and small dark speckles on nape, snout, chin, and pectoral fin. Head pores surrounded by black rings. Dorsal fin origin well behind gill opening, above tip of well-developed pectoral fin. Eye behind middle of upper jaw. Teeth stout and conical, in single row on roof of mouth. TL to 4'7"–7' (1.4–2.1 m).

Habitat: Loose sand bottoms to depths of 165' (50 m).

Range: Both sides of Atlantic; w Atlantic from Bermuda, Florida, Cuba, Lesser Antilles, Colombia to Brazil.

Notes: The Spotted Snake Eel often lies buried with only its head exposed. It is often seen by divers who pay attention to the sandy areas in and around reefs. At night it emerges to hunt for food.

Similar Species: Palespotted Eel *(O. puncticeps)* has pale spots on dark background. Spoon-nose eels (genus *Echiophis*) have pointed snouts that are somewhat concave dorsally. Blackspotted Snake Eel also has bold patterns of dark spots but has very small pectoral fin.

Other *Ophichthus* species

Shrimp Eel *(O. gomesi)* Rather robust. Dorsal fin origin over rear third of pectoral fin. Grayish brown to slate gray above, abruptly paler on lower side and belly. Head dark, sometimes with dark patch on throat;

fins dark edged. Small individuals have yellowish tinge. Bermuda, South Carolina to Florida, n Gulf of Mexico, Campeche Bank, Puerto Rico, Jamaica, Trinidad. Common off Brazil.

Tentacle-nose Eel	*(O. cylindroideus)* Uniformly plain colored. Tubular anterior nostril with fleshy tentacle extending from its rim. Trinidad, Panama, Guyana to s Brazil.
Margined Snake Eel	*(O. cruentifer)* Plain colored. Dorsal fin origin well behind tip of pectoral fin. New England to Florida, n Gulf of Mexico; 1 record each from Venezuela and Suriname.
Palespotted Eel	*(O. puncticeps)* Gray to brown, paler below, with 18–20 pale spots about as large as eye along lateral line; large individuals have less-distinct spots and reddish-brown stripes along side. North Carolina to Florida, n Gulf of Mexico, Colombia to Suriname.
King Snake Eel	*(O. rex)* Very large (TL to 7'10"/2.4 m). Dorsal fin origin well behind tip of pectoral fin. Pale yellowish brown or slate gray, abruptly lighter ventrally; 14–15 dark olive-brown, saddle-shaped markings along back. Dorsal and anal fins striped at bases; pectoral fin darker on dorsal half. N Gulf of Mexico, Florida Keys, Campeche Bank.
Spinefin Snake Eel	*(O. spinicauda)* Dark saddles on pale tan or gray background. Almost identical externally to King Snake Eel; differentiated by number of vertebrae: King 118, Spinefin 145. Deep water. Puerto Rico, s Caribbean.

Other species of snake eels

Tail ends in hard, fleshy, finless point.

Tusky Eel	*(Aplatophis chauliodus)* Stout, compressed. Dorsal fin origin behind tip of pectoral fin. Light tan, with small dark spots above. Jaws elongate; fang-like front teeth extend well outside closed mouth;

fleshy projections on tongue may also protrude. Nw Gulf of México, Puerto Rico, Panama, n South America.

Twostripe Snake Eel — *(Callechelys bilinearis)* Large (TL to 5′7″/ 1.7 m), head and body longer than tail. Pale (yellow in life) with 2 dark brown stripes on side and another on outer part of dorsal fin. Dorsal fin high and long, origin on head. Snout pointed, protruding over mouth. Anterior nostril directed downward, its tubular opening small. Teeth long, slender, and sharp. Bermuda, Bahamas, Lesser Antilles, offshore islands along Caribbean and South American coasts. Also s Brazil, s Atlantic islands.

Shorttail Snake Eel — *(Callechelys guineensis;* formerly *C. perryae)* Pale tan with dark brown spots of varying sizes. Florida, Bahamas, Puerto Rico, Lesser Antilles, Venezuela; also e Atlantic.

Spotted Spoon-nose Eel — *(Echiophis intertinctus)* Snout pointed. Pale tan with large brown spots on head and body. Dorsal fin origin behind tip of pectoral fin by less than pectoral fin length. North Carolina to Florida, ne Gulf of Mexico, Campeche Bank, Puerto Rico, St. Thomas, Brazil.

Snapper Eel — *(Echiophis punctifer)* Snout pointed. Pale tan with small brown spots. Dorsal fin origin behind tip of pectoral fin by more than pectoral fin length. N Gulf of Mexico west of Mobile Bay; also off South America, s Brazil.

CONGER EELS
Family Congridae

Congridae is a large and diverse family of scaleless eels with well-developed eyes, tubular anterior nostrils, and round or elliptical posterior nostrils that are usually in front of the eyes. Conger eels have elongate bodies that range from cylindrical to compressed posteriorly. The dorsal and anal fins are continuous with the caudal fin. In some genera the dorsal and anal fin rays are unsegmented, continuous rods; in others the dorsal and anal rays consist of short segments delimited by thin dark lines. The caudal fin is well developed but short and stiff in some genera. All congrids have pectoral fins, although in the garden eels they are reduced in size. The gill openings are on the sides, in contact with the pectoral fins. The upper and lower lips are well defined, sometimes with flanges. For some species the number, pigmentation, and location of sensory pores on the head and lateral line are important identification features.

This family has 21 genera and about 125 species, including the very large *Conger conger,* which is a valuable food fish in Europe. Fourteen genera and 32 species occur in the western Atlantic, but most are from deep water. Five genera and six species might be seen in shallow water.

Genera of family Congridae

Heteroconger	Body extremely long and slender (more so than other genera in our region). Pectoral and caudal fins very small. Eye large. Snout short; mouth oblique, lower jaw projecting beyond upper. Dorsal and anal fin rays unsegmented.
Ariosoma	Mouth nearly horizontal. Dorsal and anal fin rays unsegmented. Dorsal fin origin near level of pectoral fin base. Upper end of gill opening at level of middle of pectoral fin base. Posterior nostril below level of middle of eye. Teeth in bands, not forming cutting edge.
Paraconger	Mouth nearly horizontal. Dorsal and anal fin rays unsegmented. Teeth in 1–2 rows; outer teeth form cutting edge. Upper end of gill opening at or above upper end of pectoral fin base. Posterior nostril below level of middle of eye.
Conger	Mouth nearly horizontal. Dorsal and anal fin rays segmented. Upper lip with flange. Teeth in row, forming cutting edge. Posterior nostril at or above level of middle of eye.
Rhynchoconger	Mouth inferior, snout projecting beyond lower jaw, longitudinal fleshy keel on underside. Upper lip flange rudimentary. Jaw teeth small, in bands, not forming cutting edge. Posterior nostril at or slightly above level of middle of eye.

80 Brown Garden Eel
Heteroconger longissimus

Identification: A very long, slender eel with a tiny pectoral fin and a reduced caudal fin with no externally visible rays; tail ends in a blunt point. Brown anteriorly, with tiny pale flecks; paler posteriorly. *Eye large. Lower jaw longer than upper.* Free upper lip continuous across snout. Anterior nostril in upper lip at tip of snout. Throat has grooves or folds. 157–169 vertebrae. TL to 19″ (48 cm).

Habitat: Loose sand bottoms, at depths of 33–165′ (10–50 m).

Range: Bahamas, Florida Keys, Antilles, Yucatán, Belize, and Honduras; not in Gulf of Mexico.

Notes: Brown Garden Eels live in dense colonies, which are spectacular sights for divers. The eels spend daylight hours partway out of their burrows, feeding on plankton and detritus drifting by. As the diver approaches, the eels slowly withdraw into burrows in the sand.

Similar Species: Yellow Garden Eel *(H. luteolus),* from n Gulf of Mexico, is pale yellow and has fewer vertebrae (139–148).

81 Manytooth Conger
Conger triporiceps

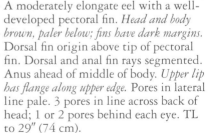

Identification: A moderately elongate eel with a well-developed pectoral fin. *Head and body brown, paler below; fins have dark margins.* Dorsal fin origin above tip of pectoral fin. Dorsal and anal fin rays segmented. Anus ahead of middle of body. *Upper lip has flange along upper edge.* Pores in lateral line pale. 3 pores in line across back of head; 1 or 2 pores behind each eye. TL to 29″ (74 cm).

Habitat: Fine white sand around coral reefs, at depths of 13–50′ (4–15 m).

Range: Bermuda, se, s, nw Florida, Bahamas, Antilles, and w Caribbean; also Brazil.

Notes: This is the only species of *Conger* in our area that lives around coral reefs.

Similar Species: Both Conger Eel *(C. oceanicus),* which
occurs along Atlantic coast and in e
Gulf of Mexico, and Antillean Conger
(C. esculentus), known from Bermuda
and Greater Antilles, have wide flange
on upper lip, 1 supratemporal pore, and
no postorbital pores. Yellow Conger
(Rhynchoconger flavus), found from n Gulf
of Mexico to n South America, has small
flange on upper lip, 1 supratemporal
pore, and no postorbital pores.

Other species of conger eels

Margintail Eel   *(Paraconger caudilimbatus)* Gray or brown
above, paler below. Dorsal and anal fins
of larger individuals dark with pale margins. Tip of lower jaw dusky. Gill opening long. Pectoral fin well developed,
close to gill opening. Reduced caudal
fin. 40–43 preanal pores in lateral line.
Anterior nostril tubular. Bermuda, s
Florida, n Bahamas, n Gulf of Mexico,
Yucatán, e Colombia.

Paraconger   Similar to Margintail Eel but with 31–36
guianensis   preanal pores in lateral line. French
Guiana, n Brazil.

Bandtooth   *(Ariosoma balearicum)* Brown with silvery
Conger   or golden overtones. Pectoral fin red;
margins of dorsal and anal fins dark. 3
sensory pores behind eye. Upper end of
gill opening at middle of pectoral fin base.
Bermuda, North Carolina, Gulf of Mexico, n coast of South America to Brazil;
also e Atlantic, Mediterranean.

Longtrunk Eel   *(Ariosoma anale)* Yellowish brown; dark
edges on dorsal and anal fins. Head and
body longer than tail. No pores behind
eye. S Florida, Panama to French Guiana;
also e Atlantic.

ORDER CLUPEIFORMES

Clupeiforms, the herrings and anchovies, are rather primitive fishes united by a number of internal features, including a peculiar connection between the swim bladder and the

ear, and special characteristics in the part of the skeleton that supports the caudal fin. Herrings and anchovies are usually silvery, more or less compressed fishes that travel in schools. They have no lateral line on the body, although in some species the *sensory canals* on the head extend onto the shoulder region. The head canals are elaborately branched and probably are used to detect the positions of other fish in the schools. Although there is no lateral line, scale size can still be determined by counting the number of vertical rows of scales across the side, exactly as if there were a lateral line (this is referred to as the number of scales in the *lateral series*). The scales are easily shed in a number of species.

Clupeiform fishes have no spines in their fins and no adipose fin. There is a single dorsal fin. The pelvic fins are abdominal, and the pectoral fins are low on the sides of the body with their bases nearly horizontal. The pelvic and pectoral fins may have large modified scales called *axillary processes* along the dorsal side of their bases. Clupeiforms have a single pair of nostrils (most fishes have an anterior and a posterior nostril on each side of the head). Most species have numerous long, fine *gill rakers,* bony rods on the front of the gill arches, which they use to strain plankton from water passing over the gills. Some species that feed on larger food items have fewer and shorter gill rakers. The number of *branchiostegal rays,* flattened bony rods that support the membrane along the lower edge of the gill cover, is useful for the identification of some species.

This order includes four families and nearly 300 species. Three families occur in our area: Clupeidae, Pristigasteridae, and Engraulidae.

HERRINGS
Family Clupeidae

Herrings of the family Clupeidae are silvery fishes that travel in schools. Most are marine, some are anadromous (ascending rivers from the sea to spawn), and a few are landlocked, occurring only in fresh water. They are generally fusiform (tapering toward both ends), and range in shape from slender and oval in cross section to deepbodied and strongly compressed (flattened from side to side). The mouth is moderate in size and terminal or inferior. Rather primitive fishes, herrings have no spines in their fins. The single dorsal fin is short and located near the middle of the body. The anal fin originates farther back, usually well behind the dorsal fin base. It is usually short, although in some species it is long, with as many as 38 rays. Most herrings have modified scales called *scutes* along the belly,

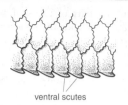

ventral scutes

although the Round and Dwarf herrings have only a single scute between the pelvic fins. The posterior wall of the gill opening, normally covered by the operculum (gill cover), is supported by the *pectoral* (or shoulder) *girdle.* In some herrings two fleshy tabs extend forward into the gill chamber; in others the tabs are lacking. Members of the genus *Jenkinsia* can be distinguished in part by the shape of the *isthmus,* the part of the underside of the body that extends forward between the gill openings.

Clupeids have some "extra" bones forming the outer upper jaw. Many species have one or more *supramaxillae,* additional bones along the upper edge of the maxillary bone. Species of *Sardinella* (two species in our area) have a characteristic paddle-shaped supramaxilla. Members of the genus *Harengula* have a *hypomaxilla,* a small, toothed bone at the edge of the upper jaw between the premaxilla and the maxilla.

Approximately 20 species of clupeids in nine genera are found in our region.

Genera of family Clupeidae

Etrumeus	Large (SL to 10″/25 cm). 1 W-shaped scute between pelvic fins. 11–15 branchiostegal rays.
Jenkinsia	Small (SL to 2½″/6.5 cm). 1 W-shaped scute between pelvic fins. 6–7 branchiostegal rays.
Sardinella	Many scutes along belly. 2 fleshy lobes on front of shoulder girdle. Last ray of dorsal fin not elongate. Last 2 anal rays slightly elongate.
Harengula	Many scutes along belly. 2 fleshy tabs on front of shoulder girdle. Toothed hypomaxilla between premaxilla and maxilla.
Dorosoma	Many scutes along belly. Snout rounded, projecting. Mouth terminal or inferior; lower jaw fits inside upper when mouth is closed. Last dorsal ray filamentous.
Opisthonema	Many scutes along belly. 2 fleshy lobes on front of shoulder girdle. Last dorsal ray extended as filament. No hypomaxilla.

Lile	Many scutes along belly. No fleshy lobes on shoulder girdle. Last dorsal ray not filamentous. 6 pelvic fin rays.
Alosa	Many scutes along belly. Front of upper jaw has distinct notch into which lower jaw fits. Last dorsal ray not elongate.
Brevoortia	Many scutes along belly. Enlarged paired scales in front of dorsal fin.

82 Dwarf Herring
Jenkinsia lamprotaenia

Identification: A small, slender herring, oval in cross section, without visible ventral scutes. Single, inconspicuous, W-shaped scute between pelvic fins. Transparent olive above, with *silver stripe along side that does not narrow toward front.* Belly pale and nearly transparent in life. Pelvic fin origin directly below origin of dorsal fin. Isthmus narrows abruptly toward front. Small teeth on premaxilla. SL to 2½″ (6.5 cm).

Habitat: Shallows around coral reefs, in schools not particularly close to either surface or bottom.

Range: Bermuda, Bahamas, Florida, Gulf of Mexico, and around Caribbean, Antilles.

Notes: Dwarf Herrings live in very large schools and are often seen close to shore around piers and jetties. The species of *Jenkinsia* are difficult to distinguish in the field from one another and from schools of silversides (family Atherinidae), although the silversides tend to be a brighter transparent green.

Similar Species: Little-eye Herring (*J. majua*), of Bahamas, Cuba, Hispaniola, and Yucatán to Costa Rica, also has abruptly narrowing isthmus and silver side stripe that does not narrow toward front, but has no teeth on premaxilla. Short-striped Round Herring (*J. parvula*) of Venezuela also has teeth on premaxilla, but isthmus tapers smoothly and silver side stripe narrows and disappears toward front. Shortband Herring (*J. stolifera*), found

in Florida and from Honduras to
Venezuela, also has teeth on premaxilla
and silver side stripe that does not
narrow toward front, but has smoothly
narrowing isthmus.

83 False Pilchard
Harengula clupeola

Identification: A moderately small, compressed, deep-
bodied herring, with 2 fleshy tabs on front
edge of shoulder girdle and prominent
ventral scutes. Blue-green above,
pale silvery white below, with faint
longitudinal dusky streaks on upper
side and back. Small dark spot behind
gill opening. *Scales rather firmly attached,
not easily shed.* Moderately wide oval
plate on tongue bears patch of blunt
teeth; tooth plate behind it on floor of
mouth supports patch of teeth that
widens gradually anteriorly. SL to 4–6″
(10–15 cm).

Habitat: Near surface in coastal waters, estuaries,
and lagoons.
Range: Bahamas, entire coast of Gulf of Mexico,
Antilles, and Caribbean coasts of Central
and South America to Brazil.
Notes: The False Pilchard occurs in schools, and
the young are sometimes abundant
along sandy beaches. This species can
tolerate a broad range of salinity levels.
Similar Species: Scaled Sardine *(H. jaguana)* is very
similar and also has firm scales, but
tooth plates on tongue and floor of
mouth are very broad; found in coastal
waters of Bermuda, New Jersey to s
Brazil, Gulf of Mexico, and Caribbean,
including Bahamas and Antilles.

84 Redear Sardine
Harengula humeralis

Identification: A moderately small, compressed, deep-
bodied herring, with 2 fleshy tabs on
front edge of shoulder girdle and
prominent ventral scutes. Brownish

olive above, silver to white on side, with faint dusky longitudinal streaks on upper side and back. *Tips of anterior dorsal fin rays always dark. In life, reddish or orange spot behind upper end of gill opening.* Tooth plates on tongue and floor of mouth slender. Scales thin and easily shed. SL to about 4″ (10 cm).

Habitat: Near surface in coastal waters. Schools often seen around mangrove shorelines.

Range: Bermuda, both coasts of peninsular Florida, Bahamas, Antilles, and Central and South American coasts from Yucatán to Guianas.

Notes: The Redear Sardine is frequently seen by snorkelers, often in large schools around roots of red mangroves and around docks and jetties.

Similar Species: Both Scaled Sardine and False Pilchard have firmer scales and broad tooth plates on floor of mouth, and lack black on tips of front dorsal fin rays and orange spot behind gills.

Other species of clupeid herrings

Round Herring *(Etrumeus teres)* Slender, elongate, oval in cross section. 1 W-shaped scute between pelvic fins. Blue-green above, silvery on side and belly. Nova Scotia to Florida, Gulf of Mexico to Yucatán, Colombia to Guianas. Not in Bahamas or Antilles.

Atlantic Thread Herring *(Opisthonema oglinum)* Compressed, deep-bodied. Small head. Blue-green above, shading to silver-white below; 5–6 dark stripes on back; dark spot behind upper end of gill opening. Appears to avoid brackish water but occurs in fresh water in St. Johns River, Florida. Maine to s Brazil, Bermuda, Bahamas, Gulf of Mexico, Caribbean, including Antilles.

Gizzard shads *(Dorosoma)* Last ray of dorsal fin extended as filament. Mouth inferior, with bulbous snout protruding in front of lower jaw. Primarily fresh water; occasionally strays into brackish or salt water.

Spanish Sardine	*(Sardinella aurita)* Dark blue above, silvery on side. Supramaxilla paddle-shaped; no hypomaxilla. Gill rakers on lower limb of second and third arches nearly flat. Bermuda, Cape Cod to Argentina, including Bahamas, Antilles, Gulf of Mexico, Caribbean coast.
Brazilian Sardine	*(Sardinella brasiliensis)* Similar to Spanish Sardine. Downward-curving gill rakers on second and third arches. Coasts of Gulf of Mexico, n South America to Uruguay; Antilles.
Atlantic Piquitinga	*(Lile piquitinga)* Moderately compressed. Prominent ventral scutes. Blue-black above, with very distinct silvery stripe along side. Coast of Venezuela east to Trinidad; Brazil from Recife to Espírito Santo.
Alabama Shad	*(Alosa alabamae)* Large (SL 15¾–19¾″/ 40–50 cm), compressed, deep-bodied. Green-blue above, shading to silver on side. Front of upper jaw has deep notch into which lower jaw fits. 41–48 gill rakers on lower limb of first arch (fewer in young). Adults in coastal waters, Gulf of Mexico from Mississippi Delta to Florida, move well up Mississippi River and its tributaries to spawn.
Skipjack Herring	*(Alosa chrysochloris)* Large (SL to 19¾″/50 cm); more slender than Alabama Shad. 20–24 gill rakers on lower limb of first arch. Far up Mississippi River and along Gulf coast from Florida to Texas.
Gulf Menhaden	*(Brevoortia patronus)* Deep-bodied, compressed. Large head. Double row of modified scales in front of dorsal fin. Blue-gray above, brassy green on side; large dark shoulder spot behind gill cover followed by 1–2 rows of smaller spots. Front of upper jaw has notch into which lower jaw fits. 29–31 prominent ventral scutes. 42–48 lateral scale rows. Rounded pelvic fin with inner and outer rays about equally long. Coastal waters of Gulf of Mexico from Florida to Yucatán; not in Caribbean.

Finescale Menhaden	(*Brevoortia gunteri*) Pointed pelvic fin with inner rays shorter than outer. 28–30 ventral scutes. 60–77 lateral scale rows. W Gulf of Mexico from Louisiana to Yucatán.
Yellowfin Menhaden	(*Brevoortia smithi*) Pointed pelvic fin with inner rays shorter than outer. 30–32 ventral scutes. 60–70 lateral scale rows. North Carolina south to Florida; e Gulf of Mexico.
Atlantic Menhaden	(*Brevoortia tyrannus*) Inner and outer pelvic rays about equal in length. 31–34 ventral scutes. Up to 6 rows of spots behind larger shoulder spot. 45–52 lateral scale rows. Nova Scotia to s Florida.

PRISTIGASTERIDS
Family Pristigasteridae

The herrings of this family are separated from those of the family Clupeidae on the basis of internal features of the skeleton. Pristigasterids are small, compressed, silvery fishes, some of which lack pelvic fins or dorsal fins or both. They have long anal fins with 30 to 92 rays (the only clupeid with more than 30 rays is *Dorosoma,* which can be distinguished by its inferior mouth). Most have large, upward-slanting, superior mouths with the lower jaw longer than the upper, and some have strong, canine-like teeth. Sometimes there is a *hypomaxilla* (a small toothed bone between the premaxilla and the maxilla). The ventral margin of the body has prominent scutes from the isthmus to the anus. Worldwide there are nine genera with 34 species; four genera are found in our region.

Genera of family Pristigasteridae

Chirocentrodon	Pelvic fin present. No hypomaxilla. Canine-like teeth in both jaws.
Neoopisthopterus	No pelvic fin. No hypomaxilla. Maxilla short, not reaching behind rear margin of eye.
Odontognathus	No pelvic fin. No hypomaxilla. Maxilla long, reaching to or beyond gill opening. Anal fin very long; dorsal fin small and far back on body.
Pellona	Toothed hypomaxilla. Pelvic fin present.

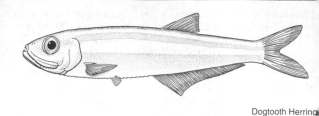

Dogtooth Herring

Dogtooth Herring
Chirocentrodon bleekerianus

Identification: A small, rather elongate, compressed species, easily recognized by *large, canine-like teeth in both jaws.* Yellow to light brown above, white below, with silvery stripe on side. Anal fin moderately long, with 38–44 rays, its origin at level of dorsal fin origin. Mouth terminal, lower jaw not projecting. SL to 3½″ (9 cm).

Habitat: Inshore waters to depths of 200′ (60 m); enters lagoons and river mouths. Probably spawns in open ocean.

Range: Antilles and s Caribbean from Yucatán to Santos, Brazil.

Notes: The Dogtooth Herring is taken in trawls at the mouth of the Orinoco River, but because of its small size it is not a species of great commercial importance.

Similar Species: No other herring in our region has canine-like teeth. Cuban Longfin Herring is similar in general appearance but lacks pelvic fin and is restricted to Cuban waters.

Other species of pristigasterids

Cuban Longfin Herring
(Neoopisthopterus cubensis) Elongate. Pale with silvery stripe along side; small dark dots on top of head. No pelvic fin. Dorsal fin well behind mid-body. Anal fin long, with 40–50 rays, its origin at level of dorsal fin origin. Cuba, possibly other parts of Caribbean.

Caribbean Longfin Herring
(Odontognathus compressus) Elongate, strongly compressed. Mouth slants obliquely upward. Pale overall, slightly

darker above, with silver stripe about same width as eye along side. Head profile concave. Dorsal fin small and well behind origin of anal fin. Anal fin long, with 55–61 rays. No pelvic fin. Ventral scutes serrate, in continuous row. Upper jaw long, maxilla tapering posteriorly. Panama to French Guiana.

Guiana Longfin Herring	*(Odontognathus mucronatus)* Elongate, strongly compressed. Row of ventral scutes with gap below pectoral fin; scutes not serrate. Anal fin very long, with 70–85 rays. Trinidad to Guianas; also s Brazil.
American Coastal Pellona	*(Pellona harroweri)* Rather deep-bodied, compressed. Bluish gray above, silvery on side; in life, tip of snout and lower jaw dusky, and dorsal and anal fins yellow. Anal fin long, with 36–42 rays; origin under middle of dorsal fin base. Small pelvic fin; no elongate axillary scale above its base. Eye large. Costa Rica to Brazil.

ANCHOVIES
Family Engraulidae

Anchovies are rather small, compressed fishes, the largest reaching about 8 inches (20 cm) in standard length (SL). In life they are silvery and translucent, often with a bright silvery stripe along each side. They are most easily recognized by their very large mouths and overhanging conical snouts. In most species the maxillary bone reaches to the preopercle, and in some it extends well beyond the gill opening. They have a single, inconspicuous ventral scute between the pelvic fins. In most anchovies the right and left *branchiostegal membranes* (gill membranes) are separate for their entire length. In *Cetengraulis* species they are broadly joined in midline, covering the entire isthmus. Most anchovies strain plankton from the water using their long and numerous gill rakers.

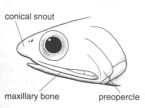

conical snout

maxillary bone   preopercle

Anchovies are difficult to identify; it is often necessary to count the vertebrae on X-rays. The length of the *pseudo-branch,* a patch of gill filaments on the inside of the upper part of the outer wall of the gill chamber and often extending onto the inside of the opercu-lum near its upper end, can be

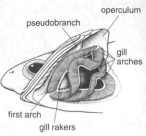

an important tool for identification, as can gill raker and anal fin ray counts. *Gill raker* counts given here are the number of rakers on the lower half of the first *gill arch* (see illustration above). Anal ray counts are the number of branched rays, not counting the short splints at the front of the fin. It is probably not possible to identify anchovies down to the species level underwater, but because they live near shore and are used for food and bait, it is often possible to examine specimens. Currently, 16 genera and 139 species of anchovies are recognized worldwide. Six genera and about 20 species occur in the Caribbean and the Gulf of Mexico.

Genera of family Engraulidae

Engraulis

Body oval in cross section. Maxilla short and blunt, not reaching edge of preoper-cle. Anal fin origin under or behind last dorsal ray. Pseudobranch longer than eye.

Anchoviella

Body moderately compressed. Maxilla short and blunt, not reaching edge of preopercle. Pseudobranch shorter than eye, not extending onto inner face of operculum.

Anchoa

Body moderately to strongly com-pressed. Maxilla long, reaching beyond front edge of preopercle, its rear tip pointed. Pseudobranch longer than eye.

Anchovia

Body strongly compressed. Dorsal origin near center of body, well in front of anal origin. Anal fin origin in front of base of last dorsal fin ray. Gill membranes separate.

Cetengraulis	Body strongly compressed. Right and left branchiostegal membranes broadly joined, covering isthmus.
Lycengraulis	Body compressed. Large, canine-like jaw teeth.

Genus *Anchoa*

There are about 13 species of *Anchoa* in the West Indies, divided into two subgenera. Two species are placed in the subgenus *Anchovietta,* distinguished by a long pseudobranch that extends onto the inside of the gill cover, and by the anal fin origin, which is below or behind the last ray of the dorsal fin. The rest are in the subgenus *Anchoa;* they have a shorter pseudobranch that does not extend onto the inside of the operculum, and their anal fin origin is below the base of the dorsal fin, well in front of the last dorsal ray. We cover one *Anchoa* species, the Bigeye Anchovy, in detail; others are briefly discussed in the table further below.

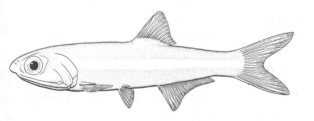

Bigeye Anchovy

Bigeye Anchovy
Anchoa lamprotaenia

Identification: An elongate, somewhat compressed anchovy with *a long, pointed maxilla.* Translucent greenish above, with silver stripe along side. Anal fin origin under dorsal fin base; 18–23 anal fin rays. Anus well in front of origin of anal fin, nearer to tips of pelvic fin rays. 17–21 slender gill rakers. SL to 3½" (8.9 cm).

Habitat:	Coastal waters; enters brackish lagoons in some areas.
Range:	Bahamas, s Florida, and around Caribbean. Does not occur in Gulf of Mexico.
Notes:	The Bigeye Anchovy travels in schools, feeding on plankton. Around Miami the species sometimes occurs in mixed schools with the Bay Anchovy, which is similar but usually has more gill rakers.

Other *Anchoa* species

Shortfinger Anchovy	*(Anchovietta lyolepis)* Lacks extended pectoral fin ray. Bermuda, w Gulf of Mexico, Antilles, Caribbean to mouth of Amazon; also s Brazil.
Longfinger Anchovy	*(Anchovietta filfera)* Upper ray of pectoral fin extended as filament; reaches to level of dorsal fin origin in large individuals. Antilles, Nicaragua to Brazil.
Cuban Anchovy	*(Anchoa cubana)* Anus well in front of anal fin origin. 16–21 anal rays. 24–30 gill rakers. North Carolina to Mississippi, Caribbean to Santos, Brazil.
Bermuda Anchovy	*(Anchoa choerostoma)* Anus well in front of anal fin origin. 19–22 anal rays. 24–30 gill rakers. Bermuda endemic.
Belize Anchovy	*(Anchoa belizensis)* Anal fin origin under front of dorsal fin. 17–20 gill rakers. Fresh water. Belize, Guatemala, Honduras.
Bay Anchovy	*(Anchoa mitchilli)* Anal fin origin below front of dorsal fin base. 21–25 gill rakers. Estuaries and river mouths. Maine to Florida, n and w Gulf of Mexico to Yucatán.
Striped Anchovy	*(Anchoa hepsetus)* Very similar to Bigeye but has anus farther forward. 16–20 anal rays. 19–25 gill rakers. Gulf of Maine to Florida north of Fort Pierce, n Gulf of Mexico, Venezuela to Uruguay.
Narrow-striped Anchovy	*(Anchoa colonensis)* 17–21 anal rays. 19–22 gill rakers. Replaces Striped Anchovy in Caribbean.

Key Anchovy   *(Anchoa cayorum)* 21–26 anal rays. 16–19 gill rakers. Honduras, Yucatán, Florida Keys, Bahamas, Antilles to Trinidad.

Little Anchovy   *(Anchoa parva)* 17–22 anal rays. 25–27 gill rakers. Greater Antilles, Caribbean coast from Yucatán to Trinidad; absent from Lesser Antilles.

Spicule Anchovy   *(Anchoa spinifer)* Long anal fin, with 31–37 rays. 12–19 gill rakers. Small triangular projection on subopercle. Panama to s Brazil; also e Pacific.

Trinidad Anchovy   *(Anchoa trinitatus)* 23–27 anal rays. 18–23 gill rakers. Colombia to Trinidad.

Other species of anchovies

Silver Anchovy   *(Engraulis eurystole)* Slender, elongate. Blue-green above, silvery on side, sometimes with broad, silver, mid-lateral stripe. 13–15 anal fin rays. Pseudobranch extends onto inside of gill cover. 27–43 gill rakers. Massachusetts south around Florida to Mississippi; Venezuela to mouth of Amazon. Distribution in w Gulf of Mexico and rest of Caribbean not known.

Flat Anchovy   *(Anchoviella perfasciata)* Bluntly rounded snout. Anal fin with 10–15 rays, origin below last dorsal ray. Gill membranes separate. 24–30 gill rakers. Ne Gulf of Mexico from Florida Keys to Mississippi; Antilles to Trinidad; Panama.

Blackburn's Anchovy   *(Anchoviella blackburni)* Anal fin origin below rear half of dorsal fin base. 15–18 gill rakers. Venezuela, Suriname.

Elongate Anchovy   *(Anchoviella elongata)* Anal fin origin below rear half of dorsal fin base. 21–24 gill rakers. Belize to Colombia.

Cayenne Anchovy   *(Anchoviella cayennensis)* Anal fin with 12–14 rays, origin below or behind last dorsal ray. 29–35 gill rakers. French Guiana to Brazil.

Zabaleta Anchovy   *(Anchovia clupeoides)* Body deep (depth 3–4 in SL). Anal fin long (25–32 rays), far forward. Maxilla short, reaching only to margin of preopercle. Gill rakers numerous, 40 in juveniles to more than 100 in adults. Antilles, coasts from Guatemala to north of Rio de Janeiro.

Surinam Anchovy	(*Anchovia surinamensis*) Similar to Zabaleta Anchovy but with 20–25 anal fin rays. Rivers and estuaries from Trinidad to Brazil.
Atlantic Anchoveta	(*Cetengraulis edentulus*) Body deep (depth about 3 in SL). Numerous fine gill rakers: 45 in juveniles to more than 100 in adults. 18–24 anal fin rays. Juveniles have silvery stripe. Antilles, Central and South American coasts from Costa Rica to Santa Catarina, Brazil.
Atlantic Sabertooth Anchovy	(*Lycengraulis grossidens*) Large canine-like teeth, especially in lower jaw. Maxilla long. Curved row of small dark spots across upper part of gill cover. 16–27 short gill rakers. Dorsal fin origin behind mid-body. Anal fin long (21–26 rays), origin below middle of dorsal fin. Juveniles have silvery stripe. Belize; Lake Maracaibo, Venezuela coast south to Argentina.
Bates's Sabertooth Anchovy	(*Lycengraulis batesii*) Similar to Atlantic Sabertooth Anchovy but with 12–15 even shorter gill rakers. Mostly in fresh water in Orinoco and Amazon Rivers.

SUPERORDER OSTARIOPHYSI

This major group of fishes includes such diverse forms as the carps, the tetras, the electric eels, and the catfishes. It encompasses more than 8,000 species, nearly all of which live in fresh water except for a few families of catfishes.

The ostariophysans are characterized by a modification of the anterior part of the vertebral column (the third to seventh vertebrae) called a Weberian apparatus, which includes a chain of small bones that connects the swim bladder with the ear. This provides these fishes with sensitive hearing and is probably a main reason they are so successful.

ORDER SILURIFORMES

Fishes of the order Siluriformes, the catfishes, are probably the most distinctive of the ostariophysans. They are easily identified by the presence of prominent barbels on the maxilla and chin, and sometimes the snout. They have an adipose fin and no scales.

There are about 33 families and 2,500 species of catfishes, but only a few families have members that venture into salt water. In addition to the Ariidae, covered below, five other families (Auchenipteridae, Hypopthalmidae, Pimelodidae, Aspredinidae, and Loricariidae) include species that sometimes stray into brackish water near river mouths. They are not discussed here.

SEA CATFISHES
Family Ariidae

Ariids are rather "typical" catfishes that resemble the familiar North American freshwater catfishes of the family Ictaluridae. Ariids have smooth skin (no scales or plates), tapering bodies, forked tails, and two dorsal fins, the second of which is an *adipose fin,* a small fatty flap without bony supporting rays. The first dorsal fin has a short base but rather long rays. The anal fin is small, and its posterior margin is usually concave. The anterior rays of the dorsal and pectoral fins are spine-like—hardened and with sharp points—but they are not true spines, for they are composed of short segments, although the segments are firmly joined to one another.

Most catfishes are bottom dwellers and have small eyes; thus they depend on touch and chemical senses rather than sight. Like almost all other catfishes, ariids have prominent *barbels* on the head. These are long, mobile, fleshy filaments that are used for exploring the environment, serving as sensitive organs of touch and bearing taste buds as well. Ariids have two or three pairs of barbels: one pair at the ends of the maxillary bones and one or two pairs on the chin called *mental barbels.*

Mostly marine species, ariids differ from other catfish families in that their anterior and posterior nostrils are close together, and the posterior nostrils are shielded by a flap of skin. The bones of the top of the skull, easily visible through the skin in most species, form a rough, pitted *head shield,* the extent and shape of which are used to distinguish the species. The rear of the head shield extends backward, forming the *supraoccipital process,* a bony ridge connecting the skull with another externally visible plate at the base of the dorsal spine called the *predorsal shield.* Catfishes have fine, bluntly pointed teeth in patches on the jaws and the roof of the mouth. Some species have molar-like teeth. Male sea catfishes carry the marble-size eggs, and later the young, in their mouths.

The family Ariidae contains 14 genera and 120 species. About 20 species in three genera occur in our area; we include here only the most common representative species. One additional genus, *Potamarius,* is restricted to fresh water of Central and South America.

Genera of family Ariidae

Bagre	1 pair of chin barbels; maxillary barbels and first rays of dorsal and pectoral fins elongate and flattened, strap-like. Teeth not molar-like.
Arius	2 pairs of chin barbels. Teeth on palate small, not molar-like.
Cathorops	2 pairs of chin barbels. Molar-like teeth on palate.

85 Gafftopsail Catfish
Bagre marinus

Identification: A rather large catfish, blue-gray to dark brown above, shading to silvery on side and white below. Anal fin white or pale blue and rather short (22–28 rays), with high anterior lobe. *Maxillary barbels, first ray of dorsal fin, and first ray of pectoral fin extended as long, flat filaments. 1 pair of barbels on chin.* TL commonly to 17¾″ (45 cm), maximum 3′3″ (1 m).

Habitat: Coastal marine waters; sometimes in estuaries and brackish or fresh water in tropics.

Range: Atlantic coast from Carolinas to Brazil, Gulf of Mexico, mainland coasts of Caribbean, and w Cuba.

Notes: Although the Gafftopsail is a good food fish, it is not used much for food in the United States. Its name, an allusion to the upper sail of a fishing boat, is said to come from the fact that its dorsal filament sometimes sticks out of the water as it swims near the surface. Gafftopsails feed on fishes and small invertebrates. Up to 55 eggs, each of which may be up to an inch (2.5 cm) in diameter, are carried in the mouth of the male. The young are just under 2 inches (5 cm) long when they hatch and may be carried until they are about 4 inches (10 cm) long. The males do not feed while they are carrying the eggs or the young.

Similar Species: Coco Sea Catfish *(B. bagre),* which lives in coastal areas from Colombia to Brazil, has long anal fin with 29–60 rays, dark spot on front anal fin rays, and even longer strap-like extensions of maxillary barbels and dorsal and pectoral rays. Other sea catfishes have 2 pairs of barbels on chin.

---

86 Hardhead Catfish
Arius felis

Identification: A rather small sea catfish with *4 chin barbels and a longitudinal groove in a depression on midline of head,* extending from about middle of head shield forward to between eyes. Head shield very rough. Brown to dark brown or dark blue above, shading to silvery on side and white below. Adipose fin black. 13–16 gill rakers on first arch. TL to about 14″ (35 cm).

Habitat: Coastal waters and lower reaches of estuaries; rarely in fresh water. Usually over mud bottoms.

Range: North Carolina to Florida, and Gulf of Mexico to Yucatán.

Notes: The Hardhead Catfish is common along the coast and is taken by anglers and in trawls. It is not considered an especially valuable food fish, although it is sometimes eaten.

Other species of sea catfishes

Mayan Sea Catfish *(Arius assimilis)* Longitudinal median groove in depression on top of head short, not reaching to between eyes.

	16–18 gill rakers on first arch. Yucatán to Honduras.
New Granada Sea Catfish	*(Arius bonillai)* Longitudinal median groove in depression on top of head longer, reaching forward to rear of eye. 17–20 gill rakers on first arch. Colombia to Venezuela.
Crucifix Sea Catfish	*(Arius proops)* Rather large (SL to 3′3″/1 m). Large, shield-shaped predorsal plate; spine from rear of head shield fits into notch in front edge of predorsal shield. Maxillary barbels short, extending only to pectoral fin. 3 tooth plates on palate, with bluntly conical, villiform teeth. Lacks groove in depression on midline of top of head. Brackish lagoons and estuaries. Colombia to Brazil.
Madmango Sea Catfish	*(Cathorops spixii)* Rather small (TL to 12″/30 cm; usually smaller). Bluish black to dark brown above, paler below. Single patch of molar-like teeth on each side of palate. Maxillary barbels reach to pectoral fin. Well-developed gill rakers on rear of first gill arch. Marine and brackish waters; lower reaches of rivers. Belize to Brazil; also Trinidad.

ORDER AULOPIFORMES

This is a small order of soft-rayed fishes, most of which live in deep ocean waters. They are defined by technical details of the gill arches, and at this time there is some debate over their classification. The order as currently understood includes 12 families, only one of which, Synodontidae, has shallow-water representatives in our area.

LIZARDFISHES
Family Synodontidae

Lizardfishes are tapering fishes that are round in cross section and moderate in size, reaching 6 to 18 inches (15–46 cm) in total length. A pointed scaly head and conspicuous teeth give them a distinctive lizard-like appearance. The mouth is large, extending well behind the eye. The maxilla is rudimentary, and the upper jaw is bordered entirely by the premaxilla, which bears several rows of needle-like teeth. The scales are smooth, and the fins lack spines. The pelvic fins are abdominal, located far back on the body, well behind the pectoral fins. A distinguishing feature of lizardfishes is a very small, nearly transparent, adipose (fatty) fin between the single dorsal fin and the upper base of the tail. The caudal fin is forked.

Adult lizardfishes spend much of their time resting motionless on the ocean bottom, where they are well camouflaged. Once a lizardfish is seen, however, it can be approached closely for a good look. Post-larval lizardfishes are often attracted to lights at the surface. Unlike adults, they are transparent except for their eyes, with a very dark bar at the base of the tail, and a series of black spots in the lining of the body cavity that show through the body wall. The number, position, and shape of these spots are useful for identifying the species.

The family contains five genera and about 55 species, some of which are common around coral reefs; three genera and 10 species occur in our region.

Genera of family Synodontidae

Synodus	Inner pelvic rays much longer than outer rays. Eye over middle of mouth. 1 pair of longitudinal tooth bands (palatine teeth) in roof of mouth. Teeth not visible when mouth closed.
Trachinocephalus	Thick, blunt head. Eye far forward, over anterior part of mouth. Inner pelvic rays longer than outer rays. 1 pair of tooth bands in roof of mouth. Teeth not visible when mouth closed.
Saurida	Inner and outer pelvic rays of equal length. Teeth visible along side of jaw when mouth closed. 2 pairs of tooth bands in roof of mouth. Eye over middle of mouth.

87 **Sand Diver**
Synodus intermedius

Identification: A typical lizardfish with an elongate, terete, tapering body. Brownish above, pale below, back crossed by about 8 darker bars that are widest at lateral line. Yellow lines on upper side. *Externally visible dark shoulder patch at*

upper end of pectoral girdle under gill cover.
Lower jaw rounded, without fleshy
knob. Scales rather large, 43–52 in
lateral line. 3 rows of scales between
lateral line and base of dorsal fin. Front
rays of dorsal fin do not extend beyond
tips of following rays when fin is laid
back. Anal fin origin closer to caudal fin
base than to pelvic fin origin. 10–12
anal fin rays. SL to about 15″ (38 cm).

Habitat: Inshore waters to depths of more than
1,000′ (300 m).

Range: Bermuda, North Carolina to Brazil,
Bahamas, s and e Gulf of Mexico, and
Caribbean.

Notes: Common in shallow waters, usually on
sand but also on rocky bottoms, the
Sand Diver is often seen by snorkelers
and divers. It is sometimes caught by
fishermen trolling in shallow water.

Similar Species: Red Lizardfish has 4 reddish bands
across back, indistinct shoulder spot,
and dark spot at tip of snout. Snakefish
has eye near tip of snout and anal fin
base longer than dorsal fin base.

88 Red Lizardfish
Synodus synodus

Identification: A rather small species with *4 prominent
reddish bands across back,* extending to
below lateral line. Small dark spot just
behind tip of snout; inconspicuous
dusky spot on upper part of pectoral
girdle under gill cover. Fins dusky with
red bands. Scales small; 54–59 in lateral
line, 4–6 rows between lateral line and
dorsal fin base. Tip of pectoral fin
reaches well beyond pelvic fin origin.
Anal fin origin closer to caudal fin base
than to pelvic fin origin. 8–10 anal fin
rays. SL to 6″ (15 cm).

Habitat: Inshore waters, often around coral reefs,
to depths of 100′ (30 m) or greater.

Range: Bahamas, e Gulf of Mexico, Jamaica,
Antilles, w Caribbean, and South
American coast from Colombia to
Uruguay. Also in e Atlantic.

Notes: Commonly seen by snorkelers, the Red Lizardfish rests on sand or rock and can be approached closely because it relies on its camouflaged color pattern for protection. It is a small species, rarely caught by fishermen and of no commercial interest.

Other *Synodus* species

Offshore Lizardfish

(*S. poeyi*) Knob at tip of lower jaw. Obscure blotches along lateral line. 43–48 scales in lateral line; 3 rows of scales between lateral line and dorsal fin base. North Carolina to Florida, n and s Gulf of Mexico, Greater Antilles, w Caribbean, n South American coast.

Inshore Lizardfish

(*S. foetens*) Grayish brown or olive above, pale below; may have about 8 indistinct blotches on side. 56–65 scales in lateral line; 4–6 rows of scales between lateral line and dorsal fin base. 11–13 anal fin rays. Massachusetts to Florida, Bahamas, Gulf of Mexico, Caribbean south to Brazil.

Bluestripe Lizardfish

(*S. saurus*) Blue and salmon lines along body. 57–60 scales in lateral line; 3 rows of scales between lateral line and dorsal fin. Bermuda, Bahamas, Lesser Antilles.

89 Snakefish
Trachinocephalus myops

Identification: An elongate, tapering, terete, yet rather robust lizardfish with *a very short snout and eye far forward.* Greenish brown above, with about 7 darker cross bands; side has yellow stripes alternating with pale blue stripes with darker edges. Oblique dark spot at upper end of gill opening (not under gill cover). Anal fin base much longer than dorsal fin base; anal fin origin closer to pelvic fin origin than to caudal fin base. 14–16 anal rays. 54–58 scales in lateral line. SL to about 10″ (25 cm).

Habitat: Inshore waters to depths of more than 1,200′ (360 m), over sand, rock, and mud, and around coral reefs.

Range: Circumtropical except for e Pacific.
In w Atlantic: Bermuda, Cape Cod
to Florida, Bahamas, Gulf of Mexico,
Antilles, and Caribbean south to
Brazil.

Notes: The Snakefish is a solitary species that
sometimes buries itself in the sand
bottom with only its eyes exposed. It is
occasionally sold in markets but is not
a highly valued food fish. No other
lizardfish in our area has the eye so near
the tip of the snout.

Lizardfishes of genus *Saurida*

Shortjaw Lizardfish	(*S. normani*) Rather slender. Lower jaw shorter than upper. Grayish brown, with 5–6 dusky blotches along side and dusky spot near middle of anterior rays of pelvic fin. More than 50 scales in lateral line; 4 rows of scales between lateral line and dorsal fin base. South Carolina to Florida, w Bahamas, e Gulf of Mexico, w Caribbean, Guianas.
Largescale Lizardfish	(*S. brasiliensis*) Lower jaw longer than upper. Dark submarginal band on dorsal fin. 43–47 scales in lateral line; 3 rows of scales between lateral line and dorsal fin. North Carolina to Florida, Gulf of Mexico, Central and South American coasts to Brazil; also e Atlantic.
Smallscale Lizardfish	(*S. caribbaea*) Lower jaw longer than upper. 54–60 scales in lateral line; 4 rows of scales between lateral line and dorsal fin. Ne Florida, w Bahamas, Cuba, Gulf of Mexico to Brazil.
Suspicious Lizardfish	(*S. suspicio*) Lower jaw longer than upper. 52–53 scales in lateral line; 3 rows of scales between lateral line and dorsal fin. Bahamas, Antilles, w Caribbean.

ORDER MYCTOPHIFORMES

This order contains only two families, the Myctophidae, or
lanternfishes, with about 235 species, and the Neoscopeli-
dae, or blackchins, with five or six species. Both families are

widespread in deep ocean waters. Their diagnostic characteristics are technical features of the gill arches that are beyond the scope of this field guide.

LANTERNFISHES
Family Myctophidae

Small deep-sea fishes usually less than 6 inches (15 cm) long, generally with tapering and somewhat compressed bodies, lanternfishes are distinguished by a series of eye-like luminescent organs called *photophores* on their heads and along their bodies. They have a short dorsal fin, an adipose fin, abdominal pelvic fins, no fin spines, and large eyes. Nearly all species are black or silvery black, with silvery sides. Lanternfishes are a major component of the so-called "deep scattering layer," an aggregation of animals that reflects sonar signals and gives the appearance of a false bottom on the ocean floor. Many lanternfishes travel up toward the surface at night; it may be possible to catch some with a dip net by hanging a light near the surface over deep water. They play a major role in distributing energy and materials in the deep ocean because they feed at the surface, then move into deep water where they are preyed on by larger organisms that do not make vertical migrations.

This is a large family with 32 genera and 235 species, all in deep water. Although identification of lanternfishes, based largely on the arrangement of the photophores and other luminous tissue, is a job best left for the experts, we include one species here for completeness.

90 Metallic Lanternfish
Myctophum affine

Identification: A small, tapering, somewhat compressed lanternfish with *ctenoid scales and upper part of opercle rounded.* Black with silvery scales. Photophores in groups on side and in rows along lower jaw, lower side of belly, anal fin base, and lower side of caudal peduncle. Females have 3 luminous scales on lower part of caudal peduncle; males have 7 or 8 luminous scales on top part. SL to 2⅜" (6 cm).

Habitat: Open ocean, usually beyond edge of continental shelf, but sometimes in water less than 660' (200 m) deep. Moves to surface at night.

Range: Bermuda, s Canada to Florida, Gulf of
Mexico, and s Caribbean.

Notes: Many other genera and species of
lanternfishes occur in our area, and
most of them come to the surface at
night and can be caught in dip nets
around lights. Lanternfishes feed on
plankton and in turn fall prey to larger
deep-water fishes.

Similar Species: *M. nitidulum,* sharing virtually the same
geographical range, is very similar but
has cycloid scales, and upper edge of
operculum has a definite angle.

ORDER GADIFORMES

This is a diverse order of soft-rayed fishes—including the
codfishes—with smooth scales and pelvic fins that are situated far forward, below or in front of the pectoral fins. They
are generally elongate, tapering, or fusiform fishes, with
long dorsal and anal fins. In some species the dorsal fin is
nearly or completely divided into two or three separate fins,
and the anal fin is divided into two separate fins. Sometimes
the dorsal and anal fins are joined to the caudal fin. The caudal fin is supported by spines of the posterior vertebrae in
addition to the usual bones of the caudal skeleton. The edge
of the upper jaw is formed by the premaxillary bones alone.
The smooth scales are often embedded in the thick skin.

The order Gadiformes contains about 12 families, 85 genera, and 482 species. The relationships, and therefore the
classification, of cods and their relatives are poorly understood. Some ichthyologists put the Fourbeard Rockling, the
Southern Hake, and the Spotted Hake in the family Phycidae; others consider them members of the family Gadidae.
Only one gadiform species is confined to fresh water; the
rest are marine, although a few enter estuaries. Most occur
in colder waters, either in temperate regions or in very deep
water. Only a few occur in the shallow waters of our region.

PHYCID HAKES
Family Phycidae

Phycid hakes are small to moderate-size
elongate fishes with a single long anal fin. The family includes the rocklings and the hakes. Rocklings occur in the
Atlantic Ocean and Mediterranean Sea in the Northern
Hemisphere and off New Zealand and Tasmania in the

Southern Hemisphere. Hakes live in the Atlantic Ocean, the Gulf of Mexico, and the Mediterranean Sea.

The family Phycidae contains five genera and 27 species; two genera and five species might be seen in our region.

Genera of family Phycidae

Enchelyopus	Barbels on snout and lower jaw. Dorsal fin in 3 segments: first a single stout ray, second consisting of short unsegmented rays in a groove, third a normal elongate fin. Pelvic fin far forward, in front of pectoral fin, with 5–7 rays.
Urophycis	No barbels on snout. Dorsal fin divided into 2 segments. Pelvic fin reduced to 1–2 filament-like rays.

91 Southern Hake
Urophycis floridana

Identification: An elongate, tapering, moderately compressed codfish with 1 short barbel at tip of chin. Reddish brown above, shading to white below. *Lateral line alternately black and white. Series of black spots above and behind eye.* 2 long pelvic fin rays originate below gill cover and extend nearly to anus. First dorsal fin short, with about 13 rays (none elongate); second dorsal fin longer, with 54–59 rays. TL to 12″ (30 cm).

Habitat: Normally an offshore species in waters as deep as 1,320′ (400 m); moves into bays and coastal waters during colder weather. Juveniles occur in estuaries.

Range: North Carolina to s Florida, and Gulf of Mexico from Florida to c Mexico.

Notes: The Southern Hake is fairly common in the northern Gulf of Mexico. When in shallow water it feeds on worms, crustaceans, and small fish.

Similar Species: Spotted Hake also has black and white lateral line but has dusky streaks from eye to pectoral fin and conspicuous black and white pattern on first dorsal fin. It and other phycid hakes are discussed in the table below.

Other species of phycid hakes

Spotted Hake	*(Urophycis regia)* 1 short barbel on chin. Brown above, paler below, with irregular dark markings. Lateral line dark, with white spots breaking it into series of dark dashes. First dorsal fin short, with white band near base, black central area, and white margin. No elongate dorsal rays. Pelvic rays not reaching to anus. Massachusetts to ne Florida, ne Gulf of Mexico.
Gulf Hake	*(Urophycis cirrata)* Long pectoral fin (reaching nearly to middle of anal fin). Pale brown with blotches and spots, pale lateral line, and dark-edged dorsal and anal fins. Deep water in n Gulf of Mexico.
Longfin Hake	*(Urophycis chesteri)* Dark edges on dorsal and anal fins. Long thread-like dorsal fin ray. Nova Scotia to s Florida.
Fourbeard Rockling	*(Enchelyopus cimbrius)* 4 barbels: at tip of snout, on lower jaw, and on each anterior nostril. Color varies from pale to dark brown. First dorsal ray well forward, followed by row of short fleshy filaments; rest of fin extends along back almost to tail. Newfoundland to n Gulf of Mexico.

ORDER OPHIDIIFORMES

Ophidiiform fishes are elongate, soft-rayed fishes with long dorsal and anal fins that are joined to the caudal fin in many genera. The pelvic fins are far forward, situated under the chin in some species; they are long and filamentous and look like barbels. Most ophidiiforms live in deep-ocean environments, although a few are shore fishes and some live in fresh water in caves.

This order, which is divided into two suborders, includes five families, 92 genera, and 355 species. Members of the suborder Ophidioidei (represented in our area by the families Carapidae and Ophidiidae) are oviparous, or egg-laying, and the males lack external copulatory organs. The front nostril is high on the side of the snout, well above the upper lip. The fishes of the suborder Bythitoidei, which has three families (one of which, Bythitidae, is covered here), are viviparous, bearing live young, and the males have external copulatory organs. Their anterior nostril is close to the upper lip.

PEARLFISHES
Family Carapidae

Pearlfishes are small, elongate, scaleless fishes with very long dorsal and anal fins (the anal fin rays are longer than the opposing dorsal fin rays), and no pelvic fins. They have pointed tails, but the caudal fin nearly always disappears during development, although it is not known whether this is because it is lost or simply fails to develop. The anus is far forward, located in the throat region, ahead of the pectoral fin base. Some pearlfishes are free-living, but most live as inquilines, residing within the bodies of other animals, usually sea cucumbers but sometimes sea stars or oysters. Inquiline species normally use the host only for shelter, but some pearlfishes actually feed on the host's internal organs.

Pearlfishes have two specialized planktonic larval stages: In the first stage (the vexillifer), the larval pearlfish has a dorsal appendage that looks like a plant stem with small leaves. In the second stage (the tenuis), it is extremely elongate and ribbon-like, reaching almost 8 inches (20 cm). After it enters the host it actually shrinks to about one-third the length of the tenuis, then begins to grow again. It is not certain how long each of these stages lasts, but the length of the larval period is probably somewhat variable so that, within limits, an individual can delay transformation until it finds a suitable host.

There are two subfamilies of pearlfishes containing seven genera and 32 species. Two species of two genera occur in our area, but only one lives in shallow water.

Genera of family Carapidae

Carapus	No enlarged fangs on premaxilla.
Echiodon	Prominent fang-like canine teeth on premaxilla, followed by a space, then a row of smaller conical teeth.

92 Pearlfish
Carapus bermudensis

Identification: A slender, elongate, tapering, transparent fish with a series of silver blotches along anterior part of side. *Anal fin rays longer than dorsal fin rays.* No enlarged fangs on premaxilla. Tail pointed; caudal fin usually missing; when present it is small

and joined with dorsal and anal fins. TL
to about 8″ (20 cm).

Habitat: Shallow water less than 3′ (1 m) deep to
depths of more than 700′ (210 m); in
bodies of sea cucumbers.

Range: Bermuda, North Carolina to Florida,
Bahamas, Gulf of Mexico, and Caribbean
to Brazil.

Notes: The Pearlfish inhabits the body cavity
of a sea cucumber, leaving the host to
feed, probably mostly at night. It
enters through the anus of its host,
tail first, and pushes itself into the
body cavity. Although it has been
reported from several species of sea
cucumbers, its most common host in
shallow water is *Actinopyga agassizii.*
The Pearlfish lays free-floating eggs in
gelatinous masses.

Similar Species: Chain Pearlfish (*Echiodon dawsoni*), a
free-living (non-inquiline) species with
fang-like canine teeth, occurs at depths
of 80–900′ (25–275 m) in Straits of
Florida and e Gulf of Mexico.

CUSK-EELS and BROTULAS
Family Ophidiidae

Cusk-eels and brotulas are slender, elon-
gate fishes similar to pearlfishes but with scales and with the
dorsal fin rays equal to or longer than the opposing anal fin
rays. The dorsal and anal fins are joined to the caudal fin, and
most species have pelvic fins, although they are reduced to two
filamentous rays inserted far forward on the body (below the
operculum or even below the eye). The anus is behind the tip
of the pectoral fin. They have a supramaxilla, a small supple-
mentary bone along the upper margin of the

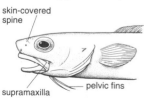

skin-covered
spine

supramaxilla　pelvic fins

maxillary bone. Some species
have a spine under the skin of
the snout. Males lack an external copulatory organ. Cusk-eels
and brotulas do not go through
a vexillifer larval stage, as the
pearlfishes do.

There are about 46 genera
and 209 species of cusk-eels and brotulas. Six genera and
about 40 species occur in shallow water in our area; we describe some of the more common species below.

Genera of family Ophidiidae

Brotula	Many long barbels on head. Pelvic fin inserted behind corner of mouth, beneath preopercle or opercle. 10 caudal fin rays.
Petrotyx	No barbels on head, but small papillae on snout. 10 caudal fin rays. Pelvic fin inserted behind corner of mouth, beneath preopercle or opercle; pelvic rays unequal in length.
Lepophidium	Scales in regular rows. Head scaly. Spine under skin at tip of snout. Pelvic fin inserted ahead of corner of mouth; pelvic rays unequal in length. 9 caudal fin rays.
Ophidion	Scales elliptical and at oblique angles to each other, forming a herringbone pattern. Head unscaled. Snout may lack spine or have forward-projecting, skin-covered spine at tip. Pelvic fin far forward, inserted ahead of corner of mouth; pelvic rays unequal in length. 9 caudal fin rays.
Otophidium	Scales in herringbone pattern. Head unscaled. Snout with stout, triangular, upward-pointing spine. 9 caudal fin rays. Pelvic fin far forward, inserted ahead of corner of mouth; pelvic rays unequal in length.
Parophidion	Scales in herringbone pattern. Top of head scaly. Pelvic fin far forward, inserted ahead of corner of mouth; rays equal in length.

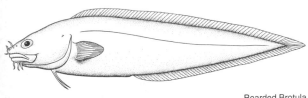

Bearded Brotula

Bearded Brotula
Brotula barbata

Identification: A slender, tapered brotula with *many long barbels on snout and lower jaw.* Reddish brown or olive, slightly paler

below, sometimes freckled or spotted.
Pelvic fin not reaching past tip of
pectoral fin. TL to 30″ (75 cm).

Habitat: Shallow waters to upper continental
slope; sometimes on coral reefs or close
to shore around jetties and bulkheads.

Range: Bermuda, Florida, Gulf of Mexico, and
w Caribbean south to n South America.

Notes: This large inshore species is sometimes
taken by angling from shore. Divers who
take care to look in holes and crevices
may see Bearded Brotulas around coral
reefs. It is the only ophidiid in our region
with long barbels on the snout and jaw.

Other species of cusk-eels and brotulas

Redfin Brotula	*(Petrotyx sanguineus)* Elongate, tapering. Entirely red: juveniles bright red, adults brownish red. Numerous small papillae on snout, but no large barbels. Mouth inferior. Scales smooth and in regular rows. Coral reefs. S Florida, Bahamas, Panama.
Blackedge Cusk-eel	*(Lepophidium brevibarbe)* Pale tan above, shading to white below. Dorsal and sometimes caudal and anal fins have black margins. Well-developed spine beneath skin of snout. No barbels on snout or chin. Ne Florida, n Gulf of Mexico south to Brazil. Not in Bahamas; scarce in Antilles.
Fawn Cusk-eel	*(Lepophidium profundorum)* Brown with row of pale spots on upper side. New England to s Florida, se Gulf of Mexico.
Mottled Cusk-eel	*(Lepophidium jeannae)* Pale with small dusky blotches; interrupted dark edge on dorsal fin. Savannah, Georgia, to Key West, w coast of Florida, Campeche Bank in s Gulf of Mexico.
Lepophidium pheromystax	Pale with conspicuous dark spots; alternating black and pale bars on dorsal fin margin. N coast of South America.
Barred Cusk-eel	*(Lepophidium staurophor)* 5 dusky bars across dorsal surface. W Caribbean, between Honduras and Jamaica to Nicaragua.
Lepophidium aporrhox	Yellowish brown; black margins on dorsal and anal fins. N South America.

Lepophidium kallion	Straw colored with 2 conspicuous brown lateral stripes. Fleshy tabs on tip of snout. Barbados.
Bank Cusk-eel	*(Ophidion holbrooki)* Pinkish to grayish brown; fins whitish; black margin on dorsal fin. Profile nearly straight from snout to dorsal origin. No spine on snout. Mouth inferior. 4 gill rakers. Pelvic fin rays rather long. North Carolina to se Brazil, Gulf of Mexico, Caribbean; not in Bahamas.
Longnose Cusk-eel	*(Ophidion beani)* Similar to Bank Cusk-eel in color. Rounded profile between snout and dorsal origin. 5–6 gill rakers. Short pelvic fin rays. South Carolina to Florida, Gulf of Mexico, Lesser Antilles.
Ghost Cusk-eel	*(Otophidium chickcharney)* Pale, without spots or blotches. Stout, upward-pointing, triangular spine under skin of snout. Slender, nearly horizontal spine on gill cover. Sandy shorelines in very shallow water to depths of 50′ (15 m). Great Bahama Bank, Bahamas.
Sleeper Cusk-eel	*(Otophidium dormitator)* No conspicuous color markings. Triangular spine under skin at tip of snout. Opercular spine stout and upward-pointing. S Florida, Bahamas.

VIVIPAROUS BROTULAS
Family Bythitidae

The viviparous brotulas are very similar to the cusk-eels and brotulas. They have long tapering bodies and long dorsal and anal fins that are joined to the caudal fin in some species. The dorsal fin rays are as long as or longer than the anal fin rays. The caudal fin is rounded or pointed, and the pelvic fins are reduced to one or two filamentous rays inserted below or in front of the pectoral fins. (The shallow-water forms covered here all have a single ray in each pelvic fin.) The scales are smooth and usually deeply embedded in the thick skin. Usually the body is completely scaled, and the head is partly scaled or unscaled. In contrast to the cusk-eels and brotulas of family Ophidiidae, the brotulas of this family are viviparous, giving birth to live young, and the males have external, rather complex copulatory organs.

There are 31 genera and about 90 species of viviparous brotulas. Though many genera occur in our geographical region, only genera that are found in shallow water are covered here.

Genera of family Bythitidae

Calamopteryx	Pectoral fin at end of arm-like base. Dorsal and anal fins joined to caudal fin. Single lateral line discontinuous, interrupted below first third of dorsal fin, then continuing to base of tail on lower side of body. Forehead not very steep.
Grammonus	2 separate lateral lines. Pectoral fin without arm-like base. Dorsal and anal fins joined to caudal fin. Forehead not very steep.
Stygnobrotula	Forehead very steep. Lateral line single but discontinuous. Pectoral fin without arm-like base. Dorsal and anal fins joined to caudal fin.
Lucifuga	Dorsal and anal fins joined to caudal fin only at their bases. Forehead not very steep. Eyes poorly developed, covered with thick skin and not visible externally in some specimens. Pectoral fin without arm-like base. Lateral line single, interrupted. Anterior nostril close to upper lip. Scales overlapping; head partly naked.
Dinematichthys	Anterior nostril high above lip. Dorsal and anal fins separate from caudal fin. Scales overlapping. Forehead not very steep. Some scales on head. Pectoral fin without arm-like base.
Gunterichthys	Scales scarcely overlapping. Anterior nostril close to upper lip. No scales on head. Dorsal and anal fins separate from caudal fin. Pectoral fin without arm-like base. Forehead not very steep.
Ogilbia	Scales overlapping. Scales on head, but not on operculum. Dorsal and anal fins separate from caudal fin. Anterior nostril close to lip. Pectoral fin without arm-like base. Forehead not very steep.

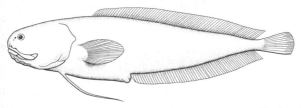

Key Brotula

Key Brotula
Ogilbia cayorum

Identification: An elongate brotula with a small eye. *Yellowish to brownish, with fins about same color as body. Head partly scaled, no scales on operculum; body completely covered with overlapping scales.* Opercle with sharp spine embedded in skin. TL to about 4″ (10 cm).

Habitat: Shallow waters around coral reefs and rocky coral debris.

Range: Bermuda, Florida, Bahamas, and Antilles to n South America.

Notes: A snorkeler may encounter the Key Brotula by turning over rocks in shallow water. Other, yet undescribed species of *Ogilbia* are known to occur in our area.

Other species of viviparous brotulas

Longarm Brotula *(Calamopteryx goslinei)* Brownish; head darker than body. Pectoral fin at end of arm-like stalk. Prominent papillae on head. Scales on head and body. 10 caudal fin rays. Coral reefs. Bahamas, Antilles.

Calamopteryx robinsorum Similar to Longarm Brotula but has 8 caudal fin rays. W Caribbean, n coast of Cuba, ne coast of Hispaniola.

Reef-cave Brotula *(Grammonus claudei)* Body moderately compressed. Dark gray to brownish black; fins black. 2 lateral lines: 1 below dorsal fin base, 1 above anal fin base. Rear edge of maxilla broad and squarish. Bermuda, Florida, Bahamas, Puerto Rico, Curaçao; possibly e Antilles.

Black Brotula	(*Stygnobrotula latebricola*) Body rather short, deep, and compressed. Dark brown to black; fins black. Snout blunt and rounded. Mouth curved downward posteriorly. Rear edge of maxilla narrow and rounded. Florida, Bahamas, Curaçao.
Bahaman Cavefish	(*Lucifuga spelaeotes*) Strongly arched profile; face concave. Eye tiny. Dark reddish brown; white margins on median fins. Body covered with small rounded scales. Caudal fin connected to dorsal and anal fins but appears distinct. Pelvic fin with single filamentous, rather short ray. 18–20 pectoral fin rays. Bahamas: New Providence, Abaco, and Grand Bahama islands.
Lucifuga subterraneus	Similar to Bahaman Cavefish but has 12–14 pectoral fin rays. Cuba.
Lucifuga dentata	15–17 pectoral fin rays. Palatine teeth. Fewer vertebrae than Bahaman Cavefish. Cuba.
Dinematichthys minyomma	Anterior nostril high on head, about midway between lip and posterior nostril. Known only from specimens collected around a coral reef in Islas de la Bahía off Honduras.

ORDER BATRACHOIDIFORMES

This small order consists of a single family of small to medium-size bottom-dwelling fishes, the toadfishes.

TOADFISHES
Family Batrachoididae

Toadfishes are robust fishes with large, broad, somewhat flattened heads and eyes that are directed upward. Slow-moving bottom dwellers, they are carnivorous (feeding mainly on mollusks and crustaceans) and have wide mouths with strong jaws and stout teeth. Most species are cryptically colored, usually mottled brown with various darker brown blotches. There are two dorsal fins: The first is short and consists of only two or three spines; the second is long, with numerous rays and no spines. The anal fin is also long and without spines. The pelvic fins originate in front of the pectoral fins; each pelvic fin consists of one spine and two or three soft rays. The gill membranes are broadly joined to the isthmus, restricting the gill openings to short slits on the sides of the body, just in front of the pectoral fins. Toadfishes have *opercular spines,* located on the opercle bone. Some species also have *subopercular spines,* which are located on the subopercle, the bone that forms the lower part of the edge of the gill cover. Some species have barbels or fleshy flaps on the head. Scales are present in some species, absent in others.

The venomous toadfishes, represented by the genus *Thalassophryne* in our area, have glands associated with hollow spines in the dorsal fin and on the gill cover that can inject venom into a would-be predator. In addition, some species have discrete glands or diffuse glandular tissue of an unspecified function on the pectoral fin membranes; others have a mass of glandular tissue on the body just behind the base of the pectoral fin; and some have a pore behind the pectoral fin that may also be associated with a gland of some type.

Toadfishes lay their eggs in shelters such as holes under stones, large shells, old tires, and similar rubble. The male guards the eggs and young until the yolk sac has been absorbed. Unlike most marine fishes, they do not have larval stages that are radically different from the adult.

Toadfishes are notorious noise-makers, producing sounds that can be detected with underwater microphones, and in some cases are loud enough to be heard through the hull of a boat anchored overhead. These sounds are produced by special muscles that vibrate the swim bladder. Rugged fishes with strong jaws, toadfishes bite vigorously when caught.

The family encompasses three subfamilies, 19 genera, and 69 species. In our area there are seven marine genera and 22 species. A few species enter or are confined to fresh water.

Genera of family Batrachoididae
Subfamily Batrachoidinae

3 dorsal spines and opercular spine solid, without associated venom glands. Subopercular spines present.

Batrachoides	Body covered with small embedded scales. 2 subopercular spines. Inner surface of pectoral fin has discrete glands between bases of upper rays. No axillary pore. 2 lateral lines.
Opsanus	Axillary pore on body behind pectoral fin. Discrete glands on inner side of pectoral fin between upper rays. No scales. 1 subopercular spine. 2 lateral lines.

Triathalassothia	Discrete glands on inner side of pectoral fin between upper rays. No axillary pore on body behind pectoral fin. 1 subopercular spine. No scales. 2 lateral lines.
Amphichthys	No glands on pectoral fin. No axillary pore on body behind pectoral fin. 1 subopercular spine. No scales. 2 lateral lines.
Sanopus	No glands on pectoral fin. Axillary pore on body behind pectoral fin. 1 subopercular spine. No scales. 2 lateral lines.

Subfamily Thalassophryninae

2 dorsal spines and opercular spine hollow, with venom glands. No subopercular spines.

| *Thalassophryne* | Pectoral fin with glandular tissue scattered distally, but no discrete glands. No scales. No pore behind pectoral fin. 1 lateral line. |

Subfamily Porichthyinae

Dorsal and opercular spines solid, without associated venom glands. No subopercular spines. Several lateral lines.

| *Porichthys* | Body with rows of photophores. 4 lateral lines. 2 dorsal spines. Discrete glands on inner side of membrane between pectoral fin rays. |

93 Gulf Toadfish
Opsanus beta

Identification: An elongate, tapering, robust toadfish with a depressed head. Head and body mottled tan, white, and brown; darker posteriorly and often with pale rosette-like spots. *Dark brown bars on pale background on caudal and pectoral fins; bars on pectoral fin irregularly joined.* Oblique alternating brown and white bars on dorsal and anal fins. 24 or 25 dorsal fin rays; 18 or 19 pectoral fin rays. TL to 12″ (30 cm).

Habitat: Shallow sea-grass beds and rocky areas near shore.

Range: Southern Florida, Little Bahama Bank, and throughout Gulf of Mexico.

Notes: On the western coast of Florida the Gulf Toadfish spawns in February and March. It is said that small individuals sometimes enter jars or cans that have been discarded on the bottom, and feed on fishes and invertebrates that attempt to enter the same shelter.

Similar Species: Oyster Toadfish *(O. tau),* a northern species that occasionally reaches s Florida, has complete pale bars across pectoral and caudal fins. Leopard Toadfish *(O. pardus),* offshore in Gulf of Mexico, is more mottled and has very irregular and incomplete bars across fins, and well-developed fleshy tabs along lower jaw. Scarecrow Toadfish *(O. phobetron)* is brown above with paler blotches forming indistinct, irregular, barred pattern; black slashes on dorsal and anal fins; and irregular bars on tail fin; mouth and gill chambers have black lining. It is found in shallow water in Bahamas and possibly Cuba.

---

94 **Coral Toadfish**
Sanopus splendidus

Identification: A spectacularly colored toadfish. Dark brown to magenta, with gray patches on body, tan and yellow lines across head and nape. *Pelvic fin all yellow; dorsal, caudal, anal, and pectoral fins have yellow margins.* Unbranched chin barbels. TL to 9½″ (24 cm).

Habitat: Sand-floored caves under rocks at depths of 25–80′ (8–25 m).

Range: Known only from Cozumel, Mexico.

Notes: During the daylight hours the Coral Toadfish rests just inside a cave with its head facing outward; at night it probably emerges partway. It feeds on small fishes, snails, and polychaete worms.

Other *Sanopus* species

S. astrifer	Dark brown with prominent light spots on head. Unbranched chin barbels. Turneffe Islands, Glovers Reef, Belize.
S. greenfieldorum	Body dark with light markings; light lines on head. Unbranched chin barbels. Belize.
Bearded Toadfish	*(S. barbatus)* Brown, with darker brown markings above; belly paler with brown mottlings. Adult's tail has conspicuous dark spots surrounded by pale rings. Numerous branched tentacles and tabs on head; no cirri between eyes. Honduras to Panama.
S. johnsoni	Brown above; belly pale with network of brown lines. Long thin cirri between eyes. Branched chin barbels. Quintana Roo, Cozumel, Mexico.
S. reticulatus	Head and body dark brown with network of pale lines. Branched chin barbels. Gulf of Mexico at Progreso, Yucatán.

Other species of toadfishes

Bocon Toadfish	*(Amphichthys cryptocentrus)* Brown and yellow markings on body; oblique brown and yellow bars on second dorsal fin; head often has small spots and white reticulations ventrally. Some individuals plain reddish brown. Plume-like tentacle on upper rim of orbit. 23–25 anal fin rays. Panama to Brazil.
Amphichthys hildebrandi	Similar to Bocon Toadfish. 26 anal fin rays. Panama.
Pacuma Toadfish	*(Batrachoides surinamensis)* Large. Brown with darker bands on upper surface of head and body; belly whitish. Top of head has fine scales posteriorly and a few fine filaments anteriorly. Molar-like jaw teeth. 28–29 rays in second dorsal fin. 25–27 anal rays. 3–11 glands on inner surface of pectoral fin between upper rays. Honduras to Brazil.
Batrachoides gilberti	Brown. Oblique dark and pale bars on dorsal and anal fins. No scales on top of

	head. 24–26 dorsal rays. 22–23 anal rays. 8 or fewer glands on inner surface of pectoral fin. Belize to Panama.
Cotuero Toadfish	(*Batrachoides manglae*) Fine filaments (but no scales) over most of top of head. 21–24 rays in second dorsal fin. 19–21 anal fin rays. Islands off Venezuela.
Atlantic Midshipman	(*Porichthys plectrodon*) Silvery with irregular rows of dark brown to bluish spots, some joining to form dark saddles across back or U-shaped marks on side. Photophores along 4 lateral lines and in rows on chin, isthmus, and belly. Large luminous area below eye. Cape Henry, Virginia, to n South America, Gulf of Mexico.
Porichthys pauciradiatus	7–8 well-defined, saddle-shaped marks on back and head. Costa Rica, Panama, Brazil.
Porichthys oculofrenum	Pale line between eyes. Known from only 2 specimens from Venezuela (at 186'/58 m) and Brazil (at 207'/63 m).
Porichthys bathoiketes	Dark with 4–6 darker blotches on upper body. W Caribbean from Honduras to Colombia.
Thalassophryne megalops	Large eye. Dorsal, anal, and pectoral fins pigmented to margins. Panama, Colombia.
Cano Toadfish	(*Thalassophryne maculosa*) Mouth large. Pale brown with darker brown spots, becoming darker with age. Fins plain. Venezuela coast and offshore islands.
Thalassophryne nattereri	Pale margins on dorsal, anal, pectoral, and caudal fins. No dark spots. Eye small. Tobago to Brazil.

ORDER LOPHIIFORMES

This is a fairly large order of fishes, collectively known as anglerfishes, with 17 families. Most occur in deep water, but three families have shallow-water representatives in our area. Anglers are characterized by a modified anterior dorsal spine that serves as a lure to attract prey. Their pectoral fins are at the ends of arm-like stalks, and their gill membranes are joined to the body, so that the gill openings are restricted to small holes near the "elbows" of each pectoral fin. Many anglerfishes have depressed heads and bodies, but some are compressed and others are globose.

GOOSEFISHES
Family Lophiidae

Goosefishes have been described as animated fish traps. They have very large heads and huge terminal mouths with projecting lower jaws and long sharp teeth. The head and anterior part of the body are depressed (except in members of the genus *Sladenia*). The pectoral fins are at the ends of long stalks, and there are prominent spines in front of the bases of the pectoral fins. The gill openings are small and located above, or even behind, the pectoral fins. The first dorsal fin consists of five or six spines. The first two spines are separate and located near the tip of the snout, and the third, also separate, is located at the back of the head. The last three dorsal spines, located behind the head, are shorter and sometimes joined by a membrane. The second dorsal fin consists of eight to 12 soft rays. The first dorsal fin spine is modified into a "fishing pole," called the *illicium*, with a lure at its tip called the *esca*. The illicium and esca are moved in a way that makes the esca look like a worm to attract small fish prey.

There are four genera and 25 species of goosefishes. Three genera occur in our area, but only one species might be encountered in moderately shallow water. Some species of goosefishes are sold commercially as monkfish.

Genera of family Lophiidae

Lophiodes	Head depressed. Gill opening behind pectoral fin, but extends around bottom of fin base to front of fin base.
Lophius	Head depressed. Gill opening entirely behind pectoral fin.
Sladenia	Head rounded, not depressed. Body compressed. Gill opening mostly in front of pectoral fin base.

Reticulate Goosefish
Lophiodes reticulatus

Identification: A stubby fish with a large, moderately depressed head and a small, anteriorly

Reticulate Goosefish

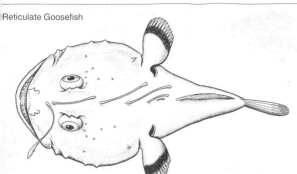

depressed body. Light to dark brown above, pale tan below. *Reticulate pattern of fine dark lines on upper surface of head, body, and pectoral fin.* 2 spines at rear of lower jaw. First dorsal fin consists of 6 separate spines; first spine with esca. Second dorsal fin has 8 soft rays. 6 anal fin rays. SL to 9¾" (25 cm).

Habitat: Continental shelf waters at depths of 210–1,200′ (64–365 m).

Range: Southern Florida, Gulf of Mexico, Puerto Rico, w and s Caribbean, Lesser Antilles to n coast of South America.

Notes: The Reticulate Goosefish is not likely to be seen by divers because it lives in deep water. Its habits are unknown, but from what is known about the similar Goosefish, it is probably a voracious carnivore that lies motionless and inhales smaller fishes that are attracted to its lure.

Similar Species: *L. monodi,* from Florida, s Gulf of Mexico, Antilles, w Caribbean, and n South America, and *L. beroe,* from e Gulf of Mexico, Lesser Antilles, w Caribbean, and n coast of South America, have fewer than 6 dorsal spines and occur only in deep water. Goosefish *(Lophius americanus),* which occurs north of n Florida, usually in very deep water, and Blackfin Goosefish *(Lophius gastrophysus),* which lives in water more than 650′ (200 m) deep along mainland coasts from Cape Hatteras to Argentina, have gill opening entirely behind pectoral fin.

FROGFISHES
Family Antennariidae

Frogfishes are wonderful little fishes with short, fat, stubby, globular bodies, pectoral fins on stalks, and very large mouths directed upward. They have small eyes, and most species are covered with highly modified scales called *dermal spinules*. All are highly camouflaged, and some are very colorful. The gill openings are restricted to small pores behind the stalked pectoral fins. They have a single dorsal fin. As in all anglerfishes, the first dorsal spine is modified into a rod, called the *illicium*, and a lure, called the *esca*. The second and third dorsal spines, which are stout and covered with thick skin, are separate from each other and from the rest of the dorsal fin. There is a web of skin behind the second dorsal spine that may be entirely covered with spinules or partly naked, depending on the species.

Frogfishes are slow swimmers and rely on their color and shape for camouflage both for defense and for feeding. They are voracious predators and ambush prey attracted to their lures. Larger individuals will even prey on smaller members of their own species. Frogfishes lay their eggs encased in floating, jelly-like rafts.

There are 41 species now placed in 12 genera. Seven species in two genera live in our area.

Genera of family Antennariidae

Antennarius	Body covered with tiny, close-set spinules. Pectoral stalk connected to body for most of its length.
Histrio	Body smooth, without spinules. Pectoral stalk free from body for most of its length.

95 Longlure Frogfish
Antennarius multiocellatus

Identification: A stubby globose frogfish. Coloring highly variable: from pale yellow to bright red or dark green to reddish brown, sometimes with irregular gray blotches and round black spots. Usually has large dark spot at dorsal fin base and dark spots of various sizes on dorsal, anal, and caudal fins. Often has white saddle on caudal peduncle. May have dark bars radiating from eye. There is a

solid black phase with no markings.
Illicium about twice as long as second dorsal spine. SL to 4⅜" (11 cm).

Habitat: Shallow water around reefs to depths of 215' (65 m), but usually in water less than 26' (8 m) deep.

Range: Bermuda, Bahamas, Antilles, coasts of Central and South America to Brazil.

Notes: The Longlure is possibly the most common frogfish in the West Indies. Its many color phases make it a delight for the snorkeler, but it is so well camouflaged that it is hard to detect. Like other frogfishes, the Longlure is an effective, voracious predator. No other species in our area has such a long illicium.

96 Ocellated Frogfish
Antennarius ocellatus

Identification: A stubby globose frogfish. Light yellow-brown, beige, brown, or gray. *3 prominent black spots on side, each surrounded by lighter ring:* one below dorsal fin, one on mid side, and one on caudal fin. Small dark spots on head, chin, belly, and fins. Illicium and second dorsal spine about equal in length; esca a dense cluster of slender filaments. Membrane behind second dorsal spine mostly naked, but has band of spinules across its middle. 13 bifurcate dorsal rays. 12 bifurcate pectoral fin rays. SL to 13" (33 cm).

Habitat: Over rubble, or mud or sand bottoms, from depths of 3–495' (1–150 m).

Range: North Carolina to Florida, Bahamas, e Gulf of Mexico, Yucatán to Venezuela.

Notes: The Ocellated is the largest species of frogfish in the western Atlantic. It is sometimes taken in shrimp trawls in deep water and sometimes collected by hand in shallow water.

Similar Species: Longlure Frogfish may have similar spots but is smaller, and its illicium is much longer than its second dorsal spine. Singlespot Frogfish *(A. radiosus),* from New Jersey to Florida Keys and

Gulf of Mexico, is similar but has 1 large ocellated spot below dorsal fin base and 13 unbranched pectoral rays; esca is a fleshy bulb with dark buds and filaments. Island Frogfish *(A. bermudensis)* has large black spot below dorsal fin base, dark bars radiating from eye, scattered short skin filaments with dark bands on head and upper body, and 10 pectoral rays; it occurs in Bermuda, Bahamas, Haiti, Puerto Rico, Colombia, and Venezuela.

97 Dwarf Frogfish
Antennarius pauciradiatus

Identification: A stubby globose frogfish with illicium distinctly shorter than second dorsal spine. Yellow overall, with tiny dark spots and irregular darker patch above pectoral fin. 9 pectoral rays. *Pair of elongate fleshy tabs near tip of second dorsal spine.* SL to 1⅜″ (4 cm).

Habitat: Depths of 19–240′ (6–73 m). In Bahamas it has been taken from patch reefs.

Range: Bermuda, Florida, Bahamas, Puerto Rico, Antigua, Honduras, Isla de Providencia, and Isla San Andrés.

Notes: This is the smallest of our frogfishes and the only one with the illicium shorter than the second dorsal spine and with fleshy tabs on the second dorsal spine. An inch-long (2.5 cm) specimen contained developing eggs. In frogfishes, the transformation from larval to adult form is triggered by contact with the bottom. Some adults can be smaller than some larvae.

98 Striated Frogfish
Antennarius striatus

Identification: A stubby globose frogfish, *pale tan with dark brown or olive elongate blotches that extend onto fins. Prominent lines radiate from eye.* Illicium about as long as second dorsal spine. *Bone supporting illicium extends in front of upper lip.* Esca consists of 2–7 elongate, worm-like appendages. Bases of dorsal and anal fins end well in front of bases of caudal fin rays. SL to about 6″ (15 cm).

Habitat: Around eelgrass and sponges on flat, open, sand bottoms from shoreline to depths of 723′ (219 m).

Range: Bermuda, New Jersey, s Florida, Bahamas, w Gulf of Mexico, Caribbean to s Brazil. Also in e Atlantic and Indo-Pacific.

Notes: With its unique color pattern and extended illicium bone, the Striated Frogfish is very distinctive and easy to recognize. Like other frogfishes, it is an ambush feeder that depends on camouflage and its lure to attract prey close enough to inhale with a quick expansion of the mouth cavity.

99 Sargassumfish
Histrio histrio

Identification: A stubby but slightly compressed frogfish. Body greenish yellow and brownish. *Skin smooth, without dermal spinules* but with numerous fleshy appendages, including 2 between upper lip and base of illicium. Illicium much shorter than second dorsal spine. *Pectoral stalk free from body for most of its length.* Pelvic fin long, more than one-quarter of body length. Outermost rays of caudal fin unbranched, 7 innermost rays branched. SL to 5½″ (14 cm).

Habitat: Open ocean in floating sargassum weed, which sometimes drifts in to shore.

Range: Widely distributed in warmer parts of Atlantic; also Indo–west Pacific area.

Notes: The Sargassumfish is a voracious feeder and grows very rapidly. It lives in sargassum weed, using its pectoral and pelvic fins to "walk" among the branches. Specimens can be collected by scooping up clumps of drifting sargassum plants and shaking them over a tub of water. Other frogfishes in our area have dermal spinules and the pectoral lobe is attached to the body for most of its length.

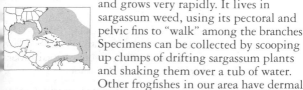

BATFISHES
Family Ogcocephalidae

Batfishes are rather bizarre bottom-dwelling fishes that "walk" on their pelvic and pectoral fins. They have depressed triangular heads with the tip of the snout projecting as a bluntly pointed *rostrum*. As in all angler-fishes, batfishes have the first (and only) dorsal fin spine modified as a rod *(illicium)* with a lure *(esca)* at its tip. Except when the batfish is actively trying to attract prey, the illicium is retracted into a cavity on the underside of the rostrum. The dorsal and anal fins are short, and the anal fin is located far behind the anus. The pectoral fins are on arm-like stalks; the pelvic fins are inserted in front of the pectoral fins. The gill openings are on the body behind the base of the stalked pectoral fins. The tail is stout and terete, with a rounded caudal fin. The skin is rough, with pointed bony tubercles on the upper surface of the body and both surfaces of the tail.

Batfishes are true bottom fishes. Their dark color and unusual flattened shape serve as camouflage, concealing them from predators and potential prey. They are ambush feeders, resting quietly and moving the lure to attract their fish and crustacean prey close enough to be captured. They also feed on snails, clams, and various kinds of worms.

Batfishes are rather difficult to identify. There are nine genera and 62 species. *Ogcocephalus,* a New World genus with two eastern Pacific species and 10 western Atlantic forms, is the only group apt to be encountered in our region *(Halieutichthys, Dibranchus,* and *Zalieutes* usually occur in somewhat deeper water here). The Shortnose Batfish and the Polka-dot Batfish are the most common species in shallow water.

Genera of family Ogcocephalidae

Ogcocephalus	Belly covered with scales. Pectoral fin stalk not attached to side of tail. No subopercular spine. Ventral surface of tail sometimes has a few tubercles in midline.
Halieutichthys	Belly without scales. Pectoral fin stalk attached to side of tail by skin. No subopercular spine.
Zalieutes	Belly covered with scales. Pectoral fin stalk not attached to tail. Ventral surface of tail has 2 rows of cone-shaped tubercles. No subopercular spine.
Dibranchus	Strong multipointed subopercular spine at rear corner of head. Belly fully scaled. Pectoral fin stalk not attached to tail.

100 Shortnose Batfish
Ogcocephalus nasutus

Identification: Head triangular; rostrum length varies from very short to longer than diameter of eye. *Dark brown above; paler brown, often reddish, below.* Warty tubercles on dorsal surface. Skin of pectoral fin thick and spongy along rays. SL to 9½" (24 cm).

Habitat: Often in sea-grass beds and around mangrove roots; from shallow water to depths of 1,000' (305 m).

Range: Southeastern Florida, Bahamas, Antilles, w Caribbean, and along South American coast to mouth of Amazon River.

Notes: The Shortnose Batfish is often encountered by snorkelers. It relies on its camouflage and remains motionless or walks slowly along the bottom using its pectoral and pelvic fins. Although it is easily caught by hand, this is a harmless species that should be treated gently. It is rarely used for food.

Similar Species: Very similar Polka-dot Batfish *(O. radiatus;* also known as *O. cubifrons)* has round dark spots on dorsal surfaces of head and pectoral fin; it ranges from North Carolina to s Florida, w Florida north to Pensacola; also Campeche Bank and n Bahamas. Pancake Batfish *(Halieutichthys aculeatus)* has round, flattened body with network of fine reddish lines on gray background; its eyes are on dorsal surface; it normally lives in deep water but sometimes comes close to shore; occurs in North Carolina, Bahamas, n Gulf of Mexico, and Lesser Antilles.

ORDER GOBIESOCIFORMES

This order consists of a single family, Gobiesocidae, whose members are identified by the presence of a ventral suction disk and a lack of fin spines.

Most ichthyologists consider these fishes to be Paracanthopterygians, a group that also includes the cod-like fishes, but some authorities now think that they are related to the dragonets, and that fin spines were present in their ancestors but have been lost.

CLINGFISHES
Family Gobiesocidae

Clingfishes are small, scaleless, tadpole-shaped fishes that have a complex sucker-like disk on the ventral surface composed of modified pelvic fins and parts of the pectoral fins. They use the disk mostly to attach themselves to the rocky bottom in the wave zone, but sometimes they cling to plants. The disk has short papillae in patches; the arrangement of these patches is useful for identification (see illustrations in the genus table below). Clingfishes have single dorsal and anal fins with few rays and no spines. Most are small, less than 2 inches (5 cm) long, but two species reach about 12 inches (30 cm) long.

This family of distinctive fishes contains about 36 genera and 120 species. In our region there are six genera that might be encountered in shallow water.

Genera of family Gobiesocidae

Illustrations show ventral disks, including patches of papillae.

Acyrtops

Upper lip narrow, same width at center as at sides. Lower jaw smooth. Papillae in central part of disk in a single median patch. Papillae flattened. Head large, nearly one-third SL. Gill membranes free from isthmus.

Rimicola

Upper lip narrow, same width at middle as at sides. Lower jaw with fleshy lobe-like structures. Upper end of gill opening opposite fifth or sixth pectoral ray. Single elongate patch of papillae on midline of central part of disk. Head short. Gill membranes free from isthmus.

Gobiesox

Upper lip broadest at middle. Papillae in central part of disk in 2 widely separated patches. Fleshy pad on base of pectoral fin with a distinct free posterior edge. Gill membranes free from isthmus.

Acyrtus

Lower jaw with fleshy papillae across its width. Upper lip broadest at middle. Papillae in central part of sucking disk either absent *(rubiginosus)* or in 2 patches *(artius)* close together, each with 3–9 rows of flattened papillae. Gill membranes free from isthmus.

Tomicodon

Lower jaw with only 2 widely spaced fleshy projections. Upper lip broadest at middle. No papillae in central region of disk. Body slender; head short. Color pattern consisting of transverse bars. Gill membranes free from isthmus.

Derilissus

Gill membranes fused to isthmus. Upper lip broadest at middle. Several large papillae in central area of disk.

101 Red Clingfish
Acyrtus rubiginosus

Identification: A short broad clingfish. Purplish red with tiny blue spots. Upper lip widest at middle. *No papillae in central part of disk.* TL to 1⅜″ (3.5 cm).

Habitat: Rocky shorelines from tide pools to depths of 12′ (3.6 m).

Range: Bahamas, Antilles, Grand Cayman, Isla de Providencia, w Caribbean from Mexico to Honduras.

Notes: The Red Clingfish lives under rock-boring sea urchins, which carve short channels in limestone in the wave zone. Its color closely matches the deep reddish purple of the urchin, and it even has tiny blue spots that mimic the light-sensing organs of the sea urchin.

Similar Species: Papillate Clingfish *(A. artius),* a rather stubby reddish species with 3 prominent gray cross bands, has upper lip wider at center than on side; forked flap on anterior nostril; and 2 patches of short papillae, side by side and near center of sucking disk, each with 3–5 rows of papillae; it lives in Bahamas, Antilles to Curaçao, Yucatán, Belize, Grand Cayman, and Isla de Providencia.
Padded Clingfish *(A. macrophthalmus),* probably same species as Papillate, has 7–9 rows of papillae in each patch on central part of disk, fleshy pad on lower part of pectoral base, and multibranched tentacle on anterior nostril; it occurs in Bahamas and Antilles.

102, 103   Skilletfish
Gobiesox strumosus

Identification:

A rather flat, broad clingfish. Olive-brown with irregular dark mottlings and dark band at base of caudal fin. *About 6 faint lines radiate from eye. 2 widely separated patches of papillae* in central part of sucking disk. Upper edge of groove above upper lip wavy but without definite barbels. Dermal flap on anterior nostril bilobed, but each branch smooth. TL to 3⅛" (8 cm).

Habitat: Shallow water in grassy areas that have some hard bottom. Often in water less than 3' (1 m) deep, but sometimes to depths of 110' (33 m).

Range: Bermuda, New Jersey to Florida, Gulf of Mexico, and St. Martin (Lesser Antilles). Not in Bahamas.

Notes: The Skilletfish ranges farther north than other western Atlantic clingfishes. In the Chesapeake Bay region it spawns in April and May. It clings to pilings and objects such as rocks and shells.

Other *Gobiesox* species

Bahama Skilletfish
(G. lucayanus) Rather stubby; TL to 2⅜" (6 cm). Pale red, with dark dots and dashes on dorsal surface. Head broad, flat. 3 low lobes separated by shallow indentations in middle of upper lip. 24–26 pectoral fin rays. Great Bahama Bank, Bahamas.

G. barbatulus
Very similar to Skilletfish. Lobe-like papillae on central margin of upper lip. Well-developed barbels on suborbital region. Fringed dermal flaps on anterior nostrils. About 12 dark lines radiate from eye. Belize to Brazil.

G. nudus
Pale gray with pale flecks on upper part of head and body; dark spot at front of dorsal fin base; dark bar near caudal fin base. Freshwater streams of Cuba, Dominica, Honduras, Costa Rica, Panama, Venezuela.

| Stippled Clingfish | (*G. punctulatus*) Small dark spots. No lobes on upper lip. 20–22 pectoral fin rays. Florida, Bahamas, Antilles, Texas, Belize, Honduras, Grand Cayman, Isla de Providencia, Panama, Venezuela. |

Other species of clingfishes

Emerald Clingfish	(*Acyrtops beryllinus*) Tiny, rather slender. Small disk. Usually brilliant emerald green above, sometimes brownish, paler below. Florida, Bahamas, w Caribbean, Lesser Antilles.
Acyrtops amplicirrus	Similar to Emerald Clingfish; may be the same species. Virgin Islands.
Rimicola brevis	Single elongate patch of papillae on midline of central part of disk. Panama, U.S. Virgin Islands.
Barred Clingfish	(*Tomicodon fasciatus*) Pale green, shading to white below, darker green bars across back, extending to lower side. 21 pectoral rays. *T. f. fasciatus:* Bahamas, Antilles, Curaçao, Grand Cayman, Isla de Providencia, Belize, Honduras to Venezuela. *T. f. australis:* Brazil.
Tomicodon rhabdotus	Narrow yellow bars on dark green background. 18 pectoral fin rays. Dominica.

ORDER ATHERINIFORMES

There is a great deal of uncertainty about the classification of fishes that are now placed in this order. It is sometimes expanded to include the fishes of the orders Beloniformes and Cyprinodontiformes as well as the Atheriniformes, but because these related fishes are quite different in appearance, we have kept them in their separate orders.

Atheriniform fishes usually have two dorsal fins, the first rather small, with slender, weak spines. The anal fin has a single spine at the front, and the pelvic fins are usually abdominal or subabdominal (sometimes thoracic). The lateral line is often poorly developed.

The order Atheriniformes includes eight families, 47 genera, and 285 species. Only one family, Atherinidae, is found in our region.

SILVERSIDES
Family Atherinidae

      Most members of this family are rather small, slender, elongate, and slightly compressed fishes; most have a distinct silvery line along each side. The eyes are large, and the smallish mouth is terminal and often directed upward. The pelvic fins are abdominal or subabdominal, located rather far back on the abdomen, and the pectoral fins are high on the sides. There are two well-separated dorsal fins, the first short, with about four slender spines. The anal fin has a single slender spine at its front, followed by a number of soft rays. The tail is forked. The scales may be smooth or have scalloped edges. Atherinid fishes are classified partly on the basis of the length of the swim bladder and other features that are not visible externally; therefore, species that appear similar may not be closely related at all.

    This is a large family, with 25 genera and 165 species. Six genera are found in our region.

Genera of family Atherinidae

Melanorhinus	Body deep, compressed, mullet-like. No silver stripe. Anal fin long; 22–24 rays.
Atherinomorus	Head broad. Body slender, not compressed. Posterior half of lower jaw without high lobe. Anal fin short; 8–14 rays.
Hypoatherina	Posterior half of lower jaw with high lobe. Head rather narrow. Body slender, not compressed. Anal fin short; 8–13 rays.
Membras	4 gland-like depressions on top of snout. Origin of first dorsal fin above or in front of anal fin origin. Anal fin long; 13–28 rays. Body slender, not compressed.
Atherinella	Origin of first dorsal fin behind anal fin origin. No gland-like depressions on top of head. Anal fin long; 13–28 rays. Body slender, not compressed.
Menidia	Origin of first dorsal fin above or in front of anal fin origin. No gland-like depressions on top of head. Anal fin long; 13–28 rays. Body slender, not compressed.

106 Reef Silverside
Hypoatherina harringtonensis

Identification: A slender species. *Head rather narrow, not conspicuously wider than body.* Dusky pigment on back separated from silvery stripe on side by transparent space that appears as pale stripe. Lower side pale transparent yellow, without black spots. Top edge of rear half of lower jaw extends upward as high lobe. Anus well in front of anal fin. Anal fin short, with 11 or 12 rays. TL to 4″ (10 cm).

Habitat: Near surface in coastal and offshore waters. Often around coral reefs.

Range: Bermuda, s Florida, Bahamas, Antilles, and w Caribbean from Yucatán to n South America.

Notes: This common reef species occurs in large schools in very shallow waters close to shore. Snorkelers delight in swimming through the schools, which open to allow the swimmer to pass through and then close again.

Similar Species: Other silversides lack clear band separating dusky color of back from silvery lateral stripe. Hardhead Silverside is similar but has broad head.

107 Hardhead Silverside
Atherinomorus stipes

Identification: A slender, elongate species with *head wider than body.* Pale transparent greenish above; silvery lateral stripe; lower side silvery white with dusky streaks. Tips of caudal lobes dark. Anus well in front of anal fin. Anal fin short, with 9–13 rays. TL to about 4″ (10 cm).

Habitat: Shallow waters and coral reefs.

Range: Southern Florida, Bahamas, and coasts from Yucatán to Brazil.

Notes: Often traveling in large schools, the Hardhead Silverside is a familiar sight for snorkelers.

Similar Species: Reef Silverside has narrower head and clear stripe above silvery lateral stripe, and lacks dusky streaks on lower side.

Other species of silversides

Querimana Silverside	(*Melanorhinus microps*) Tiny, terminal mouth. Silvery. Dorsal fin origin well ahead of anal origin. 22–24 anal fin rays. Bahamas, Cuba, Antilles, Panama.
Sardina	(*Atherinella milleri*) Abdomen compressed, forming a keel. Origin of first dorsal fin over middle of anal fin base. Anal fin has 23–27 rays; no scaly sheath along base. Honduras, Costa Rica.
Beach Silverside	(*Atherinella blackburni*) Silvery lateral stripe bordered by black line above. Anal fin long, with 22–26 rays, and scaly sheath along base. Scales smooth-edged. Coasts of Central and South America from Costa Rica to Brazil.
Rough Silverside	(*Membras martinica*) Bright silvery stripe on mid-side. Scales have scalloped edges, rough to touch. 4 gland-like depressions on top of snout. 15–21 anal fin rays. New York to Florida, including St. Johns River, n Gulf of Mexico to n Mexico.
Inland Silverside	(*Menidia beryllina*) Pale straw yellow with bright silver stripe. Edge of anal fin strongly curved. 16–19 anal rays. Massachusetts to Florida, e Gulf of Mexico, drainage of Rio Grande and Mississippi Rivers.
Atlantic Silverside	(*Menidia menidia*) Edge of anal fin straight. 23–26 anal rays. Canada to n Florida.
Tidewater Silverside	(*Menidia peninsulae*) Straight edge on anal fin; 13–19 rays. First and second dorsal fins well spaced. Peninsular Florida and w Gulf of Mexico.
Key Silverside	(*Menidia conchorum*) 12–15 anal rays. May be a local variant of Tidewater Silverside. S Florida Keys.

ORDER BELONIFORMES

This order currently includes five families and 38 genera, with about 191 species. In our region it is represented by the families Hemiramphidae (halfbeaks), Exocoetidae (flyingfishes), and Belonidae (needlefishes). The fishes of this order are united by certain skeletal characteristics that are beyond the scope of this field guide. The three families in our region have several features in common. They are slender fishes with abdominal pelvic fins, dorsal and anal fins well back on the body, and the lateral line low on the side. They lack fin spines. The lower half of the caudal fin has more rays than the upper half (in most fishes it is the other way around).

HALFBEAKS
Family Hemiramphidae

The halfbeaks are slender, elongate, surface-dwelling fishes. Most have elongate lower jaws and very short upper jaws, although the jaws are of approximately equal length in one genus. The nostrils are in a depression, or *nasal pit*. Some species have distinct bony ridges in front of the eyes. All have a single dorsal fin. The dorsal and anal fins are placed far back on the body, the pectoral fins are high on the sides, and the pelvic fins are abdominal, located far back on the belly. All fins lack spines. The lower lobe of the caudal fin is usually longer than the upper, an adaptation that enables halfbeaks to propel themselves along the surface of the water. Another adaptation for living at the surface is that the lateral line, which contains sensory pores, runs low on the body, probably so it can remain underwater and thus minimize noise from the air–water interface. Halfbeaks swim at or just below the surface and sometimes skip along the surface to avoid predators.

Some ichthyologists consider halfbeaks to belong to the same family as the closely related flyingfishes; here we treat them as separate families. The halfbeak family contains 12 genera and about 85 species, some of which occur in fresh water. There are five species and two genera in our area.

Genera of family Hemiramphidae

Hemiramphus	Caudal fin deeply forked. No scales on snout. No bony ridge in front of eye. 10–13 anal fin rays.
Hyporhamphus	Caudal fin only slightly forked, but lower lobe longer than upper. Snout scaled. Bony ridge in front of eye. 14–17 anal fin rays.

108 Ballyhoo
Hemiramphus brasiliensis

Identification:
A slender species with an elongate lower jaw. Transparent green above, silvery white below. Tip of lower jaw and upper lobe of tail orange-red. *No ridge between nostril and eye.* No scales on upper jaw or dorsal and anal fins. Pectoral fin short, not reaching nasal pit when folded forward. Pelvic fin extends past dorsal origin. Lower caudal fin lobe much longer than upper. 28–36 gill rakers on first arch. 13 or 14 dorsal rays; 12 or 13 anal rays. TL to 15¾" (40 cm).

Habitat:
Near surface in inshore waters.

Range:
Massachusetts south to Brazil, including Gulf of Mexico and Caribbean.

Notes:
The most common halfbeak species around coral reefs, the Ballyhoo is frequently used as bait for big-game fishing.

Similar Species:
Bermuda Halfbeak *(H. bermudensis),* a Bermuda endemic, is very similar but has 37–45 gill rakers on first arch. Balao *(H. balao)* has longer pectoral fin (reaching beyond front of nasal pit when folded forward) and has upper lobe of caudal fin bluish; it occurs from New York to Brazil, including Bahamas, Gulf of Mexico, and Caribbean.

Other species of halfbeaks

Silverstripe Halfbeak
(Hyporhamphus unifasciatus) Bony ridge between eye and nostril. Transparent green above, to silvery white below. Fleshy tip of elongate lower jaw red. Caudal fin pale with dark edge. Scaly sheaths along bases of dorsal and anal fins. Bermuda, peninsular Florida, s Bahamas, se Gulf of Mexico, Antilles, Caribbean south to Uruguay.

Slender Halfbeak
(Hyporhamphus roberti) Smaller and more slender than Silverstripe. Lacks scaly sheaths at bases of dorsal and anal fins. Rhode Island to Florida, Gulf of Mexico.

FLYINGFISHES
Family Exocoetidae

Flyingfishes are closely related to the halfbeaks, and the two groups are sometimes included in the same family (Exocoetidae). Unlike the halfbeaks, flying-fishes usually have short jaws, equal in length. The pectoral fins—and sometimes the pelvic fins as well—are greatly enlarged and resemble wings in most genera. As in the half-beaks, the lateral line runs low on the sides of the body, the lower lobe of the tail fin is longer than the upper lobe, and the fins lack spines. The pelvic fins are abdominal. The elongate pectoral fins serve as wings when the fishes glide through the air, although they do not actually flap their "wings." The flight is almost surely used solely for defense, for once they are in the air, flyingfishes become invisible to predators below the surface.

Flyingfishes generally live near the surface of open oceans, but a few species come in over the continental shelf and approach the drop-off at the edge of coral reefs. In keeping with their oceanic habitat, these flying fishes are blue above, shading to silvery on the sides and white on the belly.

Flyingfishes, which are abundant over deep water, are commercially important food fishes in the Lesser Antilles, where there is little shallow-water shelf area.

There are nine or 10 genera and 52 species of flyingfishes; eight genera and 16 species occur in our area. Another genus, *Fodiator,* has been reported from the southern Caribbean, but the records are doubtful. Three genera are four-winged, with large pelvic as well as pectoral fins; two are two-winged, with small pelvic fins; and three have pectoral fins that are not wing-like.

Genera of family Exocoetidae

Euleptorhamphus	Lower jaw much longer than upper. Pectoral fin long but not wing-like; does not reach pelvic fin origin. Dorsal and anal fins long; 21–24 dorsal fin rays, 19–24 anal fin rays. Body very compressed.
Chriodorus	Jaws short, equal in length. Silvery stripe along side. Pectoral fin short, not wing-like; reaches less than halfway to pelvic fin origin.
Oxyporhamphus	Pectoral fin expanded but not wing-like; reaches to pelvic fin origin. Jaws short, equal in length. Side without definite silver stripe.

Exocoetus	2-winged, with only pectoral fin expanded. Pectoral fin reaches well beyond anal fin base. Dorsal fin low and without black spot.
Parexocoetus	2-winged, with only pectoral fin expanded. Pectoral fin reaches only to posterior part of anal fin base. Dorsal fin has middle rays longer than others, and large black spot.
Cypselurus	4-winged, with pectoral and pelvic fins expanded. 1 unbranched ray at front of pectoral fin. Origin of anal fin below or behind base of third dorsal ray. Dorsal fin has 2–5 more rays than anal fin.
Prognichthys	4-winged, with pectoral and pelvic fins expanded. 2 unbranched rays at front of pectoral fin. Dorsal fin has 2–5 more rays than anal fin.
Hirundichthys	4-winged, with pectoral and pelvic fins expanded. Anal fin origin in front of dorsal fin origin, or at least not behind base of third dorsal ray. Pectoral fin has 1–2 unbranched rays at front. Dorsal and anal fins have same number of rays, or do not differ by more than 2 rays.
Fodiator	2-winged, only pectoral fin enlarged. Body compressed. Snout longer than eye diameter.

104, 105   Spotfin Flyingfish
Cypselurus furcatus

Identification: A 4-winged flyingfish. Dorsal fin lightly pigmented. *Pectoral fin dark with pale margin and pale, curved, transverse stripe.* 27–33 predorsal scales. TL to 12″ (30 cm).

Habitat: Near surface.

Range: Tropical and subtropical Atlantic, Gulf of Mexico, and Caribbean.

Notes: Like other flyingfishes, the Spotfin leaves the water and glides for long distances when disturbed. Flyingfishes often renew their flight by making "touch and go" landings on the tops of waves, giving a few quick sculls with the elongate lower lobes of their tails to propel themselves back into the air to continue their flight. Juvenile four-winged flyingfishes can be difficult to identify; juveniles of several species are orange, as shown in plate 105.

Other species of flyingfishes

Pectoral fin not wing-like.

Hardhead Halfbeak	*(Chriodorus atherinoides)* Silvery stripe along side that widens below dorsal fin. Upper and lower jaws equal in length. Pectoral and pelvic fins short, not expanded. S Florida, n Gulf of Mexico to Cuba and Yucatán.
Smallwing Flyingfish	*(Oxyporhamphus micropterus)* Jaws equal in length. Pectoral fin large, reaching front of pelvic fin, with 11–13 rays. No silver stripe along side. Off South Carolina, Lesser Antilles.
Flying Halfbeak	*(Euleptorhamphus velox)* Long pectoral fin with 7–9 rays. Lower jaw much longer than upper. Massachusetts to Florida, n Gulf of Mexico, Antilles to Brazil.

2-winged, only pectoral wing expanded.

Tropical Two-wing Flyingfish	*(Exocoetus volitans)* Pelvic fin short, not reaching anus. Body rather slender. 24–39 gill rakers on first arch. Tropical and subtropical Atlantic, e Gulf of Mexico, Caribbean; also Indian and Pacific Oceans.
Oceanic Two-wing Flyingfish	*(Exocoetus obtusirostris)* Pelvic fin short, not reaching anus. Body rather deep. 24–29 gill rakers. Tropical and subtropical Atlantic, Gulf of Mexico, Caribbean; also Indian and Pacific Oceans.
Sailfin Flyingfish	*(Parexocoetus brachypterus)* Dorsal fin large with large black area. Pelvic fin reaches anus, but is not large and wing-like. Tropical and subtropical w Atlantic, Gulf of Mexico, Caribbean.

4-winged; pelvic and pectoral fins expanded.

Atlantic Flyingfish	*(Cypselurus melanurus)* Dorsal fin low and transparent, without black spot. Pectoral fin dusky with pale central triangular area extending from middle of anterior rays to rear margin of fin. Massachusetts to Suriname, Bahamas, Gulf of Mexico, Caribbean, including Antilles; also s Brazil and e tropical Atlantic.
Mediterranean Flyingfish	*(Cypselurus heterurus)* Dorsal fin pale, without dark spot. Pectoral fin very lightly pigmented. More than 30 predorsal scales. Bermuda, Mediterranean Sea.
Clearwing Flyingfish	*(Cypselurus comatus)* Dorsal fin pale, without black spot. Pectoral fin uniformly dusky. Atlantic coast, s Gulf of Mexico, n Caribbean; also s Brazil.
Margined Flyingfish	*(Cypselurus cyanopterus)* Prominent black spot on dorsal fin. Pectoral fin uniformly dark. Florida to ne South America, Gulf of Mexico, Caribbean.
Bandwing Flyingfish	*(Cypselurus exiliens)* Prominent black spot on dorsal fin. Pectoral fin dark with pale transverse band. Upper caudal lobe lightly pigmented. W Atlantic; not in Caribbean.
Fourwing Flyingfish	*(Hirundichthys affinis)* Pectoral fin dusky with pale triangle at base and narrow clear margins; first ray unbranched. Tropical and subtropical Atlantic, including Gulf of Mexico, Caribbean.
Mirrorwing Flyingfish	*(Hirundichthys speculiger)* Pectoral fin dusky with clear triangle at base and broad, clear marginal band; first ray unbranched. Tropical and subtropical Atlantic south of 25° N latitude; uncommon in Caribbean, Gulf of Mexico.
Blackwing Flyingfish	*(Hirundichthys rondeleti)* Pectoral fin has first 2 rays unbranched, narrow clear margin; no pale triangle at base. Subtropical w Atlantic north of 25° N latitude, n Bahamas, n Gulf of Mexico.

| Bluntnose Flyingfish | *(Prognichthys gibbifrons)* Snout very short and blunt. First 2 pectoral rays unbranched. Pectoral fin transparent with dark central area. Tropical and subtropical Atlantic, Gulf of Mexico, Caribbean. |

NEEDLEFISHES
Family Belonidae

Needlefishes are large, very elongate fishes that are slightly tapered at both ends. Both jaws extend into a sharp beak that has numerous small, but very sharp, canine-like teeth. During the fish's development the lower jaw becomes elongate first, producing a halfbeak stage; later the upper jaw grows faster until it is as long as the lower jaw. The single dorsal and anal fins are set far back on the body, the pectoral fins are short and set high on the side of the body, and the pelvic fins are small and abdominal. There are no fin spines. As in the flyingfishes and halfbeaks, the lateral line runs low on the sides, and the lower lobe of the caudal fin is somewhat longer than the upper lobe. The scales are small and smooth. Offshore species tend to be blue above and silvery on the sides and belly. Inshore species are green above and transparent silvery on the sides and belly, and usually have a dusky or blue stripe along the sides. In some species the bones, visible on the top of the head and elsewhere through the transparent skin and flesh, are blue or green. In many species the top of the eyeball is opaque, apparently protecting the eyes from bright sunlight.

Needlefishes are carnivorous; their long jaws and needle-like teeth are adaptations for catching and holding prey, usually small fishes. Surface-dwellers, needlefish sometimes skip along the surface of the water and can make spectacular jumps. On rare occasions large needlefish have actually impaled people wading or in small boats.

The family includes 10 genera and about 32 species, 11 of which are restricted to fresh water. In our area there are four genera.

Genera of family Belonidae

| *Ablennes* | Body strongly compressed, with a series of well-spaced dark vertical bars. High lobe at rear of dorsal fin. |
| *Platybelone* | Body cylindrical. Caudal peduncle strongly depressed, with a well-developed keel on each side. |

Strongylura	12–17 dorsal rays. Caudal peduncle not strongly depressed. No keels on caudal peduncle. No posterior dorsal fin lobe.
Tylosurus	19–25 dorsal fin rays. Caudal peduncle not strongly depressed. A weak, darkly pigmented keel on each side of caudal peduncle. Juveniles have elongate posterior dorsal fin rays, forming a lobe that is black in color.

109 Flat Needlefish
Ablennes hians

Identification: A long, compressed needlefish. Blue or green above, silvery white on side and belly, with a broad blue stripe and *15–20 well-spaced dark gray, vertical bars on side.* Scales and bones green. Rear one-fourth of dorsal fin has long rays that form a high, darkly pigmented lobe in both young and adults. TL to 3'7" (1.1 m).

Habitat: Oceanic; sometimes in inshore areas.

Range: Worldwide in tropical waters. Bermuda, Massachusetts to Florida Keys, Bahamas, Gulf of Mexico, entire Caribbean, including Antilles, and South American coast to Rio de Janeiro.

Notes: In females of this species only the left gonad is developed, and in males the right gonad is small or absent. This is the only needlefish in our area with a strongly compressed body and bold vertical bars.

110 Atlantic Needlefish
Strongylura marina

Identification: A slender, elongate, terete needlefish. Greenish above, paler below. *Black pigment behind eye, not extending below level of middle of eye.* Dark blue stripe along side of body. Caudal fin blue. Scales and bones green. Maxilla only partly covered by preorbital region when mouth closed. 14–17 dorsal fin rays. 16–20 anal fin rays. TL to 24" (61 cm).

Habitat: Inshore waters; moves into estuaries and up into fresh water.

Range: Maine to Florida, around Gulf of Mexico, and along Central and South American coasts to Rio de Janeiro. Absent from Bahamas and Antilles.

Notes: The Atlantic Needlefish is often seen around lights shining on the water at night. In this species, only the right gonad is developed, but in the Redfin Needlefish and the Timucu, both left and right gonads are present.

Similar Species: Timucu (*S. timucu*) has broad dusky stripe on side of head and body, dusky pigment behind eye extending down to lower margin of eye, and maxilla not completely covered by preorbital region when mouth is closed; it occurs from se and w Florida to Florida Keys, Bahamas, Antilles, Yucatán Peninsula, and w Caribbean south to Rio de Janeiro. Redfin Needlefish (*S. notata*) has distinct vertical bar at posterior margin of preopercle, red or orange dorsal, caudal, and anal fins, and maxilla that slips under preorbital region and is completely covered when the mouth is closed; it occurs in Bermuda, Bahamas, and Antilles.

111 Houndfish
Tylosurus crocodilus

Identification: A large needlefish with *a relatively short beak* (length about 1½ times distance between back of eye and gill cover). Dark blue above, pale silvery white below, with dark blue stripe along side. *Weak, darkly pigmented keel on each side of caudal peduncle.* 19–22 dorsal fin rays; 22–24 anal fin rays. SL to more than 4′4″ (1.3 m).

Habitat: Surface waters, usually well offshore.

Range: Worldwide in tropical and warm temperate waters. In w Atlantic from New Jersey to Florida Keys, Bahamas, Gulf of Mexico, Antilles, and along Central and South American coasts to Salvador, Brazil.

Notes: Houndfishes have been known to cause serious injuries and even death by leaping out of the water and impaling people wading or in small boats near lights. Both gonads are present in the Houndfish, but in the Agujon the left gonad is absent or greatly reduced.

Similar Species: Agujon *(T. acus)* is smaller, has longer beak (about twice the distance from eye to edge of gill cover), more dorsal fin rays, and fewer anal fin rays; it occurs in Bermuda, Massachusetts to Florida Keys, Bahamas, around Gulf of Mexico, Antilles, and along Central and South American coasts to Rio de Janeiro.

ORDER CYPRINODONTIFORMES

This order of eight families and about 807 species includes many of the popular aquarium fishes. Four families are represented in our region.

As with the beloniforms, the defining characteristics of this order are internal and too technical to be useful here. The fishes of this family are rather small, with either no lateral line or a series of shallow pits. The pelvic fins are abdominal (sometimes absent). There are no fin spines. The mouth is terminal or superior, with a protrusible upper jaw.

RIVULINS
Family Aplocheilidae

Rivulins are small, nearly terete fishes that are closely allied to the killifishes; until quite recently they were placed in the same family (Cyprinodontidae). They have a single dorsal fin placed far back on the body, abdominal pelvic fins with their bases close together, and a rounded tail; there are no fin spines. They are quite small, reaching only 2 or 3 inches (5–8 cm). Many species are brightly colored and attractive to aquarists. Some are annuals; that is, they live in habitats that become dry during part of the year and die when the water disappears. Only the eggs, which are laid in areas that remain moist, survive the dry period.

There are 12 genera and about 125 species in this family. Nearly all live in fresh water, but one species, the Mangrove Rivulin, can tolerate brackish as well as full-strength sea water and is sometimes found around offshore mangrove islands.

112 Mangrove Rivulus
Rivulus marmoratus

Identification: An elongate, almost cylindrical fish,
only very slightly compressed. Reddish
brown with dark flecks, paler on lower
side, and abruptly white on belly. Dark
spot above pectoral fin base; *another dark
spot surrounded by yellow ring on side of
caudal peduncle, just ahead of upper part of
caudal fin base.* Mouth terminal; teeth
conical and pointed. Scales small and
smooth; head scaled. Dorsal fin origin
above or behind the second or third anal
fin rays. TL to about 2⅜″ (6 cm).

Habitat: Usually in brackish or marine water,
though sometimes in fresh. Often in
holes with crabs.

Range: Florida, Bahamas, and throughout
Caribbean to Brazil.

Notes: This species is usually hermaphroditic
and lays fertilized eggs. Under some
conditions functional males are
produced, but this is rare. Several other
rivulins occur along the Central
American coast, but no other species is
found in salt water.

Fundulinae

Cyprinodontinae

KILLIFISHES
Family Cyprinodontidae

Killifishes are sometimes called "top
minnows" or "egg-laying tooth carps"
because of their resemblance to true
minnows, which are also called carps.
However, killifishes are not at all related
to true minnows but are cyprinodonti-
forms, related to silversides, needlefishes, and halfbeaks.
They are most closely related to livebearers (family Poeciliidae), but lay eggs and therefore lack the male copulatory
organ that characterizes the livebearers.

Killifishes are relatively small fishes, with scaly heads and
upturned mouths that have pointed or incisor-like teeth.
They have a single dorsal fin that may be situated well back
on the body, abdominal pelvic fins with their bases well separated, and rounded or squared-off caudal fins; there are no
fin spines. The lateral line is reduced to a series of pits along
the sides.

Often the sexes are differently colored, and the breeding males may be quite colorful. Some species lay their eggs in places that remain moist but are flooded only during spring tides, so that the eggs that are deposited during one spring tide hatch two weeks later on the next high tide.

The family is divided into two subfamilies, the Fundulinae, which has five genera and 48 species, and the Cyprinodontinae, which has nine genera and about 100 species. Many cyprinodontids live in fresh water, but there are numerous species in our area that occasionally or regularly enter brackish or marine coastal waters. A full treatment is beyond the scope of this field guide so we have selected a few representative genera and species that are most likely to be encountered.

Genera of family Cyprinodontidae
Subfamily Fundulinae

Jaw teeth conical.

Lucania	Body moderately elongate; pale straw colored, dark outlines on scales. Jaw teeth in 1 row. 26 scales along mid-side. 10–12 dorsal fin rays.
Adinia	Body short and deep. 25 scale rows along side. 9–10 dorsal fin rays.
Fundulus	Body elongate. 30 or more scales along mid-side.

Subfamily Cyprinodontinae

Jaw teeth tricuspid.

Cyprinodon	Body deep and compressed. Large humeral scale behind gill cover and above pectoral fin base.
Floridichthys	Body deep and compressed. No enlarged humeral scale. 11–13 dorsal fin rays.
Jordanella	Body deep and compressed. No enlarged humeral scale. More than 13 dorsal fin rays.

113　Gulf Killifish
Fundulus grandis

Identification:　A large killifish with an elongate, cylindrical body; rather blunt snout. Dark greenish or bluish above, slightly yellowish on lower side and belly. *Small pearly spots on side.* Females olive above, silvery below, with 12–15 narrow bars on side. Breeding males orange-yellow below, with dark cheek. *31–35 scales in lateral line.* 11 or 12 dorsal fin rays; 10–12 anal rays. TL to about 7″ (18 cm).

Habitat: Coastal waters, brackish bays, and estuaries into fresh water.

Range: Both coasts of peninsular Florida, west along n Gulf of Mexico to Texas, and ne Mexico where there is an inland, freshwater population. Also in Cuba.

Notes: The Gulf Killifish is a locally abundant species that is highly adaptable and can survive in fresh water as well as in water that has higher salinity than sea water. It feeds on small crustaceans and other invertebrates.

Other *Fundulus* species

Marsh Killifish	(*F. confluentus*) 14–18 dark bars on side; small dark spots on upper side. Chesapeake Bay to s Florida and ne Gulf of Mexico.
Bayou Killifish	(*F. pulvereus*) No vertical bars. Females have numerous dark spots on side as large as pupil of eye. Gradually intergrades with Marsh Killifish along Gulf coast west of Mobile Bay to Texas but appears to be distinctive.
F. grandissimus	Similar to Gulf Killifish but with 37–42 scales in lateral line. Yucatán.
Saltmarsh Topminnow	(*F. jenkinsi*) 12–30 small spots on side of body, often in 2 rows above lateral line. W Florida to Louisiana; disjunct population in Texas.
Striped Killifish	(*F. majalis*) Long, pointed snout. Males have 15–20 dark bars on side; females have 2–3 longitudinal stripes. 14–15 dorsal rays. New England to n Florida, n Gulf of Mexico.
Longnose Killifish	(*F. similis*) Long, pointed snout. 12 or more bars on side, but no longitudinal lines. 12–13 dorsal fin rays. May be subspecies of Striped Killifish. Florida Keys and adjacent areas of s Florida.

114 Sheepshead Minnow
Cyprinodon variegatus

Identification: *A short, deep-bodied, compressed fish. Scales large,* with smooth or slightly wavy margins. *Dorsal profile straight from tip of snout to front of dorsal fin.* Males dark olive-gray to iridescent blue-green above with indistinct dark bars on side. Breeding males have lower parts of head and body yellow to bright orange, and *dark marginal band on tail;* no vertical bands on side. Females olive-brown above, shading to white below, with dark ocellus at rear of dorsal fin but no dark margin on caudal fin. TL to 3⅛" (8 cm).

Habitat: Coastal brackish and marine waters.

Range: Cape Cod to Florida, Bahamas, Antilles, Gulf of Mexico, Yucatán, and Venezuela.

Notes: The classification of this species is uncertain; several species have been named that are probably only variants of a single wide-ranging species. This fish is often found in isolated tide pools, where it tolerates extremes of temperature and salinity.

Similar Species: Bahama Pupfish *(C. laciniatus),* found in Bahamas, has smaller scales with lobed margins.

115 Diamond Killifish
Adinia xenica

Identification: A short, compressed killifish with *concave dorsal profile from tip of snout to front of dorsal fin.* Males have deep body and high dorsal fin; dorsal, pelvic, and anal fins dusky with pale spots. Dark greenish olive above, yellowish below, with 8 *dark bands on side, each with pale center.* Females more slender, with fewer and broader bands, and unmarked fins. TL to about 1⅝" (4.1 cm).

Habitat: Along coastline from tidal flats and mangrove shorelines to brackish water.

Range: Northern Gulf of Mexico from s Florida to Texas.

Notes: This very pretty little fish is locally abundant in shallow areas of tidal marshes. Other deep-bodied killifishes have the dorsal profile either straight or convex, and different color patterns.

Other species of killifishes

Rainwater Killifish
(Lucania parva) Males have dark spot on anterior rays of dorsal fin, and orange anal and pelvic fins. Dorsal fin origin before anal fin origin. 11–12 dorsal rays. New England to s tip of Florida, Gulf of Mexico from Florida Keys to Mexico.

Jordanella pulchra
Olive above; side silvery with dark vertical bars; dark spot above pectoral fin. In females, bars become narrower and more defined with age; in males, bars become more numerous and then break into reticulated pattern. In larger males, scales of back develop silvery centers. 15–17 dorsal fin rays. 8–10 anal fin rays. 12–15 caudal fin rays. W Caribbean from Yucatán to Belize.

Flagfish
(Jordanella floridae) Very similar to *J. pulchra.* Thickened, spine-like first dorsal ray. 11–13 anal fin rays. Fresh water in Florida.

Goldspotted Killifish
(Floridichthys carpio) Profile convex from tip of snout to front of dorsal fin. Dark olive above, with irregular dark and light bands on lower side. Breeding males have golden-orange spots on side of head and body. S Florida, and Yucatán Peninsula south to Honduras.

male

female

LIVEBEARERS
Family Poeciliidae

Livebearers are characterized by a modification of the male's front anal fin rays into a complex copulatory structure called the *gonopodium,* which is used to transfer sperm to the female's reproductive tract, enabling them to bear live young. They are small fishes with abdominal pelvic fins, pectoral fins placed rather high on the sides of the body, and

a squarish or rounded caudal fin; there are no fin spines.
Scales are smooth; the mouth is small and terminal; the lateral line is a series of pits. Males are usually smaller than females. Classification and identification of poeciliids is based
largely on the structure of the gonopodium and thus requires examination under a microscope.

This is primarily a freshwater family with a few representatives that are able to tolerate brackish or salt water. The
family is restricted to the New World and contains more
than 300 species, including the familiar guppies, mollies,
and platyfishes, all popular aquarium fishes. Three genera
have marine or brackish-water representatives in our area.

Genera of family Poeciliidae

Poecilia	Pelvic fin of males highly modified, with fleshy swelling on first ray and distinct notch behind second ray.
Gambusia	Pelvic fin of males not modified. Upper pectoral rays thickened and curved upward in most species. Jaws not elongate.
Belonesox	Jaws elongate, beak-like. Pelvic fin of males not modified.

116 Pike Killifish
Belonesox belizanus

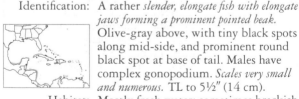

Identification: A rather *slender, elongate fish with elongate
jaws forming a prominent pointed beak.*
Olive-gray above, with tiny black spots
along mid-side, and prominent round
black spot at base of tail. Males have
complex gonopodium. *Scales very small
and numerous.* TL to 5½" (14 cm).

Habitat: Mostly fresh water; sometimes brackish
and even highly saline environments.

Range: Southern Gulf of Mexico, s Yucatán
Peninsula, and along Central American
coast south to Nicaragua. Introduced in
fresh water in Florida.

Notes: The Pike Killifish is a spectacular mini-
predator that may be hurting native
fishes in southern Florida. With its
elongate jaws, it looks like a tiny
barracuda. No other livebearer has
elongate jaws and small scales.

Genus *Gambusia*

The species of the genus *Gambusia* are very similar and can be distinguished only by microscopic examination of the gonopodia and several internal features. They are small fishes (TL to about 2⅜"/6 cm) with superior mouths. The body is translucent grayish, with the scales of the upper sides outlined in black. Some species have small dark spots and may have a dark bar below the eye. In some species the breeding males are blue above with an orange dorsal fin.

Most species of this genus are confined to fresh water but a few live in brackish or salt water. The following species are recorded from salt water in our area: *G. yucatana*, from fresh and salt water of the Yucatán Peninsula; Mangrove Gambusia *(G. rhizophorae)*, from brackish and salt water around mangrove areas of southeastern Florida and Cuba; *G. puncticulata*, from Cuba, Isla de la Juventud, Jamaica, and Cayman Islands (and possibly the Bahamas). The Bahama Gambusia *(G. manni)*, from lakes on New Providence Island, and *G. hubbsi*, from Cuba and several Bahaman localities, are considered separate species by some ichthyologists and as forms of *G. puncticulata* by others.

Other species of livebearers

Sailfin Molly	*(Poecilia latipinna)* Grayish olive above, paler below, with dark longitudinal lines. Scales of upper side outlined in black. Males have long, high, sail-like dorsal fin. Breeding males yellow, with metallic-blue tail with orange-yellow center and yellow below. North Carolina to Florida Keys, coastal Gulf of Mexico.
Poecilia vivipara	Dark bar with white border on side. Virgin Islands to Martinique; Venezuela to Argentina; introduced in Puerto Rico.

FOUREYED FISHES
Family Anablepidae

Primarily freshwater species that occasionally inhabit estuarine and coastal waters, the foureyed fishes are remarkable little surface-dwelling fishes that can see above and below the water at the same time. Their eyes, which protrude upward, are divided by a wall of opaque tissue into two parts, the upper for aerial vision and the lower for aquatic vision. They have elongate, slightly tapered bodies, flat heads, and rather small scales. The pelvic fins are abdominal, and the dorsal and anal fins are set far back on the body; there are no fin spines. Foureyed fishes are viviparous (bearing live young); the anterior parts of the male's anal fin are modified into a scale-covered tubular copulatory organ called a *gonopodium*. The reproductive structures of both males and females are asymmetrical; males have the gonopodium located on the right or left side, and females have modified scales on the right or left of the urogenital opening. It has been suggested that individuals can mate only with members of the opposite sex that have the appropriate asymmetry, but this has not been confirmed.

The family Anablepidae contains a single genus with three species, although some authorities place the foureyed fishes into an expanded family with two other South American genera that do not have the divided eyes.

---

117   Striped Foureyed Fish
Anableps anableps

Identification: A slender, elongate, tapering fish, grayish in color. *Eye divided into aerial and aquatic parts.* Distance between eyes greater than diameter of eye. Dorsal fin far back on body, behind anal fin. Pelvic fin abdominal. Anal fin of males modified as a tubular copulatory organ. No fin spines. *Fewer than 80 scales in row above lateral line.* TL to about 12″ (30 cm).

Habitat: Primarily fresh water, sometimes brackish parts of lagoons and mangrove coastlines.

Range: Venezuela to Brazil.

Notes: The Striped Foureyed Fish can remain on mud bottoms exposed to air during low tide. It often travels in schools.

Similar Species: Finescale Foureyed Fish *(A. microlepis)* has more than 80 scales in row above lateral line, and distance between eyes is equal to or smaller than diameter of eye; it occurs from Venezuela to Brazil.

ORDER BERYCIFORMES

Beryciforms are extremely spiny fishes that have one spine and more than five soft rays in each pelvic fin. They tend to be red or black in color and have very large eyes. The order includes seven families, 28 genera, and 123 species; six families occur in our region. The relationships among the fishes of this group are uncertain, and classification is changing as more information becomes available. The family Holocentridae is well represented in shallow waters, and Anomalopidae has one shallow-water species in our range; both of these families are discussed here. The other four families are confined to deeper water and are not covered in this guide. The family Berycidae contains two genera and nine species, one of which occurs in deep water in our area. The family Trachichthyidae contains seven genera and 33 species and is of special interest because some members are marketed as Orange Roughy (genus *Hoplostethus*) and the spectacular Big Roughy *(Gephyroberyx darwini)*.

FLASHLIGHTFISHES
Family Anomalopidae

The members of this family are small fishes with a spectacular light-producing organ below each eye. The dorsal fin has two to six spines and 14 to 19 soft rays, with a deep notch between the spines and rays. There are five genera and six species, one of which is found in our area.

The light is produced by symbiotic bacteria that live in special compartments within the fish's light organ. The organ can be rotated and covered by a black membrane to turn the light on and off, and the fishes probably communicate and confuse predators by blinking their lights.

118 Atlantic Flashlightfish
Kryptophanaron alfredi

Identification: A compressed fish with *a large head and a very large light-producing organ beneath eye.* Generally black, with white scutes on dorsal and ventral surfaces, and row of white spots along lateral line. Rows of enlarged scutes along sides of the bases of dorsal and anal fins. TL to 5⅛″ (13 cm).

Habitat: Outer wall of areas with steep drop-off.

Range: Greater Antilles and Cayman Islands.

Notes: Apparently the Atlantic Flashlightfish migrates to deep water during the day and ascends to near the top of the drop-off at night. Divers can spot it by descending to the drop-off without lights and remaining quiet. No other species in our area has the similar light-producing organ under the eye.

SQUIRRELFISHES
Family Holocentridae

Most squirrelfishes are small to moderate-size, elongate, and compressed, although some are quite robust with rather deep bodies. They have large eyes, terminal mouths, and are usually red in color. They are very spiny fishes, with heavy spines in the dorsal, anal, and pelvic fins (11–13 dorsal spines). Most genera also have large spines on the preopercle and other bones of the head, and even the scales have heavy spines. The pelvic fins are thoracic, inserted below the pectoral fins, and each has a strong spine and usually seven rays. The dorsal fin is usually single, and has a deep notch that divides the spiny anterior part from the soft-rayed posterior part. In the genus *Sargocentron* the separation is complete because there is a short space between the two parts. In the soldierfishes the last dorsal spine is behind the notch, so the second part of the dorsal fin has an anterior spine followed by a number of soft rays. The anterior spiny part is always much longer than the soft-rayed portion.

Common in most coral reef habitats, squirrelfishes are primarily nocturnal—for which their big eyes are adapted—although many species are also active in and around caves during daylight hours. They have special sound-producing muscles associated with the swimbladder.

There are eight genera and 65 species of squirrelfishes. Seven genera and 11 species are recognized here as occurring in our area, although many ichthyologists prefer to unite *Holocentrus, Neoniphon,* and *Sargocentron* as one genus, *Holocentrus.*

Genera of family Holocentridae

Holocentrus	Large preopercular spine. Upper lobe of caudal fin longer than lower lobe. Anterior dorsal soft rays elongate.
Neoniphon	Last dorsal spine connected to first soft ray by membrane. Caudal lobes equal. Anterior dorsal soft rays not elongate. Large preopercular spine.
Sargocentron	Last dorsal fin spine separated from first dorsal soft ray by short space. Strong preopercular spine.
Plectrypops	No preopercular spine. Circumorbital bones behind and below eye have prominent spines, those below eye forward pointing.

Myripristis No preopercular spine. No spines on suborbital bone. First dorsal fin has 10 spines; second has 1 spine and 13 soft rays.

Ostichthys No preopercular spine, but short triangular projection at angle of preopercle. No spines on suborbital bones.

Corniger 2 spines at angle of preopercle. Suborbital bone has large, backward-pointing spines.

119 Squirrelfish
Holocentrus adscensionis

Identification: A fairly elongate squirrelfish with a slender caudal peduncle. Preopercular spine about half as long as diameter of eye. Mouth terminal; upper and lower jaws nearly equal in length. Maxilla reaches beyond center of eye. Silvery reddish or pink, darker red above, shading to silvery white ventrally. *Dorsal fin clear, yellow in center, spines with yellow tips. Spiny and soft parts of dorsal fin nearly separate, but connected by low membrane.* Anterior soft rays of dorsal fin and upper lobe of caudal fin elongate. 47–49 scales in lateral line. 4 anal fin spines, longest spine shorter than longest soft rays. TL to about 12″ (30 cm).

Habitat: Coral reefs with caves and holes. Sometimes to depths of 600′ (180 m).

Range: Bermuda, North Carolina to Florida, Bahamas, e Gulf of Mexico (with scattered records in n and nw Gulf), Antilles, w Caribbean from Yucatán along Central and South American coasts to Brazil. Also in e Atlantic.

Notes: The Squirrelfish usually stays close to caves in the daytime, becoming more active when the sun is covered by clouds. At night it moves out to sandy areas and sea-grass beds where it feeds on small crustaceans.

Similar Species: Longspine Squirrelfish is sometimes
brighter red with white spots behind
tips of dorsal fin spines, and has longer
preopercular spine. Longjaw Squirrelfish
has lower jaw projecting beyond upper,
and very long anal spine, but anterior
dorsal soft rays not elongate.

120   Longspine Squirrelfish
Holocentrus rufus

Identification: A moderate-size squirrelfish with a
slender caudal peduncle and long
preopercular spine (about three-fourths as
long as diameter of eye). Maxilla reaches
to below middle of eye. Red overall,
darker above, shading to silvery white
below. *Conspicuous white spot behind tip of
each dorsal spine.* Sometimes has white
zones outlining a diamond-shaped reddish
patch on side. Dorsal fin deeply notched,
but spiny and soft parts connected by low
membrane. Anterior soft rays of dorsal
fin and upper lobe of caudal fin elongate.
51–54 scales in lateral line. Longest anal
fin spine shorter than longest anal soft
rays. TL to 10″ (25 cm).

Habitat: Coral reefs.

Range: Bermuda, e and s Florida, Bahamas,
Antilles, nw Gulf of Mexico, w Caribbean
from Yucatán to Colombia, and Venezuela
to Brazil.

Notes: The Longspine is a common and easily
identified squirrelfish, often seen by
divers. It keeps close to the mouths of
caves and holes, but comes out farther
when the sun goes under a cloud. At
night it moves out to sandy areas and
sea-grass beds to feed on crustaceans and
other invertebrates.

Similar Species: Squirrelfish has 47–49 scales in lateral
line, shorter preopercular spine, and no
white spots behind tips of dorsal spines.
Longjaw Squirrelfish has very long anal
spine and projecting lower jaw. Members
of genus *Sargocentron* have separate spiny
and soft dorsal fins. Other squirrelfishes
lack large preopercular spine.

121 Longjaw Squirrelfish
Neoniphon marianus

Identification: A rather small squirrelfish with a prominent lower jaw that extends beyond tip of upper jaw. Strong preopercular spine. *Body striped with red, yellow, and silver; often anterior third of body more yellow than remainder.* Spiny part of dorsal fin largely yellow, with scattered white spots. Dorsal fin deeply notched, but spiny and soft parts connected by low membrane. *Third anal fin spine very long and stout,* longer than longest soft rays. TL to 7″ (18 cm).

Habitat: Coral reefs, most often at depths greater than 45′ (14 m).

Range: Florida Keys, Bahamas, Antilles south to Trinidad, and throughout Caribbean.

Notes: Easily recognized by its color pattern, elongate anal fin spines, and prominent lower jaw, the Longjaw Squirrelfish is often seen by divers. It is a nocturnal species but is somewhat active during the day.

122 Dusky Squirrelfish
Sargocentron vexillarius

Identification: A small, stout squirrelfish with jaws equal in length. *Side dusky red with faint grayish stripes and rows of white spots.* Dorsal fin grayish with red spots; spiny and soft parts of fin completely separate. Caudal fin lobes about equal in length. Preopercular spine moderately long. 40–44 scales in lateral line. TL to 7″ (18 cm).

Habitat: Shallow waters, often between branches of finger coral and other branched corals.

Range: Bermuda, s Florida, Bahamas, Antilles, nw Gulf of Mexico, and coasts from Yucatán to Venezuela.

Notes: The Dusky Squirrelfish is a common but secretive species, easily overlooked unless searched for carefully between coral branches. It is a nocturnal species that seldom ventures out during daylight hours.

Similar Species: Squirrelfish and Longspine Squirrelfish
have anterior dorsal soft rays and upper
lobe of caudal fin elongate. Longjaw
Squirrelfish has lower jaw longer than
upper. Reef Squirrelfish is more elongate
in shape, and has prominent black blotch
at front of dorsal fin. Other squirrelfishes
lack single strong preopercular spine.

123 Reef Squirrelfish
Sargocentron coruscus

Identification: A small, slender, *red-and-white-striped*
squirrelfish with a prominent black blotch
between first and third, or first and fourth,
dorsal spines. Preopercular spine well
developed. Last dorsal spine separated
from first soft dorsal ray. Caudal fin lobes
equal in length. TL to about 4″ (10 cm).
Habitat: Coral reefs.
Range: Bermuda, Florida Keys, Bahamas, s Gulf
of Mexico, Antilles, and Central and
South American coasts.
Notes: This secretive species can be found deep
in crevices between branches of live
corals. It is nocturnal, coming out after
dark to forage.
Similar Species: Deepwater Squirrelfish *(S. bullisi)* has
smaller spot on dorsal fin; it is known
from deep waters of Bermuda, South
Carolina, ne Gulf of Mexico, and Lesser
Antilles. Saddle Squirrelfish *(S. poco)* has
dark spot on membranes between first
and fourth dorsal spines and black saddle
on body below soft part of dorsal fin and
another on caudal peduncle; it lives in
Bahamas, Gulf of Mexico off Texas, and
Cayman Islands. Dusky Squirrelfish has
dusky dorsal fin with red spots.

124 Cardinal Soldierfish
Plectrypops retrospinis

Identification: *A small, chunky squirrelfish without a*
preopercular spine. Circumorbital bones have
slender spines, those below eye forward-
pointing. Bright red overall, not paler

below, and no black spots. Spiny and
soft parts of dorsal fin joined by
membrane; soft parts of dorsal and anal
fins rounded. TL to 5″ (13 cm).

Habitat: Holes and caves in coral reefs.

Range: Bermuda, Bahamas, s Florida, n and
se Gulf of Mexico, and Caribbean,
including Antilles.

Notes: Although the Cardinal Soldierfish is a
common species in coral reefs, it is
seldom seen because of its secretive,
nocturnal habits. Apparently it lives
deep within the reef structure and
almost never ventures into parts of caves
that can be seen by divers.

Similar Species: Spinycheek Soldierfish *(Corniger spinosus)*
is similar in shape and color but has
larger, backward-pointing spines on
circumorbital bones; it lives in deep
water from South Carolina to Brazil.

125 Blackbar Soldierfish
Myripristis jacobus

Identification: A short, compressed, rather deep-bodied
species. Eye very large. Red above,
without lines or stripes, silvery pink
below. *Dark brown vertical bar runs along
gill opening to pectoral fin.* Front margins
of pelvic, dorsal, anal, and caudal fins
bright white. Soft parts of dorsal and
anal fins have scales. Dorsal fin deeply
notched, but connected by membrane; 10
spines in first dorsal. SL to 8¼″ (21 cm).

Habitat: Coral reefs to depths of 300′ (90 m).

Range: Bermuda, Georgia to Florida, Bahamas,
Gulf of Mexico, and Caribbean, including
Antilles, to n Brazil. Also in e Atlantic.

Notes: Blackbar Soldierfish are common and
attractive reef fish, easily seen by
snorkelers. They often hover in groups
in caves and are sometimes seen upside
down near the top of a cave, moving
along the roof as if it were the sea floor.

Similar Species: Squirrelfishes have strong preopercular
spines. Other soldierfishes of genera
Plectrypops and *Corniger* have spines
around each eye. Bigeye Soldierfish

(Ostichthys trachypoma), from Long Island
to Florida, Gulf of Mexico, and Greater
Antilles to Brazil, has 11 spines in first
dorsal fin.

ORDER SYNGNATHIFORMES

This is an order of elongate fishes with tiny mouths at the
end of a long tubular face. Syngnathiforms are closely related to the sticklebacks and are often included in the same
order, the Gasterosteiformes. The order includes five families in two suborders. Three families are included here:
Aulostomidae, Fistulariidae, and Syngnathidae.

TRUMPETFISHES
Family Aulostomidae

With their slim elongate bodies; long,
drawn-out, tubular faces; and small upturned mouths,
trumpetfishes are unmistakable. They have a single chin
barbel and rather small, rough scales. Their short, widely
spaced dorsal fin spines are not connected to one another by
a membrane. The tail is bluntly pointed. Trumpetfishes feed
by sucking in their prey, in a manner called pipette feeding.
They feed on small invertebrates and often take fishes that
seem to be too large to pass through their tubular mouths.
They are among the most abundant predators on many
West Indian reefs.

The family consists of one genus with three or four
species; one species occurs in the western Atlantic.

131 Trumpetfish
Aulostomus maculatus

Identification: Elongate, stick-like body; long tubular
face with small, almost vertical mouth
at end. Head long, nearly one-third total
body length. *Prominent barbel at tip of
lower jaw.* Usually brownish, with 2 or 3
dusky longitudinal stripes, and scattered
small dark spots on dorsal surface. Some
individuals yellow or green with blue
head. Dorsal and anal fins similar in size
and shape, each with 21–25 soft rays.
*Dorsal fin preceded by 8–13 well-spaced,
isolated spines.* Pelvic fin well back on

body. Scales small and rough. TL to at
least 30″ (75 cm).

Habitat: Coral reefs and associated habitats.

Range: Bermuda and coastal waters from
Florida Keys to Brazil, Bahamas, Gulf
of Mexico, and Caribbean, including
Antilles.

Notes: Trumpetfishes spend much of their
time hovering with their heads pointed
downward, their bodies aligned with
linear objects such as sea whips and
even large fishes. This enables them to
blend in with their surroundings and
catch their prey unawares.

Similar Species: Cornetfishes (family Fistulariidae) are
similar but have the central rays of the
caudal fin extended as long filaments.

CORNETFISHES
Family Fistulariidae

Cornetfishes resemble trumpetfishes in
their long, slender, terete body shape and their small upturned mouths at the tips of long tubular faces. Unlike the
trumpetfishes, however, they have the two middle rays of
the caudal fin extended into a long filament, and they lack
scales, chin barbels, and dorsal spines. The dorsal and anal
fins are located far back on the body, and are similar in shape
and opposite each other. The pelvic fins are abdominal. Cornetfishes are transparent reddish or grayish green, some
species with bright blue spots. They tend to be somewhat
larger than the trumpetfishes.
The family contains one genus with four species; two
species occur in our area.

---

132 Bluespotted Cornetfish
Fistularia tabacaria

Identification: A very slender, elongate, terete fish with
*middle caudal rays extended as a long
filament.* Upturned mouth at end of long
tubular face. Translucent gray-green to
translucent brownish, with rows of blue
spots on upper side and snout. Dorsal
and anal fins high and far back on body.
*No scales or fin spines. No barbel at tip of
lower jaw.* TL to more than 6′6″ (2 m).

Habitat: Coral reefs and sea-grass beds.

Range: Bermuda, Georges Bank, and coastal areas from s Canada to Florida, Bahamas, Gulf of Mexico, Antilles, Central and South American coasts to Venezuela. Also in e Atlantic.

Notes: The Bluespotted Cornetfish feeds on small fishes and shrimps. Unlike the more common Trumpetfish, it lives in open areas and does not align itself with objects. Nevertheless, its coloration serves as a surprisingly effective camouflage.

Similar Species: Red Cornetfish *(F. petimba),* which lives over soft bottoms at depths greater than 33′ (10 m), is pink to red in color, and has elongate bony plates embedded in skin along middle of back; it occurs from se Florida to Central America and in n South America.

PIPEFISHES and SEAHORSES
Family Syngnathidae

seahorse

pipefish

This family includes two subfamilies: the Syngnathinae, or pipefishes, and the Hippocampinae, or seahorses. Both have tiny snouts at the end of a tubular face, bodies encased in bony rings, and pectoral but no pelvic fins; both lack fin spines. Pipefishes are rather small, elongate, very slender, stiff-bodied fishes with the axis of the head in a continuous line with the axis of the body; they usually have caudal fins. Seahorses have the head bent at a right angle to the axis of the body. They lack caudal fins, but have prehensile tails that they use to wrap around objects to hold themselves in place.

Identification of pipefishes depends to a large extent on the pattern of longitudinal ridges on the bony rings of the body (see illustration below), the number of rings around

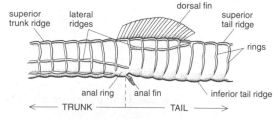

the body and the tail, the length and ornamentation of the snout, the number of rays in the dorsal fin, and the presence or absence of an anal fin. Seahorses are generally identified by size, color, length of snout, and number of rays in the fins. They do not have longitudinal ridges on the bony rings.

In both seahorses and pipefishes it is the male that guards the eggs. Male seahorses have a completely enclosed brood pouch with a small opening on the abdomen, but in male pipefishes the brood pouch can be on the abdomen or tail, and can vary from low ridges along the sides to overlapping flaps that completely cover the eggs and embryos.

The family is divided into two subfamilies with 52 genera and 215 species. Ten genera and more than two dozen species are found in our area.

Genera of family Syngnathidae

Hippocampus	No caudal fin. Tail prehensile. Head at right angle to body axis.
Acentronura	Caudal fin present. Tail prehensile. Lateral trunk ridge continuous with inferior tail ridge. Superior tail ridge begins on anal ring. Anal fin present. Snout short; 3.1 in head length.
Penetopteryx	Superior trunk ridge continuous with superior tail ridge. Lateral trunk ridge continuous with inferior tail ridge. Anal fin may be present or absent. No dorsal or pectoral fins. Snout very short; 3.2–4.0 in head length.
Microphis	More than 30 dorsal fin rays. Lateral trunk ridge continuous with inferior tail ridge. Superior tail ridge begins on anal ring. Anal fin present. Snout long; 1.5–2.0 in head length.
Micrognathus	Lateral trunk ridge continuous with inferior tail ridge. Superior tail ridge begins on anal ring. Anal fin present. Snout very short; 2.7–3.7 in head length.
Anarchopterus	Lateral trunk ridge continuous with inferior tail ridge. Superior tail ridge begins on anal ring. No anal fin. Snout very short; 3.0–3.8 in head length.
Syngnathus	Lateral trunk ridge ends on anal ring; superior tail ridge begins on anal ring. Anal fin present. No supraopercular ridge,

	lateral snout ridge, or dermal flaps. Snout moderate to long; 1.4–2.7 in head length.
Pseudophallus	Lateral trunk ridge continuous with superior tail ridge. Inferior trunk ridge continuous with inferior tail ridge. No anal fin. Mature females have a large urogenital papilla with spines. Snout moderate; 2.6 in head length.
Bryx	Lateral trunk ridge ends on anal ring; superior tail ridge begins on anal ring. No anal fin. Has supraopercular ridge, lateral snout ridge, or dermal flaps. Snout short to moderate; 2.4–3.7 in head length.
Cosmocampus	Lateral trunk ridge ends on anal ring; superior tail ridge begins on anal ring. Anal fin present. Has supraopercular ridge, lateral snout ridge, or dermal flaps. Snout length variable; 1.2–3.8 in head length.

130 Lined Seahorse
Hippocampus erectus

Identification: A fairly large seahorse with a moderately long snout. Brown, orange, or yellow, with pale blotches and *dark lengthwise lines*. Sometimes fleshy tabs on much of body. 18–21 dorsal fin rays. TL to 6″ (15 cm).

Habitat: Coastal waters; often around man-made structures and other objects it can attach itself to.

Range: Bermuda, Nova Scotia to Florida, Bahamas, Gulf of Mexico, Caribbean, including Antilles, and South American coast to Argentina.

Notes: Because of its bizarre appearance, the Lined Seahorse is a favorite of divers. It is a poor swimmer, seeming to glide along propelled by its pectoral and dorsal fins. It feeds by sucking in small organisms, using its long face as a pipette.

Similar Species: Longsnout Seahorse *(H. reidi)* has longer snout, and spots rather than lines; it ranges from North Carolina to Bahamas.

Dwarf Seahorse *(H. zosterae)* is smaller, has
16–19 dorsal fin rays, and no conspicuous
color pattern; it occurs in Bermuda,
Florida, Bahamas, and Gulf of Mexico.

126 Dusky Pipefish
Syngnathus floridae

Identification: Snout long and slender (1.6–2.1 in head
length). *Preorbital bone appears as broad
plate in front of eye.* Brown or white with
various markings. Often with narrow
longitudinal dark lines on tail. 26–35
dorsal rays. 16–19 trunk rings. 29–39
tail rings. SL to 9¾" (25 cm).

Habitat: Most common on sea-grass beds, usually
to depths of 15' (4.5 m) or less,
occasionally to 73' (22 m).

Range: Bermuda, Chesapeake Bay to South
Carolina, Florida, Bahamas, n Gulf of
Mexico to Texas, parts of coast of Central
America from Mexico to Panama.

Notes: This is one of the most common species
of pipefish along mainland coasts.
Northern populations move offshore
during the colder months.

Similar Species: No other pipefish of this genus has
broad, distinctive preorbital bone. Other
species of *Syngnathus* with long snouts:
Bull Pipefish *(S. springeri)* has 22–24
trunk rings and narrow preorbital bone;
it occurs from North Carolina to Florida
Keys, n Bahamas, and e Gulf of Mexico.
Chain Pipefish *(S. louisianae)* has 20
trunk rings; it occurs from New Jersey
to Florida Keys and around Gulf of
Mexico. Northern Pipefish *(S. fuscus)* has
19 trunk rings; it occurs from Gulf of
St. Lawrence to se Florida.

127 Gulf Pipefish
Syngnathus scovelli

Identification: A slender pipefish with *a moderately long
snout (1.9–2.7 in head length).* 25–37
dorsal fin rays. 16 trunk rings. 28–34
tail rings. SL to 7⅛" (18 cm).

Habitat: In vegetation, usually in water less than
20' (6 m) deep; sometimes in fresh water.

Range: Florida, Gulf of Mexico, Caribbean
coasts of Central and South America.

Notes: The Gulf Pipefish is very common in
Florida and the eastern Gulf of Mexico.

Similar Species: *S. makaxi* usually has 14 trunk rings and
22–27 dorsal rays; it is known only from
Quintana Roo, Mexico. Texas Pipefish
(*S. affinis*) usually has 18 trunk rings,
35–41 dorsal rays; it is known from
Louisiana to Texas in n Gulf of Mexico.

Gulf Pipefish range

S. dawsoni has 16–18 trunk rings and
25–34 dorsal rays; it is known from
Antilles, from Puerto Rico to Martinique.

---

128 **Sargassum Pipefish**
Synganthus pelagicus

Identification: A slender pipefish with a long snout
(1.4–1.7 in head length). Brown overall,
with blotches or 11–13 darker brown
bars. *28–31 dorsal fin rays. 15–18 trunk
rings.* 30–34 tail rings. SL to 7⅛" (18 cm).

Habitat: Usually associated with floating
sargassum weed.

Range: Nova Scotia to Florida, Gulf of Mexico,
Antilles, and w Caribbean from Yucatán
to Colombia.

Notes: Shaking clumps of floating sargassum
weed is almost sure to yield a few
individuals of this species. Its distribution
is very similar to that of floating
sargassum weed in the Atlantic, Gulf
of Mexico, and Caribbean.

Similar Species: Similar Caribbean Pipefish (*S. caribbaeus*)
is plain brown, lacking blotches or bars;
it occurs around Caribbean, Antilles,
and coasts of Central and South America
to Trinidad.

---

129 **Whitenose Pipefish**
Cosmocampus albirostris

Identification: A rather stout pipefish, almost square in
cross section. Dark brown, sometimes
with irregular darker bars. *Snout white*

and short (2.2–2.8 in head length). 21–24 dorsal fin rays. 24–31 tail rings. SL to 8¼" (21 cm).

Habitat: Coastal waters from shoreline to depths of 165' (50 m).

Range: Bermuda, South Carolina to Florida, Bahamas, parts of Gulf of Mexico and Caribbean.

Notes: The Whitenose Pipefish avoids areas of low salinity. It is most abundant along the mainland coast from South Carolina to Alabama, and there have been scattered sightings in the western Gulf of Mexico and parts of the Caribbean.

Similar Species: Deepwater Pipefish *(C. profundus)* has long snout (1.7 in head length), and 38 or 39 tail rings; it lives in deep water off Florida, Yucatán, and Virgin Islands. Dwarf Pipefish *(C. hildebrandi)* has short snout (2.6–3.2 in head length), 19–22 dorsal fin rays, and 33 tail rings; it occurs off North Carolina and w Florida from Pensacola to Key West. Crested Pipefish *(C. brachycephalus)* has very short snout (2.9–3.8 in head length), 22 dorsal fin rays, and 25 or 26 tail rings; it occurs from s Florida, Bahamas, and around Caribbean. Shortfin Pipefish *(C. elucens)* has long snout (1.2–2.5 in head length), 30–33 tail rings, and lacks well-developed ridges on head; it occurs in Bermuda, Bahamas, e Gulf of Mexico, Caribbean, including Antilles, South American coast to n Brazil, and s Brazil.

Other species of pipefishes

Pipehorse   *(Acentronura dendritica)* Head slightly angled from axis of body. Snout short. Generally greenish brown, with indistinct transverse darker bars. Clusters of small fleshy tabs on body. Bermuda, North Carolina to Florida, Bahamas, Brazil.

Finless Pipefish   *(Penetopteryx nanus)* Dark brown. Snout very short. Dorsal and pectoral fins only in very young. Bahamas, Isla de Providencia in w Caribbean.

Opossum Pipefish	(*Microphis brachyurus*) Snout long. Tan to dark brown, plain or mottled, sometimes with dark stripe above lateral trunk ridge. Ridges prominent; spine at end of ridge on each ring. Brood pouch entirely on trunk. 9 caudal fin rays. Atlantic coast of Florida, Bahamas, n and s Gulf of Mexico, Antilles, Central and South American coasts to Brazil. Occasionally strays as far north as New Jersey.
Banded Pipefish	(*Micrognathus crinitus*) Prominent bony ridges on head. Snout very short. 17–18 trunk rings. Pale brown to almost black; may have 10 or more diffuse bands on side and back. Some individuals have striking bands of yellow and purplish brown (sometimes considered a separate species called Harlequin Pipefish, *M. ensenadae*). Bermuda, Florida Keys, Bahamas, Antilles, coasts from Yucatán Peninsula to Venezuela; also s Brazil.
Micrognathus erugatus	20 trunk rings. Occurs only in Brazil.
Fringed Pipefish	(*Anarchopterus criniger*) Snout short and conical; dorsal profile of head almost straight. Light tan to brown with variable markings. 6–9 pectoral fin rays. 14–16 trunk rings. 35–39 tail rings. North Carolina, s Florida, Bahamas, e Gulf of Mexico, Yucatán; absent west of Mississippi Delta and in Caribbean.
Insular Pipefish	(*Anarchopterus tectus*) 10–12 pectoral fin rays. 17–18 trunk rings. 31–35 tail rings. Florida Keys, Bahamas, Belize, Honduras, Panama, Venezuela.
Pugnose Pipefish	(*Bryx dunckeri*) SL to 4″ (10 cm). Snout short (2.8–3.7 in head length). 11 pectoral fin rays. Bermuda, Cape Hatteras, s Florida, Bahamas, w and s Caribbean, Lesser Antilles, Brazil.
Ocellated Pipefish	(*Bryx randalli*) Longer· snout than Pugnose Pipefish (2.4–2.8 in head length). Usually 13 pectoral fin rays. Belize, Isla de Providencia, Lesser Antilles.

ORDER SYNBRANCHIFORMES

This is a small order of eel-shaped fishes, most of which live in fresh water. Their relationships are not clear, but at present the order encompasses three families, 12 genera, and 87 species. In addition to the Synbranchidae, the order includes the spiny eels of Africa and Asia as well as the Chaudhuriidae, a family of about five species from India and east Asia to Borneo.

SWAMP EELS
Family Synbranchidae

Although swamp eels resemble the true eels (order Anguilliformes)—in that they lack pectoral and pelvic fins and have small eyes positioned well forward on the head—the two groups are not related. Swamp Eels are related to the perch-like fishes (order Perciformes), with which they share a number of internal characteristics. Externally, swamp eels can be recognized by their gill slits, which are fused into a single small opening on the mid-ventral line of the throat area. The family contains four genera and 15 species, most of which live in fresh water in the tropics.

Fatlips Swamp Eel

Fatlips Swamp Eel
Ophisternon aenigmaticum

Identification: A large species with an elongate, eel-like body. Uniformly pinkish gray, with speckles or small inconspicuous blotches; sometimes with 1 or 2 dusky streaks behind eye. Eye small and far forward, visible but covered by thick protective skin. *Gill opening far forward on underside of head. No paired fins.* Dorsal and anal fins reduced to ray-less folds joined to much-reduced tail fin. Anus in rear part of body. TL to 28″ (70 cm).

Habitat: Fresh water and mangrove swamps along coasts.

Range: Atlantic drainages of Mexico, Belize, Honduras, and Guatemala; Cuba; and Trinidad.

Notes: A specimen of swamp eel was taken in a soil sample in peat around mangrove roots at Twin Cays off Belize.

Similar Species: Marbled Swamp Eel *(Synbranchus marmoratus)* has more distinct blotches; it occurs in fresh water of both Atlantic and Pacific drainages of Central America and south in Atlantic drainages of South America to Argentina.

ORDER DACTYLOPTERIFORMES

Flying Gurnards are distinctive, spectacular fishes, but their relationships are not clear. Some ichthyologists consider them to be related to the seahorses and pipefishes; others believe that they are related to the scorpionfishes because, like them, they are "mail-cheeked" fishes, so called because one of the bones surrounding the eye has an extension that crosses the cheek and connects with the preopercle. Because there is no clear evidence supporting their relationship to other mail-cheeked fishes, they are placed in a separate order containing only one family.

FLYING GURNARDS
Family Dactylopteridae

Flying Gurnards are easily recognized by their huge pectoral fins and heavily armored heads. Moderate-size fishes, their bodies are covered with heavy scales, most of which have longitudinal keels on their outer surface. They have two dorsal fins and thoracic pelvic fins. Contrary to their name, they do not fly, although the huge pectoral fins look like wings. Juveniles are pelagic, drifting in the open sea; adults are bottom dwellers.

The family contains two genera and about seven species; one species lives in our area.

133, 134   **Flying Gurnard**
Dactylopterus volitans

Identification: Terete, elongate, tapering body. Blunt face; mouth low and horizontal. *Pectoral fin very large and fan-like, with front 6 rays separated as small lobe.* Dark gray, often with irregular dark blotches, lighter below. Blue spots and lines on pectoral fin membranes. Head enclosed in bony casque, with very long preopercular spines, and another long spine on each side extending backward from top of skull to below middle of first dorsal fin. First 2 dorsal spines separate; spiny dorsal fin clearly separate from soft dorsal rays. Pelvic fins thoracic, each with 1 spine and 4 soft rays. Scales with bony keels that together form very rough longitudinal ridges along body. 2 sharp keels on each side of caudal peduncle near base of tail. TL to about 17¾" (45 cm).

Habitat: Coral reefs and other shallow-water habitats.

Range: Bermuda and coastal waters from Massachusetts to Argentina. Bahamas, Gulf of Mexico, and Caribbean, including Antilles.

Notes: With its enlarged pectoral fins, the Flying Gurnard sometimes resembles a ray when seen underwater. Some searobins also have enlarged pectoral fins, but they do not have keeled scales. Flyingfishes have enlarged pectoral fins but have abdominal pelvic fins.

ORDER SCORPAENIFORMES

This is a large and diverse group of bottom-dwelling fishes that are united by the presence of a bony stay, or extension, of the third circumorbital bone, which crosses the cheek and attaches to the preopercle. The order contains 24 families, 264 genera, and 1,265 species, currently placed in six suborders. Two families are covered here; the rest live outside our area or in deep water.

SCORPIONFISHES
Family Scorpaenidae

Scorpionfishes are robust, heavy-bodied fishes. They have large heads with numerous spines; some species have a deep pit, called the *occipital pit,* on top of the head behind the eyes; some also have a deep pit or ridge

below the eyes. A strut of bone
extends across each cheek from
below the eye to the preopercle,
and the bones around the eyes
may bear spines and ridges.
Both the preopercle and the operculum have strong spines.
Most species have fleshy tabs on
the head and body, and sometimes there is a complex fleshy
tentacle over the eye.

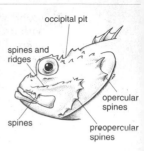

occipital pit

spines and
ridges

opercular
spines

spines

preopercular
spines

The dorsal fin is single with a deep notch between the
spiny and soft-rayed parts. The pectoral fins are large and
fan-like; the pelvic fins are thoracic, with one spine and usually five soft rays. The anal fin usually has three spines and
five soft rays. The dorsal, pelvic, and anal spines are stout and
sharp; some have venom cells in the overlying skin that can
produce a painful wound. The tail is round or square. Most
scorpionfishes are cryptically colored: Superficially they are
red to brownish gray to black, but a closer look reveals complex patterns of red, black, brown, and white spots, lines,
and swirls. A few have distinct spots and bars. Scorpionfishes
are ambush feeders, lying motionless on the bottom until
prey ventures near, then snapping it up with a quick pounce.

The family includes 56 genera and 388 species. In the
western Atlantic there are about 30 species representing 11
genera. Two genera occur in shallow water in our region:
Scorpaena, with 12 species, and *Scorpaenodes,* with two species.

Genera of family Scorpaenidae

Scorpaena	12 dorsal fin spines. Cycloid scales on body.
Scorpaenodes	13 dorsal fin spines. Ctenoid scales on body.

135 Barbfish
Scorpaena brasiliensis

Identification: A heavy-bodied, tapering scorpionfish
with a large head. Camouflaged
brownish, mottled with red, orange, and
blue; brown spots on pale background in
pectoral axil and along body to anal fin.
Usually 2 or 3 large brown spots
behind head. Preorbital bone with 2 spines
directed downward over maxilla.

Occipital pit well developed. Suborbital ridge has 3 spinous points; first 2 may be blunt. *50–60 scales in lateral line.* 18–20 pectoral rays; 9 dorsal soft rays. SL to 6⅜″ (16 cm).

Habitat: Shore to depths of 300′ (90 m) over various types of bottoms.

Range: Virginia to Florida, Gulf of Mexico, Caribbean, and south to s Brazil.

Notes: The Barbfish is a common species along the Atlantic coast and in the Gulf of Mexico. Its toxic spines can produce a painful wound. Most other species of the genus *Scorpaena* have fewer than 50 scales in the lateral line.

Similar species

Other Scorpaena *species with 2 spines on preorbital bone and well-developed occipital pit.*

Longfin Scorpionfish	*(S. agassizi)* Large eye. Elongate pectoral fin reaches to rear of anal fin. Atlantic and Gulf coasts south to Guianas.
Goosehead Scorpionfish	*(S. bergi)* Black spot on spiny dorsal fin. 1–3 points on suborbital ridge. 16–17 pectoral fin rays. Florida, Panama, Colombia, Venezuela.
Smoothcheek Scorpionfish	*(S. isthmensis)* Black spot on spiny dorsal fin. No points on suborbital ridge. 18–19 pectoral fin rays. South American coast from Panama to Rio de Janeiro.
Plumed Scorpionfish	*(S. grandicornis)* Long supraorbital tentacle (twice as long as diameter of eye). White flecks on pectoral axil. Bermuda, Florida to s Brazil.
Dwarf Scorpionfish	*(S. elachys)* Small, pale. 1 spine on suborbital ridge. 16–17 pectoral rays. Deep water off Florida, Antilles, Panama.
Shortfin Scorpionfish	*(S. brachyptera)* Short pectoral fin (does not reach to base of first anal spine). 19–20 pectoral rays. 8 soft dorsal rays. Florida, Panama, Colombia, Venezuela.
Coral Scorpionfish	*(S. albifimbria)* Nasal spines. 18–19 pectoral rays; plain color in pectoral axil. Usually 9 anal soft rays. Florida, Bahamas, Antilles, Curaçao, Isla San Andrés.

136 Mushroom Scorpionfish
Scorpaena inermis

Identification: A small, robust scorpionfish *without an occipital pit.* Reddish brown with dark mottlings; 2 indistinct bands across tail. Preorbital bone has 2 spines directed downward over maxilla. *Eye has mushroom-shaped tabs on cornea* at boundary between upper opaque area and lower, transparent part of cornea. Usually 8 dorsal soft rays. SL to 4⅜" (11 cm).

Habitat: Shore to depths of 240′ (73 m). Clear water over sand and turtle grass; less common around coral reefs.

Range: Florida, Bahamas, Antilles, Yucatán, Isla San Andrés, and Netherlands Antilles.

Notes: Although the Mushroom Scorpionfish is quite common in the Bahamas, little is known of its life history.

Similar Species: Smoothhead Scorpionfish *(S. calcarata),* which also lacks occipital pit, has no corneal tabs and usually 9 dorsal soft rays. It occurs from Carolinas around Gulf of Mexico, in w and s Caribbean, and along South American coast to Brazil. Not in Bermuda or Bahamas.

137, 138 Spotted Scorpionfish
Scorpaena plumieri

Identification: A large, robust scorpionfish with a broad head and well-developed occipital pit. Brownish to dark gray with various darker spots and blotches on paler background; caudal peduncle paler than anterior part of body. *Pectoral axil has conspicuous white spots on black background. Preorbital bone has 3 or 4 spines extending downward over maxilla.* SL to 13¾" (35 cm).

Habitat: Shoreline to depths of 180′ (55 m). Around reefs and over rock, grass, and sand.

Range: Bermuda, New York to Florida, Bahamas, Gulf of Mexico, Caribbean, including Antilles, south to Brazil.

Notes: When disturbed, the Spotted Scorpionfish confuses predators by displaying the white spots in the pectoral axil as it moves slowly away, then suddenly turns, stops, and dives to the bottom, often stirring up a cloud of silt. As it does so, it turns the pectoral fin to cover the markings. By the time the silt clears, the fish is so well camouflaged that it has virtually disappeared.

Similar Species: No other species in our area has large white spots on black background on pectoral axil. Hunchback Scorpionfish *(S. dispar),* which ranges from South Carolina to Florida, Gulf of Mexico, Yucatán, and Venezuela to Brazil, also has 3 or 4 spines on preorbital bone over maxilla but lacks markings in pectoral axil.

---

139 Reef Scorpionfish
Scorpaenodes caribbaeus

Identification: A small, robust, rather colorful scorpionfish without an occipital pit. Reddish brown, with various spots and blotches. Often has *conspicuous dark spot on rear dorsal fin spines,* and pale bar across caudal peduncle. 18–20 pectoral fin rays. TL to about 4″ (10 cm).

Habitat: Shoreline to depths of 60′ (18 m) over various kinds of bottom, from limestone to turtle grass to live coral.

Range: Florida, Bahamas, s Gulf of Mexico, Antilles, w and s Caribbean.

Notes: This pretty scorpionfish is quite common but is small and hard to see. It is said to be the most common species in the Bahamas and sometimes occurs in tide pools.

Similar Species: Deepreef Scorpionfish *(S. tredecimspinosus)* has 16 or 17 pectoral fin rays, and single row of spiny points on suborbital area.

SEAROBINS
Family Triglidae

Searobins are moderate-size, slender, tapered, terete fishes. The bones of the head are at the surface, with pits and grooves that are covered only by a thin skin. The snout is broad and flat, the mouth wide and terminal or subterminal; there are no barbels. The pectoral fins are large and wing-like, with the lower three rays free (not connected by membrane) and finger-like. Searobins use these free rays to walk along the bottom and probe the sediment for food. They are known to produce sound using special muscles that cause the swim bladder to vibrate. The pelvic fins are thoracic. There are two separate dorsal fins, the first all spines, the second all rays. The anal fin is long, with 10 to 13 widely spaced soft rays. The caudal fin is truncate or slightly emarginate.

This family contains 14 genera and about 100 species. There are two genera with about 18 species in our range. Most are continental species; few are found around coral reefs. The armored searobins, family Peristediidae, are sometimes included in this family. They have bodies encased in large bony plates, two long projecting bony lobes on the snout, and long barbels on the lower jaw. Because they occur in deep water, we do not include them here.

Genera of family Triglidae

Bellator	Dorsal fin has spines, 11 soft rays. No scales on gill membranes. 12 pectoral fin rays.
Prionotus	Dorsal fin has spines, usually 12–13 soft rays. Scales on gill membranes. 13–14 pectoral fin rays.

140 Horned Searobin
Bellator militaris

Identification:

A rather elongate searobin. Snout blunt with horn-like bony projections at each corner. *Males have first 2 dorsal spines extremely long, reaching to tip of tail.* 3 free pectoral fin rays; main pectoral fin rays banded black and white. Front half of abdomen behind pelvic fin scaleless;

chest and rest of body covered with scales. 55–67 scales in lateral line. TL to about 5⅛" (13 cm).

Habitat: Continental shelf waters at depths of 130–360' (40–110 m).

Range: From Cape Lookout, North Carolina, to Gulf of Mexico.

Notes: The Horned Searobin is most commonly observed when taken in trawls; otherwise it is unlikely to be seen.

Similar Species: *B. ribeiroi,* which occurs from Colombia to Brazil, has only first dorsal spine elongate. Streamer Searobin *(B. egretta)* has 95–112 scales in lateral line, and only first dorsal spine thread-like; Shortfin Searobin *(B. brachychir)* has 62–70 scales in lateral line, and lacks elongate dorsal spines; both occur in deeper waters in n Gulf of Mexico.

---

141 **Bandtail Searobin**
Prionotus ophryas

Identification: A moderate-size searobin with a tapering, terete body and a very steep front profile. Body covered with scales. Pale coppery orange with broad black bars. *Caudal fin has 3 dark vertical bars. Long filament on nostril. Fleshy tentacle above eye.* No barbels on chin. Lower 3 pectoral fin rays free; pectoral fin usually unspotted, long, its tip reaching end of anal fin base, its outer margin rounded. TL to 9" (23 cm).

Habitat: Sand bottoms at depths of 60–300' (18–90 m).

Range: Carolinas to Florida, Bahamas, and Gulf of Mexico to Venezuela.

Notes: The Bandtail Searobin is a distinctive and easily identified species. No other searobin has filaments on the nostril and fleshy tentacles above the eye. It is not common in the Bahamas, having been recorded only twice from the Great Bahama Bank and Cay Sal Bank.

Other *Prionotus* species

Spiny Searobin
: (*P. alatus*) Black spot at edge of first dorsal fin. Black bands on pectoral fin. Pectoral fin margin concave (lower rays longest). Small spine at nostril. Atlantic and Gulf coasts from Cape Hatteras to Louisiana.

Mexican Searobin
: (*P. paralatus*) Pectoral fin margin emarginate (upper and lower rays equally long). Black bands on pectoral fin. W Gulf of Mexico from Louisiana to Bay of Campeche.

Bean's Searobin
: (*P. beani*) Distal margin of pectoral fin emarginate. Black blotch between fourth and fifth dorsal spines. Trinidad, Gulf of Mexico to Brazil.

Northern Searobin
: (*P. carolinus*) Dorsal fin has black spot surrounded by transparent or white zone between fourth and sixth spines. Branchiostegal membranes black. Atlantic coast from Bay of Fundy to Palm Beach, Florida, Gulf of Mexico.

Striped Searobin
: (*P. evolans*) Reddish to olive-brown; narrow dark line along lateral line; incomplete narrow stripe below lateral line. Narrow black lines on pectoral fin. Atlantic coast from Bay of Fundy to Palm Beach, Florida.

Bigeye Searobin
: (*P. longispinosus*) Very large eye. Pectoral fin short and black. Black spot with white ring on first dorsal fin. Gulf of Mexico, Cuba, Venezuela.

Barred Searobin
: (*P. martis*) First dorsal fin has 2 black spots: between first and second spines, and fourth and fifth spines. Body plain. Gulf of Mexico, Florida to Texas.

Leopard Searobin
: (*P. scitulus*) First dorsal fin has 2 black spots. Red-brown spots on body. Atlantic and Gulf coasts, North Carolina to Florida, Texas, Venezuela.

Bluewing Searobin
: (*P. punctatus*) Pectoral fin long (reaching fourth anal ray) and dark green with small oval brown spots. Back greenish brown with small red spots. Brown spots on second dorsal and caudal fins. Cuba to

	Argentina, Antilles, Central and South America.
Bluespotted Searobin	*(P. roseus)* Pectoral fin very long (almost reaching last anal ray), usually with 4 rows of bright blue spots on outer surface. 2 dark vertical bars on caudal fin. North Carolina to Florida, Puerto Rico, Gulf of Mexico to Texas and Cabo Catoche, Yucatán, Venezuela.
Blackwing Searobin	*(P. rubio)* Pectoral fin long and dark, with blue leading edge. No dark spots in dorsal fin. North Carolina to Florida, Gulf of Mexico, Cuba.
Shortwing Searobin	*(P. stearnsi)* Pectoral fin short (barely reaches base of first anal ray). Back, pectoral fin, and outer margin of caudal fin black. Georgia to Florida, Gulf of Mexico from Dry Tortugas to Texas, Venezuela, Suriname.
Bighead Searobin	*(P. tribulus)* Head large and broad. Pectoral fin dark, crossed by lighter bands. North Carolina to Florida, Gulf of Mexico.

ORDER PERCIFORMES

The order Perciformes is a very large group of spiny-rayed fishes containing, at the present time, 18 suborders, 148 families, 1,496 genera, and 9,293 species. These fishes are being studied intensively and their classification is changing almost daily.

Perciforms are truly spiny-rayed fishes, with thoracic pelvic fins having one spine and five or fewer rays. There are spines in the dorsal and anal fins as well. The scales are usually ctenoid. The caudal fin is symmetrical. In some groups, however, the fin spines or scales or both have been lost.

SNOOKS
Family Centropomidae

Snooks are moderate-size, elongate, compressed, bass-like fishes, with silvery sides and a black lateral line that extends to the tip of the middle rays of the forked tail. They have a distinctive profile, with the front of the head straight or concave and the lower jaw projecting beyond the snout. The mouth is large, with small, bluntly pointed teeth and no enlarged canine teeth. The preopercle and the lower edge of the preorbital region (lacrimal bone) are serrate. The moderate to large scales are ctenoid. There are two nearly separate dorsal fins, the first with eight spines and the second with one spine and eight to ten rays. The anal fin is short, with three spines and five to eight rays; the second anal spine is the largest. The lateral line branches, and the branches continue to the end of the tail.

Snooks are inshore fishes, living in a variety of habitats including lagoons, estuaries, and the lower reaches of rivers. The family includes three genera and about 22 species, among them the famous Nile Perch, the largest African freshwater fish. Five or six species of one genus occur in our region.

142 Common Snook
Centropomus undecimalis

Identification: A large, slender snook with fine scales. Yellowish or greenish brown above, silvery side and belly, black lateral line. Fins dusky. Second dorsal fin has 1 spine and 10 soft rays. Anal fin has 3 spines and 6 soft rays. Tips of pectoral fin rays do not reach anus. 13–21 gill rakers (including rudiments) on first arch. *67–72 pored scales in lateral line to base of caudal fin.* TL to 4'3" (1.3 m).

Habitat: Coastal marine and brackish waters; enters fresh water.

Range: Southern Florida, Antilles, Central and South American coasts from s Gulf of Mexico to Rio de Janeiro.

Notes: The Common Snook is a valued game fish and an excellent food fish. It feeds on fish and crustaceans and spawns from May through September.

Similar Species: Swordspine Snook *(C. ensiferus),* from s Florida, Antilles, and Caribbean coast to Brazil, has very long and stout second anal spine and 48 or 49 scales in lateral line. Tarpon Snook *(C. pectinatus)* has 59–71 scales in lateral line; it ranges from s Florida, s Gulf of Mexico, Antilles, and Caribbean coast to Brazil, and on Pacific coast from Mexico to Colombia. Mexican Snook *(C. poeyi)* has

9 dorsal soft rays; it ranges from Tampico, Mexico, to Belize. Fat Snook (*C. parallelus*) has tips of pelvic fin rays reaching anus; it ranges from s Florida, s Gulf of Mexico, Antilles, and Central and South American coasts to Brazil.

SEA BASSES
Family Serranidae

The sea basses form a diverse group of spiny-rayed fishes, ranging from small to huge and from short to elongate. In spite of their differences, sea basses are united by the presence of three flat spines on the opercle (except for *Rypticus randalli,* which has only two spines) and certain technical specializations of the caudal fin skeleton. This family is so diverse that many ichthyologists suspect that it contains genera that are not as closely related as they seem.

Sea basses differ from the related snappers and grunts in that the maxilla does not slide under the preorbital region when the mouth is closed (see illustration). The pelvic fins

Sea basses   Snappers   Grunts

are thoracic, each with one spine and five soft rays. Most sea basses have no pelvic axillary process. Most species have one continuous dorsal fin, although the posterior dorsal spines may be somewhat shorter than the anterior dorsal soft rays, forming a notch or step in the fin. In a few species the dorsal fin is so deeply notched that the fin may appear to be two separate fins. Usually the interspinous membranes of the dorsal fin are incised at their tips; that is, the membrane reaches the tip of the spine in front and ends somewhat below the tip of the following spine. Nearly all sea basses have three anal fin spines followed by seven to 14 soft rays. The scales are usually *ctenoid* (rough).

Sea basses are hermaphroditic. In some species the male and female reproductive organs function simultaneously; in other species the fishes are females first, transforming into males later in life; in some species the fishes can function as one sex, then assume the opposite role a few minutes later.

Some live in social groups of one male and several females; if the male is removed, a large female will assume the male role and become a functional male within a few days. The simultaneous hermaphrodites perform courtship rituals as do fishes with separate sexes.

Sea basses are abundant in tropical seas, and many species occur around coral reefs. Some are brightly colored, but others are somber and camouflaged. Several sea basses have distinctive deep-water and shallow-water color phases: The shallow-water forms are olive-brown or gray, and those from deeper water are redder, sometimes intensely red. Apparently this is because the overlying brownish-black melanin pigment is poorly developed in dim light.

The family Serranidae includes the groupers (genera *Epinephelus, Cephalopholis, Mycteroperca,* and *Paranthias*), which are thick-skinned, moderate-size to large species that are important food fishes in tropical and subtropical areas around the world. There are 62 genera and 449 species of sea basses in three subfamilies: Serraninae, Anthininae, and Epinephelinae. Twenty-two genera are represented in our area.

Genera of family Serranidae
Subfamily Serraninae

Lateral line well below dorsal fin base. Bases of dorsal and anal fins not covered with thick skin and scales. Scales large, 39–55 in lateral line.

Bullisichthys	Pug-headed appearance. Anus forward, well ahead of anal fin.
Centropristis	Tail trilobed. Dorsal fin has small flaps at tips of spines.
Diplectrum	Preopercle has lobes of radiating spines.
Hypoplectrus	Compressed, deep-bodied (body depth more than 40 percent of SL); back highly arched. Dorsal fin continuous; no notch. Caudal fin slightly forked.
Schultzea	Body slender, fusiform. Mouth very protrusible. No teeth on jaws.
Serranus	Body elongate (depth less than 40 percent of SL). Preopercle evenly serrate, without lobes. Teeth on jaws. Dorsal fin usually slightly notched.
Serraniculus	6 branchiostegal rays (rather than 7).

Subfamily Anthininae

Lateral line close to base of dorsal fin. Bases of dorsal and anal fins not covered with thick skin and scales.

Plectranthias	Scales large. Tail square. Top of head scaled as far forward as posterior nostril.
Anthias	Top of head and maxilla scaled. Vomer tooth patch crescent shaped.
Hemanthias	Top of head and maxilla unscaled.
Holanthias	Top of head and maxilla scaled. Vomer tooth patch with extension.

Subfamily Epinephelinae

Lateral line well below dorsal fin base. Bases of dorsal and anal fins covered with thick skin and small scales. Scales small, 60–140 in lateral line.

Epinephelus	Body elongate, arched; dorsal profile noticeably more strongly curved than ventral profile (except *E. itajara*). Dorsal fin continuous, with slight notch. 10–11 dorsal spines. 7–9 anal rays.
Mycteroperca	Body elongate; dorsal profile not highly arched. Dorsal fin continuous, with slight notch. 11 dorsal spines. 10–14 anal rays.
Cephalopholis	(Often considered a subgenus of *Epinephelus*.) Dorsal fin continuous, with slight notch. 9 dorsal spines. 7–9 anal rays.
Paranthias	Tail forked. Head short. Dorsal and ventral profiles symmetrical.
Alphestes	(Often considered a subgenus of *Epinephelus*.) Dorsal fin continuous, with very slight notch. 11 dorsal spines. Preopercle has large forward-pointing spine.
Gonioplectrus	Dorsal fin continuous. 8 dorsal fin spines. Preopercle has large spine pointing downward and forward at its angle.
Liopropoma	Dorsal fin divided; spiny and soft sections separated by scaled-over space that usually has tips of 1–2 free spines protruding; 8 dorsal spines.

Bathyanthias	Dorsal fin deeply notched.
Rypticus	2–4 dorsal fin spines. Thick slimy skin on head, body, and fins. Tail rounded.
Jeboehlkia	7 dorsal fin spines; first spine elongate. No lateral line.
Pseudogramma	Tentacle on eye.

143 Sand Perch
Diplectrum formosum

Identification: An elongate, slightly compressed sea bass. *Preopercle has spines radiating from 2 centers.* Yellowish, with alternating blue and yellow stripes; dark brown bars on upper side. Dorsal fin continuous, without notch. In adults upper lobe of caudal fin is longer than lower, and uppermost ray is sometimes filamentous. TL to 12″ (30 cm).

Habitat: Inshore waters and shallow banks, usually over sea-grass bottoms.

Range: Virginia to Florida, Bahamas, Gulf of Mexico, Antilles, n South American coast to Uruguay. Occurrence in w Caribbean doubtful.

Notes: The common and colorful Sand Perch is often taken on hook and line. It spends much time in or near holes under rocks, often excavating these shelters by lying beside the rock and vibrating its body to fan the sand away. Sand Perches are simultaneous hermaphrodites.

Similar Species: Dwarf Sand Perch *(D. bivittatum)* has preopercular spines radiating from single center, triangular black spot on upper part of gill cover, and dark stripes and irregular vertical dark bars on side; it is found in Bermuda, Florida, Gulf of Mexico, and along Central and South American coasts to Brazil, but not in Bahamas or Antilles. Dwarf Sand Perch is distinguished from Bolo *(D. radiale),* which also has single center of radiating spines on preopercle, by presence of 15 (rather than 17) pectoral rays; Bolo occurs along coast of South America from Venezuela to Brazil.

144 Butter Hamlet
Hypoplectrus unicolor

Identification: A short, compressed, deep-bodied sea bass, with dorsal profile highly arched. *Yellowish tan, with large, black, saddle-shaped spot on caudal peduncle and diagonal blue stripes on side of head; sometimes with black blotch on snout in front of eye. No bars on side.* SL to about 4″ (10 cm).

Habitat: Coral reefs.

Range: Florida Keys, Bahamas, Caribbean; absent from Gulf of Mexico.

Notes: Experimental matings of the Butter Hamlet with the Blue Hamlet *(H. gemma)* produced hybrids that were unlike any known color forms. This indicates that they are true species, because if they were merely color morphs of a single species, as they had been classified previously, some of the offspring would be expected to resemble one of the parents or at least some of the known color variants.

Similar Species: Masked Hamlet (not yet officially described or named) has similar pattern but has dark upper and lower tail margins and dark bar below eye; it is known from Isla de Providencia, Cayman Islands, and Jamaica.

145 Shy Hamlet
Hypoplectrus guttavarius

Identification: *Body and fins rich yellow; rear part of body shading to black. Black area surrounded by blue on side of snout. Blue ring around eye, continuing onto cheek.* SL to about 4″ (10 cm).

Habitat: Coral reefs.

Range: Florida Keys, Bahamas, Cuba, Cayman Islands, Jamaica, Hispaniola, Puerto Rico, Virgin Islands, Lesser Antilles, and Panama.

Notes: The Shy Hamlet is a beautiful fish. Like other hamlets it usually travels in pairs and remains close to the bottom. Although hamlets are simultaneous

hermaphrodites, they exhibit courtship and pairing rituals, with one fish behaving as male and the other as female. It is not known, however, if one produces sperm and the other eggs, or if they both produce eggs and sperm.

Similar Species: Golden Hamlet *(H. gummigutta)* is orange or yellow overall, with black snout and some blue spots on side of snout; it occurs from Cuba and Hispaniola, and in w Caribbean from Honduras and Nicaragua. Yellowbelly Hamlet *(H. aberrans)* is generally yellow, with some blue markings on yellow snout; it is known from Bahamas, Greater Antilles, and Panama.

146 Barred Hamlet
Hypoplectrus puella

Identification: *Pale tan, with about 5 darker brown bars; second bar, below dorsal fin, widest. Blue lines on side of head and bordering some of bars on body.* SL to about 4" (10 cm).

Habitat: Coral reefs.

Range: Bermuda, sw Gulf of Mexico, and Caribbean, including Antilles.

Notes: The Barred Hamlet is usually solitary unless spawning. Although not as brightly colored as some of the other hamlets, it is still a pretty fish. The Indigo Hamlet has a similar pattern but is deep blue in color.

147 Indigo Hamlet
Hypoplectrus indigo

Identification: *About 5 deep blue bars of uneven width; second bar, below dorsal fin, much wider than others.* Areas between bars whitish. Snout blue. SL to about 5¾" (14.5 cm).

Habitat: Coral reefs.

Range: Southern Florida, Bahamas, Cuba, Hispaniola, Jamaica, Cayman Islands, Mexico, Islas de la Bahía, and Panama.

Notes: The Indigo Hamlet was previously considered a color variant of the Butter

Hamlet. There is considerable controversy over whether *Hypoplectris* comprises one highly variable species, or separate species differing only in color.

---

148 **Black Hamlet**
Hypoplectrus nigricans

Identification: A typically shaped hamlet. *Black overall.* SL to about 4″ (10 cm).

Habitat: Coral reefs; sometimes enters estuaries.

Range: Southern Florida, Bahamas, Antilles, and Belize to Panama.

Notes: The Black Hamlet, a sedately colored species, is usually solitary. It is often found near the bottom around soft and hard corals. It has occasionally been seen spawning with the Yellowtail Hamlet, but the two seem to be separate species.

Similar Species: Butter Hamlet is tawny brown with large, black, saddle-shaped mark on caudal peduncle, blue streaks on head, and sometimes with black blotch on snout. Yellowtail Hamlet *(H. chlorurus)* is all dark brown or black except for yellow tail; it occurs in Bahamas, Cuba, Puerto Rico, Antilles, offshore islands of Venezuela, Tobago, and Panama. Blue Hamlet *(H. gemma)* is uniformly blue with black dorsal and ventral caudal fin margins; it is known from s Florida and Florida Keys. Tan Hamlet, which has not yet been given a formal scientific name, is golden to chocolate brown with dark dorsal and ventral caudal fin margins; it is known from Florida and Panama.

---

149 **Lantern Bass**
Serranus baldwini

Identification: An elongate, slightly compressed sea bass with a square caudal fin. Brownish olive above, shading to white below. In deep water, reddish above. *Lower side has 4 square black blotches, each with red bar* (*yellowish in deep water*) *below it.* Caudal fin base has 4 black spots in vertical row. SL to 2" (5 cm).

Habitat: Areas with abundant shelter, either vegetation or coral, and shell rubble to depths of 250' (75 m).

Range: Southern Florida, Bahamas, Caribbean, including Antilles, to Suriname.

Notes: The Lantern Bass is a beautiful little fish. The blotches on the sides look as if they were applied with paint that has dripped down below them. This species is solitary but quite common. It is easily seen by divers who look carefully among plants, sponges, and small coral heads in parts of coral reefs with low relief. Juveniles have been collected from inside living queen conchs.

Similar Species: Snow Bass (*S. chionaraia*) has white belly and alternating black and white spots on upper and lower edges of caudal fin; it occurs in Florida and n Caribbean from Honduras to Puerto Rico. Orangeback Bass (*S. annularis*) has 2 square orange spots with black borders behind eye; it is known from Bermuda, s Florida, Bahamas, Virgin Islands, and Guianas to Brazil.

150 Belted Sandfish
Serranus subligarius

Identification: A rather stout, *stubby sea bass with a pointed snout.* Spiny and soft parts of dorsal fin continuous, with step, rather than notch, between them; soft rays longer than spines. Mottled brownish above and on side, with about 7 dark bars; belly white. Large black spot on front part of soft dorsal fin, continuing down onto body as dark bar. Bands of small dark spots on pectoral, dorsal, caudal, and anal fins. Pelvic fin spotted, dark in center. TL to 4" (10 cm).

Habitat: Inshore waters to depths of 60' (18 m). Not a coral-reef species.

Range: North Carolina to Florida, and e Gulf of Mexico from tip of Florida to Texas.

Notes: The Belted Sandfish is common along the west coast of Florida, where spawning pairs are easily observed. Although this species is a simultaneous hermaphrodite, its courtship is similar to that of species with separate sexes, concluding with the pair swimming up off the bottom in a "rush" that ends in actual release of the eggs and sperm.

Similar Species: Twinspot Bass *(S. flaviventris),* from Haiti, Puerto Rico, and Trinidad south to Brazil, is somewhat similar but has 2 spots at base of caudal fin and spots on spiny part of dorsal fin, and lacks bands across pectoral, anal, and caudal fins.

---

151 **Tobaccofish**
Serranus tabacarius

Identification: An elongate, slightly compressed sea bass with a forked tail. Back and side reddish brown; belly white. *Back crossed by yellow spots and saddles, some of which expand on upper side.* Dorsal fin slightly notched; black at outer edge of membranes between first and second spines, and between third and fourth spines. Caudal fin has dark submarginal streaks along top and bottom, joining at fin base to form V-shaped mark. SL to 5⅛" (13 cm).

Habitat: Sandy, rocky, and rubbly bottoms at depths of 15–230′ (4.5–70 m).

Range: Bermuda, s Florida, Bahamas, and Caribbean, including Antilles.

Notes: The Tobaccofish is commonly seen by divers, usually in open areas of reefs, close to sand and rubble bottoms. A solitary species, it sometimes follows goatfishes (family Mullidae) as they probe the sand for invertebrates. The goatfishes feed on organisms that dive into the sand, and the Tobaccofish snaps up any organisms that flee upward.

152 Harlequin Bass
Serranus tigrinus

Identification:

A small, elongate, somewhat compressed sea bass with a slightly forked tail. *Snout long and pointed.* Conspicuously white, with *black stripes and bars forming irregular rectangles on body,* and black spots of various sizes on fins; often has yellow on belly and yellow tips on caudal fin lobes. SL to 3⅛″ (8 cm).

Habitat: Around vegetation, live coral, and rubble to depths of 120′ (36 m).

Range: Bermuda, s Florida, Bahamas, Yucatán Peninsula, and Caribbean, including Antilles.

Notes: Very common and conspicuous in shallow reef areas, the Harlequin Bass is sure to be seen by snorkelers and divers. Its unique pointed snout and distinctive color pattern make it easy to identify.

153 Chalk Bass
Serranus tortugarum

Identification:

An elongate, moderately compressed, small sea bass with a slightly forked tail. Dorsal fin slightly notched. Head orange above, crossed by dusky blue bands. *Back with reddish-brown overtones, lighter below. Dorsal region crossed by series of pale blue bands.* When underwater appears entirely various shades of blue. No markings on fins. SL to 2⅜″ (6 cm).

Habitat: Rocky and rubbly bottoms from depths of 30–1,320′ (9–400 m).

Range: Southern Florida, Bahamas, and Caribbean, including Antilles.

Notes: The Chalk Bass is a common species on the deeper parts of the outer slope above the drop-off. It hovers a foot or so off the bottom, often in small groups of a few individuals. It probably feeds on plankton.

Other *Serranus* species

Vieja	*(S. dewegeri)* Heavy bodied. Yellowish gray with brownish-orange spots on upper body; about 7 reddish bars on lower side; dark spots on dorsal, caudal, and anal fins; large dark brown spot at base of pectoral fin. Third and fourth dorsal spines elongate; dorsal soft rays longer than spines. N coast of South America.
S. incisus	Small. Pale, with 2 longitudinal black stripes that end as separate spots on caudal peduncle. Dorsal fin deeply notched, spiny part with broad white margin, prominent black spot, and smaller, less distinct spot. Jamaica, Puerto Rico, Turks and Caicos Islands, possibly Curaçao.
Tattler	*(S. phoebe)* White bar on side in front of anus; dark bar from front of spiny dorsal fin down and across body just in front of white bar; longitudinal brown stripe behind dark bar; 1–2 dark saddles below soft dorsal fin. Bermuda, South Carolina, Florida, Mexico, Cuba, Haiti, Puerto Rico.
Blackear Bass	*(S. atrobranchus)* Pale tan above with black mark on gill cover. May have dark band on side under spiny part of dorsal fin. N Gulf of Mexico, Caribbean.
Saddle Bass	*(S. notospilus)* Brown above; white below. White bar on side; dark brown or black bar across soft dorsal fin and upper side of body. Florida Keys, e Gulf of Mexico, Suriname.
Crosshatch Bass	*(S. luciopercanus)* Long snout; projecting lower jaw. Dark diagonal band across body from posterior dorsal spines to mid-side. Caudal fin has dark lobes and clear central area. Deep water off Cuba, Grand Cayman, Honduras, Lesser Antilles.
S. maytagi	Uniformly colored, probably red in life, with no spots or bars. Nw Caribbean between Jamaica and Honduras.

154　Coney
Cephalopholis fulvus

Identification:　A small, rather elongate, robust grouper. Caudal fin square, with rather sharp corners. Color varies with habitat from olive-brown in shallow water to red in deeper water. *Small, prominent, electric-blue spots, each surrounded by black ring.* Individuals from deep water have fewer spots often without blue centers. *Always has 2 larger black spots at tip of lower jaw and 2 black spots on top of caudal peduncle.* 9 anal soft rays. TL to 15″ (38 cm).

Habitat:　Coral reefs and outer walls to depths of 500′ (150 m).

Range:　Bermuda, North Carolina to Florida, Bahamas, Gulf of Mexico, Caribbean, including Antilles; also Brazil.

Notes:　The color of the Coney varies from olive-brown to red with the depth of the water it inhabits. There are also a yellow color form and a transient bicolored phase, in which the fish is dark above and white below.

Similar Species:　Graysby has rounded tail and lacks both small blue spots and dark spots on lower jaw and caudal peduncle.

155　Graysby
Cephalopholis cruentatus

Identification:　A small, rather elongate, robust grouper. Caudal fin rounded. Head, body, and fins gray with small red spots; side of head reddish, with gray reticulated pattern separating background color into red spots. Usually has *4 contrasting spots, white or black, along body* below dorsal fin base. 8 anal soft rays. 16 pectoral fin rays. TL to 9″ (23 cm).

Habitat:　Coral reefs and other sheltered areas to depths of 560′ (170 m).

Range:　Bermuda, Florida, Bahamas, Gulf of Mexico (uncommon in nw Gulf), and around Caribbean, including Antilles.

Notes:　The Graysby is a common grouper that feeds on fishes, crustaceans, and mollusks.

A sequential hermaphrodite, it starts life as a female and transforms into a male.

Similar Species: Coney has square tail, small electric-blue spots on head and body, 2 black spots on lower jaw, and 2 black spots on caudal peduncle.

156 Mutton Hamlet
Alphestes afer

Identification: A small, deep-bodied, rather compressed grouper. *Prominent forward-pointing spine on lower edge of preopercle. Caudal fin rounded.* Brownish or orange, with orange spots and darker brown spots or mottling that tend to form vertical lines. 18 or 19 dorsal rays. 9 anal soft rays. SL to 10″ (25 cm).

Habitat: Coral reefs and sea-grass beds near hard-bottom outcrops.

Range: Bermuda, s Florida, Bahamas, Antilles, s Caribbean, and Brazil. Not reported from Gulf of Mexico north of Key West.

Notes: The Mutton Hamlet is a small colorful grouper. Like other groupers, it is a sequential hermaphrodite, starting out as a female and turning into a male.

Similar Species: Spanish Flag *(Gonioplectrus hispanus),* the only other sea bass in our area with prominent spine on lower edge of preopercle, has 3 spines on opercle (middle one knife-like) and only 8 dorsal fin spines, and is mostly yellow, with about 5 pinkish-red lines from gill opening to soft dorsal fin or tail and bright red spot at front of anal fin.

157 Marbled Grouper
Epinephelus inermis

Identification: A large, deep-bodied, *compressed grouper with a large pectoral fin.* Dark gray to nearly black overall, with whitish blotches and spots. Paler individuals with small dark spots. Juveniles black with prominent white spots. *Scales smooth,* except just behind pectoral fin

base. 11 dorsal fin spines; 18–20 soft
rays. 9 anal soft rays. 18 or 19 pectoral
rays. TL to 32" (80 cm).

Habitat: Usually near ledges and other sheltered
areas at depths from 70–700' (21–213 m).

Range: North Carolina to Florida, Bahamas,
Gulf of Mexico, Caribbean, including
Antilles, and s Brazil.

Notes: Although the Marbled Grouper is a
rather uncommon species, it is taken
consistently in small numbers by
commercial and sport fishers.

Similar Species: No other grouper in our area has smooth
scales, or same compressed shape and
color pattern. Speckled Hind *(E.
drummondhayi),* known from Bermuda,
North Carolina to Florida, and n and e
Gulf of Mexico, is dark with white flecks
and has rough scales.

158 Rock Hind
Epinephelus adscensionis

Identification: A moderate-size, robust, somewhat
compressed grouper. *Tan with red spots on
head, body, and fins, spots becoming larger
ventrally. Black saddle on caudal peduncle;
2 or 3 more black saddles along dorsal fin
base.* Dorsal and anal fins lack conspicuous
black margins. 11 dorsal fin spines; 16
or 17 soft rays. 8 anal soft rays. TL to
24" (60 cm).

Habitat: Coral reefs and other sheltered areas to
depths of 250' (76 m).

Range: Bermuda, Atlantic coast (strays to
Massachusetts) to Florida, Bahamas,
Gulf of Mexico, Antilles, and coasts of
Central and South America to Brazil.
Also in e Atlantic.

Notes: The Rock Hind is a common species
that is frequently seen by divers and
snorkelers. During daylight hours it is
usually seen close to sheltered areas,
such as bases of corals or near ledges.

Similar Species: Red Hind is similar but has dark
margins on dorsal, anal, and caudal fins,
and dark red spots of uniform size, and
lacks dark saddles.

159 Red Hind
Epinephelus guttatus

Identification: A moderate-size, robust, somewhat compressed grouper. Tan overall, with numerous *dark red spots of uniform size* on head and body. *Wide black margins on dorsal, anal, and caudal fins.* Yellow fleshy tabs behind dorsal fin spines. 11 dorsal fin spines; 15 or 16 soft rays. 8 anal soft rays. *No saddle-shaped blotch on caudal peduncle or along base of dorsal fin.* TL to about 24″ (60 cm), usually smaller.

Habitat: Coral reefs and other hard bottoms to depths of 330′ (100 m).

Range: Bermuda, North Carolina to Florida, Bahamas, Gulf of Mexico, Antilles, and Central and South American coasts to Venezuela.

Notes: The most common grouper in most of the West Indies, the Red Hind is an excellent food fish. Like other groupers, it is a sequential hermaphrodite, female first, transforming to male. During most of the year it is solitary.

Similar Species: Rock Hind has dark red spots that are larger ventrally and dark saddles across back, and lacks dark margins on fins.

160 Jewfish
Epinephelus itajara

Identification: A very large, robust, almost cylindrical grouper. Caudal fin rounded. Large individuals gray, greenish, or brownish yellow, with small black spots. Small individuals have relatively larger dark spots and 4 or 5 irregular, oblique, dark bars along side. Irregular spots and lines on side of head. 11 dorsal fin spines; 15 or 16 soft rays. 8 anal soft rays. In fish longer than 11′ (3.5 m) *dorsal fin spines shorter than soft rays,* and interorbital width much greater than eye diameter. TL to more than 8′ (2.4 m).

Habitat: Shallow coastal waters. Young enter estuaries and even canals; large adults sometimes taken close to shore around mangroves. Adults often found around wrecks and other sheltered areas in depths of 165' (50 m) or more.

Range: Both coasts of Florida, Bahamas, Gulf of Mexico, Antilles, and Central and South American coasts from Yucatán to Brazil. Also e Atlantic and e Pacific.

Notes: This large, rather slow-moving fish is often found in shallow water around mangroves, making it easy prey for spearfishers. It is an excellent food fish, but is now protected in U.S. waters. Its diet includes large crustaceans, such as spiny lobsters, and a variety of fishes. This species is said to reach weights of more than 700 pounds (315 kg); the sportfishing world record is 680 pounds (308 kg). The origin of the name Jewfish, which dates to the 1600s, is uncertain.

Similar Species: Only one other grouper in our area—Warsaw Grouper (*E. nigritus*)—reaches so large a size (TL to 7'6"/2.3 m; weight to 400 pounds/180 kg); it has a more compressed body, 10 dorsal fin spines, with second spine much longer than others, and is dark reddish brown to almost black (paler below). It occurs along Atlantic coast south to Florida, Gulf of Mexico west to Texas, Cuba, Haiti, Trinidad, and s Brazil.

161 **Red Grouper**
Epinephelus morio

Identification: A moderate-size, robust, somewhat compressed grouper. Reddish brown overall, slightly lighter below, with some very small black spots on side of head, and often with pale saddles on back below dorsal fin and irregular pale blotches on side of body. Outer edges of dorsal, caudal, and anal fins dusky with narrow white margins. Dorsal fin has 11 spines and 16 or 17 rays, second spine longest; *interspinous membranes not incised.* Caudal fin lunate, with sharp angles. 9 anal soft rays. TL to at least 3' (90 cm).

Habitat: Generally hard bottoms from near shore to depths of at least 360' (110 m). In e Gulf of Mexico, lives on flat limestone with pitted surfaces.

Range: Bermuda, North Carolina to Florida, Bahamas, Gulf of Mexico, Antilles, and Caribbean south to Brazil.

Notes: The Red Grouper is an important commercial food fish. It is a generalized carnivore; young feed mostly on shrimp, adults on fish, crustaceans, octopus, and similar items. Other groupers have the interspinous membranes incised.

---

162 Misty Grouper
Epinephelus mystacinus

Identification: A moderate-size, robust, somewhat compressed grouper. Rich chocolate brown with 8 or 9 *regular vertical darker brown bars on side,* last bar on caudal peduncle broader and somewhat darker, nearly black. 3 dark stripes radiate from eye across cheek to gill cover. Juveniles have very distinct bars on body, about equal in width to pale brown interspaces. Larger fish have pale blotches that break up bars. 11 dorsal fin spines; 13–15 soft rays. 9 anal soft rays. TL to 3'3" (1 m).

Habitat: Hard and soft bottoms at depths of 480–1,300' (145–400 m).

Range: Bermuda, South Carolina to Florida, n Gulf of Mexico to Yucatán, Antilles to Trinidad. Also Galápagos.

Notes: A deep-water species sometimes taken by anglers, the Misty Grouper is the only grouper in our area with a pattern of regular dark bars. It is carnivorous, feeding mainly on crustaceans and fishes.

---

163 Snowy Grouper
Epinephelus niveatus

Identification: A moderate-size, robust, somewhat compressed grouper. Adults uniformly reddish brown with *dark margin on spiny dorsal fin and dark saddle on caudal*

peduncle that extends below lateral line.
Juveniles have yellow pectoral and
caudal fins, and white spots on side of
body in regular pattern of 11 columns
and 5 or 6 rows. 11 dorsal fin spines. 9
anal soft rays. TL to 4' (1.2 m).

Habitat: Rocky bottoms at depths of 100–1,730'
(30–525 m); juveniles often found
inshore.

Range: Bermuda, Massachusetts to Florida,
Cuba, Gulf of Mexico, and Central and
South American coasts to Suriname.
Also s Brazil.

Notes: The Snowy Grouper feeds on fishes,
crustaceans, and mollusks. Although it
lives in deeper water, it is quite abundant
and a valuable commercial food fish.
Juveniles, apparently carried northward
on currents associated with the Gulf
Stream, are frequently taken along the
coast of Long Island, New York.

Similar Species: Adult Yellowedge Groupers *(E.
flavolimbatus)* have yellow margin on
dorsal fin and narrow blue line from eye
to corner of preopercle; juveniles have
blotch on top of caudal peduncle that
does not reach to lateral line. It occurs
from North Carolina to Florida, Gulf of
Mexico, Antilles, and coasts of Central
and South America to Brazil.

164 Nassau Grouper
Epinephelus striatus

Identification: A moderate-size, robust, somewhat
compressed grouper. Pale olive-tan to
reddish overall, with dark *tuning-
fork–shaped mark on front of head, several
small dark dots around eye, and dark bar
from tip of snout through eye to nape.* 5 dark
vertical bars on side of body, third and
fourth bars often joined into H-shaped
mark. Distinct *square saddle on caudal
peduncle.* Can quickly change color from
white to banded to very dark. 11 dorsal
fin spines; 13–15 soft rays. 8 anal soft
rays. TL to 3'3" (1 m).

Habitat:	Coral reefs and other hard bottoms to depths of 300′ (90 m).
Range:	Bermuda, Florida, Bahamas, s Gulf of Mexico from Dry Tortugas to Yucatán, Antilles, and Caribbean coast to Suriname. Also Brazil.
Notes:	The Nassau Grouper is a common and important food species that has recently become rare throughout much of its range. Although it is a transforming hermaphrodite, individuals pair during spawning. It forms large spawning aggregations of several thousand individuals. Its color pattern is distinctive.

Similar Species:	Misty Grouper also has vertical bars on body, but bars are more numerous and more regular.

---

165 Creole-fish
Paranthias furcifer

Identification:	A small, fusiform, moderately compressed grouper. *Head short (less than 35 percent of SL).* Dorsal fin continuous, scarcely notched. Grayish red to bright red above, paler below. Row of 3 or 4 white or black spots along base of dorsal fin, and red spot at upper base of pectoral fin. 9 dorsal fin spines; 18 or 19 soft rays. 9 or 10 anal soft rays. 69–77 scales in lateral line. SL to 12″ (30 cm).

Habitat:	Coral reefs and rocky ledges at depths of 20–210′ (6–64 m).
Range:	Bermuda, South Carolina to Florida, Gulf of Mexico, Antilles, and Caribbean coast from Costa Rica to Brazil. Also e Atlantic.
Notes:	This mid-water grouper occurs in small aggregations and is sometimes taken on hook and line. It has well-developed gill rakers and feeds above the bottom on plankton and occasionally small fishes.
Similar Species:	Yellowtail Snapper (family Lutjanidae) is similar in general shape but has larger scales and is blue and yellow.

166   Black Grouper
Mycteroperca bonaci

Identification: A robust, rather elongate grouper. Grayish to brown above, slightly lighter below. Head and lower body have hexagonal brassy spots; *side of body has rectangular dark gray blotches. Outer third of second dorsal, anal, and caudal fins black;* outer margin of pectoral fin orange. *Edge of preopercle smooth, without pronounced lobe at angle.* Caudal margin even, without exserted rays. 17–24 total gill rakers. TL to at least 4′3″ (1.3 m).

Habitat: Coral reefs and other hard bottoms at depths of 33–100′ (10–30 m).

Range: Bermuda, Florida, Bahamas, e and s Gulf of Mexico, Antilles, and Caribbean coast. Also Brazil.

Notes: The Black Grouper is an important commercial species that feeds mostly on fishes.

Similar Species: Comb Grouper *(M. acutirostris),* known from Bermuda, w Gulf of Mexico, Cuba, Jamaica, Virgin Islands, and Panama to Venezuela and s Brazil, has 48–55 total gill rakers. Gag *(M. microlepis)* is gray with darker gray vermiculations that tend to form ovals, and has even caudal margin, distinct expanded lobe at angle of preopercle with distinct notch above it, and 24 or 25 gill rakers; it is found in Bermuda, North Carolina to Florida, Gulf of Mexico to Yucatán Peninsula; also s Brazil. Venezuelan Grouper *(M. cidi),* from Jamaica and coast of Venezuela, is very similar to Gag but has more (27–36) total gill rakers on first arch.

167   Yellowfin Grouper
Mycteroperca venenosa

Identification: A robust, rather elongate grouper. Red overall in deeper water, olive in shallow water, somewhat paler below; head and body have *oval groups of dark spots;* lower side often has bright red or salmon-red spots on dusky red background. Outer third of soft dorsal, anal, and caudal fins dark with narrow white edges; *outer third of pectoral fin bright yellow.* Caudal margin even, without exserted rays. Edge of preopercle smooth, without pronounced lobe. 24–27 total gill rakers. 10–12 anal soft rays. TL to 3′ (90 cm).

Habitat: Coral reefs to depths of 450′ (137 m).

Range: Bermuda, Bahamas, s Gulf of Mexico, Antilles, Central and South American coasts to Guianas. Also e Brazil.

Notes: The Yellowfin Grouper has been implicated in cases of ciguatera poisoning. Adults feed mostly on fishes.

Similar Species: Black Grouper is similar but has squarish blotches on side and lacks yellow margin on pectoral fin.

---

168 **Yellowmouth Grouper**
Mycteroperca interstitialis

Identification: A moderately compressed, rather elongate grouper. *Tan to brown above, paler below; upper parts of head and most of body usually have small, brown, close-set spots. Sometimes uniformly brown.* Juveniles and subadults have 5 or 6 dark bands on side of body, each about as wide as pale interspaces; bands often broken into rectangular groups of spots by pale longitudinal lines. Inside and corners of mouth yellow. Dorsal, caudal, and anal fins have spots, dark submarginal bands, and narrow blue-white margins. Juveniles have large round dark spot on upper part of caudal fin base. Large adults have elongate rays near middle of soft dorsal and anal fins. Caudal fin lunate; adults have *exserted rays that are even and about equal in length,* making edge of tail regularly zig-zag. Preopercle has serrate bony lobe at angle. 23–27 total gill rakers, 11–15 on lower limb of first arch. TL to 30″ (75 cm).

caudal fin

Habitat: Coral reefs at depths of 66–495'
(20–150 m).

Range: Bermuda, Bahamas, e and w Gulf of
Mexico, Yucatán, Belize, Antilles,
Venezuela. Also s Brazil.

Notes: The Yellowmouth Grouper is more
common in island waters than along
the coast.

Similar Species: Scamp *(M. phenax)* is similarly brown
with small spots but lacks yellow at
corners of mouth, and its exserted
caudal fin rays are irregular and varying
in length, shortest in center of fin and
longer toward dorsal and ventral lobes.
It occurs along Atlantic coast from

caudal fin of Scamp

North Carolina to Florida, around
Gulf of Mexico, and along Central
and South American coasts of
Caribbean.

---

169 Tiger Grouper
Mycteroperca tigris

Identification: A robust, rather elongate grouper. Dark
greenish to almost black above, paler
below. Bronze spots on cheeks; *back
crossed by about 11 pale narrow lines that
slope downward and forward;* various
white spots and lines on tail. Inside of
mouth yellow-orange. Pectoral fin has
orange margin. Juveniles yellowish,
with dark mid-lateral band as well as
diagonal lines. Caudal fin margin
ragged, with exserted rays of various
lengths. 11 anal soft rays. Edge of
preopercle smoothly rounded, without
lobe at angle. 23–25 total gill rakers.
TL to 3'3" (1 m).

Habitat: Coral reefs and rocky bottoms to depths
of 130' (40 m).

Range: Bermuda, Florida, Bahamas, w Gulf of
Mexico, Antilles, and Caribbean coast to
Suriname. Also s Brazil.

Notes: The Tiger Grouper is commonly seen by
divers and snorkelers. No other grouper
in our area has the same pattern of
narrow pale diagonal lines.

170 Peppermint Bass
Liopropoma rubre

Identification: A small, elongate, slightly compressed sea bass, with caudal fin nearly square or very slightly forked, and 2 dorsal fins separated by scaled space. *Body yellow-orange with 5 wide black lines along side bordered by red above and below.* Fins pink; *large black spot on second dorsal fin; similar spot on anal fin; caudal fin has 2 black spots connected by black bar.* Margins of soft dorsal, caudal, and anal fins white. TL to 3½" (9 cm).

Habitat: Coral reefs at depths of 10–75' (3–23 m).

Range: Florida Keys, Bahamas, and Caribbean, including Antilles.

Notes: The Peppermint Bass is a very beautiful small fish but is seldom seen by divers because it spends the day in caves.

Similar Species: Candy Basslet *(L. carmabi)* also has 5 longitudinal stripes but lacks spot on anal fin, and 2 black spots on caudal fin are distinctly separate; it is known from Florida Keys, Puerto Rico, and Curaçao. Wrasse Bass *(L. eukrines)* is pale red with broad, dark red-brown mid-lateral stripe from tip of snout to caudal fin bordered above and below by narrow yellow stripes; found from North Carolina to Fort Pierce, Florida, and in Gulf of Mexico from Florida Keys to Texas. Cave Bass *(L. mowbrayi)* is red overall, paler ventrally, with dark spots on dorsal and anal fins, and dark submarginal band on caudal fin; it occurs in Bermuda, Florida Keys, Bahamas, Puerto Rico, Curaçao.

171 Reef Bass
Pseudogramma gregoryi

Identification: A small stout fish with a rounded tail and *a short, conspicuous tentacle on eye.* Mottled grayish overall, with conspicuous *ocellated black spot on upper part of operculum;* 2 broad dark lines behind eye; reddish fins. Dorsal fin continuous, with spines shorter than rays; 6–8 spines. Lateral line incomplete, ending below dorsal soft rays. TL to 3″ (8 cm).

Habitat: Coral reefs.

Range: Bermuda, Florida, Bahamas, Antilles, and Yucatán to n South America.

Notes: The Reef Bass is a secretive little fish unlikely to be seen by divers. It is usually seen around living corals, but little is known of its habits.

Similar Species: No other sea basses have orbital tentacles. Soapfishes (genus *Rypticus*) have only 2–4 dorsal fin spines.

---

172 Freckled Soapfish
Rypticus bistrispinus

Identification: A compressed, elongate soapfish with a large mouth and projecting lower jaw. *Dark red-brown above; side pale yellow or cream, with small, dark red-brown spots; belly creamy yellow.* 2 spines at front of long dorsal fin. *3 spines on vertical edge of preopercle.* TL to 6″ (15 cm).

Habitat: Clear shallow waters, often in old conch shells.

Range: Georgia, Florida, Bahamas, parts of Antilles, and Brazil.

Notes: The Freckled Soapfish is common in the shallow waters of the Bahamas. Like other soapfishes, it has special skin glands that produce an irritating, mildly toxic slime.

Similar Species: Brown Soapfish *(R. randalli),* an insular species from Jamaica, Puerto Rico, and Lesser Antilles to Venezuela and French Guiana, has only 2 spines on opercle (all other sea basses have 3); it is brownish gray above and paler below, with dark margins on dorsal, caudal, and anal fins but no other conspicuous markings. Blackfin Soapfish *(R. brachyrhinus),* from w and s Caribbean coasts from Honduras to Trinidad, is uniformly dark brown with pale branchiostegal membranes and dark margins on pectoral, pelvic, and anal fins.

173 Greater Soapfish
Rypticus saponaceus

Identification: A rather compressed, moderately elongate soapfish. *Blue-gray, mottled with irregular paler blotches.* Juveniles have dot-and-dash pattern. 3 dorsal fin spines. Preopercle usually has 2 spines, rarely 1 or 3. SL to about 9″ (23 cm).

Habitat: Shorelines and coral reefs.

Range: Bermuda, Florida, Bahamas, Antilles, Yucatán, Costa Rica to Brazil. Also in e Atlantic.

Notes: The Greater Soapfish is a large and very common species. Its size and color pattern, particularly of juveniles, are distinctive. Although primarily nocturnal, it is frequently seen skulking around the bases of coral colonies and near the mouths of caves.

Similar Species: Whitespotted Soapfish *(R. maculatus)* occurs from Cape Hatteras to Florida and in n and e Gulf of Mexico west to Texas; it has distinct white spots and usually 2 (sometimes 3) dorsal spines.

174 Spotted Soapfish
Rypticus subbifrenatus

Identification: A small, moderately elongate, and compressed soapfish. *Tan, olive, or red-brown above, pale below, with scattered rounded, dark red-brown to black spots on head and body.* Spots highly variable, usually more numerous on head, and restricted to head in large adults. 3 or 4 dorsal fin spines. Preopercle has 1 or 2 spines on its vertical margin. SL to 5⅛″ (13 cm).

Habitat: Holes in coral reefs in clear water.

Range: Florida, Bahamas, Antilles, Yucatán to Venezuela.

Notes: The Spotted Soapfish may be nocturnal. It is rarely seen, and nothing is known of its ecology.

Similar Species: Largespotted Soapfish *(R. macrostigmus),* known from n Bahamas and Panama, is similar but has much larger spots.

Haitian Soapfish *(R. bornoi),* known
from only one specimen from off Port-
au-Prince, Haiti, differs in number of
vertebrae, and has large spots on side
of head.

Other species of sea basses

School Bass   *(Schultzea beta)* Small. Very protrusible
                  mouth. Dorsal fin continuous, with defi-
                  nite but not very deep notch. Slightly
                  forked caudal fin bright yellow, base
                  finely blotched with dark brown, some-
                  times in form of crescent across each
                  lobe. Scales on top of head extend to rear
                  of orbit. S Florida, Bahamas, n Yucatán.

Yellowfin Bass   *(Anthias nicholsi)* Red with yellow blotches
                  on body and 2 yellow lines on side of head.
                  Tail deeply forked, with rounded lobes
                  and short trailing filaments on some rays.
                  Dorsal fin shallowly notched; in adults,
                  third spine elongate, short filaments be-
                  hind other spines. Lateral line complete,
                  with 31–34 scales. Nova Scotia to Straits
                  of Florida, Gulf of Mexico, Guyana to ne
                  Brazil.

Threadnose Bass   *(Anthias tenuis)* Rosy red with no con-
                  spicuous markings. Long slender fila-
                  ment on rim of anterior nostril. Lateral
                  line interrupted below soft dorsal fin
                  rays; 51–57 lateral-line scales. Bermuda,
                  North Carolina, se Gulf of Mexico, Yu-
                  catán, Puerto Rico, s Caribbean.

Streamer Bass   *(Hemanthias aureorubens)* Pinkish above,
                  silvery below. Scales with yellow mar-
                  gins. 44–48 scales in lateral line. Bot-
                  tom edge of maxilla smooth, without
                  hook. Filaments at tips of both lobes of
                  caudal fin. Eye large. Continental shelf of
                  se United States, ne Gulf of Mexico,
                  coasts of Venezuela, Guyana, Suriname.

Red Barbier   *(Hemanthias vivanus)* Prominent hook on
                  bottom edge of rear end of maxilla. Long
                  filaments on dorsal fins of adults. 43–52
                  lateral-line scales. South Carolina to
                  Florida, Gulf of Mexico, Venezuela.

Longtail Bass   *(Hemanthias leptus)* Prominent hook on
                 bottom edge of rear end of maxilla. Long
                 filaments on dorsal fins of adults. 54–65
                 lateral-line scales. North Carolina to
                 Florida, Gulf of Mexico.

BASSLETS
Family Grammatidae

Basslets are small to very small, elon-
gate, moderately compressed species with the lateral line interrupted or absent. They have continuous dorsal fins with
11 to 13 spines, rounded or lunate caudal fins, and elongate
first pelvic fin rays. They have moderately large scales. Some
of the more colorful species are kept as aquarium pets.

This is a small family, confined to the tropical western
Atlantic, with two genera and 10 species.

Genera of family Grammatidae

Gramma   Body elongate, less compressed. Lateral
                 line in 2 sections, first part high on side of
                 body, ending below soft dorsal rays; poste-
                 rior part on mid-side of caudal peduncle.

Lipogramma   Body deeper, more compressed. No lat-
                 eral line. 3 short spine-like rays at front
                 of upper and lower caudal fin rays.

caudal fin with
spine-like rays

175 Royal Gramma
Gramma loreto

Identification: A small, elongate fish with a very long
                 pelvic fin. *Bicolored: purple (appearing blue
                 underwater) in front, bright orange-yellow
                 behind.* Prominent black spot near front
                 of dorsal fin. TL to about 3⅛″ (8 cm).
      Habitat: Coral reefs and rocky shorelines to
                 depths of about 130′ (40 m).
        Range: Bermuda, Bahamas, Antilles, w
                 Caribbean to n South America.
        Notes: This strikingly colored fish is a popular
                 aquarium fish. In the wild it is often
                 found upside down in caves and under
                 ledges, apparently orienting itself to the
                 roof of the cave as if it were the seafloor.

Similar Species: Young Spanish Hogfish (family Labridae) is similar but has short pelvic fin. Bicolor Basslet lacks spot at front of dorsal fin and has only upper parts of head and anterior body purple.

176 Blackcap Basslet
Gramma melacara

Identification: An elongate, robust fish with a deeply lunate tail. Purple, with *sharply defined black "cap"* extending from tip of snout through eye and anterior part of dorsal fin to edge of soft dorsal fin. TL to about 4″ (10 cm).

Habitat: Beyond drop-off on vertical wall at depths greater than 40′ (12 m); most common in water more than 100′ (30 m) deep.

Range: Bahamas and Caribbean.

Notes: The Blackcap Basslet gradually replaces the Royal Gramma at depths of 50 to 100 feet (15–30 m) and is itself replaced by the Yellowcheek Basslet at greater depths. These small basslets stay close to the vertical wall and underhangs but are easily seen by divers.

Similar Species: Yellowcheek Basslet *(G. linki),* which occurs in deeper water in Bahamas, Greater Antilles, and w Caribbean, lacks black cap, and has yellow lines on head and yellow spots on scales on side.

177 Threeline Basslet
Lipogramma trilineatum

Identification: A tiny, moderately elongate, compressed fish with a lunate tail. Front of body deep yellow, shading to bluish on lower rear. *3 distinct blue lines on head and anterior body:* one in front of dorsal fin on mid-dorsal line, and one on each side extending from behind eye to below rear of spiny dorsal fin. 12 dorsal fin spines. TL to 1⅜″ (3.5 cm).

Habitat: Deep reefs and outer wall at depths from 72–228′ (22–69 m).

Range: Florida, Bahamas, scattered localities in Caribbean.

Notes: The Threeline Basslet is an attractive species to look for on deeper dives. Little is known of its behavior or life history.

Other *Lipogramma* species

Yellow Basslet	*(L. flavescens)* All yellow, with dark bar through eye and dark spot at base of soft dorsal rays extending onto body. Bahamas.
Dusky Basslet	*(L. anabantoides)* Uniformly bronze in color. Florida, Haiti, Bahamas.
Rosy Basslet	*(L. roseum)* Body rosy red. Tail yellow with black spots. 11 dorsal spines. Isla de Providencia, n Caribbean.
Bicolor Basslet	*(L. klayi)* Anterior part of body purplish red; posterior yellow. Bahamas, Jamaica, Belize, Curaçao.
Banded Basslet	*(L. evides)* Pale beige with prominent dark brown bands through eye and at front and rear of dorsal fin (last bar faint in large individuals). Dorsal, anal, and caudal fins pale blue with yellow lines and spots. Distinct ocellated dark spot on fourth and fifth dorsal soft rays. Tail rounded. Bahamas, w Caribbean, Lesser Antilles.
Royal Basslet	*(L. regium)* Pale bluish green with 4–5 dark orange bars, each with pale center. Large black spot ringed with blue on soft dorsal fin, extending onto body. 3–4 horizontal orange stripes across cheek and gill cover. Bahamas, Puerto Rico.

BIGEYES
Family Priacanthidae

The bigeyes are moderate-size red, pink, or orange fishes with very large eyes and ctenoid (rough) scales. They are deep bodied and compressed, with rounded, square, or slightly forked tails. Their mouths are large and directed obliquely upward. The dorsal fin is single, comprised of 10 spines (rarely nine or 11) and 10 to 15 soft rays; the longest soft rays are longer than the posterior spines. The anal fin has three spines and 9 to 16 soft rays. The pelvic fins are large, with the inner ray connected to the body by membrane for part or all of its length. The preopercle has a shelf overlying the sensory canal; the area behind the shelf may be scaled or unscaled (see illustration). There is usually a short spine at the angle, or lower corner, of the preopercle. The scales are small and strongly ctenoid.

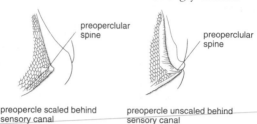

preopercle scaled behind
sensory canal

preopercle unscaled behind
sensory canal

The family Priacanthidae contains 18 species in four genera. Four species, one from each genus, occur in our area.

Genera of family Priacanthidae

Pristigenys	9–11 anal soft rays. 10–12 dorsal soft rays. 36–51 scales in lateral line. 9–12 scale rows between lateral line and dorsal fin origin. Preorbital bone coarsely serrate. Preopercle scaled behind sensory canal. Pelvic fin shorter than head, reaching to anal fin origin.
Cookeolus	More than 11 anal soft rays. More than 56 scales in lateral line. More than 16 rows of scales between lateral line and dorsal fin origin. Preorbital bone coarsely serrate. Preopercle scaled behind sensory canal. Pelvic fin usually longer than head, reaching well beyond anal fin origin.
Priacanthus	More than 11 anal soft rays. More than 56 scales in lateral line. Fewer than 16 rows of scales between lateral line and dorsal fin origin. Preorbital bone finely serrate. Preopercle scaled behind sensory canal. Pelvic fin shorter than head.
Heteropriacanthus	Similar to *Priacanthus* but lacks scales on preopercle behind sensory canal. (Other differences are internal.)

178 Short Bigeye
Pristigenys alta

Identification: *Body short and deep,* red overall, with broad, darker red bars. Dorsal, anal, and caudal fins have narrow dark edges. Pelvic fin rather long, reaching to or beyond anal fin origin. 42–45 scales in lateral line. SL to 10½" (27 cm).

Habitat: Rocky bottoms at depths of 16–410' (5–125 m).

Range: Bermuda, New England to Florida, Bahamas, Gulf of Mexico, Lesser Antilles, and w Caribbean.

Notes: As juveniles, Short Bigeyes are often carried northward on the Gulf Stream, appearing along northern shores in late summer and fall; however, they probably do not survive the cold weather. Adults are usually solitary and are associated with rocks and burrows.

Similar Species: Other bigeyes have more elongate, compressed bodies, and longer dorsal and anal fins with more rays.

179 Bulleye
Cookeolus japonicus

Identification: A large, deep-bodied, compressed fish with *a very long pelvic fin,* reaching middle of caudal fin in juveniles and almost to anal fin origin even in very large adults. Red or orange-red overall; pelvic fin dusky. Dorsal, anal, and caudal fins have dusky margins in subadults, clear margins in large adults. *Preorbital bone coarsely serrate.* Canal on preopercle mostly closed over by low shelf. 12–14 dorsal soft rays; 12 or 13 anal soft rays. 60–83 scales in lateral line. 16–20 scale rows between lateral line and dorsal fin origin. SL to 19¾" (50 cm).

Habitat: Rocky ledges at depths of 200–1,320' (60–400 m).

Range: Worldwide in warm and temperate waters. Scattered records in w Atlantic, including Bermuda, New Jersey,

Virginia, North Carolina, s Caribbean, and s Brazil.

Notes: The Bulleye is a widespread species, but because it lives in deeper water it is unlikely to be seen by divers. Young are carried northward on the Gulf Stream and occasionally stray into shallow water as far north as Nova Scotia.

Similar Species: Short Bigeye, similar in several features, is smaller and deeper-bodied, and has larger scales.

180 Glasseye Snapper
Heteropriacanthus cruentatus

Identification: A moderately elongate, compressed fish. Silvery pink to red; pelvic fin whitish, without black spot at base. Eye large, with red iris. Preopercle has prominent shelf protecting sensory canal; *section of preopercle behind canal striated and without scales.* Preopercular spine short and broadly triangular. Dorsal fin has 10 spines and 13 rays. Anal fin has 3 spines and 13 or 14 rays. Caudal fin square. 78–96 scales in lateral line. 9–12 scale rows between lateral line and dorsal fin origin. SL to 10″ (25 cm).

Habitat: Coral reefs around holes and caves; usually at depths less than 66′ (20 m).

Range: Worldwide in warm seas. Throughout our area; common in Bahamas and Caribbean. Rare along Atlantic coast and n Gulf of Mexico; a few Atlantic coast records as far north as New Jersey, presumably juveniles carried north on Gulf Stream.

Notes: The Glasseye Snapper is an island species commonly seen by snorkelers around coral reefs. Its large eye indicates that it is nocturnal, but it can be seen under ledges and in caves during the day. It feeds on a variety of invertebrates and small fishes.

Similar Species: Bigeye has scales on preopercle behind sensory canal and black spot at base of pelvic fin.

181 **Bigeye**
Priacanthus arenatus

Identification: An elongate, moderately deep-bodied, compressed species. Red overall; black spot at base of pelvic fin. *Scales present on preopercle behind shelf over sensory canal.* Preopercular spine short. Dorsal fin has 10 spines and 14 rays. Anal fin has 3 spines and 15 rays. Caudal fin lunate. 83–91 scales in lateral line. SL to 15″ (38 cm).

Habitat: Reefs and associated sand bottoms, usually at depths of 66–660′ (20–200 m).

Range: Both sides of tropical and warm-temperate Atlantic. Bermuda, North Carolina to Argentina, Bahamas, Gulf of Mexico, and Caribbean, including Antilles.

Notes: The Bigeye is less commonly seen by divers than the Glasseye Snapper. Young Bigeyes have been found as far north as Nova Scotia. This species apparently occurs in aggregations.

Similar Species: Glasseye Snapper lacks scales on preopercle behind shelf over sensory canal and does not have black spot on pelvic fin.

CARDINALFISHES
Family Apogonidae

The cardinalfishes are small, short-bodied, and somewhat compressed fishes. They range in color from pinkish, to red, to brownish. They have two well-separated dorsal fins, the first with six to eight spines, the second with one spine and eight to 14 soft rays. The pelvic fins are thoracic. The anal fin has two, rather than three, spines. The tail is moderately forked. Cardinalfishes have large eyes and terminal mouths. Most species have small villiform teeth in the jaws, and some species have enlarged pointed canine teeth as well. The scales are large, and the lateral line is complete. Cardinalfishes are nocturnal and remain in caves or underhangs during the day. Many, probably most, species are oral brooders, with the males carrying the eggs in their mouths until hatching.

There are 19 genera with 195 species in this family. Three genera and 22 species occur in our area; we cover some of the more common species below.

Genera of family Apogonidae

Apogon

Preopercle serrate, without protruding lobe. Scales ctenoid. Inner ray of pelvic fin attached to body by membrane for less than half its length. Usually 12 pectoral fin rays. Scales present on dorsal midline in front of first dorsal fin.

Phaeoptyx

Preopercle serrate, with protruding lobe at lower corner. Scales ctenoid. Inner ray of pelvic fin attached to body by membrane for less than half its length. Usually 12 pectoral fin rays. Scales present on dorsal midline in front of first dorsal fin.

Astrapogon

Preopercle smooth, without protruding lobe. Scales smooth. Pelvic fin very large and dark, inner ray attached to body by membrane for most of its length; 14–16 pectoral fin rays. No scales on dorsal midline in front of first dorsal fin.

182 Oddscale Cardinalfish
Apogon evermanni

Identification: A moderately elongate cardinalfish with *small ctenoid scales. Scales of lateral line large and well spaced* (about half as many scales in lateral line as in rows just above and below it). Reddish, with *black spot at base of last dorsal fin rays and white spot on dorsal midline just behind second dorsal fin.* Tips of first dorsal and caudal fins dusky. Dusky stripe extends from behind eye to edge of operculum. SL to 2⅜″ (6 cm).

Habitat: Caves, from shorelines to depths of 50′ (15 m).

Range: Bahamas, Cozumel to Isla de Providencia, and Curaçao.

Notes: The Oddscale Cardinalfish is known from only a few specimens found in scattered localities.

Similar Species: Whitestar Cardinalfish also has white spot behind dorsal fin but does not have enlarged scales in lateral line.

183 Flamefish
Apogon maculatus

Identification: A small, rather stubby, red cardinalfish with *a round black spot on back* just below last rays of second dorsal fin, and a *broad black saddle on caudal peduncle. Eye conspicuously marked with 2 horizontal white stripes,* one above and one below pupil, continuing to edge of operculum. Behind eye, space between lines is dark. SL to 2¾" (7 cm).

Habitat: Caves and crevices in shallow reefs from shorelines to depths of 420' (128 m).

Range: Bermuda, New England to Florida, Bahamas, ne Gulf of Mexico, and Caribbean, including Antilles, to n South America.

Notes: The Flamefish is probably the most abundant cardinalfish in the region, and is often seen in caves by divers. Males with eggs have been spotted in the Bahamas in June and July. This is a popular aquarium fish.

Similar Species: *A. americanus,* which differs only in subtle pigment and measurement features, occurs in Brazil.

184 Whitestar Cardinalfish
Apogon lachneri

Identification: A small, strikingly patterned cardinalfish. Red overall, with *black spot behind second dorsal fin, followed by brilliant white spot,* followed by dusky area. First dorsal fin black with pale leading edge; second dorsal and anal fins dark at tips; caudal lobes edged with black. SL to 2⅜" (6 cm).

Habitat: Coral reefs at depths of 12–200' (3.5–60 m).

Range: Southern Florida, Bahamas, and Caribbean, including Antilles.

Notes: The Whitestar is a spectacular but
retiring cardinalfish often seen around
caves. Although it is reasonably
common, little is known of its habits.
Similar Species: Oddscale Cardinalfish has enlarged
lateral line scales; although it also has
white spot behind dorsal fin, black area
preceding spot is farther forward, at base
of last dorsal rays.

185   Barred Cardinalfish
Apogon binotatus

Identification: A rather elongate, red cardinalfish with
2 narrow vertical black bars, one from last
rays of dorsal fin to last rays of anal fin,
one across caudal peduncle at base of
caudal fin. SL to 5⅛″ (13 cm).
Habitat: Coral reefs and associated habitats to
depths of 200′ (60 m).
Range: Bermuda, Florida, Bahamas, and
Caribbean, including Antilles.
Notes: The Barred Cardinalfish is abundant in
the Bahamas, but little is known of its
habits. It can be distinguished from
other cardinalfishes with two black bars
by the narrowness of the bar on the
caudal peduncle.

186   Belted Cardinalfish
Apogon townsendi

Identification: A relatively deep-bodied, red cardinalfish
with a narrow vertical bar from last rays
of dorsal fin to last rays of anal fin and a
*broad vertical bar across caudal peduncle
that is dusky in center but noticeably darker
along its anterior and posterior edges.* SL to
2½″ (6.5 cm).
Habitat: Coral reefs at depths of 8–90′ (2.5–27 m).
Range: Florida, Bahamas, and Caribbean,
including Antilles.
Notes: The Belted Cardinalfish is a common and
distinctive fish often seen hovering in the
spines of the long-spined urchin. None
of the other cardinalfishes with dark bars
has black edges on the peduncular bar.

187 Pale Cardinalfish
Apogon planifrons

Identification: A moderately elongate, pale red cardinalfish with *a broad dark saddle on caudal peduncle.* Narrow vertical black bar from last rays of dorsal fin to last rays of anal fin; bar has approximately parallel sides, narrowing only slightly toward belly. SL to 4⅛" (10.5 cm).

Habitat: Coral reefs and associated habitats to depths of 60' (18 m).

Range: Florida, Bahamas, Antilles, Yucatán to Venezuela.

Notes: This species is fairly common in shallow water, where it is often seen by divers and snorkelers.

Similar Species: Mimic Cardinalfish *(A. phenax)* is similar, but bar between dorsal and anal fins tapers, becoming noticeably narrower toward belly; it occurs from Florida Keys, Bahamas, and islands off Venezuelan coast. Bigtooth Cardinalfish *(A. affinis),* a pale pink species with dusky stripe from snout through eye to preopercle, lacks dark saddle and bar, and has prominent canine jaw teeth; it lives from Florida Keys and Bahamas to Venezuela.

188 Sawcheek Cardinalfish
Apogon quadrisquamatus

Identification: *A small, stubby, plain pale red cardinalfish with a smudgy bar (sometimes tiny) on caudal peduncle.* Small black melanophores on head and body. Triangular dark streak from lower rear corner of eye. May have triangular streak across second and third dorsal spines and dark streaks at bases of dorsal and anal fins. 11–13 pectoral fin rays. SL to 2⅜" (6 cm).

Habitat: Coral reefs to depths of 165' (50 m).

Range: Florida, Bahamas, and Caribbean.

Notes: The Sawcheek Cardinalfish sometimes associates with sea anemones, possibly as shelter from predators; it also lives in tubular sponges.

Similar Species: Dwarf Cardinalfish *(A. mosavi)* has more distinct peduncular bar and 14 or 15 (rather than 11–13) gill rakers; it occurs in Bahamas, Haiti, and Jamaica.

189 Freckled Cardinalfish
Phaeoptyx conklini

Identification: A rather short-bodied cardinalfish. Head and body brownish, with *enlarged melanophores that form large stellate or squarish spots, usually more than 1 per scale below lateral line.* Dark stripes near bases of second dorsal and anal fins, slightly separated from body by pale space. Caudal fin has narrow dark edges and dark blotch at base. 11–13 pectoral fin rays. SL to about 3½" (9 cm).
Habitat: Coral reefs to depths of 73′ (22 m).
Range: Bermuda, Florida, Bahamas, and Caribbean, including Antilles.
Notes: The Freckled Cardinalfish is one of the most common cardinalfishes in the Bahamas.
Similar Species: Dusky Cardinalfish lacks stripes at bases of second dorsal and anal fins and black margins on tail. Sponge Cardinalfish *(P. xenus),* which ranges from Bahamas to Curaçao, has indistinct black streaks at very bases of second dorsal and anal fins.

190 Dusky Cardinalfish
Phaeoptyx pigmentaria

Identification: A rather short-bodied cardinalfish. Head and body brownish, with *large melanophores that form star-shaped spots, usually 1 per scale below lateral line.* Dark blotch at base of caudal fin. Second dorsal and anal fins lack dark streaks at bases. 11–13 pectoral fin rays. SL to about 3⅛" (8 cm).
Habitat: Coral reefs and associated habitats to depths of 140′ (43 m).
Range: Bermuda, se and w Florida, Bahamas, and Caribbean, including Antilles.

Notes: The Dusky Cardinalfish seems to be less
common than the Freckled Cardinalfish
(which has dark stripes slightly above the
bases of the second dorsal and anal fins),
although the two are often seen together.

191 Conchfish
Astrapogon stellatus

Identification: Body short and deep, generally bronze,
with dark bars radiating from eye.
Pelvic fin black and long, reaching
almost to, or beyond, end of anal fin
base. *Preopercle smooth. Scales smooth; no
scales on midline in front of dorsal fin. 15
pectoral rays. 10 or 11 gill rakers on lower
limb of first arch.* SL to 3⅛″ (8 cm).

Habitat: Lives in mantle cavity of queen conch,
which in turn lives in sea-grass beds and
around reefs from shorelines to depths of
130′ (40 m) or more.

Range: Bermuda, Florida Keys, Bahamas, and
Caribbean, including Antilles.

Notes: This species apparently lives only in the
mantle cavities of living conchs. An
inquiline, it uses the conch for shelter
and emerges at night to feed on small
crustaceans. Like other cardinalfishes,
males brood the eggs in their mouths.

Similar Species: Very similar Blackfin Cardinalfish has
12–14 gill rakers on lower limb of first
arch. Bronze Cardinalfish *(A. alutus)* has
shorter pelvic fin reaching only to first
third of anal fin base; it lives along
Atlantic coast from North Carolina to
Florida and in Gulf of Mexico, but not
in Bahamas.

192 Blackfin Cardinalfish
Astrapogon puncticulatus

Identification: A short, deep-bodied cardinalfish.
Brownish, with *black pelvic fin and black
lines radiating from eye.* Pelvic fin reaches
to about middle of anal fin base. 16
pectoral rays. 12–14 gill rakers on lower
limb of first arch. SL to 3⅛″ (8 cm).

Habitat: Holes and shells around reefs. Usually in
            water less than 20' (6 m) deep.
Range: Southern Florida, Bahamas, Antilles,
            Caribbean to Brazil.
Notes: Although very similar to the Conchfish
            (which has 10 or 11 gill rakers and a
            longer pelvic fin), this species is not
            known to be an inquiline and is never
            found in the mantle cavities of living
            conchs.

TILEFISHES
Family Malacanthidae

Tilefishes, comprising five genera and 39
species, are a rather diverse group. There are, however, some
unifying characteristics, including gill membranes free from
the isthmus, a stout spine or a fleshy tab on the opercle, and
ctenoid scales on the body. These are moderately large to
large, elongate, tapering or fusiform fishes with long dorsal
and anal fins. The dorsal origin is above the gill opening.

Some authorities separate tilefishes into two families:
Branchiostegidae, whose members have a mid-dorsal cranial
ridge, fewer than 36 spines and rays in the dorsal fin, and
fewer than 29 spines and rays in the anal fin; and Malacan-
thidae, whose members lack a ridge on top of the head, have
more than 58 spines and rays in the dorsal fin, and more
than 49 spines and rays in the anal fin. We treat them here
as a single family. Three genera are found in our area, but
Lopholatilus occurs only in deep water.

Genera of family Malacanthidae

Malacanthus	Body elongate and little compressed. Head rather flat on top, without predorsal ridge. Dorsal fin has 4–5 spines and 54–60 rays. Anal fin has 1 spine and 48–55 rays.
Caulolatilus	Body compressed, tapering, elongate but not eel-like. Head has predorsal ridge but lacks prominent fleshy crest. Dorsal fin has 7–8 spines and 23–27 rays. Anal fin has 1 spine and 20–28 soft rays.
Lopholatilus	Body compressed. Head has prominent high crest. Dorsal fin has 7 spines and 15 rays. Anal fin has 1 spine and 13–14 rays.

275 Sand Tilefish
Malacanthus plumieri

Identification: A slender, elongate, almost *eel-like* fish with a conical snout and long, continuous dorsal and anal fins. *Corners of tail fin extended as filaments* in larger fish. Greenish or blue-green, darker dorsally, with yellowish wash on side; belly bluish white. Dorsal fin blue with yellow margin. Lips, snout, chin, and gill membranes yellowish; some individuals have blue lines behind eye. Caudal fin has some yellow-orange on both lobes and dusky spot on upper rays. Scales small, rough over most of body, smooth on head. Large flat spine on gill cover. TL to about 24″ (60 cm).

Habitat: Shallow areas around reefs with rock rubble; usually in water less than 120′ (37 m) deep.

Range: Bermuda, North Carolina to Florida, throughout Bahamas, n Gulf of Mexico, Antilles, Yucatán, Honduras, Colombia, Venezuela, and south of Amazon to Santos, Brazil. Also Ascension Island in e Atlantic.

Notes: From piles of coral fragments, the Sand Tilefish builds nests that may be several feet across. It uses its mouth to pick up the fragments, one at a time, then spends much time rearranging them. When threatened, it will disappear into a hole beneath the nest.

Similar Species: Other species of tilefishes have shorter anal fins, deeper bodies, and median ridge or flap on top of head.

Other species of tilefishes

Blackline Tilefish *(Caulolatilus cyanops)* Electric-blue chain-like pattern on upper side. Spiny part of dorsal fin brilliant yellow; black line along base of entire dorsal fin. Yellow area at base of each lobe of caudal fin. Large dark area above pectoral fin. Dorsal fin has 7 spines and 23–24 rays. North Carolina to South America.

Goldface Tilefish *(Caulolatilus chrysops)* Broad gold patch under each eye. 8 dorsal spines. North Carolina to Caribbean.

Bankslope Tilefish *(Caulolatilus dooleyi)* About 22 vague yellow bars on upper body; no dark markings. Dusky pectoral axil; no dark blotch above pectoral base. Deep water around Bahama Banks.

Bermuda Tilefish *(Caulolatilus bermudensis)* Low dorsal fin. Known only from 2 specimens found in deep water (900'/275 m) off Bermuda.

Blueline Tilefish *(Caulolatilus microps)* Dark brown above, lighter below. Blue and yellow stripe from snout to eye. North Carolina to Florida, Gulf of Mexico.

Anchor Tilefish *(Caulolatilus intermedius)* Light gray-brown with dark, anchor-shaped patch on nape. No other prominent markings. Gulf of Mexico, Cuba.

Yellow-bar Tilefish *(Caulolatilus williamsi)* Tail doubly emarginate, with broad yellow patch on lower caudal fin lobe. 17–20 light yellow bars on body. Cay Sal Bank, Bahamas, to Virgin Islands.

Reticulate Tilefish *(Caulolatilus guppyi)* Dark reticulations on upper body. Dark bar from eye to middle of upper jaw. Venezuela, Trinidad, Guyana, Suriname.

BLUEFISH
Family Pomatomidae

This family has only a single wide-spread species, the well-known Bluefish (although some authorities include another little-known genus, *Scombrops* here). Large and streamlined with a forked tail, the Bluefish has two contiguous dorsal fins: a rather small and low spiny dorsal, and a long, higher second dorsal. The pectoral fins are high on the sides and rather short, and the anal fin are long. A membranous flap extends ventrally from the preopercle.

271 Bluefish
Pomatomus saltatrix

Identification: A rather large, elongate, streamlined fish with a deeply forked tail, large mouth, and small eye. Greenish blue, shading to silvery on side and belly; pectoral fin dark at base. Small spiny *dorsal fin has 7 or 8 slender spines,* closely followed by long second dorsal fin, with 1 spine and 23–28 rays. *Anal fin long, with 2 spines and 23–27 soft rays.* Head, body, second dorsal, caudal, and anal fins covered with small scales. Lateral line nearly straight. *Teeth bluntly pointed and flattened,* blade-like. TL to 3'7" (1.1 m).

Habitat: Mid-water; coastal waters, sometimes close to shore but often far offshore.

Range: Bermuda, Nova Scotia to Florida, Gulf of Mexico, and South American coast from Colombia to Argentina. Also in e Atlantic, Mediterranean, and Indo–west Pacific regions.

Notes: A valued food and game fish, the Bluefish is a voracious predator that travels in schools and has a reputation for killing more smaller fish than it can eat. Occasionally, a Bluefish will attack a swimmer and can cause severe lacerations. This species makes long migrations, following warm water north in the summertime and retreating south as the temperature drops.

Similar Species: Amberjacks (family Carangidae) are somewhat similar in shape but have small teeth and transverse grooves at bases of upper and lower caudal fin rays.

COBIA
Family Rachycentridae

This family contains a single species, the Cobia, a large fish with short dorsal spines that are not connected to one another by a membrane. The head is flat and the lower jaw projects. The tail fin is forked in adults but long and pointed in small juveniles. The Cobia bears a remarkable resemblance to some remoras, except that the Cobia is larger and lacks a sucking disk on top of the head.

272 Cobia
Rachycentron canadum

Identification: A large terete fish with a broad, rather flat head. Mouth large; lower jaw projects, with small jaw teeth. Dark brown above, shading to yellowish brown below; 2 narrow silver bands on side. *7–9 dorsal spines, not connected by membrane.* Second dorsal and anal fins long, their front rays longest. Tail lunate in adults, with upper lobe longer than lower. Scales small and smooth. TL to about 6'6" (2 m).

Habitat: Open seas and coastal waters around obstructions such as pilings, shipwrecks, and rocky outcrops on bottoms.

Range: Bermuda, Atlantic coast from Massachusetts to Argentina, Gulf of Mexico, and entire Caribbean.

Notes: The Cobia feeds on crabs, squids, and fishes. In some areas it is a valued food fish and is also caught for sport. Some remoras (family Echeneidae) are similar in shape and color but have a sucking disk on top of the head.

REMORAS
Family Echeneidae

Remoras are fascinating fishes that have their first dorsal fin modified into a sucking disk located on the top of the head. The sucker has pairs of wall-like transverse plates, called *laminae,* that are somewhat reminiscent of venetian blinds. Remoras have long second dorsal and anal fins without spines, and rather large pectoral and pelvic fins. The tail is lunate in adults.

Remoras accompany other animals such as turtles, marine mammals, and large fishes, including sharks and manta rays, probably conserving their own energy and depending on the host for transportation. Much of the time the sucker is not in direct contact with the host's skin but is a few millimeters away. At such times the remora is probably riding on a layer of water that moves with the host. Some species associate only with specific hosts, but the Sharksucker, which is the species most frequently encountered by divers and snorkelers, can be found on a wide variety of fishes from trunkfishes to parrotfishes.

The family includes four genera and eight species, all of which occur in our region. All are worldwide except the Whitefin Sharksucker *(Echeneis neucratoides),* which is confined to the western Atlantic.

Genera of family Echeneidae

Echeneis	Body very elongate. 18–28 laminae on disk. 29–41 anal rays.
Phtheirichthys	Body elongate. 9–11 laminae on disk. 29–41 anal rays.
Remora	Body moderately elongate. 15–27 laminae on disk. 18–28 anal rays.
Remorina	Body moderately elongate. 12–14 laminae on disk. 26 anal rays.

273 Sharksucker
Echeneis naucrates

Identification: A slender, elongate remora with *a dark mid-lateral stripe bordered by narrow white stripes above and below.* Tips and edges of dorsal, anal, and caudal fins white; white edging becomes narrower with increasing size. Usually 23 laminae in sucking disk. 39 dorsal fin rays. 36 anal fin rays. TL to 3′ (90 cm).

Habitat: Open water; enters shallow water and is commonly seen near shore and around coral reefs. Frequently seen without a host.

Range: Worldwide in warm waters; in w Atlantic from Bermuda and Nova Scotia to Uruguay.

Notes: The Sharksucker occasionally strays into estuaries and is commonly caught by anglers. It feeds on small fishes as well as bits of its host's prey and the host's parasites.

Similar Species: Whitefin Sharksucker *(E. neucratoides)* usually has 21 laminae, 36 dorsal rays, and 33 anal rays; it is similarly colored but has more white on fins at all sizes; it occurs along Atlantic coasts from New England to South America, and in Gulf of Mexico. Slender Suckerfish *(Phtheirichthys lineatus),* a more slender species with only 10 laminae in its short disk, is often attached to Great Barracuda; in our region it ranges from South Carolina through Gulf of Mexico and Caribbean to n South America. Members of genera *Remora* and *Remorina* have chunkier bodies and uniform coloration.

274 Remora
Remora remora

Identification:	An elongate but somewhat chunky remora. Blackish overall. Pelvic fin broadly attached to abdomen by membrane. Pectoral fin flexible, with 26–29 rays. *17–20 laminae in sucking disk.* TL to 30″ (75 cm).
Habitat:	Open waters; attaches to large fishes and sea turtles.
Range:	Worldwide in warm waters; in w Atlantic from Nova Scotia to Argentina.
Notes:	The host preference of the Remora is less restrictive than that of some other members of this family. It attaches to a variety of hosts, including sharks, mantas, billfishes, and sea turtles. Younger individuals are more active as parasite pickers.

Similar Species:	Whalesucker *(R. australis)* has very long disk with 25–27 laminae; it attaches to whales and porpoises. Spearfish Remora *(R. brachyptera)* has 15–17 laminae in disk and flexible pectoral fin with 28–33 rays; it attaches to swordfishes, Ocean Sunfishes, and marlins. Marlinsucker *(R. osteochir)* has 17–20 laminae in disk and stiff bony pectoral fin with 23 rays; it attaches to marlins, sailfishes, spearfishes, and wahoos. White Suckerfish *(Remorina albescens)* has pelvic fin narrowly attached to body and small disk with 12–13 lamellae; it attaches to mantas, sharks, and barracudas. All are open-water fishes that occur offshore throughout our area.

JACKS
Family Carangidae

Jacks are silvery, rather compressed fishes with very narrow caudal peduncles and deeply forked tails. Their dorsal fins are nearly or completely divided, the anterior part composed only of spines and the posterior part composed of one spine followed by soft rays. In the anal fins, the first two spines are separate from the rest of the fin. Some species have the anterior soft rays of both the dorsal and anal fins elongate, forming high lobes. In most species the pectoral fins are long and falcate. The scales are usually small and smooth. In most jacks the lateral line is arched anteriorly and straight posteriorly. Many genera have some or all scales in the posterior part of the lateral line vertically elongated into plate-like *scutes,* sometimes with a prominent keel ending in a sharp point; a few genera also have scutes on part or all of the anterior portion. Because jacks have stiff, deeply forked tails, their length is often given as fork length (FL), which is measured from the tip of the snout or lower jaw (whichever is longer) to the tip of the shortest middle rays of the tail.

This is a large and variable family, with 32 genera and 140 species; 15 genera and 32 species occur in our region. We cover the more common shallow-water species.

Genera of family Carangidae

Decapterus	Body elongate. Scutes along posterior part of lateral line, sometimes also on rear of anterior part. Last ray of dorsal fin and anal fin detached as separate finlets. Pectoral fin pointed, equal to head length. Adipose eyelid well developed.
Selar	Body elongate. Scutes along posterior part of lateral line; sometimes a few scutes on anterior part. Shoulder girdle under gill cover has fleshy tabs, with deep furrow below. Pectoral fin falcate, shorter than head. Adipose eyelid well developed.
Trachurus	Body elongate, slender, nearly tcrete. Scutes along entire lateral line. Pectoral fin equal to head length. Adipose eyelid well developed.
Caranx	Body moderately elongate, compressed. Scutes on posterior part of lateral line only. Lining of mouth pale. Spiny dorsal fin low. Pectoral fin falcate, longer than head. Caudal peduncle has short auxiliary

keels above and below lateral line on each side. Adipose eyelid moderate.

Uraspis   Body moderately elongate, compressed. Scutes on posterior part of lateral line. Upper jaw elongate. Lining of mouth black, with white on tongue, roof, and floor of mouth. Anal spines reduced or resorbed in adult. Pectoral fin falcate, longer than head. Eye small; adipose eyelid weakly developed.

Pseudocaranx   Body elongate and compressed. Scutes on posterior part of lateral line. Spiny dorsal fin higher than soft dorsal fin. Pectoral fin falcate, longer than head. Adipose eyelid weakly developed.

Hemicaranx   Body deep and compressed. Posterior part of lateral line longer than anterior part, with 38–56 large scutes. Upper lobe of tail longer than lower lobe. Pectoral fin falcate, longer than head. Adipose eyelid weakly developed.

Chloroscombrus   Body compressed, deep, with lower profile more strongly curved than upper. Upper lobe of tail longer than lower. Posterior part of lateral line has 5–15 small scutes. Pectoral fin falcate, longer than head. Adipose eyelid weakly developed.

Alectis   Body deep, diamond shaped. Scales very small, so fish appears naked. Pelvic fin filamentous in young, moderately long (longer than upper jaw) in adults. Scutes small, 12–30 in posterior part of lateral line. First 2 anal spines resorbed as fish grows. Caudal peduncle has short keels above and below lateral line on each side. Pectoral fin strongly falcate, longer than head. Adipose eyelid well developed.

Selene   Body very deep and strongly compressed. Scales very small, almost invisible. Pelvic fin short, less than one-third as long as upper jaw in adults. Scutes in posterior part of lateral line small, only a little larger than scales in rest of lateral line. First 2 anal spines resorbed with growth. Pectoral fin falcate, longer than head.

Elagatis Body elongate, fusiform, moderately compressed. No scutes. Last 2 rays of dorsal and anal fins detached, forming separate finlets. Caudal peduncle has transverse grooves at upper and lower bases of caudal fin. Pectoral fin pointed, shorter than head. 2 anal fin spines.

Naucrates Body elongate, fusiform, compressed. No scutes in lateral line. Fleshy keel on each side of caudal peduncle. Caudal peduncle has dorsal and ventral transverse grooves.

Seriola Body elongate, moderately compressed. No scutes in lateral line. Caudal peduncle has dorsal and ventral transverse grooves; no keel. First 2 anal spines reduced, covered with skin in large adults. Pectoral fin shorter than head. Adipose eyelid moderate.

Oligoplites Body elongate, fusiform, compressed. No scutes in lateral line. First 4–5 dorsal spines separate from one another. 11–15 partially detached finlets at rear of dorsal and anal fins. Scales needle-like. Pectoral fin pointed, shorter than head.

Trachinotus Body short, deep, and highly compressed. No scutes in lateral line. No finlets. Snout rounded. Pectoral fin falcate, longer than head. Adipose eyelid present.

252 Round Scad
Decapterus punctatus

Identification: A slender, elongate, terete jack with *last ray of dorsal and anal fins separated as finlets.* Greenish or blue above, shading to silvery and white ventrally, with 1–14 well-spaced small black spots on curved part of lateral line. Body scales small and smooth. 77–98 total scales and scutes in lateral line: 37–56 scales and 0–6 scutes in arched anterior part, 0–2 scales and 32–46 scutes in straight posterior part. Dorsal fin has 29–34 soft rays. FL to 8⅜" (21 cm).

Habitat: Schools in mid-water and near bottom to depths of 300' (90 m); occurs near surface farther offshore.

Range: Bermuda, Massachusetts to Florida, Bahamas, Gulf of Mexico, entire Caribbean, including Antilles, and South American coast to Rio de Janeiro.

Notes: The Round Scad is caught commercially and used mainly for bait. A plankton feeder, it eats a wide variety of free-swimming invertebrates. It probably spawns well offshore year-round.

Similar Species: Mackerel Scad *(D. macarellus)* has 31–37 dorsal fin rays and 23–32 scutes in posterior part of lateral line; it ranges from New England to Brazil but is not in Gulf of Mexico. Redtail Scad *(D. tabl)* lacks spots on lateral line, has 34–44 scutes in posterior part of lateral line, and 29–34 dorsal soft rays; it lives in Bermuda, Atlantic coast off North Carolina and Florida, and along coast of South America from Colombia and Venezuela.

253 Bigeye Scad
Selar crumenophthalmus

Identification: An elongate and moderately compressed jack. Blue or green above, shading to silvery white below. Eye very large, with well-developed adipose eyelid. *Deep furrow near lower end of shoulder girdle, with fleshy tab (papilla) just above furrow;* a second papilla near upper end of shoulder girdle under gill cover. 83–94 total scales and scutes in lateral line: 48–56 scales and 0–4 scutes in arched anterior part; 0–11 scales and 29–42 scutes in straight posterior part. FL to 11" (28 cm), possibly longer.

shoulder girdle

Habitat: Shallow, sometimes turbid, coastal waters; sometimes over shallow reefs.

Range: Worldwide in tropical and subtropical marine waters. Bermuda, Atlantic coast from Nova Scotia to Rio de Janeiro; throughout Bahamas, Gulf of Mexico, and Caribbean.

Notes: The Bigeye Scad is sold for food and as live bait for billfishes. It lives in large schools and feeds on planktonic invertebrates and small fishes.

Similar Species: No other jacks have furrow across lower part of pectoral girdle. Other scads with similar shapes either have detached finlets behind dorsal and anal fins (*Decapterus* species) or scutes along entire lateral line.

254 Yellow Jack
Caranx bartholomaei

Identification: A rather slender, compressed jack. Pale greenish blue above, shading to silvery below. Juveniles have about 5 vertical dark bars on body. Adipose eyelid moderate, with large central opening. *Upper jaw does not reach to anterior margin of eye.* Small scales over most of body; 22–28 scutes along straight part of lateral line. FL usually to 17¾" (45 cm); may reach 3' (90 cm).

Habitat: Open marine waters and offshore reefs.

Range: Bermuda, Atlantic coast from Massachusetts to Maceió, Brazil; throughout Bahamas, Gulf of Mexico, and Caribbean, including Antilles.

Notes: Young Yellow Jacks sometimes associate with sargassum weed or with jellyfish. This species forages near the bottom, where it feeds on small, bottom-dwelling fishes. It probably spawns offshore from February to October.

Similar Species: Bar Jack, which also has maxilla ending in front of eye, has dark stripe along back, crossing to lower margin of tail. In other species of *Caranx,* maxilla extends to below eye. Other jacks have longer jaws, finlets, and longer dorsal spines, or lack lateral-line scutes.

255 Blue Runner
Caranx crysos

Identification: A *slender,* compressed jack with a moderately pointed snout. Olive to bluish green above, shading to silvery gray to white with a brassy cast below. *Maxilla ends below middle of eye.* Small scales over most of body. *46–56 scutes along straight part of lateral line.* FL to 13¾" (35 cm).

Habitat: Inshore waters over smooth bottoms, usually in schools; seldom around reefs.

Range: Bermuda, Atlantic coasts from Nova Scotia to São Paulo, Brazil; throughout Bahamas, Gulf of Mexico, and Caribbean, including Antilles.

Notes: Although not a highly rated food fish, the Blue Runner is often used for bait. It feeds on fishes, crustaceans, and other invertebrates, and spawns offshore from January through August.

Similar Species: Other species of *Caranx* have deeper bodies and fewer lateral-line scutes.

256 Crevalle Jack
Caranx hippos

Identification: A rather deep-bodied, compressed jack with a blunt head. Greenish to blue-black above, side and belly silvery with yellow overtones. *Large dark spot on upper margin of operculum; large dark oval blotch on lower part of pectoral fin.* Maxilla ends behind posterior margin of eye. Small scales over most of body; *chest scaleless except for median patch of scales in front of pelvic fin.* 23–35 scutes along straight part of lateral line. FL to at least 24" (60 cm); may reach 3'3" (1 m) or more.

Habitat: Shallow flats and nearshore waters. Ascends rivers. Larger individuals are found in open waters, well offshore.

Range: Atlantic coast from Nova Scotia to Uruguay; common throughout Gulf of Mexico and Caribbean, including Greater Antilles; rare in Bahamas, absent from e Lesser Antilles.

Notes: The Crevalle Jack is commonly caught by anglers. No other jack has a spot on the lower rays of the pectoral fin or a patch of scales on the chest. Smaller

Crevalle Jacks travel in schools, large individuals are solitary. These fish produce grunting or croaking sounds.

257 Horse-eye Jack
Caranx latus

Identification:
A rather elongate, deep-bodied, compressed jack. Dark blue or blue-gray above, silvery white below; yellowish wash on tail. Anterior lobe of second dorsal fin black. Sometimes an irregular dark spot on upper margin of opercle, but no spot on pectoral fin. Posterior lateral-line scutes may be dark gray. Maxilla ends below posterior margin of eye. Small scales over most of body; *chest fully scaled.* 32–39 scutes along straight part of lateral line. FL to 31″ (80 cm).

Habitat:
From sandy beaches to well offshore. Enters brackish water in lower reaches of estuaries.

Range:
Through w Atlantic from New Jersey to Rio de Janeiro, Gulf of Mexico, and entire Caribbean. Also off w Africa.

Notes:
In some areas the Horse-eye Jack is avoided because of the possibility that it is ciguatoxic. It travels in schools and feeds on small fishes and invertebrates.

Similar Species:
Crevalle Jack has scaleless area on chest and dark spot on lower rays of pectoral fin. Black Jack is darker, and has maxilla ending below middle of eye. Bar Jack and Yellow Jack are more slender, have fewer scutes, and have maxilla ending before front of eye.

258 Black Jack
Caranx lugubris

Identification:
An elongate, deep-bodied, rather slender, compressed jack. *Gray to dark brown or black overall; fins and posterior scutes black.* Snout bluntly pointed; anterior profile of head steep and straight or slightly concave. Second

dorsal and anal fins have high anterior lobes. Maxilla ends below anterior half to middle of eye. Small scales over most of body. Chest fully scaled. 26–32 scutes along straight part of lateral line. FL to about 3' (90 cm).

Habitat: Uncommon in shallow areas but sometimes seen near drop-off at outer edge of reefs.

Range: Worldwide in tropical marine waters; throughout our area.

Notes: The Black Jack is a distinctive species with an unusual circumtropical distribution. Young individuals seem to be unknown, probably because they live in deep-water habitats.

Similar Species: Other species of *Caranx* are paler overall and lighter below. Horse-eye Jack has maxilla ending behind eye. Yellow Jack has maxilla ending in front of eye. Crevalle Jack has scaleless area on chest and dark spot on lower rays of pectoral fin.

259 Bar Jack
Caranx ruber

Identification: A rather slender, compressed jack. Silvery, blue, or blue-gray dorsally, shading to white with yellowish tone ventrally; *dark line along back extending from below second dorsal fin across caudal peduncle to tip of lower lobe of tail fin. Maxilla ends in front of eye.* Small scales over most of body; chest fully scaled. 23–29 scutes along straight part of lateral line. FL to at least 15¾" (40 cm).

Habitat: Coral reefs and other clear, shallow-water areas.

Range: Bermuda, Atlantic coast from New Jersey to Venezuela, Bahamas, Gulf of Mexico, and throughout Caribbean.

Notes: The Bar Jack is the most common jack in the West Indies and is often seen close to coral reefs alone or in small schools. It feeds on small fishes and invertebrates.

Similar Species: Yellow Jack also has maxilla ending in front of eye but lacks dark line on back and lower lobe of tail.

260 **Atlantic Bumper**
Chloroscombrus chrysurus

Identification: A rather small, compressed jack with *lower profile more strongly curved than upper.* Silvery, darker above (metallic blue in life), with *dark saddle across top of caudal peduncle close to upper base of tail fin.* Upper lobe of caudal fin slightly but noticeably longer than lower. First dorsal fin has 8 spines; second has 1 spine and 25–28 soft rays. Anal fin has 25–28 soft rays. 6–12 small scutes on straight part of lateral line far back on caudal peduncle. FL to 10¼″ (26 cm).

Habitat: Shallow coastal waters and estuaries.

Range: Bermuda, Massachusetts to Florida, Bahamas, Gulf of Mexico, Antilles, and along Central and South American coasts to Uruguay.

Notes: Young Atlantic Bumpers often occur in association with jellyfish, sometimes far offshore, where they are apparently protected by the stinging tentacles of the jellyfish. Adults travel in schools, and spawn in spring and summer.

Similar Species: Bluntnose Jack *(Hemicaranx amblyrhynchus)* also has upper lobe of tail longer than lower but has dorsal and ventral profiles equally curved, and 38–56 large scutes in straight part of lateral line. It occurs in w Cuba and along Atlantic, Gulf, and Caribbean coasts from North Carolina to Brazil.

261 **African Pompano**
Alectis ciliaris

Identification: *Body diamond shaped,* compressed, and deep (body depth 2–2.8 times in FL). *Dorsal spines and separate anterior anal fin spines present in juveniles but not in adults.* Generally silvery, metallic blue above, shading to white below. 12–30 small scutes on posterior straight part of lateral line. Scales small and smooth, difficult to see. Juveniles have 7 dorsal spines, which disappear by about 7″ (18

cm) FL, extremely long and filamentous
second dorsal and anal lobes, very
elongate pelvic fin, and 3–5 chevron-
shaped dark bars on body. FL to at least
4′3″ (1.3 m).

Habitat: Juveniles drift near surface; adults near
bottom to depths of 200′ (60 m).

Range: Worldwide in tropical waters. Bermuda,
w Atlantic from Massachusetts to Santos,
Brazil, Bahamas, most of Gulf of Mexico,
and Caribbean.

Notes: The African Pompano is a solitary fish
valued by sport fishermen as a good
fighter. The young drift in the open
ocean, their long fins trailing. This is the
only species in the family that does not
have dorsal fin spines throughout life.

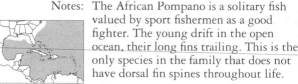

---

262   **Atlantic Moonfish**
      Selene setapinnis

Identification: *A very deep-bodied, short, and strongly
compressed fish* (body depth 1.8–2.2 in
FL). *Facial profile nearly vertical and
concave. Pelvic fin very short.* Silvery, with
faint dark spot along upper margin of
operculum. Juveniles have oval black
spot over straight part of lateral line.
7–17 small scutes in straight part of
lateral line. *Usually 36–42 gill rakers on
first arch.* FL to 13″ (33 cm).

Habitat: Near bottom from shoreline to waters as
deep as 180′ (55 m). Juveniles in bays
and river mouths.

Range: Bermuda, Nova Scotia to Florida,
throughout Antilles, along coasts of
Gulf of Mexico, Caribbean, and South
America to Argentina. Apparently not
in Bahamas.

Notes: The Atlantic Moonfish is sold for food
in Venezuela, although it is not a high-
quality food fish. Adults travel in
schools near the bottom; juveniles tend
to be nearer the surface.

Similar Species: Lookdown and Full Moonfish *(S. brownii)*
have deeper bodies. Lookdown has long
lobes at front of dorsal and anal fins. Full
Moonfish has 34–44 gill rakers; it occurs

in Antilles from Cuba to Guadeloupe,
along Central American coast from
Yucatán to Colombia, and along South
American coast from Guianas to Brazil.

 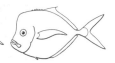

Atlantic Moonfish   Lookdown   Full Moonfish

263, 264 Lookdown
Selene vomer

Identification: A short, silvery, very deep-bodied fish
(body depth 1.4–1.7 in FL) with *high
anterior lobes on second dorsal and anal fins.*
Facial profile nearly vertical and
somewhat concave. Eye small (5.5–6.0
times in head length). Scales smooth,
absent from upper side in front of
second dorsal fin. Pelvic fin elongate in
juveniles, very small in adults. 33–35
gill rakers. FL to 15¾" (40 cm).

Habitat: Shallow coastal waters, over sand or hard
bottoms, often around pilings and
bulkheads.

Range: Bermuda, Maine to Florida, around Gulf
of Mexico, and along coasts of Central
and South America to Uruguay. Rare in
Greater Antilles.

Notes: The Lookdown occurs in schools,
feeding on and near the bottom on fish,
crustaceans, and other invertebrates. It is
reported to be an excellent food fish.

Similar Species: Atlantic Moonfish and Full Moonfish
have lower lobes on second dorsal and
anal fins. Atlantic Moonfish has less
deep body.

---

265 Rainbow Runner
Elagatis bipinnulata

Identification: A slender, fusiform jack *without scutes in
lateral line.* Dorsal surface olive, blue, or
green; ventral surface white; 2 pale blue

stripes along side with broader olive or yellow stripe between them. *Dorsal and anal fins followed by separate 2-rayed finlets.* Anal fin has 2 spines, first separate from rest of fin. FL to 3′3″ (1 m).

Habitat: Near surface in open waters, sometimes close to reefs.

Range: Circumtropical. In w Atlantic from Massachusetts to Brazil.

Notes: The Rainbow Runner is an excellent food fish and a valued game fish that gives good sport on light tackle. It feeds on small fish and invertebrates.

Similar Species: Scads (genus *Decapterus*) are smaller, have scutes in lateral line, and dorsal and anal finlets with 1 ray each. Other jacks lack detached finlets. Pilotfish *(Naucrates ductor)* also lacks scutes but has a fleshy keel on each side of caudal peduncle, 5–7 prominent dark bands, white tips on caudal lobes, first 2 anal spines short and separated from rest of fin, and very small dorsal fin with 4 or 5 spines. It travels in open water with large sharks and other fishes, in our region from Nova Scotia and Bermuda south to Argentina.

266 Greater Amberjack
Seriola dumerili

Identification: An elongate, moderately deep, and somewhat compressed fish. Olive-brown above, shading to pale silvery white below, *usually with diffuse yellow stripe along side. Dark nuchal bar through eye extending to dorsal origin. Second dorsal and anal fins with low anterior lobe.* Anal fin base long (1.4–1.7 in dorsal fin base). Pelvic fin longer than pectoral fin. Supramaxilla (a small bone along upper edge of posterior end of maxilla) very broad. FL to 5′ (1.5 m).

Habitat: Found at all levels, from near surface to bottom, in nearshore waters close to deep reefs. Usually in schools.

Range: Bermuda, Nova Scotia to Brazil, Gulf of Mexico, and Caribbean. Also in e Atlantic, Mediterranean, and Pacific.

Notes: The largest of our amberjacks, this is a valued game and food fish, although it has been reported to cause ciguatera in some areas. The Greater Amberjack feeds on fishes and some invertebrates and will take dead bait.

Similar Species: Almaco Jack *(S. rivoliana)* has higher anterior lobe on second dorsal fin; it occurs in Bermuda, Massachusetts to Florida, Bahamas, Gulf of Mexico, and Caribbean, including Antilles, and south to Argentina. Banded Rudderfish *(S. zonata)* has shorter anal fin base (1.6–2.1 in dorsal fin base); juveniles smaller than 12″ (30 cm) have 6 solid bars on body. It ranges from Maine to Florida, Gulf of Mexico, Cuba, and south to Brazil. Lesser Amberjack *(S. fasciata)* has narrow supramaxilla and nuchal bar not reaching origin of dorsal fin; juveniles have 7 irregular dark bars. It occurs in Bermuda, Massachusetts to Florida, e, n, and w Gulf of Mexico, Cuba, and Puerto Rico.

267 Leatherjack
Oligoplites saurus

Identification: A slender, compressed fish with a nearly straight lateral line (slightly arched over pectoral fin). Dusky blue above, silvery below; sometimes has indistinct bars along side. *Scales needle-like and embedded in skin. Dorsal fin has 5 nearly separate spines* followed by 1 spine and 19–21 soft rays. Anal fin has 2 strong spines separated from remaining spine and 19–22 soft rays. Posterior 11–15 soft rays of dorsal and anal fins form semi-detached finlets. Maxilla ends below posterior margin of eye. FL to about 12″ (30 cm).

Habitat: Sandy beaches in bays and river mouths. Favors rather turbid water.

Range: Massachusetts to Brazil, throughout Gulf of Mexico and Caribbean; not in Bahamas.

Notes: These fast-moving fish travel in schools, feeding on fish and small crustaceans.

The anal spines of Leatherjacks are
venomous and cause painful wounds.
Juveniles have incisor-like outer teeth
and serve as cleaners for other fish; as the
fish grow, their teeth become conical and
their diet changes.

Similar Species: Maracaibo Leatherjack *(O. palometa)* and
Castin Leatherjack *(O. saliens)* both have
end of maxilla extending behind
posterior margin of eye, and usually have
4 spines in dorsal fin. Maracaibo ranges
from Guatemala to São Paulo, Brazil;
Castin from Honduras to Uruguay.

---

268 Florida Pompano
Trachinotus carolinus

Identification: *A deep-bodied, compressed fish with a blunt
snout.* Dusky gray to blue-green above,
shading to silvery below. *First dorsal fin
low, with about 6 separate spines;* first spine
may be resorbed in larger fish. Second
dorsal and anal fins have low anterior
lobes. 20–24 anal fin rays. FL to at least
13¾" (35 cm).

Habitat: Along beaches and sandy shores to
depths of 120′ (37 m) or more.

Range: Atlantic coast from Massachusetts to
Brazil, Gulf of Mexico, and Central and
South American coasts; scattered
localities in West Indies.

Notes: The Florida Pompano is a highly rated
food fish. It feeds on mollusks,
crustaceans, and small fishes. It travels
in schools and moves north in the
summer.

Similar Species: Permit has fewer anal fin rays and high
dorsal and anal fin lobes. Palometa has
deep body, trailing dorsal and anal fin
lobes, and vertical bars on side.

---

269 Permit
Trachinotus falcatus

Identification: *A deep-bodied, compressed fish with a blunt
snout.* Silvery gray, darker above; often
has circular black patch on side near

pectoral fin. First dorsal fin low, with about 6 separate spines; first spine may be resorbed in larger fish. Second dorsal and anal fins have high anterior lobes that do not reach base of caudal fin. 16–19 anal fin rays. FL to at least 3′3″ (98 cm).

Habitat: Shallow waters to depths of more than 100′ (30 m), often over flats and in channels and holes.

Range: Bermuda, Atlantic coast from Massachusetts to s Brazil, Bahamas, Gulf of Mexico, and Caribbean.

Notes: The Permit is a highly esteemed game fish caught on light tackle. It feeds on mollusks and crustaceans, usually travels in small schools, and apparently spawns offshore.

Similar Species: Palometa has vertical bars on side, and longer dorsal and anal fin lobes that reach to caudal fin. Florida Pompano has 20–24 anal fin rays and lower dorsal and anal fin lobes. Cayenne Pompano (*T. cayennensis*) is more slender, has more than 20 anal soft rays, 5 dorsal fin spines, and rather low dorsal and anal fin lobes. It ranges from Venezuela to Paraíba, Brazil.

---

270 Palometa
Trachinotus goodei

Identification: A deep-bodied, compressed fish with a blunt snout. Silvery gray, darker above, with about 4 narrow contrasting vertical bars along side, usually dark but sometimes changing to white. *Dorsal and anal fins have very long, dark anterior lobes* that reach well beyond caudal base. First dorsal fin low, with 6 separate spines. 16–18 anal fin rays. FL to at least 13¾″ (35 cm).

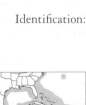

Habitat: Shallow water around reefs and along sandy beaches, often in surf zone.

Range: Bermuda, Atlantic coast from Massachusetts to Argentina, Bahamas, Antilles, and along continental shelf of Gulf of Mexico and Caribbean.

Notes: The Palometa is a strikingly graceful
fish that often travels in small schools,
feeding on small invertebrates and
fishes. Juveniles move north in summer.

Similar Species: The Permit and other pompanos have
lower dorsal and anal lobes and lack
prominent bars on the body.

DOLPHINS
Family Coryphaenidae

Dolphins are large, elongate, compressed
fishes of open water. Their bodies taper evenly from the
head to the base of the deeply forked tail. The single long
dorsal fin begins on the top of the head and extends the
length of the body. The dorsal fin spines are slender and
flexible, not clearly differentiated from the rays. There are
one to three spines at the front of the anal fin. The forehead
is very steep—almost vertical in males, less so in females.

The family contains one genus and two species, both of
which are found in our region.

276   Dolphin
Coryphaena hippurus

Identification: Body compressed, tapering, deepest just
behind head, and elongate (body depth
4 in SL). Brilliant blue-green in life,
with golden sheen on side. Small black
spots on head and body. Dorsal, anal,
and pelvic fins black, anal fin with white
edge; pectoral fin pale. *Dorsal fin very
long, beginning on nape and extending nearly
to tail, with 55–65 rays.* Anal fin very
long, with margin concave in outline.
Caudal fin deeply forked. Small oval
tooth patch on tongue. TL to 6'6" (2 m).

Habitat: Coastal and pelagic waters of open seas.

Range: Worldwide in tropical and subtropical
waters. Occurs throughout our area.

Notes: Both species of dolphin follow ships and
form aggregations around floating
objects, feeding mainly on fishes, squids,
and crustaceans. The dolphin is an
excellent food fish usually marketed
under the Hawaiian name Mahi-mahi.

The brilliant colors fade almost immediately after death.

Similar Species: Pompano Dolphin *(C. equiselis)* has 48–55 dorsal fin rays, unpigmented pelvic fin, convex anal fin margin, and broader and more squarish tooth patch on tongue. It occurs in most tropical and subtropical seas.

SNAPPERS
Family Lutjanidae

Snappers are moderate-size to large fishes with moderately deep, compressed bodies. The dorsal fin is continuous, with 10 to 12 spines and nine to 15 soft rays; sometimes there is a slight notch between the spiny and soft parts (deep notch in the genus *Etelis*). In most species the tail is moderately forked. The scales are ctenoid and rather large; there are no scales on the snout and preorbital region. Most species have a scale-like process at the pelvic fin base. When the mouth is closed the maxillary bone is nearly covered by the lacrimal bone in the preorbital region. Many species have large fang-like teeth at the front of the upper jaw. Some snappers have crescent-shaped or V-shaped patches of vomerine teeth; others have a posterior extension of the vomerine teeth along the midline, making the tooth patch anchor shaped. This distinction is useful for separating some species that otherwise resemble each other.

The family contains 21 genera and 125 species. In our area there are seven genera and 22 species. *Pristipomoides* and *Symphysanodon* are found only in deep water.

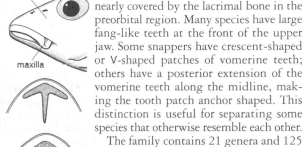

lacrimal

maxilla

vomerine teeth patches

Genera of family Lutjanidae

Etelis   Interorbital region flattened. Last ray of dorsal and anal fin slightly elongate. Dorsal fin deeply notched; 10 spines. Scales present on maxilla.

Pristipomoides   Interorbital region flattened. Last ray of dorsal and anal fins slightly elongate. Dorsal fin not deeply notched; 10 spines. No scales on maxilla.

Apsilus	Interorbital region convex. 10 dorsal fin spines. No scales on bases of dorsal and anal fins. Color uniformly dark.
Lutjanus	Interorbital region convex. 10 dorsal fin spines. Caudal fin moderately forked. Dorsal profile more strongly curved than ventral. Scales present on bases of soft dorsal and anal fins.
Ocyurus	Interorbital region convex. Dorsal fin not deeply notched; 10 spines. Caudal fin deeply forked. Dorsal and ventral profiles about equally curved. Scales present on bases of soft dorsal and anal fins.
Rhomboplites	Interorbital region convex. 12–13 dorsal spines.
Symphysanodon	Interorbital region convex. Dorsal fin without notch, 9 spines. Preorbital region narrow, covering only dorsal edge of maxilla. Probably belongs in its own family.

203 Lane Snapper
Lutjanus synagris

Identification: Body oblong, relatively deep, and moderately compressed. Reddish above, paler below, with 8–10 yellow stripes on side. *Black spot below anterior dorsal soft rays, above but touching lateral line.* Dorsal fin continuous, with slight notch between spines and rays. Anal fin rounded. Vomerine tooth patch V shaped or crescent shaped, sometimes anchor shaped with a short posterior extension. 12 dorsal soft rays. 8 anal soft rays. TL to 19¾" (50 cm).

Habitat: Shallow waters around reefs and sea-grass beds.

Range: North Carolina to se Brazil, throughout Bahamas, Gulf of Mexico, and Caribbean, including Antilles.

Notes: Common in shallow waters, the Lane Snapper is an excellent food fish. This species feeds at night on small fish, crustaceans, and cephalopods. It is often found in large aggregations.

Similar Species: Ambiguous Snapper *(L. ambiguus),* which may actually be a hybrid, has 13 dorsal soft rays and 9 anal soft rays; it is known from Florida and Cuba. Mahogany Snapper has spot on side bisected by lateral line and lacks yellow stripes.

204 Mahogany Snapper
Lutjanus mahogoni

Identification: Body oblong, relatively deep, and moderately compressed. Gray above, shading to silvery below, usually with reddish tinge overall. *Conspicuous spot centered on lateral line below front of soft part of dorsal fin.* Caudal fin has dusky margin. Dorsal fin continuous, with slight notch; 12 soft rays. Anal fin rounded. Vomerine tooth patch anchor shaped. TL to 19″ (48 cm).

Habitat: Shallow water around reefs and sea-grass beds.

Range: North Carolina to Venezuela, Bahamas, Gulf of Mexico, and Caribbean, including Antilles. Rare in U.S. waters.

Notes: An attractive small species, the Mahogany Snapper is common on shallow reefs and often encountered by snorkelers. It feeds at night on fish and small invertebrates, and often forms large aggregations.

Similar Species: Similar Lane Snapper has conspicuous yellow lines on side and spot mostly above lateral line. Black Snapper *(Apsilus dentatus),* a robust, compressed species with a continuous dorsal fin, resembles a *Lutjanus* species but is black to dark brown (paler below) and lacks scales on bases of dorsal and anal fins. It occurs in s Florida, Bahamas, and Antilles, below drop-off, usually near outer wall.

205 Mutton Snapper
Lutjanus analis

Identification: Body oblong, relatively deep, and moderately compressed. Back and upper side greenish, lower side paler with reddish tinge. *Small dark spot* below anterior soft dorsal fin rays just above lateral line. 2 blue lines on side of snout and cheek, uppermost extending through eye to upper margin of gill cover. *Soft dorsal and anal fins have middle rays elongate, making fins pointed.* Pectoral fin long, reaching level of anus. Vomerine tooth patch crescent shaped; no posterior extension. TL to 31″ (80 cm).

Habitat: Over vegetated sandy bottoms in bays and estuaries and along mangrove shores. Also over reefs.

Range: Massachusetts to Brazil, Bahamas, and much of Gulf of Mexico and Caribbean. Introduced in Bermuda.

Notes: This large snapper is an excellent food fish. It feeds day and night on small fishes, crustaceans, and mollusks.

Similar Species: No other snapper with small lateral spot has pointed second dorsal and anal fins. Lane Snapper and Mahogany Snapper are smaller, and have larger spot on side and rounded dorsal and anal fin lobes.

206 Schoolmaster
Lutjanus apodus

Identification: Body oblong, relatively deep, and moderately compressed. Grayish brown above, suffused with yellow, with *about 8 narrow pale bars on side,* paler below. Fins yellow. Blue line, sometimes broken, under eye. Dorsal fin continuous, with slight notch between spines and rays. Anal fin rounded. Scales large, 5 or 6 rows between lateral line and dorsal fin origin. Snout long and pointed. Pair of large canine teeth at front of upper jaw. Vomerine tooth patch anchor shaped with posterior extension. TL to 13¾″ (35 cm); may reach 25″ (63 cm).

Habitat: Shallow waters around mangroves and coral reefs.

Range: Bermuda, Atlantic coast (straying north to Massachusetts), Bahamas, n, s, e Gulf of Mexico, Antilles, and Caribbean to Brazil.

Notes: The Schoolmaster is very common close to shore and around mangroves. It often travels in aggregations during the day, and feeds on fishes and invertebrates, mostly at night.

Similar Species: Dog Snapper looks similar but has larger teeth, smaller scales, and prominent white inverted triangle below eye.

207 Dog Snapper
Lutjanus jocu

Identification: A rather large, oblong, moderately compressed, deep-bodied snapper with *large canine teeth and a tapering bright white bar extending downward from eye to corner of mouth.* Upper side olive to bronze, sometimes with pale bands; lower side reddish, sometimes with coppery tinge. Young have line of blue spots below eye. Dorsal fin continuous, with slight notch between spines and rays. Anal fin rounded. Vomerine tooth patch anchor shaped with posterior extension. TL commonly to 24″ (60 cm); may reach 30″ (75 cm).

Habitat: Shallow waters around coral reefs.

Range: Bermuda, coastal waters from Florida to Brazil, throughout Bahamas, Gulf of Mexico, Caribbean, and Antilles.

Notes: The Dog Snapper is a large and distinctive species whose protruding canine teeth give it a fierce look. It feeds on fishes and invertebrates.

Similar Species: Schoolmaster is somewhat similar but generally smaller and more yellowish, and lacks white marking below eye.

208 Gray Snapper
Lutjanus griseus

Identification: Body oblong, relatively deep, and moderately compressed. Back and upper side grayish; lower side often has reddish tinge. Young have dark band from snout through eye to upper opercle, and blue line below eye. *Margin of spiny part of dorsal fin black.* Dorsal fin continuous, with slight notch between spines and rays. Anal fin rounded. Vomerine tooth patch anchor shaped with posterior extension. TL to 35″ (88 cm).

Habitat: Mangroves and coral reefs to depths of 600′ (180 m); fresh water in Florida.

Range: Bermuda, coastal areas from Carolinas to Brazil, Bahamas, Gulf of Mexico, and Caribbean.

Notes: The Gray Snapper is a valued food fish that is often seen in large aggregations. It feeds mainly at night on fishes and small invertebrates, and spawns in summer around full moon.

Similar Species: Cubera Snapper is larger, lacks posterior extension of vomerine teeth, and lacks black margin on spiny part of dorsal fin.

---

209 Cubera Snapper
Lutjanus cyanopterus

Identification: Body oblong, relatively deep, and moderately compressed. Back and side dark gray with reddish tinge. Somewhat paler below. Anal fin rounded. *Vomerine tooth patch crescent shaped; no posterior extension.* TL to 3′ (90 cm); may reach 5′ (1.5 m).

Habitat: Shallow waters to depths of 130′ (40 m) around reefs and other rocky bottoms.

Range: Atlantic coast from Florida to Brazil, occasionally farther north; throughout Bahamas, Gulf of Mexico, and Caribbean, including Antilles.

Notes: The largest of our snappers, the Cubera feeds on fishes and crustaceans.

Similar Species: Very similar Gray Snapper is smaller and has posterior extension on vomerine tooth patch and black margin on spiny part of dorsal fin.

---

210 Red Snapper
Lutjanus campechanus

Identification: Body oblong, relatively deep, and moderately compressed. Pinkish red, shading to white below. Eye red. *No black blotch at base of pectoral fin, but young have black spot on lateral line.* Dorsal fin continuous, with slight notch between spines and rays. Anal fin pointed, with 9 soft rays. Scales below anterior part of lateral line larger than those farther back. Vomerine tooth patch anchor shaped with moderately short posterior extension. TL to 3′3″ (1 m).

Habitat: Rock bottoms at depths of 33–330′ (10–100 m).

Range: Atlantic coast from North Carolina (rarely Massachusetts), both coasts of Florida, and throughout Gulf of Mexico.

Notes: The Red Snapper feeds on fishes and invertebrates.

Similar Species: Caribbean Red Snapper *(L. purpureus),* which replaces Red Snapper in West Indies and Caribbean, has 8 anal soft rays and larger scales. Silk Snapper *(L. vivanus)* is brilliant red with conspicuous yellow eye; it lives in deeper waters near edge of continental and insular shelves from Bermuda, North Carolina to Brazil, Gulf of Mexico, and Caribbean. Blackfin Snapper *(L. buccanella)* has black blotch at base of pectoral fin; it occurs in Bermuda, North Carolina to Florida, Bahamas, Gulf of Mexico, and Caribbean south to n Brazil.

211 Yellowtail Snapper
Ocyurus chrysurus

Identification: An elongate snapper with *symmetrical dorsal and ventral profiles, and a deeply forked tail.* Upper side blue-gray with scattered yellow spots; lower side pale with reddish overtones. Yellow line along mid-side, narrow at head, becoming wider posteriorly, and encompassing entire tail. Anal fin rounded. Vomerine tooth patch V shaped with posterior extension. 46–49 scales in lateral line. TL to 28″ (70 cm).

Habitat: Coral reefs in shallow waters to depths of 30–60′ (10–20 m).

Range: Bermuda, Atlantic coast straying north
to Massachusetts, Bahamas, throughout
Gulf of Mexico, Caribbean, including
Antilles, and South American coast to
Brazil.

Notes: A mid-water species, the Yellowtail
Snapper is a common and valued food
and sport fish. It feeds on fishes and a
variety of invertebrates. Spawning
occurs throughout most of the year, with
peaks at different times in different
areas.

Similar Species: Creole-fish (family Serranidae) is similar
in shape but is red and has small scales.

212   Vermilion Snapper
Rhomboplites aurorubens

Identification: An elongate and moderately compressed
snapper with a blunt snout and slightly
projecting lower jaw. Vermilion above,
shading to silvery pinkish below. Upper
side has narrow diagonal blue lines
along rows of scales; lower side has
horizontal yellow lines. Dorsal and
caudal fins yellow; anal and pelvic fins
whitish. Last rays of dorsal and anal fins
not elongate. Scales on bases of dorsal
and anal fins. Tail moderately forked.
*Dorsal fin has 12 spines and 10 or 11 soft
rays.* Vomerine tooth patch diamond
shaped. Patch of blunt granular teeth on
tongue. TL to 24″ (60 cm).

Habitat: Moderately deep water (usually more than
330′/100 m) over rock bottoms. Young
in water less than 82′ (25 m) deep.

Range: Bermuda, Atlantic coast from North
Carolina to s Brazil, throughout Gulf of
Mexico, Caribbean, and West Indies.

Notes: The Vermilion Snapper is a valued
commercial species. It lives in large
schools and feeds on fishes and benthic
invertebrates. Spawning takes place over
most of the year.

Similar Species: Other snappers (except members of
genus *Symphysanodon,* which occur in
deep water) have 10 dorsal spines.
Queen Snapper *(Etelis oculatus),* a species

found in deep water (between 440–
1,475'/135–450 m) from North Carolina
to Florida, Gulf of Mexico, Antilles, and
Central and South American coasts to
Brazil, is red in color and has large eyes,
scales on maxilla, and deep notch in
dorsal fin between spiny and soft parts.

TRIPLETAILS
Family Lobotidae

Tripletails are rather large, compressed
fishes with continuous dorsal fins and rounded caudal fins.
The rear of the dorsal and anal fins are symmetrical and extend well back, giving the appearance of a trilobed tail. The
margin of the preopercle is strongly serrate.

The family contains one genus with four species; one
species is found in our area.

193 Tripletail
Lobotes surinamensis

Identification: A robust, deep-bodied, compressed fish
with rounded symmetrical dorsal and
anal fins and *rounded caudal fin that
appear as single 3-lobed fin.* Brownish to
gray, with irregular bars and blotches.
*Young yellowish with brown markings;
they resemble floating leaves.* Preopercle
strongly serrate. Mouth oblique; upper
profile of head concave. No teeth on roof
of mouth. TL to at least 3' (1 m).

Habitat: Usually in open water, sometimes comes
close to shore.

Range: Worldwide in warm seas. In w Atlantic
from Bermuda and New England to
Argentina.

Notes: The Tripletail looks like a grouper, but
its shape and the lack of teeth on the
roof of the mouth are distinctive. It
often drifts near the surface, sometimes
on its side or head down. This may
serve to attract small fishes to it, as if it
were an inanimate floating object. It
presumably eats such fishes. Occasionally
young Tripletails are found in tide pools
along the shore.

MOJARRAS
Family Gerreidae

The mojarras are small to moderately large, compressed, diamond-shaped silvery fishes with large eyes. The dorsal fin is continuous, usually with a shallow but definite notch between the spines and rays. There is a scaly sheath on each side of the dorsal and anal fins. Small juveniles have two anal spines, and in most species the first ray becomes a third spine as the individual grows. The tail is moderately forked. The scales are smooth. The profile of the lower jaw is usually somewhat concave. Mojarras have

extremely protrusible jaws, meaning that they can be extended downward and forward as a short tube. The top of the snout has a median scaleless groove (called the *premaxillary groove*) that runs from the tip of the snout to between the nostrils. This groove in turn covers a trough in the top of the skull

protrusible jaw

that houses parts of the premaxillary bones when the mouth is not protruded. In one species the premaxillary groove is interrupted by a transverse band of scales.

Mojarras have sensitive hearing. They feed by cruising along a few inches above the sand bottom. When they hear a potential meal, they dip down, extend their mouths, and slurp the prey.

The family includes eight genera and about 40 species; five genera and about 12 species are found in our area.

Genera of family Gerreidae

Diapterus	Body deep (depth 1.7–2.4 in SL). Preorbital smooth. Preopercle serrate. Body plain, without longitudinal stripes. 2–3 anal spines, second spine very large and stout.
Eugerres	Body deep (depth 1.7–2.4 in SL). Preorbital serrate. Preopercle serrate. Body has longitudinal stripes. 3 anal spines, second one very large.
Eucinostomus	Body elongate (depth 2.3–3.5 in SL). Preorbital smooth. Preopercle smooth. 3 anal spines as adults, second one not enlarged. Side plain or with irregular bars.

Ulaema Body elongate (depth 2.3–3.3 in SL). Preorbital smooth. Preopercle smooth. 2 anal spines as adults, second spine not enlarged. No distinct markings.

Gerres Body moderately deep (depth 2.3–2.6 in SL), diamond shaped, with well-spaced short vertical dark bars on side. Preorbital smooth. Preopercle smooth. 3 anal spines, second one not enlarged.

Comparison of preorbital areas and preopercles in Gerreidae genera. Left: *Diapterus,* preorbital smooth, preopercle serrate. Center: *Eugerres,* preorbital serrate, preopercle serrate. Right: *Gerres* (also *Eucinostomus* and *Ulaema),* preorbital smooth, preopercle smooth.

213 Spotfin Mojarra
Eucinostomus argenteus

Identification: Body compressed, rather slender. Silvery, without conspicuous markings; *tip of dorsal fin dusky.* V-shaped pigmented area on top of snout in front of nostrils. Preorbital smooth; *premaxillary groove continuous but narrow, bordered by scales anteriorly.* 3 anal spines, 7 anal rays; second anal spine shorter than distance from end of anal fin base to middle of caudal fin base. TL to 8″ (20 cm).

Habitat: Inshore waters, sometimes in estuaries.

Range: Bermuda, Atlantic coast from New Jersey to Brazil, Bahamas, Gulf of Mexico, and Caribbean, including Antilles.

Notes: The Spotfin Mojarra is common throughout our region, but little or nothing is known of its ecology. It probably feeds on bottom-dwelling invertebrates.

Similar Species: Most other species of mojarras have deeper bodies. Slender Mojarra *(E. jonesi),* from Bermuda and Florida to Brazil, and Tidewater Mojarra *(E. harengulus),* from Florida, are extremely similar to

Spotfin and can be identified only by average counts and measurements taken from a series of specimens. Silver Jenny *(E. gula)* is deeper bodied and more robust and has bridge of scales across premaxillary groove, isolating upper end as scaleless pit; it occurs in shallow water from Bermuda, Massachusetts to Argentina, Bahamas, Gulf of Mexico, and Caribbean.

214 Bigeye Mojarra
Eucinostomus havana

Identification: Compressed, moderately slender, with large eye. Silvery, darker above but without conspicuous markings; tip of dorsal fin dark. 3 anal spines, second shorter than distance from end of anal fin base to middle of caudal fin base. *Pectoral fin scaled* (completely scaled in adults; developing on base first in young). TL to 7″ (18 cm).

Habitat: Inshore waters over sand shallows and mud bottoms near mangroves.

Range: Bermuda, Florida, Bahamas, Antilles, and South American coast from Venezuela to ne Brazil.

Notes: The Bigeye Mojarra is a fairly common species, but not much is known of its ecology. It sometimes travels in aggregations, and probably feeds on bottom-dwelling invertebrates.

Similar Species: No other mojarra in our area has scales on pectoral fin. Flagfin Mojarra *(E. melanopterus)* has dorsal fin with black outer margin, white middle, and dusky base, and pelvic fin with dark tip; it occurs in w Gulf of Mexico, Caribbean, and south to Brazil.

215 Yellowfin Mojarra
Gerres cinereus

Identification: Body diamond shaped, compressed, and moderately deep. Silvery, somewhat darker above, with 7 *or* 8 *widely spaced*

vertical bars along side. Pelvic and anal
fins yellow in life. 3 anal spines, second
shorter than distance from end of anal
fin base to middle of caudal fin base. TL
to 15½″ (39 cm).

Habitat: Shallow areas around reefs and over sea-
grass beds.

Range: Bermuda, Florida, Bahamas, n Gulf of
Mexico, around Caribbean, including
Antilles, and South American coast to
Brazil. Also in e Pacific from Baja
California to Brazil.

Notes: The Yellowfin is probably the most
distinctive and easily recognized species
of mojarra snorkelers will encounter (no
other mojarra has vertical bars along the
side). It feeds on bottom-dwelling
invertebrates, but little is known of its
ecology.

Other species of mojarras

Irish Pompano — (*Diapterus auratus*) Body deep; TL to
13½″ (34 cm). Plain silvery. Anterior
dorsal spines long, forming high lobe.
Anal fin with 3 spines and 8 soft rays;
second spine very large. North Carolina
ro Florida, Bahamas, Gulf of Mexico,
Caribbean.

Caitipa Mojarra — (*Diapterus rhombeus*) 2 anal spines, 9
anal soft rays. West Indies, Central and
South American coasts from Mexico to
Brazil.

Striped Mojarra — (*Eugerres plumieri*) Preorbital bone serrate.
3 anal spines, 8 anal rays. Body with nu-
merous dark longitudinal stripes. South
Carolina to w Florida, West Indies, Mexico to Colombia.

Mojarra del Brasil — (*Eugerres brasilianus*) Similar to Striped
Mojarra, but has 7 anal rays. West In-
dies, coasts from Belize to Brazil.

Mottled Mojarra — (*Ulaema lefroyi*) Silvery, darker above,
with irregular brownish diagonal marks
above lateral line. 2 anal spines in adults.
Bermuda, North Carolina to Brazil, Gulf
of Mexico, Caribbean.

GRUNTS
Family Haemulidae

Grunts are small to moderately large, elongate and compressed fishes with continuous dorsal fins and moderately forked tails. The base of the spiny part of the dorsal fin is longer than the soft part, and the soft rays are longer than the last dorsal fin spines. There are three spines in the anal fin. The dorsal profile is usually arched, highest just behind the head, and the mouth is subterminal, low, and horizontal. The maxilla slips under the lacrimal bone in the preorbital region when the mouth is closed, giving grunts a characteristic smiling appearance. The head is completely scaled except for the front of the snout. The posterior margin of the preopercle is slightly concave and serrate. Grunts have small, dense, and blunt cardiform teeth (no canines) on the jaws, but no teeth on the roof of the mouth. There are two pores near the tip of the chin. In most species of the genus *Haemulon* the lining of the mouth is bright red. These grunts are frequently seen snout-to-snout with their mouths wide open to display the red lining; these displays are probably territorial contests. Grunts also produce sound by grinding their pharyngeal teeth.

The family includes 17 genera and about 150 species. Six genera and 23 species occur in our area.

Genera of family Haemulidae

Haemulon	Body rather slender to moderately deep and compressed. Groove on midline of chin. Soft parts of dorsal and anal fins densely scaled to their margins. Preopercle finely serrate. 12–13 dorsal fin spines. Lips thin.
Anisotremus	Body deep. Groove on midline of chin. Soft parts of dorsal and anal fins without scales, or with scales only at their bases. Preopercle finely serrate. 12–13 dorsal fin spines. Lips thick.
Pomadasys	Body elongate. Anal fin short, with 6–8 soft rays; second of 3 spines somewhat enlarged. Groove on midline of chin. Preopercle coarsely serrate. Soft parts of dorsal and anal fins without scales, or with scales only at their bases. Lips thin.
Orthopristis	Body moderately deep. Anal fin long, with 9–13 soft rays; spines small. Soft

parts of dorsal and anal fins without scales, or with scales only at their bases. Preopercle finely serrate. Groove on midline of chin. Lips thin.

Conodon

Body elongate. Preopercle strongly serrate, with 2 enlarged spines at angle; serrations on lower margin directed forward. Soft parts of dorsal and anal fins with scales on interradial membranes. Groove on midline of chin. Lips thin.

Genyatremus

Body short and deep. Chin without central groove. 11 soft anal fin rays. Preopercle strongly serrate at angle. Fifth dorsal fin spine longest. Dorsal and anal fins without scales. Lips thin.

216 Black Margate
Anisotremus surinamensis

Identification: A short, deep-bodied grunt with a blunt snout and thick lips. Ventral profile nearly straight, dorsal profile strongly arched. Silver gray, lighter below; *front half of body darker than rear.* Each scale of upper side has dark spot in center; these form diagonal rows of dots. Pectoral fin clear; other fins black. Juveniles have large spot at caudal fin base. 8–10 anal soft rays. *Soft dorsal and anal fins have dense scales on bases of interradial membranes.* 50–53 scales in lateral line. TL to 24″ (60 cm).

Habitat: Shallow coral reefs and rocky areas.

Range: Florida, Bahamas, Gulf of Mexico, Caribbean, including Antilles, and South American coast to Brazil.

Notes: The Black Margate is an attractive fish, although not as gaudy as the related Porkfish. It feeds on crustaceans, small fishes, and long-spined urchins. The thick lips presumably afford it some protection from the urchin's sharp spines.

Similar Species: Torroto Grunt *(Genyatremus luteus)*, which occurs along coast of South America from Colombia to Brazil, lacks median groove on chin.

217 Porkfish
Anisotremus virginicus

Identification: A short, deep-bodied grunt with a blunt
snout and thick lips. Ventral profile
nearly straight, dorsal profile strongly
arched. *Body striped yellow and silvery blue;
fins yellow. 2 black bars: one from nape
through eye to mouth, another from origin of
dorsal fin to base of pectoral fin.* Preopercle
finely serrate. 9–11 anal soft rays. 56–60
scales in lateral line. TL to 15″ (38 cm).

Habitat: Coral reefs and associated habitats.

Range: Bermuda, Florida, Bahamas, e and s Gulf
of Mexico, Caribbean, including Antilles,
and South American coast to Brazil.

Notes: This common and striking fish is the
only grunt in our region with two
vertical black bars and yellow stripes. It
feeds on a variety of invertebrates
including mollusks, echinoderms,
crustaceans, and worms. The Porkfish
has a close relative in the eastern Pacific,
the Burrito Grunt *(A. interruptus),* that is
very similar in appearance. Such closely
related pairs, called geminate species,
were thought to have been separated
when passages across the Isthmus of
Panama closed up several million years
ago. Some authorities believe that there
may be as many as 100 such pairs of
geminate species.

218 Margate
Haemulon album

Identification: A large, deep-bodied grunt with a large
mouth; maxilla reaches to below front of
eye. Gray above, silvery white on side
and belly, with dusky spot at base of
each scale on upper side; often has 3
longitudinal black stripes along side.
Soft dorsal, anal, pelvic, and caudal fins
dark gray; pectoral fin pale with gray
rays. Black blotch beneath free margin
of preopercle faint or absent. Lining of
mouth bright red. 12 dorsal fin spines.
49–52 scales in lateral line; *scale rows*

immediately below lateral line oblique.
TL to 16½" (42 cm).

Habitat: Sand and sea-grass beds to depths of 100' (30 m).

Range: Bermuda, Florida Keys, Bahamas, Antilles, and South American coast to Brazil.

Notes: The Margate is less distinctively marked than other species in its genus. It is an excellent food fish that feeds on small invertebrates. Individuals brought up from depths of approximately 100 feet (30 m) often develop myocardial infarctions and have been suggested as models for study of heart attacks.

219 Tomtate
Haemulon aurolineatum

Identification: A small, rather slender, elongate, compressed grunt. Dorsal profile not highly arched. Pale gray above, white on side and belly, with longitudinal bronze stripe from tip of snout through eye to base of tail, ending in *large, prominent dark spot;* second, narrower longitudinal black stripe on upper side from nape to below end of last dorsal soft rays. Fins light gray; soft dorsal and anal fins dusky at their bases. Lining of mouth bright red. No black blotch beneath free margin of preopercle. 13 dorsal fin spines. 50–52 scales in lateral line; scale rows below lateral line horizontal, parallel to long axis of body. TL to 10" (25 cm).

Habitat: Shorelines and around reefs and related habitats to depths of about 80' (25 m).

Range: Bermuda, Chesapeake Bay to Florida, Bahamas, Gulf of Mexico, Caribbean, including Antilles, south to Brazil.

Notes: The Tomtate is a valued food and bait fish, and probably the most abundant member of the genus *Haemulon* along the eastern coast of Florida. It feeds on small invertebrates, algae, and plankton.

Similar Species: Striped Grunt also has 13 dorsal fin spines but is rounder in cross section and has oblique rows of scales below lateral line.

220   Caesar Grunt
Haemulon carbonarium

Identification:
: A compressed, moderately deep-bodied grunt with a large mouth (upper jaw reaches past front one-third of eye). Dorsal profile moderately arched. *Pale gray above; belly darker gray. Yellow stripes along side; bronze-yellow stripes and spots on head.* Fins dark gray to black; tail has yellowish-bronze margin. Dark spot beneath edge of preopercle. Lining of mouth bright red. Preopercle serrate in young, smooth in adults. 12 dorsal fin spines. 49 or 50 scales in lateral line; scale rows below lateral line horizontal, parallel to axis of body. TL to 13¾" (35 cm).

Habitat:
: Coral reefs and nearby habitats to depths of 80' (25 m).

Range:
: Bermuda, s Florida, Bahamas, Antilles, and Central and South American coasts from s Gulf of Mexico to Brazil.

Notes:
: The Caesar Grunt often lives in schools around reefs and is considered a good food fish. It appears to be less common in most areas than some other grunt species. Its dark belly and bronze stripes make it easily identifiable.

---

221   Smallmouth Grunt
Haemulon chrysargyreum

Identification:
: An elongate, rather slender grunt with a blunt snout and a small mouth that reaches to below front of eye. Dorsal profile not strongly arched. Pale steel blue with 6 *straight, even, and nearly equally wide bronze-yellow stripes on side.* All fins yellow except pale white pectoral fin. No dark spot beneath edge of preopercle or at base of tail. Lining of mouth bright red. 12 dorsal fin spines. 50 scales in lateral line; scale rows below lateral line horizontal. TL to 9" (23 cm).

Habitat:
: Coral reefs and associated habitats.

Range:
: Southern Florida, Bahamas, Antilles, and Central and South American coasts from s Gulf of Mexico to Brazil.

Notes: The Smallmouth Grunt is an easily recognized species that feeds on plankton as well as small crustaceans and mollusks. It travels in schools, is locally abundant, and is an excellent small food fish.

Similar Species: Similar Striped Grunt has 13 dorsal fin spines and 4 dark stripes on body.

---

222 French Grunt
Haemulon flavolineatum

Identification: A moderately deep-bodied species, with upper jaw reaching to below front of eye. Dorsal profile moderately arched. *Mostly yellow, paler below,* with darker yellow to brownish parallel stripes above lateral line, and 10 or more yellow-to-bronze oblique stripes below. Prominent dark spot beneath edge of preopercle. Lining of mouth bright red. 12 dorsal fin spines; 8 anal soft rays. 48 or 49 scales in lateral line; *scales below lateral line in oblique rows and much larger than those above lateral line.* TL to 8¾" (22 cm).

Habitat: Coral reefs and sea-grass beds from shore to depths of about 80′ (25 m).

Range: Bermuda, s Florida, Bahamas, Antilles, and Central and South American coasts from s Gulf of Mexico to Brazil.

Notes: The French Grunt is a very abundant species, and schools occur almost everywhere around coral reefs. It feeds mainly on small crustaceans. No other grunt has enlarged scales below the lateral line.

---

223 Spanish Grunt
Haemulon macrostomum

Identification: A deep-bodied grunt with *a large mouth* (upper jaw reaches to below center of eye). Dorsal profile arched. *Back and spiny dorsal fin greenish yellow;* belly dusky; alternating wide and narrow longitudinal black stripes along side.

Lining of mouth bright red. 12 dorsal
fin spines; 9 soft anal fin rays. 51 scales
in lateral line; scale rows below lateral
line oblique. TL to 17″ (43 cm).

Habitat: Coral reefs.

Range: Bermuda, s Florida, Bahamas, Antilles,
coasts of s Gulf of Mexico and Caribbean
south to Brazil.

Notes: With its greenish-yellow back and
prominent black stripes, the Spanish
Grunt is an especially pretty species.
Usually seen as a solitary individual
around reefs and nearby habitats, it is
less common than many other grunt
species. It feeds on crustaceans and
sea urchins.

224 Cottonwick
Haemulon melanurum

Identification: A compressed, deep-bodied grunt,
with upper jaw reaching to below pupil
of eye. Dorsal profile moderately arched.
Body silvery white with yellow and
black stripes and *broad black area above
line from dorsal fin origin to tip of lower
caudal fin lobe, including upper part of
caudal peduncle and both lobes of tail.*
Interradial membranes of spiny dorsal
fin pale. Often has dark spot beneath
edge of preopercle. Lining of mouth
bright red. 12 dorsal fin spines; 8 anal
soft rays. 49–51 scales in lateral line;
scale rows below lateral line slightly
oblique. TL to 13″ (33 cm).

Habitat: Coral reefs and sea-grass beds.

Range: Bermuda, s Florida, Bahamas,
Caribbean, including Antilles, and
Central and South American coasts
from Yucatán to Brazil.

Notes: The Cottonwick is a strikingly colored
species (no other grunt in our area has
a silvery body with a black back and
tail) that occurs in schools around
patch reefs during the day. Like many
other grunts, it disperses to nearby sea-
grass beds to feed on small crustaceans
at night.

225 Sailors Choice
Haemulon parra

Identification: A rather deep-bodied grunt, with upper jaw reaching to below front edge of eye. Dorsal profile arched. Gray overall, paler below; scales on side have *brown spots that form discontinuous, somewhat oblique stripes.* Black blotch beneath free edge of preopercle. Lining of mouth bright red. *Pectoral fin of adults densely scaled.* 12 dorsal spines; 8 anal soft rays. 52 scales in lateral line; scale rows below lateral line oblique. TL to 16¼″ (41 cm).

Habitat: Coral reefs and nearby habitats to depths of 100′ (30 m).

Range: Southern Florida, Bahamas, Caribbean, including Antilles, and Central and South American coasts from Yucatán to Brazil.

Notes: The Sailors Choice is an esteemed food fish. It lives in schools around reefs and feeds over sea-grass beds at night.

Similar Species: No other adult grunt in our area has scaled pectoral fin. Similar Black Grunt *(H. bonariense),* which lives in Caribbean and south to Brazil, is similar in shape and color but has continuous, oblique, dark brown stripes. Chere-chere Grunt *(H. steindachneri),* found along coasts from Panama to Brazil, has pearly gray spots in similar rows and large dark blotch at caudal fin base.

226 White Grunt
Haemulon plumieri

Identification: A fairly deep-bodied grunt, with upper jaw reaching to below front of eye. Dorsal profile moderately arched. Bluish gray above, paler on side and belly. *Side of head has narrow blue stripes.* Body scales whitish with pale blue centers. Often has broad black stripe behind pectoral fin, about halfway to tail, and usually black spot beneath edge of preopercle. Lining of mouth bright red. 12 dorsal spines; 9 anal soft rays. 50 or 51 scales in lateral line; scale rows below lateral line oblique; *scales above lateral line much larger than those below.* TL to 17¾" (45 cm).

Habitat: Coral reefs and sea-grass beds to depths of 115' (35 m).

Range: Bermuda, Maryland to Florida, Bahamas, most of coastal Gulf of Mexico, Caribbean, including Antilles, and south to Brazil.

Notes: The White Grunt is an abundant reef species that feeds on crustaceans, mollusks, and small fishes. It is a staple of West Indian subsistence fishermen. No other grunt has blue stripes restricted to the head or enlarged scales above the lateral line.

---

227 Bluestriped Grunt
Haemulon sciurus

Identification: A rather deep-bodied grunt, with upper jaw reaching to below center of eye. Dorsal profile moderately arched. *Head and body yellow with narrow blue stripes continuing along length of body; stripe under eye with distinctive arch. Spiny dorsal fin yellow; soft dorsal and caudal fins blackish; anal fin dusky yellow.* Lining of mouth bright red. Preopercle finely serrate in young, smooth in adults. 12 dorsal fin spines; 9 anal soft rays. 48–51 scales in lateral line; scale rows below lateral line almost parallel to body axis. TL to 14¾" (37 cm).

Habitat: Coral reefs and associated habitats.

Range: Bermuda, s Florida, Bahamas, s Gulf of Mexico, Caribbean, including Antilles, and south to Brazil.

Notes: The Bluestriped Grunt is a common and colorful grunt. It is one of the more abundant species in mangrove and sea-grass areas. It feeds on crustaceans and small fishes.

Similar Species: Similar White Grunt has blue stripes confined to head, enlarged scales above lateral line, and oblique scale rows below lateral line.

228 Striped Grunt
Haemulon striatum

Identification: A rather slender, elongate grunt. Dorsal and ventral profiles about equally curved. Snout short and blunt, so that mouth, although small, reaches to below front one-third of eye. Gray above, white on belly; *side yellow, with 4 narrow, dark brown stripes.* Scales above lateral line have dark margins. Tail generally dark, but with *no black area at base.* Lining of mouth bright red. No dark spot beneath edge of preopercle. 13 dorsal fin spines; 8 anal soft rays. 52 scales in lateral line; scale rows below lateral line oblique. TL to 8¾" (22 cm).

Habitat: Deeper waters, from 40–330′ (12–100 m).

Range: Bermuda, se Florida, Bahamas, Antilles, and coasts of s Gulf of Mexico and Caribbean, south to Brazil.

Notes: The Striped Grunt is a deep-water species that is less likely to be seen by divers than other grunts. It feeds on small crustaceans.

Similar Species: Similar Tomtate has large dark spot at base of caudal fin and scale rows below lateral line parallel to body axis. Smallmouth Grunt has similar longitudinal stripes, but they are brassy yellow and more equal in width; it has 12 dorsal fin spines. Bronzestripe Grunt *(H. boschmae),* which occurs from Colombia to French Guiana, has brownish or bronze stripes; large, prominent spot at base of tail; 13 dorsal fin spines; and scale rows below lateral line parallel to body axis.

229 Pigfish
Orthopristis chrysoptera

Identification: A fairly deep-bodied grunt with *a rather long snout.* Mouth small, end of maxilla not reaching to below eye. Light blue-gray above shading to silver below; *bronze-yellow spots on head.* Scales with blue centers and bronze spots on edges form oblique lines above lateral line and horizontal lines below. Sometimes has longitudinal stripes. 55–58 scales in lateral line. *Soft dorsal and anal fins unscaled;* dorsal and anal fin spines in deep scaly sheath. 12 or 13 soft anal rays. TL to 15″ (38 cm).

Habitat: Sand and mud bottoms.

Range: Bermuda, New Jersey to Florida, n Bahamas, and Gulf of Mexico to Yucatán.

Notes: The Pigfish feeds on small bottom-dwelling invertebrates and small fishes. A temperate species, it sometimes becomes common in southern Florida during especially cool winters, then disappears when temperatures return to normal.

Similar Species: Corocoro Grunt *(O. ruber),* found along coasts from Honduras to Brazil, has 9–11 soft anal rays and orange-brown spots on upper body. More slender Cuban Grunt *(O. poeyi),* from Cuba, is pale metallic grayish blue without darker spots and has 53–55 scales in lateral line.

Other species of grunts

Burro Grunt

(Pomadasys crocro) Olive above, shading to silvery white below, small dusky spots on side. Pelvic and anal fins yellow. Distinct scaly sheath at base of anal soft rays. 53–55 scales in lateral line. S Florida, e Gulf of Mexico, Antilles, South American coast to Brazil.

Roughneck Grunt

(Pomadasys corvinaeformis) Dark lines on lower side. Larger scales than Burro Grunt (49–52 in lateral line). Antilles, Caribbean from Mexico to Brazil.

Barred Grunt

(Conodon nobilis) Brown with pale yellow streaks on side and 7–8 dark vertical bands that narrow toward belly. Fins yellow. Deep notch in dorsal fin. 50–53 scales in lateral line. W Gulf of Mexico from Texas to Yucatán; Jamaica, Hispaniola, Puerto Rico, Lesser Antilles, Central and South American coasts to Brazil.

BONNETMOUTHS
Family Inermiidae

Bonnetmouths are slender, elongate, terete fishes with either a deeply notched dorsal fin (genus *Inermia*) or two separate dorsal fins (genus *Emmelichthyops*). They have forked tails, and the caudal lobes fold in a scissor-like fashion. They lack teeth on the jaws and the roof of the mouth, but the mouth is extremely protrusible, meaning the upper jaws can slide forward to form a short tube. The top of the head is scaled forward to the tip of the snout. Bonnetmouths are fast-swimming, mid-water fishes that feed on plankton and small fishes. Although they have long gill rakers, they don't strain plankton; they are plankton croppers, feeding on individual organisms. Our local species are frequently seen over coral reefs.

The family contains about 10 genera and 16 species; two genera and two species occur in our area.

Genera of family Inermiidae

Inermia	Dorsal fins close together.
Emmelichthyops	Dorsal fins widely separated.

---

231 **Boga**
Inermia vittata

Identification:	A small *spindle-shaped fish with a deeply forked tail and an extremely protrusible mouth.* Metallic blue above, whitish below, with broad greenish stripe from eye to tail, and 3 dark stripes on upper side. *Dorsal fins close together,* first fin with 14 spines. TL to 9″ (23 cm).
Habitat:	Coral reefs.
Range:	Southern Florida, Bahamas, and Caribbean, including Antilles.
Notes:	The Boga feeds on plankton, usually well above the bottom. These fast-moving fishes are difficult to catch and are rare in museum collections, but they are probably much more widespread than records indicate.
Similar Species:	Bonnetmouth is similar but smaller, and has well-separated dorsal fins.

230   **Bonnetmouth**
Emmelichthyops atlanticus

Identification: A slender, fusiform fish with *dorsal fins widely separated.* Blue-brown above, shading to white below. Narrow stripe from top of eye to upper part of caudal peduncle; another stripe from tip of snout through eye to below space between dorsal fins. TL to 4½" (11.5 cm).

Habitat: Swims in schools above bottom. Often over coral reefs to depths of 210' (64 m).

Range: Florida Keys, Bahamas, Virgin Islands, and n South America.

Notes: Because it feeds on plankton and does not take a hook, the Bonnetmouth is rarely caught by anglers.

Similar Species: Boga has dorsal fins close together.

PORGIES
Family Sparidae

Porgies are moderate-size, compressed, spiny-rayed fishes with continuous dorsal fins and forked tails. The dorsal profile is usually more highly arched than the ventral. The rather small mouth is terminal, usually low and horizontal, and the maxilla slips under the preorbital region when the mouth is closed. The snout and suborbital region lack scales; the cheek and operculum have scales. In most species the eyes are large and high on the sides of the head, which gives porgies a characteristic "vacuous" look. Many porgies have incisor-like teeth at the front of the jaws and molar-like teeth at the sides of the jaws. The nostrils are close together, immediately in front of the eyes; the anterior nostril is usually round, without a raised rim, and the posterior nostril may be round, oval, or slit-like. The anal fins have three spines; the pelvic fins have well-developed scaly axillary processes at their bases.

The family contains 29 genera with 100 species; six genera and 19 species occur in our region. We cover those most likely to be seen.

Genera of family Sparidae

Archosargus   Front teeth incisor-like, not notched. Forward-pointing spine embedded in skin in front of dorsal fin. 10 soft anal rays. Posterior nostril slit-like.

Lagodon	Front teeth incisor-like, notched at tips. Forward-pointing spine in front of dorsal fin. 11 soft anal rays. Posterior nostril oval.
Calamus	Front teeth slender, canine-like. 10–11 soft anal rays. No embedded spine in front of dorsal fin. Posterior nostril slit-like. Body deep (deepest behind head), compressed, tapering, with back strongly arched.
Diplodus	Front teeth incisor-like. No embedded spine in front of dorsal fin. Saddle-shaped blotch on caudal peduncle. 13–15 soft anal rays. Posterior nostril round.
Pagrus	Front teeth canine-like. 8 soft anal fin rays. No embedded spine in front of dorsal fin. Posterior nostril oval.
Stenotomus	Front teeth incisor-like, narrower at base. No embedded spine in front of dorsal fin. Posterior nostril slit-like.

232 Sheepshead
Archosargus probatocephalus

Identification: Body deep and compressed; dorsal profile strongly arched. *Gray overall, with dark bar at nape and 5 or 6 broad dark bars on side.* Incisor-like teeth at front of jaws broad, not notched at tips, and not narrower at bases. 3 rows of lateral molar-like teeth in upper jaw, 2 rows in lower jaw. 12 dorsal spines. TL to 3′ (91 cm).

Habitat: Shallow coastal waters and estuaries; sometimes enters fresh waters.

Range: New York to s Florida, Gulf of Mexico, and Central and South American coasts to Brazil. Absent from Bermuda and West Indies to Grenada. Occasionally strays as far north as Cape Cod.

Notes: The Sheepshead is an excellent, highly valued food fish that is caught by trawlers and also on hook and line. It feeds on mollusks and crustaceans.

Similar Species: Sea Bream has dark shoulder spot below beginning of lateral line, and lacks dark vertical bars.

233 Sea Bream
Archosargus rhomboidalis

Identification: Body moderately elongate and
compressed; dorsal profile strongly
arched. Olivaceous above; side
shading to silvery with longitudinal
yellow streaks. *Large dark spot (about
same size as eye) below lateral line just
behind gill opening.* Incisor-like teeth
at front of jaws flat. 3 rows of lateral
molar-like teeth in upper jaw, 2
rows in lower jaw. Slit-like posterior
nostril. 13 dorsal fin spines. TL to
12¾" (32 cm).

Habitat: Mangrove shorelines and nearby
habitats. Enters brackish waters.

Range: Atlantic coast, occasionally as far north
as New Jersey, to s Florida, Gulf of
Mexico, Antilles, and Central and South
American coasts to Brazil. Absent from
Bahamas.

Notes: The Sea Bream is abundant in some
localities. It feeds on a variety of
invertebrates and consumes some plant
material. Although it is caught for food,
its flesh is not considered to be of high
quality.

Similar Species: Sheepshead has 5 or 6 conspicuous
vertical black bars on side and lacks dark
spot on shoulder. Pinfish is quite similar
overall but has notched incisor-like teeth
and dark shoulder spot centered on
lateral line.

234 Pinfish
Lagodon rhomboides

Identification: Body moderately compressed. Ventral
profile arched, but less so than dorsal
profile. Silvery, olive dorsally, with
yellow stripes on side, *shoulder spot
centered on lateral line,* and 4–6 indistinct
vertical bars on body. Front teeth flat,
incisor-like, and *deeply notched; side teeth
molar-like.* TL to 15¾" (40 cm), but
usually smaller.

Habitat: Shallow waters in vegetated areas. Enters estuaries, sometimes fresh waters.

Range: Bermuda, Massachusetts to Florida, around Gulf of Mexico, and n coast of Cuba. Apparently not in Bahamas or rest of Antilles.

Notes: The Pinfish is a common shallow-water species that often occurs in large aggregations. In the northern parts of its range, it may move offshore during the winter. Its diet includes crustaceans, mollusks, worms, small fishes, and some plant material.

Similar Species: Sea Bream is similar but has larger, more diffuse shoulder spot below lateral line, slit-like posterior nostril, and unnotched incisor-like front teeth.

235 Grass Porgy
Calamus arctifrons

Identification: Light olive dorsally, shading to silvery white below, with 7 or 8 indistinct dark bars on side that are narrower than spaces between them and broken into series of vertical blotches. *Usually has dark spot (larger than pupil) on lateral line just behind gill opening.* Top of head between eyes sometimes yellow. No lines on unscaled area below eye, but sometimes indistinct pearly streaks below and in front of eye. Lateral teeth molar-like; 2 rows in lower jaw, 3 rows in upper. 16 pectoral fin rays; pectoral fin does not reach anal fin origin. 43–49 scales in lateral line. TL to 8¾″ (22 cm).

Habitat: Sea-grass beds to depths of 75′ (22 m).

Range: Florida Keys and e Gulf of Mexico to Louisiana.

Notes: A valued food fish, the Grass Porgy appears to be replaced by the Campeche Porgy off the Yucatán Peninsula.

Similar Species: Campeche Porgy *(C. campechanus)* has light and dark lines below eye and lacks dark shoulder spot. It is known only in Gulf of Mexico off n coast of Yucatán Peninsula.

236 Saucereye Porgy
Calamus calamus

Identification: Bluish silvery overall, darker above; scales have blue centers and yellow edges. *Rows of orange spots on unscaled part of cheek. Blue line under each eye.* Lips and isthmus blue; blue spot at upper end of gill opening and at upper pectoral fin base. Third and fourth teeth on either side of upper jaw enlarged and curved outward. Lateral teeth molar-like. Prominent bony tubercle in front of each eye. 14 pectoral fin rays; pectoral fin reaches to anal fin origin. 51–55 scales in lateral line. TL to 14″ (36 cm).

bony tubercle

Habitat: Coral reefs and associated habitats at depths of 20–250′ (6–75 m).

Range: Bermuda, North Carolina to Florida, Bahamas, ne and se Gulf of Mexico, Antilles, Central and South American coasts to Brazil.

Notes: The Saucereye Porgy is moderately common in the West Indies. Adults are found around coral reefs, and the young are seen in sea grass and in sandy areas. This species feeds on mollusks, crustaceans, and echinoderms, including brittle stars and sea urchins.

Similar Species: Whitebone Porgy has larger scales, 16 pectoral fin rays, and purplish-gray cheek without spots. Knobbed Porgy has scattered yellow spots on cheek and longer pectoral fins.

237 Knobbed Porgy
Calamus nodosus

Identification: *Rosy silver with blue centers on scales of upper side;* lighter below. Snout purplish. Bronze-yellow spots on cheek; horizontal blue line below eye. Well-developed tubercle in front of eye. 52–57 scales in lateral line. 14 pectoral fin rays. 11 anal soft rays. TL to 16¾″ (43 cm).

Habitat: Usually over hard bottoms at depths of 23–300′ (7–90 m).

Range: North Carolina to Florida Keys, e Gulf of Mexico to Pensacola, and w Gulf from Texas to Campeche Bank.

Notes: The Knobbed Porgy is sometimes taken in trawls and by hook and line. It is a tasty food fish.

Similar Species: Saucereye Porgy has similar counts and coloring but has enlarged, outward-curving teeth in upper jaw. Other *Calamus* species have 43–49 lateral-line scales, 15 pectoral rays, or 10 anal rays.

238 Jolthead Porgy
Calamus bajonado

Identification: Silvery overall, scales with blue centers and brassy margins. Cheek brassy, with no markings, but appears crossed by white stripes when seen underwater. *Blue line under each eye. Corner of mouth and isthmus have orange cast.* Lateral teeth molar-like. 15 pectoral fin rays; pectoral fin reaches past anal origin. 50–57 scales in lateral line. TL to 27″ (68 cm).

Habitat: Sand and coral bottoms at depths of 20–150′ (6–45 m), occasionally deeper, to at least 660′ (200 m).

Range: Atlantic coast from Carolinas to Brazil, Bahamas, n Gulf of Mexico from Florida Keys to Rio Grande, s Gulf around Yucatán Peninsula, and Caribbean, including Antilles. Absent from w Gulf of Mexico. Occasionally strays north to Rhode Island.

Notes: The Jolthead Porgy is a large and wide-ranging species that feeds on sea urchins, crabs, and mollusks. It is a good food fish caught by trawls, longlines, and hook and line.

Similar Species: Red Porgy *(Pagrus pagrus)* is similar in shape and also has canine-like teeth, but is pinkish with blue spots and has oval posterior nostril; it lives on continental shelf of Atlantic coast from New York to Argentina.

Other *Calamus* species

Whitebone Porgy *(C. leucosteus)* Silvery with irregular purplish-gray blotches on side. Blue lines above and below eye. Dorsal and anal fins dusky with yellowish tinge. Bony tubercle in front of eye not well developed. 16 pectoral fin rays. 44–49 scales in lateral line. Carolinas to Florida Keys, Gulf of Mexico.

Littlehead Porgy *(C. proridens)* Bluish rectangular bars across upper end of gill opening; wavy blue lines below eye. Florida, Yucatán, Greater Antilles.

Pluma Porgy *(C. pennatula)* Bluish rectangular bars across upper end of gill opening; wavy blue lines below eye. Small reddish spot at upper end of pectoral fin base. Bahamas, Caribbean, south to Brazil.

Sheepshead Porgy *(C. penna)* Silvery with indistinct yellow stripes. Dark or dusky vertical bar from eye to corner of mouth; sometimes blue-gray line under eye. Small black spot at upper end of pectoral fin base. 15 pectoral fin rays. W Florida, Bahamas, Antilles, Panama to Brazil.

Spotfin Porgy *(C. cervigoni)* Prominent black area on last dorsal spines and first soft rays. Coast of Venezuela.

---

239 Silver Porgy
Diplodus argenteus

Identification: Body moderately elongate and compressed; dorsal and ventral profiles evenly curved. Silvery overall, darker above with 8 or 9 faint vertical bars that disappear in largest fish. Opercular membrane black. *Large, black, saddle-shaped blotch on upper caudal peduncle* that ends at about lateral line. Front teeth flattened, broad, and incisor-like; lateral teeth molar-like. 56–65 scales in lateral line. 12–14 soft anal rays. Pectoral fin long, reaching to first anal spine. TL to 11″ (28 cm).

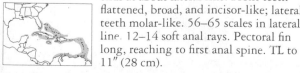

Habitat:	Shallow water around rocky shores and coral reefs.
Range:	Southern Florida, Bahamas, Antilles, and coast of South America from Colombia to n Brazil.
Notes:	The southern population of the Silver Porgy, ranging from southern Brazil to Argentina, is recognized as a different subspecies, *D. argenteus argenteus.*
Similar Species:	Bermuda Porgy *(D. bermudensis),* a Bermuda endemic, has 62–67 scales in lateral line and more slender body. Spottail Pinfish *(D. holbrooki),* which ranges from Chesapeake Bay, around Florida, to ne Gulf of Mexico, has saddle-shaped blotch on caudal peduncle extending below lateral line, but is otherwise similar.

DRUMS
Family Sciaenidae

Drums are moderate to large, slender fishes. The dorsal fin is separated by a deep notch that nearly divides it into two contiguous fins, the first with seven to 13 spines and the second, which is much longer, with one spine and 17 to 40 soft rays. The anal fin has one or two spines and six to 13 rays (except in *Isopisthus,* in which it has 16 to 20). Large sensory canals on the head produce a honeycomb appearance in many species. The lateral line continues to the tip of the caudal fin rays, and the tail is often asymmetrically pointed, with some of the lower rays longer than the upper rays. If not pointed, the tail is truncate or lunate, but never really forked. Some species have one or more barbels on the lower jaw.

Drums are, in general, bottom-dwelling, continental shelf fishes with relatively few representatives in coral reef areas. Many species enter brackish water, but few are truly freshwater fishes. Some are highly valued food or game species. Drums get their name from the low drumming or croaking sounds they produce with special muscles that cause the swim bladder to vibrate. In some species, the swim bladder is highly modified with special diverticulae; these structures provide clues to generic relationships.

There are about 70 genera and 270 species of drums worldwide; about 22 genera and about 58 species occur in our area. We cover only those species that might be seen by divers or caught by anglers.

Genera of family Sciaenidae

Cynoscion	Mouth strongly oblique. Pair of large, non-lanceolate canines at tip of upper jaw.
Macrodon	Mouth strongly oblique. Pair of large, curved, lanceolate canines at front of upper and lower jaws, those of upper jaw larger.
Isopisthus	Mouth strongly oblique. Pair of large, non-lanceolate canines at tip of upper jaw. Body slender. 2 well-separated dorsal fins. 16–20 anal fin rays.
Larimus	Mouth strongly oblique. Jaw teeth minute. Body short and deep. Gill rakers long and slender, 34–36 on first gill arch.
Nebris	Mouth strongly oblique. Body terete. Eye tiny (8–11 in head length).
Odontoscion	Mouth slightly oblique. Enlarged canine-like teeth in upper and lower jaws, pair of very large teeth at tip of lower jaw. Distinct blotch on pectoral fin base.
Bairdiella	Mouth slightly oblique and terminal. Teeth small. Preopercle serrate. Caudal fin rounded to slightly pointed. Top of head not cavernous.
Stellifer	Mouth inferior to slightly oblique. Top of head cavernous and broad (up to 3.4 in head length).
Ophioscion	Mouth inferior to slightly oblique. Top of head not especially cavernous and not quite as broad as in *Stellifer*. Caudal fin asymmetrically pointed.
Sciaena	Mouth subterminal, not strongly oblique; lower jaw slightly shorter than upper. Back not elevated. No canines. Tail pointed. Eye very large (3.5 in head length).
Leiostomus	Mouth low and horizontal. Back elevated. Tail forked. Body short and deep, with oblique dark bars; dark spot behind upper corner of gill cover.
Pareques	Mouth low and nearly horizontal. Dorsal profile highly arched. First dorsal fin moderately high, second dorsal fin with fewer than 40 rays.

Equetus	Mouth low and nearly horizontal. Dorsal profile highly arched. First dorsal fin high, second dorsal fin with more than 45 soft rays.
Sciaenops	Mouth inferior to slightly oblique. No large canines. Body elongate, with 1 or more dark spots on side.
Ctenosciaena	Single barbel at tip of lower jaw with no pore at tip. Anal fin has 2 spines.
Umbrina	Single barbel at tip of lower jaw with pore at tip. Anal fin has 2 spines.
Menticirrhus	Single barbel at tip of lower jaw. Anal fin has single spine. Margin of caudal fin S-shaped, pointed dorsally, rounded ventrally.
Lonchurus	2 barbels at tip of lower jaw, each longer than diameter of eye. Pectoral fin long.
Paralonchurus	3 pairs of barbels in tuft at tip of lower jaw, followed by more than 10 pairs of barbels along inner edges of lower jaw.
Micropogonias	No tuft of barbels at tip of lower jaw; several pairs of barbels along inner edge of lower jaw. Preopercle serrate.
Pogonias	No tuft of barbels at tip of lower jaw; several pairs of barbels along inner edge of lower jaw. Preopercle smooth. Tail truncate or slightly emarginate.

194 Jackknife-fish
Equetus lanceolatus

Identification: A small, elongate, tapering drum with *a very high first dorsal fin with a short base.* Body tan, with 3 broad black bands: first from top of head through eye to corner of mouth; second from nape across pectoral fin base to tip of pelvic fin; *third and widest band from tip of high dorsal fin, curving along length of body to tip of tail.* Second and third stripes edged with white. Rear half (really outer margin) of first dorsal fin white; second dorsal and anal fins pale. Young have similar color pattern, but proportionally much longer caudal, pelvic, and first dorsal fins. TL to 10″ (25 cm).

Habitat: Shallow inshore waters around coral reefs to depths of 180′ (55 m).

Range: Bermuda, North Carolina to Florida, Bahamas, parts of Gulf of Mexico, Caribbean, including Antilles, and south to Brazil.

Notes: The elongate fins of juvenile Jackknife-fish are truly spectacular. The first dorsal and pelvic fins are longer than the standard length of the fish, and the caudal fin is so long that it makes the fish appear eel-like.

Similar Species: No other drum has this distinctive color pattern. Spotted Drum has second dorsal and caudal fins dark with white spots.

---

195 Spotted Drum
Equetus punctatus

Identification: An elongate, tapering drum. *First dorsal fin very high with short base.* Black and white with both bands and spots. 3 broad black bands: first from top of head through eye to corner of mouth; second from nape to tip of pelvic fin and also along belly; third and widest from tip of high dorsal fin, curving along side to base of tail. Longitudinal dark stripes on upper and lower side. Tip of snout dark. Pectoral, pelvic, and anal fins black. Rear half (really outer margin) of first dorsal fin white. *Second dorsal and caudal fins dark with white spots and dashes.* Young have extremely elongate dorsal and pelvic fins, pale dorsal and anal fins, and dark spot on snout. TL to 10″ (25 cm).

Habitat: Coral reefs.

Range: Bermuda, Florida, Antilles, and Yucatán to Brazil.

Notes: The Spotted Drum is often seen during the day around the bases of corals. Its high dorsal fin and striking black and white color pattern make it a favorite of snorkelers and divers.

Similar Species: Similar Jackknife-fish has pale second dorsal and anal fins and 3 broad black bands on tan body, but lacks side stripes and white spots on median fins.

---

196 Cubbyu
Pareques umbrosus

Identification: An elongate, compressed drum. *Pale brown with about 7 parallel narrow dark stripes on side.* All fins dark. Lower lobe of caudal fin rounded and longer than upper. *Young do not have excessively elongate fins.* TL to 10″ (25 cm).

Habitat: Coastal waters from shore to depths of 300′ (90 m).

Range: Chesapeake Bay to Florida, Gulf of Mexico, and Venezuela.

Notes: The Cubbyu is sometimes caught on hook and line, but it is small and not important as either a sport or food fish.

Similar Species: High-hat is also pale but has alternating narrow and wide dark stripes.

---

197 High-hat
Pareques acuminatus

Identification: An elongate, tapering drum. *Black and white stripes on pale head and body; dark stripes more or less alternate in width, with wide bands slightly wider than diameter of pupil.* All fins dark. First dorsal fin moderately elongate in adults. First dorsal and pelvic fins elongate in juveniles, with fewer parallel stripes. TL to 9″ (23 cm).

Habitat: Coral reefs and adjacent habitats, often under eroded edges of sea-grass beds.

Range: Bermuda, North Carolina (occasionally Chesapeake Bay) to Bahamas, Gulf of Mexico, most of Caribbean, and south to Brazil.

Notes: Divers and snorkelers should look for this species along undercut edges of patches of sea grass where the black-and-white pattern serves as camouflage.

Similar Species: Cubbyu has narrow, more regular stripes.

198 Gulf Kingfish
Menticirrhus littoralis

Identification: An elongate drum with a low, horizontal mouth. *Grayish brown above, shading to silvery below; no prominent bars.* Tip of tail blackish; tip of first dorsal fin dusky. Lower jaw has *single, stout, peg-like barbel with pore at tip.* No enlarged teeth in jaws. *Scales on belly smaller than those on side.* TL to 18″ (46 cm).

Habitat: Surf zone along sandy beaches.

Range: Atlantic coast from Chesapeake Bay to Florida, Gulf of Mexico, Caribbean, and South American coast to Brazil.

Notes: A fairly common species, the Gulf Kingfish feeds on bottom-dwelling invertebrates. It is an excellent food fish often caught by sport fishers.

Similar Species: Northern Kingfish *(M. saxatilis)* and Southern Kingfish *(M. americanus)* have diagonal black bands on sides. Northern Kingfish ranges from Gulf of Maine to Florida and around Gulf of Mexico; Southern Kingfish occurs from Cape Cod to Buenos Aires, with a few records in Greater Antilles.

199 Atlantic Croaker
Micropogonias undulatus

Identification: A moderately elongate drum with a small, inferior mouth and *many small barbels on lower jaw.* Silvery gray, darker above. Side with dark spots on scales forming *diagonal dotted rows (but not continuous streaks)* below soft dorsal fin. 8 or 9 rows of scales between lateral line and dorsal fin origin. Preopercle serrate, with strong spine at its angle. TL to 20″ (51 cm).

Habitat: Inshore waters over sand and mud to depths of 330′ (100 m). Also estuaries, where it enters fresh water.

Range: Cape Cod to Florida, n and w Gulf of Mexico, Greater Antilles, and along South American coast from Suriname to Argentina. Its range in s Gulf of Mexico,

Lesser Antilles, and s Caribbean is uncertain.

Notes: An excellent food fish that is taken by commercial fishing boats as well as sport fishers, the Atlantic Croaker feeds on bottom-dwelling invertebrates and fishes.

Similar Species: Black Drum also has many barbels, but preopercle is smooth. Whitemouth Croaker *(M. furnieri),* from Antilles and South American coast from Venezuela to Argentina, has 6 or 7 rows of scales between lateral line and dorsal fin origin, and spots on scales forming continuous diagonal streaks.

---

200 Reef Croaker
Odontoscion dentex

Identification: A moderately elongate drum with *a square caudal fin.* Brownish silver, lighter below, with conspicuous *dark blotch at base of pectoral fin. Mouth large, terminal, slightly oblique, with 1 row of canine-like teeth* in each jaw and pair of larger canines at tip of lower jaw. Preopercular margin smooth. TL to 8″ (20 cm).

Habitat: Coral reefs.

Range: Florida, Antilles, and Central and South American coasts from Costa Rica to Bahia, Brazil.

Notes: A fairly common species, the Reef Croaker is sometimes seen in the day but is more active at night. It feeds mainly on crustaceans and small fishes. Its large terminal mouth and the single series of canine-like teeth with large canines at the tip of the lower jaw are unique in our region.

---

201 Black Drum
Pogonias cromis

Identification: A large, rather deep-bodied, robust drum with a low and horizontal mouth. Silver-gray to almost black, often with brassy cast. Young have 4 or 5 dark

vertical bars; these disappear in adults as
fish get larger and darker. *Many small
barbels along inner margins of lower jaw
bones.* Tail truncate. TL to 5'6" (1.7 m).

Habitat: Coastal waters over sand and mud
bottoms, often near mouths of large rivers
where considerable fresh water enters
sea. Juveniles sometimes enter estuaries.

Range: Gulf of Maine to Gulf of Mexico. Rare
in Antilles and southward.

Notes: The large Black Drum is a popular sport
fish but is not valued as a food fish. It
preys on oyster beds, using its triangular
patch of large molar-like pharyngeal teeth
(located in the throat just behind the
gills) to crush the shells. The combination
of large body size, smooth preopercular
margin, and many small barbels in a row
along side of lower jaw distinguish this
species from other drums.

202 Red Drum
Sciaenops ocellatus

Identification: Body elongate, moderately compressed,
with back not particularly elevated.
Silvery gray to dark bronze above,
shading to paler below, with reddish
overtones. *1 or more conspicuous dark spots
on upper side below end of second dorsal fin or
on caudal peduncle;* number and position
of spots sometimes varies from one side
to other. Mouth low and horizontal,
with lower jaw shorter and fitting inside
upper. No barbels. Caudal fin round in
young, nearly square in adults. TL to
4'11" (1.5 m).

Habitat: Coastal waters and estuaries over sand
and mud bottoms.

Range: Massachusetts to s Florida, and Gulf of
Mexico to n Mexico.

Notes: Also known as "Redfish," this important
sport and commercial fish underwent a
significant decline in numbers when
"blackened redfish" became a popular
dish. Stricter conservation laws have
resulted in some recovery of the

population. It can be distinguished from other drums with inferior mouths and no barbels by its more elongate body and lower dorsal profile.

Other species of drums

Blue Croaker
(*Bairdiella batabana*) Silvery with blue-gray tones. Dark stripes below lateral line, scattered dark spots above. 25–29 soft dorsal rays. 2 anal spines; 8–10 anal soft rays; second spine much shorter than first soft ray. Tail rounded. S Florida, Bay of Campeche, Antilles.

Silver Perch
(*Bairdiella chrysoura*) Similar to Blue Croaker but lacks stripes and spots. Second anal fin spine nearly as long as first soft ray. Connecticut to Florida, Gulf of Mexico from tip of Florida to Texas.

Ground Croaker
(*Bairdiella ronchus*) Gray with faint, narrow longitudinal stripes. Very large second anal fin spine. Caribbean to Brazil.

Striped Croaker
(*Bairdiella sanctaeluciae*) Grayish silver with faint dusky stripes. Second anal spine short. Antilles, s Caribbean to Guyana; isolated population in se Florida.

Silver Seatrout
(*Cynoscion nothus*) Pale silvery gray above, abruptly white below. Protruding lower jaw. Dorsal fin has 26–31 soft rays, small scales covering two-thirds of base. 8–10 anal soft rays. Caudal fin truncate in adults, lower lobe longer in young. Chesapeake Bay to Florida, n Gulf of Mexico to Bay of Campeche.

Sand Seatrout
(*Cynoscion arenarius*) Uniformly yellowish gray, with dusky blotch at pectoral fin base. Second dorsal fin has scales on one-third of base. 25–29 soft dorsal rays. 11 soft anal rays. Tail bluntly pointed, with lower rays longer than upper. Florida, Gulf of Mexico, Campeche Banks.

Southern Weakfish
(*Cynoscion jamaicensis*) Brownish above, silvery below; faint streaks along scale rows above lateral line. 68–73 scales in lateral series above lateral line. Second

dorsal fin scaled more than halfway to edge. 23–27 soft dorsal rays. Tail truncate to lunate. Jamaica, Puerto Rico, Lesser Antilles, Panama to Argentina.

Spotted Seatrout *(Cynoscion nebulosus)* Dark gray above with conspicuous large spots on back and upper side; white below. No scales on second dorsal fin. Tail truncate to lunate. New York to Florida, Gulf of Mexico to Laguna Madre.

Weakfish *(Cynoscion regalis)* Small spots forming oblique lines on back and upper side. Second dorsal fin scaled on one-third of base. 26–28 soft dorsal rays. Tail truncate to lunate. Nova Scotia to s and sw Florida.

Acoupa Weakfish *(Cynoscion acoupa)* Brownish gray to silvery. Bases of dorsal and pectoral fins dark. Dark margins on first dorsal and caudal fins. 80–90 scales in lateral series above lateral line. 17–22 soft dorsal rays. Panama to Argentina.

Smooth Weakfish *(Cynoscion leiarchus)* Bluish or brownish above, silvery below, sometimes with inconspicuous tiny dark spots. Smooth scales; more than 110 scales in lateral series above lateral line. 22–25 soft dorsal rays. Panama to Brazil.

Smallscale Weakfish *(Cynoscion microlepidotus)* Gray above, silvery below. Scales more than halfway up dorsal fin. More than 110 scales in lateral series above lateral line. Venezuela to Brazil.

Tonkin Weakfish *(Cynoscion similis)* Brownish gray above. Dark edges on first dorsal fin. Large ctenoid scales; 55–58 in lateral series above lateral line. Venezuela to n Brazil.

Green Weakfish *(Cynoscion virescens)* More than 110 scales in lateral series above lateral line. 27–31 dorsal soft rays. Panama to Santos, Brazil.

Shorthead Drum *(Larimus breviceps)* Silvery; yellow pelvic fin; brownish spot at base of pectoral fin. Eye moderately large. Antilles, Honduras to Rio de Janeiro.

Banded Drum

(Larimus fasciatus) Dark bars on upper side. No spot at base of pectoral fin. Massachusetts to Florida, Gulf of Mexico west to Texas.

Spotted Croaker

(Ophioscion punctatissmus) Brownish, paler below, with small dark spots on belly. Margin of first dorsal fin dark. 23–24 soft dorsal fin rays. Preopercle serrate. 52–53 pored scales in lateral line. Panama to Brazil.

Ophioscion panamensis

Lacks small dark spots. 20–21 soft dorsal fin rays. 47–49 pored scales in lateral line. Panama.

Banded Croaker

(Paralonchurus brasiliensis) Brownish silvery with about 7 vertical dark bars. Dark spot on lateral line above pectoral fin base. Tuft of short barbels at tip of lower jaw, several pairs of barbels along side. 28–31 soft dorsal rays. 8 soft anal rays. Pectoral fin small. Tail pointed. Venezuela to Argentina.

Blackfin Croaker

(Paralonchurus elegans) Large black pectoral fin. Small eye. Suriname to Brazil.

Longtail Croaker

(Lonchurus lanceolatus) Similar to Banded Croaker. 2 long barbels and 38–40 soft dorsal fin rays. S Lesser Antilles, Venezuela to Amazon.

Deepwater Drum

(Sciaena bathytatos) Light to dark brown. First dorsal and caudal fins have dark margins. Eye large. 21–23 soft rays in second dorsal fin. Colombia, adjacent Caribbean islands.

New Granada Drum

(Sciaena trewavasae) Very similar to Deepwater Drum (shares same range), but has 24–26 rays in second dorsal fin.

Star Drum

(Stellifer lanceolatus) Brownish above, shading to silvery below. Head broad and flat on top; interorbital region twice as wide as eye diameter. Snout blunt. Mouth large, somewhat oblique; lower jaw shorter than upper. 4–5 fairly strong spines on preopercle. Tail pointed. Chesapeake Bay to Florida, e and n Gulf of Mexico to Texas.

Stellifer colonensis	Similar to Star Drum but has less oblique mouth; snout projects slightly beyond lower lip. Panama, Puerto Rico, Haiti.
Sand Drum	(*Umbrina coroides*) Silvery with narrow dark lines that run diagonally above lateral line and horizontally below; may also have obscure dark bars. About 8 rows of scales in oblique rows between spiny dorsal fin and lateral line. 26–31 dorsal soft rays. Florida, Bahamas, w Gulf of Mexico, Antilles, n South America from Panama.
Umbrina milliae	Relatively long pectoral fin. Large eye. Single chin barbel laterally flattened with large pore at middle of anterior edge. Deep water off Colombia.
Umbrina broussonnetii	Similar to Sand Drum but with larger scales (usually 6 rows between dorsal origin and lateral line). Antilles; deep water off Hispaniola, Puerto Rico, Costa Rica to Colombia.

GOATFISHES
Family Mullidae

Goatfishes are medium-size, rather slender, terete fishes with two well-separated dorsal fins and forked tails. They have large heads and a pair of long, slender barbels under the lower jaw. In some genera there is a spine on the opercle near the upper end of the gill cover. The first dorsal fin has seven or eight spines; the second dorsal fin has one spine and seven or eight rays. The anal fin has one spine and six or seven rays.

Goatfishes are rather colorful fishes, usually with reds and yellows. They are bottom dwellers that feed by stirring sand with their barbels as they search for small invertebrates. Feeding goatfishes are often followed by wrasses and other fishes that crop any prey that escapes upward. Goatfishes are capable of rapid changes in pattern and coloration (some change when undergoing a "cleaning" by smaller fishes), and like many other fishes they look quite different at night. Some goatfish species are caught for food and are said to be of high quality.

The family contains six genera and about 55 species worldwide; four genera and four species occur in our area.

Genera of family Mullidae

Mulloidichthys	Opercular spine. Yellow stripe along side. 34–39 scales in lateral line.
Pseudupeneus	Opercular spine. 3 blotches along side. 27–31 scales in lateral line.
Mullus	No opercular spine. No teeth in upper jaw. 8 dorsal spines.
Upeneus	No opercular spine. Teeth in upper and lower jaws. 7 dorsal fin spines.

281 Yellow Goatfish
Mulloidichthys martinicus

Identification: A slender goatfish with a rather short snout and convex head profile. *Body pale tan with distinctive yellow stripe from eye to caudal fin; tail yellow.* TL to 15″ (38 cm).

Habitat: Sandy areas near coral reefs. Often in schools.

Range: Bermuda, Florida, Bahamas, Gulf of Mexico, Antilles, and Caribbean south to Brazil.

Notes: During the daylight hours, schools of Yellow Goatfish are often seen hovering in the shade of sea fans and high coral structures. This goatfish is less brightly colored than other species and is the only one with a single yellow stripe along the side.

Similar Species: Red Goatfish *(Mullus auratus),* a bright red species with head silvery on side, has 2 yellowish side stripes, orange stripe at base of first dorsal fin, and yellow stripe near middle of fin; it lives in slightly deeper water over sand and mud bottoms from Florida to Guyana, Gulf of Mexico, and Caribbean.

283, 284 Spotted Goatfish
Pseudupeneus maculatus

Identification: A slender goatfish with a long snout. Head profile in front of eye straight or very slightly convex. *Body tan to pale pinkish with 3 mid-lateral dark spots* (eye appears as fourth spot). Coloration can change rapidly to nearly all red. TL to 12″ (30 cm).

Habitat: Coral reefs and associated habitats.

Range: Bermuda, Atlantic coast from New Jersey to Brazil, Bahamas, Gulf of Mexico, and Caribbean, including Antilles.

Notes: The Spotted Goatfish is very common on coral reefs. When it visits cleaning stations to be groomed by small shrimps or gobies, it undergoes a dramatic color change—vertical bars appear below each of the spots on the sides of the body. Other goatfishes in our area have convex snouts in profile.

282 Dwarf Goatfish
Upeneus parvus

Identification: A small goatfish with a short convex snout. Color variable: tan to bright red above, shading into silvery white below. Conspicuously marked with *oblique dark bars across both lobes of caudal fin* and dark horizontal bars on both dorsal fins. TL to 12″ (30 cm).

Habitat: Probably over smooth (sand or mud) bottoms to depths of 60–240′ (18–73 m).

Range: North Carolina to s Florida, Gulf of Mexico, Antilles, and Colombia to Brazil. Apparently absent from Bermuda, Bahamas, and w Caribbean.

Notes: The Dwarf Goatfish feeds on bottom-dwelling invertebrates. It is caught in trawls and used for food. No other goatfish in our area has oblique bars across the caudal fin lobes.

SWEEPERS
Family Pempheridae

Sweepers are deep-bodied, compressed fishes with a ventral profile that is much more curved than the dorsal profile. They have large eyes and a single short dorsal fin with four to seven graduated spines. The anal fin is very long, and the caudal fin is forked. Most species are red with brassy or coppery overtones. The lateral line curves upward and runs high on the sides for most of its length, then curves down to the middle of the caudal base, and continues out to the end of the middle caudal fin rays. At first glance, sweepers might be mistaken for some kind of herring because of their deep, compressed bodies and short dorsal fins, but herrings have no spines in the fins. Schools of sweepers are found in caves and shaded areas, often in very shallow water.

The family contains two genera and 25 species worldwide; two species occur in our area.

277 Glassy Sweeper
Pempheris schomburgki

Identification: Body deep and strongly compressed. Dorsal profile gently arched; *ventral profile deeply curved in front of anal fin, tapering upward to slender caudal peduncle. Mouth very oblique.* Coppery brown, shading to silvery red below, with dark line along base of anal fin. Juveniles transparent red. Anal fin long, with 32–34 soft rays. TL to 5⅜" (13.5 cm).

Habitat: Caves and large shaded holes in coral reefs.

Range: Bermuda, se Florida, Bahamas, Antilles, and Caribbean south to Brazil.

Notes: The Glassy Sweeper usually occurs in schools in shaded areas, often in caves and under boulders very close to shore. Its name probably refers to the juveniles, which are so transparent that the backbone can be seen in the living fish.

Similar Species: Shortfin Sweeper *(P. poeyi),* which ranges from Bahamas to Lesser Antilles, has only 23 or 24 soft anal fin rays and lacks line at base of anal fin.

SEA CHUBS
Family Kyphosidae

Sea chubs are deep-bodied, compressed, moderately large fishes with slightly notched dorsal fins and forked caudal fins. The spiny part of the dorsal fin is in a deep groove; the pectoral fin is short. The head is short, the snout blunt, the mouth small, not reaching the anterior margin of the eye. The maxilla slips under the preorbital region when the mouth is closed. The teeth have long horizontal bases, bending upward and ending in incisor-like tips.

The family contains 15 genera and 42 species; one genus and two species occur in our area.

312 Bermuda Chub
Kyphosus sectatrix

Identification: A compressed, heavy-bodied fish with evenly curved dorsal and ventral profiles. Caudal fin V shaped. *Gray overall, with faint yellow lines on side and yellow line* *from corner of mouth to preopercle.* Mouth small; teeth with long bases and incisor-like tips. Head and dorsal and anal fins scaly. 11 or 12 soft dorsal fin rays; 11 soft anal fin rays. TL to 13¾" (35 cm).

Habitat: Reefs and sea-grass beds.

Range: Bermuda, Cape Cod to Florida, Bahamas, Gulf of Mexico, Antilles, and Central and South American coasts to Brazil.

Notes: A common herbivorous fish, the Bermuda Chub is often seen in shallow water near the algal crest at the outer edges of reefs. The horizontal bases of the jaw teeth form a flat striated surface that presumably is used to process the macroalgae that make up its diet.

Similar Species: Yellow Chub *(K. incisor)* has same range, but has brassy-colored lines on body, 13 or 14 soft dorsal rays, and 12 or 13 soft anal rays.

SPADEFISHES
Family Ephippidae

These are moderate-size, deep-bodied and compressed, disk-shaped fishes with blunt snouts and small mouths. They resemble angelfishes but have deeply notched dorsal fins and no spine at the angle of the preopercle. Gill membranes are united to the isthmus, and the upper part of the first gill arch has a comb-like series of short gill rakers. The anterior dorsal spines are long in juveniles, but short in adults.

The family contains seven genera and 23 species; one species occurs in our area.

313 Atlantic Spadefish
Chaetodipterus faber

Identification: *A very deep-bodied, compressed, disk-shaped fish with a very blunt snout.* Pale gray with 3–7 somewhat *irregular, bold, blackish, vertical bands that fade with age.* Preopercle finely serrate without spine at angle. First dorsal fin nearly separate; *second dorsal and anal fins have high anterior lobes.* Caudal fin has slight indentation. TL to 3′ (91 cm).

Habitat: Coastal waters, often on seaward side of reefs; also close inshore and around obstructions.

Range: Bermuda, Massachusetts to Brazil, Bahamas, Gulf of Mexico, and Caribbean.

Notes: Adults are often seen in large schools along the edge of the drop-off. Smaller young are nearly jet black and are often found on white sand bottoms, where they resemble fallen blossoms of mangrove trees. Larger young, which have a high spiny dorsal fin and are brownish without prominent bars, resemble fallen leaves in the water.

Similar Species: Angelfishes (family Pomacanthidae) are similar but have strong spines at corner of preopercle and continuous dorsal fin.

BUTTERFLYFISHES
Family Chaetodontidae

Butterflyfishes are small, very deep-bodied and strongly compressed, disk-shaped fishes with very small, terminal mouths. The teeth are small and brush-like, and there is no spine on the pre-opercle, but there is a scaly axillary process at the base of the pelvic fin. The dorsal fin is continuous, sometimes with a shallow notch between the spines and rays; membranes between spines are deeply notched. The scales are ctenoid and small to moderate-size, extending to the bases of the dorsal, anal, and caudal fins.

Butterflyfishes are extremely colorful, and the species can be identified on the basis of color patterns alone, but the observer should be aware that tiny juveniles may differ in color patterns from adults. The delight of snorkelers, butterflyfishes travel in pairs or small groups over reefs, the individuals keeping track of their partners and interacting with other pairs they encounter.

This family contains 10 genera and 114 species; one genus, *Chaetodon,* and seven species occur in our region.

314 Longsnout Butterflyfish
Chaetodon aculeatus

Identification:

A small butterflyfish with *a long snout.* Yellowish tan above, shading to pale yellow below; dorsal fin dark brown. Dark bar from nape to eye, another from eye forward along snout. No dark bar below eye. TL to 2⅞" (7.5 cm).

Habitat: Deeper parts of coral reefs to depths of 200′ (60 m); occasionally in shallow waters.

Range: Southern Florida, n and s Gulf of Mexico, Bahamas, Antilles, and Caribbean to n South America.

Notes: The Longsnout Butterflyfish is a pretty little fish more often seen by divers than by snorkelers. All other butterflyfishes in our area have a dark bar below the eye.

315 Bank Butterflyfish
Chaetodon aya

Identification:

A rather large butterflyfish with a moderately long snout. Pale tan overall with narrow dark bar extending from dorsal fin origin through eye to behind lower jaw; *broad dark bar slopes down and backward from middle of spiny dorsal fin to base of rear part of anal fin.* Pelvic, anal, and caudal fins yellowish. TL to 6″ (15 cm).

Habitat: Rocky ledges at depths of 66–550′ (20–168 m).

Range: North Carolina to Florida and ne Gulf of Mexico, Yucatán.

Notes: The Bank Butterflyfish is a strictly coastal form that does not occur in the Bahamas or Antilles. Little is known of its life habits.

Similar Species: Guyana Butterflyfish *(C. guyanensis)* has dark line on snout and additional dark bar from rear dorsal spines to top of caudal peduncle. It occurs in se Bahamas and Greater Antilles to Guyana. Other butterflyfishes in our area have vertical dark lines or lack dark bars entirely.

---

316 Foureye Butterflyfish
Chaetodon capistratus

Identification: A small butterflyfish with a short snout and *a large black spot surrounded by a white ring on body below rear of dorsal fin.* Body whitish, with *narrow, dark, diagonal lines that meet at mid-side, forming series of forward-pointing chevrons.* Dark band from nape through eye to lower edge of gill cover. TL to 2⅞" (7.5 cm).

Habitat: Common on coral reefs and related inshore habitats.

Range: Bermuda, Atlantic coast from Massachusetts to n South America, Bahamas, Gulf of Mexico, and Caribbean, including Antilles.

Notes: A delight for snorkelers, the Foureye Butterflyfish is often seen in pairs or in larger groups on reefs. Like other butterflyfishes, if a pair gets separated, one partner will swim upward for a better view in an effort to locate and rejoin its partner. This is the only species in our region with converging lines along the side.

---

317 Spotfin Butterflyfish
Chaetodon ocellatus

Identification: A large butterflyfish with a short snout. *Body plain whitish yellow;* dark bar from nape through eye to behind lower jaw. Fins yellow; soft dorsal and anal fins with narrow submarginal blue bands; large dusky spot at base of soft dorsal fin *lacks white ring.* Males have second spot on rear edge of dorsal fin. TL to 8" (20 cm).

Habitat: Coral reefs and other inshore habitats.
Range: Atlantic coast from Massachusetts to Brazil, Bahamas, Gulf of Mexico, and Caribbean, including Antilles.
Notes: The Spotfin Butterflyfish travels in pairs and is commonly seen by snorkelers and divers. It is the only local species that has a spot without a white ring on the dorsal fin.

---

318 Reef Butterflyfish
Chaetodon sedentarius

Identification: A moderate-size butterflyfish with a short pointed snout. Body yellow above, shading to white below, without spots. *2 dark vertical bands:* first from dorsal fin origin through eye to gill membranes; second, less defined, along rear of dorsal fin, across caudal peduncle, and along rear of anal fin. Caudal fin white at base, shading to dark brown toward edge. TL to 6″ (15 cm).
Habitat: Deeper parts of coral reefs.
Range: Southern Florida, Bahamas, Gulf of Mexico, and Caribbean, including Antilles.
Notes: The Reef Butterflyfish is a very pretty species that seems to be less common than other butterflyfishes in our area. Nothing is known of its habits other than its preference for deeper parts of coral reefs.
Similar Species: Spotfin Butterflyfish has dark spot on dorsal fin and lacks band at rear of dorsal and anal fins.

---

319 Banded Butterflyfish
Chaetodon striatus

Identification: A moderate-size butterflyfish with a short pointed snout. Body whitish with *4 dark bands:* first from near dorsal origin through eye to edge of gill cover, second from front part of dorsal fin to belly, third from rear dorsal fin spines to middle of anal fin, and last from base of soft dorsal

fin across caudal peduncle to soft anal fin. Also narrow dark diagonal lines on mid-side that converge anteriorly. Soft dorsal, caudal, and anal fins have dark band across middle and white edges. Pelvic fin dark with white leading edge. Juveniles (TL to 2"/5 cm) have black ocellus at base of soft dorsal fin. TL to 6" (15 cm).

Habitat: Shallow waters around coral reefs.

Range: Bermuda, Atlantic coast from New Jersey to Brazil, Gulf of Mexico, Bahamas, and Caribbean, including Antilles. Also in e Atlantic.

Notes: The Banded Butterflyfish is one of the most common butterflyfishes in the West Indies. It travels in pairs and is often seen in very shallow water. No other butterflyfish in our area has four dark bands.

ANGELFISHES
Family Pomacanthidae

Angelfishes and butterflyfishes were once grouped in the same family. They are both deep bodied, strongly compressed, and disk shaped, with scaly dorsal and anal fins, but the angelfishes have a large spine at the angle of the preopercle and lack a pelvic axillary process. Most angelfishes are bigger than butterflyfishes, but members of the genus *Centropyge* are generally much smaller. The juveniles of some angelfishes have quite different color patterns from the adults.

This family contains nine genera and 74 species; there are three genera and seven species in our region.

Genera of family Pomacanthidae

Centropyge	14–15 dorsal fin spines. Suborbital with spines. No trailing lobes on dorsal or anal fins.
Holacanthus	14–15 dorsal fin spines. No spines on suborbital. Dorsal and anal fins of adults have long, slender, trailing lobes.
Pomacanthus	9–10 dorsal fin spines. No spines on suborbital. Dorsal and anal fins of adults have long, slender, trailing lobes.

320 Cherubfish
Centropyge argi

Identification: A *very small, oval angelfish* with 2 conspicuous spines below eye and a large preopercular spine. *Body blue; face, chest, and pectoral fin orange; blue ring around eye.* Dorsal and anal fins lack trailing lobes. TL to 2″ (5 cm).

Habitat: Rubble areas around coral reefs, more common at depths over 100′ (30 m).

Range: Bermuda, Florida, Bahamas, Yucatán, and Central American coast to n South America.

Notes: A small but spectacular angelfish, the Cherubfish was once thought to be rare and was actually unknown in the Bahamas until 1959, when the use of self-contained, underwater breathing apparatus (scuba) became common and enabled divers to descend to greater depths.

Similar Species: Flameback Pygmy Angelfish *(C. aurantonotus)* has orange or yellow back and head. It lives in Lesser Antilles to Curaçao.

321 Blue Angelfish
Holacanthus bermudensis

Identification: A large angelfish with lobes of dorsal and anal fins trailing backward, and corners of tail rounded. Body bluish tan; scales on side have yellow edges; *soft parts of dorsal and anal fins and caudal fins have wide yellow margins.* Margins of spiny parts of dorsal and anal fins blue. No blue spot at base of pectoral fin. *Dark spot on forehead lacks electric blue ring.* Juveniles blue, banded, with *last prominent band straight.* TL to 17½″ (44 cm).

Habitat: Coral reefs.

Range: Bermuda, North Carolina to Florida, Bahamas, and Gulf of Mexico to Yucatán.

Notes: The Blue Angelfish is a spectacular coral-reef fish. The Queen Angelfish and Blue Angelfish sometimes hybridize, and the hybrids were at first thought to be a separate species. Hybridization among marine fish species is quite uncommon.

Similar Species: Queen Angelfish has yellow tail and bright blue ring around black spot on forehead.

322 Queen Angelfish
Holacanthus ciliaris

Identification: A large angelfish with dorsal and anal lobes trailing backward. Body bluish green; scales on side have orange centers; *tail and pectoral fins entirely yellow.* Black spot on forehead has electric blue spots and is *surrounded by narrow, electric blue ring. Large blue spot at base of pectoral fin.* Juveniles have blue vertical bands; last prominent band is curved. TL to 12″ (30 cm).

Habitat: Coral reefs and associated habitats.

Range: Florida, Bahamas, Gulf of Mexico, Caribbean, including Antilles, and South American coast.

Notes: The Queen Angelfish is one of the most stunning fishes of the coral reef. Hybrid angelfish also have the entirely yellow tail and a blue spot on the base of the pectoral fin, but they have an indistinct ocellus on the forehead.

Similar Species: Blue Angelfish has duller spot without bright blue ring on forehead; only margin of tail yellow.

323 Rock Beauty
Holacanthus tricolor

Identification: A moderately large angelfish with tips of caudal fin lobes extended as short points, upper lobe usually longer. *Front of body yellow; remainder of body, most of dorsal fin, and all but front of anal fin black. Caudal fin entirely yellow.* Lips black. Edges of dorsal and anal fins have narrow orange margins. Juveniles entirely yellow with black spot on side below dorsal fin; spot surrounded by blue ring in individuals less than 1″ (2.5 cm) long. Spot loses blue ring with growth and expands until it covers most of body and dorsal and anal fins. TL to 12″ (30 cm).

Habitat: Coral reefs. Often seen in quite shallow waters.

Range: Bermuda, Georgia to Florida, Bahamas, Caribbean, including Antilles, and South American coast to Brazil.

Notes: The color changes the Rock Beauty undergoes as it matures are remarkable. This is an abundant species that is easily seen and identified by snorkelers.

324 French Angelfish
Pomacanthus paru

Identification: A medium-size angelfish; high dorsal and anal fins give it a somewhat triangular profile. Caudal fin rounded. Blackish; *some scales on side have crescent-shaped yellow margins.* Yellow ring around eye, and yellow bar at base of pectoral fin. Lips, chin, and tip of snout yellow. Juveniles black with yellow bars and yellow edges on tail encircling central black area, but no yellow crescents on side. TL to 13½″ (34 cm).

Habitat: Coral reefs. Often in shallow waters.

Range: Bermuda (where it may have been introduced), Atlantic coast from New England to s Brazil, Bahamas, Gulf of Mexico, and Caribbean, including Antilles.

Notes: The French Angelfish is a common reef species that allows divers and snorkelers to approach quite closely. It is a favorite subject for underwater photographers.

Similar Species: Gray Angelfish is grayish brown, lacks yellow crescent-shaped scale margins on side, and does not have yellow bar at base of pectoral fin. Juvenile Gray Angelfish has triangular black area on tail, and yellow chin.

325 Gray Angelfish
Pomacanthus arcuatus

Identification: A medium-size angelfish; high dorsal and anal fins give it a somewhat triangular profile. Grayish brown; paler edges on scales give side *a marbled* appearance. *Pale gray around mouth, and pale gray margin on caudal fin. Inside of pectoral fin yellow.* Caudal fin truncate with sharp corners. Juveniles black with vertical yellow bars and yellow on caudal fin surrounding *a semicircular dark center.* TL to 14″ (36 cm).

Habitat: Coral reefs.

Range: Atlantic coast from New England (strays) to Brazil, Bahamas, Gulf of Mexico, and Caribbean, including Antilles.

Notes: Perhaps even more common than the French Angelfish, the Gray Angelfish is easily approachable.

Similar Species: French Angelfish is similar in shape, but is black with scale margins forming yellow crescents on side, and has bright yellow bar at base of pectoral fin. Juvenile French Angelfish has nearly round black area on tail, and black chin.

DAMSELFISHES
Family Pomacentridae

Damselfishes are rather small, compressed, deep-bodied fishes with forked tails and a single nostril on each side of the head. They have a continuous dorsal fin with a shallow notch in front of the soft rays. The bases of the dorsal and anal fins are densely scaled. The lateral line ends below the soft part of dorsal fin, then continues as a row of pits on the mid-sides of the caudal peduncle. They have strong fin spines, with 10 to 14 in the dorsal fin and three in the anal fin. Damselfishes have small, terminal mouths with teeth that are flexible and brush-like, conical, or incisor-like, but never fang-like. Some species produce sound.

There are 28 genera and 321 species in this family; four genera and about 20 species occur in our area.

Genera of family Pomacentridae

Abudefduf	Preopercular margin smooth. Jaw teeth flat, incisor-like. No spines at base of caudal fin.
Microspathodon	Preopercular margin smooth. Jaw teeth flexible, brush-like. Notch in preorbital bone. No spines at base of caudal fin.
Chromis	Preopercular margin smooth. Jaw teeth conical. 2–3 spines on upper and lower margins of caudal peduncle just ahead of base of caudal fin rays.
Stegastes	Preopercular margin serrate. Jaw teeth conical. No spines at base of caudal fin.

241 Yellowtail Damselfish
Microspathodon chrysurus

Identification: A rather large, heavy-bodied damselfish. Teeth of upper jaw numerous, close-set, and brush-like, attached to bones but movable. Teeth of lower jaw broader and more rigid. Body and dorsal, anal, and pelvic fins of adults brown with some blue overtones. *Tail bright yellow.* Juveniles dark blue with transparent tail and *electric blue spots* on side. TL to 8″ (20 cm).

Habitat: Very shallow waters of coral reefs, usually near top of outer edge where there are caves, holes, and abundant fire coral. Occasionally to depths of 30′ (9 m).

Range: Southern Florida, Bahamas, Gulf of Mexico, and Caribbean, including Antilles, to Venezuela.

Notes: The only damselfish in our region with a dark brown body and bright yellow tail, the Yellowtail Damselfish is a very aggressive, territorial species. The striking blue-spotted young— known as "jewelfish"—are favorites of snorkelers and saltwater aquarists. This species feeds to a large extent on filamentous algae.

242 Sergeant Major
Abudefduf saxatilis

Identification: A deep-bodied, strongly compressed damselfish with a single row of incisor-like teeth. *Greenish yellow above, shading to white below, with 5 prominent vertical black bars that narrow toward belly.* Dark spot at pectoral fin base. As breeding male guards eggs, he becomes bluish overall, with dark bars less prominent. TL to 8″ (20 cm).

Habitat: Around shoreline structures and to depths of about 45′ (14 m).

Range: Bermuda, Atlantic coast from North Carolina to Brazil, Bahamas, Gulf of Mexico, and Caribbean, including Antilles.

Notes: The Sergeant Major is a conspicuous species that can be seen around piers and bulkheads and in tide pools. Males guard patches of purple ovoid eggs on vertical hard surfaces. Presumably, its name comes from the dark bars or stripes that resemble the traditional insignia of the military rank.

Similar Species: Night Sergeant is larger and heavier bodied, with broader and often more numerous bars.

---

243 Night Sergeant
Abudefduf taurus

Identification: *A heavy-bodied, compressed species* with a single row of incisor-like teeth in each jaw. *Tawny yellow above, paler below, with 5 or 6 dark bars wider than interspaces between them.* Dark spot on upper base of pectoral fin. TL to 9½″ (24 cm).

Habitat: Very shallow waters along rocky shores. Young in tide pools. Rarely at depths greater than 15′ (4.5 m).

Range: Southern Florida, Bahamas, Gulf of Mexico, Antilles, and Caribbean to Suriname.

Notes: The Night Sergeant is a much heavier-bodied fish than the Sergeant Major and is more restricted in its habitat.

Although both species occur along rocky shores, the Night Sergeant seems to thrive where there is stronger wave action and is therefore less likely to be seen by snorkelers.

Similar Species: Sergeant Major is more compressed, with narrower dark bars that taper ventrally and a smaller spot on upper pectoral fin base.

---

244 Blue Chromis
Chromis cyanea

Identification: A rather elongate damselfish with a deeply forked tail. *Body bright blue, scarcely paler below, with black stripe* from head along back to tip of upper lobe of tail; another black stripe along lower margin of tail. 2–4 rows of conical teeth. TL to 4¾" (12 cm).

Habitat: Coral reefs.

Range: Bermuda, Florida, Bahamas, Gulf of Mexico, Antilles, and Caribbean to Venezuela.

Notes: The Blue Chromis is a striking species, usually seen in large aggregations. This plankton picker works the water column above reefs. Because it feeds by sight, it is inactive at night.

Similar Species: Brown Chromis also has deeply forked tail, but is gray or brown.

---

245 Brown Chromis
Chromis multilineata

Identification: A moderately elongate damselfish with a deeply forked tail. Grayish brown overall, with *conspicuous yellow spot just behind end of dorsal fin base. Margin of dorsal fin and tips of caudal lobes yellow.* Dark bar at base of pectoral fin. TL to 5⅜" (13.5 cm).

Habitat: Coral reefs.

Range: Carolinas to Florida, Bahamas, Gulf of Mexico, Antilles, and Central and South American coasts to Brazil.

Notes:	A plankton picker, the Brown Chromis occurs in aggregations with the Blue Chromis and the Bicolor Damselfish along edges of reefs. Like those species, it is a daytime feeder that seeks shelter in the reef at night.
Similar Species:	Blue Chromis also has deeply forked tail, but is blue and lacks yellow spot at end of dorsal fin base.

Other *Chromis* species

The following species have deep bodies and occur in fairly deep water.

Yellowfin Chromis	*(C. flavicauda)* Bright blue. Tail and outer halves of dorsal, anal, and pelvic fins yellow. Large black spot at base of pectoral fin. Bermuda, Brazil.
Yellowtail Reeffish	*(C. enchrysurus)* Blue above to gray or dusky below. Bright blue V-shaped lines on top of head continuing behind eye to below spiny dorsal fin. Bermuda, Florida, Texas, Bahamas, Antilles.
Sunshinefish	*(C. insolata)* Olive-gray. Large dark spot on pectoral fin base. V-shaped lines on top of head and at rear of eye. Young are lime green above and abruptly dull olive below. Bermuda, s Florida, Bahamas, s Gulf of Mexico, Caribbean coast.
Purple Reeffish	*(C. scotti)* Dark to bright blue. Spot at base of pectoral fin small or absent. Bermuda, North Carolina to Florida, Gulf of Mexico, Jamaica, Belize, Colombia, Curaçao.

246 Dusky Damselfish
Stegastes adustus

Identification:	A short, deep-bodied damselfish with dorsal profile slightly convex from snout to dorsal origin. Short, rounded anal fin does not reach caudal fin base. Caudal fin slightly forked, with rounded lobes. Dark brown overall, with dark margins on scales that form vertical lines on side;

median fin borders sometimes blue. *Juveniles are reddish orange above, with small bright blue spots on forehead* and dark spots at upper pectoral fin base, in dorsal fin, and on caudal peduncle; colors disappear as fish grows larger. TL to 6″ (15 cm).

Habitat: Coral reefs and associated shallow habitats.

Range: Bermuda, Florida, Bahamas, Gulf of Mexico, Caribbean, including Antilles, to Venezuela.

Notes: The Dusky Damselfish is a common, but not flashy, damselfish. There is a possibility that the Brazilian species *S. fuscus* and *S. adustus* are the same species, in which case this species would take the name *S. fuscus*.

Similar Species: Juvenile Dusky Damselfishes are very distinctive. *S. fuscus* from Brazil is very similar but has slightly smaller scales on side. Adult Longfin Damselfishes are similar but have longer anal fin.

---

247 Longfin Damselfish
Stegastes diencaeus

Identification: A short, deep-bodied damselfish with convex profile from snout to dorsal fin. Caudal fin slightly forked, with rounded lobes. *Anal fin long and pointed, reaching well beyond base of tail.* Body of adults uniformly dark brown with little countershading. Juveniles yellow with large black spot on dorsal fin, no spot on caudal peduncle, and blue lines on head that continue as rows of spots on upper part of body and dorsal fin. TL to 5″ (12.5 cm).

Habitat: Coral reefs and associated habitats.

Range: Florida, Bahamas, Antilles, and Yucatán to Venezuela.

Notes: The young Longfin is called "Honey Damselfish" or "Honey Gregory" and for a time was thought to be a separate species called *Pomacentrus mellis*.

Similar Species: Juveniles of Cocoa Damselfish and Beaugregory are similar to Longfin Damselfish juveniles but have less yellow on dorsal surface and lack electric blue stripes on top of head.

248 Threespot Damselfish
Stegastes planifrons

Identification: A short, deep-bodied damselfish with *dorsal profile almost straight from tip of snout to dorsal fin origin.* Caudal fin slightly forked, with rounded lobes. Anal fin long and pointed, tip reaching beyond base of caudal fin. Front of body brownish gray; narrow, dark, slightly oblique vertical lines on side; tail and rear parts of dorsal and anal fins yellow. Dark spots on pectoral base and top of caudal peduncle become less distinct as entire fish becomes dark. Juveniles yellow with large spots on dorsal fin and on top of caudal peduncle. TL to 5″ (12.5 cm).

Habitat: Coral reefs, often in tangles of staghorn coral; anywhere there is abundant algae on reefs.

Range: Bermuda, Florida, Bahamas, Gulf of Mexico, and Caribbean, including Antilles.

Notes: The Threespot Damselfish is a fiercely territorial species that attacks almost any fish that enters its territory. It will attempt to bite the diver who approaches too closely, although it is too small to do any harm. This fish kills corals within its territory by eating the polyps, and then feeds on algae that grow on the dead coral.

Similar Species: No other species has such a flat profile. Dusky Damselfish and Longfin Damselfish lack spots on top of caudal peduncle.

249 Cocoa Damselfish
Stegastes variabilis

Identification: A small, deep-bodied damselfish with head profile curved from snout to dorsal origin. Caudal fin slightly forked, with rounded lobes. *Dark brown or blue above,*

shading to yellow below. *Narrow, dark, obliquely vertical lines on side. Snout and forehead have bright blue lines.* Small dark spot in pectoral axil, *another on top of caudal peduncle.* Juveniles blue above and yellow below, with blue spots and lines on top of head and ocellated spot low on dorsal fin that becomes diffuse and disappears in adults. TL to 5″ (12.5 cm).

Habitat: Shallow waters around coral reefs and associated habitats.

Range: Southern Florida, n Gulf of Mexico, Bahamas, Caribbean, including Antilles, to Brazil.

Notes: The Cocoa Damselfish is a very common and attractive fish.

Similar Species: *S. rocasensis* is larger and has distinctive line of pigment from pelvic fin base to anal fin that forms a ring around anus. It is known only from Atol das Rocas, Brazil, but probably occurs on other Brazilian offshore islands as well. Beaugregory lacks spot on top of caudal peduncle and has spot in dorsal fin toward rear of and well above its base, not spreading onto its back.

250 Beaugregory
Stegastes leucostictus

Identification: A somewhat elongate damselfish. Dorsal profile markedly convex from snout to dorsal fin origin. Caudal fin slightly forked, with rounded lobes. *Dark blue or brown above, yellow below, without obvious narrow vertical lines.* No spot on top of caudal peduncle. 2 prominent electric blue lines on forehead. *Dark spot near back of dorsal fin well above its base becomes smaller in larger fish.* Large dark spot in pectoral fin axil.

Large individuals uniformly dusky with yellowish tail. Juveniles blue above, yellow below, with prominent electric blue lines and spots on head and back. TL to 4″ (10 cm).

Habitat: Shallow waters around mangrove shores and sponge beds. Less common on flourishing coral reefs.

Range: Bermuda, Atlantic coast from Maine (strays) to Brazil, Bahamas, Gulf of Mexico, and Caribbean, including Antilles.

Notes: The Beaugregory is a common and attractive species, often seen in aquariums.

Similar Species: *S. otophorus* lives in waters of reduced salinity in Jamaica and Panama, has black "ear spot" on upper angle of gill cover, and lacks spot on dorsal fin.

251 Bicolor Damselfish
Stegastes partitus

Identification: A rather short and deep-bodied damselfish with head profile curved from snout to dorsal fin origin. Caudal fin slightly forked, with rounded lobes. *Body dark in front, becoming abruptly yellow between last dorsal spine and anal fin origin;* exact delineation varies with locality. Belly sometimes bright yellow. Pectoral fin clear or yellowish; large black spot in axil. No spot in dorsal fin. TL to 4″ (10 cm).

Habitat: Coral reefs.

Range: Southern Florida, Bahamas, Gulf of Mexico, and Caribbean, including Antilles.

Notes: The Bicolor Damselfish is a plankton picker that feeds in mid-water above coral reefs, chasing down individual plankton organisms, often with aggregations of Blue Chromis and Brown Chromis.

Similar Species: *S. pictus* from Brazil is very similar, but upper lobe of tail is pale, lower lobe dark.

HAWKFISHES
Family Cirrhitidae

Hawkfishes are robust small fishes. The lower rays of the pectoral fins are thickened and free at their tips, and extend beyond the margin of the upper part of the fin. The membrane between the dorsal fin spines is deeply incised, and there is a tuft of filaments at the tip of each dorsal fin spine.

There are nine genera and 32 species in this family, but hawkfishes are primarily fishes of the Indo-Pacific region; only one species occurs in our area.

240   Redspotted Hawkfish
Amblycirrhitus pinos

Identification: A small, moderately compressed fish with a rather sharp snout. Body has dark bands on olive background. Upper part has scattered bright red spots. Black spot below soft dorsal fin, and black band around caudal peduncle. Dorsal fin spines have tufts of filaments at their tips. *Lower pectoral rays unbranched and longer than upper rays.* TL to 3⅛″ (8 cm).

Habitat: Coral reefs.

Range: Southern Florida, Bahamas, Gulf of Mexico, Caribbean, including Antilles, and n South America.

Notes: This rather secretive fish will be seen only by the careful observer willing to spend time looking closely at the reef. It is the only species in our area with a combination of tufted dorsal spines and thickened, unbranched lower pectoral fin rays.

JAWFISHES
Family Opistognathidae

Jawfishes are small, rather robust fishes with large heads, large eyes, and large mouths. The dorsal fin is continuous, and the caudal fin is either rounded (*Opistognathus*) or pointed (*Lonchopisthus*). The fin spines are rather flexible and are fully scaled with thick skin. The lateral line is incomplete, ending near mid-body.

As bottom dwellers, jawfishes live in holes they build, either in sand with burrows protected by stones placed like small walls, or in rocky crevices augmented by small stones. Some jawfishes spend much of the day hovering a few inches above the opening of their burrows; others remain in their burrows waiting for prey.

Jawfishes are oral brooders, with males carrying the eggs in their mouths until they hatch.

The family contains three genera and about 90 species. Two genera and about eight species may be encountered in our area; we cover those that are reasonably common in shallow waters.

Genera of family Opistognathidae

Lonchopisthus	Tail pointed.
Opistognathus	Tail rounded.

349 Yellowhead Jawfish
Opistognathus aurifrons

Identification: A rather slender jawfish with *a yellow head. Front of body yellow, shading to blue in rear.* Elongate pelvic fin reaches past origin of anal fin. Area around and above pectoral fin base scaleless. Tail rounded. Bahaman specimens have pair of black spots on chin. TL to 4″ (10 cm).

Habitat: Shallow sand and rubble areas.

Range: Southern Florida, Bahamas, Cuba, and Caribbean, including Antilles, to n South America.

Notes: The Yellowhead Jawfish builds a burrow lined with small rocks in sand bottoms. It is sometimes kept in aquariums.

Similar Species: Swordtail Jawfish *(Lonchopisthus micrognathus),* from s Florida and Gulf of Mexico, has pointed caudal fin and lacks yellow head.

350 Banded Jawfish
Opistognathus macrognathus

Identification: An elongate, heavy-bodied fish with a large head and large mouth. Body light brown with small pale blotches; 2 rows of dark blotches nearly fused to form vertical bars on mid- and upper sides. *Black spot on upper half of dorsal fin from sixth or seventh to ninth spines.* Tail rounded. *Males have long, upcurved extension of maxillary bone marked with black bands.* TL to 8″ (20 cm).

Habitat: Shallow waters over sand and rubble or rocky bottoms.

Range: Southern Florida, Bahamas, Antilles (not in Jamaica), and Venezuelan coast.

Notes: The black bands on the inside of the male's upper jaw are probably used in territorial or courtship displays.

Similar Species: Mottled Jawfish *(O. maxillosus),* from s Florida, Bahamas, and Caribbean, including Antilles, lacks spot in dorsal fin, and has black lining in mouth. Yellow Jawfish *(O. gilberti)* from Bahamas is yellow, and males have dark spot on fifth to seventh dorsal spines. Dusky Jawfish *(O. whitehursti),* from s Florida and Bahamas to coast of South America, has larger scales.

WRASSES
Family Labridae

Wrasses may be small, moderate-size, or large fishes. They vary considerably in body shape; many species are compressed and rectangular, with square tails. There is a single dorsal fin with eight to 14 spines and usually only a slight notch between the spines and rays. The scales are smooth. The lateral line may be continuous, with or without an abrupt curve below the posterior part of the dorsal fin, or it may be interrupted in the same region of the dorsal fin. Wrasses are closely related to parrotfishes, but their teeth—strong and canine-like, and sometimes protruding—are never fused into beak-like structures. Most species have one or two pairs of teeth that are enlarged as canines at the front of the jaws, and some genera have an isolated posterior canine tooth on each side of the upper jaw near the corner of the mouth. This posterior canine points outward and forward, rather than downward. Unlike parrotfishes, wrasses do not have a pharyngeal mill.

Most wrasses are brightly colored, and many have three distinct color phases: those of juveniles, those of the young adults of both sexes and older females, and those of *terminal males,* also called *supermales.* The supermale spawns with an individual female, while non-terminal males spawn in groups with similarly colored females. Some species of wrasses have two kinds of males: those that start life as males, and those that complete a female phase before transforming into males.

The family contains about 60 genera and 500 species; eight genera and about 18 species occur in our area.

Genera of family Labridae

Bodianus

12 dorsal fin spines. Snout pointed, with large canine teeth in front of jaws. Posterior canine on upper jaw near corner of mouth. Lateral line continuous, without abrupt curve.

Lachnolaimus

14 dorsal fin spines; first 3 filamentous, with deeply incised membranes. Lateral line continuous, without abrupt curve.

Clepticus

12 dorsal fin spines. Snout blunt, with small and weak canine teeth in front of jaws. No posterior canine. Lateral line continuous, without abrupt curve.

Decodon

11 dorsal fin spines. No scales on dorsal or anal fin base. Red above, paler below; no conspicuous color pattern, but head and side have yellow lines.

Doratonotus

9 dorsal fin spines. Lateral line interrupted. Side of head covered with scales. Posterior canine present. Body very small.

Thalassoma

8 dorsal fin spines. Lateral line continuous, with abrupt curve below soft dorsal fin. No posterior canine.

Halichoeres

9 dorsal fin spines. Lateral line continuous, with abrupt curve below soft dorsal fin. Posterior canine present.

Xyrichtys

9 dorsal fin spines. Lateral line interrupted. Side of cheek unscaled. No posterior canine. Head and body strongly compressed. (This genus was formerly known as *Hemipteronotus*.)

285 Spanish Hogfish
Bodianus rufus

Identification: A robust, elongate fish with tips of tail, pelvic fin, and central rays of dorsal and anal fins extended as pointed lobes. *Head, upper front part of body, and front of dorsal fin blue if from shallow water, red if from deep; rest of body and tail yellow. Dorsal, anal, and pelvic fins mostly blue or red-yellow at rear.* Black spot on front of dorsal fin. Pectoral fin unmarked, transparent. 17–19 gill rakers on first arch. TL to 15″ (38 cm).

Habitat: Coral reefs and associated habitats from shoreline to depths of 200′ (60 m).

Range: Eastern and w Atlantic. Bermuda, s Florida, Bahamas, Gulf of Mexico, Antilles, and Central and South American coasts; also Brazil.

Notes: The Spanish Hogfish is a common and conspicuous species on coral reefs. The blue and yellow young strongly resemble the Royal Gramma (family Grammatidae) and often serve as cleaners of larger fish. This species feeds on crabs, brittle stars, sea urchins, and snails.

Similar Species: Spotfin Hogfish is similar, but its dark parts are red, and it has dark blotch on upper lobe of pectoral fin and white stripe on lower side.

286 Spotfin Hogfish
Bodianus pulchellus

Identification: Body elongate, moderately compressed. Snout pointed. *Red with white stripe on lower side.* Rear of dorsal fin, upper part of caudal peduncle, and caudal fin yellow. *Black spot at base of anterior dorsal spines.* Black blotch at tip of upper part of pectoral fin. TL to 9½″ (24 cm).

Habitat: Deep reefs and rocky areas at depths of 50–400′ (15–120 m).

Range: Bermuda, South Carolina to n Florida, n and w Gulf of Mexico, Yucatán, and Caribbean, including Antilles, to Brazil.

Notes: This is a very distinctive and colorful species that feeds mainly on crustaceans.

Similar Species: Spanish Hogfish is blue and yellow, and lacks spot at tip of pectoral fin.

287 Hogfish
Lachnolaimus maximus

Identification: A large, compressed, *deep-bodied wrasse with a strongly arched dorsal profile. First 3 dorsal spines filamentous;* middle soft rays of dorsal and anal fins form high, pointed lobes. Color highly variable: reddish brown to pale gray with red vermiculations on side of head. Large individuals have dark face and nape. Usually prominent black blotch at base of last dorsal soft rays. Snout pointed; jaws very protrusible, with thick lips. TL to 3′ (91 cm).

Habitat: Coral reefs and shallow habitats.

Range: Bermuda, Nova Scotia to s Florida, Bahamas, Gulf of Mexico, Antilles, and w Caribbean to Guianas.

Notes: The Hogfish is a spectacular fish and the only wrasse with elongate dorsal spines and such a highly arched profile. Sometimes sold as "Hog Snapper" or "Hognose Snapper," the Hogfish is an excellent food fish.

288 Creole Wrasse
Clepticus parrae

Identification: A moderately elongate, compressed fish with *equally curved upper and lower profiles.* Caudal fin deeply lunate. Color somewhat variable: usually blue or dark purple above shading to purple below, and yellowish on lower part of rear of body. Pelvic fin, rear of dorsal fin, anal fin, and margin of tail yellow. Large adults often have black face. Juveniles have dark submarginal bands along upper and lower margins of tail; smaller juveniles have about 6 dusky bands on upper side. Mouth small. TL to 12″ (30 cm).

Habitat: Mid-water over reefs, especially near drop-off.

Range: Bermuda, s Florida, Bahamas, and Caribbean, including Antilles.

Notes: The Creole Wrasse feeds in schools in mid-water along the edges of reefs and is often seen in mixed schools with the Blue Chromis. A plankton cropper, it snatches individual organisms one at a time.

Similar Species: Blue Chromis (family Pomacentridae) is similar in habits and coloration but is smaller, deeper bodied, and blue rather than purple.

---

289 Bluehead
Thalassoma bifasciatum

Identification: An elongate, compressed fish with a blunt snout and *8 dorsal spines.* Juveniles, young adults of both sexes, and older females *yellow with broad dark stripe along side,* dark bands along upper and lower edges of tail, and prominent spot in front of dorsal fin. *Supermales have blue head separated from green body by 2 vertical black bars with pale blue band between them;* caudal fin with dark upper and lower margins and elongate lobes. Upper and lower jaws have conical teeth that are progressively longer toward front. TL to 5″ (12.5 cm).

Habitat: Coral reefs and associated habitats; most abundant near top of reef in shallow waters.

Range: Bermuda, Atlantic coast of Florida, Bahamas, Gulf of Mexico, and Caribbean, including Antilles, to n South America.

Notes: The Bluehead is a very common species that can be seen spawning at midday throughout the year. Supermales establish harems and spawn with individual females. Yellow-phase males and females spawn in groups. No other wrasse in our region has eight dorsal fin spines.

290 Slippery Dick
Halichoeres bivittatus

Identification: A moderately large, elongate, and compressed wrasse. No distinct juvenile or supermale color phases. Greenish gray overall, with *2 narrow dark stripes:* first from snout through eye to base of caudal fin; second from lower end of pectoral fin base to lower part of caudal peduncle (lower stripe fades in large individuals). Small black spot at rear base of dorsal fin; black spot also within upper stripe near margin of operculum. Ends of caudal fin lobes black in large fish. 2 pairs of enlarged teeth at front of lower jaw. 12 anal soft rays. TL to 7″ (18 cm).

Habitat: Coral reefs and associated habitats.

Range: Bermuda, North Carolina to Florida, Bahamas, Gulf of Mexico, Antilles, and coasts of Central and South America to Brazil.

Notes: The Slippery Dick, easily distinguished by its stripes, is very common in a variety of shallow-water habitats. It feeds on crabs, sea urchins, polychaetes, mollusks, and brittle stars.

291 Yellowcheek Wrasse
Halichoeres cyanocephalus

Identification: Body elongate and compressed. Juveniles, young adults of both sexes, and females *yellow with broad blue stripe* from eye to center of caudal fin. Black spots on nape behind eye; narrow lines radiate from rear of eye; dark streak from upper hind part of eye to dorsal fin origin. Dorsal fin black with narrow blue margin; in supermales blue stripe is very dark, almost black, and extends onto dorsal surface of body and dorsal fin. 12 dorsal soft rays. 2 pairs of enlarged canine teeth in lower jaw. TL to 8″ (20 cm).

Habitat: Coral reefs and associated habitats. Usually at depths of 90–300′ (27–90 m), but seen at 30′ (9 m) in Belize.

Range: Florida, Antilles, and Central and South
         American coasts to Brazil.

Notes: The blue and yellow young adults of the
         Yellowcheek Wrasse are especially
         beautiful. This is the only *Halichoeres*
         species in our region with 12 dorsal rays;
         all others have 11.

292 Yellowhead Wrasse
Halichoeres garnoti

Identification: A moderate-size, elongate, and
                 compressed wrasse with 3 distinct color
                 phases: *Juveniles yellow with silvery blue
                 stripe along side;* larger juveniles, young
                 adults of both sexes, and females almost
                 all yellow with various blue lines in dorsal
                 and caudal fins, and anal fin orange-red
                 with blue margin. *Supermales have black
                 vertical bar behind tip of pectoral fin, merging
                 with broad black area on upper side,
                 continuing to top of caudal peduncle and upper
                 caudal fin;* head and body bright yellow
                 in front of black bar; scales behind black
                 bar green with dusky centers. 2 pairs of
                 enlarged canines at front of lower jaw. 12
                 soft anal fin rays. TL to 6½″ (16.5 cm).

Habitat: Coral reefs and associated habitats to
          depths of 200′ (60 m).

Range: Bermuda, Florida, Bahamas, Caribbean,
          including Antilles, to Brazil.

Notes: A very common and attractive fish, the
          Yellowhead Wrasse is easily distinguished
          by its color pattern. Both the blue-
          striped juveniles and the supermales are
          spectacular sights for snorkelers and
          divers. This is one of the easiest wrasses
          to identify at all its stages.

293 Clown Wrasse
Halichoeres maculipinna

Identification: Body elongate, compressed. Juveniles,
                 young adults of both sexes, and adult
                 females pale with prominent *wide black
                 stripe through eye to base of tail, bordered
                 above by prominent gold line.* Small distinct

black spot at end of dorsal fin base, another at upper end of pectoral fin base. Larger juveniles have dark spot on middle dorsal fin spines. Supermales green above, abruptly paler below, with *large black spot on mid-side* above origin of anal fin and orange-red spots and lines on head. Single pair of enlarged canine teeth at front of lower jaw. Anal fin has 3 spines and 11 soft rays. TL to 5½" (14 cm).

Habitat: Reefs and associated habitats to depths of at least 80' (25 m).

Range: Bermuda, North Carolina to Florida, Bahamas, Caribbean, including Antilles, and Natal, Brazil.

Notes: A common and easily observed species, the Clown Wrasse tends to be solitary and wary, and can be difficult to approach.

Similar Species: Other *Halichoeres* species in our area have 2 pairs of enlarged canines and 12 soft anal rays. Bluehead juveniles resemble Clown Wrasse young adults and females but have narrower side stripe without prominent golden line.

---

294 Rainbow Wrasse
Halichoeres pictus

Identification: *An elongate, slender fish, less compressed than other wrasses.* Juveniles, young adults of both sexes, and females brown above, shading to white below, with yellowish-brown stripe from snout through eye to caudal fin base, separated from dark dorsal region by narrow pale stripe; fins pale. Supermales blue-green above, shading to pale green behind; lower half of body pale blue; head has longitudinal blue stripes. Large dark spot on caudal peduncle. TL to 3¾" (9.5 cm).

Habitat: Coral reefs at depths of 20–70' (6–21 m).

Range: Bahamas and Caribbean, including Antilles.

Notes: The Rainbow Wrasse is a beautiful wrasse that feeds in mid-water above coral reefs. Easily confused with Slippery Dick and Clown Wrasse juveniles, it is not often recognized and is probably less common than other wrasses that live at comparable depths.

Similar Species: All other species of genus *Halichoeres* are deeper bodied and more compressed. Young Blueheads are similar to juvenile Rainbow Wrasses but have prominent spot in dorsal fin and broader mid-lateral stripe.

---

295 Blackear Wrasse
Halichoeres poeyi

Identification: An elongate and compressed wrasse. Juveniles, young adults of both sexes, and adult females *green with conspicuous, usually dark spot behind eye.* Small black spot at rear of dorsal fin base. Supermales have greenish background, some scales on side with orange spot ringed with blue. Head has orange-red bars. Large black spot behind eye somewhat obscure. 2 pairs of enlarged teeth at front of lower jaw. 12 soft anal rays. Caudal fin bluntly pointed or slightly trilobed in large adults. Several pores on each lateral-line scale. TL to 6¾" (17 cm).

Habitat: Turtle grass, sometimes on coral reefs. Often in very shallow water.

Range: Florida, Bahamas, and Caribbean, including Antilles, to Bahia and Rio de Janeiro, Brazil.

Notes: The green color of the young adults of this species is remarkably similar to the color of turtle grass. Little is known of the ecology of the Blackear Wrasse.

Similar Species: Painted Wrasse *(H. caudalis)* has small, faint blue spot behind eye and single opening on each lateral-line scale. It occurs from North Carolina to Florida, Gulf of Mexico, and Antilles to Suriname.

---

296 Puddingwife
Halichoeres radiatus

Identification: A large, *strongly compressed, rather deep-bodied wrasse.* Juveniles orange above, with 4 saddle-shaped blotches along dorsal fin base and large prominent dark spot at caudal fin base. Third blotch largest, extending onto dorsal fin. 2 bright orange stripes: first from eye to middle of caudal fin base, second from pectoral fin base to lower edge of caudal peduncle. Head and cheeks yellow with blue lines. Large adults greenish, paler below; scales on side have blue spots and paler margins. Back crossed by about 5 indistinct, narrow, pale vertical bars. Small black spot at upper pectoral fin base. 12 anal soft rays. TL to 20″ (51 cm).

Habitat: Coral reefs and associated habitats.

Range: Bermuda, North Carolina to Florida, Gulf of Mexico, Bahamas, Caribbean, including Antilles, and Brazil.

Notes: The Puddingwife is the largest species of *Halichoeres* in the western Atlantic. A good food fish, it feeds on mollusks, sea urchins, crabs, and brittle stars.

Similar Species: Some parrotfishes (family Scaridae) are similar but are thick bodied and have teeth fused into beaks.

---

297 **Pearly Razorfish**
Xyrichtys novacula

Identification: *An elongate, very compressed fish with front of head forming a sharp edge. Snout very blunt; profile steep. Pale greenish, usually with no conspicuous markings on body* (some Atlantic coast individuals have dusky blotch just below lateral line over tip of pectoral fin). Cheek has alternating pale and gray vertical lines. Dorsal, anal, and caudal fins rosy. Anal fin has diagonal lines; caudal fin has faint vertical bars. 9 dorsal fin spines, first 2 more flexible than others. Lateral line discontinuous; 5 scale rows between lateral line and origin of dorsal fin. Pelvic fin not greatly elongate. TL to 7⅛″ (18 cm).

Habitat: Over sandy bottoms at depths of 4–270′ (1.2–80 m).

Range: Carolinas to s Florida, Bahamas, n Gulf of Mexico, Antilles, n South America, and Brazil. Also in e Atlantic.

Notes: The Pearly Razorfish dives into the sand when alarmed, and a diver or snorkeler can often hear the fish swimming through the sand. If the diver remains quiet the fish will cautiously emerge, the head and eyes appearing first, as if it were checking to see if it is safe.

Similar Species: Adult males of Green Razorfish (*X. splendens*), from s Florida and Antilles to Brazil, and Rosy Razorfish (*X. martinicensis*), from Bahamas, Cuba, Yucatán, and Antilles, have elongate pelvic fins and 3 or 4 scale rows between lateral line and dorsal fin origin.

Other species of wrasses

Red Hogfish (*Decodon puellaris*) Plain reddish, paler below; yellow lines on side of head. Conspicuous canine teeth at front of upper and lower jaws. Last dorsal soft rays noticeably longer than front rays. S Florida, Gulf of Mexico, Antilles to n South America.

Dwarf Wrasse (*Doratonotus megalepis*) Snout pointed. First dorsal fin spines form high lobe. Usually green, sometimes yellowish below or with green, red, black, or white spots. Oblique white bar from eye to preopercle. Lateral line interrupted under soft dorsal fin rays, continuing on caudal peduncle. Bermuda, s Florida, Bahamas, Lesser Antilles, w Caribbean to South America.

PARROTFISHES
Family Scaridae

Parrotfishes are distinctive small to large fishes with large, smooth scales and teeth that are fused into beak-like structures. They are heavy bodied, have square or slightly forked tails, and have a single dorsal fin without a distinct notch. The lateral line is interrupted below the rear of the dorsal fin. Many parrotfishes are colorful and, like wrasses, have several distinct color phases, including juvenile, young adult male and female, older female, and *terminal male*, or *supermale*. Some species also have two kinds of males—those that start life as males, and those that complete a female phase before transforming into males. As with wrasses, the supermale spawns with an individual female, while the other males spawn with females in groups. Adult parrotfishes are easily identified if one takes into account the different color phases, but several species have striped juveniles that are difficult to distinguish.

Parrotfishes often travel in groups, and, like terrestrial grazers, they crop from various locations and thus do not destroy their food source. They use their beaks to nip pieces of large algae and to scrape algae and other encrusting organisms such as sponges from rocky bottoms. In the process they ingest large quantities of rock and coral, which is ground to a fine powder by their highly specialized pharyngeal teeth (also called the *pharyngeal mill*). When parrotfishes feed, the noise of their teeth scraping rock is easily heard. Parrotfishes are active strictly during the day; at night they find a crevice in which to sleep, and many species are able to secrete a mucous envelope around themselves, presumably for protection from predators.

This family contains nine genera and about 83 species worldwide; four genera and 14 species occur in our area.

Genera of family Scaridae

Cryptotomus	Jaw teeth fused at base, but distinct at tips. Body slender; SL less than 4″ (10 cm). No membranous flap on anterior nostril.
Nicholsina	Jaw teeth fused at base, but distinct at tips. Anterior nostril has membranous flap on its posterior edge. Body moderately deep; SL nearly 12″ (30 cm).
Scarus	Teeth completely fused into beaks, individual teeth not visible. Upper beak fits over lower when mouth is closed.
Sparisoma	Teeth completely fused, but individual teeth can be distinguished. Lower beak fits over upper when mouth is closed.

300 Bluelip Parrotfish
Cryptotomus roseus

Identification:	A small, slender, elongate parrotfish (body depth 4–4.6 times in SL). Snout rather pointed. Pale blue-green, with salmon-colored stripe on side and dark spot at pectoral fin base. *Jaw teeth fused only at bases. Anterior nostril without membranous flap.* TL to 4″ (10 cm).

Habitat: Shallow vegetated areas.
Range: Bermuda, South Carolina to s Florida,
          Bahamas, Antilles, and Central and
          South American coasts to Brazil.
Notes: The slender shape and partially free teeth
          make the Bluelip Parrotfish resemble a
          wrasse more than a parrotfish. It burrows
          in the sand at night like a wrasse, but
          within the sand it secretes a mucous
          envelope like a parrotfish.

Similar Species: Emerald Parrotfish *(Nicholsina usta)* also
          has teeth free at tips but is larger and
          deeper bodied (depth 3–3.2 times in
          SL), with membranous flap at rear edge
          of front nostril. It occurs in Bermuda,
          North Carolina to Florida Keys, s Gulf
          of Mexico, Antilles, Panama, and Brazil.

298, 299   Queen Parrotfish
Scarus vetula

Identification: Body rather deep and somewhat
          compressed. Young adults of both sexes
          dark gray overall, with *broad white stripe
          slightly below mid-side.* Juveniles have 2
          white stripes and white belly.
          Supermales blue-green, with orange
          edges on scales, alternating stripes of
          orange and blue-green on sides of snout
          and chin, and dorsal and anal fins orange
          at base but otherwise blue-green.
          Supermales also have *upper pectoral fin
          margin and upper and lower margins of tail
          dusky with submarginal band of brownish
          orange.* 4 scale rows on cheek below eye.
          7 mid-dorsal scales in front of dorsal fin.
          12 pectoral fin rays. TL to 20″ (51 cm).
Habitat: Coral reefs and associated habitats.
Range: Bermuda, Bahamas, Antilles, and
          around Central and South American
          coasts from Yucatán to Trinidad.
Notes: Beautiful and abundant, the Queen
          Parrotfish is often seen in groups of one
          supermale with several young adults,
          most of which are probably females.
Similar Species: No other parrotfish in our area has
          young adult dark gray with white stripe.
          Supermales of Princess Parrotfish are

similar but have broad orange area above pelvic fin and 2 dark lines behind eye, and lack orange stripe in pectoral fin.

301, 302 Princess Parrotfish
Scarus taeniopterus

Identification: Body rather deep and somewhat compressed. *Juveniles and young adults dark olive above with 2 broad dark stripes: upper from tip of snout through eye to middle of caudal fin base, lower from chin through pectoral fin base to lower caudal fin base; white area above upper stripe continues around front of head above eye.* Upper and lower edges of tail dark. 2 white lines on side of belly. Supermales greenish with 2 dark green stripes on head, above and below eye, continuing in back of eye slightly past edge of operculum; scales on side have orange edges. Broad yellow area behind pectoral fin; center of dorsal and anal fins orange, margins with broad blue-green band; caudal fin has orange submarginal bands along upper and lower edges; pectoral fin clear, without orange submarginal band. 3 rows of scales on cheek below eye. 7 mid-dorsal scales in front of dorsal fin. 12 pectoral fin rays. TL to 13″ (33 cm).

Habitat: Coral reefs and associated habitats.
Range: Bermuda, s Florida, Bahamas, Caribbean, including Antilles, and south to Brazil.
Notes: The Princess Parrotfish is a common and beautiful fish that travels in schools.
Similar Species: Striped Parrotfish is similar, but white band usually stops above gill opening; supermales lack orange-yellow band behind pectoral fin.

---

303 Striped Parrotfish
Scarus iserti

Identification: Body rather deep and somewhat compressed. Young dark olive above with 2 broad dark stripes: upper from eye to middle of caudal base, lower from cheek through pectoral fin base to lower caudal fin base; *white stripe above upper dark stripe ends at gill opening; upper and lower caudal margins pale.* Supermales blue-green; scales on side have orange edges. Top of head sometimes yellow, with dark lines on side above and below eye, ending at gill opening, pale salmon-colored blotch behind gill opening and above clear pectoral fin. Dorsal and anal fins have orange centers with blue streaks and spots, margins dark green; upper and lower caudal fin margins dark without submarginal orange stripes, central rays with orange and blue lines. 3 scale rows on cheek below eye. 7 mid-dorsal scales in front of dorsal fin. 12 pectoral rays. TL to 11″ (28 cm).

Habitat: Coral reefs and associated habitats.

Range: Bermuda, s and w Florida, Bahamas, Caribbean, including Antilles, and south to Brazil.

Notes: The Striped Parrotfish, also known as *S. croicensis,* travels in schools and is one of the most common parrotfishes on coral reefs.

Similar Species: Princess Parrotfish is similar but differs in details of color: white band above eye continues around front of head; supermales have orange submarginal bands on caudal fin, broad yellow area behind pectoral fin, and orange center of dorsal and anal fins without blue streaks and spots.

---

304 Blue Parrotfish
Scarus coeruleus

Identification: Body rather deep and somewhat compressed. Juveniles pale with 3 dark longitudinal stripes. *Adults uniformly blue, with yellow area on top of head that disappears in larger fish.* Snout blunt; mouth low. *Large fish develop prominent bulging snout and extended upper and lower caudal fin lobes.* 3 scale rows on cheek below eye. 6 mid-dorsal scales in front of dorsal fin. 13 pectoral fin rays. TL to 3' (91 cm), possibly larger.

Habitat: Coral reefs and adjacent habitats.

Range: Bermuda, Maryland to Florida, Bahamas, Caribbean, including Antilles, and South American coast to Brazil. Not in Gulf of Mexico.

Notes: The Blue Parrotfish is a beautiful fish. Large males are seldom seen and probably live in deeper water than most divers frequent.

Similar Species: No other species has this uniform blue color in adults. Striped juveniles can be identified by scale and fin ray counts: usually 6 mid-dorsal scales in Blue Parrotfish, and usually 7 in Striped Parrotfish and Princess Parrotfish.

305 Rainbow Parrotfish
Scarus guacamaia

Identification: A large, heavy-bodied, somewhat compressed parrotfish with *bright green teeth.* Adults bronze-orange in front and green behind. Scales on side of body green with orange edges. Young have 2 longitudinal stripes on pale tannish-gray background. 3 scale rows on cheek below eye, lowest row with single scale. 6 mid-dorsal scales in front of dorsal fin. 14 pectoral fin rays. Caudal fin lobes extended as filaments in large individuals. TL to 4' (1.2 m).

Habitat: Coral reefs and associated habitats; mangrove shorelines.

Range: Bermuda, s Florida, Bahamas, Antilles, Central and South American coasts to Argentina.

Notes: The spectacular Rainbow Parrotfish has home shelters under ledges to which it returns at night and when threatened. It has been shown that this species uses the angle of the sun to find its way home.

Similar Species: Midnight Parrotfish also has green teeth, but body is dark and bright blue.

306 **Midnight Parrotfish**
Scarus coelestinus

Identification: A large dark parrotfish with *blue-green teeth.* Body rather deep and somewhat compressed. *Adults generally black or blue-black, with centers of scales and unscaled part of head bright blue, and blue band between eyes.* Fins have blue margins. Juveniles mostly dull gray, not striped. 3 scale rows on cheek below eye, lowest row with 2 scales. 6 mid-dorsal scales in front of dorsal fin. 14 pectoral fin rays. TL to 30″ (76 cm).

Habitat: Coral reefs and other hard-bottom areas.

Range: Bermuda, s Florida, Bahamas, Antilles, and Caribbean to Rio de Janeiro.

Notes: The Midnight Parrotfish is the only large black or blue-black parrotfish in our area. It sometimes schools with surgeonfishes.

Similar Species: Rainbow Parrotfish also has green teeth, but body is green or green-orange and bronze in adults, striped in juveniles.

307 **Bucktooth Parrotfish**
Sparisoma radians

Identification: A small parrotfish with a deep and somewhat compressed body. Mottled red and greenish overall. Pectoral fin has black base but lacks saddle-shaped spot at upper base. Largest adults have blue stripe from eye to angle of mouth, and broad black margin on tail. Young have 5 or 6 indistinct pale stripes and considerable red on side. *Front of upper jaw has horizontal canine-like tusks.* Unbranched fleshy flap protrudes from rim of anterior nostril. Single row of scales on cheek below eye. 4 mid-dorsal scales in front of dorsal fin. *2 scales between bases of pelvic fins.* TL to 8″ (20 cm).

Habitat: Sea-grass beds in shallow waters.

Range: Bermuda, Georgia to Florida, Bahamas, Gulf of Mexico, Antilles, and Caribbean.

Notes: When fleeing, this species will suddenly stop and dive into the sea grass, where

its mottled colors serve as effective camouflage.

Similar Species: Greenblotch Parrotfish *(S. atomarium),* from Bermuda, Florida, Bahamas, Antilles, and Caribbean, is similar but has black blotch above pectoral fin and single scale between pelvic fins.

---

308 Redband Parrotfish
Sparisoma aurofrenatum

Identification: Body rather deep and somewhat compressed. Adults of both sexes have *distinct white spot behind base of dorsal fin;* sometimes have white blotch on gill cover. Supermales green with red fins; dark tips on caudal fin lobes and dark margin on anal fin; *red line from corner of mouth to below back of eye; and 2 or more jet-black spots on side above pectoral fin* that look like scars or parasite cysts but are normal pigmentation. Young mottled grayish above with broad stripe along mid-side that intensifies anteriorly into dark 4-sided blotch; no white spots on body. Single row of scales on cheek below eye. Fleshy flap on rim of anterior nostril has several lobes and points. 4 mid-dorsal scales in front of dorsal fin. TL to 11″ (28 cm).

Habitat: Coral reefs and associated habitats.
Range: Bermuda, Florida, Bahamas, Antilles, and Central and South American coasts to Brazil.
Notes: The Redband Parrotfish is a common species, but little is known about its ecology.
Similar Species: Young Stoplight Parrotfish are similar to juvenile phases but have white spots in orderly vertical and horizontal rows.

---

309 Redtail Parrotfish
Sparisoma chrysopterum

Identification: Body rather deep and somewhat compressed. Young adults of both sexes mottled gray to reddish brown overall, with *black saddle-shaped marking at upper end of pectoral fin base; often vague, pale saddle-shaped area on top of caudal peduncle; and dorsal, anal, and pelvic fins red or orange.* Supermales green above and blue below; dorsal, anal, and pelvic fins light red; red crescent at tips of middle caudal rays; base of pectoral fin red-orange with large purple spot at upper end. Red-phase supermale has distinct saddle-shaped spot on upper end of pectoral fin and yellow crescent in tail. Fleshy flap on rim of anterior nostril undivided or with a few lobes. Single row of scales on cheek below eye. 4 mid-dorsal scales in front of dorsal fin. TL to 18″ (46 cm).

Habitat: Shallow sandy areas with sea grasses.

Range: Bermuda, s Florida, Bahamas, Antilles, and Central and South American coasts to Brazil.

Notes: The Redtail Parrotfish is capable of rapid color changes to blend in with its surroundings.

Similar Species: Redfin Parrotfish *(S. rubripinne)* is very similar in coloration and also has pectoral saddle in supermales (young lack dark saddle), but has brush-like tentacle on rim of anterior nostril, completely yellow tail, and dark margins on scales; it lives in Bermuda, s Florida, Bahamas, Antilles, and Central and South American coasts to Brazil.

310, 311 Stoplight Parrotfish
Sparisoma viride

Identification: Body rather deep and somewhat compressed. Young adults and females gray above, with *scales outlined in darker gray; often bright red below.* Juveniles have regular vertical and horizontal rows of white spots, and dark blotch behind pectoral fin. *Supermales green, with bright yellow spot at upper edge of gill cover, yellow bar at base of tail, curved orange-yellow mark on caudal fin rays,* dull red streak below eye from corner of mouth to upper part of operculum, and red along lower

edge of gill cover. Single row of scales on cheek below eye. 4 mid-dorsal scales in front of dorsal fin. TL to 22″ (55 cm).

Habitat: Coral reefs and associated habitats.

Range: Bermuda, s Florida, Bahamas, e and w Gulf of Mexico, Antilles, and Central and South American coasts to Brazil.

Notes: The Stoplight Parrotfish is a distinctive, colorful, and abundant fish. The gray-and-red phase of the young adults and females was for a long time thought to be a different species and was called *S. abildgaardi.*

Similar Species: Color patterns of adults are distinctive. Juvenile phase of Redband Parrotfish has similar black blotch above pectoral fin but lacks white spots in regular rows on body.

MULLETS
Family Mugilidae

Mullets are elongate, nearly terete, moderately large fishes. They have two well-separated dorsal fins, the first consisting of four slender spines, the second of one spine and eight or more rays. The pelvic fins are subabdominal, located rather far forward on the belly, although still well behind the pectoral fins, and have one spine and five soft rays. The caudal fin is moderately forked. Juveniles have two anal fin spines, and in some species the third ray becomes a spine as the fish matures. Mullets have no lateral line on the body, and the scales are counted in a line from the gill opening to the base of the tail. Members of some genera have *adipose eyelids*—transparent fleshy extensions of the anterior and posterior rims of the eye socket that cover most of the eye, except for a vertical oval area near the center. Some mullets regularly enter fresh water during part of their life cycle. Most mullets are bottom feeders that consume organic detritus or microorganisms.

The family consists of about 17 genera, with at least 66 and possibly as many as 80 species. Three genera and about 10 species occur in our region.

Genera of family Mugilidae

Mugil	Well-developed adipose eyelid. Lips thin. Mouth terminal. Head nearly flat on top; appears triangular in cross section. 3 anal fin spines in adults.

Agonostomus	No adipose eyelid. Lips thin. Mouth terminal. 2 anal fin spines in adults. Head not flat on top.
Joturus	No adipose eyelid. Lower lip very thick. Mouth inferior. 2 anal fin spines in adults. Head not flat on top.

279 Striped Mullet
Mugil cephalus

Identification: A rather stout mullet. Lower lip has bump at tip. Dusky gray, shading to white below, with dark lines along side. Dark blotch at pectoral fin base. Second dorsal and anal fins nearly scaleless; only few scales along bases and partway up anterior rays. *8 soft anal fin rays. 38–42 scales in lateral series.* TL to 24″ (60 cm).

Habitat: Coastal waters, including estuaries; moves into fresh water.

Range: Worldwide in tropical and temperate waters. In w Atlantic, continental waters from Cape Cod to s Gulf of Mexico.

Notes: The Striped Mullet is a very important commercial species in many parts of the world.

Similar Species: Other species of mullets with adipose eyelids differ in color, number of anal fin rays, or scale counts. Similar Liza *(M. liza)*, from Bermuda, s tip of Florida, Bahamas, Antilles, and South American coast to Brazil, has larger scales, 31–36 in lateral series.

280 White Mullet
Mugil curema

Identification: A medium-size mullet. Olive above, shading to silvery white below; no dark stripes on side. Black blotch in and above axil of pectoral fin. Dark margin on caudal fin. Origin of first dorsal fin midway between tip of snout and caudal fin base. *Usually 38 or 39 scales in lateral series. Scales on side covered with smaller secondary scales.* Second dorsal and anal fins covered with scales. *9 or 10 soft anal fin rays.* TL to 15″ (38 cm).

Habitat: Coastal waters and estuaries; rarely in fresh water.

Range: Bermuda, Atlantic coast from Massachusetts to Brazil, Bahamas, Gulf of Mexico, and around Caribbean, including Antilles.

Notes: The White Mullet is a common and important commercial species that is marketed both fresh and salted. The roe is considered a delicacy.

Other *Mugil* species

Second dorsal and anal fins densely scaled. No stripes on body.

Fantail Mullet
: (*M. gyrans*) Dark spot at base of pectoral fin. Tail has dusky margin. 8 soft anal rays. 29–31 scales in lateral series. Bermuda, Bahamas, Gulf of Mexico, Antilles, Caribbean coast, south to Brazil.

Redeye Mullet
: (*M. gaimardianus*) Dusky area at tip of second dorsal fin. Tail large. Eye red. 9–10 soft anal rays. 36–37 scales in lateral series. E Florida, Cuba.

Hospe Mullet
: (*M. hospes*) 9 soft anal rays. 38–40 scales in lateral series. Venezuela to Brazil. Also e Pacific.

Parassi Mullet
: (*M. incilis*) Second dorsal and caudal fins have dusky edges. 9 soft anal rays. 42–45 scales in lateral series. Colombia to Brazil.

Dwarf Mullet
: (*M. curvidens*) Teeth bent near tips, nearly at right angle. Black blotch at base of pectoral fin. 8 soft anal rays. 36–38 scales in lateral series. West Indies, Colombia to Brazil. Also Ascension Island.

Other species of mullets

Mountain Mullet
: (*Agonostomus monticola*) Mouth terminal; lower lip thin. Freshwater streams, often well into mountains. North Carolina to Venezuela, Bahamas, Greater Antilles.

Bobo Mullet
: (*Joturus pichardi*) Mouth inferior; lower lip very thick. Fresh water, sometimes estuaries. Central America, n South America.

THREADFINS
Family Polynemidae

Threadfins are medium-size, moderately elongate, and moderately compressed fishes. They have a rounded snout that overhangs the mouth, two well-separated dorsal fins, and a deeply forked tail. Their name comes from the fact that the lower three to eight pectoral fin rays are long and free, not connected by membranes. The pelvic fin is subabdominal, located well behind the pectoral fin, but not far back on the belly. The lateral line divides at the caudal fin base and its branches continue to the end of the fin.

The family contains seven genera and 33 species. One genus, *Polydactylus,* and three species occur in our area.

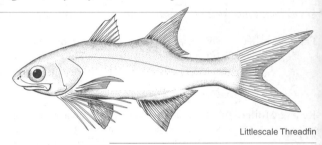

Littlescale Threadfin

Littlescale Threadfin
Polydactylus oligodon

Identification:	A fairly large fish with a protruding snout, a deep caudal peduncle, and a deeply forked tail. Pale silvery gray overall, darker above, with blackish pectoral and pelvic fins. *7 free pectoral fin rays. Scales small: 68–74 in lateral line to caudal fin base.* TL to 18″ (46 cm).
Habitat:	Inshore waters, sandy or muddy shores.
Range:	Southern Florida, Bahamas, Jamaica, Trinidad, and Brazil.
Notes:	A striking but little-known species, the Littlescale Threadfin is probably taken as a food fish in beach seines but is not of great commercial importance.
Similar Species:	Atlantic Threadfin *(P. octonemus),* which lives along coasts from New York to Brazil but not in Bermuda, Bahamas, or Antilles, has 8 free pectoral rays. Barbu *(P. virginicus)* also has 7 free pectoral rays but has 53–63 scales in lateral line; it is found in Bermuda, along Atlantic coast

from Chesapeake Bay (occasionally New Jersey) to Florida Keys, Antilles, and Yucatán to Uruguay.

STARGAZERS
Family Uranoscopidae

Stargazers are rather small, moderately elongate fishes that spend most of their time partially buried in the bottom with only their eyes showing. The head is cuboidal (rectangular in cross section), and the small eyes are located on the flat upper surface of the head, which is probably why these fishes are called stargazers. The mouth is nearly vertical and the lips are fringed. Some species have a spiny dorsal fin with three to five spines; others lack the spiny dorsal fin. The soft dorsal fin has 12 to 15 rays, and the anal fin has 12 to 17 soft rays. The pectoral fin is large; the pelvic fin is jugular, with one spine and five soft rays. There is a strong grooved spine called a *cleithral spine* on the shoulder girdle above the pectoral fin; a poison gland is associated with this spine. The caudal fin is either truncate or rounded. Members of the genus *Astroscopus* produce electricity in special organs derived from eye muscles and located immediately behind the eyes.

The family contains eight genera and about 50 species. Three genera and four species occur in our area, only one of which lives in shallow waters. Juveniles of deep-water species are sometimes taken in shallow waters.

Genera of family Uranoscopidae

Astroscopus	Spiny dorsal fin with 3–5 spines. Scales present. Electric organ marked by smooth plate behind each eye. No cleithral spine.
Kathetostoma	No spiny dorsal fin. No scales. Prominent, pointed cleithral spine at upper end of shoulder girdle. No electric organs.
Gnathagnus	No spiny dorsal fin. No scales. Cleithral spine flat. No electric organs.

346, 347	**Southern Stargazer**	
	Astroscopus y-graecum	

Identification: A moderately small, tapering stargazer. Eyes on upper side of head. *Smooth area behind each eye covers electric organ; smooth*

areas separated by Y-shaped superficial bone. Marbled sand color overall, with large white spots on head and side. 2 black bars on second dorsal fin. Mouth almost vertical. *Spiny dorsal fin small, with 3–5 short spines.* TL to 17¼" (44 cm).

Habitat: Soft-bottom areas inshore.

Range: Cape Hatteras and n Gulf of Mexico to Yucatán and Venezuela.

Notes: The Southern Stargazer can deliver an uncomfortable electric shock with its modified eye muscles.

Similar Species: Northern Stargazer *(A. guttatus),* found north of Cape Hatteras, has dark stripe on side of caudal peduncle.

SAND STARGAZERS
Family Dactyloscopidae

Sand stargazers are small fishes of sand and reef habitats, mostly in shallow waters. Their bodies are moderately elongate, tapering, and compressed posteriorly. The eyes are on top of the head, on stalks in many species. Most species have strongly oblique mouths with fleshy projections called *fimbriae* on the gill cover and usually on the lips. They have a long, continuous dorsal fin that sometimes is divided by a deep notch; in some species the anterior dorsal spines are not connected by membranes. The anal fin is long, with two spines and 22 to 35 soft rays. The pectoral fin is rather large. The pelvic fins, which have one spine and three unbranched soft rays, are jugular and are directed outward from the ventral midline. The lateral line is high anteriorly, then curves abruptly downward and continues along the mid-side. The males of several genera carry clusters of developing eggs beneath the pectoral fin.

This family contains nine genera and about 46 species; six genera and 16 species occur in our region. It is one of the few fish families that is confined to the New World.

The genera of sand stargazers in our area fall into three groups based on the configuration of the dorsal fin: those with very deeply notched interspinous membranes, making the spines essentially separate; those with the first spines connected by membrane but forming a separate finlet; and those with a continuous dorsal fin.

Genera of family Dactyloscopidae

Interspinous membranes deeply notched; first 1–4 dorsal spines nearly or completely separate.

Dactyloscopus	Dorsal fin origin on nape, well in front of anal fin origin. Well-developed fimbriae on both lips. 10 caudal fin rays.

First 3–4 dorsal spines connected but forming separate finlet.

Leurochilus	No fimbriae on upper and lower lips. Lateral line bends downward at middle of pectoral fin. Dorsal fin origin on nape, in front of anal fin origin. 10 caudal fin rays.
Gillellus	No fimbriae on upper lip, but 2–8 fleshy lobes on lower lip. Lateral line bends abruptly downward behind tip of pectoral fin. Dorsal fin origin on nape, in front of anal fin origin. Belly and pectoral fin base scaleless. 10 caudal fin rays.
Platygillellus	Fimbriae on both lips. Dorsal fin origin on nape, in front of anal fin origin. Pectoral fin base and belly scaled. Lateral line bends downward behind tip of pectoral fin. 11 caudal fin rays.

Dorsal fin continuous; fimbriae on both lips.

Dactylagnus	Head truncate. Dorsal fin origin above anal fin origin. 10 caudal fin rays.
Myxodagnus	Head conically pointed, with lower jaw strongly projecting. Dorsal fin origin above anal fin origin. 10 caudal fin rays.

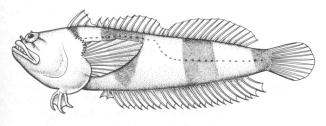

Saddle Stargazer

Saddle Stargazer
Platygillellus rubrocinctus

Identification: *Pale tan or white with 4 broad reddish-brown bands on side between nape and caudal fin base. Dorsal and caudal fin rays have dark spots.* 3 spines in dorsal finlet. Fimbriae on both lips. SL to 2" (5 cm).

Habitat: Rock or coral to depths of 100' (30 m).

Range: Southeastern Florida, Bahamas, Antilles, and w Caribbean from Mexico to Panama.

Notes: The reddish-brown bands along the sides of the Saddle Stargazer serve as camouflage when the fish partially buries itself in sand that has reddish particles (skeletons of a common foraminiferan, a marine protozoan).

Similar Species: Sailfin Stargazer *(P. smithi),* known only from a single specimen from Little Inagua Island, Bahamas, is similar but has 4 spines in a much higher anterior dorsal finlet.

Other species of sand stargazers

Bigeye Stargazer	*(Dactyloscopus crossotus)* Eye large, on very short stalk. 41–42 total dorsal fin elements. 12–15 fimbriae on upper part of opercular flap. Pale tan, without conspicuous markings. Se Bahamas, Antilles, Brazil.
Sand Stargazer	*(Dactyloscopus tridigitatus)* Eye small, on long slender stalk. 10–16 fimbriae on upper part of opercular flap. Pale tan, without conspicuous markings; sometimes dark brown flecks on upper side and 11–14 irregular brown bars across back. Bermuda, Florida, Bahamas, Gulf of Mexico, coasts of Central and South America to Brazil.
Shortchin Stargazer	*(Dactyloscopus boehlkei)* 10 dorsal spines; 40 total dorsal elements. 17–20 fimbriae on upper part of opercular flap. Pale tan, without conspicuous markings. Bahamas, Cuba to Lesser Antilles.

Dactyloscopus foraminosus	10 dorsal spines; 41 total dorsal elements. Upper side flecked with brown; 10 irregular brownish bars on back. Se Florida, mouth of Amazon River.
Dactyloscopus comptus	11 dorsal spines; 37–38 total dorsal elements. 28–30 soft anal rays. Pale tan, without persistent markings. Bahamas, provisionally Puerto Rico and Virgin Islands.
Speckled Stargazer	*(Dactyloscopus moorei)* Dorsal fin continuous, all 11 spines connected by membrane; 38–41 total elements. 30–35 soft anal rays. Upper side flecked with dark brown, often with hint of longitudinal stripes. North Carolina to Florida, Gulf of Mexico west to Texas.
Dactyloscopus poeyi	Dorsal fin has 11 spines, 40–43 total elements; 2–3 anterior spines usually not connected by membrane. 33–34 soft anal rays. Pale tan, with brown flecks on back, 10–13 brownish bars on upper side. May have mid-lateral stripe. W Caribbean to Brazil.
Warteye Stargazer	*(Gillellus uranidea)* Eye ringed with short fleshy papillae. Dorsal fin has 11–15 spines, 14–17 soft rays. Florida Keys, Bahamas, Central American coast.
Masked Stargazer	*(Gillellus healae)* Broad dark band across eye. Dorsal fin has 11–15 spines, 27–29 soft rays. South Carolina to Florida Keys, e Gulf of Mexico north to Pensacola.
Gillellus jacksoni	17–20 dorsal spines. 28–30 soft anal rays. 6–7 narrow, poorly defined dark bars across back and extending down to midside. Anguilla, St. Barthélemy, Union Island, Aruba.
Arrow Stargazer	*(Gillellus greyae)* White with 6–8 dark bars. 17–20 dorsal spines. 31–35 soft anal rays. Florida, Bahamas, Antilles, Venezuela.
Smoothlip Stargazer	*(Leurochilus acon)* No fimbriae on lips. Mouth nearly terminal, lower jaw slightly longer than upper. Bahamas, Virgin Islands, Antigua.

Dactylagnus peratikos	Body stout. Head broadly rounded in front. Pale tan speckled with irregular small dark markings. Costa Rica, Panama.
Dartfish	*(Myxodagnus belone)* Body slender. Snout conical; lower jaw protrudes noticeably. Bahamas, Puerto Rico.

TRIPLEFINS
Family Tripterygiidae

Triplefins are small, elongate, robust fishes with large rough scales and three distinct dorsal fins. The first and second dorsal fins have only spines, the third has only soft rays. All triplefins are similar in appearance but differ in details of scale, proportion, and color. They have cryptic coloration and are detectable only by carefully searching the reef surface and among algae and coral branches.

The family includes 20 genera with 115 species; one genus, *Enneanectes,* and five species occur in our area.

---

329 Redeye Triplefin
Enneanectes pectoralis

Identification: A small, tapering, terete fish with a rather pointed head. Grayish tan, often with red tint, with 5 dark saddle-shaped bars on body; *last bar, located on caudal peduncle, wider and darker than others.* Dark bar on cheek below eye. *No dark bars on anal fin. Iris red.* Short spines on anterior rim of eye socket. Scales on belly and pectoral fin base. Usually 13 pored scales in lateral line. SL to 1¼″ (3.2 cm).

Habitat: Coral reefs to depths of at least 35′ (10.6 m).

Range: Florida, Bahamas, Virgin Islands, Martinique, Yucatán, Belize, Honduras, Nicaragua, Venezuela.

Notes: The Redeye Triplefin is fairly common in the Bahamas, but hard to spot because of its camouflaged coloration.

Similar Species: Mimic Triplefin *(E. jordani),* occurring in Bahamas, Puerto Rico, Belize, Honduras, and Venezuela, has scales on belly and spines on front rim of eye socket, but has 6 or 7 dark bars on anal fin. Lofty Triplefin *(E. altivelis),* from Bahamas, Yucatán, and Belize to Nicaragua, has scales on belly, but has smooth front edge of eye orbit and higher first dorsal fin. Roughhead Triplefin *(E. boehlkei),* from Florida, Bahamas, Puerto Rico, Virgin Islands, Yucatán, Belize to Costa Rica, and Venezuela, lacks scales on belly and has blunter snout and 15 pored scales in lateral line. Blackedge Triplefin *(E. atrorus),* occurring in Bahamas, Turneffe Islands, Glovers Reef, Belize, and Honduras, lacks scales on belly and has 12 or 13 pored scales in lateral line.

PIKEBLENNIES
Family Chaenopsidae

The term *blenny* is applied to members of three closely related families: Chaenopsidae, Labrisomidae, and Blenniidae. All are small fishes with pelvic fins that are reduced to a minute embedded spine and two or three soft rays. Nearly all blennies have large eyes, rather small mouths, and *cirri,* or fleshy tentacles, on the head. The closely related triplefins (family Tripterygiidae) are sometimes called "triplefin blennies."

The pikeblennies, family Chaenopsidae, usually have cirri above the eye (supraorbital), on the rim of the nostril (nasal), and on the side of the nape (nuchal). Species exhibit many variations of size, color, and shape. They are usually scaleless *(Stathmonotus stahli* is an exception) and without a lateral line. The dorsal fin is continuous, often with more spines than rays. For identification purposes, the number of total elements comprising the fin (spines plus soft rays) is sometimes more important than separate counts of the number of spines or rays. All fin rays are unbranched. The pelvic fins are jugular and consist of an embedded spine and two or three segmented rays.

The family consists of 11 genera and 56 species; 10 genera and about 39 species are found in our area.

Genera of family Chaenopsidae

Stathmonotus	Dorsal fin consists of 41–53 spines; no soft rays. Body elongate, almost eel-like.

Acanthemblemaria	Top of head usually spiny.
Ekemblemaria	Head rugose (knobby) anteriorly.
Chaenopsis	45–57 total dorsal fin elements; rays more numerous than spines. Dorsal and anal fins joined to caudal fin.
Lucayablennius	38–42 total dorsal fin elements; spines and rays equal in number or varying by no more than 1. Lower jaw protrudes, with fleshy projection.
Hemiemblemaria	Lower jaw protrudes. Dark line along side. No supraorbital cirri. Dorsal fin has more spines than rays.
Emblemaria	13–17 soft dorsal rays; 30–38 total dorsal fin elements. Head smooth anteriorly. Males have cirrus on eye longer than eye diameter.
Coralliozetus	Cirri on each eye arise from 2 separate bases; cirri not branched. 29–30 total dorsal fin elements; 11 dorsal soft rays.
Protoemblemaria	Cirri on each eye arise from 2 separate bases; cirri branched. 34–37 total dorsal fin elements; 13–17 dorsal soft rays.
Emblemariopsis	Cirrus on eye single and unbranched, or absent. 30–38 total dorsal fin elements; 10–13 dorsal soft rays.

330 Papillose Blenny
Acanthemblemaria chaplini

Identification: An elongate, tapering pikeblenny with *soft papillae on top of head between eyes and on snout. Well-developed fleshy flap on anterior margin of first dorsal spine.* Body orangish to brown, darker posteriorly, with 3 longitudinal rows of dark spots on side and row of dark spots at base of dorsal fin. Spiny dorsal fin dark with row of pale spots. Anterior half of anal fin has longitudinal line. Dorsal fin has 21–23 spines, 38–44 total elements. Single supraorbital cirrus with side branches. SL to 1⅝″ (4.1 cm).

Habitat: Limestone slopes at depths of 6–40′ (2–12 m).

Range: Florida, n Bahamas, and Cay Sal Bank.
Notes: Like other species of *Acanthemblemaria*, the Papillose Blenny lives in holes. Divers should look for this fish in small holes in limestone areas.

Other *Acanthemblemaria* species

Secretary Blenny (*A. maria*) Bony spines extend from top of head almost to dorsal fin origin. Spines on rear rim of eye socket. Conspicuous vertical bands or oval spots on side. Bahamas, Grand Cayman, Puerto Rico, Lesser Antilles to Tobago, Belize.

Spinyhead Blenny (*A. spinosa*) Strong bony spines extend from top of head almost to dorsal origin. Dusky, with small, round dark spots along side. Supraorbital cirrus has few short branches. Bahamas, Caribbean, including Antilles.

Spotjaw Blenny (*A. rivasi*) Short blunt spines on top of head in front of rear margin of eye. Rear margin of orbit smooth. Supraorbital cirrus unbranched. 5–10 vertical bands on side, anterior bands extending from dorsal fin base to belly, posterior bands diamond shaped. Panama, Costa Rica.

Dwarf Spinyhead Blenny (*A. paula*) Bony spines extend from top of head to well behind eye. Supraorbital cirrus complexly branched. Pale, without prominent markings. Belize.

False Papillose Blenny (*A. greenfieldi*) Poorly developed spines on top of head. Dorsal rim of orbit has a few spines; rear margin of eye socket smooth. Supraorbital cirrus branched. Pale, with rows of small distinct spots. Jamaica, Yucatán, Isla de Providencia.

Roughhead Blenny (*A. aspera*) Well-developed spines without papillae on top of head. Supraorbital cirrus has long branches. Pale; male has dark ocellus between third and fourth dorsal spines. Florida, Bahamas, Antilles, w Caribbean.

Medusa Blenny (*A. medusa*) Spines with slender, tapering papillae on top of head. Supraorbital cirrus has long branches. Brown with faint blotches; spot behind eye. Lesser Antilles; Los Roques Islands off Venezuela.

Speckled Blenny *(A. betinensis)* 2 parallel rows of spines between eyes on top of head. Supra-orbital cirrus branched. Dark brown with rows of small, pale, elongate spots. Costa Rica to Colombia.

331 Bluethroat Pikeblenny
Chaenopsis ocellata

Identification: Body elongate. *Snout V shaped when viewed from above.* Mature males sand colored dorsally with variable number of dark bars that merge into very dark side; head dark with *blue gill membranes;* comma-shaped spot in first dorsal fin between first and second spines partly enclosing orange spot. Females and juveniles also bicolored but lack conspicuous markings on dorsal fin; gill membranes dark but not blue. 13 pectoral fin rays. Usually 21 spines and 34 or fewer soft dorsal rays; 51 or more total dorsal fin elements. TL to 5″ (12.5 cm).

Habitat: Worm tubes in sea-grass beds and sandy areas in very shallow waters, occasionally to depths of 40′ (12 m).

Range: Florida, Bahamas, and Antilles from Cuba to Virgin Islands.

Notes: Divers and snorkelers should examine any tube-like structures for the Bluethroat Pikeblenny.

Similar Species: Yellowface Pikeblenny *(C. limbaughi),* from Bahamas and Caribbean, has similar dorsal fin counts, 12 pectoral rays, and U-shaped snout; it has pale yellow head, black gill membranes, and ocellated spot in dorsal fin between first and second spines.

Other *Chaenopsis* species

C. resh Greenish gray with dark mid-lateral stripe, 16 dark brown blotches above stripe, and dark inverted L-shaped mark behind eye. Males have ocellus on first

	dorsal fin between second and third spines. Dorsal fin has 35–37 soft rays, more than 51 total elements. Venezuela.
C. stephensi	Pale, with 6 diamond-shaped blotches along mid-side. Dorsal fin has 28 soft rays, 45 total elements. Venezuela.
Flecked Pikeblenny	(*C. roseola*) Pale straw color with 8 black blotches along side; first 6 inverted triangles, last 2 horizontally elongate. Males have dark blotch between first and fourth dorsal spines. Dorsal fin has 26–28 soft rays; 44–45 total elements. North Carolina, ne Gulf of Mexico.

332 Arrow Blenny
Lucayablennius zingaro

Identification: A slender little fish with an *emarginate caudal fin,* deep caudal peduncle, and dorsal and anal fins not connected to caudal fin. *Reddish tan, with 3 large dark spots along rear of dorsal fin base, and 2 similar spots along rear of anal fin base.* No supraorbital cirri. TL to 1½" (3.8 cm).

Habitat: Deeper parts of coral reefs, especially outer slopes near drop-off; usually at depths over 30' (9 m).

Range: Bahamas and Caribbean, including Antilles.

Notes: The Arrow Blenny hovers with its body curved like a question mark. This distinctive species is often seen with schools of Masked Gobies.

333 Wrasse Blenny
Hemiemblemaria simulus

Identification: A slender, elongate fish. *Yellow, with dark mid-lateral stripe from snout to base of tail, and dark spot near edge of dorsal fin from fourth to sixth spines.* No supraorbital cirri; nasal cirri rudimentary. TL to 4" (10 cm).

Habitat: Coral reefs; often in abandoned holes of Christmas tree worms.

Range: Dry Tortugas, Bahamas, Cuba; in w Caribbean, Belize and Honduras.

Notes: This species bears a remarkable resemblance to juveniles, females, and young mature males of the Bluehead, a member of the wrasse family (although wrasses have scales). The Bluehead sometimes acts as a cleaner of other fish, and it is presumed that the resemblance allows the Wrasse Blenny to approach and prey on fishes that would not flee a Bluehead. Unlike other pikeblennies, the Wrasse Blenny often swims off the bottom.

334 Sailfin Blenny
Emblemaria pandionis

Identification: An elongate, moderately compressed blenny. *Males have very high, sail-like dorsal fin.* Males dark in front, irregularly mottled behind, little lighter below. Females irregularly mottled with much lower dorsal fin. 3 obvious pelvic fin rays. Supraorbital cirrus short, often slightly forked, but not much longer than diameter of eye. No fleshy flap on base of first dorsal spine; first dorsal soft ray longer than last dorsal spine. 32–37 total dorsal elements. 13 pectoral fin rays. TL to 2″ (5 cm).

Habitat: Coral rubble in sandy areas.
Range: Southern Florida, Bahamas, Gulf of Mexico from Florida to Texas, Caribbean, including Antilles.
Notes: Male Sailfin Blennies signal intensely in the morning and afternoon, emerging from their nest holes and rapidly raising and lowering their dorsal and anal fins. It is postulated that this signal attracts both males and females to a suitable environment.

Other *Emblemaria* species

3 obvious pelvic fin rays.

Twospot Blenny *(E. biocellata)* Females have 2 well-developed ocelli on dorsal fin (fourth and fifth interspinal membranes). Supraorbital cirrus not banded, about twice as long as eye diameter. Dorsal fin has 22 spines, 15 soft rays. 13 pectoral rays. Venezuela, French Guiana.

Banner Blenny

(E. atlantica) Supraorbital cirrus banded, up to 3 times as long as eye diameter. Dorsal fin has 22 spines, 14 soft rays. 22 anal soft rays. 14 pectoral rays. Bermuda, Georgia, Florida.

Venezuelan Blenny

(E. diphyodontis) Dorsal fin of males very large, with flag-like flaps on base of first spine. 19–21 dorsal spines, 14–16 soft rays. 22–24 anal soft rays. Palatine teeth in 2 rows. Venezuela.

Colombian Blenny

(E. caycedoi) Dorsal fin of males very large, with flag-like flaps on base of first spine. Dorsal fin has 19–21 spines, 14–15 soft rays. 22–23 anal rays. 13 pectoral rays. Palatine teeth in 1 row. Isla de Providencia, Colombia.

Ridge Blenny

(E. culmensis) Pair of obvious bony ridges on rear half of interorbital region. Supraorbital cirrus slender, long (2½ times eye diameter). Dorsal fin has 22 spines, 15 soft rays. 24 anal soft rays. Venezuela.

2 obvious pelvic fin rays (third ray vestigial).

Pirate Blenny

(E. piratula) 17–20 dorsal spines. 20–21 anal soft rays. 13 pectoral rays. Supraorbital cirrus of males unpigmented, large, usually flattened. W Florida, Belize.

Caribbean Blenny

(E. caldwelli) 21–23 dorsal spines. 22–23 anal soft rays. 14 pectoral rays. Supraorbital cirrus slender, speckled with melanophores. Bahamas, Jamaica, Belize.

Filament Blenny

(E. hyltoni) 21–23 dorsal spines; first 2 spines filamentous (extending more than two-thirds SL). 23 anal soft rays. 14 pectoral rays. Supraorbital cirrus long, unbranched. Roatán, Honduras.

Other species of pikeblennies

Blackbelly Blenny

(Stathmonotus hemphilli) No scales. No cirri on head. Dorsal and anal fins connected to tail by membrane. 2 color phases: one

pale; other nearly all black with pale slash marks on dorsal and anal fins, light margins on dorsal and caudal fins. Florida, Bahamas, Haiti, Puerto Rico, St. Croix, Antigua; w Caribbean from Yucatán to Corn Islands off Nicaragua.

Naked Blenny

(*Stathmonotus gymnodermis*) No scales. Cirri on nostril, eye, nape, and behind and below eye. Dorsal and anal fins nearly or completely separate from caudal fin. Pale, with mid-lateral row of dots. Bahamas, Puerto Rico, Virgin Islands, Glovers Reef off Belize, Venezuela.

Eelgrass Blenny

(*Stathmonotus stahli*) Scales present. Cirri on nostril, eye, preopercle, and nape. Pale greenish. *S. s. stahli:* Puerto Rico, Virgin Islands, Martinique, Bonaire, Venezuela. *S. s. tekla:* Dry Tortugas, Bahamas, Cuba, Yucatán, Belize, Honduras, Isla de Providencia.

Moth Blenny

(*Ekemblemaria nigra*) Supraorbital cirrus feather-like. Body uniformly dark brown. Males have dark dorsal fin; females have series of unpigmented blotches along base. 20–22 dorsal spines, 17 dorsal soft rays. 24 anal soft rays. Pelvic fin has 1 spine, 3 obvious rays. Panama.

Twinhorn Blenny

(*Coralliozetus cardonae*) Males pale reddish with dark head, irregular markings on body, and black-edged pale stripe from eye to pectoral fin base. Females reddish with black spots on underside of head; front part of dorsal fin nearly black. Bahamas, Puerto Rico, Virgin Islands, Curaçao, Belize.

Estuarian Blenny

(*Protoemblemaria punctata*) 2 fleshy ridges on top of head in males, sometimes females. Fleshy flap on anterior edge of first dorsal spine. Males have black ocellus on outer part of front of dorsal fin. Venezuela.

Flagfin Blenny

(*Emblemariopsis signifera*) Males have first 2 dorsal spines elongate, first reaching halfway to first soft ray, second about two-thirds as long as first. Has supraorbital cirrus. Bahamas, Cayman Islands, Lesser Antilles, Belize, Honduras, Curaçao to Rio de Janeiro.

Redspine Blenny *(Emblemariopsis occidentalis)* Females transparent, no dark markings; first 2 dorsal spines nearly equal in length, elongate but not reaching halfway to first soft ray. Dorsal fin of males lacks elongate spines; dark anteriorly, with margin clear in first 5 spines, pigment not reaching edge of fin until sixth spine. Soft dorsal fin transparent. Base of anal fin dark brown. Has supraorbital cirrus. Bahamas, Lesser Antilles.

Emblemariopsis leptocirris First 2 dorsal spines nearly equal in length, not elongate. Head and anterior body evenly covered with large melanophores. Anterior part of dorsal fin dark; pigment reaching distal edge of anterior spines. Anal fin base dark. Has supraorbital cirrus. Bahamas, Grand Cayman, Haiti, Puerto Rico to Antigua, Belize, Honduras.

Hornless Blenny *(Emblemariopsis randalli)* Pectoral fin has 14 rays; pelvic fin much shorter. Head depth 4.5–5.0 in SL. No supraorbital cirri. Venezuela.

Seafan Blenny *(Emblemariopsis pricei)* 14 pectoral fin rays. Head depth 8.0–8.4 in SL. No supraorbital cirri. Glovers Reef, coasts of Belize and Honduras.

Glass Blenny *(Emblemariopsis diaphana)* 13 pectoral fin rays. First dorsal spine longer than second. No supraorbital cirri. Florida Keys.

Blackhead Blenny *(Emblemariopsis bahamensis)* 13 pectoral fin rays. First dorsal spine slightly shorter than second. Head length 3.0–4.0 in SL. No supraorbital cirri. Bahamas, Antilles, w Caribbean, South American coast.

Emblemariopsis bottomei 13 pectoral fin rays. First dorsal spine slightly shorter than second. Head length 4.2–5.0 in SL. No supraorbital cirri. Los Roques Islands off Venezuela.

LABRISOMIDS
Family Labrisomidae

The labrisomids are similar to the pike-blennies except that they have scales and lateral lines. They have elongate, usually tapering bodies and a single continuous dorsal fin that is usually composed of spines and rays (the deep-water genus *Haptoclinus* is an exception). The pelvic fins are thoracic and have two or three visible rays, and the caudal fin may be truncate or rounded. There may be fleshy cirri on the eyes and nostrils. Some species have one or more fleshy cirri on each side of the nape; sometimes a row of cirri forms a *nuchal comb* on each side.

This is one of the few families confined to the New World, although two species also occur in the eastern Atlantic, and a few species occur in the northwestern Pacific. As currently recognized, the family contains 16 genera and 102 species. Six genera and 38 species occur in our area, but two genera, *Haptoclinus* and *Nemaclinus,* are found only in deep water and are not covered here.

Genera of family Labrisomidae

Labrisomus	Nuchal combs widely separated. Maxilla exposed posteriorly. 40–74 lateral-line scales.
Malacoctenus	Nuchal combs close together. Maxilla mostly covered by preorbital bone. 40–66 lateral-line scales.
Paraclinus	Dorsal fin composed of all spines, or spines and 1 soft ray. Nasal, supraorbital, and nuchal cirri usually present. 27–40 lateral-line scales.
Starksia	Males have copulatory organ consisting of tubular genital papilla usually attached to anterior anal fin spine. First anal spine separate from rest of fin. Nasal, supraorbital, and nuchal cirri usually present. 41 or fewer scales in lateral line.

335 Hairy Blenny
Labrisomus nuchipinnis

Identification: A rather large blenny with a tapering, moderately compressed body. Operculum has dark spot surrounded by paler ring; body yellowish green to olive, mottled

with brown and gray, with irregular dark bars. Spot on anterior dorsal fin spines, becoming less prominent in larger fish. Anterior dorsal spines not elongate. *65–67 scales in lateral line.* SL to 7″ (18 cm).

Habitat: Coral and rock areas in shallow waters.

Range: Bermuda, Florida, Bahamas, Gulf of Mexico, Caribbean, including Antilles, to Brazil. Also e Atlantic.

Notes: The Hairy Blenny is a common species often encountered near reef tops in quite shallow waters. It is usually seen resting in a hole or crevice, and when disturbed it quickly moves to another crevice. This species is the largest of the labrisomids in our region.

Other *Labrisomus* species

Quillfin Blenny — (*L. filamentosus*) Large ocellus on operculum. 65 scales in lateral line. First 3 dorsal spines elongate. Bahamas, Hispaniola, Nicaragua.

Longfin Blenny — (*L. haitiensis*) No ocellus on operculum. Longest pelvic ray twice as long as shortest. 43–46 scales in lateral line. Body brownish with indistinct, irregular darker bars. All fins barred or speckled. Lining of body cavity pale. Florida, Bahamas, e Gulf of Mexico, Antilles, w Caribbean from Yucatán to Honduras.

Spotcheek Blenny — (*L. nigricinctus*) Very prominent ocellus on operculum. Head and snout narrow, pointed. Males pale yellowish with marbling on fins. Females tan with 8–9 rather regular dark bands extending onto dorsal and anal fins. 40–44 scales in lateral line. Florida, Bahamas, Antilles, Caribbean to Brazil.

Whitecheek Blenny — (*L. albigenys*) No ocellus on operculum. 41–44 scales in lateral line. Head blunt. Haiti, Antigua, Campeche Banks, Belize, Honduras, Venezuela.

Mimic Blenny — (*L. guppyi*) Ocellus on operculum. Head blunt. 48–53 scales in lateral line. Florida, Bahamas, Antilles, Yucatán, Belize to

Nicaragua, Curaçao, Venezuela, Fernando de Noronha, Brazil.

Puffcheek Blenny   *(L. bucciferus)* No ocellus on operculum. Shortest pelvic ray more than half as long as longest. 45–48 scales in lateral line. Lining of body cavity dark gray or black. Bermuda, Florida, Bahamas, Antilles, Yucatán, Belize to Nicaragua.

Palehead Blenny   *(L. gobio)* No ocellus on operculum. Lining of body cavity pale with scattered tiny spots. Anal and pectoral fins never heavily spotted. 48–53 scales in lateral line. Bahamas, Antilles, Yucatán, Belize to Nicaragua.

Downy Blenny   *(L. kalisherae)* No ocellus on operculum (young have dark smudge). Anal and pectoral fins usually heavily spotted. 48–53 scales in lateral line. Florida, coasts from Veracruz, Mexico, to Venezuela, Tobago, Fernando de Noronha, Brazil.

336   Saddled Blenny
Malacoctenus triangulatus

Identification: A tapering, moderately compressed labrisomid. Pale tan with *3–5 dark brownish-red bands in form of inverted triangles along side.* Dark spot at base of first dorsal fin spine. 14 pectoral rays. 52–61 scales in lateral line. TL to 3″ (7.6 cm).

Habitat: Patch reefs and eroded limestone areas in waters to depths of 45′ (14 m).

Range: Bahamas, s Florida, sw Gulf of Mexico, and Caribbean, including Antilles. Also reported from Fernando de Noronha, Brazil.

Notes: The Saddled Blenny is a rather common shallow-water species frequently seen by divers and snorkelers and often found in very shallow waters. No other labrisomid has this distinctive color pattern.

337   Diamond Blenny
Malacoctenus boehlkei

Identification: A tapering, compressed labrisomid with a long, pointed snout. Pale tan with various irregular spots. Upper side has series of dark blotches; *lower side has series of diamond-shaped markings.* Dark spot near middle of second, third, and fourth dorsal fin spines. Longest pelvic fin ray more than 4 times as long as shortest. No scales on fin membranes. 15 pectoral fin rays. 58–66 scales in lateral line. TL to 2½″ (6.4 cm).

Habitat: Coral reefs at depths of 25–70′ (7.5–21 m).

Range: Bahamas to Virgin Islands, Belize, Honduras, and Cayos de Albuquerque off Nicaragua.

Notes: The Diamond Blenny is a conspicuous and easily recognized species. It is more apt to be seen by divers than snorkelers because it lives in slightly deeper parts of the reef.

Similar Species: Related species lack diamonds on lower sides and have longest pelvic fin ray less than 4 times as long as shortest. Saddled Blenny also has spot at base of anterior dorsal spines but has series of large triangular saddles on body.

338   Rosy Blenny
Malacoctenus macropus

Identification: A moderately compressed labrisomid. *No conspicuous spots or ocelli.* Males dark grayish with broad darker gray stripe along upper third of body, and white blotches along dorsal fin base, sometimes interrupted by about 6 narrow paler bands. Females paler, darker above than below, with small dark spots on pale gray background. No spot on last dorsal spines. Usually 15 pectoral rays. 40–45 scales in lateral line. TL to 2⅛″ (5.6 cm).

Habitat: Sponge beds in shallow waters and grassy areas to depths of 25′ (7.5 m).

Range: Bermuda, Florida, Bahamas, Antilles to
Venezuela, Yucatán, Belize to Panama.

Notes: The Rosy Blenny is a common but
rather plain species often abundant in
very shallow water around the bases of
sponges and finger corals. It is the only
member of its genus that does not have a
conspicuous color pattern.

---

339   Goldline Blenny
Malacoctenus aurolineatus

Identification: A tapering, moderately compressed
labrisomid. Body pale with dark bars;
*first two bars connected to form an H, last two
bars remote from first.* In life, lower side of
body has golden yellow lines. No scales
on membranes of fins. 48–53 scales in
lateral line. 14 pectoral fin rays. TL to
2¼" (5.8 cm).

Habitat: Along shorelines, over shallow reefs
and beach rock in water to depths of 20'
(6 m).

Range: Florida, Bahamas, Antilles, Campeche
Banks, Yucatán, Belize, Honduras, Isla
San Andrés, Serrana Bank, Venezuela.

Notes: The Goldline Blenny is often associated
with rock-boring sea urchins along rocky
shorelines where there is considerable
wave action.

Other *Malacoctenus* species

Imitator Blenny   *(M. erdmani)* Dark spot below last dorsal
spines that does not extend onto fin. 16
pectoral rays. Bahamas, Antilles, Honduras, Nicaragua.

Dusky Blenny   *(M. gilli)* Dark ocellated spot at base of
last dorsal spines extends onto fin. Dark
ocellus on anterior dorsal spines. 14 pectoral rays. Bahamas, Antilles, w Gulf of
Mexico, Yucatán to Venezuela, Curaçao.

M. delalandei   Evenly spaced irregular dark bands on
body extending less than halfway up dor-
sal and anal fins. No dark spots at base of
dorsal fin. 4 dark bars radiate from eye.
48–54 lateral-line scales. 14 pectoral

rays. Caribbean, including Greater Antilles and Tobago; Natal, Brazil.

M. versicolor   Dark bands on body extending onto dorsal and anal fins nearly to fin margins. No dark spots at base of dorsal fin. 59–64 scales in lateral line. Bahamas, Antilles, Belize.

340 Blackcheek Blenny
Starksia lepicoelia

Identification: A robust blenny with unbranched nasal, nuchal, and supraorbital cirri. More or less uniformly reddish brown, sometimes with pale vertical bands. Males have dark blotch on cheek. Belly completely scaled. 2 visible pelvic fin rays. *Adult males have genital papilla not attached to first anal spine.* SL to 1¼" (3.2 cm).

Habitat: Coral reefs at depths of 26–66′ (8–20 m).
Range: Bahamas, Grand Cayman, Virgin Islands, Antigua, Arrecife Alacrán, Banco Chinchorro, Turneffe Islands and Lighthouse Reef off Belize, Honduras, Isla de Providencia, and Cayos de Albuquerque off Nicaragua.
Notes: The Blackcheek Blenny is a distinctive but secretive species unlikely to be seen.

Other *Starksia* species

S. hassi   3 visible rays in pelvic fin (2 in all other *Starksia*). Bahamas, Puerto Rico, Virgin Islands, Antigua, Guadeloupe, Belize, Panama, Venezuela.

Smootheye Blenny   (*S. atlantica*) Dark overall with pale lines between irregular dark patches. Prominent round spot around base of last dorsal rays; smaller spot at base of last anal rays. Bahamas, Haiti, Antigua, Yucatán; Turneffe Islands, Lighthouse and Glovers Reefs, off Belize; Isla de Providencia, Honduras, Courtown Cays, Nicaragua, Curaçao, Venezuela.

Key Blenny   (*S. starcki*) Body has 8–9 widely spaced, sometimes broken, vertical dark bars;

posterior bars sometimes replaced by broken horizontal line. Belly fully scaled. Florida Keys, Honduras.

Dwarf Blenny

(S. nanodes) Body pale with 2 dark L-shaped marks at base of tail. Bahamas, Haiti, Grand Cayman, Virgin Islands, Turneffe Islands off Belize, Honduras, Cayos de Albuquerque off Nicaragua, Isla de Providencia, Colombia.

Blackbar Blenny

(S. fasciata) Body pale with 7–8 vertical bars about as wide as interspaces. Males have dark blotch on cheek. Belly unscaled. Genital papilla of males longer than first anal spine and bound to it for entire spine length. Bahamas, Cuba, Dominica, Antigua.

Checkered Blenny

(S. ocellata) Head and body dark, often with 3 rows of indistinct and irregular spots separated by pale lines. Side of head has small circular spots but no Y-shaped bar. North Carolina to Florida; sw Florida.

S. guttata

Side of head has circular spots and pale horizontal line that branches into Y posteriorly. Body pale with numerous round dark spots. No distinct vertical bars on lips. Tobago Cays and Grenadines to Trinidad and Curaçao.

S. culebrae

Side of head has pale, unbranched, horizontal line from eye to opercle. Vertical black bars on lips. Haiti, Puerto Rico, Lesser Antilles south to St. Vincent.

S. variabilis

Side of head has net-like pattern of dark lines. Vertical bars on lips. Santa Marta, Colombia.

S. occidentalis

Side of head has pale line that branches into Y posteriorly. Lips have vertical black bars. Yucatán, Belize, Honduras, Isla de Providencia, Panama.

S. sluiteri

Body pale with 3 rows of dark blotches, rounded in middle row, squarish in upper and lower rows. Antigua, Dominica, Yucatán, Glovers Reef off Belize, Nicaragua, Isla de Providencia, Bon-

	aire, Curaçao, Los Roques Islands off Venezuela.
S. elongata	Body pale with 7 vertical dark bars, each half as wide as pale interspaces. Genital papilla only slightly longer than, and joined to, first anal spine. S Bahamas, Belize, Honduras.
S. y-lineata	Dark above, pale below. Upper side has narrow, pale, Y-shaped vertical lines. Grand Cayman, Courtown Cays off Nicaragua.

Paraclinus species

1 spine and 3 soft rays in pelvic fin; last element of dorsal fin a soft ray.

Horned Blenny	(*P. grandicomis*) Supraorbital cirrus flat, fringed, and long, reaching beyond dorsal origin. Florida, Bahamas, Lesser Antilles.
Blackfin Blenny	(*P. nigripinnis*) Opercular spine ends in complex lobe with 2–5 points. Bermuda, Florida Keys, Bahamas, Antilles, Belize to Costa Rica, Isla de Providencia, Venezuela, Brazil.
Marbled Blenny	(*P. marmoratus*) Opercular spine long, reaching beyond base of third dorsal spine, ending in single point. 2–3 ocelli on dorsal fin. 1 ocellus on anal fin. Florida, Bahamas, Cuba, Glovers Reef off Belize, Venezuela.
Bald Blenny	(*P. infrons*) Anterior nostril tubular. No nasal or nuchal cirri. Bahamas, Glovers Reef and Carrie Bow Cay off Belize.
Goatee Blenny	(*P. barbatus*) Prominent barbel at tip of chin. Bahamas, Virgin Islands, Belize, Colombia.

1 spine and 2 soft rays in pelvic fin; dorsal fin all spines.

Banded Blenny	(*P. fasciatus*) Nuchal cirrus paddle-like, usually with 3 tiny points. 28–31 dorsal fin spines. Pale to dark brown, usually with some darker bars. 0–4 ocelli on

dorsal fin. Base of pectoral fin scaled. S Florida, Bahamas, Gulf of Mexico, Antilles, Belize, Guatemala, Honduras, Isla de Providencia, Panama, Colombia, Venezuela.

Surf Blenny	(*P. naeorhegmis*) Nuchal cirrus has several finger-like lobes. 26–27 dorsal fin spines. Anal fin has 2 spines, 16–17 rays. Base of pectoral fin scaled. Bahamas.
Coral Blenny	(*P. cingulatus*) No scales on pectoral fin base. Anal fin has 2 spines, 15–16 rays. 12 pectoral rays. Dry Tortugas, Bahamas, Cuba, Puerto Rico, Honduras.

COMBTOOTH BLENNIES
Family Blenniidae

Combtooth blennies are small, slender, scaleless fishes, usually with blunt heads. Most species have fleshy cirri or tabs on the eyes and sometimes on the nostrils and nape. The mouth is low and the upper jaw is not protrusible. Both jaws have a row of small, close-set teeth like those of a comb, and some species have large fangs at the rear of the jaws. The eyes are high on the sides of the head. The dorsal fin is usually continuous and has fewer spines than rays; sometimes it is notched between the spines and soft rays. Soft rays of all fins except the caudal fin are unbranched. The pectoral fins are large, and the pelvic fins are jugular, with a very small hidden spine and two to four rays.

This family includes 53 genera and 345 species worldwide; eight genera and 15 species occur naturally in our region, and one species from an additional genus (*Omobranchus*) has been introduced.

Genera of family Blenniidae

Gill membranes broadly joined to each other, but not to isthmus; gill openings continuous across ventral surface of head.

Entomacrodus	Dorsal fin deeply notched, nearly or completely separated. Supraorbital and nasal cirri branched. Single nuchal cirrus on each side.
Ophioblennius	Lateral line discontinuous, its two segments overlapping. Supraorbital cirri

	unbranched. Single nuchal cirrus on each side. Fangs in rear of mouth.
Scartella	Cirri on midline of head. Supraorbital cirri branched. No nuchal cirri.
Parablennius	Supraorbital cirri branched; several on each eye. No nuchal cirri.
Lupinoblennius	Supraorbital cirrus unbranched; one on each eye. No nuchal cirri.

Gill membranes broadly fused to isthmus, confining gill openings to sides of body.

Hypleurochilus	Enlarged canine teeth near rear of one or both jaws. No nuchal cirri; 4–15 supraorbital cirri on each eye.
Hypsoblennius	No enlarged canine teeth on jaws. No nuchal cirri; supraorbital cirrus branched.
Chasmodes	No cirri on head. Some caudal rays branched. 12 pectoral fin rays.
Omobranchus	All caudal rays unbranched. 2 pelvic fin rays. No cirri on head.

341 Striped Blenny
Chasmodes bosquianus

Identification: An elongate, rather heavy-bodied blenny. Head pointed, profile straight from snout to dorsal fin origin. *Brown with wavy dark and light lines and spots along side.* SL to 3⅛″ (8 cm).

Habitat: Oyster beds and other hard bottoms to depths of 100′ (30 m).

Range: New York to ne Florida, and n Gulf of Mexico from Florida panhandle to Texas.

Notes: The Striped Blenny has a discontinuous range, and the Atlantic population and the Gulf of Mexico population are now recognized as separate subspecies. The similar Florida Blenny populates the area between the two, where Striped Blennies are absent.

Similar Species: Florida Blenny *(C. saburrae)* is similar but lacks body stripes; it occurs in s Florida and e Gulf of Mexico as far west as Louisiana.

342 Redlip Blenny
Ophioblennius atlanticus

Identification:
An elongate, tapering species with *head profile in front of eyes vertical; forehead projects in front of snout. Head, body, and anal fin dark reddish brown, sometimes pale pinkish gray; lips and parts of pectoral and tail fins red.* Body color extends onto base of dorsal fin; outer two-thirds of dorsal fin clear pink with red edge. Dark spot on side of head behind eye. Young sometimes barred. Mouth low, upper lip with lobes or papillae across its entire width. Dorsal fin continuous with shallow notch between spines and rays. TL to 4½" (11.5 cm).

Habitat:
Rocky shorelines where there is considerable wave action, to depths of about 26' (8 m).

Range:
Bermuda, North Carolina to Florida, Bahamas, and Caribbean, including Antilles, to Brazil. Rare in n Gulf of Mexico. Also in e Atlantic.

Notes:
The Redlip Blenny is very common and easily seen by snorkelers as it flits over rock surfaces. Because the body color extends onto the dorsal fin, the fish appears larger than it really is. No other blenny in our region has this color pattern.

343 Seaweed Blenny
Parablennius marmoreus

Identification:
An elongate, tapering blenny with a large eye and blunt head profile. Color variable, usually pale tan with scattered brown spots, and dusky stripe on mid-side from behind head to below last dorsal fin spines. Dark spot on anterior spines of dorsal fin. Lower half of head white. Upper lip smooth. *No median row of cirri;* supraorbital cirri branched. TL to 3⅜" (8.5 cm).

Habitat:
Rocky and sandy areas to depths of 20' (6 m). Sometimes around mangrove roots.

Range: New York to Florida, Bahamas, Gulf of Mexico, and Caribbean, including Antilles.

Notes: The Seaweed Blenny is said to seek shelter in crevices and sometimes to make its own hiding place by removing sand from under a stone. The young are sometimes found in floating sargassum weed.

Similar Species: Molly Miller is similar but has median row of cirri on head.

---

344 Molly Miller
Scartella cristata

Identification: An elongate, tapering blenny. Greenish gray with scattered groups of vertical dashes and sometimes pearly white spots. May have broad, dark, vertical bands. Upper lip smooth. *Median longitudinal row of cirri forms fringe on top of head.* Supraorbital cirri with multiple branches. TL to 4″ (10 cm).

Habitat: Tide pools and shallow waters along rocky shorelines, generally in water to depths of 10′ (3 m).

Range: Bermuda, North Carolina to Florida, Bahamas, Gulf of Mexico, Caribbean, including Antilles, to Brazil. Also in e Atlantic.

Notes: The Molly Miller is easily observed by snorkelers and can be seen from the surface when it is in tide pools.

Similar Species: Seaweed Blenny is similar but lacks row of cirri on head.

---

345 Tessellated Blenny
Hypsoblennius invemar

Identification: A stout, rather deep-bodied blenny. Greenish brown; *head and usually pectoral fin base have orange spots on dark background. Black spot on side of head behind eye.* Orbital cirri well developed. Teeth comb-like. 4 pelvic fin rays. SL to 1⅞″ (4.7 cm).

Habitat: In Gulf of Mexico, barnacle shells on oil platforms. Elsewhere, in old barnacle shells and other holes.

Range: Gulf of Mexico off Louisiana, St. Barthélemy, Colombia, and Venezuela.

Notes: The Tessellated Blenny is a strikingly colored blenny that guards its eggs in the shells of barnacles.

Other *Hypsoblennius* species

Longhorn Blenny *(H. exstochilus)* Elongate posterior flap on lower lip. Dorsal spines flexible. Very long, branched orbital cirrus. Bahamas, Jamaica, Mona Island, St. Croix.

Freckled Blenny *(H. ionthas)* Upper lip separated by continuous groove around snout. Lower lips broad, fleshy, separated by shield-shaped central lobe; no elongate flap. North Carolina to n Florida, n Gulf of Mexico.

Feather Blenny *(H. hentz)* Upper lip connected to snout by bridge of tissue. Smooth area, but no shield-shaped lobe, between thin lower lips; no elongate flap. Nova Scotia to n Florida, n Gulf of Mexico.

Other species of combtooth blennies

Pearl Blenny *(Entomacrodus nigricans)* Deep notch between spiny and soft dorsal fins. Bermuda, Florida, Bahamas, Antilles, Curaçao, Yucatán, Belize to Venezuela.

Highfin Blenny *(Lupinoblennius nicholsi)* First 4 dorsal spines of adult males elongate, free at tips. Dorsal and anal fins connected to caudal fin by low membrane. Florida; Gulf of Mexico at Tamaulipas, Mexico.

Mangrove Blenny *(Lupinoblennius dispar)* No high lobe on dorsal fin of males. 8–9 prominent but sometimes interrupted dark bars on side. Jamaica, Antigua, Trinidad, Yucatán, Belize to Panama.

Oyster Blenny *(Hypleurochilus aequipinnis)* Greenish gray with dark spots grouped into 5 squarish blotches on upper side. Black spot at front of dorsal fin. Florida, Bahamas, Antilles, Yucatán, Belize to Honduras, Venezuela. Also e Atlantic.

Crested Blenny	*(Hypleurochilus geminatus)* Squarish spots on side not grouped into bars or blotches. Black spot at front of dorsal fin. North Carolina to s Florida; Gulf of Mexico west to Texas.
Orangespotted Blenny	*(Hypleurochilus springeri)* 5 groups of spots on side. No spot on dorsal fin. Florida Keys, Bahamas, Antilles, Los Roques Islands off Venezuela.
Barred Blenny	*(Hypleurochilus bermudensis)* 6 dark saddles across back. No spot on dorsal fin. Bermuda, Bahamas, s and w Florida.
Omobranchus punctatus	All rays in caudal fin unbranched. Gill openings on side of head above level of upper end of pectoral fin base. Indo-Pacific; introduced at Trinidad and Panama Canal near Atlantic end.

DRAGONETS
Family Callionymidae

Our local species of dragonets are small, slender, terete fishes with depressed heads and small, terminal, protrusible mouths. The eyes are large and protrude dorsally. Dragonets have two dorsal fins; in adult males the spiny dorsal is short but high and colorful. The pelvic fins are rather large, and inserted ahead of the pectoral fins. The gill opening is small and restricted to the upper side of the head. The preopercle has a strong, complexly hooked and barbed spine.

The family contains 18 genera and about 130 species. Three genera occur in our region, but only two live in shallow water. The closely related family Draconettidae has only two deep-water species in our region, and is not covered.

Genera of family Callionymidae

Diplogrammus	Longitudinal dermal fold on lower side. Only last dorsal fin rays branched at tips.
Paradiplogrammus	No dermal fold on side. Most dorsal rays unbranched.
Foetorepus	No dermal fold on side. Most dorsal rays branched.

348 Lancer Dragonet
Paradiplogrammus bairdi

Identification: Body reddish, mottled. *Preopercular spine has 3 or more teeth on top and 1 forward-projecting spine on bottom.* Second dorsal fin has 8 rays; anal fin has 7 rays. First dorsal fin twice as high as second in adult males. TL to 4½" (11.5 cm).

Habitat: On sand around shallow reefs to depths of 300' (90 m).

Range: Bermuda, w Florida, Bahamas, and Caribbean, including Antilles.

Notes: The Lancer Dragonet was formerly known as *Callionymus bairdi.*

Similar Species: Spotfin Dragonet *(Foetorepus agassizi),* which occurs off Florida coast at depths of 300–2,100' (90–640 m), has 2 upturned spines on preopercle. Spotted Dragonet *(Diplogrammus pauciradiatus)* has dermal fold on side, 6 dorsal rays, and 4 anal rays; it occurs in Bermuda, North Carolina to Florida, Bahamas to Colombia.

GOBIES
Family Gobiidae

With more species than any other family in tropical waters, the family Gobiidae encompasses fishes of extremely diverse structures and habits. Gobies range in size from tiny (less than 1 inch/2.5 cm long) to moderate (up to 19 inches/48 cm long). Most species have moderately elongate, terete bodies with two dorsal fins. Because the second dorsal and anal fins usually have a weak spine at the front followed by soft rays, the total fin elements (spines plus soft rays) are counted. In most species the inner rays of the pelvic fins are connected by a membrane, forming a suction disk with which the gobies cling to the bottom. There may be another membrane, called a *frenum,* across the front of the disk between the pelvic fin spines. Sometimes the inner pelvic rays are shorter than the outer rays, so that the disk is notched at the back. In some species the pelvic fins are almost, or even completely, separate. The tail ranges from rounded to pointed; in a few species it is slightly forked.

Gobies vary from scaleless to fully scaled. They have no lateral lines on the body; scale counts are made along the side of the body as if there were a lateral line and are given as "scales in lateral series." Most species have sensory canals on the head with pores opening to the surface, but a few genera lack these pores. The presence and structure of these sensory canals and their pores are important genus and species characteristics.

Some gobies live in fresh water, but their young are carried out to sea where they spend their early larval period. The family includes about 212 genera and 1,875 species in five subfamilies. The classification of gobies is under active study, and name changes can be expected. At present about 30 genera are recognized from our region. We also include here the genus *Ptereleotris,* which belongs to the family Microdesmidae (subfamily Ptereleotrinae), because of its superficial resemblance to the six-spined gobies.

Genera of family Gobiidae

6 spines in first dorsal fin.

Gobioides	Only goby in our region with single continuous dorsal fin. Body large, long, and slender, eel-like. Pelvic fins completely united.
Awaous	Front edge of shoulder girdle with 2 fleshy tabs under gill cover. Pelvic fins completely united.
Bathygobius	Upper pectoral rays free, not connected by membrane. Pelvic fins completely united.
Sicydium	Pelvic fins completely united. Pelvic disk joined to abdominal wall for much of its length.
Gnatholepis	Body fully scaled; cheek and opercle scaled. Pelvic fins completely united. Mouth inferior.
Coryphopterus	Body fully scaled; cheek and opercle unscaled. Mouth terminal. Second dorsal fin has same number of rays as, or 1 more than, anal fin. Caudal fin rounded. Pelvic fins separate to completely united.
Gobionellus	Body fully scaled; predorsal area and nape may have scales; cheek and opercle unscaled. Second dorsal fin has 1 less ray than anal fin. Caudal fin pointed. Pelvic fins completely united.
Lophogobius	Body fully scaled; cheek and opercle unscaled. Head has prominent mid-dorsal crest. Pelvic fins completely united.

Evorthodus	Snout short and rounded, mouth inferior. Body completely scaled. Pelvic fins completely united.
Lythrypnus	No head pores. Head, nape, chest, and pectoral fin base unscaled. Mouth terminal. Pelvic fins completely united; inner pelvic rays shorter than outer, making rear edge of disk indented.
Priolepis	No head pores. Occiput, nape, chest, and pectoral fin base scaled. 17–19 pectoral fin rays. Pelvic fins completely united.
Vomerogobius	Dorsal fins well separated, with interspace longer than base of spiny part; second dorsal fin has 1 spine and 11 rays. Pelvic fins completely united, inner rays longer than outer rays; no frenum. Caudal fin deeply emarginate. Vomer and jaws have large canine-like teeth.
Ptereleotris	Pelvic fins separate. 24 elements in second dorsal fin. 22–24 elements in anal fin.

7 spines in first dorsal fin.

Psilotris	Pelvic fins separate; no frenum. No scales; no head pores.
Varicus	Pelvic fins separate, but with low membrane between inner rays; rays long, unbranched. Body scaled. No head pores.
Chriolepis	Pelvic fins completely separate, no membrane connecting inner rays; first 4 rays branched. No head pores. Scales reduced to 1–2 patches on side or to just 2 scales on each side of caudal fin base.
Pycnomma	Pelvic fins nearly separate; inner rays slightly joined at base; no frenum. No pores on preopercle. Rear of body scaled.
Nes	No scales; no head pores. Pelvic fins united, with frenum. Body pale.
Gobulus	Pelvic fins united, but indented posteriorly; frenum weak or absent. No scales; no head pores. Body dark below and pale above.

Risor	Pelvic fins united, with frenum. No pores on preopercle. Jaws have outward-curving, tusk-like teeth. 14–20 scales in lateral series.
Parrella	Pelvic fins united, with frenum. No pores on preopercle. No tusk-like teeth. 28–38 scales in lateral series.
Barbulifer	Pelvic fins united, with frenum. Head pores present. 2–3 pores on preopercle. No scales. 3 pairs of barbels on head.
Bollmannia	Pelvic fins united, with frenum. 2–3 pores on preopercle. Body fully scaled, including top of head, nape, and chest. 12–14 elements in second dorsal fin.
Microgobius	Pelvic fins united, with frenum. 2–3 pores on preopercle. Chest, nape, and top of head unscaled. Body scaled from behind pectoral fin to caudal peduncle; more than 40 scales in lateral series. Second dorsal fin long, with 15 or more elements.
Ginsburgellus	Pelvic fins united, with frenum. 2–3 pores on preopercle. No scales. Upper lip broadly joined to snout and free only near corner of mouth. Brown, with 9 narrow vertical bars.
Gobiosoma	Pelvic fins united, with frenum. 2–3 pores on preopercle. Usually no barbels. Head, chest, and nape without scales; body with or without scales. Upper lip entirely free or with narrow frenum at front.
Palatogobius	Pelvic fins united; no frenum. Posterior fourth of body scaled. Large teeth on vomer.

Different numbers of spines in first dorsal fin.

Pariah	8 dorsal spines. Pelvic fins united, with frenum. No head pores. Scales only on lower half of caudal peduncle and on caudal and anal fin bases.
Evermannichthys	3–7 dorsal fin spines. Pelvic fins united; well-developed frenum. Scales variable but only on lower posterior part of body. Elongate, very slender.

368   Violet Goby
Gobioides broussoneti

Identification:

A very large, elongate, eel-like goby with *a continuous dorsal fin, and dorsal and anal fins joined with caudal fin.* Purplish brown and mottled, often with chevron-shaped markings on side. Body fully scaled; anterior scales smaller than posterior scales. TL to 19" (48 cm).

Habitat: Tidal creeks and drainage canals.

Range: Georgia to Florida, Gulf of Mexico and Caribbean coasts to Brazil, and Greater Antilles.

Notes: The Violet Goby is the largest goby in our area, and the only one with this distinctive eel-like shape.

351   Frillfin Goby
Bathygobius soporator

Identification:

Mottled grayish brown, often with dark saddles across back. Body scaled. 20 or 21 pectoral fin rays; *uppermost rays not connected by membrane, appear fringed. 37–41 scales in lateral series.* Tip of tongue notched, not rounded. TL to 6" (15 cm).

Habitat: Tide pools and shallows, usually in water to depths of 10' (3 m).

Range: Bermuda, North Carolina to Florida, Bahamas, Gulf of Mexico, and Caribbean, including Antilles. Also in Brazil and e Atlantic.

Notes: The Frillfin Goby, named for its free upper pectoral fin rays, often jumps from isolated tide pools to open water or to other tide pools.

Similar Species: Other gobies with free upper pectoral fin rays are smaller and have fewer lateral scales. Notchtongue Goby *(B. curacao)* has 31–34 (usually 33) scales in lateral series, 16 or 17 pectoral fin rays, and deep notch at front of tongue; it is known from Bermuda, Florida, Bahamas, Antilles, and Central American coast. Island Frillfin *(B. mystacium)* has blunter head, 33–36 (usually 35) scales in lateral series, and 19 or 20 pectoral fin rays; it lives in Bahamas, Greater Antilles, and w Caribbean.

367 Goldspot Goby
Gnatholepis thompsoni

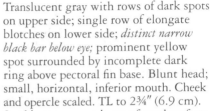

Identification: Translucent gray with rows of dark spots on upper side; single row of elongate blotches on lower side; *distinct narrow black bar below eye;* prominent yellow spot surrounded by incomplete dark ring above pectoral fin base. Blunt head; small, horizontal, inferior mouth. Cheek and opercle scaled. TL to 2¾″ (6.9 cm).

Habitat: Sand bottoms near bases of coral reefs to depths of 85′ (25 m).

Range: Bermuda, Florida, Bahamas, Antilles, and Central and South American coasts.

Notes: A very common species, the Goldspot Goby feeds on organisms and organic material by taking sand into its mouth and expelling it through the gill openings, filtering out its food in the process.

Similar Species: Gobies of genus *Coryphopterus* are similar but lack scales on cheek and opercle and have terminal mouths.

352 Colon Goby
Coryphopterus dicrus

Identification: Body pale sand color with brown spots of varying sizes; dark bar at caudal fin base; and *2 distinct dark spots, one above other, on pectoral fin base.* 10 elements each in second dorsal and anal fins. Inner rays of pelvic fins joined by membrane, branched but shorter than outer rays; no frenum. SL to 1½″ (3.8 cm).

Habitat: Coral reefs; prefers rocky areas between individual coral colonies, at depths of 3–50′ (1–15 m).

Range: Florida Keys, Bahamas, and Caribbean, including Antilles.

Notes: A common species, the Colon Goby is easily seen by divers.

Similar Species:
Spotted Goby *(C. punctipectophorus),* from w coast of Florida, has 10 elements in second dorsal fin and prominent spot on ventral half of pectoral fin base. Bartail Goby *(C. thrix)* has second dorsal fin spine extended as filament, and dark spot on dorsal part of pectoral fin base; it occurs in Bahamas.

353 Bridled Goby
Coryphopterus glaucofraenum

Identification:
Pale sand color with *black spot on side of head above gill cover* and 3 rows of round to X-shaped dark spots on body (spots often quite faint). Caudal fin base has dark, often dumbbell-shaped bar, sometimes broken into 2 spots. Branchiostegal membranes pale. 10 elements each in second dorsal and anal fins. Pelvic fins united, with well-developed frenum; inner pelvic rays branched, about as long as outer rays. SL to 2¼" (5.8 cm).

Habitat:
Sand around bases of coral reefs, to depths of more than 80' (25 m).

Range:
Bermuda, North Carolina, s Florida, Florida Keys, Bahamas, around Caribbean, including Antilles, and Brazil.

Notes:
The Bridled Goby, which has X-shaped marks and spots, occurs in both clear and more murky inshore waters, while the paler, very similar Sand Goby occurs over white sand.

Similar Species:
Sand Goby *(C. tortugae),* which also has black spot above operculum, is usually considered a pale variety of Bridled Goby; it is known from Bermuda, Bahamas, Florida, Antilles, Venezuela, and w Caribbean. Pallid Goby *(C. eidolon),* known from Florida, Bahamas, Haiti, and Virgin Islands, has 2 pale stripes on side of head and lower stripe outlined in black and extending from rear of eye socket to above pectoral fin base; it lacks black spot above operculum. *C. venezuelae,* of Venezuela,

has small round black spots on caudal
fin base, 11 elements in second dorsal fin
and 10 or 11 in anal, and small obscure
spot in lower prepectoral area.

355 Masked Goby
Coryphopterus personatus

Identification: Pale orange-red with dark mask from
snout through eye. Row of white spots
along backbone shows through almost-
transparent flesh. *Anus centered in black
ring. 2 pores between eyes.* Second dorsal fin
spine elongate. 11 elements each in
second dorsal and anal fins. Pelvic fins
nearly separate, without frenum. TL to
1⅜″ (3.5 cm).

Habitat: Hovers above bottom in caves and shaded
areas in reefs.

Range: Bermuda, Bahamas, and Caribbean,
including Antilles.

Notes: The Masked Goby often occurs in large
schools.

Similar Species: Glass Goby *(C. hyalinus),* from Florida,
Bahamas, Greater Antilles, and w
Caribbean, is similar but has anus near
front of black ring. Peppermint Goby is
yellow and has 2 or 3 horizontal dark
lines behind eye.

354 Peppermint Goby
Coryphopterus lipernes

Identification: *Rich yellow with blue snout and 2 dusky
stripes behind eye.* Anus centered in
narrow dark ring. 10 elements each in
second dorsal and anal fins. Second
dorsal fin spine elongate. Pelvic fins
nearly separate, without frenum. TL to
1¼″ (3.2 cm).

Habitat: Surface of live corals.

Range: Florida Keys, Bahamas, and Caribbean,
including Antilles.

Notes: The Peppermint Goby can be found by
examining the surface of coral colonies.

Similar Species: Masked Goby and Glass Goby are
reddish with black band through eye.

Barfin Goby *(C. alloides)*, from Bahamas
and Belize, also has pelvic fins nearly
separate but has no black ring around
anus and is pale with black blotch
on first dorsal fin and dark bar at base
of tail.

357 Darter Goby
Gobionellus boleosoma

Identification: Light tan with dark triangular shoulder
spot above pectoral fin. *About 5 round or
elongate dark blotches along mid-side, some
with diagonal marks extending upward to
form V shapes.* No circular spots on side
of head; no bands on pectoral fin. 11
elements in second dorsal fin; 12 in anal
fin. No canine teeth. Usually no scales
on predorsal area; fewer than 46 scales in
lateral series. TL to 2⅞″ (7.5 cm).

Habitat: Higher-salinity grass flats of lower
estuaries and barrier islands.

Range: Chesapeake Bay to Florida, Bahamas,
Gulf of Mexico, Cayman Islands, and
Caribbean to Brazil.

Notes: Although the Darter Goby prefers higher
salinity areas and the Freshwater Goby
lower salinity areas and fresh water, the
two species live together in mud-bottom
estuaries of the north-central Gulf of
Mexico.

358 Freshwater Goby
Gobionellus shufeldti

Identification: Pale tan with 5 *dark squarish blotches
along mid-side. No bar below eye; no shoulder
spot.* 12 elements in second dorsal fin; 13
in anal fin. 17 or 18 pectoral fin rays.
Usually a few scales in predorsal area. TL
to 3⅛″ (8 cm).

Habitat: Low salinity, upper estuarine marshes.
Often enters fresh water.

Range: North Carolina to ec Florida, n Gulf of
Mexico from Florida panhandle to c
Texas; also Venezuela and Brazil.

Notes: The Freshwater Goby and the Darter Goby are very similar, but the Darter usually does not enter fresh water.

359 Dash Goby
Gobionellus saepepallens

Identification: Pale bluish gray with reddish brown mottling on upper side. *Triangular dark blotch on operculum; 5 elongate dark blotches along mid-side; thin dark bar below eye. No shoulder spot.* Adults have canine teeth on both jaws. 12 elements in second dorsal fin; 13 in anal fin. No scales on nape. TL to 2″ (5 cm).

Habitat: Sand bottoms; shares burrow with shrimp.

Range: Southern Florida and Bahamas to Venezuela.

Notes: The Dash Goby cohabits with a nearly blind shrimp that clears sand from the burrow while the goby keeps watch for predators.

Similar Species: Comma Goby is similar but has thick, comma-shaped bar below eye.

Other *Gobionellus* species

Fewer than 46 scales in lateral series.

G. munizi	12 elements in second dorsal fin, 13 in anal fin. Possibly same species as Darter Goby. Cuba.
Comma Goby	*(G. comma)* Dark comma-shaped bar below eye. 5 indistinct elongate spots on side. Black diamond-shaped spot near tip of fourth dorsal spine; smaller spot near tips of fifth and sixth dorsal spines. 12 elements in second dorsal fin, 13 in anal fin. Venezuela.
Blackfin Goby	*(G. atripinnis)* 5 narrow elongate blotches on mid-side; small but distinct spots between posterior 3 blotches in females. Males have distinct elongate black blotches at tips of first elements of both dorsal fins. 12 elements in second dorsal fin, 13 in anal fin. W Gulf of Mexico from Texas to Veracruz.

Slashcheek Goby	(*G. pseudofasciatus*) Pale with 5 oval blotches on side. Distinct dark blotch from lower rear corner of cheek, upward and forward to behind end of maxilla. No dark bar below eye. 12 elements in second dorsal fin, 13 in anal fin. Lower se coast of Florida, Belize, Costa Rica, Trinidad.
G. fasciatus	Dark blotch on lower rear of cheek. Diagonal line from top rear of maxilla to just below and behind eye. 6–8 small spots near base of anal fin membrane. 12 elements in second dorsal fin, 13 in anal fin. Dominica, Trinidad, Costa Rica.
G. claytoni	Distinct dark blotches on side; no dark blotch on cheek. 12 elements in second dorsal fin, 13 in anal fin. Veracruz.
Emerald Goby	(*G. smaragdus*) Black circles on side of head; many green spots on side; dark spot above pectoral fin base. 11 elements in second dorsal fin, 12 in anal fin. South Carolina to Florida, Cuba (absent from rest of Antilles), Gulf of Mexico and Caribbean coasts to Brazil.
Marked Goby	(*G. stigmaticus*) 3 bars on cheek; small shoulder spot. Thread-like extensions on spines of first dorsal fin. 12 elements in second dorsal fin, 13 in anal fin. North Carolina to Florida, ne Gulf of Mexico, Cuba, Honduras, Brazil.
Spottail Goby	(*G. stigmaturus*) Dark blotches on mid-side that continue ventrally as comma-shaped marks. Faint shoulder spot. 12 elements in second dorsal fin, 13 in anal fin. Bermuda, se Florida, Cuba, Belize, and Panama.

More than 46 scales in lateral series.

Highfin Goby	(*G. oceanicus*) Thread-like extensions on second, third, and fourth dorsal spines. Light brown, paler below. Dark brown oval above pectoral fin and below rear half of first dorsal fin. 14 elements in second dorsal fin, 15 in anal fin. Caudal fin very long and pointed. Atlantic coast from North Carolina, Gulf of Mexico to Bay of Campeche.

Spotfin Goby

(G. stigmalophius) Pale with 4 large rounded spots along mid-side; conspicuous black spot at rear of first dorsal fin. 13 elements in second dorsal fin, 14 in anal fin. Bahamas, Gulf of Mexico, Suriname.

356 Lyre Goby
Evorthodus lyricus

Identification: Brown and gray with 5 or 6 narrow irregular dark bars and median blotches. Caudal fin large and bluntly pointed with *dark lyre-shaped mark on base consisting of 2 dark spots separated by pale central area.* Males have pink stripes on upper and lower lobes of caudal fin. *Snout very short, mouth small and inferior. Adults have first 3 or 4 dorsal fin spines elongate, reaching from third to sixth ray of second dorsal in females, to base of caudal peduncle in males.* 16 pectoral fin rays. *Predorsal area and top of head scaled as far forward as eye;* some scales on operculum. SL to 3″ (7.7 cm).

Habitat: Muddy areas of bays and estuaries; enters fresh water.

Range: Chesapeake Bay to Florida, Gulf of Mexico, and Greater Antilles to n South America; absent from Bahamas.

Notes: The Lyre Goby is an attractive fish that lives in a less attractive muddy habitat.

Similar Species: Species of related genus *Gobionellus* are similar looking but usually lack scales on top of head and predorsal area.

371 Rusty Goby
Priolepis hipoliti

Identification: A rather chunky little goby with a projecting lower jaw. *Orange-red with poorly defined, dusky vertical bars.* Orange spots on fins. Pelvic fins fully united, but with no frenum. Second dorsal fin spine elongate. 10 elements in second dorsal fin. Nape fully scaled. TL to 1⅝″ (4.1 cm).

Habitat: Coral reefs, usually on undersides of ledges and roofs of caves in water to depths of 425' (130 m).

Range: Florida Keys, Bahamas, and Caribbean, including Antilles.

Notes: Snorkelers and divers should look for the colorful Rusty Goby under shaded ledges. Its stout body and orange color make it distinctive.

Similar Species: *P. dawsoni* is a similar species from Brazil with wider bars on body, pigment along dorsal fin base, and 11 elements in second dorsal fin.

---

372 Hovering Goby
Ptereleotris helenae

Identification: A moderately large, slender, goby-like fish with a high first dorsal fin and long second dorsal. *Body pale bluish-gray, with lavender overtones.* Blue stripe from between eyes to dorsal origin; similar lines on side of head, yellow stripe on underside of head. *Fins paler, greenish yellow;* second dorsal, anal, and lower caudal fins have red submarginal band. *Caudal fin rounded, moderately long. Mouth very oblique. Scales very small, about 145 in lateral series;* smooth and embedded anteriorly, ctenoid posteriorly. SL to 3½" (9.1 cm).

Habitat: Sand or mud bottoms at depths of 30–200' (9–60 m).

Range: Southeastern Florida, Bahamas, and Caribbean, including Antilles.

Notes: Although the Hovering Goby belongs to the subfamily Ptereleotrinae, the dartfishes, of the family Microdesmidae, it is included here because of its resemblance to the six-spined gobies. True to its name, it hovers over its burrow, a U-shaped tunnel lined with stones.

Similar Species: Blue Goby *(P. calliurus)* of s Florida and e Gulf of Mexico has very long, pointed tail; black pigment on anal fin, lower half of caudal fin, and first dorsal fin margin; and brownish submarginal band on second dorsal fin.

Other gobies with 6 spines in first dorsal fin

River Goby
(Awaous banana) Snout conical; lips thick; eye small. Pale yellowish tan with irregular blotches and worm-like markings. Small scales (more than 60 in lateral series). Florida and Antilles to Central America and Brazil.

Sirajo
(Sicydium plumieri) Head blunt; eye small; mouth low, horizontal. Young barred. Adult color varies with habitat. Females usually dull gray or brown. Adult males longer than 4″ (10 cm) are blue with white fins. Third through fifth dorsal spines of males extended as filaments. Caudal fin squarish in adults. Cuba, Jamaica, Puerto Rico, Martinique, Guadeloupe, St. Vincent, Barbados.

Crested Goby
(Lophogobius cyprinoides) High fleshy crest on top of head ending before base of first dorsal spine. Brownish olive with vague darker markings. Distal half of first dorsal fin dark. Bermuda, Florida, Bahamas, Greater Antilles, Central American coast.

Dwarf Goby
(Lythrypnus elasson) Reddish gray, uniformly pigmented. No dark spot at pectoral fin base. First 2 dorsal spines elongate, especially in males. Bahamas.

Pygmy Goby
(Lythrypnus minimus) Body translucent with pale bars on posterior half. Bahamas, Isla de Providencia, Venezuela.

Diphasic Goby
(Lythrypnus heterochroma) First 2 dorsal spines elongate, especially in males. Pale sand color with dark bands anteriorly and longitudinal stripes posteriorly. No spots on pectoral fin base. Bahamas, Grand Cayman, Glovers Reef off Belize.

Bluegold Goby
(Lythrypnus spilus) Large spot extending full width of pectoral fin base. Blue and yellow bands on body, each blue band with darker center line. S Florida, Bahamas, Greater Antilles.

Island Goby
(Lythrypnus nesiotes) Alternating pale and dark brown bands; dark center line in pale bands. Cheek and occiput pale tan with

round dark spots. Single dark spot on lower half of pectoral fin base. Dorsal fin spines never elongate. Bahamas, Haiti, Puerto Rico, Virgin Islands, w Caribbean.

Convict Goby
(Lythrypnus phorellus) Alternating dark and pale bands; light bands have dark line in center; dark bands have pale central area. 2 indistinct blotches on pectoral fin base; lower spot larger and darker than upper. Florida Keys, Texas, w Caribbean.

Okapi Goby
(Lythrypnus okapia) Large spot on pectoral fin base. Narrow dark bands on body without dark center line. Great Bahama Bank.

Mahogany Goby
(Lythrypnus crocodilus) Dark spot covering entire pectoral fin base. 16 pectoral fin rays. Pale bands on body with dark center line. Haiti, Dominican Republic.

Lythrypnus mowbrayi
Spot on pectoral fin base confined to lower two-thirds. 17 pectoral fin rays. Pale bands with dark center line. Bermuda.

Lemon Goby
(Vomerogobius flavus) Slender. Lemon yellow in life; males without conspicuous markings, females with dark pigment on dorsal, anal, and pelvic fins and on middle of snout. Dark mid-dorsal line from rear third of head to base of tail. Bahamas.

---

369 Orangespotted Goby
Nes longus

Identification:
Moderately elongate. Grayish white or tan with *small orange spots on body and fins*. 5–7 paired dark brown lateral blotches along side. First dorsal spine elongate in both sexes. 13 or 14 elements in second dorsal fin. Body scaleless. No head pores. SL to 3¼″ (8.3 cm).

Habitat:
Soft sand and sandy mud at depths to 75′ (23 m). Shares burrow with shrimp.

Range:
Bermuda, Florida, Bahamas, s Gulf of Mexico (Arrecife Alacrán), Antilles, and Yucatán to Venezuela.

Notes:
The Orangespotted Goby is one of a few western Atlantic gobies that cohabits

with shrimp. The combination of an
elongate orange-spotted body with no
scales or head pores makes it unique.

370 Clown Goby
Microgobius gulosus

Identification: *Dark spots and blotches on body* but no
bright colors. Dark marginal band on
second dorsal fin; dark marginal or
submarginal band on anal fin. In females
both dorsal fins and upper part of caudal
fin have dark spots. Males have greatly
enlarged mouth, and second through
fifth dorsal spines extended as filaments.
16 elements in second dorsal fin, 17 in
anal fin. Pelvic fin reaches anal fin
origin. No nuchal crest. SL to 2¾"
(7.2 cm).

Habitat: Muddy estuaries with vegetation.
Sometimes moves well into fresh water.
Range: Chesapeake Bay to Florida and Gulf of
Mexico to Texas.
Notes: Large male Clown Gobies are sometimes
pale with only a few spots.

Other *Microgobius* species

Banner Goby | *(M. microlepis)* Light brown with no dark
spots on fins or body. Fleshy nuchal crest
moderate in females, weaker in males. Se
Florida (Jupiter Inlet south to Florida
Bay), Dry Tortugas, Bahamas, Yucatán,
Belize.

M. signatus | Well-developed nuchal crest. Dark spot
at upper part of caudal fin base. Females
have pale vertical bar edged in black on
shoulder. Antilles, coast of Venezuela.

M. meeki | Nuchal crest well developed in females,
smaller in males. Dark spot on body
below spiny dorsal fin origin. Caudal fin
long and pointed (2.4 in SL). Puerto
Rico, Venezuela south to Santos, Brazil.

Seminole Goby | *(M. carri)* Bright orange stripe along
body continuing to caudal fin. No dark
markings or nuchal crest. Not strongly

dimorphic. Peninsular Florida (Jacksonville south to Dry Tortugas), ne Gulf of Mexico, Lesser Antilles from St. John to Tobago.

Green Goby
(*M. thalassinus*) Body green. Chesapeake Bay to Cape Canaveral, Florida; n Gulf of Mexico to Galveston, Texas (absent from se Florida, Florida Keys).

360 Tiger Goby
Gobiosoma macrodon

Identification:
Body pale sand color, nearly translucent, with *13 dark bands narrower than pale interspaces.* 17 pectoral fin rays. Unscaled, except for 2 scales on each side of caudal fin base and patch of 4 or 5 scales on caudal peduncle. TL to 2″ (5 cm).

Habitat:
Tide pools and rocky areas; associated with red algae.

Range:
Southern Florida and Cuba to Haiti.

Notes:
The Tiger Goby is sometimes found on the surfaces of large sponges.

Similar Species:
Zebrette Goby (*G. zebrella*) has more scales and about 13 dark bands that are wider than pale interspaces; it occurs in Trinidad and Venezuela. Wall Goby (*G. pallens*), from Cayman Islands, Lesser Antilles, Belize, and Cayos de Albuquerque in w Caribbean, has fewer than 13 dark vertical bars. Frecklefin Goby (*G. gemmatum*), from Bahamas, Cayman Islands, Puerto Rico, Lesser Antilles, w Caribbean, from Belize to Isla de Providencia, and Venezuela, has fewer than 13 dark bars, and barred fins.

361 Leopard Goby
Gobiosoma saucrum

Identification:

Translucent sand color; small dark spots on head and body; *side of belly has 2 squarish red spots bordered in white figure 8-shaped mark.* 2 scales on side near base of caudal peduncle, and 4 or 5 rows of scales on side of caudal peduncle; body otherwise unscaled. SL to ⅝″ (1.6 cm).

Habitat: Living coral colonies.

Range: Florida Keys, Bahamas, Jamaica, Virgin Islands, and Belize.

Notes: The Leopard Goby is one of several small fishes that lives among the tentacles of living corals.

Similar Species: Orangeside Goby *(G. dilepis)* has bars on rear of body and 2 orange spots on side separated by white bar with black edges; it occurs in Bahamas, Grand Cayman, Lesser Antilles, and Belize.

362 Greenbanded Goby
Gobiosoma multifasciatum

Identification: *Dark green, with 17–23 pale green bars. Brownish stripe through eye interrupted by bright red spot.* Body scaleless. 20 or 21 pectoral fin rays. TL to 1¾″ (4.4 cm).

Habitat: Rocky shorelines, usually among spines of rock-boring sea urchins.

Range: Bahamas, Cuba, Cayman Islands, Antilles, and Caribbean coast from Panama to Venezuela.

Notes: Snorkelers can find this beautiful species by looking carefully around rock-boring sea urchins in shallow water. No other goby in our area has this combination of colors.

363 Neon Goby
Gobiosoma oceanops

Identification: Nearly black above, pale gray below; *electric blue stripe from front of eye to end of caudal fin. Pale stripe in front of each eye, not reaching tip of snout.* Black stripe below blue stripe from tip of snout to tip of caudal fin rays. Mouth inferior; snout overhangs upper lip, to which it is connected by frenum. Body scaleless. SL to 1⅝″ (4.1 cm).

Habitat: Living coral colonies.

Range: Southern Florida, Florida Keys, Texas coast, Yucatán, and Belize.

Notes: The Neon Goby is a well-known cleaner, removing parasites and bits of dead

tissue from fishes that come to its
cleaning stations.

Similar Species: Yellowline Goby also lacks markings
on tip of snout but has terminal mouth
and pale yellow stripe behind eye.

364 Yellowline Goby
Gobiosoma horsti

Identification: Dark gray above, paler below. Snout
dusky, tip unmarked. *Narrow, pale yellow
or white line extending from eye to caudal fin
base.* Individuals from Belize have white
bar on snout. Mouth terminal; upper lip
separated from snout by groove, not
connected by frenum. Body scaleless. SL
to 1⅞″ (4.7 cm).

Habitat: Tubular sponges to depths of 100′ (30 m).

Range: Southern Florida, n Bahamas, Cayman
Islands, Jamaica, Haiti, Belize, islands
off Nicaragua, Panama, and Curaçao.

Notes: Look for the Yellowline Goby in large
tubular sponges.

Similar Species: Neon Goby also lacks markings on tip of
snout but has inferior mouth and blue
stripe behind eye.

365 Yellowprow Goby
Gobiosoma xanthiprora

Identification: Dark gray above, paler below. *Isolated
yellow bar on snout.* 2 stripes along side:
upper stripe pale yellow or white,
extending from behind eye to caudal fin
base; lower stripe broad, dark, continuing
to tip of caudal fin. Mouth terminal;
upper lip dusky, separated from snout by
complete groove (no frenum). 19
pectoral fin rays. Body scaleless. TL to
1¼″ (3.2 cm).

Habitat: Coral reefs; depths of 60–85′ (18–25 m).

Range: Florida Keys, Dry Tortugas, Caribbean.

Notes: The Yellowprow Goby probably lives in
sponges.

Similar Species: Yellownose Goby *(G. randalli),* from
Puerto Rico, Lesser Antilles, and islands
off Venezuela, also has isolated yellow

bar on snout and pale narrow stripe from behind eye to tip of tail but has pale upper lip and 17 pectoral fin rays. Blacknose Goby (*G. atronasum*), from Bahamas, also has terminal mouth, dark snout without frenum, and broad, dark, lateral stripe on body but has 16 pectoral fin rays.

---

366 Sharknose Goby
Gobiosoma evelynae

Identification: Dark gray above, paler below. *Yellow stripe in front of each eye, joining near tip of snout to form* V. Stripe from behind eye to caudal fin base pale yellow-white or yellow shading to pale iridescent blue. *Mouth inferior; snout overhangs upper lip, connected by frenum.* Body scaleless. SL to 1⅛" (2.9 cm).

Habitat: Live coral; to depths of 85′ (25 m).

Range: Bahamas, Virgin Islands, Antilles, and w Caribbean.

Notes: The Sharknose Goby is a cleaner that removes parasites from other fishes.

Similar Species: Neon Goby is similar, but pale stripes in front of eyes do not join. *G. prochilos*, from n Gulf of Mexico, Jamaica, Lesser Antilles, Yucatán, and Belize, has pale snout, pale stripe on upper body as wide as eye diameter continuing forward through eye and meeting on snout to form Y or V, and dark lateral stripe continuing to tip of tail. Cleaning Goby (*G. genie*), from Bahamas and Cayman Islands, also has lines in front of eye forming V and inferior mouth, but upper lip is separated from tip of snout by groove (no frenum).

Other *Gobiosoma* species

Seaboard Goby (*G. ginsburgi*) Body pale with 8 dark vertical bands separated by wide spaces. 12 elements in second dorsal fin, 11 in anal fin. 18–19 pectoral fin rays. Atlantic coast from New York to Miami.

Twoscale Goby	*(G. longipala)* 2 scales on caudal fin base; no other scales. 10 anal fin elements. 16 pectoral rays. Gulf coast of Florida.
Naked Goby	*(G. bosc)* No scales. Atlantic coast from New York to c Florida, Gulf of Mexico from Florida to Texas, south to Bay of Campeche.
Rockcut Goby	*(G. grosvenori)* 9 short horizontal dashes along mid-side, each in center of dusky band. 10 elements in second dorsal fin, 9 in anal fin. Body scaled from pectoral fin to caudal fin base; no scales on belly or on upper side above line from pectoral fin base to second dorsal origin. Se Florida, Jamaica, Venezuela.
Isthmian Goby	*(G. spilotum)* Scales on side in broad wedge-shaped patch; 26–29 scales in row on caudal peduncle. Panama.
Code Goby	*(G. robustum)* Short, chunky; scaleless. About 9 dusky bars with paler narrow interspaces on body; longitudinal row of darker dots and dashes along mid-side. 12 elements in second dorsal fin, 10 in anal fin. 16–17 pectoral fin rays. No chin barbel. S Florida from Cape Kennedy to Key West, Gulf of Mexico from Key West to Texas.
G. nudum	2 scales on caudal fin base. Bilobed barbel on chin. Both coasts of Panama near Panama Canal.
Vermiculated Goby	*(G. spes)* Patch of 7–16 transverse rows of scales on caudal peduncle; isolated patch of scales behind pectoral fin. 15–16 pectoral fin rays. Males have filamentous first dorsal fin spine. No chin barbel. Jamaica, Puerto Rico, Costa Rica, Panama, Venezuela.
G. schultzi	Patch of 7–16 transverse rows of scales on caudal peduncle; isolated patch of scales behind pectoral fin. 17–18 pectoral fin rays. No filament on first dorsal fin spine. Lake Maracaibo, Venezuela.
G. hildebrandi	Continuous wedge-shaped patch of about 30 transverse rows of scales from pectoral fin base to caudal fin base. Panama Canal.

G. yucatanum	Patch of 8–10 transverse rows of scales on caudal peduncle; isolated patch of scales behind pectoral fin. 16 pectoral rays. 9 anal fin elements. No filamentous dorsal fin spines. Caribbean side of Yucatán Peninsula.
Spotlight Goby	(*G. louisae*) Dark gray above, paler below; yellow oval spot on snout. 2 stripes along side: pale upper stripe from behind eye to caudal fin base; dark lower stripe terminating in dark ovate spot at caudal fin base. Mouth terminal, upper lip separated from snout by groove (no frenum). Bahamas, Grand Cayman.
G. illecebrosum	White stripe along upper side, sometimes with middle third yellow or blue. Pale vertical bar on snout. Groove above upper lip interrupted by frenum. W Caribbean from Mexico to Colombia.
Shortstripe Goby	(*G. chancei*) Body scaleless. Dark above, pale below; short, yellow dorso-lateral stripe from behind eye to above edge of gill cover. Tip of snout unmarked. S Bahamas, Caicos Islands, Puerto Rico, Virgin Islands, Lesser Antilles, islands off Venezuela.
Slaty Goby	(*G. tenox*) Body uniformly gray. Short dorso-lateral stripe; yellow median bar on tip of snout. N Lesser Antilles, Panama.

Other gobies with 7 spines in first dorsal fin

Toadfish Goby	(*Psilotris batrachodes*) Dark diagonal bar on pectoral fin; dark bars on dorsal fins; crescent on caudal fin base. Bahamas, Puerto Rico, Belize, Honduras, Isla de Providencia, Santa Marta, Punta de San Bernardo off Colombia.
Psilotris kaufmani	Pectoral fin dark above, pale below. Jamaica, Belize, Honduras, Isla de Providencia.
Scaleless Goby	(*Psilotris alepis*) Pectoral fin clear, with 15 rays. Bahamas, Cuba, Virgin Islands, Honduras.

Highspine Goby   *(Psilotris celsus)* Pectoral fin clear. First 2 dorsal spines elongate. Mouth small, rear of jaw not extending past rear edge of pupil. Bermuda, Bahamas, Puerto Rico, Virgin Islands, Isla de Providencia, Santa Marta, Colombia.

Psilotris boehlkei   Mouth large, rear of jaw extending past rear edge of pupil. Pectoral fin clear. St. Barthélemy.

Whiteband Goby   *(Varicus imswe)* Pelvic fin rays extend beyond base of anal fin. 8 elements in second dorsal fin. 14–15 pectoral fin rays. 24 scales in lateral series. Belly completely scaled. Eleuthera Island, Bahamas; Carrie Bow Cay, Belize.

Varicus bucca   Pelvic fin rays with fleshy tips. 9–10 elements in second dorsal fin. 16–19 pectoral fin rays. 27 scales in lateral series. Belly completely scaled or with naked central area. Greater Antilles.

Orangebelly Goby   *(Varicus marilynae)* Pelvic fin rays with fleshy tips. 9 elements in second dorsal fin. 16–18 pectoral fin rays. 18–19 scales in lateral series. Belly unscaled. Deep water off Florida.

Translucent Goby   *(Chriolepis fisheri)* Largely translucent with 6 dark bars; second through fifth bars Y shaped. Both dorsal fins have broad central dark band. Only 2 scales on each side, one each at base of upper and lower caudal fin rays. Bahamas, Barbados.

Chriolepis benthonis   Scales from caudal peduncle to point on body below seventh dorsal ray; no enlarged scales at base of caudal fin. 10 elements in second dorsal fin, 9 in anal fin. Arrowsmith Bank off Quintana Roo; deep water off Progreso, Yucatán.

Wasp Goby   *(Chriolepis vespa)* Body yellow with 4 narrow olive bars with intervening saddles. 11 elements in second dorsal fin, 8 in anal fin. No enlarged scales at caudal fin base. Ne Gulf of Mexico, possibly Guyana.

Pycnomma roosevelti   Body pale with 6 irregular bands; dark bar at base of caudal fin; oblique dark bars on dorsal fins. Body scaled from below dorsal origin to base of caudal fin; about 26 scales in lateral series. 10 elements in second dorsal fin, 9 in anal fin. 16 pectoral rays. Isla de Providencia.

Paleback Goby   *(Gobulus myersi)* Pale above, lower body dark. 11–12 elements in second dorsal fin. Pelvic fins united, without frenum. Florida, Bahamas to Venezuela.

Tusked Goby   *(Risor ruber)* Inferior mouth with prominent diverging canine teeth. Black overall or pale with dark dorsal and anal fins. Scales only on rear of body. Florida, n Bahamas, Gulf of Mexico, Antilles, South American coast to Suriname.

Parrella macropteryx   Body pale with 5 diffuse blotches on side. Pectoral fin very long (16–18 rays) reaching to below seventh or eighth dorsal ray. 13 elements in second dorsal fin, 12 in anal fin. Isla de la Juventud off Cuba (formerly Isle of Pines), Puerto Rico.

Bearded Goby   *(Barbulifer ceuthoecus)* Body greenish with pale bands above and below mid-side. Short barbels; 1 barbel below eye. S Florida, Bahamas to Venezuela.

Barbulifer   *(Barbulifer antennatus)* Mostly black. Longer barbels than Bearded Goby; 2 barbels between eye and corner of mouth. Bahamas, Jamaica, Lesser Antilles.

White-eye Goby   *(Bollmannia boqueronensis)* Head and body completely scaled; 27–30 scales in lateral series. 13 elements each in second dorsal and anal fins. S Florida, Greater Antilles, Venezuela.

Bollmannia litura   28 scales in lateral series. 12 elements each in second dorsal and anal fins. 20 pectoral fin rays. Middle dorsal spines elongate, fourth spine longest. Row of 5 faint blotches on mid-side. Bay of Samaná, Dominican Republic.

Ragged Goby   *(Bollmannia communis)* 14 elements each in second dorsal and anal fins. 22 pectoral fin rays. S Florida, Gulf of Mexico.

Ninelined Goby	*(Ginsburgellus novemlineatus)* Body dark reddish brown with 9 pale blue vertical lines. Eye red. Bahamas, Cayman Islands, Antilles to Venezuela.
Mauve Goby	*(Palatogobius paradoxus)* 19–20 elements in second dorsal fin. Virgin Islands, ne Gulf of Mexico, Panama, Venezuela.

Gobies with different numbers of spines in first dorsal fin

Peppered Goby	*(Pariah scotius)* Dark overall with large melanophores; fins paler. 8 spines in first dorsal fin. 2 scales on each side at caudal base; few scales on lower part of caudal peduncle. S Bahamas (Mayaguana Island).
Roughtail Goby	*(Evermannichthys metzelaari)* Dark saddles on body. 4–5 spines in first dorsal fin. Row of scales along base of anal fin. Bahamas, Antilles south to Curaçao.
Sponge Goby	*(Evermannichthys spongicola)* Dark saddles on body. 6–7 spines in first dorsal fin. No scales along base of anal fin. North Carolina to Fort Pierce, Florida; Dry Tortugas to Panama City; Bay of Campeche.
Pugnose Goby	*(Evermannichthys silus)* Dorsal fins connected. Head blunt. No dark saddles on body. Samana Cay, Bahamas.
Tenant Goby	*(Evermannichthys convictor)* Dorsal fins well separated. No dark saddles on body. Green Cay, Bahamas.

WORMFISHES and DARTFISHES
Family Microdesmidae

The family Microdesmidae is closely related to the family Gobiidae (the gobies). Two subfamilies are recognized: the Microdesminae, or wormfishes, and the Ptereleotrinae, or dartfishes. Like the gobies, these fishes have no lateral line on the body.

Wormfishes are elongate, somewhat compressed fishes with small eyes and embedded scales. They have a single continuous dorsal fin consisting of 10 to 28 spines and 28 to 66 soft rays, and minute pelvic fins, each consisting of one spine and two to four rays. The anal fin consists of 23 to 61 soft rays. Wormfishes are generally small burrowing fishes, reaching a maximum length of 12 inches (30 cm). Most are pale pinkish or sand colored, and they sometimes have dark lines on the body. The subfamily Microdesminae contains five genera and about 30 species; two genera and six species occur in our region.

Dartfishes are more goby-like, with two separate dorsal fins, well-developed but nearly separate pelvic fins with one spine and four rays, and one spine in the anal fin. They are placed in the family Microdesmidae on the basis of the internal structure of the pectoral girdle, but because of their close superficial resemblance to the six-spined gobies, we have included them with the gobies. The subfamily Ptereleotrinae contains four genera and about 35 species; one genus, *Ptereleotris,* and two species occur in our region (see family Gobiidae for species account).

Genera of subfamily Microdesminae

Cerdale	Gill opening in short tube. Single continuous dorsal fin.
Microdesmus	Gill opening not in tube. Single continuous dorsal fin.

Pugjaw Wormfish

Pugjaw Wormfish
Cerdale floridana

Identification: Body pale tan, freckled with tiny black melanophores; no prominent markings. *Mouth oblique, lower jaw stout and projecting.* 17 segmented soft caudal fin rays; 12–14 dorsal fin spines, 43–47 total dorsal elements. SL to 3⅛″ (8 cm).

Habitat: Coral reefs and coastal habitats to depths of 100′ (30 m).

Range: Southeastern coast of Florida, Florida Keys, Bahamas, Antilles, Nicaragua to Panama, and Isla San Andrés.

Notes: A plain species that seems to be most abundant in shallow waters over reef flats, the Pugjaw Wormfish probably gets its name from its protruding lower jaw.

Other species of wormfishes

Microdesmus carri   Mostly brown, heavily stippled with melanophores; belly white. 3 dark lines radiating from eye. Dark stripe along base of anal fin. 24–27 dorsal fin spines; more than 60 total dorsal elements. 34–40 anal fin rays. Se Mexico, Costa Rica.

Lancetail Wormfish   *(Microdesmus lanceolatus)* 12 dorsal fin spines; more than 60 total dorsal elements. 55 anal fin rays. Gulf of Mexico.

Pink Wormfish   *(Microdesmus longipinnis)* 19–22 dorsal fin spines; more than 60 total dorsal elements. 37–48 anal fin rays. Bermuda, Georgia to Florida, n Gulf of Mexico, Cayman Islands.

Microdesmus luscus   50–51 total dorsal fin elements. 35 anal fin rays. Puerto Rico, Dominica, Panama.

SLEEPERS
Family Eleotridae

Sleepers are chunky to elongate, terete, moderate-size fishes with two dorsal fins positioned rather close together and a round to pointed tail. They are similar to the gobies (family Gobiidae), but always have well-separated pelvic fins not joined by a membrane. As in the gobies, the first dorsal fin consists of spines, and the second has one spine followed by soft rays. The mouth is large and terminal. There is no lateral line on the body; scale counts are taken along the side of the body, referred to as the lateral series. Most species occur in waters of reduced salinity, in regions where salt and fresh water come together.

There are about 35 genera and 150 species in this family; six genera and seven species occur in our area.

Genera of family Eleotridae

Erotelis   Strong downward-pointing spine on preopercle. Scales cycloid, about 90 in lateral series. Caudal fin extends forward onto dorsal and ventral surfaces of caudal peduncle.

Eleotris	Strong downward-pointing spine on preopercle. Scales ctenoid. Caudal fin not extended forward onto body.
Dormitator	No preopercular spine. Body short, stocky. Head fully scaled, rather flat on top. Scales large, about 30 in lateral series.
Gobiomorus	No preopercular spine. Body slender, terete, with projecting lower jaw.
Guavina	Scales ctenoid, very small, about 110 in lateral series. No preopercular spine.
Leptophilypnus	Bones of lower jaw expanded inward as flat plates, meeting in midline as far back as angle of jaw. No preopercular spine. Fresh water.

373 Fat Sleeper
Dormitator maculatus

Identification: *A short stubby fish with a conspicuously flat head.* Dark brown, with darker blotch above pectoral fin. 7 spines in first dorsal fin. 30 ctenoid scales in lateral series. TL usually to 10″ (25 cm); sometimes to 15″ (38 cm).
Habitat: Inshore brackish and fresh waters.
Range: North Carolina (occasionally New York) to Florida, Bahamas, Gulf of Mexico, Caribbean, including Antilles, to Brazil.
Notes: The Fat Sleeper is a conspicuously large estuarine species. It is stubbier and has larger scales than other sleepers.

374 Bigmouth Sleeper
Gobiomorus dormitor

Identification: A large terete fish with *a strongly projecting lower jaw. Yellowish to brown, lighter below, with dark lines on cheek and opercle. No preopercular spine.* 6 spines in first dorsal fin. About 60 ctenoid scales in lateral series. TL to 24″ (60 cm).

	Habitat:	Coastal areas and fresh waters.
	Range:	Southern Florida, w Gulf of Mexico, and Caribbean, including Antilles, to Brazil.
	Notes:	The Bigmouth is a very large sleeper. Other species have jaws of equal length or only slightly projecting lower jaws.

Other species of sleepers

Spinycheek Sleeper	*(Eleotris pisonis)* Elongate, somewhat flattened. Prominent downward-pointing spine on preopercle. Dark brownish gray, somewhat lighter above. 50–65 scales in lateral series. North Carolina (occasionally New York) to Florida, Bahamas, Gulf of Mexico to Brazil.
Emerald Sleeper	*(Erotelis smaragdus)* Slender, elongate, terete. Prominent downward-pointing spine on preopercle. Dark brownish gray with dark spot at upper pectoral fin base. Short rays extend forward from caudal fin onto caudal peduncle. More than 90 scales in lateral series. Florida, Bahamas, n Gulf of Mexico, Antilles, Central and South American coasts to Brazil.
Guavina	*(Guavina guavina)* Heavy, stout bodied. 7 spines in first dorsal fin. Small scales, about 110 in lateral series. Mexico, Cuba, Puerto Rico, Panama to Brazil.

SURGEONFISHES
Family Acanthuridae

Surgeonfishes are some of the most conspicuous fishes on coral reefs and are seen almost everywhere. They are daytime grazers that travel in large schools, constantly moving as they crop bits of algae. The name surgeonfish refers to the large scalpel-like spine on either side of the caudal peduncle. When the body is flexed these spines extend forward at about a 45-degree angle, serving as formidable defensive weapons. In some Indo-Pacific genera the spines are nonmovable or in the form of blade-like plates, but our Atlantic species all have movable spines.

Surgeonfishes have a distinctive physiognomy: a steep frontal region, with a small terminal mouth and rather small eyes placed high on the head. The single dorsal fin has no notch between the spines and the rays. The caudal peduncle is slender, and the tail is lunate. The scales are very small. The species in our area have close-set, spatulate teeth with serrate edges that are effective for nipping pieces from macroscopic algae. All except the Blue Tang have thick-walled, gizzard-like stomachs for crushing and grinding their plant food. While many surgeonfishes are somber brown or gray, some species are very colorful; in our area, the Blue Tang is usually bright yellow when young and sometimes bright blue in adulthood.

The family includes six genera and 72 species; there are four species in our region, all in the genus *Acanthurus*.

326 Ocean Surgeon
Acanthurus bahianus

Identification: *Head and body deep and compressed* (body depth about 2.1 in SL). Rather plain yellowish to brownish gray, sometimes with faint, pale blue lines on body and alternating pale orange and bluish-green lines on dorsal fin. Anal fin has narrow bright blue margin, and blue and dark gray lines. Caudal fin has rear margin bluish white, base often abruptly paler. Groove around caudal spine edged in black. Pectoral fin long (3.4–3.7 in SL). 20–22 gill rakers. TL to 14″ (36 cm).

Habitat: Shallow waters around reefs and other hard bottoms.

Range: Bermuda, Atlantic coast occasionally as far north as Massachusetts and south to Brazil, Bahamas, and Caribbean. Also in s Atlantic: Ascension Island and St. Helena off Angola.

Notes: When observed underwater, the lines on the Ocean Surgeon's body and fins are not prominent and its coloring appears to range from gray to brown, often with a pale area on the caudal peduncle.

Similar Species: Gulf Surgeonfish *(A. randalli),* which replaces Ocean Surgeon in n Gulf of Mexico, is very similar but has shorter pectoral fin (3.8–4.4 in SL) and more shallowly lunate caudal fin. Doctorfish has narrow vertical bars on side.

327 Doctorfish
Acanthurus chirurgus

Identification: Body strongly compressed, relatively elongate. Gray, with *10 well-spaced, narrow, darker gray vertical bars on side* that are sometimes obscure. Dorsal and anal fins have longitudinal light and dark lines and pale blue margins. Caudal fin shallowly forked, lacks pale rear margin; its base paler than body. Groove around caudal spine edged in black and surrounded by blue. 16–19 gill rakers. SL to 13¾" (35 cm).

Habitat: Shallow waters over hard bottoms.

Range: Atlantic coast from Massachusetts to Rio de Janeiro, both coasts of Florida (but confined to offshore reefs in rest of Gulf of Mexico), Bahamas, and Caribbean.

Notes: The Doctorfish often travels in schools with the Ocean Surgeon; look carefully for the vertical bars on its sides, which can change in intensity as the fish swims along.

Similar Species: Ocean Surgeon, which sometimes has pale blue lines on body, and Gulf Surgeonfish are similar in shape and general coloration but lack vertical bars.

328 Blue Tang
Acanthurus coeruleus

Identification: *A deep-bodied surgeonfish* (body depth 1.7 in SL) with *a conspicuous yellow caudal spine*. Juveniles all yellow; adults range from gray to dark blue, with narrow gray longitudinal bands on body and on dorsal and anal fins. TL to 14" (36 cm).

Habitat: Around coral reefs.

Range: Bermuda, Atlantic coast (straying north to New York and south to Rio de Janeiro), Bahamas, and Caribbean; distribution in Gulf of Mexico uncertain.

Notes: The Blue Tang has the most distinctive coloration of all western Atlantic surgeonfishes. This fish has a thin-

walled stomach, whereas the other
surgeonfishes in our area have gizzard-
like stomachs.

BARRACUDAS
Family Sphyraenidae

Barracudas are moderate-size to large,
slender fishes that are terete or rectangular in cross section.
They have two well-separated dorsal fins and a forked tail.
The scales are smooth and rather small. The lower jaw projects beyond the upper jaw, and both jaws have large,
pointed, blade-like teeth. With slender, arrow-shaped bodies that are built for speed, barracudas are efficient predators. Large barracudas are often implicated in ciguatera
poisoning, but in parts of our area they are highly esteemed
food fishes.

This family consists of a single genus, *Sphyraena,* with 20
species; three or four species occur in our region.

278   Great Barracuda
Sphyraena barracuda

Identification: A large, streamlined fish, nearly round
in cross section. Brownish gray above,
with greenish cast, shading to silvery on
side, becoming white on belly. Upper
side may have 18–23 oblique darker
bars. *Conspicuous scattered black spots on
lower side. Top of head between eyes flat or
concave. Mouth large;* maxilla extends to
below front of eye. Second dorsal, anal,
and caudal fins blackish with white tips.
Young have pale reticulations on back.
Tip of pectoral fin extends to or beyond
pelvic fin origin. TL to 6′6″ (2 m).

Habitat: Mangrove shores and turbid inshore
waters to open ocean.
Range: Worldwide in warm seas. Bermuda,
Atlantic coast from Massachusetts to
Brazil, Gulf of Mexico, and Caribbean,
including Antilles.
Notes: Great Barracudas are curious and often
follow snorkelers or divers, but attacks
are rare and probably occur accidentally
when the barracudas attempt to take
speared fish.

Similar Species: Other barracudas lack black spots on lower side. Guaguanche *(S. guachancho),* from New England, Gulf of Mexico, and Caribbean to Brazil, has convex top of head, smaller scales, and last rays of second dorsal and anal fins slightly extended as short filaments. Southern Sennet *(S. picudilla)* has convex top of head and shorter pectoral fin, not reaching to pelvic fin; it occurs in Bermuda, s Florida, Bahamas, and Antilles to Uruguay. Northern Sennet *(S. borealis),* which may be same species as Southern Sennet, has smaller eye and slightly smaller scales; it occurs from Massachusetts to Florida and Gulf of Mexico.

SNAKE MACKERELS
Family Gempylidae

Snake mackerels are fairly large fishes, most species surpassing 3 feet (1 m) in total length. They have two dorsal fins, the first much longer than the second, and usually several finlets behind the dorsal and anal fins. The tail is relatively small and forked. The mouth is large, with a protruding lower jaw; the upper jaw usually has formidable fang-like teeth, but because snake mackerels live in deep water, they are not dangerous to humans. Most species are dark brown or black and silvery in color. They are closely related to cutlassfishes (family Trichiuridae), and some ichthyologists combine the two families, but they differ significantly in appearance and we have treated them separately here.

The family Gempylidae includes 16 genera and 23 species of mainly deep-water oceanic fishes. A few species of three genera come to the surface at night and are sometimes caught by fishermen in our area.

Genera of family Gempylidae

Gempylus   Elongate, compressed. Black. 26–32 dorsal fin spines. 2 lateral lines, both originating above opercle. Pelvic fin rudimentary.

Lepidocybium   Large, mackerel-like. Brown. Smooth scales. Lateral line single, sinuous. 3 keels on each side of caudal peduncle. 8–9 dorsal fin spines.

Ruvettus Large, mackerel-like. Black. Single lateral line. Skin very rough, with large scales interspersed with spiny, star-shaped bony tubercles. No keels on caudal peduncle. 12 or more dorsal fin spines.

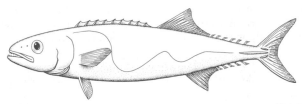

Escolar

Escolar
Lepidocybium flavobrunneum

Identification: *A uniformly dark brown fish with a low first dorsal fin and a sinuous lateral line. Prominent lateral keel on caudal peduncle, flanked by smaller accessory keels above and below.* Scales small, each surrounded by network of tubules with pores. 4 finlets behind second dorsal fin; 4 finlets behind anal fin. SL to 6′6″ (2 m).

Habitat: Over continental shelves; near surface at night.

Range: Widely distributed in tropical and temperate seas; throughout deeper waters of our area.

Notes: The Escolar is sometimes caught by tuna long-liners. It resembles the mackerels, but they are silvery blue and have a band of large scales around the front of the body.

CUTLASSFISHES
Family Trichiuridae

Cutlassfishes are named for their body shape, which is elongate and very strongly compressed like a cutlass or machete. The lower jaw projects forward, and there are very strong, blade-like, pointed teeth on both jaws; the teeth of the upper jaw (and sometimes the lower jaw as well) are fang-like. The dorsal fin, which may be continuous or divided by a shallow notch, is very long. If divided, the second part is longer than the first. In some species, the tail ends in a small fin, but the only shallow-water species found in our region has a tail tapering to a thin point. Cutlassfishes have no finlets and no scales, and the pelvic fin is either absent or rudimentary, with a scale-like spine and one ray.

The family contains nine genera and 32 species of generally deep-water fishes; one species occurs in shallow water in the western Atlantic. Many ichthyologists now combine this family with the snake mackerel family, Gempylidae.

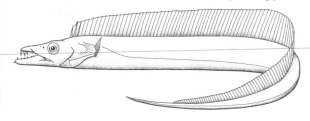

Atlantic Cutlassfish

Atlantic Cutlassfish
Trichiurus lepturus

Identification: *Elongate and very compressed, ribbon-like body, tapering to a point.* Color silvery. Barbed fangs in both jaws. No pelvic or caudal fins. Soft anal rays mostly buried in skin. TL to 4′ (1.2 m).

Habitat: Estuaries and continental shelves to depths of 1,150′ (350 m).

Range: Tropical and temperate waters worldwide; Virginia (rarely Massachusetts) to Florida, Gulf of Mexico, and Caribbean, including Antilles, to n Argentina.

Notes: This is the only cutlassfish in our region found in shallow water.

MACKERELS
Family Scombridae

The fishes of the mackerel family, which includes the tunas, are powerful swimmers with moderate-size to large, torpedo-shaped bodies. They have two dorsal fins, which in some species are separated by a wide space and in other species are very close together, or contiguous. The spiny dorsal fin is only a little longer than the soft part. There is a series of separate finlets behind the dorsal and anal fins. Scombrids have rather large, terminal mouths with rigid, non-protrusible jaws. Some species have large, thick scales in a band called a *corselet,* which encircles the body behind the head and extends backward along the lateral line. Scombrids have stiff, deeply forked tails and slender caudal peduncles with two or three short keels on each side. As in the jacks (family Carangidae), the tails are so rigid that fork length (FL) or the distance from the tip of the snout to the end of the middle caudal fin rays, is the measurement usually taken.

Most species are epipelagic, living near the surface of open waters, either over the continental shelf (neritic) or beyond the shelf in truly oceanic waters. Mackerels and tunas are among the world's most important food and game fishes. (Species of the genera *Thunnus* and *Katsuwonus,* all of which are rather stout bodied, are usually referred to as tunas.)

The family Scombridae includes 15 genera and 49 species; eight genera occur in our region.

Genera of family Scombridae

Dorsal fins widely separated.

Acanthocybium	Body covered with small scales; no corselet. Jaw teeth strong and flat. Vertical bars on upper side. 8–9 dorsal and 9 anal finlets.
Scomber	Body covered with small scales. Corselet indistinct. Snout as long as rest of head. Jaw teeth small and conical. 2 keels on each side of caudal peduncle (all other genera in our region have 3). 5 dorsal and 5 anal finlets.
Auxis	Body scaleless except for well-developed corselet. Jaw teeth conical. 2 longitudinal cartilaginous ridges on tongue. 8 dorsal and 7 anal finlets.

Dorsal fins not widely separated; close together or contiguous.

Scomberomorus	Body elongate, moderately compressed, covered with small scales. No corselet. Jaw teeth strong and flat. Posterior end of maxilla exposed (not slipping under

	preorbital bone). 6–11 dorsal and 5–12 anal finlets.
Sarda	Body elongate, fusiform, covered with small scales. Well-developed corselet. Oblique lines on upper part of body. No longitudinal ridges on tongue. 7–9 dorsal and 6–8 anal finlets.
Euthynnus	Body stout, fusiform. Scaleless except for corselet and lateral line. 2 longitudinal ridges on tongue. Complex pattern of stripes on back; several black spots between pectoral and pelvic fin bases. 8–10 dorsal and 6–8 anal finlets.
Thunnus	Body stout, fusiform, covered with small scales behind corselet. 2 longitudinal ridges on tongue. 7–10 dorsal and 7–10 anal finlets. No dark spots or stripes.
Katsuwonus	Body stout, fusiform; scaleless except for corselet and lateral line. 2 longitudinal ridges on tongue. 4–6 longitudinal stripes on lower side. 7–9 dorsal and 7–8 anal finlets.

377 Wahoo
Acanthocybium solandri

Identification:

A slender, moderately compressed mackerel with a large median keel between 2 smaller keels on each side of caudal peduncle. Bluish green, shading to silvery white below. *24–30 vertical cobalt blue bars, some double or Y shaped,* along upper side. *Snout beak-like, as long as rest of head.* Lateral line curves downward below first dorsal fin. FL to 6′10″ (2.1 m).

Habitat: Epipelagic, in open ocean.

Range: Tropical parts of Atlantic, Pacific, and Indian Oceans and Mediterranean Sea; throughout our area.

Notes: A valued game fish, this very distinctive species is unlikely to be confused with any other scombrid. Barracudas (family Sphyraenidae) have somewhat similar heads and teeth but lack finlets and have less rigid tails.

378 Spanish Mackerel
Scomberomorus maculatus

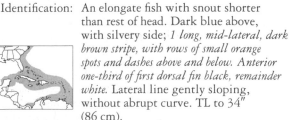

Identification: An elongate, silvery mackerel with *3 rows of elliptical or round orange spots on side. First dorsal fin black on anterior part and distal edge of posterior part. Lateral line curves gently.* 50–53 vertebrae. FL to 28" (70 cm).

Habitat: Epipelagic, over continental shelf.

Range: Bermuda, Cape Cod to Florida, and Gulf of Mexico. Not in Bahamas or Caribbean.

Notes: The Spanish Mackerel is an excellent food fish.

Similar Species: The King Mackerel *(S. cavalla)* ranges along Atlantic coast (occasionally north to Massachusetts), Bahamas, Gulf of Mexico, Antilles, and coasts of Central and South America to Brazil; it has iridescent greenish back and clear dorsal fin, and lateral line that curves abruptly downward at level of soft dorsal fin; Serra Spanish Mackerel *(S. brasiliensis),* which ranges from Belize to Brazil, is similar but has 47–49 vertebrae.

379 Cero
Scomberomorus regalis

Identification: An elongate fish with snout shorter than rest of head. Dark blue above, with silvery side; *1 long, mid-lateral, dark brown stripe, with rows of small orange spots and dashes above and below. Anterior one-third of first dorsal fin black, remainder white.* Lateral line gently sloping, without abrupt curve. TL to 34" (86 cm).

Habitat: Epipelagic, in inshore waters; frequently around coral reefs.

Range: Western Atlantic from Massachusetts to Brazil, Bahamas, Gulf of Mexico, Antilles, and Caribbean.

Notes: The Cero often comes close to snorkelers near the reef crest and over the outer slope.

Similar Species: Spanish Mackerel has 3 rows of orange spots on side.

380 Bullet Mackerel
Auxis rochei

Identification: An elongate, fusiform mackerel with *dorsal fins separated by a space equal to length of base of first dorsal.* Blue above, silvery white below; 15 nearly vertical dark bars in scaleless area above corselet. Pectoral fin short, not reaching to front margin of scaleless area above corselet. *Rear extension of corselet 10–15 scales wide* under origin of second dorsal fin. FL to 19¾" (50 cm).

Habitat: Epipelagic, over continental shelf and open oceanic water.

Range: Worldwide in warm waters; throughout our area.

Similar Species: Frigate Mackerel *(A. thazard)* has narrower corselet; only 1–5 scales wide below second dorsal fin; longer pectoral fin; 15 or more narrow, oblique to almost horizontal bars in scaleless area behind corselet; and several black spots below pectoral fin. It is found worldwide in warm waters, but there are few Atlantic records. Tunas are similar but are more stout bodied and have dorsal fins close together. *Scomber* species are covered with scales, have no corselet, and have 2 keels on each side of caudal peduncle.

381 Little Tunny
Euthynnus alletteratus

Identification: A robust fish. Blue above, shading to silvery white below, with *several broken, nearly horizontal dark bars above lateral line and 4 or 5 black spots below pectoral fin.* 37–45 gill rakers on first arch. Pectoral fin short, not reaching to end of first dorsal fin. FL to 3'3" (1 m).

Habitat: Epipelagic, neritic waters over continental shelves.

Range: Tropical and subtropical waters of Atlantic, Caribbean, and e Gulf of Mexico. Also in e Atlantic and Mediterranean.

Similar Species: Tunas of genus *Thunnus* have scales behind corselet. Skipjack Tuna has distinctive pattern of longitudinal dark lines on lower side.

382 Skipjack Tuna
Katsuwonus pelamis

Identification: A robust, elongate tuna. Dark blue above, shading to silvery white below, with *bold pattern of 4–6 dark longitudinal stripes on lower side.* 53–63 gill rakers on first arch. FL to 3'3" (1 m).

Habitat: Epipelagic oceanic waters; from surface to depths of 860' (260 m) during day, near surface at night.

Range: Worldwide in tropical and warm temperate waters; throughout our area.

Notes: A valuable commercial species, the Skipjack Tuna travels in large schools. No other species has longitudinal lines on the lower side.

383 Yellowfin Tuna
Thunnus albacares

Identification: A robust tuna with *very high second dorsal and anal fins* (in adults). *Dorsal and anal fins and finlets yellow.* Dark blue above, shading to pale silvery yellow to silver-white. Belly crossed by about 20 broken, nearly vertical, pale lines. *No dark stripes.* 26–34 (usually more than 27) gill rakers. Pectoral fin moderate, reaching to below second dorsal fin origin. FL to more than 6'10" (2.1 m).

Habitat: Epipelagic oceanic waters.

Range: Throughout offshore waters of our area. Also in warm oceans.

Notes: The Yellowfin Tuna is highly valued for sashimi. Other species of tunas have lower second dorsal and anal fins.

Other species of mackerels

Blackfin Tuna	*(Thunnus atlanticus)* Rather small. Back dark blue, belly white; sometimes pale spots in vertical rows on lower side. Second dorsal and anal fins low, about as high as longest spines in first dorsal. W Atlantic from Massachusetts to Brazil, Gulf of Mexico, Caribbean.
Albacore	*(Thunnus alalunga)* Stout. Pectoral fin long, reaching well beyond end of second dorsal fin. Blue above, white below. Dorsal and anal finlets yellow, caudal fin margin white. Worldwide in tropical and warm temperate waters; throughout our area.
Chub Mackerel	*(Scomber japonicus)* Top of head dark blue, body silvery. Oblique, dark, undulating lines on back; black spots and wavy broken lines on belly. New York to Florida, n Cuba; coast of South America east of Trinidad.
Atlantic Bonito	*(Sarda sarda)* Blue above, silvery white below; oblique dark stripes on upper side. Gulf of St. Lawrence to Florida, n Gulf of Mexico, Campeche Banks; mouth of Amazon south to Argentina. Absent from most of Caribbean; sometimes occurs in Colombia and Venezuela.

SWORDFISH
Family Xiphiidae

The Swordfish is a very large, open-water species. Its name refers to its prolonged upper jaw, which forms a long, flat, sword-shaped *rostrum,* or bill. The Swordfish has a rather short first dorsal fin, which in adults is rigid and does not fold, a tiny second dorsal fin, two anal fins, and a rigid, deeply forked tail. Although the adults are scaleless, juveniles have embedded splint-like scales. The Swordfish is usually placed in its own family, as we have done here, because it lacks scales and pelvic fins, but it is sometimes combined with the sailfishes and spearfishes in an expanded family Xiphiidae, with the Swordfish recognized as a subfamily. Like mackerels, the Swordfish is measured in fork length (FL).

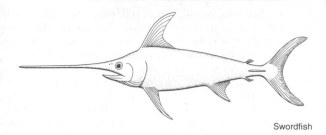

Swordfish

Swordfish
Xiphias gladius

Identification: A large, elongate, tapering fish with *a long, flat, sword-like bill and no pelvic fins.* Blackish brown overall; paler on side and belly. *Head, including bill, 2.25 in FL.* Eye very large. First dorsal fin high and relatively short, well separated from small second dorsal fin. 2 well-separated anal fins. Tail deeply forked; caudal peduncle depressed, with well-developed keel on each side. FL to 14'5" (4.4 m).

Habitat: Open ocean waters, from surface to depths of 2,130' (650 m).

Range: Newfoundland to Argentina, and offshore in Caribbean and Gulf of Mexico, where it spawns throughout year. Also throughout all warm and temperate oceans.

Notes: A valued commercial species, the Swordfish is harvested by longlines and harpoons and is prized by big-game anglers. It can reach a weight of nearly 1,200 pounds (550 kg).

Similar Species: Sailfishes and marlins (family Istiophoridae) are similar but have round bills, long first dorsal fins, little space between first and second dorsals, and pelvic fins.

BILLFISHES
Family Istiophoridae

The marlins, spearfishes, and sailfishes are collectively called billfishes. They are large fishes and represent the ultimate challenge for offshore anglers. Like the Swordfish, the billfishes have a prolonged upper jaw forming a *rostrum,* or bill, but in billfishes it is shorter and is round in cross section rather than flat. Longer than the length of the rest of the head, the rostrum varies with age: in members of the genus *Makaira* it lengthens; in members of the genera *Istiophorus* and *Tetrapturus* it shortens. Unlike the Swordfish, billfishes have pelvic fins, and throughout their lives have elongate bony scales. The base of the first dorsal fin is long, extending backward almost to the second dorsal fin. There are two anal fins. The first dorsal, first anal, and pelvic fins fold down into grooves when the fishes are swimming fast. The tail is rigid and deeply forked. There are two keels on each side of the caudal peduncle. The measurement given for billfishes is fork length (FL).

This family encompasses three genera, all represented in our region, and 11 species, four of which occur here.

Genera of family Istiophoridae

Istiophorus	First dorsal fin sail-like. Pelvic fin long, nearly reaching anus. Body tapering, moderately compressed. Lateral line unbranched.
Tetrapturus	First dorsal fin long, with higher lobe at front, but not sail-like. Pelvic fin moderate. Body tapering, compressed. Lateral line unbranched, nearly straight, and readily visible.
Makaira	First dorsal fin not sail-like, with front lobe shorter than body depth. Pelvic fin short. Body moderately compressed. Lateral line has complex chain-like pattern, usually not readily visible.

375   Sailfish
Istiophorus platypterus

Identification: A slender billfish with *a high, sail-like first dorsal fin,* its middle rays longer than depth of body. Dark blue dorsally, shading to white below, with vertical rows of pale blue spots on side. Dorsal fin membrane dark blue, with small, round, dark spots. FL to 7′10″ (2.4 m).

Habitat: Coastal waters and epipelagic waters of open oceans.

Range: Tropical and temperate waters of all oceans; throughout our area.

Notes: Atlantic and Pacific populations of the sailfishes were once considered separate species but are now regarded as one wide-ranging form (the Atlantic was formerly known as *I. albicans*). The all-tackle record weights are 135 pounds (61.4 kg) for the Atlantic Sailfish, and 221 pounds (100 kg) for the Pacific Sailfish.

Similar Species: No other billfish has such a high dorsal fin. Marlins and spearfishes have high lobes only at front of dorsal fin.

376 Blue Marlin
Makaira nigricans

Identification: A deep-bodied billfish. First dorsal fin not sail-like (height of front rays shorter than body depth). Dark blue above, lighter below, with about 15 vertical rows of round pale blue spots on side. Pectoral fin folds against body. Tips of fins pointed. *Lateral line a network of interconnecting canals.* FL to 12'1" (3.7 m).

Habitat: Near surfaces of open oceans.

Range: New England to Argentina, including Gulf of Mexico and Caribbean. Also e Atlantic from Spain southward and Pacific Ocean.

Notes: The Blue Marlin is one of the most sought-after big-game species. It can top 1,402 pounds (636 kg).

Similar Species: White Marlin *(Tetrapturus albidus),* found throughout Atlantic, Gulf of Mexico, and Caribbean, has about 15 narrow, pale vertical bars on side; tips of first dorsal, anal, and pectoral fins rounded; height of anterior dorsal fin lobe slightly greater than greatest depth of body; dorsal rays progressively shorter toward rear of fin; and anus close to anal fin origin. Longbill Spearfish *(T. pfluegeri),* found from New Jersey to Venezuela and Gulf of Mexico, has dorsal fin rays behind anterior lobe of almost equal length along most of fin, and anus well in front of anal fin origin.

SUBORDER STROMATEOIDEI

This suborder of the order Perciformes is a complex group of diverse species united by the presence of sac-like outgrowths of the esophagus just behind the last gill arch. Most stromateoids live in deep water in the open ocean, but a few occur at the surface close to land. Altogether the group includes some 16 genera and 65 species. Some icthyologists place all stromateoids in a single family, but others divide them into as many as six families. We include three families that might be seen in our area—Nomeidae, Ariommatidae, and Stromateidae.

DRIFTFISHES
Family Nomeidae

This is a small family of fishes that live near the surface of the open ocean, often in association with floating seaweed or other objects. They have two contiguous dorsal fins, the first with nine to 12 spines, the second with up to three spines and 15 to 32 soft rays. The anal fin has one to three spines and 14 to 31 soft rays. The pelvic fins may be large or small. The caudal fin is forked. The lateral line runs high on the side, along the base of the dorsal fin; there is also a system of mucous canals along the side that is usually visible through the skin.

The family contains three genera and 15 species, about five of which occur in our area.

Genera of family Nomeidae

Nomeus	Body elongate. Top of head scaled as far forward as nostrils. Pelvic fin large, inserted below or ahead of pectoral fin base. Anal fin has 1–2 spines and 24–29 soft rays.
Cubiceps	Body elongate. Top of head scaled as far forward as nostrils. Pelvic fin small, inserted below or behind pectoral fin base. Anal fin has 1–3 spines and 14–25 soft rays.
Psenes	Body deep. Scales on top of head only as far forward as eye. Pelvic fin moderate, inserted below or behind pectoral fin base. Anal fin has 3 spines and 22–31 rays.

384 Man-of-War Fish
Nomeus gronovii

Identification: A small, elongate driftfish with a deeply forked tail. *Dark blue above, side silvery with patches of dark blue. Pelvic fin black and large, with inner rays joined to abdomen by membrane for its entire length.* TL to 8″ (20 cm).

Habitat: Open seas; lives among tentacles of Portuguese Man-of-War.

Range: Worldwide in warm seas. Bermuda (occasionally n to New England) to Brazil, Bahamas, Gulf of Mexico, and Caribbean.

Notes: The Man-of-War Fish lives among the tentacles of the Portuguese Man-of-War, which are up to 33 feet (10 m) long and armed with powerful stinging cells fatal to other fishes. The Man-of-War Fish is not harmed by these cells and is thus protected by the Portuguese Man-of-War. Other driftfishes have the pelvic fin connected to the belly for less than half its length.

Other species of driftfishes

Bigeye Cigarfish (*Cubiceps pauciradiatus*) Brown above, paler on side. First dorsal and caudal fins black; ventral fins whitish. Top of head scaled as far forward as nostrils. Scattered records in Atlantic; Gulf of Mexico, Caribbean.

Freckled Driftfish (*Psenes cyanophrys*) Snout blunt. Juveniles brown with dark freckling; adults with numerous longitudinal dark lines on side. Flat, knife-like teeth in lower jaw. 24–28 soft rays in second dorsal fin; 24–28 in anal fin. Scales on top of head only as far forward as eye; temporal region unscaled. Throughout our area; warm parts of Atlantic.

Silver Driftfish (*Psenes maculatus*) Pale silver with black first dorsal fin. 22–24 soft rays in second dorsal fin; 21–23 in anal fin. Throughout our area.

Bluefin Driftfish   *(Psenes pellucidus)* 27–32 soft rays in second dorsal fin; 26–31 soft rays in anal fin. Throughout our area.

ARIOMMATIDS
Family Ariommatidae

Ariommatids are similar to driftfishes (family Nomeidae), with two closely spaced dorsal fins, the first higher than the second, and a deeply forked tail. The pelvic fins are inserted behind the pectoral fins. Unlike the driftfishes they have two fleshy keels on each side of the caudal peduncle, and lack a visible mucous canal system. They travel in schools, generally over mud bottoms.

The family contains a single genus, *Ariomma,* with about six species. One species is included here.

Spotted Driftfish

Spotted Driftfish
Ariomma regulus

Identification: A moderately deep-bodied, compressed fish with a blunt snout and a forked tail. Silvery blue-gray above, paler below, with scattered small dark blue spots on upper side. Gill cover, first dorsal fin, and pelvic fin dark. Eye rather low on side of head. First dorsal fin higher than second. *Caudal peduncle slender, square in cross section, with 2 fleshy keels along each side.* TL to about 10¼″ (26 cm).

Habitat: Juveniles near surface, often around floating objects. Adults near bottom, usually offshore at depths greater than 330′ (100 m).

Range: Atlantic coast occasionally as far north
         as New Jersey, Gulf of Mexico, and
         Caribbean, including Antilles, to
         Guianas.

Notes: The Spotted Driftfish is an excellent
         food fish that feeds mainly on bottom-
         dwelling crustaceans. Other *Ariomma*
         species in our area are more slender,
         with more pointed snouts, and have
         no spots.

BUTTERFISHES
Family Stromateidae

Butterfishes are compressed silvery fishes
with short blunt snouts, forked tails, and
continuous dorsal fins. The adults have pelvic bones, but no
pelvic fins; some juveniles have pelvic fins. Some butterfishes, especially members of the genus *Peprilus,* resemble
small jacks (family Carangidae).

This family includes three genera and about 13 species;
one genus, *Peprilus,* with three species, is found in our area.

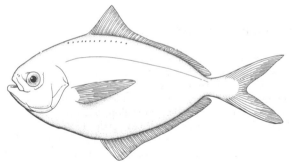

Butterfish

Butterfish
Peprilus triacanthus

Identification: A deep-bodied, moderately compressed
                  butterfish with a deeply forked tail and
                  no pelvic fin. Pale blue above, silvery
                  below, with irregular dark spots on
                  side. *Conspicuous row of pores above lateral
                  line on anterior part of back.* Dorsal and
                  anal fins long, both with moderately
                  high front lobe. Mouth small. TL to
                  12″ (30 cm).

Habitat: Schools in inshore and continental shelf waters; occasionally enters estuaries.

Range: Nova Scotia to Florida and around Gulf of Mexico to Campeche Bank; not in Bermuda or Caribbean.

Notes: The Butterfish is a valued commercial species. Adults feed largely on jellyfishes; juveniles are plankton feeders.

Similar Species: Harvestfish *(P. alepidotus)* has much deeper body and falcate dorsal and anal fins, and lacks pores above lateral line; it occurs along Atlantic coast from Newfoundland to Florida, Gulf of Mexico, Antilles, and South American coast to Argentina, but not in Bermuda, Bahamas, or w Caribbean. Gulf Butterfish *(P. burti),* which ranges from Virginia to Florida and Gulf of Mexico, has row of pores above lateral line and higher lobes at front of dorsal and anal fins.

ORDER PLEURONECTIFORMES

This order includes the flounders, halibuts, soles, and tongue-fishes, which are collectively known as flatfishes because of their highly compressed bodies. When first hatched, flatfishes have one eye on each side of the head, like any other vertebrate, but as they develop, one eye moves to the other side of the head. Flatfishes settle on ocean bottoms, resting on their sides, with their eyes facing upward. Even when flatfishes leave the bottom they continue to swim on their sides.

In some families the eyes are on the left side; other families have the eyes on the right side. You can tell which side is which by locating the pelvic fins and the lower jaw: If they are on the left side of the fish when it is in its normal, eyes-up position, then the fish is a left-eyed flatfish; if they are on the right, it is a right-eyed species. Rarely, however, an individual that would normally be right-eyed has the eyes on the left side, or vice versa. Usually the eyed side is pigmented and the blind side is plain white or has very little pigment. Some species have distinct spots or rings on the eyed side, and many are capable of remarkable color changes to match their background.

LEFTEYE FLOUNDERS
Family Bothidae

These flounders have both eyes on the left side of the head (rare abnormal individuals have both eyes on the right side). The dorsal fin origin is over or in front of the eyes. The caudal fin is rounded or pointed, and is separate from the dorsal and anal fins, both of which are without spines. Pectoral and pelvic fins are present. The preopercle has a fold along its vertical margin. The lateral line is single, sometimes forked behind the upper eye.

There are 20 genera and 115 species of lefteye flounders. Some ichthyologists divide them into three families, but we retain them as a single family with three subfamilies, two of which are represented in our area by about 13 genera and 47 species. Twelve genera and 18 species are covered here; the others live in deep water.

Genera of family Bothidae
Subfamily Bothinae

Pelvic fin of eyed side on midline of belly, its base much longer than fin on blind side, and inserted anterior to pelvic fin on blind side. Lateral line arched anteriorly. Pectoral and pelvic fin rays unbranched.

Bothus	Mouth small, not reaching to below center of eye. Eyes widely separated (more so in males than females).
Chascanopsetta	Mouth very large, reaching to or beyond rear margin of eye. Eyes close together.
Monolene	Body elongate. No pectoral fin on blind side. Mouth moderate, reaching to below anterior third of eye.
Engyophrys	Mouth tiny, maxilla not extending beyond anterior margin of eye. Tentacles on eye. Eyes separated by narrow ridge.
Trichopsetta	Dorsal fin origin anterior to eye. Mouth moderate, maxilla reaching to below anterior part of eye. Eyes separated by ridge. No ocellated spots on body.

Subfamily Paralichthinae

Pelvic fin bases equal in length. Pectoral fin rays branched.

Ancylopsetta	Pelvic fins on sides (neither on midline of belly); pelvic rays of eyed side longer than those of blind side. Lateral line

arched anteriorly. Dorsal fin origin over or slightly anterior to eyes. Ctenoid scales on eyed side.

Gastropsetta Pelvic fins on sides; pelvic rays of eyed side longer than those of blind side. Lateral line arched anteriorly. Dorsal fin origin well in front of eye. Cycloid scales on eyed side.

Paralichthys Pelvic fins on sides; pelvic rays of eyed and blind sides equal in length. Lateral line arched anteriorly. Eyes separated by flat space without ridge. Large ocellated spots usually present.

Citharichthys Pelvic fin of eyed side on midline of belly. Lateral line nearly straight. Mouth moderate; maxilla reaching to below middle of eye; 1 row of teeth in upper jaw. Scales ctenoid.

Cyclopsetta Pelvic fin of eyed side on midline of belly. Lateral line nearly straight. Mouth large; maxilla less than 3.5 in head length, reaching to below rear margin of eye. 1 row of teeth in upper jaw. Scales cycloid.

Syacium Pelvic fin of eyed side on midline of belly. Lateral line nearly straight. Mouth large, maxilla less than 3.5 in head length, reaching to below middle of eye. 2 rows of teeth in upper jaw.

Etropus Pelvic fin of eyed side on midline of belly. Lateral line nearly straight. Mouth small, maxilla 3.5–4.2 in head length. Jaws on blind side arched.

385 Peacock Flounder
Bothus lunatus

Identification: A moderately elongate flounder (body depth more than 1.6 in SL). Mottled brownish gray, with *blue spots and blue circles on eyed side,* many incomplete. 2 or 3 dark smudges along lateral line, which is arched anteriorly. Anterior profile notched in front of lower eye; front edge of upper eye over rear edge of lower eye. Tentacles on eyes not well developed. Males have long filamentous rays in pectoral fin on eyed side. TL to 17¾″ (45 cm).

Habitat: Shallow areas around coral reefs, often in sea-grass beds.

Range: Bermuda, Florida, Bahamas, Caribbean, including Antilles, to Brazil; not in Gulf of Mexico.

Notes: The Peacock Flounder is the most common flounder around coral reefs.

Similar Species: Maculated Flounder *(B. maculiferus),* from Bahamas and Cuba to Curaçao, is similar but has well-developed tentacles on eyes and convex anterior profile.

---

386 Eyed Flounder
Bothus ocellatus

Identification: A deep-bodied flounder *(body depth less than 1.6 in SL). Eyed side mottled, with some blue rings.* Dark blotch along lateral line and 2 dark spots in vertical line at tail base. No notch above nostril. Males have filamentous rays in left pectoral fin. TL to 6″ (15 cm).

Habitat: Shallow coastal waters to depths of 360′ (110 m).

Range: Bermuda, New York to Florida, Bahamas, Gulf of Mexico, and Caribbean, including Antilles, south to Brazil.

Notes: Common in shallow waters in the Bahamas, the larvae of the Eyed Flounder are attracted to lights at night but are difficult to see because they are transparent.

Similar Species: Twospot Flounder *(B. robinsi)* is also deep bodied but has 2 dark spots aligned on tail; it occurs along Atlantic coast from New York to Florida, Gulf of Mexico, and Caribbean to Brazil.

---

387 Ocellated Flounder
Ancylopsetta quadrocellata

Identification: A moderately deep-bodied flounder. *Eyed side brownish with 4 ocelli with whitish centers: 1 on caudal peduncle, 2 in vertical line between dorsal and anal fins, and*

another above arch in lateral line. Dorsal
fin origin above front margin of eye.
Lateral line arched anteriorly. TL to
10″ (25 cm).

Habitat: Shallow inshore waters at depths of
12–360′ (3.7–110 m).

Range: North Carolina to Florida and around
Gulf of Mexico.

Similar Species: Three-eye Flounder *(A. dilecta)* is similar
but has elongate rays at front of dorsal
and pelvic fins, and only 3 ocelli with
white centers; lacks ocellus above arch in
lateral line; it occurs along Atlantic
coast south of North Carolina and
around Gulf of Mexico. *A. kumperae* has

Ocellated Flounder
range

1 dark ocellus on pelvic fin of eyed side
and ocelli with dark centers; it occurs
from Colombia to Brazil in waters at
depths of 110–300′ (33–90 m).

---

388 Gulf Flounder
Paralichthys albigutta

Identification:

A moderately large, elongate flounder
with a large mouth. *3 ocellated spots
form a triangle on eyed side.* High arch in
lateral line over pectoral fin. 80–95
dorsal fin rays. 53–63 anal rays. TL to
28″ (71 cm).

Habitat: Inshore coastal waters over hard and
sandy bottoms at depths of 60–425′
(19–130 m).

Range: North Carolina to s Florida, n Bahamas,
Gulf of Mexico, and w Caribbean to
Colombia.

Similar Species: Southern Flounder *(P. lethostigma),*
another large, elongate species, lacks
ocellated spots and has 80–95 dorsal fin
rays and 63–74 anal rays; it lives from
North Carolina to Florida and n Gulf of
Mexico to Texas. Tropical Flounder *(P.
tropicus)* lacks ocellated spots and has
73–80 dorsal rays and 57–64 anal rays; it
ranges from Colombia and Venezuela to
Trinidad and Tobago. Summer Flounder
(P. dentatus), found along Atlantic Coast
from Nova Scotia to n Florida, has 5
ocellated spots on eyed side.

Other species of lefteye flounders

Gulf Stream Flounder
(Citharichthys arctifrons) Small, elongate, with small head. Stout, forward-projecting bony protuberance on snout. Eyed side grayish brown with no conspicuous marks. Atlantic coast from Georges Bank to s Florida, Gulf of Mexico to Yucatán.

Fringed Flounder
(Etropus crossotus) Small, elongate. Very small mouth, maxilla ending below front of eye. Eyed side brown, without prominent markings. Caudal fin sometimes has dark margin. No tiny scales at base of normal scales. Chesapeake Bay to Florida, Gulf of Mexico, Antilles, Brazil. Also in e Pacific.

Mexican Flounder
(Cyclopsetta chittendeni) Moderately elongate. Large mouth. Large black blotch under slight arch in lateral line; large spots in dorsal and anal fins, 3 black spots near rear margin of tail fin. Nw Gulf of Mexico, coasts of Central and South America from Yucatán to Trinidad.

Spotfin Flounder
(Cyclopsetta fimbriata) Caudal fin has black blotch in center and 3 spots along margin. Large black blotch on outer half of pectoral fin. North Carolina to Florida, Gulf of Mexico, Greater Antilles, coasts of Central and South America to Guianas.

Channel Flounder
(Syacium micrurum) Rather elongate. Eyed side brown with dusky blotch under pectoral fin and another on lateral line below rear of dorsal fin. Upper 2 pectoral rays elongate in males. 57–68 scales in lateral line. Florida to Brazil; not in Gulf of Mexico. Also e Atlantic.

Shoal Flounder
(Syacium gunteri) Deeper bodied than Channel Flounder. 1 blotch on lateral line below rear of dorsal fin. 46–55 scales in lateral line. Florida, Gulf of Mexico, Caribbean to Guianas.

Dusky Flounder
(Syacium papillosum) Barred pectoral fin. No dark blotches on eyed side. North Carolina to Florida, Gulf of Mexico to Brazil.

AMERICAN SOLES
Family Achiridae

The American soles are rather small flatfishes with both eyes on the right side of the head. The dorsal and anal fins are separate from the caudal fin, but the right pelvic fin is joined to the anal fin. The margin of the preopercle is covered by skin, and its location is marked only by a shallow groove. The American soles were formerly included in the wide-ranging family Soleidae.

There are nine genera and about 28 species; four genera occur in our area.

Genera of family Achiridae

Achirus	Right and left gill chambers connected by interbranchial foramen (small hole through isthmus), visible when gill cover is lifted. Gill membranes separate so that gill openings are confluent ventrally. Body covered with scales.
Trinectes	No interbranchial foramen. Gill openings confluent ventrally. Body covered with scales.
Gymnachirus	Body scaleless. Gill openings confluent ventrally. No interbranchial foramen.
Aprionichthys	Gill membranes joined to isthmus so that gill openings are separate short slits.

389 Hogchoker
Trinectes maculatus

Identification: A stubby oval sole with *no pectoral fins.* Eyed side dark brown, often with narrow vertical lines. *Blind side with dark spots or blotches.* Body scaled, with scattered cirri on side, not in tufts. TL to 8″ (20 cm).

Habitat: Coastal waters. Young enter river mouths to fresh waters and move downstream as they get older.

Range: Massachusetts to Florida, Gulf of Mexico, and w Caribbean.

Notes: It is said that the Hogchoker was once so abundant in estuaries that it was used as food for pigs. Occasionally one would get stuck in a hog's throat, hence the common name.

Similar Species: Scrawled Sole *(T. inscriptus),* from s Florida and Bahamas to Venezuela, lacks cirri on side, has pectoral fins, and is pale with network of dark lines on eyed side.

---

390 **Naked Sole**
Gymnachirus melas

Identification: A small oval sole. Eyed side light brown, with 20–30 alternating wide and narrow dark bars, wider than interspaces. No cirri on lighter interspaces. *Body scaleless.* Blind side whitish, with dusky edges on dorsal, anal, and caudal fins. TL to 8½″ (22 cm).

Habitat: Coastal waters.

Range: Massachusetts to s Florida, e Gulf of Mexico, n Bahamas, Cayman Islands.

Notes: Like other soles in our area, the Naked Sole is too small to be used for food.

Similar Species: Fringed Sole *(G. texae)* has more bars, narrower than interspaces, and cirri on interspaces; in Gulf of Mexico from w Florida to Yucatán. *G. nudus* has 15–18 broader stripes and interspaces; it is known from s Gulf of Mexico, Jamaica, Virgin Islands, and south to Brazil.

TONGUEFISHES
Family Cynoglossidae

The tonguefishes are elongate, tapering flatfishes. Both eyes, which are very small, are on the left side of the head. The dorsal and anal fins are continuous with the pointed caudal fin, and there are no pectoral fins and no fin spines. There is a single pelvic fin that is joined to the anal fin by a membrane. The mouth is asymmetrical, with the right and left jaws unequally curved. A few species have distinctive color patterns, but the best way to identify tonguefishes is by counting the dorsal and anal fin rays. Species from our area have no lateral line on either side. Most tonguefishes live on mud or sand bottoms but a few small species live near coral reefs.

Even though the tonguefishes have their eyes on the left side, they are closely related to the right-eyed soles and some ichthyologists place them in the same family. However, because of their distinctive appearance, we treat them as a separate family.

The family Cynoglossidae contains three genera and about 110 species; the genus *Symphurus* has 15 species that occur in our area; we cover 11.

---

391   Blackcheek Tonguefish
Symphurus plagiusa

Identification: A moderately small, slender tonguefish. Eyed side dark brown, sometimes with narrow bars; *large blackish patch on opercle.* 10 caudal fin rays; 85–92 dorsal fin rays; 69–72 anal fin rays. 71–76 scales in lateral series. TL to 7½″ (19 cm).

Habitat: Inshore waters over mud bottoms.

Range: Atlantic coast from New York to s Florida, Bahamas, n Gulf of Mexico, and Greater Antilles.

Notes: The Blackcheek Tonguefish is an abundant species. It is replaced by the Offshore Tonguefish and the Spottedfin Tonguefish in deeper offshore waters.

Other *Symphurus* species

Caribbean Tonguefish	(*S. arawak*) Small (SL to 2″/5.1 cm); body depth about 3.3 in SL. Eyed side pale sand color with indistinct darker blotches; about 4 dark bands on side, last one chevron-shaped. 1 dark line above eye, 2 dark lines behind eye. Rear parts of dorsal and anal fins blackish. 69–75 dorsal fin rays; 56–61 anal rays; 12 caudal rays. 55–63 scales in lateral series. Florida, Bahamas, Antilles, South American coast from Colombia to Curaçao.
Longtail Tonguefish	(*S. pelicanus*) 80–81 dorsal rays; 63–67 anal rays; 12 caudal rays. 61–74 scales in lateral series. Texas to Trinidad.
Largescale Tonguefish	(*S. minor*) 72–75 dorsal rays; 56–61 anal rays; 10 caudal rays. 55–56 scales in lateral series. Nova Scotia to Florida.
Pygmy Tonguefish	(*S. parvus*) 78–84 dorsal rays; 64–68 anal rays; 10 caudal rays. 60–73 scales in lateral series. E coast of Florida.

Ocellated Tonguefish	*(S. ommospilus)* Slender, small (SL to 1⅞"/ 4.7 cm); body depth about 3 in SL. Pale with distinct, dark ocellated spots near rear of dorsal and anal fins. 76–77 dorsal fin rays; 61–62 anal fin rays; 10 caudal fin rays. 60 scales in lateral series. Bahamas, Belize.
Spottedfin Tonguefish	*(S. diomedianus)* 1–4 plain (not ocellated) spots in dorsal and anal fins. North Carolina to Florida, Gulf of Mexico, Antilles, Caribbean to Brazil.
Spottail Tonguefish	*(S. urospilus)* Conspicuous black ocellated spot on tail. 7–11 narrow dark bands across body. 84–86 dorsal rays; 68–71 anal rays; 11 caudal rays. 71–73 scales in lateral series. Georgia to Florida Keys.
Patchtail Tonguefish	*(S. rhytisma)* Posterior one-third of body abruptly black. 85 dorsal rays; 71 anal rays; 12 caudal rays. 90 scales in lateral series. Bahamas, Curaçao.
Duskycheek Tonguefish	*(S. plagusia)* Eyed side uniformly brown, sometimes with narrow darker cross bars. Dusky blotch on opercle. Posterior rays of dorsal and anal fins dusky to black. 90–101 dorsal fin rays; 76–85 anal fin rays; 12 caudal fin rays. 74–92 scales in lateral series. Antilles, South American coast from Trinidad to Brazil.
Offshore Tonguefish	*(S. civitatus)* 87–92 dorsal rays; 70–77 anal rays; 12 caudal rays. 69–80 scales in lateral series. North Carolina to Florida, n Gulf of Mexico.

ORDER TETRAODONTIFORMES

This order includes the leatherjackets (filefishes and triggerfishes, not to be confused with the Leatherjack *[Oligoplites saurus],* which is a member of the family Carangidae), boxfishes, puffers, and molas. All are highly distinctive fishes with reduced numbers of vertebrae and fin rays, tough skin, specialized teeth, and reduced or absent pelvic fins.

The closely related triggerfishes and filefishes are sometimes treated as subfamilies within one family, Balistidae. Because they are easily distinguished, we place them in two separate families, Balistidae and Monacanthidae.

TRIGGERFISHES
Family Balistidae

These are moderate-size to large, compressed, deep-bodied fishes with two well-separated dorsal fins, the first of which has three spines. The members of this family are generally called triggerfishes because the first dorsal fin spine, which is long and stout, can be locked in an upright position by the second spine, which is just over half as long as the first. Only after the second spine has been depressed can the first spine be lowered. The pelvic fins are rudimentary, represented only by a small movable bone. The mouth is small and terminal, with very strong teeth. The body and head are covered with thick, plate-like scales, and in some genera enlarged scales above the pectoral fin form a flexible tympanum that probably serves to transmit sound to the ears.

There are 11 genera and 40 species; four genera and six species occur in our area.

Genera of family Balistidae

Balistes	Patch of enlarged scales above pectoral fin; scales on posterior part of body smooth, without keels. Teeth notched.
Melichthys	Patch of enlarged scales above pectoral fin; scales on posterior part of body have keels that form longitudinal ridges. Teeth not notched.
Xanthichthys	No enlarged scales above pectoral fin. 3 naked, longitudinal grooves on cheek. Lower jaw projects. Scales smooth.
Canthidermis	No enlarged scales above pectoral fin. Lower jaw does not project. No grooves on cheek. Scales with or without keels.

392 Queen Triggerfish
Balistes vetula

Identification:　A large, compressed triggerfish. Yellowish gray to bluish green above, paler below, with *2 conspicuous bright blue curved lines on side of head, and black lines radiating from eye.* Anterior ray of soft dorsal fin and upper and lower caudal fin rays extended as long trailing filaments. TL to 19¾″ (50 cm).

Habitat: Around coral reefs to depths of 330′ (100 m).

Range: Bermuda, Atlantic coast from Massachusetts to Brazil, Bahamas, Gulf of Mexico, and throughout Caribbean. Also e Atlantic.

Notes: The Queen Triggerfish is the most colorful common triggerfish around coral reefs. It often feeds on sea urchins, flipping them over and attacking the underside. Other triggerfishes feed well above the bottom.

Similar Species: No other triggerfish in our area has elongate caudal fin rays. Gray Triggerfish *(B. capriscus)* is blotched, and lacks blue lines on head and trailing extensions of dorsal and caudal fins; it ranges from Nova Scotia to Florida, Bahamas, Gulf of Mexico, Antilles, Caribbean, and s Argentina. Black Durgon is black with blue lines at bases of soft dorsal and anal fins.

---

393 Black Durgon
Melichthys niger

Identification: *A dark greenish-black triggerfish with purplish overtones. Pale blue lines along bases of soft dorsal and anal fins.* Small, scaleless groove in front of eye. Upper and lower rays of caudal fin somewhat extended. *Scales of rear part of body have prominent keels that form longitudinal ridges.* TL to 19¾″ (50 cm).

Habitat: Along edges of drop-offs and over reefs to depths of about 330′ (100 m).

Range: Circumtropical. Southern Florida, Bahamas, and Caribbean, including Antilles, to Brazil. Not in Gulf of Mexico.

Notes: The Black Durgon is a beautiful triggerfish and is often seen by snorkelers and divers. No other triggerfish shares its distinctive color pattern.

394 Sargassum Triggerfish
Xanthichthys ringens

Identification: A colorful, predominantly brown or blue triggerfish with *dark pigment in grooves on cheek and along bases of dorsal and anal fins;* red on central caudal rays and along upper and lower margins of caudal fin. Mouth superior, with *lower jaw projecting as distinct chin.* Caudal fin lunate, upper and lower rays not extended. TL to 10″ (25 cm).

Habitat: Young associated with floating sargassum. Adults near bottom at depths over 100′ (30 m).

Range: Bermuda, North Carolina to Florida, Bahamas, Gulf of Mexico, Caribbean, including Antilles, to Brazil.

Notes: The Sargassum Triggerfish is possibly the prettiest of our local triggerfishes, although not as gaudy as the Queen Triggerfish. No other triggerfish has longitudinal grooves on the cheek.

395 Ocean Triggerfish
Canthidermis sufflamen

Identification: A large, plain gray triggerfish with diffuse dark spot at base of pectoral fin. *Dorsal and anal fins very high.* Tail somewhat lunate. Scales smooth, lacking keels in both young and adults. TL to 24″ (60 cm).

Habitat: Pelagic, but frequently seen near edges of reefs.

Range: Bermuda, Atlantic coast from Massachusetts to South America, Bahamas, Gulf of Mexico, and Caribbean, including Antilles.

Notes: The Ocean Triggerfish is a spectacular sight underwater. As it swims toward the snorkeler, the dorsal and anal fins, which provide its main propulsion, can be seen flexing in unison.

Similar Species: Rough Triggerfish *(C. maculata)* is similar but has strongly keeled scales that become smoother with age, and is dark brown or black with white spots. It lives in warm seas worldwide.

FILEFISHES
Family Monacanthidae

Filefishes are small to moderate-size, highly compressed fishes. Although some species have only one dorsal spine, most have two, and the second is tiny, always less than one-third as long as the first. Usually the first spine can be locked upright by the second. The body is covered with tiny, modified, bristle-like scales that are not discernible to the naked eye. Pelvic fins are absent or rudimentary, represented by a series of up to three scales that cover the end of the pelvic bone. Filefishes have a well-developed pelvic bone that is hinged to the pectoral girdle and supports a *ventral flap* of skin between its tip and the anus. The pelvic bone can be moved to expand or contract the ventral flap. In some species the flap is highly pigmented and probably used in courtship display.

The family contains 31 genera and 95 species; four genera and 10 species occur in our region.

Genera of family Monacanthidae

Cantherhines	Deep groove behind first dorsal spines into which spines fold when depressed. First dorsal spine inserted over front of eye. Rudimentary pelvic fin fixed, cannot be moved up and down.
Monacanthus	2–4 pairs of enlarged spine-like scales on side of caudal peduncle. Rudimentary pelvic fin capable of flexing up and down. First dorsal spine inserted over rear of eye. No groove behind dorsal spines.
Stephanolepis	No enlarged scales on side of caudal peduncle. Males have second dorsal ray extended as filament. Rudimentary pelvic fin capable of moving up and down. First dorsal spine inserted over rear of eye.
Aluterus	Body elongate, caudal fin long. No rudimentary pelvic fin at tip of pelvic bone. No enlarged scales on side of caudal peduncle. No groove between dorsal fins.

396 Whitespotted Filefish
Cantherhines macrocerus

Identification:
A rather large, heavy-bodied filefish with small scales. Brown above; yellow or orange below; scattered white spots on side of head and body. *Large, rather vague, grayish saddle-shaped band between dorsal fins, narrowing to point ventrally (band looks like fungus invasion, but is normal color pattern).* 2 dorsal fin spines; first rather stout, located over front part of eye, folds down into deep groove between dorsal fins. Large males have 4 prominent hooked spines on side of caudal peduncle. TL to 18″ (46 cm).

Habitat: Coral reefs.

Range: Bermuda, Florida, Bahamas, n Gulf of Mexico, and Caribbean, including Antilles, to Brazil.

Notes: This large, spectacular filefish is easily seen by divers and snorkelers.

Similar Species: Orangespotted Filefish is smaller, lacks white spots, and has a distinct pale spot behind dorsal fin.

397 Orangespotted Filefish
Cantherhines pullus

Identification:
A small, elongate filefish with *a stout first dorsal fin spine, located over front part of eye, that folds down into a deep groove between dorsal fins.* Greenish to dark brown overall with 2 or more transient white streaks, *conspicuous pale spot behind dorsal fin,* smaller pale spot behind anal fin, and small orange spots on body (hard to see underwater). No strong spines on side of caudal peduncle. TL to 8″ (20 cm).

Habitat: Coral reefs and associated habitats.

Range: Bermuda, Massachusetts to Bahamas, Gulf of Mexico, and Caribbean, including Antilles, south to s Brazil.

Notes: The Orangespotted Filefish is one of the most commonly seen filefishes.

Similar Species: Whitespotted Filefish is larger and has white spots.

398 Fringed Filefish
Monacanthus ciliatus

Identification: A relatively *deep-bodied filefish* (greatest body depth about 2 in SL). Greenish tan or brownish overall, with longitudinal dark stripes. Ventral flap large, dark at base, its margin bright golden yellow in males, duller greenish yellow in females. Snout concave in profile. First dorsal fin spine stout, with double row of barbs. 2–4 enlarged scales on each side of caudal peduncle. TL to 8″ (20 cm).

Habitat: Shallow waters to depths of 165′ (50 m), usually over sea-grass beds.

Range: Bermuda, Atlantic coast from Newfoundland to Argentina, Bahamas, Gulf of Mexico, and Caribbean, including Antilles. Also e Atlantic.

Notes: The Fringed Filefish is common in sea-grass beds.

Similar Species: Slender Filefish is smaller, with longer snout and less deep body. Pygmy Filefish has bristle-like scales on side of caudal peduncle and filament at front of dorsal fin.

399 Slender Filefish
Monacanthus tuckeri

Identification: *A small, slender filefish (body depth about 3 in SL) with a rather long, concave facial profile. Brownish gray with scattered small black spots.* First dorsal fin spine stout, with double row of barbs. Second dorsal fin ray without filamentous extension. Ventral flap rather small with dark base. 2–4 enlarged scales on each side of caudal peduncle. TL to 3½″ (9 cm).

Habitat: Coral reefs.

Range: Bermuda, North Carolina to Florida, Bahamas, and Caribbean, including Antilles.

Notes: The Slender Filefish is often seen among the branches of sea whips.

Similar Species: Fringed Filefish has deeper body, shorter snout, and larger ventral flap.

400 Planehead Filefish
Stephanolepis hispidus

Identification: A small, compact filefish with a stout
first dorsal spine that has a double row
of barbs. Brownish tan to greenish, with
irregular spots and blotches. Profile from
snout to origin of first dorsal fin spine
nearly straight. *31–34 dorsal fin rays;
31–33 anal fin rays.* No enlarged scales
on caudal peduncle. TL to 8″ (20 cm).

Habitat: Sea-grass beds and sand or mud bottoms
to depths of 265′ (80 m).

Range: Bermuda, Atlantic coast from North
Carolina to Brazil, Bahamas, Gulf of
Mexico, and Caribbean, including
Antilles.

Notes: The Planehead Filefish provides another
reason for divers and snorkelers to be
attentive around sea-grass beds. Some
authorities incorporate the genus
Stephanolepis into the genus *Monacanthus*.

Similar Species: Fringed Filefish and Slender Filefish
have concave faces and 2–4 enlarged
scales on each side of caudal peduncle.
Pygmy Filefish has fewer rays in dorsal
and anal fins.

401 Pygmy Filefish
Stephanolepis setifer

Identification: A small, compact filefish. Brownish tan
to greenish with irregular spots and
blotches. *Profile from snout to origin of first
dorsal spine nearly straight.* First dorsal
spine stout, with double row of barbs.
Adult males have first ray of second
dorsal fin extended as filament. 27–29
dorsal fin rays; 27–29 anal fin rays.
Caudal peduncle has patch of bristle-like
scales but no prominent enlarged scales.
TL to 8″ (20 cm).

Habitat: Offshore around seaweed and other
floating objects.

Range: Bermuda, Atlantic coast from North
Carolina to n South America, Bahamas,
Gulf of Mexico, Antilles, Caribbean.

Notes: The Pygmy Filefish is an inconspicuous member of the community of fishes that assembles around floating objects.

Similar Species: Planehead Filefish has more fin rays.

---

402 Scrawled Filefish
Aluterus scriptus

Identification: A rather elongate, strongly compressed filefish without a rudimentary pelvic fin. *Tan, with blue lines and spots.* Upper profile of snout concave. First dorsal fin spine slender and without prominent barbs, second spine minute and not easily seen externally. 43–49 dorsal fin rays; 46–52 anal fin rays. Caudal fin rounded, very long. TL to 3′ (91 cm).

Habitat: Open waters and around reefs.

Range: Worldwide in warmer seas. Bermuda, Atlantic coast from Nova Scotia to Brazil, Bahamas, Gulf of Mexico, and Caribbean, including Antilles.

Notes: The Scrawled Filefish often drifts head down, which may make it look like a piece of floating debris and thus confuse predators; or its posture may make it appear to be a potential shelter to its own prey.

Similar Species: Dotterel Filefish *(A. heudeloti)* has 36–41 dorsal rays, 39–44 anal rays, relatively short first dorsal spine with large barbs, and bluish-purple spots on body; known from both sides of Atlantic, it is rare in our area. Orange Filefish *(A. schoepfi)* has 32–40 dorsal rays, 35–41 anal rays, and brown to gray body with scattered small orange spots; it lives from Nova Scotia to Florida, Bahamas, Gulf of Mexico, and Caribbean to Brazil. Unicorn Filefish *(A. monoceros)* has gray or dark brown body with scattered small black spots, head concave below chin and followed by prominent convex ridge, 46–50 dorsal rays, and 47–52 anal rays; it occurs worldwide in warm and temperate seas but is rare in our area.

BOXFISHES
Family Ostraciidae

These spectacular fishes are named for their modified scales, which form a bony armor of hexagonal plates that enclose the body (except for the caudal peduncle) in a rigid, shell-like covering called a *cuirass.* Only the eyes, mouth, fins, and tail are free to move. Approximately triangular in cross section, at least as adults, boxfishes are small to medium-size, with no fin spines and no pelvic fins. Their caudal fins are fan shaped with rounded or convex rear margins.

The family contains 14 genera and 33 species; our five species are usually placed in two genera, *Acanthostracion* and *Lactophrys,* although some authorities group them all in the latter.

Genera of family Ostraciidae

Acanthostracion	Cuirass with prominent, horn-like spines in front of eyes.
Lactophrys	No horn-like spines in front of eyes.

403 Scrawled Cowfish
Acanthostracion quadricornis

Identification: Grayish brown to yellowish, with numerous irregular spots and lines of various shades of blue; 3 or 4 parallel horizontal blue lines on side of head below eye. *Pair of prominent spines projecting from in front of eyes suggests cow horns. Second pair of spines at lower rear corners of cuirass.* Cuirass forms bridge behind dorsal fin; no separate plate on top of caudal peduncle. 11 pectoral fin rays. TL to 13¾″ (35 cm).

Habitat: Usually in sea-grass beds in water to depths of 265′ (80 m).

Range: Bermuda, Atlantic coast from Massachusetts to Brazil, throughout Bahamas, Gulf of Mexico, and Caribbean. Also in e Atlantic.

Notes: The Scrawled Cowfish is commonly seen by snorkelers and divers. It is usually more common than the Honeycomb Cowfish.

404 Honeycomb Cowfish
Acanthostracion polygonius

Identification: A rather short boxfish. *Bold pattern of hexagons outlined by narrow dark lines; centers and areas between hexagons pale.* Usually 12 pectoral fin rays. SL to 14" (36 cm).

Habitat: Shallow water, over sea-grass beds and around coral reefs to depths of 250' (75 m).

Range: Bermuda, New Jersey to South Carolina, Bahamas, and Caribbean, including Antilles, to Brazil.

Notes: This species is sometimes confused with the Scrawled Cowfish but can be identified by its honeycomb-like pattern and 12 pectoral rays.

405 Smooth Trunkfish
Lactophrys triqueter

Identification: A rather short boxfish, triangular in cross section, *without spines on cuirass and without free plate on dorsal surface of caudal peduncle.* Dark mottled gray, with white or yellow spots. TL to 12" (30 cm).

Habitat: Coral reefs and associated habitats.

Range: Bermuda, Atlantic coast from Massachusetts to Brazil, Bahamas, Gulf of Mexico, and Caribbean, including Antilles.

Notes: A common reef fish, the Smooth Trunkfish bumps along the bottom picking up invertebrates. Other boxfishes in our area have spines at the lower posterior corners of the cuirass.

406 Spotted Trunkfish
Lactophrys bicaudalis

Identification: *A robust boxfish with large spines at lower rear corners of cuirass.* Pale gray with small black spots. Carapace forms bridge behind dorsal fin; no free plate on dorsal surface of caudal peduncle. TL to 17¾" (45 cm).

Habitat: Reefs and shallow habitats to depths of 165′ (50 m).

Range: Bermuda, Atlantic coast to Florida, Bahamas, Gulf of Mexico, and Caribbean, including Antilles to Brazil.

Notes: The Spotted Trunkfish is common around shallow reefs.

Similar Species: Trunkfish has separate plate on dorsal surface of caudal peduncle; Smooth Trunkfish has no spines; and cowfishes have spines on head as well as at lower rear corners of cuirass.

---

407 Trunkfish
Lactophrys trigonus

Identification: A fairly large, somewhat elongate boxfish with spines at lower rear corners of cuirass. Greenish to tannish, with small white spots; sometimes with network of dark, chain-like markings. *Cuirass open behind dorsal fin, with separate large oval plate on dorsal surface of caudal peduncle.* TL to 17¾″ (45 cm).

Habitat: Shallow water, often over sponge and grass beds to depths of 165′ (50 m).

Range: Bermuda, Atlantic coast from New England to Brazil, Bahamas, Gulf of Mexico, Antilles, and Caribbean.

Notes: The Trunkfish is often seen from small boats moving over shallow flats. Other boxfishes have the cuirass closed behind the dorsal fin.

PUFFERS
Family Tetraodontidae

As the name Tetraodontidae implies (*tetra* means "four" and *odont* means "tooth"), the fishes of this family have their jaw teeth fused into four plates, two in each jaw. In this way they differ from the related porcupinefishes and burrfishes (family Diodontidae), which have the tooth plates in each jaw fused into a single beak-like structure. Puffers are moderately small to large, tapering, nearly terete fishes with blunt heads. They are capable of inflating themselves with air or water until they are nearly spherical. This is presumably a defense mechanism, making them larger and difficult to swallow. Puffers lack fin spines and pelvic fins. They have short dorsal and anal fins, bluntly rounded pectoral fins, and usually truncate or slightly rounded caudal fins (lunate in one genus, *Lagocephalus*). They do not have normal scales, but part or all of the body may bear small prickles or scale-like dermal plates. Some species are completely scaleless; some have small fleshy skin tabs.

The family includes 19 genera and 121 species; four genera occur in our region. Sometimes the Sharpnose Puffer of the genus *Canthigaster* is placed in a separate family.

Genera of family Tetraodontidae

Canthigaster	Snout rather long and pointed. Low mid-dorsal keel in front of dorsal fin. Nostrils very small, nearly invisible. 10 dorsal fin rays.
Lagocephalus	Caudal fin lunate. 13 or more dorsal fin rays. Nostrils small but plainly visible. No mid-dorsal keel.
Sphoeroides	9 or fewer dorsal fin rays. Nostrils small but visible. No mid-dorsal keel. Caudal fin rounded or squarish.
Colomesus	No mid-dorsal keel. Nostrils small but visible. 10–12 dorsal fin rays. Caudal fin rounded or squarish.

408, 409   Sharpnose Puffer
Canthigaster rostrata

Identification: A rather small species with a long snout, tiny nostrils, and *a distinct mid-dorsal keel from nape to dorsal fin.* Brown above, sharply lighter below. Short blue radial lines around eye; scattered blue spots on head; blue lines on lower side of caudal peduncle. *Upper and lower margins of tail dark,* center clear. TL to 4⅜″ (11 cm).

Habitat: Coral reefs and other hard bottom areas to depths of 85′ (25 m).

Range: Bermuda, Florida and e Gulf of Mexico, Bahamas, Antilles, Caribbean to n coast of South America.

Notes: The Sharpnose Puffer is a very common reef fish. No other puffer has a mid-dorsal keel.

410   Amazon Puffer
Colomesus asellus

Identification: A rather small puffer. Pale yellow overall with 5 dark bars crossing back, including 2 on top of head. *Distinct large black spot on underside of caudal peduncle. 13–16 pectoral fin rays.* TL to 5″ (12 cm).

Habitat: Mostly fresh water and coastal streams, but can tolerate brackish water.

Range: Northern South America from lower Orinoco River to Amazon River basin.

Notes: This distinctive small puffer is sometimes kept in aquariums.

Similar Species: Corrotucho *(C. psittacus)* is somewhat larger (TL to 13″/33 cm), has 17–19 pectoral fin rays, and lacks distinct dark spot on underside of caudal peduncle; it lives in brackish and inshore marine waters from Venezuela to Brazil.

Amazon Puffer range

411   Bandtail Puffer
Sphoeroides spengleri

Identification: A rather small puffer. Olive-brown above, pale below, with *11–14 sharply defined round black spots on head and lower side of body.* Caudal fin dark at base, with dark bar across its outer third. No pale lines on cheeks. No black fleshy tabs on back midway between eye and dorsal fin. Many tan lappets on rear part of body. 9 dorsal fin rays. SL to 6″ (15 cm).

Habitat: Shallow waters over reefs and seagrass.

Range: Bermuda, Massachusetts to Brazil, Bahamas, Gulf of Mexico, and Caribbean.

Notes: The Bandtail Puffer is a common puffer around coral reefs. The numerous tan lappets on the rear part of the body and distinct spots along the lower side make it unmistakable.

412   Checkered Puffer
Sphoeroides testudineus

Identification: A moderate-size puffer. Greenish above, pale yellow to white below; *back* has series of pale lines and arcs suggesting concentric circles with intersecting lines. No black fleshy tabs on back between eye and dorsal fin. *9 dorsal fin rays.* TL to 12″ (30 cm).

Habitat: Sea-grass beds, often in very shallow waters.

Range: Florida, Bahamas, sw Gulf of Mexico from Yucatán Peninsula along w and s margins of Caribbean, Antilles, and South American coast to Brazil.

Notes: The Checkered Puffer is conspicuous in grass flats in very shallow water.

Similar Species: No other puffer has this color pattern. Marbled Puffer *(S. dorsalis)* has small black lappets behind head on either side of midline; occurs from North Carolina to Suriname, including Gulf of Mexico and Bahamas.

Other *Sphoeroides* species

Southern Puffer
(S. nephelus) Moderately small. Green to slate brown with pale blue reticulations on back. Several black spots behind pectoral fin; spot in axil very dark. Breeding males have small red spots over much of body. Small prickles on body, often embedded beneath tiny pores in skin. 9 dorsal fin rays. 14 pectoral fin rays. Florida, Bahamas, e Gulf of Mexico, Antilles, w Caribbean.

Northern Puffer
(S. maculatus) Small dark spots over dorsal surface. Vertical bars behind pectoral fin. 16 pectoral fin rays. South to Jacksonville, Florida.

Blunthead Puffer
(S. pachygaster) Uniformly gray or brown. Lacks prickles. Coastal waters from New Jersey to Argentina.

Least Puffer
(S. parvus) Snout and head entirely covered with prickles. Gulf of Mexico from Pensacola to Yucatán.

Speckled Puffer
(S. yergeri) Tiny black flecks on ventral surface. Belize to Colombia.

Bearded Puffer
(S. tyleri) 3–4 vague diagonal blotches on lower cheek. South American coast from Colombia to ec Brazil.

Other species of puffers

Smooth Puffer	*(Lagocephalus laevigatus)* Large (TL to 3′3″/1 m). Gray back, silvery side, white belly. Side and back smooth; small prickles on belly. 13 or more dorsal rays; 12 anal rays; 17–18 pectoral fin rays. No fleshy tabs. Bermuda, New England to Argentina, Bahamas, Gulf of Mexico, Caribbean.
Oceanic Puffer	*(Lagocephalus lagocephalus)* Similar to Smooth Puffer. Dorsal fin origin farther back. 13–16 pectoral rays. E Atlantic; few scattered records in our region.

PORCUPINEFISHES and BURRFISHES
Family Diodontidae

Like the related puffers, porcupinefishes and burrfishes are capable of inflating their bodies with water or air until almost spherical. Members of this family have large spines on the body that in the burrfishes are short and fixed in place and in the porcupinefishes are long, quill-like, and erectile. The porcupinefishes and burrfishes have teeth fused into a single beak-like structure in each jaw, whereas the puffers have four separate teeth. The dorsal and anal fins are short with no spines, the caudal fin is squarish or slightly rounded, and there are no pelvic fins.

The family includes six genera and 19 species; there are two genera and six species in our area.

Genera of family Diodontidae

Diodon	Body with long, quill-like erectile spines, most with 2 roots.
Chilomycterus	Body with short, rigid spines, most with 3 roots.

413   Balloonfish
Diodon holocanthus

Identification: A stout, almost globose fish with long erectile spines over most of its body, those on forehead longer than those behind pectoral fin. Body gray with small black spots; *large dark blotches on dorsal surface,* and prominent bar through eye. TL to 19¾" (50 cm); usually smaller.

Habitat: Shallow waters from mangrove shores to coral reefs.

Range: Worldwide in tropical waters. Florida, Bahamas, Gulf of Mexico, and Caribbean to Brazil.

Notes: The Balloonfish is fairly common in a variety of habitats.

Similar Species: Porcupinefish has shorter spines on forehead and lacks prominent dark blotches.

414 Porcupinefish
Diodon hystrix

Identification: A rather large, globose fish with long erectile spines over most of its body, those on forehead shorter than those behind pectoral fin. Body grayish tan, with *small black spots, but no large dark blotches. Belly white, surrounded by dusky ring.* 2 indistinct bars on side of head. TL to 24" (60 cm).

Habitat: Coral reefs and associated habitats.

Range: Worldwide in warm seas. Bermuda, Atlantic coast from Massachusetts to Brazil, Bahamas, Gulf of Mexico, and Caribbean, including Antilles.

Notes: The Porcupinefish is commonly seen in caves and holes in shallow reefs.

Similar Species: Balloonfish has dark blotches.

415 Bridled Burrfish
Chilomycterus antennatus

Identification: A rather small, stout fish with short fixed spines. Body light brownish with small dark spots; larger dark blotches across top of head and around dorsal fin; *kidney-shaped spot above pectoral fin.* Fins without spots. TL to 15" (38 cm).

Habitat: Coral reefs and related habitats.

Range: Florida, Bahamas, Antilles, and n South
America to Panama. Also in e Atlantic.

Notes: The Bridled Burrfish is not a very
common species.

Similar Species: Spotted Burrfish *(C. atinga)* also has
black spots and sometimes dark blotches,
but never has kidney-shaped spot above
pectoral fin; known from Bermuda,
Florida Keys and s to Brazil. Other
species of burrfishes lack small black
spots. Striped Burrfish *(C. schoepfi)* has
pattern of dark parallel lines on pale
greenish background; ranges from New
England to Brazil, including Gulf of
Mexico.

416 Web Burrfish
Chilomycterus antillarum

Identification: A rather small, stout species with short
fixed spines. *Body greenish to brown, with
network of fine dark lines enclosing roughly
hexagonal spaces. Black blotches on side;
dark bar below eye.* TL to 12″ (30 cm).

Habitat: Sea-grass beds in shallow waters; to
depths of 165′ (50 m) off South America.

Range: Florida, Bahamas, Antilles, and South
American coast from Colombia to n
Brazil.

Notes: The Web Burrfish is an interesting,
distinctively colored species, the only
burrfish in our area with a network of
fine dark lines.

MOLAS
Family Molidae

Molas are large, bizarre-looking fishes
that drift at the surface of the open ocean,
often on their sides, which has given them
the name ocean sunfishes. The body is
thick, deep, and compressed, and appears "incomplete" because it lacks a caudal peduncle and a true caudal fin, ending in a pseudocaudal fin, or *clavus*—a fin-like structure
formed by the rear dorsal and anal fin rays. The tail fin is absent or represented by a few bony elements embedded in a

rudder-like lobe of the clavus. The dorsal and anal fins have high lobes; there are no pelvic fins. The mouth is small, with beak-like upper and lower jaws.

There are three species, variously placed in two or three genera; all three species might be encountered in our region.

Genera of family Molidae

Ranzania	Skin with hexagonal plates.
Mola	Skin without hexagonal plates.

417   Ocean Sunfish
Mola mola

Identification: A huge, stubby, compressed fish with high dorsal and anal fins. Body gray-brown, without conspicuous markings. *Margin of clavus evenly curved, without central projection. Mouth a horizontal slit when closed.* TL to 10′ (3 m), height to 11′ (3.3 m).

Habitat: Open oceans.

Range: Worldwide.

Notes: One of the largest bony fishes in the world, the Ocean Sunfish could be encountered anywhere in our region. It can weigh up to 4,400 pounds (1,995 kg).

Similar Species: Sharptail Mola *(M. lanceolata),* which also occurs in all warm seas, has central lobe on clavus. Slender Mola *(Ranzania laevis),* which occurs throughout our area, is elongate but smaller (TL to 32″/ 81 cm), with bony hexagonal plates in skin and whitish bands on lower part of head.

GLOSSARY

Abdominal Describes the placement of the pelvic fins when they originate far back on the body, well behind the pectoral fins.

Adipose eyelid A thick, transparent membrane covering part of the eyeball in some fishes.

Adipose fin A fleshy fin, without supporting rays, behind the dorsal fin in some fishes.

Anadromous Migrating from marine waters upstream to breed in fresh water.

Anterior margin The leading edge of a fin.

Axil The inner angle at which a paired fin, especially the pectoral fin, is joined to the body.

Axillary process An enlarged scaly structure along the bases of the pectoral and/or pelvic fins of some fishes.

Band A broad pigmented vertical line; also called a bar.

Barbel A fleshy projection of skin, often thread-like, usually found near the mouth, chin, or nostrils.

Base In a fin, the place where the fin joins the body.

Brackish Water that is slightly less salty than sea water.

Branchiostegal ray One of a number of flattened bony rods that support the gill membrane along the lower edge of the operculum.

Canine teeth Long, pointed, conical or lance-shaped teeth.

Catadromous Migrating from fresh water downstream to breed in salt water.

Caudal peduncle The slender part of the body just ahead of the caudal fin.

Ciguatera An illness humans get by eating fish with toxic flesh.

Circumorbital bones A ring of rather superficial bones that surrounds each eye.

Cirrus A finger-like protuberance, sometimes occurring in a fringe-like series.

Claspers Modified parts of the pelvic fins of male sharks, rays, and skates; used in copulation.

Compressed Flattened from side to side; higher than wide.

Continental shelf An underwater plain that surrounds most continents; slopes gently to depths of about 650 feet (200 m); called the insular shelf around islands.

Continental slope That part of the ocean floor beyond the edge of the continental shelf where the bottom falls away.

Corselet A girdle of enlarged scales on the anterior part of the body in mackerel-like fishes.

Ctenoid scale A scale with small spines on the exposed edge.

Cusp A pointed projection on a tooth.

Cusplet A small accessory cusp; called lateral cusplets when located on each side of the main cusp.

Cycloid scale A smooth scale without spines.

Deep-bodied Describes a fish whose depth measurement (the distance from dorsal midline to ventral midline) is high in comparison to its length.

Depressed Flattened from top to bottom; wider than high.

Distal The part of an appendage that is farthest from the body.

Dorsal Pertaining to the back or upper surface of the body.

Elongate Describes a fish whose length measurement is proportionally much greater than its depth measurement (the distance from dorsal midline to ventral midline).

Emarginate An edge that is notched but not deeply forked.

Endemic Restricted or peculiar to a locality or region.

Epipelagic Of or inhabiting that part of the open ocean from the surface to a depth of about 650 feet (200 m).

Esca The "lure" at the tip of the modified dorsal spine (the "fishing pole," or illicium) used in some fishes to attract prey.

Falcate Long and curved like a sickle.

Fin ray One of the bony or horny rods that support the fins; may be soft or spiny. *See* Fin spine and Soft ray.

Fin spine A solid, unsegmented fin ray that does not branch.

Free rear tip The tip of the last ray of a fin.

Frenum A bridge of connective tissue, such as the fleshy membrane connecting the upper lip to the snout.

Fusiform Spindle shaped, or tapering at both ends.

Gill arch A bony or cartilaginous structure that supports the gills.

Gill cover *See* Operculum.

Gill filaments Finger-like projections along the posterior surface of the gill arch that take oxygen from the water that passes over them; the "lungs" of a fish.

Gill membrane An external tissue along the edge of the operculum that prevents water from entering the gills through the gill opening.

Gill opening The opening through which the water used in respiration leaves the body.

Gill rakers A row of slender bony or hardened finger-like structures along the front of the gill arch in some fishes.

Gills The filamentous respiratory organs of fishes.

Gill slits Gill openings; often used for the multiple gill openings of sharks and batoids.

Gular plate A bony plate on the throat, between the lower jaw bones, of certain fishes.

Heterocercal Describes a caudal fin in which the spinal column extends into the larger upper lobe.

Homocercal Describes a caudal fin that is nearly or completely symmetrical and that is supported by a complex internal V-shaped bony plate.

Hypomaxilla A small, toothed bone at the edge of the upper jaw between the premaxilla and the maxilla.

Illicium A dorsal fin spine that is modified in some fishes into a "fishing pole" with a lure at its tip called the esca.

Inferior Describes a mouth that is on the underside of the head, with the upper jaw, or snout, projecting.

Inner margin The rear edge of a fin, bounded by its last ray.

Inquiline Residing within the body of another animal.

Insular shelf *See* Continental shelf.

Interorbital Pertaining to the area between the eyes.

Intrauterine cannibalism When one or more embryos of a litter of a live-bearing species develop faster and eat other embryos while they are in the uterus.

Isthmus The triangular part of the underside of the body that extends forward between the gill covers of bony fishes.

Keel A sharp ridge located on the back, belly, or caudal peduncle in some fishes; called lateral keels when located on either side of the caudal peduncle.

Labial furrows Grooves that extend forward from the corners of the mouths of some sharks.

Lateral line A series of tubes or pored scales associated with the sensory system that runs along the length of a fish at mid-side.

Leptocephalus Transparent, ribbon-shaped planktonic larva.

Lunate Crescent shaped.

Mandibular On the lower jaw.

Maxilla One of two bones, along with the premaxilla, that support the upper outer jaws on each side.

Nape The area behind the back of the head.

Nictitating membrane An inner eyelid in several families of sharks that can be pulled protectively across the eye.

Occipital pit A deep pit on top of the head behind the eyes.

Occiput The hindmost part of the top of the head.

Ocellus A spot with a margin of contrasting color.

Opercle The uppermost of the two main bones that support the operculum.

Operculum A movable bony plate covering the gills of bony fishes; also called the gill cover.

Origin The forward-most limit of the fin base.

Oviparous Producing young by means of eggs that hatch after being laid, outside the mother's body.

Ovoviviparous Producing live young by means of eggs that are retained and hatched within the body of the female but receive no nutrients from her.

Palatine teeth Teeth on the palatine bones, a pair of bones on the roof of the mouth.

Pectoral girdle A series of bones that support the pectoral fin; also called the shoulder girdle.

Pelagic Of or inhabiting the waters of the open ocean.

Pharyngeal teeth Teeth, sometimes molar-like, located on the bones of the pharynx, the passage between the mouth and the esophagus; also called the pharyngeal mill.

Photophore A light-emitting organ or spot on certain fishes.

Placoid scale A scale with a flat base and one or more spines; each scale has a dentine core and an enamel surface like a tiny tooth.

Plankton Microscopic plants and animals that drift near the surface of open waters.

Polychaete worms A class of mainly marine annelid worms.

Pored scale One of a series of scales with a small opening into a sensory system; usually found along the lateral line.

Posterior margin The edge of a fin formed by the tips of the rays.

Precaudal pits Deep grooves or squarish indentations in some sharks marking the beginning of the tail.

Predorsal Pertaining to the area on the back between the occiput and the dorsal fin origin.

Premaxilla One of the two bones, along with the maxilla, that support the upper outer jaws on each side.

Preopercle A J- or L-shaped bone on each side of the head.

Preorbital The anterior part of the suborbital area (which is below the eyes).

Protrusible A type of mouth that allows the premaxillae to slide forward, displacing the upper jaw into a kind of tube.

Pseudobranch A patch of gill filaments inside the gill chamber; often extends onto the inside of the operculum.

Reticulate Marked with a net-like or chain-like pattern.

Rostrum An extended snout.

Saddle A blotch or patch of pigment that extends across the midline of the back and onto the sides.

Sargassum A brown seaweed; often refers to a free-floating species.

Scute A modified scale, often large and shield-like, with one or more ridges.

Sensory pore A small opening leading to the lateral line on the head and/or body of some fishes.

Soft ray A flexible fin ray that is usually segmented and branched toward the tip.

Spawn To release eggs and sperm into the water.

Spine A sharp, bony projection, usually on the head or in a fin; *see also* Fin spine.

Spiracle A respiratory opening behind each eye of skates and rays and some sharks.

Subabdominal Describes the placement of the pelvic fins when they are behind the pectoral fins (not as far back as abdominal pelvic fins).

Subopercle The lower of the two main bones that support the operculum.

Suborbital The area below the eyes.

Subspecies Population of a species that usually differs in appearance (and is usually geographically isolated), but whose individuals can still interbreed and produce fertile offspring with other members of the species; also called race.

Subterminal Describes a mouth in which the upper jaw projects only slightly beyond the lower.

Sucking disk An adhesive structure; a disk formed by the union of paired fins or a modification of the dorsal spines.

Superior Describes a mouth in which the lower jaw projects beyond the upper.

Supramaxilla An additional bone or bones along the upper edge of the maxilla in some species.

Supraorbital Above the eyes.

Swim bladder A gas- or fat-filled sac found in bony fishes that provides buoyancy.

Tapering Deepest at the front, tapering toward the tail.

Terete Round in cross section.

Terminal Describes a mouth placed at the very front of the head.

Thoracic Describes the placement of the pelvic fins when they are below or ahead of the pectoral fins.

Truncate An edge, as of a tail fin, that is straight and vertical.

Ventral Pertaining to the underside or lower part of the body.

Vermiculations Fine, wavy lines.

Villiform teeth Minute, slender teeth in compact patches.

Viviparous Bearing live young that have received nutrients from the mother during embryonic development.

Vomer teeth The teeth on the vomer bone, located in the front part of the roof of the mouth behind the upper jaw.

PHOTO CREDITS

The photo credits are listed by plate number. All photographers hold the copyright for their images.

212 John E. Randall
213 Fred Rohde/Visuals Unlimited
214 John E. Randall
215 Stephen Frink/WaterHouse
216 Bob Bowdey
217 Steffen Mittelhaeuser
218 Graeme Teague
219 Fred McConnaughey/ Photo Researchers, Inc.
220 Joyce Burek/Azure Computer and Photographic Services, Inc.
221 Joyce Burek/Azure Computer and Photographic Services, Inc.
222 Steve Simonsen
223 Fred McConnaughey/ Photo Researchers, Inc.
224 Gregory S. Boland
225 Stephen Frink/WaterHouse
226 Michael Cardwell
227 Andrew J. Martinez
228 Fred McConnaughey/ Photo Researchers, Inc.
229 John G. Shedd Aquarium
230 Stephen Frink/WaterHouse
231 Doug Perrine/Innerspace Visions
232 Herb Segars
233 Edward G. Lines, Jr./ John G. Shedd Aquarium
234 Fred McConnaughey/ Photo Researchers, Inc.
235 David B. Snyder
236 Paul H. Humann
237 Frank Burek/Azure Computer and Photographic Services, Inc.
238 Susan Blanchet/Blanchet Photographics
239 David B. Snyder
240 Steve Simonsen
241 Steffen Mittelhaeuser
242 Andrew J. Martinez
243 John E. Randall
244 Wayne & Karen Brown/ Brown & Company Photography
245 Doug Perrine/Innerspace Visions
246 Herb Segars
247 Fred McConnaughey/ Photo Researchers, Inc.
248 Charles V. Angelo/Photo Researchers, Inc.
249 Joyce Burek/Azure Computer and Photographic Services, Inc.
250 Joyce Burek/Azure Computer and Photographic Services, Inc.
251 Michael Cardwell
252 Gregory S. Boland
253 John E. Randall
254 Doug Perrine/Innerspace Visions
255 Gregory S. Boland
256 Varin-Visage/Jacana/ Photo Researchers, Inc.
257 Stephen Frink/WaterHouse
258 Joyce Burek/Azure Computer and Photographic Services, Inc.
259 Frank Burek/Azure Computer and Photographic Services, Inc.
260 John G. Shedd Aquarium
261 Joyce Burek/Azure Computer and Photographic Services, Inc.
262 Randal D. Sanders
263 Joyce Burek/Azure Computer and Photographic Services, Inc.
264 David S. Addison/Visuals Unlimited
265 Wayne & Karen Brown/ Brown & Company Photography
266 Frank Burek/Azure Computer and Photographic Services, Inc.
267 David S. Addison/Visuals Unlimited
268 Gilbert S. Grant/Photo Researchers, Inc.
269 Stephen Frink/WaterHouse
270 Joyce Burek/Azure Computer and Photographic Services, Inc.
271 Tom McHugh/Steinhart Aquarium/Photo Researchers, Inc.
272 Herb Segars
273 Bob Cranston
274 Bob Cranston
275 Michael Cardwell

INDEX

Numbers in boldface type refer to color-plate numbers. Numbers in italic type refer to page numbers.

NATIONAL AUDUBON SOCIETY

The mission of NATIONAL AUDUBON SOCIETY, *founded in 1905, is to conserve and restore natural ecosystems, focusing on birds, other wildlife, and their habitats for the benefit of humanity and the earth's biological diversity.*

One of the largest, most effective environmental organizations, AUDUBON has nearly 550,000 members, numerous state offices and nature centers, and 500+ chapters in the United States and Latin America, plus a professional staff of scientists, educators, and policy analysts. Through its nationwide sanctuary system AUDUBON manages 160,000 acres of critical wildlife habitat and unique natural areas for birds, wild animals, and rare plant life.

The award-winning *Audubon* magazine, which is sent to all members, carries outstanding articles and color photography on wildlife, nature, environmental issues, and conservation news. AUDUBON also publishes *Audubon Adventures,* a children's newsletter reaching 450,000 students. Through its ecology camps and workshops in Maine, Connecticut, and Wyoming, AUDUBON offers nature education for teachers, families, and children; through *Audubon Expedition Institute* in Belfast, Maine, AUDUBON offers unique, traveling undergraduate and graduate degree programs in Environmental Education.

AUDUBON sponsors books and on-line nature activities, plus travel programs to exotic places like Antarctica, Africa, Baja California, the Galápagos Islands, and Patagonia. For information about how to become an AUDUBON member, subscribe to *Audubon Adventures,* or to learn more about any of our programs, please contact:

NATIONAL AUDUBON SOCIETY
Membership Dept.
700 Broadway
New York, NY 10003
(800) 274-4201
(212) 979-3000
http://www.audubon.org/

NATIONAL AUDUBON SOCIETY
FIELD GUIDE SERIES

Also available in this unique all-color,
all-photographic format:

African Wildlife • **Birds** *(Eastern Region)* • **Birds**
(Western Region) • **Butterflies** • **Fishes** • **Fossils**
• **Insects and Spiders** • **Mammals** • **Mushrooms** •
Night Sky • **Reptiles and Amphibians** • **Rocks
and Minerals** • **Seashells** • **Seashore Creatures** •
Trees *(Eastern Region)* • **Trees** *(Western Region)* •
Weather • **Wildflowers** *(Eastern Region)* •
Wildflowers *(Western Region)*

Prepared and produced by Chanticleer Press, Inc.

Founding Publisher: Paul Steiner
Publisher: Andrew Stewart

Staff for this book:

Editor-in-Chief: Amy K. Hughes
Managing Editor: Edie Locke
Art Director: Drew Stevens
Production Manager: Alicia Mills
Photo Editor: Teri Myers
Editors: Kathryn Clark, Lisa Leventer, Miriam Harris
Assistant Editor: Kristina Lucenko
Editorial Assistant: Michelle Bredeson
Production Assistant: Elizabeth Gaynor
Photo Assistant: Christine Heslin
Illustrations: John Norton
Silhouettes: Dolores R. Santoliquido
Endpaper Maps: Ortelius Design
Range Maps: Sam Shaw, Nicholas Vitiello, Deidre Freeman
Original series design by Massimo Vignelli

All editorial inquiries on this title should be addressed to:
Field Guides
P.O. Box 479
Woodstock, VT 05091
editors@thefieldguideproject.com

To purchase this book, or other National Audubon Society
illustrated nature books, please contact:
Alfred A. Knopf
1745 Broadway
New York, NY 10019
(800) 733-3000
www.randomhouse.com

Gulf
of
Mexico

Florida

Grand
Bahama

Abaco

New
Providence

Eleuthe

Florida Keys

Dry
Tortugas

Straits of Florida

Andros

Cay Sal
Bank

Exuma

Matanzas

CUBA

Long
Island

Isla de la
Juventud

Cayman
Islands

Caribbean
Sea

JAMAICA

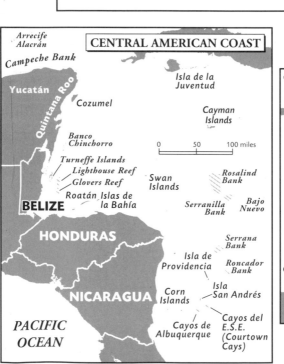

Arrecife
Alacrán

CENTRAL AMERICAN COAST

Campeche Bank

Yucatán

Quintana Roo

Isla de la
Juventud

Cozumel

Cayman
Islands

HAITI

Banco
Chinchorro

Turneffe Islands
Lighthouse Reef
Glovers Reef

0   50   100 miles

Swan
Islands

Rosalind
Bank

BELIZE

Roatán Islas de
la Bahía

Serranilla
Bank

Bajo
Nuevo

Península
de la
Guajira

HONDURAS

Serrana
Bank

Isla de
Providencia

Roncador
Bank

COLOMB

NICARAGUA

Corn
Islands

Isla
San Andrés

PACIFIC
OCEAN

Cayos de
Albuquerque

Cayos del
E.S.E.
(Courtown
Cays)